American
Actors and Actresses

PERFORMING ARTS INFORMATION GUIDE SERIES

Series Editor: Louis A. Rachow, Librarian, The Walter Hampton-Edwin Booth Theatre Collection and Memorial Library, New York

Also in this series:

AMERICAN AND ENGLISH POPULAR ENTERTAINMENT—*Edited by Don B. Wilmeth*

THE AMERICAN STAGE TO WORLD WAR I—*Edited by Don B. Wilmeth*

GUIDE TO DANCE IN FILM—*Edited by David Parker and Esther Siegel*

PERFORMING ARTS RESEARCH—*Edited by Marion K. Whalon*

STAGE SCENERY, MACHINERY, AND LIGHTING—*Edited by Richard Stoddard*

THEATRE AND CINEMA ARCHITECTURE—*Edited by Richard Stoddard*

THEATRICAL COSTUME—*Edited by Jackson Kessler*

The above series is part of the
GALE INFORMATION GUIDE LIBRARY

The Library consists of a number of separate series of guides covering major areas in the social sciences, humanities, and current affairs.

General Editor: Paul Wasserman, Professor and former Dean, School of Library and Information Services, University of Maryland

Managing Editor: Denise Allard Adzigian, Gale Research Company

American Actors and Actresses

A GUIDE TO INFORMATION SOURCES

Volume 8 in the Performing Arts Information Guide Series

Stephen M. Archer

Professor of Speech and Dramatic Art
University of Missouri
Columbia

Preface by Barnard Hewitt

Professor of Theatre Emeritus
University of Illinois
Urbana

Gale Research Company
Book Tower, Detroit, Michigan 48226

Library of Congress Cataloging in Publication Data

Archer, Stephen M.
    American actors and actresses.

    (Performing arts information guide series ; v. 8)
(Gale information guide library)
    Includes indexes.
        1. Moving pictures actors and actresses—United States—
Biography—Bibliography. 2.Moving pictures actors and
actresses—United States—Biography—Sources—Bibliog-
raphy. I. Title. II. Series.
Z5784.M9A7   016.79143'028'0922   82-15685
[PN1998.A2]
ISBN 0-8103-1495-9

To the Players

VITA

Stephen M. Archer is professor of speech and dramatic art at University of Missouri, Columbia. Since 1971 he has been teaching theatre history and directing theatre productions at the university.

Archer received his B.A., B.S. in Education, and M.S. in Education from Emporia State University, and Ph.D. from the University of Illinois. He has published articles and reviews in such journals as THEATRE JOURNAL, PLAYERS, DRAMATICS, CENTRAL STATES SPEECH JOURNAL, and ASSOCIATION FOR COMMUNICATION ADMINISTRATION BULLETIN. He is the author of HOW THEATRE HAPPENS, the second edition of which is forthcoming. He is a member of the Freedley Jury of the Theatre Library Association and a member of the Players Club.

CONTENTS

Contents

Contents

Contents

Contents

Contents

PREFACE

The literature on American actors and actresses is voluminous. The professional and private lives of men and women who earn their living on the stage have a perennial fascination for their fellows in other walks of life. Acting appears to them a glamorous profession. Consequently, since early in the history of this country, biographies and autobiographies of the stars and of lesser lights of the stage have found a ready market; books and articles designed to appeal to the general public constitute a considerable part of the literature on American actors and actresses.

Added relatively recently to the popular literature in the field are scholarly studies which seek to define an actor's art and to place him in the history of American theatre. Such studies had to wait for the appearance of the history of American theatre, distinct from the history of American drama, as a field for study in our colleges and universities. And that is a recent development as such things go in higher education.

In 1946 when I was invited to teach a course in the history of American theatre in Erwin Piscator's Dramatic Workshop at the New School for Social Research, I doubt if there was another such course offered anywhere in the country. No textbook was available. The nearest thing to one was Coad and Mims's THE AMERICAN STAGE in the Yale University Press Series The Pageant of America. Now long out of print, it remains an excellent study profusely illustrated, but because it was intended for the general reader, it lacks supporting bibliography and references to specific sources. There was also Arthur Hobson Quinn's HISTORY OF AMERICAN DRAMA, which contained full bibliographical support, including useful entries on leading actors and actresses, but as its title indicated, focused on plays rather than on the larger subject of theatre.

Until I undertook to teach that course in Piscator's Dramatic Workshop, I had given very little attention to the history of our theatre. I was excited instead by developments in the European theatre growing out of the theory and practice of Gordon Craig, Adolphe Appia, Georg Fuchs, Stanislavsky, Meierhold, and Tairov, to which I had been introduced by Professor Alexander Drummond at Cornell University. So I had to do some exploring in a field new to me. My interest was aroused and grew as I prepared my lectures for the Dramatic Workshop. It continued to grow after that course was finished, and when I joined the faculty of the University of Illinois in 1948, it was to teach not only modern theories of theatre art, but also the history of the American theatre.

Similar courses began to appear elsewhere, and the subject was given some attention in the fast growing numbers of courses in western and world theatre. Glenn Hughes's A HISTORY OF AMERICAN THEATRE was published in 1951, my THEATRE U.S.A. 1668-1957 in 1959, and Garff B. Wilson's THREE HUNDRED YEARS OF AMERICAN DRAMA AND THEATRE in 1973. Graduate studies in various aspects of American theatre appeared, including actors and acting, Garff Wilson's A HISTORY OF AMERICAN ACTING was published in 1966 and William C. Young's two-volume FAMOUS ACTORS AND ACTRESSES OF THE AMERICAN STAGE in 1975. Graduate studies of American actors and acting proliferated. The products of scholarly research joined the books and articles intended for the general public to swell the volume of literature on American actors and acting.

Dr. Stephen Archer is very familiar with that literature and has long been aware of the need for a comprehensive bibliographical guide to the field. He has taught history of the American theatre, as well as history of world theatre, for nearly twenty years, and he has occasionally taught a seminar in the history of acting. He has been collecting materials on actors and acting since his years as a graduate student.

Five years in the making, this bibliographical guide is unique in its field. It contains over 3,200 entries of books and serial articles containing information about 226 American actors and actresses. Each entry is carefully annotated. The performers range in time from Anthony Aston and Lewis Hallam, Sr., in the eighteenth century to Helen Hayes and Morris Carnovsky today; alphabetically, from Edwin Adams and Maude Adams to William B. Wood and Blanche Yurka; and in celebrity, from Susanna Rowson and John Durang to Charlotte Cushman and John Barrymore. Most of today's stars have been excluded.

A complete entry for each major source appears under each actor's name. For Stella Adler there is 1 such entry; for Edwin Booth there are 102. In addition, one is keyed by number to other sources, for example, for Stella Adler to 5 other sources, for Edwin Booth to over 100.

For these other sources, more than 1,000 books and serial articles have been surveyed. They include 520 general reference works, dictionaries, encyclopedias, and biographical guides; 81 bibliographies and indexes; 113 general and specialized histories, surveys, and regional studies; 254 general sources: books and serials; and 80 biographies and autobiographies.

Obviously, this guide is an indispensable tool for study and research in the history of American actors and acting. It will be useful to the undergraduate student in courses in the history of the American theatre, to the graduate student engaged in research in the field, and to the authors of biographies, both popular and scholarly, of American performers. Not so obviously, it will be useful to students of other aspects of American theatre history for many of its entries contain information about the larger field, and each entry is fully annotated.

Barnard Hewitt
University of Illinois
Urbana-Champaign

INTRODUCTION

This volume lists and describes major published sources of information about American actors and actresses from the beginning of professional theatre in this country to the present. In order to contain such an examination in a single volume, several substantial restrictions and definitions were necessary.

The term "American" in most cases restricts the coverage to performers born in this country. Since, however, the stage in this country was dominated until about the 1820s by English colonials and expatriates, I included such performers as the Hallams, Aston, Wignell, Warren, Douglass, and the others who forged a theatrical tradition in North America. As the nineteenth century progressed, fewer stars of foreign birth were included unless they had substantial and influential careers in the United States, such as Boucicault, Modjeska, or Janauscheck. Visiting stars who substantially retained their national identities, such as Charles and Edmund Kean, Sarah Bernhardt, Constant Coquelin, Henry Irving, Ellen Terry, Fanny Kemble, and Laurence Olivier, while deserving of such bibliographical studies, could not be included in this volume.

A further restriction limited the persons covered to those performers associated primarily with the legitimate stage, omitting those who worked only or primarily in variety entertainments, minstrel shows, musical theatre, vaudeville, film, video, and the like. I intend no elitism here, only a clarification of restrictions. Categorizations are not always clear; performers often worked in two or more facets of the entertainment industry, especially since the advent of film and the subsequent migration of major performers from the stage to the screen.

Given the restrictions listed above, one doubts that any two scholars of the American theatre would draw up exactly the same list of performers for coverage. Those included in this volume represent actors and actresses with substantial careers who have attracted the attention of scholars, those for whom substantial material is available, and a few persons whose influence upon American acting has been notable. Augustin Daly, David Belasco, and Lee Strasberg may not be considered primarily as actors, but their influence and interaction with the performers of their times has been such that their inclusion seemed potentially helpful for those seeking information sources.

Items included are restricted to books and periodical articles published in English, primarily though not exclusively from the United States. Some types of materials were excluded:

1. Dissertations and theses, which may be located through existing indexes and guides.

2. Newspaper articles, obituaries, and reviews, the multiplicity and relative inaccessability of which made inclusion impossible. After some consideration, VARIETY, BILLBOARD, and NEW YORK DRAMATIC MIRROR were excluded, although the Witham item (no. 112) will lead the researcher to a number of major interviews in the MIRROR.

3. Materials in regularly appearing columns in periodicals, a valuable source of information, but one requiring additional volumes and compilers.

4. Photographs, engravings, and other graphic representations of performers; such materials are indexed to a large extent in existing guides.

5. Most film fan magazines, which regularly published articles about stage personalities working in the film industry. The usefulness of such items varies considerably; a few are included as representative of such materials rather than as a definitive listing.

6. Collections of personal papers, diaries, manuscripts, play bills, and unpublished materials relevant to individual performers. Indexes to such collections of which I was aware are included.

7. Review and critiques of specific performances. While such materials are invaluable primary materials for the assessment of performers, literally thousands of such reviews are in print, making their inclusion in a volume such as this impossible.

The items are entered in seven categories, as follows:

1. General references, dictionaries, encyclopedias, and biographical guides, listing reference works not restricted to the theatre.

2. Bibliographies and indexes, both theatrical and nontheatrical.

3. General and specialized histories, surveys, and regional studies. I have omitted histories of the world theatre, many of which mention American actors and actresses in varying degrees, but I have included histories of the American theatre.

4. General sources: books. This section includes book-length works which cover several American actors and actresses and which seemed more appropriately placed in this section than under an individual performer. While the volume's full entry is made here, references to the entry number will be found after the individual section on each actor substantially covered in the volume.

5. General sources: serials. This section contains periodical articles relevant to several performers; again, each entry is cross-indexed under the relevant individual.

6. Relevant biographies and autobiographies. This section contains biographical works by or about individuals not included in the individual actor or actress sec-

tions, but which contains material about varying numbers of performers. Each entry is cross-indexed under individual performers.

7. Individual performers. Performers are listed alphabetically; within each section, items are listed alphabetically by author. At the end of each individual's section, entry numbers of relevant items are listed for additional reference.

Each entry contains the traditional bibliographical information and indications as to illustrations, indexes, or bibliographies. Where available, information concerning multiple editions is included. Indexes are not included in determining the number of pages of a book, unless the volume is basically an index.

ACKNOWLEDGMENTS

No such undertaking as this volume is possible without the kindness of strangers. The enormous pantheon of performers made the work necessary; hundreds of critics, scholars, interviewers, and writers of all sorts supplied the material. To them all, I offer my highest regard and deepest gratitude.

During the years of examination of materials, many persons gave freely of their time and expertise. Chief among them was Jeaneice Brewer of Ellis Library at the University of Missouri and her most capable and affable staff of Gina Mares, Melissa Poole, and James Blair, who somehow managed large numbers of interlibrary loan requests with efficiency, dispatch, and accuracy.

At the other end of the process, librarians across the United States processed the requests, located the materials, and made them available to me; without them, no such project can be undertaken. Libraries employed included those of the Universities of Alabama, Arizona, Bradley, Bryn Mawr, California, Case Western Reserve, Chicago, Cincinnati, Cleveland State, Colorado, Colorado State, Columbia, Cornell, Dayton, DePaul, Drake, Duke, Eastern Kentucky, Emory, Emporia (Kans.) State, Ft. Hayes (Kans.) State, Georgia, Grand View College, Hamilton College, Harvard, Idaho, Illinois, Indiana, Iowa, Iowa State, Kansas, Kansas State, Kent State, Kentucky, Knox College, Lake Forest College, Louisiana State, Miami, Michigan, Michigan State, Minnesota, Mississippi, Mississippi State, Missouri–Kansas City, Missouri Western State, Montana, Morningside College, Nebraska, New York University, North Carolina, North Carolina State, Northeast Missouri State, Northern Illinois, Northwestern, Oakland, Ohio, Ohio State, Oklahoma, Oklahoma State, Old Dominion, Pennsylvania, Pepperdine, Pittsburgh, Princeton, Rochester, Rutgers, St. Louis, South Carolina, South Florida, Southeast Missouri State, Southwest Louisiana, Southwest Missouri State, Southern California, Southern Illinois, SUNY-Binghamton, SUNY-Brockport, SUNY-Stonybrook, Tennessee, Texas, Tulane, Vassar, Virginia, Wake Forest, Washington, Washington University (St. Louis), West Texas, West Virginia, Westminster College, Wisconsin, and Yale. Libraries unaffiliated with educational institutions included Boston Athenaeum, Boston Public, Buffalo and Erie County, Center for Research Libraries, Chicago Public, Cleveland Public, Detroit Public, Enoch Pratt Free Library, Free Library of Philadelphia, Johnson County (Mo.) Library, Kansas City Public, Kansas State Historical Society, Library Company of

Acknowledgments

Philadelphia, Library of Congress, Los Angeles Public, Michigan State Library, Milwaukee Public, Mississippi Library Commission, Montana Historical Society, New Brunswick Theological Seminary, New York State Library, Newberry Library, Omaha Public, St. Louis Public, Seattle Public, and Wisconsin State Historical Society. To all those involved, my gratitude.

Friends, colleagues, and students frequently and freely offered their assistance; the contributions of Carla Waal, Larry Clark, Weldon Durham, Tom Hellie, Michael Mooney, and Michael Shapiro were substantial and appreciated. Throughout the entire project, the advice and friendship of Don Wilmeth sustained the effort.

Grants from the University of Missouri Research Council enabled me to visit several research centers for varying amounts of time. I there enjoyed the assistance of gracious and talented professionals such as Louis Rachow of the Players Club, Paul Meyers at the Lincoln Center Collection, and the staffs of the New York Public Library, including the 43d Street Annex and the Rare Book Room, St. Louis Public, Library of Congress, and British Library, whose operation must be a standard by which research libraries are to be judged.

In spite of such spendid assistance, such a work as this will contain errors and omissions; I invite the reader to bring those to my attention as they are discovered.

Valuable advice and encouragement were offered by Barnard Hewitt and Loren Reid, scholars and gentlemen both. The Gale Research Company editors, specifically Denise Allard Adzigian and Pamela Dear, were both patient and professional; my thanks to both.

As always, my family, Kelly and Steven, supplied essential support and understanding in full measure.

GENERAL INFORMATION SOURCES

GENERAL REFERENCES, DICTIONARIES, ENCYCLOPEDIAS, AND BIOGRAPHICAL GUIDES

1   Adams, W[illiam]. Davenport. A DICTIONARY OF THE DRAMA: A GUIDE TO THE PLAYS, PLAYWRIGHTS, PLAYERS AND PLAYHOUSES OF THE UNITED KINGDOM AND AMERICA, FROM THE EARLIEST TIMES TO THE PRESENT. Only Volume 1 (A-G) published. Philadelphia: Lippincott, 1904. London: Chatto and Windus, 1904. viii, 627 p.

Encyclopedic entries on major actors and actresses. The intended second volume never appeared as a publication, but the manuscript is available from University Microfilms Library Service.

2   Amory, Cleveland, ed. CELEBRITY REGISTER: AN IRREVERENT COMPENDIUM OF AMERICAN QUOTABLE NOTABLES. New York, Evanston, and London: Harper and Row, 1963. vi, 676 p. Illus.

A biographical dictionary composed of a paragraph and a photograph for each of approximately 2,800 celebrities, among them many performers. Amory edited an earlier edition in 1959, the INTERNATIONAL CELEBRITY REGISTER, U.S. EDITION, and in 1973 Earl Blackwell edited the comparable CELEBRITY REGISTER.

3   Brown, John Howard, ed. LAMB'S BIOGRAPHICAL DICTIONARY OF THE UNITED STATES. 7 vols. Boston: James H. Lamb, Co., 1900-1903. Illus.

A biographical dictionary of wide scope, unfortunately undocumented. Most of the performers who had achieved substantial reputations by the turn of this century are included.

4   Campbell, Oscar James, and Quinn, Edward G. THE READER'S ENCYCLOPEDIA OF SHAKESPEARE. New York: Thomas Y. Crowell, 1966. xv, 1,014 p. Illus., bibliog.

The authors compiled this work in "the hope of offering in a single volume all the essential information about every feature of Shakespeare's life and works." They include brief biographies of the major Shakespearean actors, including those in the United States.

5   CURRENT BIOGRAPHY: WHO'S NEWS AND WHY. New York: H.W. Wilson Co., 1940-- . Annual. Index, illus., bibliog.

An annual volume of celebrity biographical sketches, including the following performers--1941: Judith Anderson, Tallulah Bankhead, Ethel Barrymore, Katharine Cornell, Lynn Fontanne, Alfred Lunt. 1942: Ilka Chase, Helen Hayes, Eva Le Gallienne, Cornelia Otis Skinner, Peggy Wood. 1943: Lionel Barrymore, Laura Crews, Ruth Gordon, Fredric March, Zero Mostel. 1944: Elsie Ferguson, Dorothy Gish, Lillian Gish, Paul Muni. 1945: Laurette Taylor. 1949: Walter Huston. 1952: Katharine Cornell. 1953: Tallulah Bankhead, Walter Hampden, Josephine Hull. 1954: Ina Claire. 1955: Eva Le Gallienne. 1956: Joseph Schildkraut. 1960: Lee Strasberg. 1963: Zero Mostel. 1964: Cornelia Otis Skinner. 1972: Ruth Gordon. 1978: Lillian Gish.

6   Duyckinck, Evert A. PORTRAIT GALLERY OF EMINENT MEN AND WOMEN OF EUROPE AND AMERICA. EMBRACING HISTORY, STATESMANSHIP, NAVAL AND MILITARY LIFE, PHILOSOPHY, THE DRAMA, SCIENCE, LITERATURE AND ART WITH BIOGRAPHIES. 2 vols. New York: Johnson, Wilson and Co., 1873. 640, 638 p. Illus.

Includes brief sketches of Edwin Booth and Charlotte Cushman, accompanied by handsome steel engravings.

7   ENCICLOPEDIA DELLO SPETTACOLO. 9 vols., 3 vols. of supplements. Rome: Casa Editrice le Maschere, 1954-68.

Although the entries are written in Italian, this encyclopedia of spectacle contains valuable bibliographies for many actors and actresses, the citation printed in the language in which they were written. A mammoth work.

8   Fitzhugh, Harriet, and Fitzhugh, Lloyd. THE CONCISE BIBLIOGRAPHICAL DICTIONARY OF FAMOUS MEN AND WOMEN. New York: Grosset and Dunlap, 1935. 760 p. Index. Rev. and enl. ed. 1949.

Brief and undistinguished essays on celebrities, among them Edwin Booth, Mrs. Fiske, and Joseph Jefferson III.

9   Gallico, Paul. THE REVEALING EYE: PERSONALITIES OF THE 1920'S IN PHOTOGRAPHS BY NICKOLAS MURAY AND WORDS BY PAUL GALLICO. New York: Atheneum, 1967. xxviii, 301 p. Index, illus.

A photographic study with each subject briefly described by

Gallico; among those covered are Tallulah Bankhead, Ethel Barrymore, David Belasco, Alice Brady, Billie Burke, Ina Claire, Katharine Cornell, Jane Cowl, Jeanne Eagles, Lynn Fontanne, Dorothy Gish, Lillian Gish, Walter Hampden, Helen Hayes, Eva Le Gallienne, Alfred Lunt, Nazimova, Florence Reed, Paul Robeson, Otis Skinner, Fred Stone, Louis Wolheim, and Blanche Yurka.

10   Graham, Peter John. A DICTIONARY OF THE CINEMA. London: Tantivy Press; New York: A.S. Barnes, 1964. 116 p. Index, illus.

Includes one-paragraph entries on film stars, some of whom had worked on the legitimate stage.

11   Hines, Dixie, and Hanaford, Harry Prescott. WHO'S WHO IN MUSIC AND DRAMA: AN ENCYCLOPEDIA OF BIOGRAPHY OF NOTABLE MEN AND WOMEN IN MUSIC AND THE DRAMA, 1914. New York: H.D. Hanaford, 1914. 558 p. Illus., appendix.

A substantial encyclopedia of performers with a capsule biography for each of an estimated thousand subjects. Cast lists for metropolitan premieres from June 1910 through August 1913 are appended.

12   Iles, George, ed. THE POCKET UNIVERSITY. 21 vols. Garden City, N.Y.: Doubleday, Page and Co., 1924.

Volume 21, part 2, is subtitled AUTOBIOGRAPHY: ACTORS. In it, Iles reprints sections of Joseph Jefferson's autobiography, some of Edwin Booth's letters, Richard Mansfield's essay, "Man and the Actor," from ATLANTIC MONTHLY, and several essays on European performers.

13   James, Edward T.; James, Janet Wilson; and Bayer, Paul S., eds. NOTABLE AMERICAN WOMEN 1607-1950 A BIOGRAPHICAL DICTIONARY. 3 vols. Cambridge, Mass.: Belknap Press of Harvard University Press, 1971. Index, bibliogs.

Includes essays on ninety-one American actresses, indexed on page 709 of volume 3. Each entry concludes with a brief bibliography, often including the location of unpublished materials and major collections. See no. 26.

14   Johnson, Allen, ed. DICTIONARY OF AMERICAN BIOGRAPHY. 21 vols., 4 vols. of supplements. New York: Charles Scribner's Sons, under the auspices of the American Council of Learned Societies, 1928.

Capsule biographies of important American citizens, including performers, with a brief bibliography for each.

15   Johnson, Allen, and Malone, Dumas, eds. DICTIONARY OF AMERICAN
      BIOGRAPHY. 11 vols., with 5 vols. of supplements. New York: Charles
      Scribner's Sons, 1930.

      A revised version of the previous entry (no. 14).

16   Johnson, Rossiter, ed.-in-chief. THE TWENTIETH CENTURY BIOGRAPHI-
      CAL DICTIONARY OF NOTABLE AMERICANS: BRIEF BIOGRAPHIES OF
      AUTHORS, ADMINISTRATORS, CLERGYMEN, COMMANDERS, EDITORS,
      ENGINEERS, JURISTS, MERCHANTS, OFFICIALS, PHILANTHROPISTS,
      SCIENTISTS, STATESMEN, AND OTHERS WHO ARE MAKING AMERICAN
      HISTORY. Boston: Biographical Society, 1904. Reprint. Detroit: Gale
      Research Co., 1968. 10 vols. Illus.

      Includes brief essays on the leading American players up to the
      turn of the twentieth century.

17   Kunitz, Stanley Jasspon, and Haycraft, Howard, eds. AMERICAN AU-
      THORS, 1600-1900: A BIOGRAPHICAL DICTIONARY OF AMERICAN
      LITERATURE: COMPLETE IN ONE VOLUME WITH 1300 BIOGRAPHIES
      AND 400 PORTRAITS. New York: H.W. Wilson, 1938. vi, 846 p.
      Illus., bibliogs.

      Coverage includes brief biographies of several American play-
      wrights, such as Augustin Daly, James A. Herne, and Anna
      Cora Mowatt.

18   Leonard, John William, ed.-in-chief. WOMAN'S WHO'S WHO OF
      AMERICA, A BIOGRAPHICAL DICTIONARY OF THE CONTEMPORARY
      WOMEN OF THE UNITED STATES AND CANADA, 1914-1915. New
      York: American Commonwealth Co., 1914. 961 p.

      Capsule biographies, including actresses.

19   Morello, Theodore, ed. THE HALL OF FAME FOR GREAT AMERICANS
      AT NEW YORK UNIVERSITY. New York: New York University Press,
      1962. 192 p. Illus.

      The official handbook of the Hall of Fame, established at the
      turn of this century. Two American performers are included, with
      photographs of their statues and brief biographies: Edwin Booth
      (p. 139) and Charlotte Cushman (p. 193).

20   THE NATIONAL CYCLOPEDIA OF AMERICAN BIOGRAPHY BEING THE
      HISTORY OF THE UNITED STATES AS ILLUSTRATED IN THE LIVES OF
      THE FOUNDERS, BUILDERS AND DEFENDERS OF THE REPUBLIC, AND
      OF THE MEN AND WOMEN WHO ARE DOING THE WORK AND MOULD-
      IND THE THOUGHT OF THE PRESENT TIME. 70 vols. New York: James
      T. White and Co., 1892-1977.

      An immense resource which includes many American performers.
      An index was published separately by White and Co. in 1975.

21   Pasco, Ch[arles]. Eyre, ed. THE DRAMATIC LIST: A RECORD OF THE PRINCIPAL PERFORMANCES OF LIVING ACTORS AND ACTRESSES OF THE BRITISH STAGE; WITH CRITICISMS FROM CONTEMPORARY JOURNALS. London: Hardwicke and Bogue, 1879; Boston: Roberts Brothers, 1879. Reprints. St. Clair Shores, Mich.: Scholarly Press, 1971. New York: Benjamin Blom, 1969. 428 p. Index.

A biographical encyclopedia, including some international figures with significant careers in the United States, such as Dion Boucicault, Daniel Bandmann, John Brougham, John Sleeper Clarke, Rose Coghlan, Joseph Jefferson III, E. A. Sothern, and Charles Fechter.

22   Phillips, Laurence B. A DICTIONARY OF BIOGRAPHICAL REFERENCE CONTAINING OVER ONE HUNDRED THOUSAND NAMES TOGETHER WITH A CLASSED INDEX OF THE BIOGRAPHICAL LITERATURE OF EUROPE AND AMERICA. Graz, Austria: Akademische Druck, 1966. x, 1,038 p.

Lists only each subject's profession, birth date, and death date.

23   THE PICTUREGOER'S WHO'S WHO AND ENCYCLOPEDIA OF THE SCREEN TODAY. London: Odhams Press, 1933. 608 p. Illus.

A guide to film actors with brief biographies of stage stars who had cinematic careers, such as the Barrymores and the Gishs. Superseded by later publications.

24   Plarr, Victor G. MEN AND WOMEN OF THE TIME. A DICTIONARY OF CONTEMPORARIES. 14th ed. London: George Routledge and Sons, 1895. 986 p. 15th ed. London: George Routledge and Sons, 1899.

Includes short biographies of performers; of minimal value.

25   Ross, Paul L., ed. PLAYERS' GUIDE. New York: Players' Guide, 1953-- . Annual. Illus.

Pictorial directory of stage, screen, radio, and television performers, sponsored by Actors Equity, Chorus Equity, and the American Federation of Television and Radio Artists.

26   Sicherman, Barbara, and Green, Carol Hurd. NOTABLE AMERICAN WOMEN. THE MODERN PERIOD. A BIOGRAPHICAL DICTIONARY. Cambridge, Mass.: Belknap Press of Harvard University, 1980. 773 p. Bibliogs.

A companion volume to no. 13. Includes a number of actresses, each entry including a brief bibliography. Among those included are Maude Adams, Tallulah Bankhead, Ethel Barrymore, and Blanche Yurka.

27 Sobel, Bernard, ed. THE NEW THEATRE HANDBOOK AND DIGEST OF PLAYS. New York: Crown Publishers, 1959. 749 p. Bibliog.

An encyclopedia of the theatre, more useful for references to dramatists than to performers.

28 Storms, A. D., comp. THE PLAYERS BLUE BOOK. Worcester, Mass.: Sutherland and Storms, 1901. 303 p. Index, illus.

A series of one-page biographical sketches and full-page illustrations of various stage celebrities, among them Maude Adams, Viola Allen, Margaret Anglin, Ethel Barrymore, Blanche Bates, Amelia Bingham, Mrs. Carter, William Collier, Ida Conquest, William H. Crane, Henrietta Crosman, E.L. Davenport, Jefferson DeAngelis, J.E. Dodson, Marie Dressler, John Drew, Maxine Elliott, Effie Ellsler, William Faversham, Mrs. Fiske, Grace George, William Gillette, Nat Goodwin, James K. Hackett, Virginia Harned, Joseph Haworth, James A. Herne, E. M. Holland, DeWolf Hopper, Isabel Irving, May Irwin, Herbert Kelcey, Wilton Lackaye, Sarah Cowell Le Moyne, Edna May, Louis Mann, Mary Mannering, Richard Mansfield, Robert Mantell, Julia Marlowe, Henry Miller, Modjeska, Chauncey Olcott, James O'Neill, Ada Rehan, Stuart Robson, Annie Russell, Sol Smith Russell, Otis Skinner, Hilda Spong, E. H. Sothern, Fay Templeton, Denman Thomson, Blanche Walsh, Frederick Warde, and Francis Wilson.

29 THE THESPIAN DICTIONARY; OR, DRAMATIC BIOGRAPHY OF THE PRESENT AGE; CONTAINING SKETCHES OF THE LIVES, LISTS OF THE PRODUCTIONS, VARIOUS MERITS, &C, &C, OF ALL THE PRINCIPAL DRAMATISTS, COMPOSERS, COMMENTATORS, MANAGERS, ACTORS, AND ACTRESSES OF THE UNITED KINGDOM; INTERSPERSED WITH NUMEROUS ORIGINAL ANECDOTES FORMING A COMPLETE MODERN HISTORY OF THE ENGLISH STAGE. 1st ed. 1802. 2d ed. London: James Cundee, 1805. 390 p. Illus.

Of use in identifying British performers in this country, such as Anthony Aston or Mrs. Merry. The first edition was unavailable for examination.

30 WHO'S WHO IN THE THEATRE: A BIOGRAPHICAL RECORD OF THE CONTEMPORARY STAGE. 1st ed., 1912; 2d ed., 1914; 3d ed., 1916; 4th ed., 1922; 5th ed., 1926; 6th ed., 1930; 7th ed., 1933; 8th ed., 1936; 9th ed., 1939; 10th ed., 1947; 11th ed., 1952, edited by John Parker; 12th ed., 1957, edited by John Parker, Jr.; 13th ed., 1961; 14th ed., 1967, edited by Freda Gayle; 14th ed., 1967, edited by Ian Herbert et al., London: Sir Isaac Pitman and Sons. 16th ed., 1977, edited by Ian Herbert et al. Detroit: Gale Research Co. 17th ed., 1981, edited by Ian Herbert et al. 2 vols. Detroit: Gale Research Co.

Immensely useful biographical sketches on the leading performers of the time. Considerable information concerning productions, theatres, family trees, etc., are found in the various editions.

Myers, which includes annotated biographical entries on American stars, restricted to readily available works. Useful, if limited.

38   Baker, Blanche M. DRAMATIC BIBLIOGRAPHY; AN ANNOTATED LIST OF BOOKS ON THE HISTORY AND CRITICISM OF THE DRAMA AND STAGE AND ON THE ALLIED ARTS OF THE THEATRE. New York: H. W. Wilson Co., 1933. ix, 320 p. Index.

Extremely useful, containing entries on acting and the speech arts (pp. 47-60), actors, criticism, biography, autobiography (pp. 60-70), and a bibliography of bibliographies (pp. 246-263).

39   _____. THEATRE AND ALLIED ARTS: A GUIDE TO THE BOOKS DEALING WITH THE HISTORY, CRITICISM, AND TECHNIC OF THE DRAMA AND THEATRE AND RELATED ARTS AND CRAFTS. New York: H.W. Wilson Co., 1952. viii, 459 p. Index.

An expansion of the previous entry Index. Section 4 (pp. 212-74) covers general and specific works on actors and actresses of all countries. Each entry is annotated.

40   BIBLIOGRAPHIC GUIDE TO THEATRE ARTS. Boston: G.K. Hall and Co., 1975-- . Annual.

Index to theatre publications.

41   "A Bibliography of Speech and Theatre in the South for the Year 1954-- ." SOUTHERN SPEECH JOURNAL, 1955-- . Annual. Compiler varies.

Became the SOUTHERN SPEECH COMMUNICATION JOURNAL in 1968. Bibliography includes theatrical subjects.

42   BIOGRAPHY INDEX. New York: H.W. Wilson Co., 1947-- . Quarterly.

An index to books and articles, classified by subject. Now consists of eleven volumes; supplements are issued quarterly.

43   Blitgen, Sister Carol. "An Index to: A RECORD OF THE BOSTON STAGE by William W. Clapp, Jr." THEATRE DOCUMENTATION 1 (Fall 1968): 35-68.

See Clapp's RECORD OF THE BOSTON STAGE, no. 136.

44   Brockett, O[scar]. G. "The Theatre of the Southern United States from the Beginnings through 1865: A Bibliographic Essay." THEATRE RESEARCH 2 (1960): 163-74.

An annotated bibliography of general works, contemporary accounts, biographies, local histories, specialized accounts, and doctoral dissertations. Useful.

45 BULLETIN OF BIBLIOGRAPHY AND MAGAZINE NOTES. Boston: F.W. Faxon Co., 1897-- . 3/year.

> Contains various special interest bibliographies and lists changes or cessations of periodical publications. Includes the Dramatic Index through 1953. (See no. 57).

46 Busfield, Roger M., Jr. THEATRE ARTS PUBLICATIONS AVAILABLE IN THE UNITED STATES. 1953-1957 A FIVE YEAR BIBLIOGRAPHY. Washington, D.C.: American Educational Theatre Association, 1964. xiii, 165 p. Index.

> Compiled by the Bibliography Project of the American Educational Theatre Association. Pages 38-41, section 2-A, deals with actors and acting.

47 Carson, William G[lasgow]. B[ruce]. "The Theatre of the American Frontier: A Bibliographical Essay." THEATRE RESEARCH 1 (March 1958): 14-23. Bibliog.

> A gracefully written essay surveying the major published primary sources for the American theatre. A one and one-half page bibliography is appended.

48 A CATALOGUE OF THE ALLEN A. BROWN COLLECTION OF BOOKS RELATING TO THE STAGE IN THE PUBLIC LIBRARY OF THE CITY OF BOSTON. Boston: Published by the Trustees, 1919. viii, 952 p.

> Brown donated his 3,500-volume theatrical library to the Boston Public Library. This volume identifies that collection as well as listing all the other books in the Boston Public Library of interest to the theatre historian.

49 Cok, Wendell. "Early Theatre in America West of the Rockies." THEATRE RESEARCH 4 (1962): 36-45.

> The bibliography is divided by state: California, Utah, Nevada, Oregon, and Washington. Useful, if not extensive.

50 COMPREHENSIVE DISSERTATION INDEX: 1861-1972. 37 vols. Ann Arbor, Mich.: University Microfilm, 1973.

> An index to DISSERTATION ABSTRACTS; volume 31 includes theatrical subjects.

51 COMPREHENSIVE DISSERTATION INDEX: 1973 SUPPLEMENT. 5 vols. Ann Arbor, Mich.: University Microfilm, 1974.

> Volumes 3 to 5 cover the humanities and include an author index.

52 Conolly, L[eonard]. W., and Wearing, J.P. (since 1978, Wearing alone)

"Nineteenth Century Theatre Research 1972-- . "In NINETEENTH CEN-
TURY THEATRE RESEARCH, 1973-- . Annual.

Annotated bibliography of theatre publications involving the
nineteenth century.

53   Cooperman, Gail B., and Shea, Maureen. "Index to the Journal of the
      OSU Theatre Research Institute, 1954-1974." THEATRE STUDIES, no. 20
      (1973-74), pp. 64-70.

      Indexes 135 essays in THEATRE STUDIES AND O[hio] S[tate]
      U[niversity] THEATRE COLLECTION BULLETIN by author,
      chronology, and nation.

54   Cornyn, Stan. A SELECTIVE INDEX TO THEATRE MAGAZINE. New
      York: Scarecrow Press, 1964. 289 p. Bibliog.

      Indexes the major articles and interviews of the periodical pub-
      lished from March 1901 to April 1931.

55   CUMULATED DRAMATIC INDEX, 1909-1949. 2 vols. Boston: G. K.
      Hall and Co., 1915.

      More than a third of a million entries from 150 periodicals cited
      in Faxon's DRAMATIC INDEX, originally published in forty-one
      annual volumes.

56   In "Doctoral Projects in Progress in Theatre Arts." [1948--] EDUCA-
      TIONAL THEATRE JOURNAL, 1949-- . Annual.

      Compiled by various persons, a list of dissertations in progress,
      divided by topic, including actors and acting.

57   THE DRAMATIC INDEX FOR [1909-49]: COVERING ARTICLES AND
      ILLUSTRATIONS CONCERNING THE STAGE AND ITS PLAYERS IN THE
      PERIODICALS OF AMERICA AND ENGLAND; WITH A RECORD OF BOOKS
      ON THE DRAMA AND OF TEXTS OF PLAYS PUBLISHED 41
      vols. Boston: Boston Book Co., 1909-17; F. W. Faxson Co., 1918-49.

      Edited by Frederick Winthrop Faxon from 1909 through 1935,
      by Mary E. Bates from 1936 through 1940, by Mary E. Bates and
      Anne C. Sutherland from 1941 through 1943, by Anne C. Su-
      therland and John F. Shea in 1949. A valuable guide, attempt-
      ing to list every portrait, article, or book dealing with the
      theatre or film annually. Indexed by name, script title, or
      topic, although not adequately cross-indexed. Extremely useful
      for the period covered, although containing frequent errors, omis-
      sions, and mis-citations.

58   Elliott, Agnes M. CONTEMPORARY BIOGRAPHY: REFERENCES TO
      BOOKS AND MAGAZINE ARTICLES ON PROMINENT MEN AND WOMEN

OF THE TIME. Pittsburgh: Carnegie Library, 1903. 167 p.

> Contains a section of actors and actresses (p. 90 f.) including Maude Adams, Mary Anderson, Lawrence Barrett, Edwin Booth, Fanny Davenport, John Drew, Mrs. Fiske, William J. Florence, William Gillette, Nat Goodwin, Joseph Jefferson III, Richard Mansfield, Julia Marlowe, Modjeska, Clara Morris, Olga Nethersole, Ada Rehan, Sol Smith Russell, E. H. Sothern, and Edward S. Willard.

59   Farrell, Nancy Lee. "A Subject Index to: THE THEATRE ANNUAL, 1942-1969." THEATRE DOCUMENTATION 2 (1969-70): 125-34.

> Includes a section on performance aspects for the United States on pages 126-27 in which performers are indexed.

60   Gilder, Rosamond. A THEATRE LIBRARY: A BIBLIOGRAPHY OF ONE HUNDRED BOOKS RELATING TO THE THEATRE. New York: Theatre Arts, 1932. xiv, 61 p. Index.

> Drama is treated by nationality; specific players are not often named. Superseded by more recent work.

61   Gilder, Rosamond, and Freedley, George. THEATRE COLLECTIONS IN LIBRARIES AND MUSEUMS. AN INTERNATIONAL HANDBOOK. New York: Theatre Arts, 1936. 165 p. Index.

> A valuable albeit now out-of-date index to collections.

62   Gohdes, Clarence. LITERATURE AND THEATRE OF THE STATES AND REGIONS OF THE U.S.A.: AN HISTORICAL BIBLIOGRAPHY. Durham, N.C.: Duke University Press, 1967. ix, 276 p.

> A useful checklist for local studies, divided by state and region. Each section is divided into literature and theatre.

63   _____. "The Theatre in New York: A Tentative Checklist." NEW YORK PUBLIC LIBRARY BULLETIN 69 (April 1965): 232-46.

> A bibliography intended to cover books and articles dealing with the history of the theatre in the state and city of New York. Biographies and autobiographies are for the most part omitted by design. A valuable work, taken with Carl J. Stratman's addenda published in the same serial, 70 (June 1966): 389-407.

64   Gray, Giles Wilkeson, comp. "An Index to SPEECH MONOGRAPHS, Volumes 1-26 (1934-1959). " SPEECH MONOGRAPHS 27 (1960): 155-200.

> Acting and actors are indexed on page 156.

65 _____. INDEX TO THE QUARTERLY JOURNAL OF SPEECH, VOLUMES I TO XL, 1915-1954. Dubuque, Iowa: Speech Association of America, 1956. ix, 338 p.

Articles relevant to the theatre are listed separately.

66 Hall, Lillian Arrilla. CATALOGUE OF DRAMATIC PORTRAITS IN THE THEATRE COLLECTION OF THE HARVARD UNIVERSITY LIBRARY. 4 vols. Cambridge, Mass.: Harvard University Press, 1930-34.

The collection numbers approximately forty thousand, chiefly of American and British actors. The collection is restricted to engravings and does not include photographs, drawings, or process prints.

67 Hamar, Clifford E. "American Theatre History: A Geographical Index." EDUCATIONAL THEATRE JOURNAL 1 (December 1949): 164-94.

Sixty-eight cities in thirty-nine states are covered in this bibliographic guide to books, serials, dissertations, and special collections pertaining to local theatre history in the United States. Dated, but useful.

68 INDEX TO THE PORTRAITS IN ODELL'S ANNALS OF THE NEW YORK STAGE TRANSCRIBED FROM THE FILE IN THE THEATRE COLLECTION AT PRINCETON UNIVERSITY. Introduction by Alan S. Downer. New York: American Society for Theatre Research, 1963. iv, 178 p.

A useful guide for locating photographs and engravings in Odell's fourteen-volume work.

69 Knower, Franklin H., comp. TABLE OF CONTENTS OF THE QUARTERLY JOURNAL OF SPEECH, 1915-1960, SPEECH MONOGRAPHS, 1934-1960, AND THE SPEECH TEACHER, 1952-1960. [Bloomington, Indiana]: Speech Association of America, 1961. 86 p.

Many theatre articles are included in these publications.

70 Larson, Carl F. W. AMERICAN REGIONAL THEATRE HISTORY TO 1900: A BIBLIOGRAPHY. Metuchen, N.J., and London: Scarecrow Press, 1979. xi, 167 p. Indexes.

A valuable guide to materials excluding those dealing with the New York stage. The compilation includes 1,481 items, including books, articles in periodicals, essays in anthologies, theses, dissertations, sections of local history books, newspaper articles, and some manuscripts. The "Persons as Subject Index" lists many American performers.

71 Litto, Fredric M. AMERICAN DISSERTATIONS ON THE DRAMA AND THE THEATRE. Kent, Ohio: Kent State University Press, 1969. ix, 519 p. Index.

American and Canadian dissertations up to 1965; some 4,565
authors are listed. Indexed by title, author, key words, and
subject. Projected annual supplements have not materialized.

72   Long, E. Hudson. AMERICAN DRAMA FROM ITS BEGINNING TO
      THE PRESENT. New York: Appleton-Century-Crofts, 1970. xi, 64 p.
      Index.

      A bibliography mainly focused upon the drama, but with occa-
      sional references to works by or about actors or actor-playwrights.

73   Lowe, Claudio Jean. A GUIDE TO REFERENCE AND BIBLIOGRAPHY
      FOR THEATRE RESEARCH. Columbus: Office of Educational Services,
      Ohio State University Libraries, 1971. 137 p. Indexes.

      A guide seeking to provide the theatre student or researcher
      with a basic list of both generalized and specialized sources of
      reference and bibliographical information. The work is divided
      into two major sections: (1) general reference, and (2) theatre
      and drama. While actors are not the primary focus, many
      useful references are included.

74   Lowe, Robert W. A BIBLIOGRAPHICAL ACCOUNT OF ENGLISH THE-
      ATRICAL LITERATURE FROM THE EARLIEST TIMES TO THE PRESENT DAY.
      London: John C. Nimmo, 1888. x, 384 p.

      A relatively early theatrical bibliography, still of value, but
      superseded and incorporated by Arnott. See no. 36.

75   McDowell, John H., and McGraw, Charles J. "A Bibliography on Theatre
      and Drama in American Colleges and Universities, 1937-1947." SPEECH
      MONOGRAPHS 16 (November 1949): 1-124.

      Includes a section (pp. 11-14) on "Actors: Criticism and Biog-
      raphy."

76   Marder, Carl J., III. "An Index to: PERSONAL RECOLLECTIONS OF
      THE DRAMA by Henry Dickinson Stone." THEATRE DOCUMENTATION
      3 (Fall 1970-Spring 1971): 65-80.

      See Stone, PERSONAL RECOLLECTIONS, no. 249

77   Marshall, Thomas F[rederic]. "Beyond New York: A Bibliography of the
      19th Century American Stage from the Atlantic to the Mississippi." THEATRE
      RESEARCH 3 (1961): 208-17.

      A useful if not extensive bibliography, most of it annotated.
      Divided by states, actor and manager, and general references.

78 Matlon, Ronald J., comp. INDEX TO JOURNALS IN COMMUNICA-
TION STUDIES THROUGH 1979. Annandale, Va.: Speech Communication Association, 1980. 531 p. Index.

An index to fourteen scholarly journals; articles on acting and
actors are indexed on pages 385-86.

79 Matlon, Ronald J., and Matlon, Irene R. INDEX TO JOURNALS IN
COMMUNICATIONS STUDIES THROUGH 1974. Falls Church, Va.:
Speech Communication Association, 1975. 365 p. Index.

An index to thirteen scholarly journals. "Actors, Acting, and
Roles" is indexed on page 297.

80 Melnitz, William W., ed. THEATRE ARTS PUBLICATIONS IN THE
UNITED STATES 1947-52 A FIVE YEAR BIBLIOGRAPHY. Washington,
D.C.: American Educational Theatre Association, 1957. 79 p.

Part of a project by the AETA, unhappily abandoned in recent
years. Contains a section for actor biographies and related
work.

81 Meserve, Walter J. "The American Periodical Series: Source Material
for Theatre and Drama Research." EDUCATIONAL THEATRE JOURNAL
20 (October 1968): 443-48.

A description of the series of American periodicals from the
eighteenth and nineteenth centuries placed on film. Meserve
describes the resources thus available for research in theatre.

82 Milner, Anita Cheek. NEWSPAPER INDEXES: A LOCATION AND
SUBJECT GUIDE. 2 vols. Metuchen, N.J., and London: Scarecrow
Press, 1977, 1979.

An index of indexes to newspapers. Potentially useful in tracing tours by performers.

83 THE NEW YORK TIMES DIRECTORY OF THE THEATER. New York:
Arno Press, in cooperation wit the Quadrangle, New York Times Book
Co., 1973. 1,009 p. Illus.

An index to New York TIMES articles and reviews printed from
1920 to 1970, indexed by names of people and titles of productions. Also includes a section on New York TIMES theatre
critics, a listing of theatre awards, and reprints of TIMES articles on theatre awards.

84 THE NEW YORK TIMES INDEX. New York: New York Times Book Co.,
September 1851-- . Annual.

Extremely useful in tracing the New York activities of performers.

85   NEW YORK TIMES OBITUARIES INDEX, 1858-1968. New York: New York Times Co., 1970. 1,136 p.

An index to nearly a third of a million obituaries, including those of prominent performers.

86   Pence, James H. THE MAGAZINE AND THE DRAMA: AN INDEX. New York: Dunlap Society, 1896. xiii, 190 p.

An index of articles about the theatre from 1800 to 1896.

87   Perry, Jeb H. VARIETY OBITS: AN INDEX TO OBITUARIES IN VARIETY, 1905-1978. Metuchen, N.J., and London: Scarecrow Press, 1980. x, 311 p.

An index to some fifteen thousand people who worked in motion pictures, television, radio, minstrelsy, vaudeville, and the legitimate theatre. The index covers issues of VARIETY from 16. December 1905 to 21 June 1978, inclusive.

88   Roorbach, Orville Augustus, comp. BIBLIOTHECA AMERICANA: CATALOGUE OF AMERICAN PUBLICATIONS, INCLUDING REPRINTS AND ORIGINAL WORKS, FROM 1820 TO 1852, INCLUSIVE; TOGETHER WITH A LIST OF PERIODICALS PUBLISHED IN THE UNITED STATES. 4 vols. New York: 1852-61. Reprint. New York: Peter Smith, 1939.

A standard bibliographical source. The first supplement covers 1852-55; the second 1855-58, and the third 1858-61.

89   Salem, James M. A GUIDE TO CRITICAL REVIEWS: PART I--AMERICAN DRAMA, 1909-1969. Vol. 1 of 5 vols. 2d ed. Metuchen, N.J.: Scarecrow Press, 1973. xiv, 591 p. Indexes.

Entries are listed by playwright and title. Scholarly criticism is omitted, but popular magazines and the New York TIMES are included.

90   Santaniello, A.E. THEATRE BOOKS IN PRINT. New York: Drama Book Shop, 1963. 266 p. 2d ed. New York: Drama Book Specialists, 1966. xiii, 509 p. 3d ed. New York: Drama Book Specialists, 1973. 761 p. Indexes.

An annotated bibliography of books on all aspects of the theatre published through 1966. Author, editor, and title indexes.

91   Schneider, Ben Ross, Jr. INDEX TO THE LONDON STAGE 1660-1800. Carbondale and Edwardsville: Southern Illinois University Press, 1979. xx, 939 p.

See Van Lennep et al., THE LONDON STAGE, no. 254.

92   Schoolcraft, Ralph Newman. PERFORMING ARTS BOOK IN PRINT:

AN ANNOTATED BIBLIOGRAPHY. New York: Drama Book Specialists, 1973. xiii, 761 p. Indexes.

A substantial bibliography, containing sections on "Biographies of Stage Personalities," (pp. 261-78 and 561-67). Film actors, some of whom had earlier stage careers, are listed separately.

93 Shaw, Ralph R., and Shoemaker, Richard H., comps. AMERICAN BIBLI-OGRAPHY: A PRELIMINARY CHECKLIST FOR [1801--]. New York: Scarecrow Press, 1958--. Index.

A twenty-two volume set of bibliographies covering U.S. publications from 1801 through 1819.

94 Sherman, Robert Lowery. DRAMA CYCLOPEDIA: A BIBLIOGRAPHY OF PLAYS AND PLAYERS. Chicago: The Author, 1944. 612 p. Illus.

An undocumented work seeking to list every play produced in America from 1750 to 1940 with a leading player listed for each.

95 Shipton, Clifford K. THE AMERICAN BIBLIOGRAPHY OF CHARLES EVANS: A CHRONOLOGICAL DICTIONARY OF ALL BOOKS, PAM-PHLETS, AND PERIODICAL PUBLICATIONS PRINTED IN 1639 TO AND INCLUDING THE YEAR 1820; WITH BIBLIOGRAPHICAL NOTES. Vol. 13, 1799-1800. Worcester, Mass.: American Antiquarian Society, 1955. 281 p.

A useful bibliographical reference. A supplementary list can be found in the HUNTINGTON LIBRARY BULLETIN, no. 3 (1933): 1-95.

96 Slocum, Robert B., ed. BIOGRAPHICAL DICTIONARIES AND RELATED WORKS: AN INTERNATIONAL BIBLIOGRAPHY OF COLLECTIVE BI-OGRAPHIES, BIBLIOGRAPHIES, COLLECTIONS OF EPITAPHS, SELECTED GENEALOGICAL WORKS, DICTIONARIES OF ANONYMS AND PSEU-DONYMS, HISTORICAL AND SPECIALIZED DICTIONARIES, BIOGRAPH-ICAL MATERIALS IN GOVERNMENT MANUALS, BIBLIOGRAPHIES OF BIOGRAPHY, BIOGRAPHICAL INDEXES, AND SELECTED PORTRAIT CATALOGS. Detroit: Gale Research Co., 1967. xxiii, 1,056 p. Index.

A monumental work, more than doubled by ensuing supplements. In this volume, pages 440-52 are specifically theatrical entries.

97 _____. BIOGRAPHICAL DICTIONARIES AND RELATED WORKS. SUP-PLEMENT. Detroit: Gale Research Co., 1972. x, 852 p.

See previous entry.

98 _____. BIOGRAPHICAL DICTIONARIES AND RELATED WORKS. SE-COND SUPPLMENT. Detroit: Gale Research Co., 1978. xviii, 922 p.

See nos. 96 and 97.

99   Srnka, Alfred. "An Index to: PERSONAL RECOLLECTIONS OF THE
      STAGE by William Burke Wood." THEATRE DOCUMENTATION 1 (Spring
      1969): 51-73.

      See Wood's PERSONAL RECOLLECTIONS, no. 3208.

100   Stallings, Roy, and Myers, Paul, under the editorial supervision of George
      Freedley. A GUIDE TO THEATRE READING. New York: National
      Theatre Conference, 1949. ix, 123 p. Index.

      A selected bibliography with a section on biography. Dated.

101   Stoddard, Richard, and Kozuch, Frances Knibb, eds. "The Theatre in
      American Fiction, 1774-1850: An Annotated List of References." In
      PERFORMING ARTS RESOURCES, vol. 1., pp. 173-212. New York:
      Drama Book Specialists, 1975. Index.

      Stoddard and Kozuch examined 1,815 items, of which 350 had
      substantial references to the theatre, then selected for annota-
      tion 116 titles. Specific actors mentioned include John Howard
      Payne, Thomas Abthorpe Cooper, the elder Booth, James Fennell,
      the Hallams, Edwin Forrest, Clara Fisher, Henry Placide, Sol
      Smith, Charlotte Cushman, Frank Chanfrau, James H. Caldwell,
      John Hodgkinson, William Warren, Joseph Jefferson I, James
      Henry Wallack, Mrs. Duff, Thomas Wignell, John Henry, Tyrone
      Power, and Anna Cora Mowatt.

102   Stratman, Carl Joseph. AMERICAN THEATRICAL PERIODICALS, 1798-
      1967; A BIBLIOGRAPHICAL GUIDE. Durham, N.C.: Duke University
      Press, 1970. xxii, 106 p. Index.

      A listing of 685 theatrical periodicals, published in 122 cities
      in thirty-one states. Eighty-five of the periodicals could not
      be located, and 171 of them existed only in incomplete runs. Lo-
      cations of issues are given for 137 libraries. A valuable resource
      volume.

103   _____. BIBLIOGRAPHY OF THE AMERICAN THEATRE EXCLUDING
      NEW YORK CITY. Chicago: Loyola University Press, 1965. xv, 397 p.
      Index.

      A valuable reference, listing 3,856 entries with an index of
      references to specific performers.

104   _____. "The New York Stage: A Check List of Unpublished Dissertations
      and Theses." BULLETIN OF BIBLIOGRAPHY 24 (September-December
      1963): 41-44.

      Includes 125 items on the New York City theatre.

105   _____. "The Theatre in New York: Addenda." NEW YORK PUBLIC

LIBRARY BULLETIN 70 (June 1966): 389-407.

Addenda to Clarence Gohdes's work published in April 1965 in the same periodical.

106 THEATRE/DRAMA AND SPEECH INDEX. Pleasant Hill, Calif.: Theatre/ Drama and Speech Information Center, 1974-- . Three times a year.

A survey of sixty journals from fifteen countries, omitting popular periodicals.

107 Waters, Willard W., comp. "American Imprints, 1648-1979, in the Huntington Library, Supplementing Evan's AMERICAN BIBLIOGRAPHY." HUNTINGTON LIBRARY BULLETIN 3 (1933): 1-95. Index.

A total of 736 additional items arranged by year of publication. See no. 95.

108 Wearing, P. O. AMERICAN AND BRITISH THEATRICAL BIOGRAPHY: A DIRECTORY. Metuchen, N.J., and London: Scarecrow Press, 1979. v, 1,007 p.

Wearing surveyed the major biographical dictionaries, a total of 172 volumes, and indexed them by English, American, and foreign actors and actresses, as well as other theatre personnel. A valuable work.

109 Welker, David, ed. EDUCATIONAL THEATRE JOURNAL: A TEN-YEAR INDEX, 1949-1958. East Lansing, Mich.: American Educational Theatre Association, 1959. 81 p.

"Acting," "Actors," and individual performers are indexed separately.

110 Wilmeth, Don B., ed. THE AMERICAN STAGE TO WORLD WAR I: A GUIDE TO INFORMATION SOURCES. Performing Arts Series, vol. 4. Detroit: Gale Research Co., 1978. xxi, 225 p. Index.

An annotated bibliography of 1,461 items, cross-indexed, covering all theatrical and paratheatrical forms up to 1915.

111 _____. "Index to William Dunlap's LIFE OF GEORGE FREDERICK COOKE." THEATRE DOCUMENTATION 2 (1969): 109-20.

See Dunlap's LIFE, no. 553.

112 Witham, Barry B. "An Index to MIRROR 'Interviews.'" In PERFORMING ARTS RESOURCES, edited by Ted Perry, pp. 153-55. New York: Drama Book Specialists, 1975.

Witham indexes approximately one hundred interviews published in THE NEW YORK DRAMATIC MIRROR between May 1894 and

May 1899. Those covered by this bibliography include Maurice
Barrymore, David Belasco, Georgia Cayvan, Kate Claxton, Rose
Coghlan, William H. Crane, Jefferson DeAngelis, J. E. Dodson,
John Drew, Mrs. John Drew, Mrs. William J. Florence, William
Gillette, Edward Harrigan, Joseph Haworth, E. M. Holland,
Joseph Holland, DeWolf Hopper, Louis James, Janauschek, Wil-
ton Lackaye, Clara Fisher, Frank Mayo, Modjeska, Clara Morris,
James O'Neill, Augustus Pitou, Stuart Robson, Annie Russell,
Sol Smith Russell, Mary Shaw, E. H. Sothern, James H. Stoddart,
Denman Thompson, and Francis Wilson.

113   Young, William C. AMERICAN THEATRICAL ARTS: A GUIDE TO MANU-
SCRIPTS AND SPECIAL COLLECTIONS IN THE UNITED STATES AND
CANADA. Chicago: American Library Association, 1971. ix, 166 p.
Index.

Young indexes holdings in 138 collections of various primary
materials, including the manuscripts, private papers, and memorabilia collections of many American actors and actresses. Unfortunately, the work is untrustworthy and stimulated considerable
controversy when it appeared, the author having omitted many
substantial collections and included numerous errors of fact (the
St. Louis and Missouri Historical Societies are reversed, for
example). Still useful when corroborated.

GENERAL AND SPECIALIZED HISTORIES, SURVEYS, AND REGIONAL STUDIES

114 THE AMERICAN THEATRE: A SUM OF ITS PARTS: A COLLECTION OF THE DISTINGUISHED ADDRESSES PREPARED EXPRESSLY FOR THE SYM-POSIUM, "THE AMERICAN THEATRE--A CULTURAL PROCESS," AT THE FIRST AMERICAN COLLEGE THEATRE FESTIVAL, WASHINGTON, D.C., 1969. New York: Samuel French, 1971. 431 p. Bibliogs.

A collection of sixteen essays by leading theatre scholars. It includes two essays on American acting; see Moody, Richard, no. 210.

115 Anderson, John. THE AMERICAN THEATRE. New York: Dial Press, 1938. 424 p. Index, illus., bibliog.

The first one hundred pages offer a brief history of the American theatre, making mention of the leading actors, although in no significant depth.

116 Atkinson, Brooks. BROADWAY. New York: Macmillan Co., 1970. 461 p. Index, illus.

Atkinson deals only with the New York theatre of this century and concentrates on scripts rather than performers, but he does include a chapter on the Barrymores.

117 _____. BROADWAY SCRAPBOOK. New York: Theatre Arts, 1947. x, 303 p. Index, illus.

A collection of seventy articles on various aspects of the theatre, reprinted from the Sunday editions of the New York TIMES. Among the performers described are Katharine Cornell, Helen Hayes, Laurette Taylor, the Lunts, and Ruth Gordon.

118 Baker, Henry Barton. HISTORY OF THE LONDON STAGE AND ITS FA-MOUS PLAYERS 1576-1903. New York: Dutton, 1904. Reprint. New York and London: Benjamin Blom, 1969. 646 p. Index, frontispiece.

A substantial treatment of the subject including descriptions of the Booths, Jeffersons, Botherns, Boucicaults, and the Wallacks.

119 _____. THE LONDON STAGE: ITS HISTORY AND TRADITIONS FROM 1576 TO 1889. London: W. H. Allen and Co., 1889. xiv, 296; 308 p. Index.

> An English historian's perceptions of Edwin Forrest, Charlotte Cushman, Dion Boucicault, Charles Fechter, and Joseph Jefferson III on the London stage.

120 Ball, Robert Hamilton. THE AMAZING CAREER OF SIR GILES OVER-REACH BEING THE LIFE AND ADVENTURES OF A NEFARIOUS SCOUNDREL. WHO FOR THREE CENTURIES PURSUED HIS SINISTER DESIGNS IN ALMOST ALL THE THEATRES OF THE BRITISH ISLES AND AMERICA, THE WHOLE COMPROMISING A HISTORY OF THE STAGE. Princeton, N.J., and London: Princeton University Press, 1939. ix, 438 p. Index, illus., bibliog.

> A stage history of Massinger's play, A NEW WAY TO PAY OLD DEBTS (1625), with descriptions of major actors in the role of Overreach, among them the elder and Edwin Booth, Thomas Abthorpe Cooper, E. L. Davenport, Edwin Forrest, and Walter Hampden.

121 Blake, Charles. AN HISTORICAL ACCOUNT OF THE PROVIDENCE STAGE; BEING A PAPER READ BEFORE THE RHODE ISLAND HISTORICAL SOCIETY, OCTOBER 25TH, 1860 (WITH ADDITIONS). Providence: George H. Whitney, 1868. 297 p.

> An account of the Providence theatre from 1745 to 1860, with descriptions of engagements by the Hallams, David Douglass, John Henry, John Hodgkinson, Thomas Abthorpe Cooper, John Howard Payne, James Wallack, Edwin Forrest, Clara Fisher, and the elder Booth, as well as many lesser performers. Admittedly incomplete, but nevertheless valuable.

122 Blum, Daniel. A PICTORIAL HISTORY OF THE AMERICAN THEATRE. New York: Greenberg, 1950. 276 p. New York: Greenberg, 1951. 304 p. New York: Grosset and Dunlap, 1953. 304 p. New York: Greenberg, 1956. 319 p. Philadelphia: Chilton; New York: Bonanza, 1960. 384 p. New York: Crown, 1969. 416 p. New York: Crown, 1981. 448 p. Index, illus.

> Primarily a compilation of theatrical photographs arranged chronologically, these volumes have brief texts and comprehensive indexes.

123 Bost, James. MONARCHS OF THE MIMIC WORLD OR THE AMERICAN THEATRE OF THE EIGHTEENTH CENTURY THROUGH THE MANAGERS-- THE MEN WHO MADE IT. Orono: University of Maine at Orono Press, 1977. xii, 194 p. Index, illus., notes.

> A lively and unusually arranged volume describing managerial practices in early America. Among those described are John

Bernard, Thomas Abthorpe Cooper, David Douglass, John Durang, James Fennell, the Hallams, John Henry, John Hodgkinson, Mrs. Merry, Lester Wallack, Thomas Wignell, and William Wood.

124   Briscoe, Johnson. THE DRAMATIC RECORD AND GUIDE FOR 1912. Brooklyn: Printed for the Guide Printing and Publishing Co., 1913. 64 p.

Verified in the National Union Catalog, but unavailable for examination.

125   Brown, Thomas Allston. HISTORY OF THE AMERICAN STAGE, CONTAINING BIOGRAPHICAL SKETCHES OF NEARLY EVERY MEMBER OF THE PROFESSION THAT HAS APPEARED ON THE AMERICAN STAGE, FROM 1733 TO 1870. New York: Dick and Fitzgerald, 1870. Reprint. New York: Benjamin Blom, 1969; New York: Burt Franklin, 1969. 421 p. Illus.

An encyclopedic treatment. The entries are usually quite brief, and the illustrations are poorly done.

126   _____. HISTORY OF THE NEW YORK STAGE, FROM THE FIRST PERFORMANCE IN 1732 TO 1901. New York: Dodd, Mead, 1903. 3 vols. Reprint. New York: Benjamin Blom, 1964.

Brown attempted to document completely the New York stage for the period named with deeper coverage than that of Joseph Norton Ireland. Useful, but superseded by Odell's ANNALS, no. 218.

127   Buell, William Ackerman. THE HAMLETS OF THE THEATRE. New York: Aston-Honor, 1968. 175 p. Illus., bibliog.

Contains descriptions, quotations, and graphic materials describing eighteen of the more successful portrayers of the Dane, among them Edwin Forrest, Edwin Booth, Charles Fechter, E. H. Sothern, Walter Hampden, and John Barrymore. Buell devotes only a few pages to each, but includes useful illustrations.

128   Bunner, H.C., et al. A PORTFOLIO OF PLAYERS WITH A PACKET OF NOTES THEREON BY H.C. BUNNER, E.A. DITHMAR, LAURENCE HUTTON, BRANDER MATTHEWS, AND WILLIAM WINTER. New York: J. W. Bouton, 1888. Unpaged. Illus.

A tribute to Augustin Daly's company, including Ada Rehan, James Lewis, Mrs. Gilbert, John Drew, and Charles Fisher. Edition limited to 110 copies.

129   Cahn, William. THE LAUGH MAKERS: A PICTORICAL HISTORY OF AMERICAN COMEDIANS. New York: G. P. Putnam's Sons, 1957. Rev. ed. A PICTORIAL HISTORY OF THE GREAT COMEDIANS. New

York: Grosset and Dunlap, 1970. 190 p. Index, illus., bibliog.

A popularized theatre history including brief descriptions of Joseph Jefferson III, Harrigan and Hart, May Irwin, John E. Owens, and Thomas Wignell.

130   Carlisle, Carol Jones. SHAKESPEARE FROM THE GREEN ROOM: ACTORS' CRITICISM OF FOUR MAJOR TRAGEDIES. Chapel Hill: University of North Carolina Press, 1969. xiv, 476 p. Index, notes.

A well-researched compilation of Shakespearean criticism by English and American performers about HAMLET, OTHELLO, KING LEAR, and MACBETH. American performers quoted substantially include Mary Anderson, Daniel Bandmann, Lawrence Barrett, John Barrymore, Edwin Booth, the elder Booth, Dion Boucicault, Thomas Abthorpe Cooper, Charlotte Cushman, Charles Fechter, James H. Hackett, Joseph Jefferson III, Eva Le Gallienne, Julia Marlowe, Clara Morris, James E. Murdoch, Otis Skinner, E. H. Sothern, Frederick B. Warde, and William Wood.

131   Carroll, David. THE MATINEE IDOLS. New York: Arbor House, 1972. 155 p. Index, illus.

A volume more useful for its many photographs than for its undocumented text. Actors discussed include John Wilkes Booth, Harry Montague, Charles Fechter, Frank Mayo, Maurice and John Barrymore, Wilton Lackaye, Robert Mantell, John Drew, James K. Hackett, Henry Miller, and William Faversham.

132   Carson, William G[lasgow]. B[ruce]. MANAGERS IN DISTRESS; THE ST. LOUIS STAGE, 1840-1844. St. Louis Historical Documents Foundation, 1949. xv, 313 p. Index, illus., bibliog.

A sequel to Carson's THE THEATRE ON THE FRONTIER covering five seasons of unrest and misfortune on the St. Louis stage. Substantial references to Noah Ludlow, Sol Smith, Edwin Forrest, and Joseph Jefferson III.

133   _____. THE THEATRE ON THE FRONTIER; THE EARLY YEARS OF THE ST. LOUIS STAGE. Chicago: University of Chicago Press, 1932. xi, 335 p. Index, illus., bibliog.

An exemplary piece of theatrical scholarship, this volume examines the St. Louis theatre from the beginning to about 1839. Important actresses and actors described include Noah Ludlow, the Drakes, the Caldwells, Sol Smith, and Edwin Forrest.

134   Churchill, Allen. THE GREAT WHITE WAY: A RE-CREATION OF BROADWAY'S GOLDEN ERA OF THEATRICAL ENTERTAINMENT. New

York: E. P. Dutton and Co., 1962. 304 p. Index, illus., bibliog.

An undocumented history of the New York stage from 1900 to 1919, including the formation of Actors' Equity and the resulting strike.

135 _____. THE THEATRICAL 20'S. New York: McGraw-Hill Book Co., 1975. 316 p. Index, illus., bibliog.

A heavily illustrated, year-by-year account of the major events in the New York entertainment industry during the 1920's. Primarily focused on popular entertainment and musical comedy, but contains some information about the legitimate stage and some of its stars, such as the Barrymores, David Belasco, Ina Claire, the Lunts, Helen Hayes, Joseph Schildkraut, and Eva Le Gallienne.

136 Clapp, William, Jr. A RECORD OF THE BOSTON STAGE. Boston and Cambridge, Mass.: James Munroe and Co., 1853. xiii, 479 p. Reprint. New York: Greenwood Press, 1969.

A detailed history, originally published in the Boston EVENING GAZETTE. For index, see no. 43.

137 Clurman, Harold. THE FERVENT YEARS: THE STORY OF THE GROUP THEATRE AND THE THIRTIES. New York and London: Harcourt Brace Jovanovich, 1945. 320 p. Index, illus.

Richly descriptive of Clurman's work with Lee Strasberg. Others described include Stella Adler and Morris Carnovsky.

138 Coad, Oral Sumner. "The American Theatre in the 18th Century." SOUTH ATLANTIC QUARTERLY 17 (July 1918): 190-97.

Brief documentation of the Hallams, David Douglass, and Thomas Wignell.

139 _____. "Stage and Players in Eighteenth Century America." JOURNAL OF ENGLISH AND GERMANIC PHILOLOGY 19 (1920): 201-3.

A gracefully written account of early American theatre with evaluations of Mr. and Mrs. Hodgkinson, Mrs. Merry, and Thomas Abthorpe Cooper. Also describes scenic practices and dramaturgy.

140 Coad, Oral Sumner, and Mims, Edwin, Jr. THE AMERICAN STAGE. Pageant of America Series, vol. 14. New Haven, Conn.: Yale University Press, 1929. 342 p. Index, illus.

Remarkable for its profuse illustrations. Contains brief biographical and critical accounts of most of the leading players of the eighteenth and nineteenth century. Basic to any collection.

141 Crawford, Mary Caroline. THE ROMANCE OF THE AMERICAN THEATRE. Boston: Little, Brown and Co., 1913. xiv, 400 p. Index, illus.

An unexceptional history of the American theatre with brief sections on Edwin Forrest, Charles Fechter, and Edwin Booth.

142 Crowther, Bosley. THE LION'S SHARE: THE STORY OF AN ENTERTAIN-MENT EMPIRE. New York: E. P. Dutton and Co., 1957. 312 p. Index, illus.

While primarily a history of the Hollywood cinema, this volume deals with a few of the stage stars who settled there; for example, the Barrymores, Marie Dressler, and Lillian Gish.

143 Daly, Charles P. FIRST THEATRE IN AMERICA: WHEN WAS THE DRAMA FIRST INTRODUCED IN AMERICA? AN INQUIRY. New York: Dunlap Society, 1896. Reprint. Port Washington, N.Y.: Kennikat Press, 1968. 115 p. Frontispiece.

Daly attempts to clarify the origin of American theatre and deals to a limited extent with the Hallams and David Douglass.

144 Dithmar, Edward A[ugustus]. MEMORIES OF ONE THEATRE, WITH PAS-SING RECOLLECTIONS OF MANY OTHERS, INCLUDING A RECORD OF PLAYS AND ACTORS AT THE FIFTH AVENUE THEATRE, 1869-1877. 1891, 1893.

Verified in NATIONAL UNION CATALOG, but unavailable for examination.

145 Donohue, Joseph W., Jr., ed. THE THEATRICAL MANAGER IN ENG-LAND AND AMERICA: PLAYERS OF A PERILOUS GAME: PHILIP HENSLOWE, TATE WILKINSON, STEPHEN PRICE, EDWIN BOOTH, CHARLES WYNDAM. Princeton, N.J.: Princeton University Press, 1971. xii, 216 p. Illus.

Five essays, the third of which, "'King Stephen' of the Park and Drury Lane," (pp. 87-141), by Barnard Hewitt, describes Stephen Price's management and his relationship with Thomas Abthorpe Cooper. The fourth, "The Theatrical Management of Edwin Booth" (pp. 143-88), by Charles Shattuck, examines Booth's managerial failures.

146 Dorman, James H., Jr. THEATRE IN THE ANTE-BELLUM SOUTH, 1815-1861. Chapel Hill: University of North Carolina, 1967. 309 p. Index, illus., bibliog.

A well-documented, scholarly history containing relevant material concerning the elder Booth, Edwin Booth, James Caldwell, Thomas Abthorpe Cooper, Julia Dean, Samuel Drake, Edwin Forrest,

James H. Hackett, the Hallams, the Hollands, Joseph Jefferson III, Noah Ludlow, Dan Marble, Anna Cora Mowatt, the Placides, Sol Smith, James Wallach, and Francis Wemyss.

147 Dunlap, William. HISTORY OF THE AMERICAN THEATRE AND ANECDOTES OF THE PRINCIPAL ACTORS. New York: J. and J. Harper, 1832. Reprint. New York: Burt Franklin, 1963. 387 p. Frontispiece.

While not completely trustworthy, Dunlap was the first to publish an American theatre history. The Franklin edition includes a twenty-three page work by John Hodgkinson, A NARRATIVE OF HIS CONNECTION WITH THE OLD AMERICAN COMPANY, 1792-1797, first published in 1797.

148 Dunn, Esther Cloudman. SHAKESPEARE IN AMERICA. New York: Macmillan Co., 1939. xiv, 306 p. Index, illus.

An attempt to combine cultural history with the establishment of the Shakespearean tradition in the United States. Among the performers described are the Booths, the Chapmans, Thomas Abthorpe Cooper, David Douglass, Edwin Forrest, James H. Hackett, the Hallams, Joseph Jefferson III, Noah Ludlow, Sol Smith, William B. Wood, and William Warren.

149 Eaton, Walter Prichard. THE ACTOR'S HERITAGE: SCENES FROM THE THEATRE OF YESTERDAY AND THE DAY BEFORE. Boston: Atlantic Monthly Press, 1924. 287 p. Index, illus.

A highly selective but eminently readable history of the theatre, lacking documentation. Substantial quotations from Olive Logan's APROPOS OF WOMEN AND THEATRES.

150 _____. THE AMERICAN STAGE OF TO-DAY. Boston: Small, Maynard and Co., 1908. 338 p.

A sprawling collection of critical essays, focused more on the drama than acting, but containing evaluations of Henry Miller, Mrs. Fiske, Otis Skinner, Robert Mantell, David Belasco, George M. Cohan, Nazimova, and E. H. Sothern.

151 _____. AT THE NEW THEATRE AND OTHERS. THE AMERICAN STAGE: ITS PROBLEMS AND PERFORMANCES 1908-1910. Boston: Small, Maynard and Co., 1910. 359 p.

A series of reprinted critical accounts of such performers as John Drew, Ethel Barrymore, Mrs. Fiske, Nazimova, William Faversham, and Otis Skinner.

152 _____. THE THEATRE GUILD: THE FIRST TEN YEARS. New York:

Brentano's, 1929. Reprint. Freeport, N.Y.: Books for Libraries Press, 1970. 299 p. Illus.

A detailed history of the Guild from 1919 to 1929.

153   Ernst, Alice Henson. TROUPING IN THE OREGON COUNTRY: A HISTORY OF FRONTIER THEATRE. Portland: Oregon Historical Society, 1961. xviii, 182 p. Index, illus., bibliog.

Undocumented but well-researched, this volume describes such frontier theatrical personnel as Lotta Crabtree, Julia Dean, James A. Herne, and David Belasco.

154   Estavan, Lawrence, ed. "San Francisco Theatre Research Monograph." 20 vols. Mimeographed. San Francisco: WPA Project, 1938-42. Index, illus., bibliog.

A series of pamphlets, of which several deal with U.S. performers: Vol. 3: biographies of the Starks, the Bakers, and the Chapmans. Vol. 4: the Booth family. Vol. 5: biographies of Lola Montez, Adah Isaacs Menken, and Mrs. Judah. Vol. 6: biographies of Lotta Crabtree and John McCullough. Vol. 11: biographies of Edwin Forrest and Catherine Sinclair. Vol. 20: biography of James O'Neill.

155   Field, Edwin A. THROUGH THE STAGE-DOOR: A COMPLETE HANDBOOK OF THE THEATRE. N.p.: n.p., 1896. 36 p. Illus.

A brief description of the commercial theatre practices of the day. Includes a brief chapter on acting from Joseph Jefferson III's autobiography and a list of the major theatres of the United States, their owners and managers.

156   Filon, Pierre Marie Augustin. THE ENGLISH STAGE. BEING AN ACCOUNT OF THE VICTORIAN DRAMA. Trans. by Frederic Whyte. London: John Milne, 1897. New York: Dodd, Mead and Co., 1897. 314 p. Index.

Contains brief descriptions of the London careers of E. A. Sothern and Dion Boucicault, the latter treated only as a dramatist.

157   Fiske, Harrison, Grey, ed. THE NEW YORK MIRROR ANNUAL AND DIRECTORY OF THE THEATRICAL PROFESSION FOR 1888. New York: New York Mirror, 1888. vi, 194 p. Index, illus., bibliog.

Most of the volume is devoted to a chronological dramatic record for 1887, to which are appended a necrology, a dramatic bibliography, a list of star, combination, and stock companies, and a directory for the theatrical profession in the United States.

158   Ford, Paul Leicester. WASHINGTON AND THE THEATRE. New York: Dunlap Society, 1899. Reprint. New York: Benjamin Blom, 1967. 68 p. Illus.

Describes several of the leading actors Washington saw, such as the Hallams, Thomas Wignell, and John Henry. Appended is a script of DARBY'S RETURN, as played by Wignell 24 November 1789.

159   Foster, Lois M. ANNALS OF THE SAN FRANCISCO STAGE: 1850-1880. San Francisco: Federal Theatre, 1937. 307 p. Bibliog.

The first of two volumes (see no. 209), giving an overview of the subject with brief accounts of the major stars who worked the West Coast during this period.

160   Fox, Dixon Ryan. "The Development of the American Theatre." PROCEEDINGS OF THE NEW YORK STAGE HISTORICAL ASSOCIATION 17 (January 1936): 22-41. Illus.

The text of an address given 30 September 1935 at the society's annual meeting. A solid overview with only passing references to specific performers, but a useful description of early conditions for actors in the United States.

161   Francis, John W[akefield]. OLD NEW YORK OR, REMINISCENCES OF THE PAST SIXTY YEARS, BEING AN ENLARGED AND REVISED EDITION OF THE ANNIVERSARY DISCOURSE DELIVERED BEFORE THE NEW YORK HISTORICAL SOCIETY (NOVEMBER 17, 1857). New York: Charles Roe, 1858. 384 p. Reprint. New York: Benjamin Blom, 1971. cxxxvi, 400 p. Index.

Beginning on page 191, Francis describes the early American stage, for which he has no great admiration. Among the performers he describes are John Howard Payne and Thomas Abthorpe Cooper.

162   Frohman, Daniel. ENCORE. New York: Lee Furman, 1937. 282 p. Index, illus., bibliog. Reprint. Freeport, N.Y.: Books for Libraries, 1970.

A compendium of anecdotes with some historical pretension. Substantial mention is made of Edwin Booth and Dion Boucicault.

163   Fuller, Edward, ed. THE DRAMATIC YEAR [1887-88]: BRIEF CRITICISMS OF IMPORTANT THEATRICAL EVENTS IN THE UNITED STATES WITH A SKETCH OF THE SEASON IN LONDON, BY WILLIAM ARCHER. Boston: Ticknor and Co., 1889. v, 268 p.

Contains several relevant articles, such as George Edgar Montgomery's "The Last Year of 'Wallack's'" J. Ranken Towse's "The Wallack Testimonial," Montgomery's "Daly's Theatre,"

C. T. Copeland's "Mr. Harrigan's Latest Play," Edward Fuller's "Mdme. Janauschek," Howard Malcom Ticknor's "The Two Tragedians, Booth and Barrett," and C. T. Copeland's "Mr. Boucicault and Irish Drama," "Miss Morris in 'Renee de Moray,'" "Mr. Frederick Warde," and "Mr. Sothern's First Tour."

164   Gagey, Edmond M. THE SAN FRANCISCO STAGE: A HISTORY. New York: Columbia University Press, 1950. 233 p. Index, illus., bibliog. Reprint. Westport, Conn.: Greenwood Press, 1970.

A well-documented history with substantial accounts of many players and theatrical figures, among them Maude Adams, Lawrence Barrett, Blanche Bates, David Belasco, the Booths, Dion Boucicault, the Chapmans, Lotta Crabtree, Augustin Daly, the Drews, Mrs. Fiske, Laura Keene, Walter Leman, John McCullough, Frank Mayo, Adah Issacs Menken, Catherine Sinclair, and the Wallacks.

165   Gallegly, Joseph. FOOTLIGHTS ON THE BORDER: THE GALVESTON AND HOUSTON STAGE BEFORE 1900. The Hague: Mouton and Co., 1962. 236 p. Index, illus., bibliog. New York: Humanities Press, 1962.

A well-documented account developed chronologically. Several performers are described, among them Edwin Booth, Lawrence Barrett, Joseph Jefferson III, Louis James, Richard Mansfield, Clara Morris, and James O'Neill.

166   Gard, Robert E., and Semmes, David. AMERICA'S PLAYERS. New York: Seaborg Press, 1967. 152 p. Illus., bibliog.

A simplistic history of U.S. acting, written for children, offering superficial accounts of the Hallams, the Drakes, Noah Ludlow, James H. Caldwell, the Chapmans, Charlotte Cushman, Lotta Crabtree, Edwin Forrest, Joseph Jefferson III, Edwin Booth, David Belasco, Modjeska, Richard Mansfield, and William Gillette.

167   Garfield, David. A PLAYER'S PLACE: THE STORY OF THE ACTOR'S STUDIO. New York: Macmillan Publishing Co., 1980. xii, 300 p. Index, illus., bibliog.

A history of the institution, dealing with the contributions of Stella Adler and Morris Carnovsky, as well as Lee Strasberg, from whom Garfield obtained most of his information and insights.

168   Gilbert, Douglas. AMERICAN VAUDEVILLE ITS LIFE AND TIMES. New York and London: Whittlesey House, 1940. 410 p. Index, illus.

This volume describes several performers who had careers on the legitimate stage as well, among them May Irwin and Elsie Janis.

169   Glover, Lyman B[eecher]. THE STORY OF A THEATRE. Chicago: R. R. Donnelley, [1898]. 129 p. Illus.

Scraps of information concerning performers who appeared at Power's (formerly Hooley's) Theatre in Chicago from 1871 to about the turn of the century.

170   Graham, Franklin. HISTRIONIC MONTREAL: ANNALS OF THE MONTREAL STAGE WITH BIOGRAPHICAL AND CRITICAL NOTICES OF THE PLAYERS OF A CENTURY. Montreal: John Lovell and Son, Publishers, 1902. 303 p. Index, illus.

A biographical encyclopedia which includes capsule sketches of many nineteenth-century American performers.

171   Grebanier, Bernard. THEN CAME EACH ACTOR: SHAKESPEAREAN ACTORS, GREAT AND OTHERWISE, INCLUDING PLAYERS AND PRINCES, ROGUES, VAGABONDS AND ACTORS MOTLEY, FROM WILL KEMPE TO OLIVIER AND GIELGUD AND AFTER. New York: David McKay Co., 1975. xii, 591 p. Index, illus., bibliog.

An ambitious attempt, drawn from an impressive bibliography. Contains substantial sections of Edwin Forrest and Edwin Booth, lesser ones on Modjeska, McCullough, and E. L. Davenport.

172   Green, Abel, ed. THE SPICE OF VARIETY. New York: Henry Holt and Co., 1952. viii, 277 p.

A series of reprinted articles from VARIETY, including "How Ethel Barrymore, 26, Interviewed Ashton Stevens, 33," and an essay, "George M. Cohan," by Charles B. Cochran.

173   Green, Abel, and Laurie, Joe, Jr. SHOW BIZ FROM VAUDE TO VIDEO. Garden City, N.J.: Doubleday and Co., 1953. 531 p. Index.

This volume is written in "Varietyese" and "is intended to be breezy and gay as well as informative." The legitimate stage is included in the coverage from 1905 to the 1950s; a useful glossary of entertainment terms is appended.

174   Green, Roger Lancelyn. FIFTY YEARS OF PETER PAN. London: Peter Davies, 1954. xiii, 244 p. Index, illus., bibliog.

A stage history of the conception, execution, and staging of Barrie's PETER PAN, with brief sections on Maude Adams and Eva Le Gallienne.

175   Hagan, John S. G. RECORDS OF THE NEW YORK STAGE FROM 1860- 1870 . . . CONTAINING ILLUSTRATIONS . . . SCENES FROM PLAYS,

VIEWS, & C., COLLECTED AND ARRANGED BY GEORGE P. ELDER.
4 vols. New York: 1880.

Located at Cornell University Library, but unavailable for examination.

176   Hall, [William T.] "Biff." THE TURNOVER CLUB. TALES TOLD AT
        THE MEETINGS OF THE TURNOVER CLUB, ABOUT ACTORS AND
        ACTRESSES. Chicago and New York: Rand McNally and Co., 1890.
        234 p.

        The Turnover Club was a social organization which met weekly
        in Chicago, beginning in 1885. Hall describes the conversations
        during the meetings, some of which concerned performers, among
        them Nat Goodwin, William Crane, Louis James, Stuart Robson,
        Edwin Booth, John McCullough, and John T. Raymond. The
        remarks are anecdotal and frivolous.

177   Hapgood, Norman. THE STAGE IN AMERICA 1897-1900. New York:
        Macmillan Co., 1901. 396 p. Index.

        A perceptive analysis of the theatre of the time, focused on
        dramaturgy for the most part, but including descriptions of the
        following performers: Maude Adams, Augustin Daly, Mrs. Fiske,
        William Gillette, Nat C. Goodwin, Joseph Jefferson III, Richard Mansfield, Ada Rehan, E.H. Sothern, and Francis Wilson.

178   Harding, Alfred. THE REVOLT OF THE ACTORS. New York: William
        Morrow and Co., 1929. xiii, 570 p. Index, illus.

        A detailed account of the formation of Actors' Equity. Contains
        substantial sections on Ethel Barrymore, David Belasco, George
        M. Cohan, Marie Dressler, E. H. Sothern, and Francis Wilson.

179   Hewitt, Barnard. THEATRE U.S.A. 1665 TO 1957. New York, Toronto,
        and London: McGraw-Hill Book Co., 1959. xi, 513 p. Index, illus.,
        bibliog.

        For many years, this was the most popular history of the American theatre. About 75 percent of the volume is quoted source
        material, the remainder commentary and continuity. Most major
        performers are included.

180   Hill, West T., Jr. THE THEATRE IN EARLY KENTUCKY 1790-1820.
        Lexington: University Press of Kentucky, 1971. 192 p. Index, illus.,
        bibliog.

        A well-documented account of frontier theatre, including substantial accounts of John Bernard, the Chapman family, Joe
        Cowell, the Drake family, the Jefferson family, and Noah Ludlow.

181   Hodge, Francis. YANKEE THEATRE: THE IMAGE OF AMERICA ON THE
       STAGE, 1825–1850. Austin: University of Texas Press, 1964. 296 p.
       Index, illus., bibliog.

       Hodge, in analyzing American comedy between 1825 and 1850,
       focuses upon Yankee specialists: James H. Hackett, George H.
       Hill, and Dan Marble. Outstanding scholarship is supported by
       a valuable bibliography.

182   Hoole, William Stanley. THE ANTE-BELLUM CHARLESTON THEATRE.
       Tuscaloosa: University of Alabama Press, 1946. xx, 230 p. Index, illus.

       An encyclopedic treatment of the subject, useful for specifying
       the activities of the Placides, the Booths, Thomas Abthorpe
       Cooper, Julia Dean, and James H. Hackett.

183   Hornblow, Arthur. A HISTORY OF THE THEATRE IN AMERICA FROM ITS
       BEGINNINGS TO THE PRESENT TIME. 2 vols. Philadelphia: J. B.
       Lippincott and Co., 1919. 356, 351 p. Index, illus.

       A useful detailed account of the American theatre. Chapters
       and partial chapters on many leading performers, among them
       the Hallams, David Douglass, the elder Wallack, the Hacketts,
       Edwin Forrest, the Hollands, Mrs. Drew, Joseph Jefferson III
       Charlotte Cushman, Dion Boucicault, and Edwin Booth.

184   Hoyt, Harlowe R. TOWN HALL TONIGHT. Englewood Cliffs, N.J.:
       Prentice-Hall, 1955. 279 p. Index, illus.

       Hoyt describes in lively prose the nature of the provincial thea-
       tre in this country in the nineteenth century, specifically that
       operated by his father in Beaver Dam, Wisconsin. Corraboration
       required.

185   Huggett, Richard. SUPERNATURAL ON STAGE: GHOSTS AND SUPER-
       STITIONS OF THE THEATRE. New York: Taplinger Publishing Co.,
       1975. 215 p. Illus.

       A gracefully written volume of theatrical superstitions, including
       those practiced by the Barrymores, the Lunts, and Tallulah Bank-
       head. John Wilkes Booth, Jeanne Eagels, and David Belasco
       are given brief attention.

186   Hughes, Glenn. A HISTORY OF THE AMERICAN THEATRE 1700-1950.
       New York and London: Samuel French, 1951. ix, 514 p. Index, illus.,
       bibliog.

       A relatively traditional approach to the subject, useful for an
       overview of American theatre history, with coverage of most
       leading performers.

187 Hutton, Laurence. CURIOSITIES OF THE AMERICAN STAGE. New York: Harper and Brothers, 1891. xv, 330 p. Index, illus.

Hutton mentions practically every U.S. performer of note from the Hallams to the date of publication. Substantial sections include the Indian drama, war dramas, frontier drama, "stage Americans," stage blacks, and American Hamlets. Edwin Booth and G. L. Fox are treated with some substance.

188 Ireland, Joseph Norton. [H.N.D.] FIFTY YEARS OF A PLAY-GOER'S JOURNAL; OR, ANNALS OF THE NEW YORK STAGE, FROM A. D. 1798 to A. S. 1848. WITH BIOGRAPHICAL SKETCHES OF THE PRINCI-PAL PERFORMERS. 3 vols. in 1 vol. New York: Samuel French, Publisher, 1860. vi, 288 p.

Valuable insights into the Hallams, John Hodgkinson, Joseph Jefferson III, Thomas Abthorpe Cooper, James Fennell, Mrs. Merry, the Placides, Thomas Wignell, William Wood, William Warren, Elizabeth Poe, John Durang, John J. Holland, and others. In spite of the title, coverage only goes through the 1818-19 season. See next entry.

189 _____. RECORDS OF THE NEW YORK STAGE, FROM 1750 TO 1860. 2 vols. New York: T. H. Morrell, 1866. Reprint. New York: Benja-min Blom, 1966. 668, 708 p. Index.

An amplified version of the previous entry.

190 Isaacs, Edith J. R. THE NEGRO IN THE AMERICAN THEATRE. New York: Theatre Arts, 1947. 143 p. Illus.

Among the black stars of the legitimate stage described are Ira Aldridge, Charles Gilpin, and Rose McClendon.

191 Isman, Felix. WEBER AND FIELDS: THEIR TRIBULATIONS, TRIUMPHS AND THEIR ASSOCIATES. New York: Boni and Liveright, 1924. xii, 345 p. Illus.

A richly detailed but undocumented account of the variety team, including descriptions of some of the work done in their com-pany by Lillian Russell, Fay Templeton, David Warfield, and DeWolf Hopper.

192 James, Reese Davis. CRADLE OF CULTURE, 1800-1810: THE PHILA-DELPHIA STAGE. Philadelphia: University of Pennsylvania Press, 1957. 143 p. Index, illus., bibliog.

A chronicle of productions in the Chestnut Street Theatre for the period named, drawn from periodicals and serials of that time. Includes the activities of such actors as Elizabeth Poe, Thomas Abthorpe Cooper, John Durang, the Hallams, John Hodg-kinson, Joseph Jefferson I, William Warren, Mrs. Merry, Thomas Wignell, and William Wood.

193 _____. OLD DRURY OF PHILADELPHIA. Philadelphia: University of Pennsylvania Press, 1932. xv, 635 p. Index.

James's doctoral dissertation, constituting a calendar of theatrical events from 1818 to 1835 with a useful index of scripts and performers. Includes the diary or daily account book of William Wood.

194 Johnson, James Weldon. BLACK MANHATTAN. New York: Alfred A. Knopf, 1940. viii, 284 p. Index, illus.

Johnson describes the theatrical contributions of Ira Aldridge, Charles Gilpin, and Rose McClendon.

195 Johnson, Robert Underwood. YOUR HALL OF FAME BEING AN ACCOUNT OF THE ORIGIN, ESTABLISHMENT, AND HISTORY OF THIS DIVISION OF NEW YORK UNIVERSITY FROM 1900 TO 1935 INCLUSIVE. New York: New York University, 1935. xx, 187 p. Index, illus.

Includes brief descriptions of the only two performers included, Edwin Booth and Charlotte Cushman.

196 Kendall, John S. THE GOLDEN AGE OF THE NEW ORLEANS THEATRE. Baton Rouge: Louisiana State University Press, 1952. 608 p. Index, illus., bibliog.

This substantial work contains relevant data on most American performers who had engagements in New Orleans, but is especially useful for the Caldwells and John E. Owens.

197 Kummer, George. "The Americanization of Burlesque, 1840-1860." THEATRE ANNUAL 27 (1971-72): 47-56. Illus.

Describes the contributions of William Burton and John Broughman.

198 Lahue, Kalton. LADIES IN DISTRESS. South Brunswick, N.J., and New York: A. S. Barnes and Co., 1971. London: Thomas Yoseloff, 1971. 334 p. Illus.

Superficial essays on the film careers of Pauline Frederick and Lillian Gish.

199 Leary, Lewis Gaston, comp. ARTICLES ON AMERICAN LITERATURE, 1950-1967. Durham, N.C.: Duke University Press, 1970. xxi, 751 p.

Theatre entries are grouped on pages 736-51. The work includes items relevant to such actor-playwrights as Dion Boucicault, William Gillette, and James A. Herne.

200 Lewis, Phillip C. TROUPING: HOW THE SHOW CAME TO TOWN.

New York, Evanston, San Francisco, and London: Harper and Row, 1973. 264 p. Index, illus., notes.

A popularized treatment with substantial sections on the tours of Edwin Booth, Joseph Jefferson III, James O'Neill, and Denman Thompson.

201   MacAdam, George. THE LITTLE CHURCH AROUND THE CORNER. New York and London: G. P. Putnam's Sons (Knickerbocker Press), 1925. 347 p. Illus.

A history of the Church of the Transfiguration at 1 East Twenty-ninth Street in New York, long associated with the theatre. Among the performers described are George Holland, Joseph Jefferson III, Harry Montague, Edwin Booth, and Richard Mansfield.

202   McGlinchee, Claire. THE FIRST DECADE OF THE BOSTON MUSEUM. Boston: Bruce Humphries, 1940. 362 p. Index, illus., bibliog.

Originated as a doctoral dissertation at Columbia University. Text consists of 172 pages, followed by 179 pages of day-to-day bills for the period covered, during which most leading performers appeared there.

203   MacMinn, George Rupert. THE THEATRE OF THE GOLDEN ERA IN CALIFORNIA. Caldwell, Idaho: Caxton Printers, 1941. 515 p. Index, illus., bibliog.

A history of frontier theatre and entertainment on the West Coast in the mid-nineteenth century, covering several forms of entertainment. Legitimate performers described include the Booths, Dion Boucicault, the Chapmans, Jean Davenport, Julia Dean, Matilda Heron, Laura Keene, and James E. Murdoch.

204   Marshall, Herbert, ed. HAMLET THROUGH THE AGES: A PICTORIAL RECORD FROM 1709 COMPILED BY RAYMOND MANDER AND JOE MITCHENSON. London: Rockliff, 1952. xvii, 151 p. Index, illus.

Copious notes support the 250 illustrations from various productions, arranged by scene. Most of the productions and performers are English, but material is included about John Barrymore, Lawrence Barrett, Edwin Booth, the elder Booth, Charlotte Cushman, Charles Fechter, Walter Hampden, and Eva Le Gallienne.

205   Marshall, Thomas Frederic. A HISTORY OF THE PHILADELPHIA THEATRE 1878-1890: AN ESSENTIAL PORTION OF A DOCTORAL DISSERTATION IN ENGLISH. Philadelphia: University of Pennsylvania, 1943. 54 p.

A partial reprint, representing lists of casts and productions for specific dates, useful in tracing the performers of the time.

206   Mates, Julian. THE AMERICAN MUSICAL STAGE BEFORE 1800. New
       Brunswick, N.J.: Rutgers University Press, 1962. ix, 313 p. Index,
       illus., bibliog.

       Although only examining the legitimate stage marginally, Mates
       includes biographical material on John Hodgkinson, Lewis Hal-
       lam, Jr., Joseph Jefferson I, John Durang, and minor performers.

207   May, Robin. A COMPANION TO THE THEATRE: THE ANGLO-
       AMERICAN STAGE FROM 1920. Guilford and London: Lutterworth,
       1973. New York: Hippocrene Books, 1975. 283 p. Index, illus.

       Pages 147-93 are entitled "West End and Broadway, Some Stars,
       Matinee Idols, Major Talents and Popular Favourites," and con-
       tain very brief and highly subjective descriptions of leading players.

208   Mayorga, Margaret G. A SHORT HISTORY OF THE AMERICAN DRAMA.
       New York: Dodd, Mead and Co., 1932. xxi, 472 p. Index, bibliog.

       Several actor-playwrights are discussed, among them Dion Bou-
       cicault, George M. Cohan, Harrigan and Hart, and James A.
       Herne.

209   Michael, C. Everett; Williams, Gordon; and Shapiro, Nadia. ANNALS
       OF THE SAN FRANCISCO STAGE 1880-1924. San Francisco: Federal
       Theatre, 1937. 317 p. Bibliog.

       See no. 159.

210   Moody, Richard. "American Actors and Acting Before 1900: The Making
       of a Tradition." In AMERICAN THEATRE: A SUM OF ITS PARTS, pp.
       40-81. New York: Samuel French, 1971.

       Moody offers a concise but penetrating overview of the actor's
       art in the United States, based on the work of such players as
       the Hallams, Mary Ann Duff, Thomas Abthorpe Cooper, Edwin
       Forrest, Charlotte Cushman, James Murdoch, E. L. Davenport,
       Anna Cora Mowatt, William Warren, Clara Fisher, and Edwin
       Booth.

211   _____. AMERICA TAKES THE STAGE: ROMANTICISM IN AMERICAN
       DRAMA AND THEATRE, 1750-1900. Bloomington: Indiana University
       Press, 1955. viii, 307 p. Index, frontispiece, bibliog.

       A major work by one of the outstanding American theatre scho-
       lars. Moody focuses on scripts and playwrights, but uses actors
       and others for illustrations of his ideas, among them David

Belasco, Edwin Booth, the elder Booth, Dion Boucicault, John Broughman, Augustin Daly, Edwin Forrest, William Gillette, James H. Hackett, James A. Herne, Joseph Jefferson III, Anna Cora Mowatt, John Howard Payne, Sol Smith, and the Wallacks.

212 _____. DRAMA FROM THE AMERICAN THEATRE, 1762-1909. New York: World, 1966. 973 p. Illus., bibliog.

Although the volume is a script anthology, each script is preceded by an introduction describing the playwright. Included are Anna Cora Mowatt's FASHION, John Broughman's POCA-HON-TAS, and James A. Herne's SHORE ACRES.

213 Morris, Lloyd R. CURTAIN TIME: THE STORY OF THE AMERICAN THEATRE. New York: Random House, 1953. xvi, 367 p. Index, illus.

A lively, anecdotal, and undocumented history of the American theatre, beginning in the early nineteenth century and mentioning almost all actors and actresses of note since then.

214 Moses, Montrose J. THE AMERICAN DRAMATIST. Boston: Little, Brown and Co., 1911. ix, 326 p. Index, illus., bibliog. Rev. ed. Boston: Little, Brown and Co., 1925. xiii, 459 p. Index, bibliog.

The 1911 edition gives substantial coverage to several American actor-playwrights, such as James A. Herne, David Belasco, Dion Boucicault, William Gillette, and Steele MacKaye. Moses completely revised the work for the 1925 edition, in which he again describes those listed above and adds Augustin Daly and John Howard Payne.

215 Moses, Montrose J., and Brown, John Mason. THE AMERICAN THEATRE AS SEEN BY ITS CRITICS 1752-1934. New York: W. W. Norton and Co., 1934. 391 p. Bibliog.

A collection of critical accounts of leading players, native and foreign, on the American stage as well as critical receptions to various scripts and dramatists. Valuable in that it makes available many accounts scattered through rare and defunct serials. Major articles on players are cross-indexed. Also contains thirty-six pages of brief biographical sketches of actors, playwrights, and critics mentioned in the text.

216 Nagler, A.M. A SOURCE BOOK IN THEATRICAL HISTORY. New York: Dover, 1952. xxiii, 601 p. Index, illus.

The twelfth section, "The American Theatre" (pp. 509-75) contains sections on Lewis Hallam, Sr., Edwin Forrest, William B. Wood, Edwin Booth, and David Belasco.

217   Norton, Elliott. BROADWAY DOWN EAST: AN INFORMAL ACCOUNT
       OF THE PLAYS, PLAYERS AND PLAYHOUSES OF BOSTON FROM PURI-
       TAN TIMES TO THE PRESENT. Boston: Boston Public Library, 1978.
       145 p. Index, illus., bibliog.

       Based on a series of lectures given at the Boston Public Library
       beginning 7 April 1977. Exceptionally well illustrated; written
       in a lively style. Most leading players are mentioned, though
       not in great detail.

218   Odell, George C[linton]. D[ensmore]. ANNALS OF THE NEW YORK
       STAGE. 15 vols. New York: Columbia University Press, 1927-49.
       Index, illus.

       An enormous landmark piece of scholarship which chronicles
       stage activity in New York from the beginning through Septem-
       ber 1894. Occasional errors, but of enormous value for any
       study of eighteenth- or nineteenth-century American theatre.

219   Ormsbee, Helen. BACKSTAGE WITH ACTORS FROM THE TIME OF
       SHAKESPEARE TO THE PRESENT DAY. New York: Thomas Y. Crowell
       Co., 1938. Reprint. New York and London: Benjamin Blom, 1969.
       343 p. Index, illus.

       Ormsbee attempts to survey almost all the acting tradition in
       the English language; in so doing, she describes to various degrees
       several of the stars of the American stage, among them Maude
       Adams, Edwin Booth, Arnold Daly, Mrs. Fiske, James A. Herne,
       Joseph Jefferson III, and Richard Mansfield.

220   Phelps, Henry Pitt. ADDENDA TO PLAYERS OF A CENTURY. A RECORD
       OF THE ALBANY STAGE. INCLUDING NOTICES OF PROMINENT
       ACTORS WHO HAVE APPEARED IN AMERICA. Albany, 1887.

       An addition to Phelps's earlier work, containing brief notices
       of the various actors appearing in Albany.

221   _____. HAMLET FROM THE ACTORS' STANDPOINT. ITS REPRESENTA-
       TIVES, AND A COMPARISON OF THEIR PERFORMANCES. New York:
       E.S. Werner, 1890. 170 p. Index, illus., bibliog.

       The first section, "The Hamlets of the Stage," describes the role's
       major delineators, among them the elder Booth, Edwin Forrest,
       Charles Fechter, and Edwin Booth. The second section, "A
       Comparison of Different Performers of Hamlet," describes various
       performances scene by scene.

222   _____. PLAYERS OF A CENTURY: A RECORD OF THE ALBANY STAGE.
       INCLUDING NOTICES OF PROMINENT ACTORS WHO HAVE APPEARED
       IN AMERICA. Albany, N.Y.: Joseph McDonough, 1880. Reprint. New

York: Benjamin Blom, 1972. x, 413 p. Index, frontispeice.

Phelps originally published most of this volume as a series of articles in the Albany ARGUS in 1879. He drew heavily upon newspapers, playbills, and interviews to create this chronicle, which makes references to nearly every player of note in this country from the beginning to 1880.

223 Phelps, William Lyon. TWENTIETH CENTURY THEATRE: OBSERVATION ON THE CONTEMPORARY ENGLISH AND AMERICAN STAGE. New York: Macmillan Co., 1918. ix, 144 p. Index.

Chapter 6, "Actors and Acting," describes the various contributions of Richard Mansfield and Maude Adams.

224 Phillips, Catherine Coffin. PORTSMOUTH PLAZA: THE CRADLE OF SAN FRANCISCO. San Francisco: Printed by John Henry Nash, 1932. 447 p. Index, illus., bibliog.

A regional history. Chapter 9, "Whispers in the Wings," describes early theatricals; succeeding chapters describe engagements by Catherine Sinclair, the Booths, and Julia Dean.

225 Pollock, Thomas Clark. THE PHILADELPHIA THEATRE IN THE EIGHTEENTH CENTURY TOGETHER WITH THE DAY BOOK OF THE SAME PERIOD. Philadelphia: University of Pennsylvania Press, 1933. Reprint. New York: Greenwood Press, 1968. 403 p. Index, frontispiece, bibliog.

Originally a dissertation, this volume documents the Philadelphia engagements of many outstanding performers, including the Hallams, David Douglass, Thomas Abthorpe Cooper, James Fennell, John Henry, Mr. and Mrs. Owen Morris, and William Warren.

226 Pyper, George D. THE ROMANCE OF AN OLD PLAYHOUSE. Salt Lake City: Seagull Press, 1928. 342 p. Illus.

A history of Salt Lake City theatre with substantial sections on Maude Adams and Julia Dean. Considerable detail.

227 Quinn, Arthur Hobson. A HISTORY OF THE AMERICAN DRAMA FROM THE BEGINNING TO THE CIVIL WAR. New York and London: Harper and Brothers, 1923; New York: F.S. Crofts and Co., 1943, 1944; New York: Appleton-Century-Crofts, 1951. xvi, 497 p. Index, bibliog.

An excellent general history, well documented. Although focused on dramaturgy, Quinn includes substantial accounts of the Hallams, John Howard Payne, Edwin Forrest, James H. Hackett, Anna Cora Mowatt, Lester Wallack, Julia Dean, E. L. Davenport, Lawrence Barrett, Otis Skinner, and Dion Boucicault.

228 _____. A HISTORY OF THE AMERICAN DRAMA FROM THE CIVIL WAR TO THE PRESENT DAY. New York and London: 1927; New York: Appleton-Century-Crofts, 1936; New York: F.S. Crofts, 1936; London: I. Pitman, 1937; New York: F.S. Crofts, 1937; New York: Crofts, 1943; New York: F.S. Crofts, 1945; New York: Appleton, 1955. xvi, 404 p. Index, illus., bibliog.

> Again centered upon the evolution of the American drama, with substantial sections on Augustin Daly, Edward Harrigan, James E. Murdoch, James E. Herne, David Belasco, Lawrence Barrett, E.H. Sothern, Otis Skinner, Richard Mansfield, William Gillette, George M. Cohan, and Frank Bacon.

229 Rahill, Frank. THE WORLD OF MELODRAMA. University Park and London: Pennsylvania State University Press, 1967. vii, 325 p. Index, bibliog.

> Chapter 30, "Uncle Tom's Cabin," repeats standard descriptions of the Howards, and chapter 32, "Melodrama Comes of Age," describes the contributions of David Belasco and William Gillette.

230 Rankin, Hugh F. THE THEATRE IN COLONIAL AMERICA. Chapel Hill: University of North Carolina Press, 1960, 1965. xiii, 223 p. Index, illus., bibliog.

> A meticulous scholarly work with substantial references to the Hallams, David Douglass, John Henry, and Mr. and Mrs. Owen Morris. Substantial and useful bibliography.

231 Rooker, Henry Grady. AN ABSTRACT OF THE STAGE HISTORY OF THE PORTRAYAL OF SHAKESPEARE'S CHARACTER, HAMLET. Contributions to Education Series, no. 205. Nashville: George Peabody College for Teachers, 1932. 35 p. Frontispiece.

> This dissertation abstract indicates coverage of the elder Booth, Edwin Forrest, Charles Fechter, Edwin Booth, and John Barrymore.

232 Rourke, Constance. THE ROOTS OF AMERICAN CULTURE AND OTHER ESSAYS. New York: Harcourt, Brace and Co., 1942. xii, 296 p. Index.

> In a lengthy essay, "The Rise of Theatricals," Rourke devotes a subsection (pp. 75-87) to Susanah Rowson and another (pp. 141-60) to the elder Booth.

233 Ryan, Kate. OLD BOSTON MUSEUM DAYS. Boston: Little, Brown and Co., 1915. xii, 250 p. Index, illus.

> Somewhat self-centered, but a nevertheless evocative account of the actress's life. Filled with anecdotes and reminiscences of such performers as Edwin Booth, Dion Boucicault, Janauschek, Richard Mansfield, Mrs. Vincent, and William Warren, Jr.

234 Sayler, Oliver Martin. OUR AMERICAN THEATRE. New York: Brentano's, 1923. xiv, 369 p. Index, illus.

An examination of theatrical conditions in the early 1920s with brief references to the leading actors and actresses of the time.

235 _____. REVOLT IN THE ARTS: A SURVEY OF THE CREATION, DISTRIBUTION AND APPRECIATION OF ART IN AMERICA. New York: Brentano's, n.d. [1930]. ix, 341 p. Index.

Sayler addresses the entire field of fine arts and includes the following theatrically oriented essays: David Belasco's "The Theatre--Art and Instinct"; Alfred Lunt's "The Actor as Artist"; Eva Le Gallienne's "The Repertory Theatre"; Lillian Gish's "On Behalf of the Silent Film," and Ruth Chatterton's "The Player in the Films."

236 Scott, Clement. THE DRAMA OF YESTERDAY AND TO-DAY. 2 vols. New York and London: Macmillan Co., 1899. xviii, 607, 558 p. Index, illus.

A history of the London stage from 1840 to 1899, containing substantial analyses of such visitors as Joseph Jefferson III, Dion Boucicault, Genevieve Ward, E.S. Willard, Edwin Booth, Charles Fechter, J.S. Clarke, Ada Rehan, and E.A. Sothern.

237 Seilhamer, George O. A HISTORY OF THE AMERICAN THEATRE. 3 vols. Philadelphia: Globe Printing House, 1888-91. Reprint. New York: Benjamin Blom, 1968. Index.

Volume 1 is subtitled "Before the Revolution"; volume 2, "During the Revolution and After," and volume 3, "New Foundations." Coverage terminates in the 1796-97 season. An immensely detailed study, invaluable for the study of this period.

238 Shattuck, Charles. SHAKESPEARE ON THE AMERICAN STAGE FROM THE HALLAMS TO EDWIN BOOTH. Washington, D.C.: Folger Shakespeare Library, 1976. xiv, 162 p. Index, illus., bibliog.

Shattuck examines and describes the work of every significant performer during the period indicated by the title. Exemplary documentation supports a clear and succinct style.

239 Sherman, Robert Lowery. "Chicago Stage: Its Record and Achievements; Volume One: Gives a Complete Record of all Entertainments and, Substantially, The Cast of Every Play Presented in Chicago, on its First Production in the City, From the Beginning of Theatricals in 1834 Down to the Last Before the Fire of 1871." Mimeographed. Chicago: Robert L. Sherman, 1947. 760 p.

A privately distributed volume. Sherman apparently intended three volumes, the second to cover Chicago theatre from 1871 to 1900 and the third to cover this century. The second and third volumes seem never to have appeared. Volume 1 documents engagements of most of the leading players of the time and includes lists of the Chicago theatres of the period.

240   Shockley, Martin Staples. THE RICHMOND STAGE 1784-1812. Charlottesville: University Press of Virginia, 1977. 420 p. Index, illus., bibliog.

Annals of the Richmond stage from the first professional company to the theatre fire of 1811. Meticulously researched. Performers recorded include George Barrett, the Hallams, John Henry, John Howard Payne, the Placides, Elizabeth Poe, Suzannah Rowson, Thomas Wade West, and Thomas Wignell.

241   Silverman, Kenneth. A CULTURAL HISTORY OF THE AMERICAN REVOLUTION: PAINTING, MUSIC, LITERATURE, AND THE THEATRE IN THE COLONIES AND THE UNITED STATES FROM THE TREATY OF PARIS TO THE INAUGURATION OF GEORGE WASHINGTON, 1763-1789. New York: Thomas Y. Crowell, 1976. 674 p. Index, illus., bibliog., notes.

The Hallams, David Douglass, John Henry, John Durang, and Thomas Wignell figure prominently in this exceptional scholarly work. Extremely useful.

242   Simon, Louis M. A HISTORY OF THE ACTORS' FUND OF AMERICA WITH SPECIAL CONTRIBUTIONS BY RUTH GORDON, NEDDA HARRIGAN LOGAN, CORNELIA OTIS SKINNER, AND JEAN LOGGIE. New York: Theatre Arts Books, 1972. x, 268 p. Index, illus.

The fund was founded in 1882. This volume has sections on Henry Miller, Lester Wallack, Ethel Barrymore, David Belasco, and Edwin Booth, as well as essays by Skinner and Gordon.

243   Smith, Cecil. MUSICAL COMEDY IN AMERICA. New York: Theatre Arts Books, 1950. x, 354 p. Index, illus. Rev. ed. by Smith, Cecil, and Litton, Glenn, 1981. 348 p. Index, illus.

Several players from the legitimate stage figure prominently in this history, among them George M. Cohan, Augustin Daly, Jefferson DeAngelis, George L. Fox, Edward Harrigan, DeWolf Hopper, Lillian Russell, Fred Stone, and Francis Wilson.

244   Smither, Nelle. "A History of the English Theatre at New Orleans, 1806-1842." LOUISIANA HISTORICAL QUARTERLY 28 (January-April 1945): 85-276, 361-572. Bibliog.

A published version of Smither's dissertation from Pennsylvania in 1942. The first section is a historical narrative, the latter the tabular material. Noah Ludlow, Sol Smith, James H. Caldwell, Thomas Abthorpe Cooper, the elder Booth, George Holland, and the Placides figure prominently.

245 Sprague, Arthur Colby. SHAKESPEARE AND THE ACTORS: THE STAGE BUSINESS IN HIS PLAYS (1660-1905). Cambridge, Mass.: Harvard University Press, 1944. xxv, 430 p. Index, illus., bibliog.

World War II prevented Sprague from using materials outside the United States when he prepared this volume, but it is a valuable compendium. Descriptions are made of the work of Maude Adams, Mary Anderson, Lawrence Barrett, Edwin Booth, the elder Booth, William E. Burton, Thomas Abthorpe Cooper, Charlotte Cushman, E.L. and Fanny Davenport, William Davidge, Mrs. Duff, Charles Fechter, James Fennell, Edwin Forrest, James H. Hackett, Walter Hampden, Louis James, Janauschek, James Lewis, John McCullough, Richard Mansfield, Julia Marlowe, Modjeska, James E. Murdoch, Ada Rehan, Kate Reignolds-Winslow, Otis Skinner, E.H. Sothern, George Vandenhoff, James W. Wallack, Genevieve Ward, Frederick Ward, and William Warren.

246 _____. SHAKESPEAREAN PLAYERS AND PERFORMANCES. Cambridge, Mass.: Harvard University Press, 1953. viii, 216 p. Index, illus., notes. Reprint. With a new preface by the author. New York: Greenwood, 1969.

A brief history of Shakespearean acting, including a chapter on Edwin Booth as Iago, originally published in THEATRE ANNUAL. Other performances substantially treated are the elder Booth, Edwin Forrest, and Walter Hampden.

247 Steinberg, Mollie B. THE HISTORY OF THE FOURTEENTH STREET THEATRE. New York: Dial Press, 1931. 105 p. Illus.

This theatre, built in 1866, fell into neglect in 1901. In 1926, Eva Le Gallienne reopened it as the Civic Repertory Theatre. Besides Le Gallienne, Steinberg briefly examines the engagements of Jean Davenport, Edwin Forrest, Laura Keene, Charles Fechter, Edwin Booth, Fanny Davenport, Modjeska, Robert Mantell, Clara Morris, Chauncey Olcott, and Nazimova.

248 Stirling, Edward. OLD DRURY LANE: FIFTY YEARS' RECOLLECTIONS OF AUTHOR, ACTOR, AND MANAGER. 2 vols. London: Chatto and Windus, 1881. 363, 356 p. Index.

Includes brief accounts of the elder Booth and Dion Boucicault and their careers in London.

249 Stone, Henry Dickinson. PERSONAL RECOLLECTIONS OF THE DRAMA OR THEATRICAL REMINISCENCES, EMBRACING SKETCHES OF PROMINENT ACTORS AND ACTRESSES, THEIR CHIEF CHARACTERISTICS, ORIGINAL ANECDOTES OF THEM AND INCIDENTS CONNECTED THEREWITH. Albany, N.Y.: C. van Benthuysen, 1873. Reprint. New York: Benjamin Blom, 1969. 316 p. Illus.

Stone's account is amusing but not especially accurate. Dozens of anecdotes permeate the work, especially concerning Edwin Forrest and Charlotte Cushman. See no. 76 for index.

250   Taubman, Howard. THE MAKING OF THE AMERICAN THEATRE. New York: Coward McCann, 1965. 372 p. Index, illus.

An undocumented general history, somewhat focused upon dramaturgy but including brief descriptions of most major players.

251   Toll, Robert C. ON WITH THE SHOW: THE FIRST CENTURY OF SHOW BUSINESS IN AMERICA. New York: Oxford University Press, 1976. 355 p. Index, illus., bibliog.

A general history of the American entertainment industry, including the legitimate stage. Includes a useful chronology.

252   Tompkins, Eugene, and Kilby, Quincy. HISTORY OF THE BOSTON THEATRE, 1854-1901. Boston and New York: Houghton Mifflin Co., 1908. xv, 483 p. Index, illus.

Tompkins was manager of the Boston Theatre from 1878 to 1901, and Kilby was treasurer from 1886 to 1901. This volume is heavily illustrated and well indexed, facilitating its use. Most of the major figures of the American theatre for this period are mentioned.

253   Turner, Vivian. "Our Colonial Theatre." QUARTERLY JOURNAL OF SPEECH 27 (December 1941): 559-73.

An overview which uses standard secondary sources to trace the Hallam and Douglass companies, adding little.

254   Van Lennep, William, et al. THE LONDON STAGE 1660-1880: A CALENDAR OF PLAYS, ENTERTAINMENTS, & AFTERPIECES TOGETHER WITH CASTS, BOX-OFFICE RECEIPTS AND CONTEMPORARY COMMENT COMPILED FROM THE PLAYBILLS, NEWSPAPERS AND THEATRICAL DIARIES OF THE PERIOD. 5 vols. Carbondale: Southern Illinois University Press, 1965. Index, illus., bibliog.

A monumental work with value to students to American acting for the English backgrounds of players who settled here. A separately published index (see no. 91) renders the material more accessible.

255   Watson, Ernest Bradlee. SHERIDAN TO ROBERTSON; A STUDY OF THE NINETEENTH-CENTURY LONDON STAGE. Cambridge, Mass.: Harvard University Press, 1926. xix, 455 p. Index, illus., bibliog.

Substantial accounts of E.A. Sothern and Dion Boucicault and their work in London.

256   Weidenthal, Leo. FROM DIS'S WAGON, A SENTIMENTAL SURVEY
       OF A POETS' CORNER--THE SHAKESPEARE GARDEN OF CLEVELAND.
       Cleveland: Weidenthal Co., 1926. 70 p. Illus.

       A description of the creation of a Shakespeare memorial, involv-
       ing such stage celebrities as Julia Marlowe, E.H. Sothern, Effie
       Ellsler, David Belasco, Ethel Barrymore, Richard Mansfield, Mary
       Anderson, Clara Morris, Joseph Haworth, and Jane Cowl.

257   Whitney, Horace G. THE DRAMA IN UTAH: THE STORY OF THE
       SALT LAKE THEATRE. Salt Lake City: Deseret News, 1915. 48 p.
       Illus.

       A brief pamphlet based on an address by the author, later serial-
       ized. Valuable and rare illustrations.

258   Willard, George O. HISTORY OF THE PROVIDENCE STAGE 1762-1891.
       Providence: Rhode Island News Co., 1891. 288 p. Index.

       A detailed chronicle, useful in verifying appearances of major
       stars during the period covered.

259   Willis, Eola. THE CHARLESTON STAGE IN THE XVIII CENTURY WITH
       SOCIAL SETTINGS OF THE TIME. Columbia, S.C.: State Co., 1924.
       464 p. Index, illus.

       A detailed study, including descriptions of Elizabeth Poe, David
       Douglass, the Hallams, and the Placides.

260   Wilson, Arthur Herman. HISTORY OF THE PHILADELPHIA THEATRE,
       1835-1855. Philadelphia: University of Pennsylvania Press, 1935.
       London: Oxford, n.d. 724 p. Index, bibliog.

       A catalog of play titles, actors, and engagements, useful for
       tracing theatrical activities during this period.

261   Wilson, Garff B. A HISTORY OF AMERICAN ACTING. Bloomington
       and London: Indiana University Press, 1966. 301 p. Index, illus.,
       notes.

       An excellent study, now out of print. Every performer of major
       rank is described, and the notes constitute a useful source of
       further information.

262   _____. THREE HUNDRED YEARS OF AMERICAN DRAMA AND THEATRE
       FROM YE BEAR AND YE CUBB TO HAIR. Englewood Cliffs, N.J.:
       Prentice-Hall, 1973. viii, 536 p. Index, illus., bibliog.

       A highly regarded general history, frequently used as a text for
       university classes. Discusses and describes almost every major
       performer on the American stage.

263   Wingate, Charles E[dgar]. L[ewis]. THE PLAYGOER'S YEARBOOK, FOR 1888. STORY OF THE STAGE THE PAST YEAR, WITH ESPECIAL REFERENCE TO BOSTON. Boston: Stage Publishing Co., [1888]. 87 p. Illus.

> A monthly account of the Boston stage, describing such performers as Modjeska, Lawrence Barrett, Louis James, Dion Boucicault, Joseph Haworth, Genevieve Ward, Fanny Davenport, Janauschek, Richard Mansfield, E.H. Sothern, Frederick Warde, and Edwin Booth.

264   Winter, William. SHAKESPEARE ON THE STAGE. 3 vols. New York: Moffat, Yard and Co., 1911. First Series: 564 p.; Second Series: 630 p., index; Third Series: 516 p., index. Illus. Reprint. 3 vols. New York: Benjamin Blom, 1969.

> Winter has written a history of the acting, primarily by British and American performers, of Shakepeare's scripts from the Elizabethan age to the time of publication. Most major players are described and evaluated. The first series covers RICHARD III, MERCHANT OF VENICE, OTHELLO, HAMLET, MACBETH, and HENRY VIII; the second series, TWELFTH NIGHT, ROMEO AND JULIET, AS YOU LIKE IT, KING LEAR, THE TAMING OF THE SHREW, and JULIUS CAESAR; the third series deals with CYMBELINE, LOVE'S LABORS LOST, CORIOLANUS, MIDSUMMER NIGHT'S DREAM, HENRY IV, HENRY II, THE MERRY WIVES OF WINDSOR, ANTONY AND CLEOPATRA, and KING JOHN. Winter's criticism is clearly prejudicial. Six of the plays were treated in a series of articles in CENTURY MAGAZINE, volumes 69 to 71.

265   Wright, Richardson. HAWKERS AND WALKERS IN EARLY AMERICA: STROLLING PEDDLERS, PREACHERS, LAWYERS, DOCTORS, PLAYERS, AND OTHERS, FROM THE BEGINNING TO THE CIVIL WAR. Philadelphia: J.B. Lippincott Co., 1927. 289 p. Index, illus., bibliog.

> A lively account of commerce and entertainment in colonial America, including a chapter, "Circus and Theatre Starts on Tour."

266   _____. REVELS IN JAMAICA 1682-1838: PLAYS AND PLAYERS OF A CENTURY, TUMBLERS AND CONJURORS, MUSICAL REFUGEES AND SOLITARY SHOWMEN, DINNERS, BALLS AND COCKFIGHTS, DARKY MUMMERS AND OTHER MEMORIES OF HIGH TIMES AND MERRY HEARTS. New York: Dodd, Mead and Co., 1937. 357 p. Index, illus., bibliog.

> Among the performers described are the Hallams, John Henry, and David Douglass before his company visited the mainland.

GENERAL SOURCES: BOOKS

267   ACTORS AS THEY ARE: A SERIES OF SKETCHES OF THE MOST EMI-
NENT PERFORMERS NOW ON THE STAGE. New York: O.A. Roorbach, 1856. 85 p.

Verified in the NATIONAL UNION CATALOG, but unavailable for examination.

268   THE AMERICAN STAGE. SCHILLER THEATRE SOUVENIR. Chicago:
American Stage Publishing, [1895]. Unpaged.

Sixty-one portraits with brief biographical sketches.

269   AMERICAN STAGE CELEBRITIES. Chicago: Hunt and Wall, 1894.
137 p. Illus.

Sixty-six portraits of leading performers with very brief biographical sketches.

270   THE AMERICAN STAGE OF TODAY. BIOGRAPHIES AND PHOTOGRAPHS
OF ONE HUNDRED LEADING ACTORS AND ACTRESSES WITH AN IN-
TRODUCTION BY WILLIAM WINTER. New York: P.F. Collier and Son,
1910. Unpaged. Illus.

A pictorial portfolio including capsule biographies of leading
players, among them Maude Adams, Viola Allen, Margaret Ang-
lin, Ethel and John Barrymore, Blanche Bates, Billie Burke,
Marie Cahill, Mrs. Carter, Marguerite Clark, Rose Coghlan,
George M. Cohan, William Collier, Ida Conquest, W. H.
Crane, Henrietta Crosman, Arnold Daly, J.E. Dodson, Marie
Doro, John Drew, Maxine Elliott, William Faversham, Elsie
Ferguson, Mrs. Fiske, Grace George, William Gillette, Nat
Goodwin, James K. Hackett, Virginia Harned, Crystal Herne,
Raymond Hitchcock, E.M. Holland, DeWolf Hopper, Isabel
Irving, May Irwin, Louis James, Elsie Janis, Bertha Kalich,
Doris Keane, Herbert Kelcey, Wilton Lackaye, Cecelia Loftus,
Louis Mann, Mary Mannering, Robert Mantell, Julia Marlowe,
John B. Mason, Henry Miller, Nazimova, Chauncy Olcott,

James O'Neill, Ada Rehan, Annie Russell, Lillian Russell,
Julia Sanderson, Otis Skinner, E.H. Sothern, Rose Stahl,
Frances Starr, Blanche Walsh, David Warfield, and Francis
Wilson.

271   THE AMERICAN THEATRE: A SUM OF ITS PARTS. COLLECTION OF THE
      DISTINGUISHED ADDRESSES PREPARED EXPRESSLY FOR THE SYMPOSIUM;
      "THE AMERICAN THEATRE--A CULTURAL PROCESS," AT THE FIRST AMERI-
      CAN COLLEGE THEATRE FESTIVAL, WASHINGTON, D.C., 1969. New
      York: Samuel French, 1971. 431 p. Bibliogs.

      Sixteen essays by leading theatre scholars, including one by
      Richard Moody (see no. 210). An essay (no. 1204) by Helen
      Krich Chinoy describes Boucicault's contributions to U.S. direct-
      ing.

272   Amory, Cleveland, and Bradlee, Frederic, eds. VANITY FAIR: SELEC-
      TIONS FROM AMERICA'S MOST MEMORABLE MAGAZINE: A CAVAL-
      CADE OF THE 1920'S AND 1930'S. New York: Viking Press, 1960.
      324 p. Index, illus.

      Includes such essays as Joseph H. Choate's "Early Memories of
      DeWolf Hopper," Stark Young's "David Garrick to John Barry-
      more: An Imaginary Letter from One Celebrated Hamlet to
      Another," Gilbert Selde's "Fred Stone and W.C. Fields: A
      Comparison of the Comic Art of These Two Popular Exponents
      of the Old School," and Mary Cass Canfield's "Mrs. Fiske:
      An Artist and a Personality."

273   Aronson, Rudolph. THEATRICAL AND MUSICAL MEMOIRS. New York:
      McBride, Nast and Co., 1913. 268 p. Index, illus.

      Primarily concerned with Aronson's musical career, but contains
      some material on Lillian Russell.

274   Arthur, Sir George C.A. FROM PHELPS TO GIELGUD. REMINISCENCES
      OF THE STAGE THROUGH SIXTY-FIVE YEARS. London: Chapman and
      Hall, 1936. Reprint. Freeport, N.Y.: Books for Libraries Press, 1967.
      248 p. Index, illus.

      Among the Shakespearean performers selected for analysis are
      Mary Anderson and Helena Modjeska.

275   Beaton, Cecil. THE FACE OF THE WORLD: AN INTERNATIONAL
      SCRAPBOOK OF PEOPLE AND PLACES. New York: John Day Co.,
      n.d. 240 p. Illus.

      Pages 146-53 describe several performers, among them Ina Claire,
      the Lunts, Ethel Barrymore, Ruth Gordon, Katharine Cornell,
      and Laurette Taylor.

276   Blum, Daniel. GREAT STARS OF THE AMERICAN STAGE: A PICTORIAL
RECORD. New York: Greenburg; Toronto: Ambassador, 1952. 151 p.
Index, illus.

A compilation of 150 profiles of leading players, each consisting
of a one- or two-page photographic collage and a capsule biography.

277   Bodeen, De Witt. LADIES OF THE FOOTLIGHTS. Pasadena, Calif.:
Pasadena Playhouse Association, 1937. 133 p. Illus.

A series of twenty brief essays on leading actresses, undocumented
and illustrated by drawings. The actresses include Adah Issacs
Menken, Lotta Crabtree, Catherine Sinclair, Modjeska, Ada
Rehan, Julia Dean, Laura Keene, Fanny Davenport, Matilda
Heron, Julia Marlowe, Clara Morris, Mary Anderson, and Lillian
Russell. Of minimal value.

278   Brazier, Marion Howard. STAGE AND SCREEN. Boston: M.H. Brazier,
1920. 130 p. Illus.

The author refers to her work as "wayside jottings," rather than
the work of a professional critic. She devotes chapters to Charlotte Cushman, Mary Anderson, and Kate Reignold. Briefer
sections deal with Rose Coghlan, Mary Shaw, E.H. Sothern,
Julia Marlowe, the Barrymores, Viola Allen, Margaret Anglin,
Nance O'Neill, and Maude Adams.

279   Brereton, Austin, ed. GALLERY OF PLAYERS FROM THE ILLUSTRATED
AMERICAN. 12 vols. New York: Illustrated American Publishing Co.,
1894-- . Illus.

The volumes are composed of one-page biographies and full-page
plates. Among those included are: (volume 1) E.H. Sothern,
Edwin Booth, Modjeska, Cora Urquhart Potter, Joseph Jefferson
III, Lillian Russell, Ada Rehan, Henry Miller, Richard Mans-
field; (volume 2) Nat Goodwin, Francis Wilson, Herbert Kelcey,
Julia Marlowe, Effie Ellsler, Edward Harringan, James A. Herne;
(volume 3) Lotta Crabtree, Robert Mantell, Isabell Irving, James
Lewis, Mrs. John Drew, William H. Crane, Viola Allen, Mau-
rice Barrymore, DeWolf Hopper, Georgia Cayvan, John Drew,
Otis Skinner, Maude Adams; (volume 4) E.S. Willard, Elsie
DeWolfe, Sol Smith Russell, William Gillette, Annie Russell;
(Volume 5) Mary Anderson, Fanny Davenport, Rose Coghlan,
Maxine Elliott; (volume 6) Mrs. Gilbert, Wilton Lackaye, Marie
Burroughs, Kate Claxton, William Faversham, Virginia Harned,
May Irwin; (volume 7) Clara Morris, William Warren, E.L. Daven-
port, Joseph Haworth, James O'Neill, Joseph Holland, Odette
Tyler; (volume 8) Mrs. Carter, Louis James, Janauschek, Chaun-
cey Olcott, James K. Hackett, Jefferson DeAngelis; (volume 9)
Mrs. Fiske, Mary Shaw, Mrs. Whiffen, Frank Mayo, Fay Tem-
pleton; Agnes Booth; (volume 12) Maude Adams. The editorship
varies; Brereton edited the first volume; Charles F.D.C. Nird-

linger edited the second; volumes 3 through 6 were edited by Marwell Hall; Henry Austin did volumes 7 through 9, and Arthur Hoeber edited the rest of the series.

280 _____. SHAKESPEAREAN SCENES AND CHARACTERS: WITH DE-SCRIPTIVE NOTES ON THE PLAYS, AND THE PRINCIPAL SHAKESPEAREAN PLAYERS, FROM BETTERTON TO IRVING. London, Paris, New York, and Melbourne: Cassell and Co., 1887. 96 p. Illus.

An overview of the subject, primarily concerned with English performers, but occasionally mentioning American players of note.

281 _____. SOME FAMOUS HAMLETS FROM BURBAGE TO FECHTER. London: David Bogue, 1884. 74 p.

Brief critical and biographical essays on various performers, among them the elder Booth and Fechter.

282 Briscoe, Johnson. THE ACTORS' BIRTHDAY BOOK, AN AUTHORITA-TIVE INSIGHT INTO THE LIVES OF THE MEN AND WOMEN OF THE STAGE BORN BETWEEN JANUARY 1 AND DECEMBER 31. First Series: New York: Moffat, Yard and Co., 1907. 285 p. Illus. Second Series: New York: Moffat, Yard and Co., 1908. 285 p. Index, illus. Third Series: New York: Moffat, Yard and Co., 1909. 296 p. Illus.

Briscoe intended this work as an "artistic souvenir" rather than a reference work and gathered his biographical material from various secondary sources. The first volume contains 345 brief biographies, the second 363, and the last 400.

283 Brown, John Mason. DRAMATIS PERSONAE: A RETROSPECTIVE SHOW. New York: Viking Press, 1963. xii, 542 p. Index.

A collection of critical pieces drawn primarily from the SATUR-DAY REVIEW after 1942. Coverage includes Katharine Cornell and Helen Hayes.

284 _____. LETTERS FROM GREENROOM GHOSTS. New York: Viking Press, 1934. 207 p. Toronto: Macmillan, 1934.

Inspired by Stark Young, Brown composed a series of imaginary letters from players of the past to those in 1934. The first is from Sarah Siddons to Katharine Cornell; the second from Peg Woffington to Ina Claire.

285 _____. UPSTAGE: THE AMERICAN THEATRE IN PERFORMANCE. New York: W.W. Norton and Co., 1930. xi, 276 p.

Brown deals with the major figures of the U.S. stage in a series of essays. Among those described are Mrs. Fiske, Otis Skinner, Walter Hampden, the Lunts, Pauline Lord, Lenore Ulric, Katharine Cornell, and Eva Le Gallienne.

286   Browne, Walter, and Koch, E. De Roy, eds. WHO'S WHO ON THE
       STAGE; THE DRAMATIC REFERENCE BOOK AND BIOGRAPHICAL DIC-
       TIONARY OF THE THEATRE. CONTAINING RECORDS OF THE CAREERS
       OF ACTORS, ACTRESSES, MANAGERS, AND PLAYWRIGHTS OF THE
       AMERICAN STAGE. New York: Walter Browne and F.A. Austin, 1906.
       232 p. Illus. New York: Dodge and Co., 1908. 467 p. Illus.

       A biographical dictionary of performers arranged alphabetically
       from Maude Adams to Florence Ziegfeld, Jr. Almost every
       performer of any significance at the time is represented by a
       capsule biography.

287   Broxam, Pearl Bennett. GLIMPSES OF STAGE FOLK: AN OUTLINE
       FOR STUDY CLUBS BASED ON AUTOBIOGRAPHIES OF THEATRE PEOPLE.
       Iowa City: University of Iowa, 1933. 48 p. Bibliog.

       A pamphlet prepared by the Extension Division of the University
       of Iowa, containing brief biographies and bibliographies for John
       Barrymore, Marie Dressler, John Drew, Joseph Jefferson III,
       Otis Skinner, E.H. Sothern, and Francis Wilson.

288   Buck, Mrs. Lillie (West) Brown. [Amy Leslie]. SOME PLAYERS: PER-
       SONAL SKETCHES. Chicago and New York: Herbert S. Stone and Co.,
       1899. 624 p. New York: Duffield, 1906. 436 p. Illus.

       "Leslie" was the drama critic for the Chicago NEWS for many
       years. In this volume, she assesses nearly sixty leading performers,
       among them Viola Allen, Maurice Barrymore, Edwin Booth, W.H.
       Crane, Fanny Davenport, Mrs. Fiske, William Gillette, Nat Good-
       win, James A. Herne, May Irwin, Joseph Jefferson III, Richard
       Mansfield, Julia Marlowe, Modjeska, Clara Morris, Cora Ur-
       quhart Potter, Ada Rehan, Stuart Robson, Annie Russell, Lillian
       Russell, Otis Skinner, E.H. Sothern, James H. Stoddart, and Fay
       Templeton. Allen, Irwin, and Lillian Russell are omitted from
       the 1906 edition.

289   Burroughs, Marie. THE MARIE BURROUGHS ART PORTFOLIO OF STAGE
       CELEBRITIES: A COLLECTION OF PHOTOGRAPHS OF THE LEADERS OF
       DRAMATIC AND LYRIC ART. Chicago: A.N. Marquis and Co., 1894.
       Unpaged. Illus.

       A collection of nearly three hundred black and white photographs
       of the leading performers of the late nineteenth century, each
       with a brief biographical-critical paragraph. While other per-
       formers have only one photograph included, Burroughs has eight.

290   Clapp, John, and Edgett, Edwin Francis. PLAYERS OF THE PRESENT
       (1899-1901). New York: Dunlap Society, 1901. Reprint. New York:
       Benjamin Blom, 1969. New York: Burt Franklin, 1970. vi, 405 p.
       Index, illus.

       This was to be the first volume of a projected series, intended
       "to give reliable statistics . . . and not to enter upon the domain

of criticism." Over 150 capsule biographies are included, most including considerable specific information.

291   Cole, Toby, and Chinoy, Helen Krich, eds. ACTORS ON ACTING:
       THE THEORIES, TECHNIQUES, AND PRACTICES OF THE GREAT ACTORS
       OF ALL TIMES AS TOLD IN THEIR OWN WORDS. New rev. ed. New
       York: Crown Publishers, 1970. 732 p. Index, bibliog.

       A collection of essays on acting from the time of Plato to the
       present, with twenty-five entries in the American section, each
       containing a brief biographical sketch. Among those quoted or
       discussed are Edwin Forrest, Dion Boucicault, Joseph Jefferson
       III, Edwin Booth, William Gillette, Richard Mansfield, E.H.
       Sothern, Julia Marlowe, David Belasco, Mrs. Fiske, Otis Skinner,
       Nazimova, John Barrymore, Laurette Taylor, Walter Huston,
       Stella Adler, the Lunts, Morris Carnovsky, and Lee Strasberg.

292   Cook, Edward Dutton. HOURS WITH THE PLAYERS. 2 vols. London:
       Chatto-Windus, 1881. vi, 277, 263 p.

       Chapter 8 of volume 2 describes Charlotte Cushman; chapter 11
       of the same volume deals with Charles Fechter. The elder Booth's
       London career is outlined in chapter 3.

293   Dale, Alan. [Pseud.] FAMILIAR CHATS WITH THE QUEENS OF THE
       STAGE. New York: G.W. Dillingham, 1890. 399 p. Illus.

       Dale assembled twenty-nine "gossipy sketches, or interviews,"
       as he calls them. Among his subjects are Lillian Russell, Rose
       Coghlan, Fanny Davenport, Lotta Crabtree, Modjeska, Georgia
       Cayvan, Mary Ellsler, Ada Rehan, Georgie Drew Barrymore, and
       Clara Morris.

294   Eaton, Walter Prichard. PLAYS AND PLAYERS, LEAVES FROM A CRI-
       TIC'S SCRAPBOOK. Cincinnati: Steward and Kidd Co., 1916. xii,
       413 p. Index, illus.

       A collection of essays previously published in various serials.
       Among the players discussed are David Belasco, George M.
       Cohan, Mrs. Fiske, Maude Adams, and Margaret Anglin.

295   Eustis, Morton. PLAYERS AT WORK; ACTING ACCORDING TO THE
       ACTORS WITH A CHAPTER ON THE SINGING ACTOR. New York:
       Theatre Arts, 1937. 127 p. Illus.

       Analyses of the work of Helen Hayes, the Lunts, Nazimova,
       Katharine Cornell, Ina Claire, and lesser performers.

296   Fabian, Monroe H. ON STAGE: 200 YEARS OF GREAT THEATRICAL
       PERSONALITIES. New York: Mayflower Books, 1980. 222 p. Index, illus.

       Brief commentaries and illustrations of seventy-seven great names

in American performing arts, assembled by the research and cura-
torial staff of the National Portrait Gallery of the Smithsonian
Institution. Among those included are Nancy Hallam, John
Durang, William Burke Wood, the elder Booth, James H. Hackett,
Edwin Forrest, Ira Aldridge, Clara Fisher, Charlotte Cushman,
Dion Boucicault, John McCullough, Joseph Jefferson III, Edwin
Booth, Richard Mansfield, Otis Skinner, Julia Marlowe, Mrs.
Fiske, Maude Adams, Ethel Barrymore, Nazimova, Walter
Hampden, John Barrymore, Jeanne Eagels, the Lunts, Fay Bain-
ter, Katharine Cornell, Paul Robeson, Helen Hayes, Tallulah
Bankhead, and Zero Mostel.

297   FAMOUS PLAYERS OF TO-DAY. New York: Geo. A. Melbourne,
        1904. Unpaged. Illus.

        A large portrait book, each actor represented by a full-page
        portrait preceded by a one-page critical commentary. Included
        are Mrs. Carter, Blanche Bates, E.H. Sothern, Maude Adams,
        David Warfield, Tyrone Power, Rose Coghlan, Marie Cahill,
        Mrs. Fiske, and Henry Miller.

298   Funke, Lewis, and Booth, John E., eds. ACTORS TALK ABOUT ACTING.
        2 vols. New York: Avon Book Division, 1961. 221, 221 p.

        A series of interviews and discussions of acting with noted per-
        formers, among them Helen Hayes, Morris Carnovsky, the Lunts,
        Katharine Cornell, and Paul Muni.

299   Gassner, John, and Quinn, Edwards, eds. THE READER'S ENCYCLO-
        PEDIA OF WORLD DRAMA. New York: Crowell, 1969. 1,030 p.

        Includes brief essays on such actor-playwrights as Herne and Bou-
        cicault.

300   Geller, James Jacob. GRANDFATHER'S FOLLIES. New York: Macaulay
        Co., 1934. xiv, 211 p. Illus.

        Sections on Augustin Daly and Joseph Jefferson III. Each short
        chapter concerns a specific script, such as Daly's LEAH, THE
        FORESAKEN; RIP VAN WINKLE with Joseph Jefferson III,
        Boucicault's THE COLLEEN BAWN and THE SHAUGHRAUN;
        Chanfrau's KIT, THE ARKANSAS TRAVELER; Mayo in DAVY
        CROCKETT, Harrigan's OLD LAVENDER; MacKaye's HAZEL
        KIRKE; James O'Neill in THE COUNT OF MONTE CRISTO;
        Herne's SHORE ACRES; Belasco's THE HEART OF MARYLAND,
        and William Gillette's SECRET SERVICE.

301   Entry deleted.

302 GREEN ROOM YARNS. New York: J. Haney and Co., 1876. 64 p. Illus.

A collection of undocumented theatrical anecdotes, with stories about Edwin Forrest, James Wallack, the Davenports, the elder Sothern, Joseph Jefferson III, Edwin Booth, Clara Morris, William J. Florence, Julia Dean, Stuart Robson, and John E. Owens.

303 Hamm, Margherita Arlina. EMINENT ACTORS IN THEIR HOMES: PERSONAL DESCRIPTIONS AND INTERVIEWS. New York: James Pott and Co., 1902. 336 p. Index.

The author presents leading actors of the time as reasonably domestic when not on tour. Brief biographical sketches are combined with detailed descriptions of the actors' homes. Those selected include E.H. Sothern, Virginia Harned, Richard Mansfield, Elsie de Wolfe, Mrs. Fiske, David Warfield, Viola Allen, Julia Marlowe, Chauncey Olcott, James K. Hackett, Mary Mannering, Joseph Jefferson III, Otis Skinner, Nat C. Goodwin, and Maxine Elliott.

304 Hartnoll, Phyllis, ed. THE OXFORD COMPANION TO THE THEATRE. 3d ed. London: Oxford University Press, 1967. xv, 1,088 p. Illus., bibliog.

A basic encyclopedia of the theatre with articles on all aspects of the profession, including capsule biographies of leading performers. In some cases, earlier editions had different material. The first edition was published in 1951, the second in 1957.

305 Highfill, Philip W.; Burnim, Kalman A.; and Langhans, Edward A. A BIOGRAPHICAL DICTIONARY OF ACTORS, ACTRESSES, MUSICIANS, DANCERS, MANAGERS, & OTHER STAGE PERSONNEL IN LONDON, 1660-1800. Carbondale and Edwardsville: Southern Illinois Press, 1973-- .

A projected series of volumes, of which six have been published. Extremely useful for English actors who had substantial careers in the United States, such as Anthony Aston and Thomas Abthorpe Cooper. Impeccable scholarship.

306 Hopkins, Arthur Melancthon. REFERENCE POINT: REFLECTIONS ON CREATIVE WAYS IN GENERAL WITH SPECIAL REFERENCE TO CREATIVE WAYS IN THE THEATRE. New York: Samuel French, 1948. 135 p.

A strangely aphoristic volume with descriptive sections on John, Ethel, and Lionel Barrymore.

307   Horne, Charles F., ed. GREAT MEN AND FAMOUS WOMEN; A SERIES
      OF PEN AND PENCIL SKETCHES OF THE LIVES OF MORE THAN 200
      OF THE MOST PROMINENT PERSONAGES IN HISTORY. 8 vols. New
      York: Selmar Hess, 1894. Illus.

      Capsule biographies of small value, including Edwin Booth,
      Charlotte Cushman, and Joseph Jefferson III.

308   Horton, William E. DRIFTWOOD OF THE STAGE. Detroit: Press of Winn
      and Hammond, 1904. 369 p. Index, illus.

      A conglomeration of biographical scraps about leading nineteenth-
      century players, including a full chapter on John Wilkes Booth.
      Includes a valuable chapter on stage slang and superstitions.

309   Hubert, Philip G., Jr. THE STAGE AS A CAREER, A SKETCH OF THE
      ACTOR'S LIFE; ITS REQUIREMENTS, HARDSHIPS, AND REWARDS. THE
      QUALIFICATIONS AND TRAINING ESSENTIAL TO SUCCESS--EXPERT
      OPINIONS FROM FAMOUS ACTORS, INCLUDING SIR HENRY IRVING,
      LAWRENCE BARRETT, DION BOUCICAULT, JOSEPH JEFFERSON, HELENA
      MODJESKA, MARY ANDERSON, AND MAGGIE MITCHELL--DISAPPOINT-
      MENTS AND PITFALLS--THE ACTOR AND SOCIETY--HOW TO BEGIN--
      DRAMATIC SCHOOLS AND TEACHERS--CONTRACTS AND SALARIES.
      New York and London: G.P. Putnam's Sons, 1900. v, 187 p. Index.

      Hubert describes theatre as a way of life in a manner designed to
      discourage applicants. He quotes from the players mentioned in
      the title, as well as others, mostly from articles from the NORTH
      AMERICAN REVIEW.

310   Hughes, Elinor. FAMOUS STARS OF FILMDOM (MEN). Boston: L.C.
      Page, 1932. 327 p. Index, illus.

      A collection of brief critical and biographical sketches; among
      them are essays on John Barrymore and Walter Huston.

311   _____. FAMOUS STARS OF FILMDOM (WOMEN). Boston: L.C. Page,
      1931. 327 p. Index, illus.

      A companion volume to the previous entry (no. 310); includes
      Ruth Chatterton and Marie Dressler.

312   Hunt, Brampton, ed. THE GREEN ROOM BOOK OR WHO'S WHO ON
      THE STAGE: AN ANNUAL BIOGRAPHICAL RECORD OF THE DRAMATIC,
      MUSICAL, AND VARIETY WORLD. New York: Frederic Warne and Co.,
      1906. 452 p. Illus. London: T. Sealey and Co., 1907. xliv, 556 p. Illus.
      1908. xxxvi, 705 p. Illus. 1909. lvi, 832 p. Illus.

      A valuable encyclopedic compendium of biographies, plus sub-
      stantial additional material. By the fourth edition, some two
      thousand actors and actresses were included.

313 Hutton, Laurence. PLAYS AND PLAYERS OF THIS CENTURY. New York:
Dutton, 1875; New York: Hurd and Houghton, 1875. 265 p. Index.

Hutton's reminiscences include descriptions of E.A. Sothern, John
Brougham, the Wallacks, Laura Keene, William R. Blake, William
Davidge, Edwin Forrest, Julia Dean, E.L. Davenport, Matilda
Heron, Joseph Jefferson III, Dion Boucicault, and Charlotte Cush-
man.

314 THE ILLUSTRATED AMERICAN STAGE. A PICTORIAL REVIEW OF THE
MOST NOTABLE RECENT THEATRICAL SUCCESSES, TOGETHER WITH
MANY DRAWINGS AND PORTRAITS OF CELEBRATED PLAYERS. New
York: R.H. Russell, 1901. Unpaged. Illus.

This volume is almost entirely pictorial. Specific players and
productions include Ethel Barrymore in CAPTAIN JINKS OF THE
HORSE MARINES, Julia Marlowe in WHEN KNIGHTHOOD WAS
IN FLOWER, Maude Adams in L'AIGLON, John Drew in RICH-
ARD CARVEL, Edna May in THE GIRL FROM UP THERE, and
Amelia Bingham and her company.

315 Isaacs, Edith J.R., ed. THEATRE: ESSAYS ON THE ARTS OF THE THEA-
TRE. Boston: Little, Brown and Co., 1927. xxiii, 331. Index, illus.

A series of essays by various authors on the actor, the playwright,
the director, scenic design, costumes, dance, architecture, and
innovations in the theatre. Several references are indexed for
John Barrymore and Edwin Booth.

316 Izzard, Forrest. HEROINES OF THE MODERN STAGE. New York: Sturgis
and Walton Co., 1915. ix, 379 p. Illus., bibliog.

Includes short biographical sketches of Modjeska, Ada Rehan,
Mary Anderson, Mrs. Fiske, Julia Marlowe, and Maude Adams.
The final section, "American Actresses of Today," contains shorter
descriptions of Ethel Barrymore, Margaret Anglin, Nazimova,
Grace George, Laura Hope Crews, Margaret Illington, and several
lesser figures.

317 Jennings, John T. THEATRICAL OR CIRCUS LIFE; OR SECRETS OF THE
STAGE, GREEN ROOM AND SAWDUST ARENA, EMBRACING A HISTORY
OF THE THEATRE FROM SHAKESPEARE'S TIME TO THE PRESENT DAY,
AND ABOUNDING IN ANECDOTES CONCERNING THE MOST PROMI-
NENT ACTORS AND ACTRESSES BEFORE THE PUBLIC; ALSO, A COMPLETE
EXPOSITION OF THE MYSTERIES OF THE STAGE, SHOWING THE MAN-
NER IN WHICH WONDERFUL SCENIC AND OTHER EFFECTS ARE PRO-
DUCED; THE ORIGIN AND GROWTH OF NEGRO MINSTRESLY; THE
MOST ASTONISHING TRICKS OF MODERN MAGICIANS, AND A HIS-
TORY OF THE HIPPODROME, ETC., ETC. St. Louis: M.S. Barnett,
1882. 608 p. Illus.

Apparently also published in Brandon, Vermont, by Sidney M.

Southard in 1884. A sprawling, slangy, no doubt then sensational treatment of the entire entertainment industry. Includes anecdotes on most of the leading U.S. actors from the Hallams to the time of publication, but to be used warily and only with corroboration. Hundreds of illustrations, some in color.

318 Kean, Charles, and Kean, Ellen. LETTERS OF MR. AND MRS. CHARLES KEAN RELATING TO THEIR AMERICAN TOURS. Edited by William G[lasgow]. B[ruce]. Carson. St. Louis: Washington University Press, 1945. ix, 173 p. Index, illus.

Carson supplied a thirty-nine page introduction to the eighty-five letters he edited for this volume. A great deal of the correspondence is to Noah Ludlow and Sol Smith, and some general remarks are made about Edwin Forrest.

319 Keese, William L. A GROUP OF COMEDIANS. New York: Dunlap Society, 1901. Reprint. New York: Burt Franklin, 1970. 91 p. Illus.

A series of brief and undocumented biographical sketches of such performers as Henry Placide, William R. Blake, John Brougham, George Holland, and Charles Fisher.

320 Kennedy, Harold J. NO PICKLE, NO PERFORMANCE: AN IRREVERENT THEATRICAL EXCURSION FROM TALLULAH TO TRAVOLTA. New York: Doubleday and Co., 1977. 262 p. Illus.

Rambling, gossipy reminiscences of Kennedy's thirty-eight years as an actor and director. Almost entirely anecdotal, concerning such performers as Jane Cowl, Florence Reed, Tallulah Bankhead, and Helen Hayes.

321 Kobbé, Gustav. FAMOUS ACTORS & ACTRESSES AND THIER HOMES. Boston: Little, Brown and Co., 1903. ix, 360 p. Illus.

Breezy descriptions of the residences and home lives of Ethel Barrymore, John Drew, William Gillette, Richard Mansfield, Julia Marlowe, Annie Russell, E.H. Sothern, Virginia Harned, and Francis Wilson. Also included are descriptions of the Players Club and the Lambs Club. See nos. 322-23.

322 _____. FAMOUS ACTORS AND THEIR HOMES. Toronto: Musson, 1905. x, 221 p. Illus.

See nos. 321 and 323.

323 _____. FAMOUS ACTRESSES AND THIER HOMES. Boston: Little, Brown and Co., 1905. x, 243 p. Illus.

An expansion of entry no. 321. Mrs. Fiske is added in this particular volume.

324   Lawrence, Boyle. CELEBRITIES OF THE STAGE. London: George Newnes, n.d. Unpaged. Illus.

A series of color plates of various English and American players, with one-page critical-biographical sketches. Included are Edna May and Ada Rehan.

325   Lease, Rex, and Harlan, Kenneth, comps. WHAT ACTORS EAT--WHEN THEY EAT. Los Angeles: Lyman House, 1939. 241 p. Index, illus.

A compilation of the favorite recipes of film and stage stars, including John Barrymore (ham loaf), Lionel Barrymore (fettucini Alfredo), Melvyn Douglas (chicken chinese and chicken caccitore), and Walter Huston (vegetable soup).

326   McGill, Raymond D., ed. NOTABLE NAMES IN THE AMERICAN THEATRE. Clifton, N.J.: James T. White and Co., 1976. ix, 1,250 p.

A valuable volume for (1) encyclopedic treatments of the major figures of the contemporary U.S. theatre, and (2) a biographical bibliography, listing the major sources of information about past and present leading theatre artists. This is a more recent edition of THE BIOGRAPHICAL ENCYCLOPEDIA & WHO'S WHO OF THE AMERICAN THEATRE (no. 362).

327   McGRAW-HILL ENCYCLOPEDIA OF WORLD DRAMA. 4 vols. New York: McGraw-Hill Book Co., 1972. Index, illus., bibliogs.

Capsule biographies, not covering actors as such, but including some who were also playwrights, such as Dion Boucicault, George M. Cohan, and James A. Herne.

328   McKay, Frederick Edward, and Wingate, Charles E.L., eds. FAMOUS ACTORS OF TO-DAY. 2 vols. New York: Thomas Y. Crowell and Co., 1896. viii, 220, 179 p. Illus.

A series of forty-one essays by various authors, including Henry A. Clapp, Lewis C. Strang, Edward A. Dithmar, Laurence Hutton, Harrison Grey Fiske, and others, on the leading actors of the time. Each essay is cross-listed in this bibliography.

329   Mammen, Edward William. THE OLD STOCK COMPANY SCHOOL OF ACTING; A STUDY OF THE BOSTON MUSEUM. Boston: Trustees of the Public Library, 1945. 89 p. Illus., bibliog.

Reprinted with additions from Mammen's article in MORE BOOKS (no. 467).

330   Mantle, Burns, ed. THE BEST PLAYS OF [1919-20--]. New York: Dodd, Mead and Co., 1921-- . Published annually, editors, and titles vary.

Volumes in 1933, 1934, and 1955 have additional material to extend coverage back to 1894. Each volumes lists all plays produced on Broadway by season, including casts.

331   Entry deleted.

332   Marinacci, Barbara. LEADING LADIES: A GALLERY OF FAMOUS
       ACTRESSES. New York: Dodd, Mead and Co., 1961. 306 p. Index,
       bibliog.

       Marinacci presents twelve chapters, each describing a major actress
       from the past, among them four Americans: Charlotte Cushman,
       Mrs. Fiske, Ethel Barrymore, and Laurette Taylor.

333   Marks, Edward B. THEY ALL HAD GLAMOUR: FROM THE SWEDISH
       NIGHTINGALE TO THE NAKED LADY. New York: Julian Messner,
       1944. 448 p. Index, illus.

       Marks describes the American popular stage from THE BLACK
       CROOK to Adah Issacs Menken, focusing primarily on singers
       and variety artists, but including a full chapter each on G.L.
       Fox and Menken. Marks appends lengthy lists of old-time
       slang terms, ballad and song titles, and a "Roll of Honor" of
       outstanding foreign and native performers.

334   Marshall, Thomas. LIVES OF THE MOST CELEBRATED ACTORS AND AC-
       TRESSES. London: E. Appleyard, 1847. 232 p. Illus.

       Although prepared as biographical-critical accounts of the leading
       London players, this volume includes sections of interest on Bri-
       tish actors who had substantial careers in America: James Wallack,
       William Davidge, and Dion Boucicault.

335   Marston, [John] Westland. OUR RECENT ACTORS: BEING RECOLLEC-
       TIONS CRITICAL, AND, IN MANY CASES, PERSONAL, OF LATE DIS-
       TINGUISHED PERFORMERS OF BOTH SEXES. WITH SOME INCIDENTAL
       NOTICES OF LIVING ACTORS. 2 vols. Boston: Roberts Brothers, 1888.
       xviii, 288; xix, 310. London: S. Low, Marston, Searle, and Rivington,
       1890. 393 p.

       Marston surveys British acting from 1834 to approximately 1880.
       Some inclusions relevant to the American theatre include the
       Vandenhoffs (chapter 1), Charlotte Cushman (chapter 13), Charles
       Fechter (chapter 21), E.A. Sothern (chapter 22), and James
       Wallack (chapter 26).

336   Matthews, Brander. MACREADY AND FORREST AND THEIR CONTEM-
       PORARIES. Boston: L.C. Page, 1900. 304 p. Index, illus.

       Biographical and critical sketches of nineteenth-century British
       and American performers, among them Edwin Forrest, E.L. Daven-

port, Charlotte Cushman, Anna Cora Mowatt, Charles Fechter, Matilda Heron, E.A. Sothern, and John McCullough.

337   _____, ed. PAPERS ON ACTING. New York: Dramatic Museum, Columbia University, 1915-26. New York: Hill and Wang, 1958. viii, 303 p. Index.

A collection of important essays on acting: William Gillette's "The Illusion of the First Time in Acting"; Dion Boucicault's "The Art of Acting"; Coquelin, Irving, and Boucicault's paper debate, "Actors and Acting"; and Edwin Booth's "Edmund Kean and Junius Brutus Booth."

338   _____. PLAYWRIGHTS ON PLAYMAKING AND OTHER STUDIES OF THE STAGE. New York and London: Charles Scribner's Sons, 1923. xiii, 315 p.

A series of essays on various theatrical subjects, including Matthews's "Memories of Actors," in which he recalls John Brougham, John T. Raymond, and Nat Goodwin.

339   _____. RIP VAN WINKLE GOES TO THE PLAY AND OTHER ESSAYS ON PLAYS AND PLAYERS. New York and London: Charles Scribner's Sons, 1926. 256 p.

Included is Matthews's "Memories of Actresses," in which he describes seeing Clara Morris, Mrs. Gilbert, Mrs. Drew, and Ada Rehan.

340   Matthews, Brander, and Hutton, Laurence, eds. ACTORS AND ACTRESSES OF GREAT BRITAIN AND THE UNITED STATES; FROM THE DAYS OF DAVID GARRICK TO THE PRESENT TIME. 5 vols. New York: Cassell and Co., 1886.

A substantial series of essays which, while not illustrated, usually conclude with specific descriptions of performances by the performer. Players important to the American theatre are distributed as follows:
Vol. 1: Lewis Hallam, Jr.
Vol. 2: Thomas Abthorpe Cooper
Vol. 3: John Howard Payne, James W. Wallack, Mary Ann Duff, the elder Booth, Henry Placide, James H. Hackett, William E. Burton, Clara Fisher, and John Brougham.
Vol. 4: Edwin Forrest, E.L. Davenport, Charlotte Cushman, Anna Cora Mowatt, Charles Fechter, Matilda Heron, E.A. Sothern, and John McCullough.
Vol. 5: Mary Anderson, Lawrence Barrett, Edwin Booth, Dion Boucicault, J.S. Clarke, Mr. and Mrs. Florence, Joseph Jefferson III, Modjeska, Clara Morris, John T. Raymond, and Lester Wallack.

341   . THE LIFE AND ART OF EDWIN BOOTH AND HIS CON-
TEMPORARIES. Boston: L.C. Page and Co., 1886. 317 p. Index,
illus.

> Matthews and Hutton assembled a series of articles and essays
> by various authors covering such performers as Mary Anderson,
> Lawrence Barrett, Edwin Booth, Dion Boucicault, J.S. Clarke,
> William Florence, Joseph Jefferson III, Modjeska, Clara Morris,
> John T. Raymond, and Lester Wallack. Each chapter contains
> a series of critical assessments of the specific player.

342 Moody, William Vaughn. LETTERS TO HARRIETT. Edited, Intro. and Conclusion by Percy MacKaye. Boston and New York: Houghton Mifflin,
1935. 443 p. Index, illus., bibliog.

> Moody, in his letters to his wife, commented freely on such
> players as Margaret Anglin, Ethel Barrymore, Julia Marlowe,
> and Henry Miller.

343 Moore, Isabel. TALKS IN A LIBRARY WITH LAURENCE HUTTON. New
York and London: G.P. Putnam's Sons, 1905. ix, 447 p. Index, illus.

> Moore recorded a series of informal reminiscences by Hutton
> shortly before his death and published them as a biographical
> volume. Hutton's friendship with and observations of several ac-
> tors are included, with descriptions of Edwin Booth, Frederick
> Warde, Lawrence Barrett, Joseph Jefferson III, Lester Wallack,
> Henry J. Montague, William Florence, John McCullough, and
> Mary Anderson.

344 Morgan-Powell, S. MEMORIES THAT LIVE. Toronto: Macmillan Co.,
1929. 282 p.

> A haphazard collection of vignettes and sketches on various sub-
> jects and personalities, among them Margaret Anglin, E.H.
> Sothern, and Julia Marlowe.

345 Morley, Henry. JOURNAL OF A LONDON PLAYGOER. London: George
Routledge and Sons, 1891. 316 p. Index. Reprint. Leicester, Engl.:
Leicester University Press, 1974.

> London theatre criticisms, including coverage of several visiting
> performers, such as Charles Fechter, Dion Boucicault, and John
> Drew.

346 Morrissey, James W. NOTED MEN AND WOMEN, A PROFUSELY ILLUS-
TRATED BOOK CONTAINING THE HUMOR, WIT, SENTIMENT, AND
DIPLOMACY IN THE SOCIAL, ARTISTIC, AND BUSINESS LIVES OF THE

PEOPLE SET FORTH. New York: Klebold Press, 1910. 262 p. Illus.

A rambling, disconnected, and undocumented discourse, describing the many celebrities Morrissey had known, among them Mary Anderson, Rose Coghlan, Joseph Jefferson III, Richard Mansfield, DeWolf Hopper, Edwin Booth, and Fanny Davenport.

347   Moses, Montrose. FAMOUS ACTOR-FAMILIES IN AMERICA. New York: Thomas D. Crowell and Co., 1906. viii, 341 p. Illus., bibliog. Reprint. New York: Benjamin Blom, 1968.

Based on a series of articles in THEATRE MAGAZINE (N.Y.) in 1904 and 1905. Not completely accurate; some dates are inaccurate, but still a valuable source of information with an extensive bibliography. Coverage includes the Booths, the Jeffersons, the Sotherns, the Boucicaults, the Hacketts, the Drews, the Barrymores, the Wallacks, the Davenports, the Hollands, and the Powers.

348   Nathan, George Jean. COMEDIANS ALL. New York: Alfred A. Knopf, 1919. 267 p.

Various critical essays, including "Belasco" (pp. 70-71), a few remarks on Otis Skinner (pp. 155-56), "The Belasco Technic" (pp. 217-18), and comments on George M. Cohan (pp. 252-53).

349   Newquist, Roy. SHOWCASE. Caricatures by Irma Selz. New York: William Morrow and Co., 1966. 412 p. Illus.

A collection of twenty-five interviews by Newquist with various celebrities, among them Helen Hayes (pp. 195-209).

350   NEW YORK THEATRE CRITICS' REVIEWS. New York: Critics Theatre Reviews, 1940-- . Weekly.

A publication compiling reviews of Broadway productions. The first two years were published as CRITICS' THEATRE REVIEWS, thereafter by the present title.

351   Oppenheimer, George, ed. THE PASSIONATE PLAYGOER: A PERSONAL SCRAPBOOK. New York: Viking Press, 1958. 612 p. Index, illus.

A collection of essays on various aspects of the theatre, including acting. Includes Ethel Barrymore's "A Memory," Robert E. Sherwood's "The Lunts," Ruth Gordon's "Those Years after YEARS AGO," Charles Brackett's "Jane Cowl," Alexander Woollcott's "Miss Kitty Takes to the Road," Tallulah Bankhead's "It's Not 'The Road'--It's Detours," and Percy Hammond's "The Barrymore Hamlet."

352   Osmun, Thomas Embley [Ayres, Alfred]. ACTING AND ACTORS: ELOCUTION AND ELOCUTIONISTS: A BOOK ABOUT THEATRE FOLK AND

THEATRE ART. New York: D. Appleton and Co., 1894. 287 p. Index.
2d ed. with supplement. New York: D. Appleton and Co., 1894. 293 p.

A series of essays discussing elocution and acting with descriptions
of leading players in specific roles, including Edwin Forrest, McKee
Rankin, Lawrence Barrett, Charlotte Cushman, Edwin Booth, and
Julia Marlowe.

353   Oxberry, William. OXBERRY'S DRAMATIC BIOGRAPHY AND HISTRONIC
ANECDOTES. 7 vols. London: G. Virtue, 1825-27.

Volume 4, pages 181-96, is an early assessment of the elder Booth's
acting, which Oxberry considered inferior to Kean's, Macready's,
and Charles Kemble's; volume 5 and pages 181-92 considers
James Wallack.

354   Parish, James Robert, and Bowers, Ronald L. THE MGM STOCK COMPANY:
THE GOLDEN ERA. New Rochelle, N.Y.: Arlington House, 1973. 818 p.
Index, illus.

Filmographies and brief biographical sketches of film stars, among
them Ethel, John, and Lionel Barrymore, Billie Burke, and Marie
Dressler.

355   Parker, John, ed. THE GREEN ROOM BOOK AND ANGLO-AMERICAN
DRAMATIC REGISTER. London: T. Sealey Clark and Co., 1906-09.

Superseded by WHO'S WHO IN THE THEATRE (no. 30) which
was edited by Parker up through the eleventh edition in 1952.

356   Paul, Howard, and Gebbie, George, eds. THE STAGE AND ITS STARS,
PAST AND PRESENT. A GALLERY OF DRAMATIC ILLUSTRATIONS AND
CRITICAL BIOGRAPHIES OF DISTINGUISHED ENGLISH AND AMERICAN
ACTORS FROM THE TIME OF SHAKESPEARE TILL TODAY. 2 vols. in 1.
Philadelphia: Gebbie and Co., 1887.

Among those treated are William H. Crane, Stuart Robson, Ada
Rehan, William E. Burton, J. Lester Wallack, John Drew, James
H. Hackett, the elder Booth, Richard Mansfield, Edwin Forrest,
Mary Anderson, Charles Fechter, Charlotte Cushman, James W.
Wallack, E.L. Davenport, and James E. Murdoch in the first
volume. Volume 2 includes several of the above, plus William
Warren II, Joseph Jefferson III, John McCullough, William J.
Florence, Modjeska, John Gilbert, Mrs. John Drew, John Brough-
ham, Lawrence Barrett, Janauschek, E.A. Sothern, Fanny Daven-
port, Clara Morris, Rose Coghlan, Nat Goodwin, Julia Marlowe,
James Lewis, Mrs. Gilbert, Agnes Booth, Denman Thompson,
Lotta Crabtree, and Maggie Mitchell. All are shown in success-
ful roles.

357   Pond, Maj. J[ames]. B[urton]. ECCENTRICITIES OF GENIUS: MEMORIES OF FAMOUS MEN AND WOMEN OF THE PLATFORM AND STAGE. New York: G.W. Dillingham, 1900. xxvi, 554 p. Index, illus.

> Joseph Jefferson III and Charlotte Cushman are included in brief essays of very little distinction.

358   PORTRAITS OF THE AMERICAN STAGE 1771-1971. Washington, D.C.: Published for the National Portrait Gallery by the Smithsonian Institution Press, 1971. 201 p. Index, illus.

> An exhibition catalog for an exhibition at the National Gallery in 1971. Portraits are reproduced in black and white and accompanied by a one-page biographical sketch. Those included are Nancy Hallam, John Durang, William B. Wood, the elder Booth, Ira Aldridge, Edwin Forrest, Clara Fisher, Charlotte Cushman, Edwin Booth, John McCullough, Joseph Jefferson III, Dion Boucicault, Richard Mansfield, Mrs. Fiske, Maude Adams, Julia Marlowe, Ethel Barrymore, Walter Hampden, Nazimova, Fay Bainter, Otis Skinner, Jeane Eagels, John Barrymore, Katharine Cornell, Tallaluh Bankhead, Paul Robeson, the Lunts, Zero Mostel, and Helen Hayes.

359   Rede, Leman Thomas, and Wemyss, Francis G., eds. THE GUIDE TO THE STAGE, CONTAINING CLEAR AND AMPLE INSTRUCTIONS FOR OBTAINING THEATRICAL ENGAGEMENTS, WITH A LIST OF THE PROVINCIAL THEATRES, NAMES OF THE MANAGERS, AND PARTICULARS AS TO SALARIES, RULES, FINES, & C., AND A CLEAR ELUCIDATION OF ALL THE TECHNICALITIES OF THE HISTRIONIC ART. TO WHICH IS ADDED A LIST OF THE LONDON THEATRES AND COPIES OF THEIR RULES AND ARTICLES OF ENGAGEMENT BY LEMAN THOMAS REDE. WITH ADDITIONAL INFORMATION MAKING IT APPLICABLE TO THE AMERICAN STAGE, WITH LESSONS FOR BEGINNERS, INSTRUCTING THEM HOW TO OBTAIN A FIRST APPEARANCE; HOW TO CONDUCT THEMSELVES IN THE GREEN-ROOM: HOW TO GO THROUGH A REHEARSAL AND A FIRST PERFORMANCE; THE NECESSARY DRESSES AND PROPERTIES DESCRIBED; THE PRICES; HOW AND WHERE TO OBTAIN THEM; HOW TO DRESS, PAINT, AND MAKE UP FOR A PART; SALARIES, RULES, &C., &C., &C. ALSO A LIST OF THE AMERICAN THEATRES. AND COPIES OF THEIR RULES AND ARTICLES OF ENGAGEMENT. EDITED BY FRANCIS G. WEMYSS. New York: Samuel French, 1864. 58 p.

> According to the NATIONAL UNION CATALOG, this guide went through at least ten editions. A fascinating look at the more practical aspects of the profession at the time.

360   Reid, Erskine, and Compton, Herbert. THE DRAMATIC PEERAGE, 1891: PERSONAL NOTES AND PROFESSIONAL SKETCHES OF THE ACTORS AND ACTRESSES OF THE LONDON STAGE. London: General Publishing Co., [1891]. 266 p.

> Of small value, the biographical entries being quite brief, but

including a few English actors with substantial careers in America.

361   Rice, Edw[ard]. LeRoy. MONARCHS OF MINSTRELSY, FROM "DADDY"
       RICE TO DATE. New York: Kenny Publishing, 1911. 336 p. Index,
       illus.

       Brief remarks about minstrel performers, among them some with
       later careers in the legitimate theatre, such as Otis Skinner,
       Francis Wilson, and Wilton Lackaye.

362   Rigdon, Walter, ed. THE BIOGRAPHICAL ENCYCLOPEDIA & WHO'S
       WHO OF THE AMERICAN THEATRE. New York: James H. Heineman,
       1966. xiv, 1,101 p.

       A comprehensive reference work including over seven hundred
       pages of biographical entries on American theatre personnel,
       plus a bibliographical bibliography. See McGill's NOTABLE
       NAMES IN THE AMERICAN THEATRE (no. 326) for a more recent
       version.

363   Robins, Edward. TWELVE GREAT ACTORS. New York and London: G.P.
       Putnam's Sons, Knickerbocker Press, 1900. xiv, 460 p. Index, illus.

       Somewhat idealized and undocumented biographical sketches,
       including the elder Booth, Edwin Forrest, Edwin Booth, Charles
       Fechter, William E. Burton, E.A. Sothern, and John Lester Wal-
       lack.

364   _____. TWELVE GREAT ACTRESSES. New York and London: G.P.
       Putnam's Sons, 1900. iv, 431 p. Index, illus.

       Using the same treatment as in the previous volume (no. 363),
       Robins describes Charlotte Cushman.

365   Rosenberg, C[harles]. [Q]. YOU HAVE HEARD OF THEM. New York:
       Redfield, 1854. vi, 353 p. Frontispiece.

       A series of somewhat shallow biographical sketches, among them
       essays on Dion Boucicault and Charlotte Cushman.

366   Rosenberg, Marvin. THE MASKS OF KING LEAR. Berkeley, Los Angeles,
       and London: University of California Press, 1972. 424 p. Index, bibliog.

       Rosenberg has examined, compiled, and analyzed the records of
       major productions of LEAR and devised a production history of the
       script. Among the American actors included are the elder Booth,
       Edwin Booth, Morris Carnovsky, Edwin Forrest, Robert Mantell,
       and John McCullough.

367   _____. THE MASKS OF MACBETH. Berkeley, Los Angeles, and
       London: University of California Press, 1978. xiv, 743 p. Index,
       bibliog.

See previous entry (no. 366). This volume includes coverage of Ira Aldridge, Viola Allen, Edwin Booth, the elder Booth, Charlotte Cushman, Edwin Forrest, James K. Hackett, Walter Hampden, Janauschek, Julia Marlowe, Modjeska, Clara Morris, E.H. Sothern, and George Vandenhoff.

368   . THE MASKS OF OTHELLO: THE SEARCH FOR THE IDENTITY OF OTHELLO, IAGO, AND DESDEMONA BY THREE CENTURIES OF ACTORS AND CRITICS. Berkeley and Los Angeles: University of California Press, 1961. ix, 302 p. Index, frontispiece, notes.

The first of Rosenberg's excellent series of similar studies. He describes performances by Ira Aldridge, Edwin Booth, Charles Fechter, Edwin Forrest, and Paul Robeson.

369   Ross, Lillian, and Ross, Helen. THE PLAYER: A PROFILE OF AN ART. New York: Simon and Schuster, 1962. 437 p. Index, illus.

Fifty-five autobiographical sketches, based on interviews. Includes Zero Mostel, Katharine Cornell, and Fredric March.

370   Rowlands, Walter. AMONG THE GREAT MASTERS OF THE DRAMA: SCENES IN THE LIVES OF FAMOUS ACTORS. Boston: Dana Estes and Co., 1903. 233 p. Illus.

Rowlands presents thirty-three brief (eight to ten pages) essays on various theatre artists, from Shakespeare to Mary Anderson. American stars include Edwin Forrest, William Warren II, Charlotte Cushman, Joseph Jefferson III, Edwin Booth, John McCullough, Lawrence Barrett, Modjeska, and Mary Anderson.

371   Salgado, Gamini. EYEWITNESSES OF SHAKESPEARE: FIRST HAND ACCOUNTS OF PERFORMANCES, 1590-1890. London: Cox and Wyman; New York: Harper and Row, 1975. 358 p. Index, illus.

A useful sourcebook, including descriptions of Ira Aldridge, the elder Booth, Charles Fechter, and Ada Rehan.

372   Schevichaven, Herman Diederik Johan van [Larwood, Jacob]. THEATRICAL ANECDOTES OR FUN AND CURIOSITIES OF THE PLAY, THE PLAYHOUSE, AND THE PLAYERS. London: Chatto and Windus, 1882. 323 p. Index.

Of limited value; the preface suggests "Too great a regard for truth has taken the point out of many a good story, and to weigh evidences concerning the 'flying words' of a theatrical anecdote is a waste of critical acumen equal to the feat of breaking a butterfly on the wheel." An amusing collection, needing corroboration.

373   Shaw, Dale. TITANS OF THE AMERICAN STAGE: EDWIN FORREST,

THE BOOTHS, THE O'NEILLS. Philadelphia: Westminster Press, 1971. 156 p. Index, illus., bibliog.

Brief treatments, drawing upon widely available materials for those named in the title.

374 Sherman, Robert Lowery. ACTORS AND AUTHORS WITH COMPOSERS AND MANAGERS WHO HELPED MAKE THEM FAMOUS: A CHRONO-LOGICAL RECORD AND BRIEF BIOGRAPHY OF THE THEATRICAL CELE-BRITIES FROM 1750 TO 1950. Chicago: Robert L. Sherman, 1951. 433 p.

An undocumented series of capsule biographies of theatrical cele-brities. Requires corroboration.

375 Shipman, Louis Evan. A GROUP OF THEATRICAL CARICATURES BEING TWELVE PLATES BY W.J. GLADDING WITH AN INTRODUCTION AND BIOGRAPHICAL SKETCHES BY LOUIS EVAN SHIPMAN. New York: Dun-lap Society, 1897. Reprint. Burt Franklin, 1970. viii, 78 p. Illus.

Brief essays about John Brougham, Lester Wallack, Edwin Forrest, Edwin Booth, William J. Florence, John E. Owens, Francis S. Chanfrau, and G.L. Fox, among others.

376 Skolsky, Sidney. TIMES SQUARE TIN-TYPES, BEING TYPEWRITER CARI-CATURES OF THOSE WHO MADE THEIR NAMES ALONG THE NOT SO STRAIGHT AND VERY NARROW PATH OF BROADWAY. New York: Ives Washburn, 1930. 291 p. Illus.

Three- to four-page essays of David Belasco, George M. Cohan, Dorothy Gish, Lynn Fontanne, and Eva Le Gallienne, among others.

377 Stevens, Ashton. ACTOR VIEWS: INTIMATE PORTRAITS. Chicago: Covici-McGee Co., 1923. 324 p. Index, illus.

In a breezy and informal style, Stevens addresses himself to the various aspects of the commercial theatre of his time, including brief remarks about the leading players. Performers included are John Drew, Arnold Daly, Elsie Ferguson, Ina Claire, John Barry-more, Mrs. Leslie Carter, Laurette Taylor, Louis Wolheim, Richard Bennett, Nat Goodwin, David Warfield, Lynn Fontanne, Raymond Hitchcock, E.H. Sothern, Julia Marlowe, Helen Hayes, Pauline Lord, Patricia Collinge, Frank Bacon, Jane Cowl, and Mrs. Fiske.

378 Strang, Lewis C[linton]. CELEBRATED COMEDIANS OF LIGHT OPERA AND MUSICAL COMEDY IN AMERICA. Boston: L.C. Page, 1901. 279 p. Index, illus. Reprint. New York: Benjamin Blom, 1971.

Some of Strang's subjects also had careers on the legitimate stage, among them Jefferson DeAngelis, DeWolf Hopper, and Francis Wilson.

379   _____. FAMOUS ACTORS OF THE DAY IN AMERICA. First Series.
Boston: L.C. Page, 1900. 333 p. Index, illus.

A gracefully written volume of twenty-five biographical and
critical essays, covering Joseph Jefferson III, James A. Herne,
Richard Mansfield, E.M. Holland, E.H. Sothern, John Drew,
William Faversham, John B. Mason, Nat Goodwin, James O'Neill,
William H. Crane, Wilton Lackaye, William Gillette, Henry
Miller, James K. Hackett, Stuart Robson, Sol Smith Russell,
Otis Skinner, J.E. Dodson, Robert Mantell, Joseph Haworth,
and Herbert Kelcey.

380   _____. FAMOUS ACTORS OF THE DAY IN AMERICA. Second Series.
Boston: L.C. Page, 1902. viii, 333 p. Index, illus.

This volume deals rather more with criticism of each actor than
did the first volume (no. 379). Actors described include E.H.
Sothern, John Drew, Nat Goodwin, John B. Mason, William
Gillette, Richard Mansfield, William Faversham, Stuart Robson,
James O'Neill, James A. Herne, William H. Crane, Henry
Miller, E.S. Willard, and Louis Mann.

381   _____. FAMOUS ACTRESSES OF THE DAY IN AMERICA. Boston: L.C.
Page, 1899. 338 p. Index, illus.

Thirty-one short chapters, each with an actress as its subject.
Strang admits that he has only compiled and edited the material
and that he offers very little new information. Actresses include
Maude Adams, Julia Marlowe, Sarah Cowell LeMoyne, Mrs.
Fiske, Ida Conquest, Blanche Walsh, Annie Russell, Isabel Irving,
Maxine Elliott, Ada Rehan, Virginia Harned, Viola Allen, Mary
Mannering, May Irwin, Mrs. Carter, Mary Shaw, Olga Nether-
sole, Blanch Bates, Elsie DeWolfe, Rose Coghlan, Margaret Ang-
lin, Odette Taylor, Marie Burroughs, Modjeska, and May Robson.

382   _____. FAMOUS ACTRESSES OF THE DAY IN AMERICA. Second
Series. Boston: L.C. Page, 1902. 331 p. Index, illus.

Strang focuses more on criticism than on biography and anecdote.
Those selected include Julia Marlowe, Henrietta Crosman, Mary
Shaw, Maude Adams, Amelia Bingham, Ida Conquest, Mrs. Fiske,
Hilda Spong, Annie Russell, Mary Mannering, Mrs. Carter, Sarah
Cowell Le Moyne, Ada Rehan, Grace George, Margaret Anglin,
Viola Allen, and Maxine Elliott.

383   _____. PLAYERS AND PLAYS OF THE LAST QUARTER CENTURY: AN
HISTORICAL SUMMARY OF CAUSES AND A CRITICAL REVIEW OF CON-
DITIONS AS EXISTING IN THE AMERICAN THEATRE AT THE CLOSE OF
THE NINETEENTH CENTURY. 2 vols. Boston: L.C. Page, 1903.
292, 322 p. Index, illus.

Volume 1 is subtitled THE THEATRE OF YESTERDAY; volume 2,

THE THEATRE OF TO-DAY. The first volume contains substantial descriptions of Edwin Forrest, Charlotte Cushman, Jean Davenport, John McCullough, Frank Murdoch, E.L. Davenport, Lawrence Barrett, Edwin Booth, Mrs. Duff, Anna Cora Mowatt, Mary Anderson, Modjeska, Julia Marlowe, Henry Placide, James H. Hackett, William E. Burton, John Gilbert, John E. Owens, Joseph Jefferson III, William J. Florence, and William Warren. Volume 2 deals more with drama than with performers, but includes material on Clara Morris, Mrs. Fiske, and Henrietta Crosman.

384 _____. PRIMA DONNAS AND SOUBRETTES OF LIGHT OPERA AND MUSICAL COMEDY IN AMERICA. Boston: L.C. Page and Co., 1900. 259 p. Index, illus.

Capsule biographies of twenty-two performers, among them Lillian Russell and Marie Dressler.

385 TALLIS'S DRAWING-ROOM TABLE BOOK OF THE THEATRICAL PORTRAITS, MEMOIRS, AND ANECDOTES. London and New York: J. Tallis and Co., 1851.

Includes two- or three-page sections on Mrs. Mowatt, E.L. Davenport, Ira Aldridge, James H. Hackett, and Charlotte Cushman.

386 Townsend, Margaret [Margaret]. THEATRICAL SKETCHES: HERE AND THERE WITH PROMINENT ACTORS. New York: Merriam Co., 1894. 217 p. Illus.

Twenty-five brief essays of an anecdotal nature, including "Lester Wallack Averse to the Stage. His advice to a Young Lady," "A Glimpse of the Domestic Life of Edwin Booth," "Louis James in Comedy," "Characteristics of Maurice Barrymore," "A Playwright's Interview with the Mansfields," "Letters and Lines from Louis James," "A Realistic Dream of the Late Lester Wallack," and a discussion of Lillian Russell (p. 123-f).

387 Trumble, Alfred. GREAT ARTISTS OF THE AMERICAN STAGE: A PORTRAIT GALLERY OF THE LEADING ACTORS AND ACTRESSES OF AMERICA WITH CRITICAL BIOGRAPHIES. New York: Richard K. Fox, 1882. 73 p. Illus.

A volume of steel engravings and three- to four-page capsule biographies of thirty performers, among them Joseph Jefferson III, Janauschek, Edwin Booth, Clara Morris, Lester Wallack, Fanny Davenport, John Gilbert, Lawrence Barrett, Rose Coghlan, John T. Raymond, Rose Eytinge, John McCullough, Frank Chanfrau, Maggie Mitchell, Kate Claxton, Stuart Robson, William H. Crane, J.H. Stoddart, and Agnes Booth.

388 Vardac, A. Nicholas. STAGE TO SCREEN: THEATRICAL METHOD FROM

GARRICK TO GRIFFITH. Cambridge, Mass.: Harvard University Press, 1949. xxvi, 251 p. Index, illus.

> Vardac examines the relationship between stage and film and includes substantial sections on the aesthetics of David Belasco and Steele MacKaye.

389   Wagenknecht, Edward C[harles]. MERELY PLAYERS. Norman: University of Oklahoma Press, 1966. xiv, 270 p. Index, illus., bibliog.

> Chapters are devoted to Edwin Forrest, Edwin Booth, Joseph Jefferson III, and Richard Mansfield.

390   Wagner, Frederick, and Brady, Barbara. FAMOUS AMERICAN ACTORS AND ACTRESSES. Famous Biographies for Young People Series. New York: Dodd, Mead and Co., 1961. 154 p. Index, illus., bibliog.

> Includes chapters on Edwin Forrest, Joseph Jefferson III, Edwin Booth, the Drews, the Barrymores, E.H. Sothern, Julia Marlowe, Maude Adams, George M. Cohan, the Lunts, Katharine Cornell, and Helen Hayes.

391   Walbrook, H.M. NIGHTS AT THE PLAY. London: W.J. Ham-Smith, 1911. xiv, 218 p. Index, illus.

> A collection of reviews of London stage productions, reprinted from the PALL MALL GAZETTE, including coverage of Genevieve Ward, Rose Stahl, Julia Marlowe, and E.H. Sothern.

392   Wallace, Irving; Wallace, Amy; Wallechinsky, David; and Wallace, Sylvia. THE INTIMATE SEX LIVES OF FAMOUS PEOPLE. New York: Delacorte Press, 1981. xvii, 592 p. Index, illus.

> Undocumented and sensationalized accounts of various celebrities, including John Barrymore (pp. 24–26), Lillian Russell (pp. 36–38), and Adah Isaacs Menken (pp. 503–4).

393   Wemyss, Francis Courtney. THEATRICAL BIOGRAPHY OF EMINENT ACTORS AND AUTHORS COMPARED FROM THE STANDARD AND MINOR DRAMA WITH PORTRAITS OF E. FORREST AND SIR E.L. BULWER. New York: Estate of William Taylor, [1836]. Glasgow, Scotland: R. Griffin, 1848. 324 p.

> Unavailable for examination.

394   Wharton, John F. LIFE AMONG THE PLAYWRIGHTS BEING MOSTLY THE STORY OF THE PLAYWRIGHTS PRODUCING COMPANY, INC. New York: Quadrangle, New York Times Book Co., 1974. viii, 320 p. Index, illus.

> Exactly what the title suggests, but amplified by material about specific performers, such as Katharine Cornell, Lynn Fontanne, Helen Hayes, and Alfred Lunt.

395   Whitman, Walt. THE GATHERING OF THE FORCES: EDITORIALS, ESSAYS,
        LITERARY AND DRAMATIC REVIEWS AND OTHER MATERIAL WRITTEN BY
        WALT WHITMAN AS EDITOR OF THE BROOKLYN DAILY EAGLE IN 1846
        AND 1847. 2 vols. New York: Putnam's, 1920. lxiii, 272; 386 p. Index,
        illus.

        As a drama critic, Whitman describes Charlotte Cushman, whom
        he preferred, and Edwin Forrest, whose style he considered over-
        done.

396   Whitton, Joseph. WAGS OF THE STAGE. Philadelphia: George H. Rigby,
        1902. 264 p. Illus.

        Whitton gathered together a lengthy collection of anecdotes about
        leading players of the day, among them the elder Booth, John
        Brougham, William R. Blake, Edwin Forrest, William E. Burton,
        John Drew I, William H. Florence, E.A. Sothern, and a substan-
        tial section on William Wheatley.

397   WHO WAS WHO IN THE THEATRE 1912-1976. A BIOGRAPHICAL DIC-
        TIONARY OF ACTORS, ACTRESSES, DIRECTORS, PLAYWRIGHTS, AND
        PRODUCERS OF THE ENGLISH-SPEAKING THEATRE, COMPILED FROM
        WHO'S WHO IN THE THEATRE, VOLUMES 1-15 (1912-1972). 4 vols.
        Detroit: Gale Research Co., 1978.

        A compilation from the earlier series with dates of deaths added.
        An invaluable reference, albeit dates are not always accurate.

398   Wilde, Oscar. THE LETTERS OF OSCAR WILDE. Rupert Hart-Davis, ed.
        New York: Harcourt, Brace and World, 1962. 872 p. Index, illus.

        In widely varying circumstances, references are made to Dion
        Boucicault, Clara Morris, Modjeska, and Mary Anderson.

399   Wingate, Charles E[dgar]. L[ewis]. SHAKESPEARE'S HEROES ON THE
        STAGE. 2 vols. New York: Thomas Y. Crowell and Co., 1896. vi,
        335 p. Index, illus.

        Organized by role, describing leading actors such as Edwin
        Adams, Ira Aldridge, Anthony Aston, Daniel Bandmann, Lawrence
        Barrett, the Booths, Rose Coghlan, Thomas Abthorpe Cooper,
        Charlotte Cushman, E.L. Davenport, David Douglass, William
        Davidge, Mrs. Duff, Charles Fechter, James Fennell, Clara
        Fisher, William J. Florence, Edwin Forrest, John Gilbert, the
        Hallams, Thomas Hamblin, Joseph Haworth, John Henry, John
        Hodgkinson, Louis James, Joseph Jefferson I and III, Herbert
        Kelcey, Richard Mansfield, Robert Mantell, Frank Mayo, John
        McCullough, Modjeska, James E. Murdoch, John Howard Payne,
        George Vandenhoff, the Wallacks, Frederick Warde, and E.S.
        Willard.

400   _____. SHAKESPEARE'S HEROINES ON THE STAGE. New York and
Boston: Thomas Y. Crowell and Co., 1895. 355 p. Index, illus.

Wingate's organizational approach is to examine briefly the outstanding performances of Shakespeare's heroines, including Juliet,
Beatrice, Hermione, Perdita, Viola, Imogen, Rosalind, Cleopatra,
Lady Macbeth, Queen Katherine, Portia, Katherine, and Ophelia.
After a description of leading British actresses in each role, Win-
gate examines the American stage history of the past. Among
the American performers described are Ira Aldridge, Mary Ander-
son, Lawrence Barrett, Edwin and John Wilkes Booth, Thomas Ab-
thorpe Cooper, Charlotte Cushman, E.L. and Fanny Davenport,
Julia Dean, the Hallams, Clara Fisher, Edwin Forrest, John Henry,
Janauschek, Laura Keene, Julia Marlowe, Modjeska, Anna Cora
Mowatt, Kate Reignolds, James W. Wallack, and Lester Wallack.

401   Winter, William. BRIEF CHRONICLES. New York: Dunlap Society,
1889. Reprint. New York: Burt Franklin, 1970. 339 p. Frontispiece.

A compilation of eighty-six biographical sketches by Winter of
various performers he had seen and in many cases known. All
the articles had been written for various serials, such as the New
York TRIBUNE, the WEEKLY REVIEW, ALBION, HARPER's
WEEKLY, SATURDAY PRESS, LEADER, VANITY FAIR, and the
Boston GAZETTE. Most were tributes, written shortly after the
subject's death. Among those included are Edwin Adams, Mary
McVicker Booth, John Brougham, Ada Clare, Charlotte Cushman,
Julia Dean, Charles Fechter, Edwin Forrest, James H. Hackett,
Matilda Heron, George Holland, Laura Keene, John McCullough,
H.J. Montague, Mrs. Mowatt, Henry Placide, John T. Raymond,
Sol Smith, E.A. Sothern, Mrs. C.R. Thorne, J.W. Wallack, and
Lester Wallack. Most of the essays, revised from their earlier
version, are brief.

402   _____. OTHER DAYS BEING CHRONICLES AND MEMORIES OF THE
STAGE. New York: Moffat, Yard and Co., 1908. 389 p. Index, illus.
Reprint. Freeport, N.Y.: Books for Libraries, 1970.

Winter collects nine of ten sketches originally published in the
Philadelphia SATURDAY EVENING POST. The tenth, on Richard
Mansfield, appears in Winter's biography of him. Winter adds an
introductory chapter, covering such performers as John Hodgkinson, James Fennell, Thomas Abthorpe Cooper, Edwin Forrest,
the elder Booth, and Edwin Booth. He then devotes chapters to
Joseph Jefferson III, John Brougham, Dion Boucicault, Charlotte
Cushman, E.A. Sothern, John McCullough, Lawrence Barrett,
and Mary Anderson.

403   _____. POEMS. New York: Moffat, Yard and Co., 1909. 319 p.
Frontispiece.

Winter includes poetic tributes to Edwin Booth, Lawrence Barrett,
and Joseph Jefferson III.

404 _____. SHADOWS OF THE STAGE. New York and London: Macmillan Co., 1896. 387 p. Edinburgh: D. Douglas, 1892.

The first of three volumes, originally serialized in HARPER'S WEEKLY, beginning with volume 54 (24 September 1910). Of the twenty-eight essays in this volume, separate treatments are given to Edwin Booth, Mary Anderson, Joseph Jefferson III, William J. Florence, John McCullough, Charlotte Cushman, Lawrence Barrett, Ada Rehan, Richard Mansfield, Genevieve Ward, Edward S. Willard, Charles Fisher, Mrs. Gilbert, and James Lewis.

405 _____. SHADOWS OF THE STAGE. Second Series. New York and London: Macmillan and Co., 1893. 367 p.

The second volume in a series contains essays on Mrs. Duff, the elder Booth, James H. Hackett, Edwin Forrest, John Gilbert, John Brougham, Charlotte Cushman, William Wheatley, John E. Owens, Jean Davenport Lander, Ada Rehan, Clara Morris, Lawrence Barrett, John T. Raymond, Richard Mansfield, E.S. Willard, and Modjeska.

406 _____. SHADOWS OF THE STAGE. Third Series. New York and London: Macmillan and Co., 1895. 351 p.

Winter describes specific productions by Ada Rehan, Lawrence Barrett, Augustin Daly, Richard Mansfield, Edward S. Willard, Mary Anderson, and Edwin Booth.

407 _____. VAGRANT MEMORIES: BEING FURTHER RECOLLECTIONS OF OTHER DAYS. New York: George H. Doran Co., 1915. 525 p. Index. Reprint. Freeport, N.Y.: Books for Libraries, 1970.

Winter considered this work a supplement to OTHER DAYS (no. 402), but in this case much of the material had not been previously published. Winter devotes entire chapters to William Warren, Lester Wallack, Edwin Booth, E.H. Sothern, and Julia Marlowe, and reminiscences to a lesser degree about Laura Keene, Matilda Heron, James W. Wallack, Edwin Adams, Henry Montague, the elder Booth, John Wilkes Booth, Clara Morris, Ada Rehan, Mrs. Gilbert, James Lewis, and Mary Anderson.

408 _____. THE WALLET OF TIME CONTAINING PERSONAL, BIOGRAPHICAL, AND CRITICAL REMINISCENCES OF THE AMERICAN THEATRE. 2 vols. New York: Moffat and Yard, 1913. Reprint. New York: Benjamin Blom, 1969. Freeport, N.Y.: Books for Libraries, 1969.

Winter attempted to give a "comprehensive glance at dramatic affairs in America within the period of about the last sixty years." Although Winter was an active critic during that period, his prejudices emerge in almost every essay. Among the actors he describes are Lawrence Barrett, John Brougham, Charlotte Cushman, Charles Fechter, Edwin Forrest, Mrs. Gilbert, George Holland, James Lewis, John McCullough, Modjeska, Mary Anderson, Blanche Bates, Mrs. Carter, Mrs. Fiske, Julia Marlowe, Ada Rehan, E.H. Sothern, and David Warfield.

409   WIT AND HUMOR OF THE STAGE: A COLLECTION FROM VARIOUS SOURCES CLASSIFIED UNDER APPROPRIATE SUBJECT HEADINGS. Philadelphia: George W. Jacobs, 1909. 236 p.

Anecdotes concerning various theatrical figures, among them E.A. Sothern, Nat Goodwin, Joseph Jefferson III, and John McCullough. Undocumented.

410   Woollcott, Alexander. ENCHANTED AISLES. New York and London: G.P. Putnam's Sons, 1924. 260 p.

A collection of Woollcott's essays, most of them previously published in various serials, among them recollections and descriptions of Pauline Lord, Mrs. Fiske, John Drew, William Gillette, and David Belasco.

411   _____. THE PORTABLE WOOLLCOTT. New York: Viking Press, 1946. xxviii, 729 p. Index.

A collection of various writings by Woollcott, among them "Colossal Bronze" about Paul Robeson (pp. 158-69), "Miss Kitty Takes to the Road" about Katharine Cornell (pp. 469-80), and comments on Mrs. Fiske on pages 407-17.

412   Young, Roland. ACTORS AND OTHERS. Introduction by Ashton Stevens. Chicago: Pascal Covici, 1925. 92 p. Illus.

The first edition was limited to 550 numbered and autographed copies. The volume is a collection of caricatures of celebrities, among them Ethel Barrymore, John Drew, Francis Wilson, Henry Hull, Louis Wolheim, Helen Westley, Walter Hampden, and Otis Skinner.

413   Young, William C. FAMOUS ACTORS AND ACTRESSES OF THE AMERICAN STAGE: DOCUMENTS OF AMERICAN THEATRE HISTORY. 2 vols. 602, 696 p. New York and London: R.R. Bowker Co., 1975. Illus., bibliog.

Young encapsulates the careers of 225 performers, some of them foreign or from popular entertainment forms, drawing upon source materials of various types to describe them.

GENERAL SOURCES: SERIALS

414   Adams, Mildred. "Young Ladies of the Stage." WOMAN CITIZEN 8 (19 April 1924): 36-37. Illus.

       Among others, Adams offers brief descriptive tributes and photographs of Mrs. Whiffen, Rose Coghlan, and Helen Hayes.

415   Anderson, John. "Sketches." THEATRE ARTS 15 (January 1931): 26-30.

       Brief descriptions of the acting of Paul Muni and Lynn Fontanne.

416   Archer, William. "The American Stage." PALL MALL MAGAZINE 19 (1899) 303-16, 473-88; 20 (1900) 23-37.

       An assessment of the U.S. theatre, mentioning most of the major actors of the time, albeit briefly. Well illustrated.

417   Barker, Meta. "Some Highlights of the Old Atlanta Stage." ATLANTA HISTORICAL SOCIETY BULLETIN 1 (January 1928): 33-51.

       Barker describes engagement in Atlanta by Edwin Forrest, Lawrence Barrett, Edwin Booth, Mary Anderson, John McCullough, Janauschek, and Modjeska.

418   Barrymore, John. "Heredity on the Stage." GREEN BOOK ALBUM 1 (March 1909): 626-35.

       Barrymore builds a case for the inheritance of theatrical excellence, citing as evidence the Jefferson, Booth, Boucicault, Sothern, Davenport, Herne, Drew, and Barrymore families.

419   Bates, William O. "There Were Giants in Those Days." DRAMA 11 (June 1921): 305-7, 333-34; (July 1921); 350-51, 373. Illus.

       Superficial reminiscences of Janauschek, Modjeska, Mary Anderson, Edwin Booth, Charlotte Cushman, William Florence, Richard Mansfield, and Lawrence Barrett.

420●   Beaton, Cecil. "Prince of Players." THEATRE ARTS 41 (December 1957): 32-33, 959-96. Illus.

      Taken from Beaton's THE FACE OF THE WORLD (no. 275), this article lavishes high praise on Ina Claire with briefer treatments of the Lunts and Ethel Barrymore.

421   Bernard, Bayle. "Early Days of the American Stage." TALLIS'S DRAMATIC MAGAZINE AND GENERAL THEATRICAL AND MUSICAL REVIEW.

      Bernard condensed six chapters from his father's (John Bernard) autobiography for this series of articles, as follows: chapter 1 (December 1850): 45-48; chapter 2 (January 1851): 75-79; chapter 3 (February 1851): 109-11; chapter 4 (March 1851): 138-41; chapter 5 (May 1851): 202-4; chapter 6 (June 1851): 237-39.

422   Broeck, Helen Ten. "Successful Stage Mothers." THEATRE (N.Y.) 26 (July 1917): 16. Illus.

      An article which describes the mothers of Elsie Janis and Marjorie Rambeau.

423   Burr, Eugene. "See the Players Well Bestowed." THEATRE ARTS 38 (December 1954): 68-72, 93-94.

      A monograph sketching the history of American acting, with brief mentions of the Hallams, John Henry, the elder Booth, and Edwin Booth.

424   Clapp, Henry Austin. "Reminiscences of a Drama Critic." ATLANTIC 88 (August 1901): 155-65; (September 1901): 344-54; (October 1901): 490-501; (November 1901): 622-34.

      A serialization of Clapp's autobiography (no. 538).

425   Clurman, Harold. "Actors--The Image of Their Era." TULANE DRAMA REVIEW 4 (March 1960): 38-44.

      Casual remarks about such performers as Edwin Forrest, Richard Mansfield, John Barrymore, Alfred Lunt, Edwin Booth, Joseph Jefferson III, John Drew, and Ethel Barrymore.

426   Conway, Hart. "A Theatrical Trinity." PHILHARMONIC 1 (January 1901): 49-53. Illus.

      Conway recalls meeting and working with E.L. Davenport and Charlotte Cushman at the Chestnut Street Theatre.

427   Corbin, John. "What the Actors Would Like to Do and What the Public Won't Let Them Do." LADIES' HOME JOURNAL, March 1911, pp. 9, 62. Illus.

Speculation on desired roles by various performers, among them
William Gillette, Ethel Barrymore, Grace George, David Warfield, Annie Russell, Maude Adams, and John Drew.

428   Cronin, James E. "Elihu Hubbard Smith and the New York Theatre."
NEW YORK HISTORY 31 (April 1950): 136–48.

Extracted from Smith's diary, which Cronin published separately
in 1973, this article presents the descriptions of the theatre of
the times as recorded by Smith. Mention is made of the Hallams,
John Henry, and John Hodgkinson, but not in great depth.

429   Dale, Alan. [Pseud.] "Six Effulgent Stars." COSMOPOLITAN 40 (February
1906): 429–34. Illus.

Superficial and supercilious remarks on the simultaneous successes
of Maude Adams, Blanch Bates, Grace George, Virginia Harned,
and Viola Allen.

430   Davis, Charles Belmont. "The Empty Throne." COLLIER'S 58 (28 October
1916): 22–25. Illus.

The author decries the lack of a theatrical leader after the death
of Joseph Jefferson III, suggesting no performer seemed capable
of assuming such a position. Among those he discusses and dis-
misses are E.H. Sothern, Julia Marlowe, John Drew, George M.
Cohan, Mrs. Fiske, Maude Adams, and Margaret Anglin.

431   Davis, L. "Among the Comedians." ATLANTIC 19 (June 1867): 750–61.

A comparison of the leading comic actors of the day, among them
Joseph Jefferson III, John Sleeper Clarke, John E. Owens, William Warren, Jr., with high praise for them all.

432   Davis, L. Clarke. "These Our Actors." LIPPINCOTT'S MAGAZINE 32
(October 1883): 396–406.

An overview and assessment of actors and actresses working in
New York, among them John Drew, Ada Rehan, James Lewis,
Mrs. George H. Gilbert, Augustin Daly, and Charles Fisher.

433   [Doesticks, Q.K. Philander]. "Sketches of the Actors." WILKES' SPIRIT
OF THE TIMES 5 and 6 (1862).

A series of biographical articles as follows:
John Sleeper Clark 5 (11 January 1862): 301.
E.L. Davenport 5 (25 January 1862): 324–25.
Dion Boucicault 5 (1 February 1862): 339–40.
William Evans Burton 5 (8 February 1862): 356.
James H. Hackett 5 (15 February 1862): 375–76.
Charlotte Cushman 5 (22 February 1862): 389, 396.

Laura Keene 5 (1 March 1862): 414.
James W. Wallack 6 (8 March 1862): 6-7.
Agnes Boucicault 6 (22 March 1862): 38-39.
William Rufus Blake 6 (5 April 1862): 70-71.
Lester Wallack 6 (26 April 1862): 125.
Joseph Jefferson III 6 (3 May 1862): 134-35.
Charles Fisher 6 (24 May 1862): 182.
Maggie J. Mitchell 6 (28 June 1862): 260.

434   Downer, Alan S. "Early American Professional Acting." THEATRE SURVEY
12 (November 1971): 79-96.

Originally presented as part of the American Theatre Festival at
C. W. Post College in April 1968. Includes considerations of the
Hallams, John Durang, Edwin Forrest, and Joseph Jefferson III.

435   _____. "The Private Papers of George Spelvin." PLAYERS 19 and 20
(1943, 1944).

A series of six articles on the development of the actor's art, as
follows:
May 1943, pp. 11-12: "On Romantic Acting, Principally Edmund
Kean."
October 1943, pp. 20-21: "On Romantic Acting, Principally
Junius Brutus Booth."
November 1943, pp. 7-8: "The Eminent." [William Charles
Macready.]
December 1943, pp. 7-8: "The Old School."
January 1944, pp. 7-8: "On the Survival of Classicism in Acting."
[Kemble, Young, Edwin Booth.]
February 1944, pp. 7-8, 11: "The New School."

436   Eaton, Walter Prichard. "Great Actors with Wonderful Personalities."
AMERICAN MAGAZINE 82 (August 1916): 32, 72-74.

Eaton offers his observations on Doris Keane, Mrs. Fiske, and
Maude Adams as exceptional actresses and especially attractive
persons.

437   _____. "On Some of the Old Actors." THEATRE ARTS 9 (March 1925):
154-64.

Eaton discusses the talents of Frank Bacon, Marilyn Miller, Walter
Huston, and Laura Hope Crews, having very little positive to say
of any of them.

438   _____. "The Passing of the Great Figures of the Stage." MUNSEY'S 41
(June 1909): 311-22. Illus.

Brief memorial tributes to Joseph Jefferson III, William Warren,
Richard Mansfield, Ada Rehan, Maxine Elliott, Mary Anderson,
Lawrence Barrett, and Edwin Booth.

439   . "The Six Best-Loved Characters on the American Stage." AMERI-
CAN MAGAZINE 105 (January 1928): 34-35, 96-98.

>   Brief descriptions of Joseph Jefferson III as Rip, Maude Adams
>   in THE LITTLE MINISTER, E.A. Sothern as Lord Dundreary, Frank
>   Bacon in LIGHTIN', and David Warfield in THE MUSIC MASTER.

440   . "Some Actresses Who Do More Than Act." WOMAN'S HOME
COMPANION 36 (March 1909): 17, 69. Illus.

>   Eaton lauds the managerial contributions of Mrs. Fiske, Maude
>   Adams, Julia Marlowe, and Margaret Anglin.

441   Eustis, Morton. "The Actor Attacks His Part." THEATRE ARTS 20-21
(October 1936-May 1937). Illus.

>   A series of articles in which various performers discuss role prepara-
>   tion and rehearsal procedures.
>   20 (October 1936): 798-811. Helen Hayes.
>   20 (November 1936): 857-71. The Lunts.
>   20 (December 1936): 950-60. Nazimova.
>   21 (January 1937): 37-51. Katharine Cornell.
>   22 (February 1937): 126-38. Ina Claire.
>   22 (March 1937): 227-35. Burgess Meredith.
>   22 (April 1937): 285-92. Lotte Lehman.
>   22 (May 1937): 371-86. Fred Astaire.

442   [F., G.T.] "Players of Yesterday." THEATRE 9 (September 1909): 82,
84-86, ix. Illus.

>   Brief remarks on the Booths, Lawrence Barrett, and Charlotte
>   Cushman.

443   Franklin, Irene. "The American Beauty." STAGE 16 (October 1938):
50-51. Illus.

>   Franklin, a minor actress, recalls early meetings with Lillian
>   Russell and Marie Burroughs.

444   Fyles, Vanderheyden. "The Degree of L.L.D." GREEN BOOK MAGAZINE
11 (March 1914): 490-97. Illus.

>   The title refers to leading ladies of John Drew. Fyles describes
>   Drew's acting with Ada Rehan, Maude Adams, Ethel Barrymore,
>   Isabel Irving, Ida Conquest, Margaret Illington, and Billie Burke.

445   Garrett, Kurt L. "The Flexible Loyalties of American Actors in the Eighteenth Century." THEATRE JOURNAL 32 (May 1980): 223-34.

>   The author examines some of the obstacles to professional theatre
>   in America in the latter half of the eighteenth century. Key
>   figures include David Douglass, John Henry, and Lewis Hallam,
>   Jr.

446   Goddard, Henry P. "Players I Have Known." THEATRE (N.Y.) 13
       (February 1911): 63-64, viii. Illus.

       Goddard describes seeing Edwin Forrest, Richard Mansfield, Otis
       Skinner, Louis James, and Mrs. Gilbert.

447   Goodrich, Marc. "Who is the Best American Actress?" THEATRE (N.Y.)
       42 (December 1925): 9, 56.

       Candidates include Katharine Cornell, Pauline Lord, and Laurette
       Taylor.

448   Grau, Robert. "When They Were Twenty-One." THEATRE (N.Y.) 21
       (April 1915): 191-92, 207; (June 1915): 307-8, 312. Illus.

       A brief description of the youths of Maude Adams, Mrs. Fiske,
       Annie Russell, E.H. Sothern, Julia Marlowe, David Belasco,
       Otis Skinner, John Drew, William H. Crane, May Irwin, Nat
       Goodwin, and Marie Dressler. The second section continues with
       Henry Miller, Isabel Irving, and Henrietta Crosman.

449   Graves, Ralph. "Bits That Have Made Actors Big." THEATRE (N.Y.) 21
       (July 1915): 24-27, 43. Illus.

       The author describes the "overnight successes" of Blanche Bates,
       E.H. Sothern, Clara Morris, and Ruth Chatterton.

450   "Great Actors Who Have Died in Poverty." DRAMA 10 (December 1919):
       107-9.

       Brief descriptions of the deaths of George Holland, Mary Ann
       Duff, John Brougham, and Modjeska.

451   Grey, Katherine. "Picking Up Stage Wisdom." AMERICAN MAGAZINE
       80 (July 1915): 30-34, 68-70. Illus.

       Grey describes professional influence upon her career by Augustin
       Daly, Ada Rehan, Henry Miller, Viola Allen, Maude Adams, James
       A. Herne, Richard Mansfield, Janauschek, E.M. Holland, Georgie
       Drew, James K. Hackett, David Belasco, and Nat Goodwin.

452   Harriman, Margaret Case. "Somebody's Mother." VOGUE, 15 April
       1937, pp. 94-95, 138. Illus.

       A series of brief descriptions of various celebrities' mothers,
       among them Helen Haye's and Ina Claire's.

453   Harrington, John Walker. "Old Matinee Idols." BOOKMAN 67 (March
       1928): 53-55. Illus.

       Brief remarks on the popularity of Henry J. Montague and Maurice
       Barrymore.

454 Haworth, Joseph. "A Conversation with Joseph Haworth, Embodying Personal Reminiscences of Great Actors in the Classic Drama." ARENA 25 (January 1901): 69-77.

   An imaginary interview in which Haworth discusses Edwin Booth, John McCullough, Lawrence Barrett, Mary Anderson, Modjeska, and William Warren.

455 Herbert, Joseph W. "Noted Young Men of the American Stage." COSMOPOLITAN 28 (February 1900): 419-24. Illus.

   Herbert surveys American actors, describing and praising James K. Hackett, Henry Miller, E.H. Sothern, William Faversham, and Maurice Barrymore.

456 Hewitt, Barnard. "Four Hamlets of the 19th Century American Stage." TULANE DRAMA REVIEW 6 (March 1962): 193-207; 6 (June 1962): 156-67.

   Written by a major American theatre scholar, part 1 describes Thomas Abthorpe Cooper and the elder Booth; part 2 deals with Edwin Forrest and Edwin Booth.

457 Highfill, Philip H. "Edmund Simpson's Talent Raid on England in 1818." THEATRE NOTEBOOK 12 (Spring 1958): 83-91; 12 (Summer 1958): 130-40; 13 (Autumn 1958): 7-14.

   A detailed and documented account of Simpson's search for performers for the New York stage as described in his notes, now at the Folger Shakespeare Library. Those mentioned include the Wallacks and John Howard Payne.

458 Hornblow, Arthur. "Our American Dramatists." MUNSEY'S 12 (November 1894): 139-66. Illus.

   Includes a brief description of David Belasco and William Gillette as playwrights.

459 Hunter, Frederick J. "Passion and Posture in Early Dramatic Photographs." THEATRE SURVEY 5 (May 1964): 43-63. Illus.

   Hunter describes the problems and conditions under which some early theatrical photographs were taken, with specific references to Adah Issacs Menken, Olive Logan, Mary Anderson, Bertha Kalich, and James K. Hackett. Useful study.

460 Hutton, Laurence. "A Group of Players." HARPERS 96 (January 1898): 96-210. Illus.

   Affectionate appreciations of Edwin Booth, Lawrence Barrett, Lester Wallack, Henry J. Montague, William J. Florence, and John McCullough.

461 _____. "Negro on the Stage." HARPER'S MONTHLY 79 (June 1889): 131–45. Illus.

> Includes descriptions of Ira Aldridge and others, mostly from minstrel shows.

462 Jackson, Joseph. "The Shakespeare Tradition in Philadelphia." PENNSYLVANIA MAGAZINE OF HISTORY AND BIOGRAPHY 40 (April 1916): 161–71.

> Includes brief descriptions of performances by Lewis Hallam, Jr., Mrs. Merry, Thomas Abthorpe Cooper, and Edwin Forrest.

463 Kirk, John Foster. "Shakespeare's Tragedies on the Stage." LIPPINCOTT'S 33 (May 1884): 501–10; 33 (June 1884): 604–16.

> At age sixty, Kirk recalls and describes famous players he had seen, among them Edwin Forrest and Edwin Booth, as well as foreign stars.

464 [Lady with the Lorgnettes, The.] "The Mirrors of Stageland." THEATRE (N.Y.) 36 (November 1922): 295, 332. Illus.

> Brief assessments of David Belasco and Blanche Bates. The series continued over several years, as follows: Frances Starr and John Barrymore (December 1922): 386, 418; Lenore Ulric 37 (January 1923): 12, 60; Ethel Barrymore and David Warfield 37 (February 1923): 12, 60; Joseph Schildkraut and Pauline Frederick (April 1923): 12; Henry Miller and Florence Reed 38 (August 1923): 12, 54, 60; Margaret Anglin (September 1923): 16; Mrs. Fiske, Henry Miller, and Billie Burke (November 1923): 22, 64; Walter Hampden, Julia Marlowe, and George M. Cohan 39 (April 1924): 22, 52; Katharine Cornell (May 1924): 22, 56; E.H. Sothern 40 (August 1924): 40; Ina Claire (October 1924): 18; Helen Westley 42 (October 1925): 18, 52; Louis Wolheim, Jeanne Eagels, and Lenore Ulrich 43 (January 1926): 12; Lynn Fontanne and Otis Skinner (February 1926): 30, 52; Marjorie Rambeau (June 1926): 32; Amelia Bingham 44 (September 1926); 32; Dudley Digges (October 1926): 32, 62; Helen Menken 45 (January 1927): 30.

465 McIntosh, Burr. "Actresses at Leisure." COSMOPOLITAN 31 (October 1901): 586–92. Illus.

> McIntosh interviewed several actresses about their summer vacation plans, among them Julia Marlowe, Maude Adams, Annie Russell, Mary Mannering, Ethel Barrymore, Lillian Russell, May Robson, and Viola Allen.

466 Maiden, Lewis S. "Three Theatrical Stars in Nashville, 1876–1906." SOUTHERN SPEECH JOURNAL 31 (Summer 1966): 338–47.

> The authors draws upon published criticism to describe Edwin Booth as Hamlet, Joseph Jefferson III as Rip Van Winkle, and Sarah Bernhardt as Camille.

467   Mammen, Edward William. "The Old Stock Company: The Boston Museum and Other 19th Century Theatres." MORE BOOKS 19 (January 1944): 3-18; (February 1944): 49-63; (March 1944): 100-107; (April 1944): 132-49; (May 1944): 176-95. Illus., bibliog.

       A useful evocation of acting conditions in the nineteenth century, although Mammen does not deal here or in later revisions of this work with specific actors in any significant depth.

468   Manson, George J., comp. and ed. "These Our Actors." SPIRIT OF THE TIMES 106, 107, as listed below.

       A series of biographical articles on various players: Joseph Jefferson III: 5 January 1884, p. 674. The elder Booth: 12 January 1884, p. 722. Edwin Forrest: 26 January 1884, p. 771. Edwin Booth: 9 February 1884, p. 35. E.A. Sothern: 8 March 1884, pp. 153-54. William J. Florence: 5 April 1884, p. 279.

469   Mantle, Burns. "The Price of Popularity." MUNSEY'S 51 (May 1914): 777-88. Illus.

       Mantle describes the loss of privacy for Laurette Taylor, Ruth Chatterton, Alice Brady, and Maude Adams.

470   Mason, John. "Some Memories of a Notable Career." PEARSON'S (N.Y.) 26 (July 1911): 129-36. Illus.

       Mason recalls attending Edwin Booth's first performance after Lincoln's assassination, as well as seeing Lester Wallack in ROSEDALE.

471   Matthews, Brander. "Actors and Actresses of New York." SCRIBNER'S 17 (April 1879): 767-83. Illus.

       Matthews suggests acting is the first art in which Americans could equal the work of Europeans, citing the performances of Agnes Booth, Clara Morris, Kate Claxton, Mrs. Gilbert, Charles Thorne, James Lewis, and John Gilbert.

472   _____. "The American on the Stage." SCRIBNER'S 18 (July 1879): 321-33.

       Descriptions of stage Americans, based on the work of John E. Owens, James H. Hackett, Frank Chanfrau, Frank Mayo, W.J. Florence, John T. Raymond, and Joseph Jefferson III.

473   _____. "Autobiographies of Actors." MUNSEY'S 74 (December 1920): 478-82.

       Matthews used works written by Joseph Jefferson III and Clara Morris as examples.

474 _____. "Foreign Actors on the American Stage." SCRIBNER'S 21 (February 1881): 521-34. Illus.

Matthews describes the work of Charles Fechter and Janauschek.

475 _____. "Memories of Actors." MUNSEY'S 72 (February 1921): 89-98.

Personal recollections of John Brougham, John T. Raymond, and Nat Goodwin.

476 _____. "Memories of Actresses." SCRIBNER'S 78 (November 1925): 497-504.

Matthew's somewhat superficial remarks on Clara Morris, Ada Rehan, and Mrs. Gilbert, as well as several foreign stars.

477 _____. "Recollections of a Playgoer." THEATRE (N.Y.) 25 (May 1917): 263-65. Illus.

The first in a series of articles in which Matthews discusses briefly the major performers he had seen. Succeeding articles are 25 (June 1917): 346-47; 26 (July 1917): 30, 32.

478 _____. "Sheridan's 'Rivals.'" SCRIBNER'S 21 (December 1880): 182-89. Illus.

Critical analysis of the performances of Mrs. Drew and Joseph Jefferson III.

479 Meier, Nellie Simmons. "Player's Characteristics Shown by Their Hands." THEATRE (N.Y.) 3 (July 1903): 174-76. Illus.

An exercise in palmistry using the hands of John Drew, Maude Adams, Blanche Walsh, and Otis Skinner.

480 Meltzer, Charles Henry. "An Actor's Summer Colony." COSMOPOLITAN 32 (September 1902): 545-52. Illus.

A description of a colony in Siaconset, Massachusetts, the summer home of several actresses, among them Mary Shaw, Henrietta Crosman, and Isabel Irving.

481 Miller, Llewellyn. "313 Years Behind Make-up." MOTION PICTURE MAGAZINE 46 (October 1933): 54-55, 76. Illus.

Miller describes some film actresses with previous stage careers: May Robson, Marie Dressler, Henrietta Crosman, and Laura Hope Crews.

482 Morris, Fritz. "Stage Beauties of the Last Two Decades." BURR McINTOSH MONTHLY 17 (August 1908): 16-23. Illus.

Those admired and described by Morris include Adah Isaacs Menken, Ada Rehan, Lillian Russell, Maxine Elliot, Mrs. Carter, and Mary Anderson.

483   Moses, Montrose. "The Best of Them Get Stagefright." EVERYBODY'S MAGAZINE 54 (May 1926): 95-98, 170.

A humorous article about performance anxiety with anecdotes about Jane Cowl, David Belasco, and John Barrymore.

484   Motherwell, Hiram. "The Illusion of Reality in Acting." STAGE 11 (May 1934): 15-19. Illus.

Minor observations on the acting of Helen Hayes, Walter Huston, and George M. Cohan.

485   Myers, Norman J. "A Season at the John Street: From 'The Theatrical Register.' " SOUTHERN SPEECH JOURNAL 34 (Winter 1968): 126-35.

Myers analyzes the theatre column from NEW YORK MAGAZINE from November 1794 to August 1795. Lewis Hallam, Jr., and John Hodgkinson are covered in depth.

486   Nathan, George Jean. "Best Actress?" VOGUE, 1 April 1936, pp. 67, 115-116, 144. Illus.

Nathan compares Helen Hayes, Lynn Fontanne, Ina Claire, and Katharine Cornell, considering Cornell slightly superior to Hayes and thus America's best actress.

487   _____. "Katharine Cornell Compared with Margaret Anglin." VANITY FAIR 43 (October 1934): 45-46.

Unavailable for examination.

488   Odell, George C[linton]. D[enemore]. "Some Theatrical Stock Companies of New York." THEATRE ANNUAL 9 (1951): 7-26.

An essay found in Odell's papers shortly after his death. Among the companies examined are those of William Mitchell, William E. Burton, James and Lester Wallack, and Augustin Daly. Undocumented.

489   Osmun, Thomas Embley [Ayres, Alfred]. "America's Greatest Players." THEATRE (N.Y.) 1 (December 1901): 21-22. Illus.

The first of a series of articles, this one dealing with Edwin Forrest. The series continues in volume 2 as follows: February, p. 19, Edwin Booth; March, pp. 22-24, Frank Murdoch and John McCullough; April, pp. 22-23, Lotta Crabtree, Charles Fechter, James H. Hackett, and Lawrence Barrett; May, pp. 24-25, J.E. Owens and J.W. Wallack, Jr.; June, p. 13, E.L. Davenport and John Gilbert; July, p. 18, Edwin Adams, Frank Mayo, and the elder Booth.

490   P., A. [Patterson, Ada?]. "The Three Funny Women of the Stage."
        THEATRE (N.Y.) 4 (May 1904): 117-18. Illus.

        Very brief assessments of Marie Dressler and Marie Cahill.

491   Patterson, Ada. "Players in Business." THEATRE (N.Y.) 24 (October
        1916): 202, 250. Illus.

        Patterson describes business flyers taken by such performers as
        Lillian Russell, Rose Stahl, May Irwin, and Marie Dressler.

492   _____. "What They Would Have Been if They Weren't What They Were."
        THEATRE (N.Y.) 23 (May 1916): 292, 304. Illus.

        An article speculating on alternative vocations for Ethel Barrymore,
        Wilton Lackaye, Blanche Bates, DeWolf Hopper, Lillian Russell,
        May Irwin, Clara Morris, and Julia Dean.

493   _____. "Where Are the Stars of Yesteryear." THEATRE (N.Y.) 41 (May
        1925): 12, 64, 66. Illus.

        Patterson describes various performers' decline as "the setting
        of . . . theatrical stars," among them Maude Adams, Julia
        Marlowe, Frank Bacon, Janauschek, Lotta Crabtree, Effie Ellsler,
        Virginia Harned, Lillian Russell, Ada Rehan, and others.

494   Randolph, Ann. "Personality on the Stage Discussed by Leading Actresses."
        NATIONAL MAGAZINE 38 (April 1913): 53-59. Illus.

        Jane Cowl is quoted.

495   Ross, Claire. "Music in the Theatre." MUSICAL COURIER 77 (8 August
        1918): 6-7, 18. Illus.

        Interviews about music with actresses who sang, among them
        Frances Starr, Ina Claire, Lenore Ulric, and Nazimova.

496   S., C. "Stories of Sothern." THEATRE (Engl.), o.s. 12, n.s. 3 (March
        1881): 161-69.

        A collection of anecdotes about E.A. Sothern, most of them in-
        volving Edwin Adams and William Florence.

497   "Santa Claus Time in Stageland." LESLIES WEEKLY 109 (9 December 1909):
        24, 29. Illus.

        Seven leading players recall their best-remembered Christmas,
        among them Frances Starr and Rose Stahl.

498   Savage, Richard. " 'Creating' a Part." THEATRE (N.Y.) 45 (February
        1927): 24, 58.

Remarks on role preparation by Alice Brady, Lynn Fontanne, and Frances Starr, among others.

499   Schmidt, Karl. "My Best Lines." EVERYBODY'S MAGAZINE 34 (July 1916): 495-502. Illus.

Schmidt asked several leading performers to recall their most effective line. Those recorded include Grace George, Blanche Bates, Otis Skinner, David Warfield, and Frances Starr.

500   Sherwin, Louis. "Just Arrived!" METROPOLITAN 37 (April 1913): 30-32, 63-64. Illus.

Sherwin, who considered the theatre of the past irrelevant, describes the recent successes of several actresses, among them Laurette Taylor, Jane Cowl, and Florence Reed.

501   "Some Famous Falstaffs." THEATRE (N.Y.) 25 (March 1917): 146-88. Illus.

Brief accounts of W.H. Crane, Louis James, and the elder Hackett.

502   Stovall, Floyd. "Walt Whitman and the Dramatic Stage in New York." STUDIES IN PHILOLOGY 50 (July 1953): 515-39.

A discussion of Whitman as a critic and several of the actors who influenced his conceptions of the theatre, among them the elder Booth, Thomas B. Hamblin, James H. Hackett, Edwin Forrest, and Charlotte Cushman.

503   "Success on the Stage." NORTH AMERICAN REVIEW 135 (December 1882): 580-602.

A series of articles on acting methods by John McCullough, Modjeska, Joseph Jefferson III, Lawrence Barrett, Maggie Mitchell, and William Warren.

504   "The Theatre Takes Stock." THEATRE ARTS 24 (May 1940): 327-89.

A collection of remarks by leading theatre personnel of the time as to the state of the U.S. theatre. Among those quoted are the Lunts and Katharine Cornell.

505   Van Law, H.R. "Five Actresses Whom I Have Seen as Juliet." THEATRE (N.Y.) 12 (July 1910): 23-25. Illus.

Comparisions of Julia Marlowe and Maude Adams. The author considered Marlowe superior.

506   Weisser, H. de. "If I Were to Write a Play." THEATRE (N.Y.) 22 (November 1915): 239-40.

E.H. Sothern, Julia Sanderson, George M. Cohan, William Faversham, Nazimova, Viola Allen, Wilton Lackaye, and May Robson speculate on dramaturgy.

507   West, E.J. "Revolution in the American Theatre: Glimpses of Acting Conditions on the American Stage, 1855-1870." THEATRE SURVEY 1 (1960): 43-64.

Undocumented and discovered in West's papers after his death, the monograph describes conditions faced by the major performers of the period, such as Edwin Booth, Matilda Heron, Dion Boucicault, Edwin Forrest, and Joseph Jefferson III.

508   "When You First Heard Their Names." STAGE 11 (December 1934): 30-31. Illus.

Brief comments on breakthrough roles for the Lunts, Nazimova, Ruth Gordon, Ina Claire, Alice Brady, Osgood Perkins, Maude Adams, Lenore Ulric, Katharine Cornell, and George M. Cohan.

509   "Where They Are Summering." THEATRE (N.Y.) 22 (August 1915): 60-61, 94. Illus.

Tidbits about the vacation homes of Nazimova, Billie Burke, Laurette Taylor, May Irwin, George M. Cohan, Margaret Illington, Julia Marlowe, and Elsie Janis.

510   Whitworth, Grace. "The Homes of the Players." THEATRE (N.Y.) 6 (September 1906): 242-46, vi. Illus.

Brief textual descriptions and photographs of the residences of Julia Marlowe, E.H. Sothern, Lillian Russell, Francis Wilson, Richard Mansfield, Ethel Barrymore, W.H. Crane, Otis Skinner, Margaret Anglin, and Viola Allen.

511   Williams, Edith B. "The Actors' Colony in Cohasset." THEATRE (N.Y.) 9 (November 1909): 162-64. Illus.

The author describes the formation of what was known as the Actors' Corner. Residents included Lawrence Barrett (the author's father), Stuart Robson, Charles Thorne, William H. Crane. Edwin Booth was a frequent guest.

512   Willis, Richard. "In Search of an American Siddons." THEATRE (N.Y.) 38 (December 1923): 12, 64, 66. Illus.

Willis examines the American stage and finds only four actresses of genius: Mrs. Fiske, Margaret Anglin, Helen Menken, and Eva Le Gallienne.

513   Wilson, Francis. "Jefferson and the All-Star Cast in 'The Rivals.' "
       SCRIBNER'S 39 (March 1906): 300-317. Illus.

       Part of Wilson's book on Joseph Jefferson III (no. 2274). The
       rest of the cast described include William H. Crane, Joseph Hol-
       land, Nat Goodwin, E.M. Holland, Mrs. Drew, Julia Marlowe,
       and Wilson.

514   Wilson, Garff B. "Achievement in the Acting of Comedy." EDUCATIONAL
       THEATRE JOURNAL 5 (December 1953): 328-32.

       Describes critical reception to the acting of Joseph Jefferson III
       and William Warren.

515   _____. "The Art of the Leading Actresses of the American Stage."
       QUARTERLY JOURNAL OF SPEECH 48 (February 1962): 31-37.

       An early version of the comparable section of Wilson's A HISTORY
       OF AMERICAN ACTING (1966). A great many actresses are
       mentioned in passing.

516   _____. "Versatile Tragedians: Edwin Booth and James E. Murdoch. "
       SPEECH MONOGRAPHS 19 (March 1952): 27-38.

       Wilson considers Booth, Murdoch, Lawrence Barrett, and E.L.
       Davenport all typical of this school of acting, but he describes
       only Booth and Murdoch in this monograph.

517   Winter, William. "Famous Actors of the Nineteenth Century: A Chapter
       of Theatrical History." MUNSEY'S 35 (June 1906): 347-59.

       Offers an overview of U.S. acting with specific sections describing
       John Hodgkinson, James Fennell, Thomas Abthorpe Cooper, Edwin
       Forrest, the elder Booth, Joseph Jefferson III, and Edwin Booth.

518   _____. "Memories of the Players." COLLIER'S. A series of articles as
       follows: "Henry Irving." 50 (15 March 1913): 11-12, 29, 32-33; "Mrs.
       Gilbert and James Lewis." 51 (29 March 1913): 17, 20, 27; "Edwin
       Booth." 51 (12 April 1913): 15-16, 30; "William Warren." 51 (19
       April 1913): 16-17, 35-36, 39; "Augustin Daly." 51 (26 April 1913):
       19-20, 26, 28, 31. Illus.

       Anecdotes, reminiscences, adding little to other sources.

519   _____. "Players Past and Present, Being Pictures Drawn from Life."
       SATURDAY EVENING POST. "Joseph Jefferson." 178 (23 June 1906):
       3-5; "Richard Mansfield: A Glance at a Brilliant Man." 179 (11 August
       1906): 10-11, 21; "A Glimpse of a Beautiful Life: Mary Anderson." 179
       (1 September 1906): 10-11, 22; "Great Actress and Great Woman: Char-
       lotte Cushman." 179 (29 September 1906): 10-11, 18; "John McCullough:

Tragedian, Comrade, Friend." 179 (3 November 1907): 10-11, 28; Law-rence Barrett: Character, Intellect, Genius." 179 (5 January 1907): 20-22; "Edward A. Sothern, The Yorick of the Stage." 179 (2 February 1907): 10-11, 27; "John Brougham--Comedian and Humorist." 179 (6 April 1907): 12-13, 25-27; "Dion Boucicault, The Master of the Revels." 179 (18 May 1907): 14-15, 24-25. Illus.

Affectionate reminiscences. A final article on 15 June 1907 treats Adelaide Neilson.

520   Woodbury, Lael J. "Death on the Romantic Stage." QUARTERLY JOURNAL OF SPEECH 49 (February 1963): 57-61.

A description of nineteenth-century death scenes as played by Edmund Kean, the elder Booth, Cooke, Salvini, and Edwin Forrest.

RELEVANT BIOGRAPHIES AND AUTOBIOGRAPHIES

521   Anderson, James R. AN ACTOR'S LIFE. London: Walter Scott Publishing
      Co., 1902. 347 p. Index, illus.

> The autobiography of an English actor who played several engage-
> ments in the United States. In his memoirs, he mentions and de-
> scribes to varying degrees Dion Boucicault, Charlotte Cushman,
> and Charles Fechter.

522   Bancroft, Marie, and Bancroft, Squire. THE BANCROFTS: RECOLLEC-
      TIONS OF SIXTY YEARS. New York: E.P. Dutton, 1909. Reprint. New
      York: Benjamin Blom, 1969. 440 p. Illus.

> The English performer-managers discuss at some length their work
> with Dion Boucicault and E.A. Sothern.

523   Bancroft, Squire. EMPTY CHAIRS. New York: Frederick A. Stokes Co.,
      1925. 244 p. Index, frontispiece.

> Bancroft recalls the work of Dion Boucicault, E.A. Sothern, and
> Charles Fechter.

524   Barnabee, Henry Clay. REMINISCENCES BEING AN ATTEMPT TO AC-
      COUNT FOR HIS LIFE, WITH SOME EXCUSES FOR HIS PROFESSIONAL
      CAREER. Boston: Chapple Publishing Co., 1913. 461 p. Illus.

> The author recalls having seen the elder Booth, describes Edwin
> Booth's debut (chapter 7), describes Forrest as Metamora (chapter
> 12), and devotes chapter 15 to his season with William Warren at
> the Boston Museum. Valuable for descriptions of touring condi-
> tions.

525   Barnes, Eric Wollencott. THE MAN WHO LIVED TWICE: THE BIOGRAPHY
      OF EDWARD SHELDON. New York: Charles Scribner's Sons, 1956. 358 p.
      Illus.

> The playwright's biography deals with many of the performers
> with whom he worked or with whom he became acquainted, among

them Maude Adams, the Barrymores, David Belasco, Katharine
Cornell, Ruth Draper, William Faversham, Mrs. Fiske, Grace
George, Ruth Gordon, Helen Hayes, Doris Keane, and Cornelia
Otis Skinner.

526   Barnes J[ohn]. H. FORTY YEARS ON THE STAGE: OTHERS (PRINCIPALLY)
AND MYSELF. London: Chapman and Hall, 1914. New York: E.P. Dutton, 1915. 313 p. Index, illus.

A chatty stage reminiscence with substantial sections and numerous
anecdotes about Mary Anderson, Maurice Barrymore, Dion Boucicault, the Drews, Joseph Jefferson III, and John McCullough.

527   Behrman, S.N. PEOPLE IN A DIARY: A MEMOIR BY S.N. BEHRMAN.
Boston and Toronto: Little, Brown and Co., 1972. 328 p. Index, illus.

Behrman suggests "An odd quirk of destiny has put a great many
people in my way. I want, in this book, to return to them. I
want to revive their society; to share their tribulations and their
laughter." Among those so treated are the Lunts, Ina Claire,
and Katharine Cornell.

528   Bernhard, Karl, Duke of Saxe-Weimar Eisenbach. TRAVELS THROUGH
NORTH AMERICA DURING THE YEARS 1825 AND 1826. 2 vols. Philadelphia: Carey, Lea and Carey, 1828. 212, 238 p.

Bernhard travelled extensively on this continent and described
practically everything he saw; a few items describe his theatrical
experiences in this country.

529   Blumenthal, George, as told to Arthur H. Menkin. MY SIXTY YEARS IN
SHOW BUSINESS. New York: Frederick C. Osberg, 1936. xiv, 336 p.
Illus.

An anecdotal reminiscence with occasional references to Lillian
Russell, Augustin Daly, Richard Mansfield, Viola Allen, and
Louis Mann. Somewhat frivolous.

530   Bradley, Edward Sculley. GEORGE HENRY BOKER: POET AND PATRIOT.
Philadelphia: University of Pennsylvania Press, 1927. xi, 355 p. Index,
illus., bibliog. Reprint. New York: Benjamin Blom, 1972.

The playwright's biography is studded with references to actors
with whom he worked and offers substantial sections on Lawrence
Barrett, Otis Skinner, E. L. Davenport, and Julia Dean.

531   Brady, William A. THE FIGHTING MAN. Indianapolis: Bobbs-Merrill
Co., 1916. 227 p. Illus.

Brady's reminiscences describe his career as a prize fight manager,
but include some observations about his brief acting career and
his acquaintances with E.H. Sothern, Julia Marlowe, Dion Bou-

cicault, Augustin Daly, and David Belasco.

532 _____. SHOWMAN. New York: E.P. Dutton and Co., 1937. 278 p. Illus.

Brady describes his raucous career in show business and describes his dealings with Grace George, Maude Adams, Helen Hayes, and Alice Brady. Useful for managerial practices of the time.

533 Burton, Percy. ADVENTURES AMONG IMMORTALS: PERCY BURTON-- IMPRESARIO; AS TOLD TO LOWELL THOMAS. London: Hutchinson, 1938, 1941. New York: Dodd, 1937. Toronto: McClelland, 1937. vi, 330 p.

Burton's reminiscences include his impressions of William Gillette and Richard Mansfield.

534 Calvert, Mrs. Charles. SIXTY-EIGHT YEARS ON THE STAGE. London: Mills and Boon, 1911. 373 p. Illus.

A rambling discourse with descriptions of and reactions to Edwin Booth and Mary Anderson.

535 Canary, Robert H. WILLIAM DUNLAP. New York: Twayne Publishers, 1970. 158 p. Index, bibliog.

While the author is primarily concerned with Dunlap as dramatist, he includes necessary information about Thomas Abthorpe Cooper, the Hallams, John Hodgkinson, and Thomas Wignell.

536 Carroll, Renee. IN YOUR HAT. New York: Macaulay Co., 1933. xii, 287 p. Illus., with caricatures by Gard.

Anecdotal memoirs of a hat-check girl at Sardi's restaurant with a few references to George M. Cohan and Katharine Cornell. Of minimal value, but offers an interesting look at Broadway from the fringes.

537 Case, Frank. TALES OF A WAYWARD INN. New York: Frederick A. Stokes Co., 1938. 384 p. Index.

Case was manager of the Algonquin Hotel in New York, a favorite of theatre people. Him rambling memoirs mention many of them, and he includes letters from John Barrymore and Elsie Janis.

538 Clapp, Henry Austin. REMINISCENCES OF A DRAMA CRITIC WITH AN ESSAY ON THE ART OF HENRY IRVING. Boston and New York: Houghton Mifflin and Co., 1902. 236 p. Index, illus.

Clapp surveys his three-decade career as a reviewer and includes substantial analyses of William Warren, Jr., Charlotte Cushman,

E.A. Sothern, Charles Fechter, and Edwin Booth. Clapp's style is abstract rather than specific in describing actors and acting.

539   Clarke, Joseph I[gantius].C[onstantine]. MY LIFE AND MEMORIES. New York: Dodd, Mead, 1925. xv, 404 p. Illus.

Memoirs of an expatriate Irishman who achieved a journalistic career in the United States. An avid theatregoer, his memoirs include chapters on John McCullough (30), Richard Mansfield (34), and Julia Marlowe, Margaret Anglin, and Grace George (35).

540   Clurman, Harold. ALL PEOPLE ARE FAMOUS: INSTEAD OF AN AUTO-BIOGRAPHY. New York and London: Harcourt Brace Jovanovich, 1974. 313 p. Index.

A rambling set of memoirs, describing many celebrities, among them Stella Adler (Clurman's wife), the Lunts, and Lee Strasberg.

541   Coad, Oral Sumner. WILLIAM DUNLAP: A STUDY OF HIS LIFE AND WORKS AND OF HIS PLACE IN CONTEMPORARY CULTURE. New York: Dunlap Society, 1917. Reprint. New York: Russell and Russell, 1962. xiii. 302 p. Index, illus., bibliog.

Meticulously documented with valuable appendixes and notes. Includes descriptions of Thomas Abthorpe Cooper, the Hallams, John Hodgkinson, Thomas Wignell, and Joseph Jefferson I.

542   Cochran, Charles B[lake]. COCK-A-DOODLE-DO. London: J.M. Dent and Sons, 1941. New York: Salloch, 1942. 357 p. Illus.

Anecdotes about celebrities, including such stage personalities as Billie Burke, Peggy Wood, John Barrymore, Richard Mansfield, Modjeska, Pauline Lord, and the Lunts, most of whom Cochran met or saw in London.

543   _____. THE SECRETS OF A SHOWMAN. New York: Henry Holt and Co., 1926. xx, 422 p. Index, illus.

Rambling theatrical memoirs describing Cochran's observations of Maurice Barrymore, Tyrone Power, Richard Mansfield (a substantial section as Cochran was a member of Mansfield's company and later his secretary), Elsie Janis, Laurette Taylor, Pauline Lord, Florence Mills, and George M. Cohan.

544   _____. SHOWMAN LOOKS ON. London: J.M. Dent and Sons, 1945. vii, 306 p. Index, illus., bibliog.

Cochran reminisces about friends and acquaintances from the theatre, among them Mary Anderson, Steele MacKaye, Maurice and John Barrymore, Grace George, Alice Brady, Richard Mansfield, Joseph Jefferson III, E.H. Sothern, and George M. Cohan.

545   Cocroft, Thoda. GREAT NAMES AND HOW THEY ARE MADE. Chicago, New York, and London: Dartnell Corp., 1941. 267 p. Index, illus.

Cocroft was a publicist and advance agent for twenty years. Her memoirs discuss such theatrical figures as Helen Hayes, Margaret Anglin, Mrs. Fiske, the Lunts, and Lillian Gish.

546   Coleman, John. FIFTY YEARS OF AN ACTOR'S LIFE. 2 vols. London: Hutchinson; New York: Pott and Co., 1904. 338, 389 p. Illus.

Undocumented memoirs of an English actor who describes his reactions to Charlotte Cushman, Edwin Forrest, and Otis Skinner.

547   Cooley, Winnifred Harper. I KNEW THEM WHEN . . . ! New York: Saravan House, 1940. 250 p. Illus.

An undistinguished autobiography which "drops" many names, among them Ethel Barrymore, David Belasco, Jane Cowl, Katharine Cornell, Julia Marlowe, Lillian Russell, Otis Skinner, Cornelia Otis Skinner, E.H. Sothern, and Blanche Yurka.

548   Davis, Owen. I'D LIKE TO DO IT AGAIN. New York: Farrar and Rinehart, 1931. viii, 233 p. Illus.

Rambling reminiscences with descriptions of Davis's acquaintances with Maurice Barrymore, Janauschek, Lawrence Barrett, James O'Neill, Edwin Booth, Harrigan and Hart, Augustin Daly, and David Belasco.

549   Derwent, Clarence. THE DERWENT STORY: MY FIRST FIFTY YEARS IN THE THEATRE IN ENGLAND AND AMERICA BY CLARENCE DERWENT. New York: Henry Schuman, 1953. 304 p. Illus.

Derwent, an English actor, came to the United States in 1916 for a substantial career, appearing here with Katharine Cornell, Helen Hayes, the Lunts, Tallulah Bankhead, Laurette Taylor, Grace George, Margaret Anglin, Lionel Barrymore, and others. He also functioned as president of Actors Equity and the American National Theatre and Academy.

550   Dier, Mary Caroline Lawrence. THE LADY OF THE GARDENS: MARY ELITCH LONG. Hollywood: Hollycrofters; Los Angeles: Saturday Night Publishing, 1932. 305 p.

John Elitch opened a pleasure resort in Denver in 1890 in which his widow organized a stock company in 1897. Some of the performers who received their first professional training there include Frank Mayo, Blanche Walsh, Henrietta Crosman, and David Warfield.

551   Donaldson, Walter. RECOLLECTIONS OF AN ACTOR. London: John

Maxwell and Co., 1865. 360 p. Frontispiece.

Typical of English theatrical autobiographies of the time. Contains an account of the elder Booth's unsuccessful debut and Donaldson's recollections of Ira Aldridge.

552   Dunlap, William. DIARY OF WILLIAM DUNLAP (1766-1839): THE MEMOIRS OF A DRAMATIST, THEATRICAL MANAGER, PAINTER, CRITIC, NOVELIST, AND HISTORIAN. New York: New York Historical Society, 1830. Reprint. New York and London: Benjamin Blom, 1969. 851 p. Index, illus.

Dunlap naturally came into contact with the leading players of his time, and while his accounts of them are tinged by his professional and personal relations with them and while his facts are not in every case accurate, the diary remains a valuable primary source. The Blom edition is indexed, making the material far more accessible than the original edition.

553   _____. THE LIFE OF GEORGE FRED. COOKE (LATE OF THE THEATRE ROYAL, COVENT GARDEN). COMPOSED PRINCIPALLY FROM JOURNALS AND OTHER AUTHENTIC DOCUMENTS LEFT BY MR. COOKE, AND THE PERSONAL KNOWLEDGE OF THE AUTHOR. COMPRISING ORIGINAL ANECDOTES OF HIS THEATRICAL CONTEMPORARIES, HIS OPINIONS ON VARIOUS DRAMATIC WRITINGS, &C. 2nd ed., rev. London: Henry Colburn, 1815. Reprint. New York: Benjamin Blom, 1972. 2 vols. xiii, 441 p.; vi, 410 p.

A revised edition of Dunlap's MEMOIRS OF GEORGE FREDERICK COOKE, ESQ. (no. 554).

554   _____. MEMOIRS OF GEORGE FREDERICK COOKE, ESQ. LATE OF THE THEATRE ROYAL, COVENT GARDEN. London: Henry Colburn, 1813. 2 vols. xiv, 344 p.; vi, 362 p. Frontispiece.

Dunlap traveled with Cooke in the United States from 1810 to 1812 and cites the erratic actor's interactions with players of this country, such as John Henry and Thomas Abthorpe Cooper.

555   Fitch, Clyde; Moses, Montrose J., and Gerson, Virginia, eds. CLYDE FITCH AND HIS LETTERS. Boston: Little, Brown and Co., 1924. xv, 392 p. Index, illus.

Moses and Gerson supply a biography interspersed between Fitch's correspondence. The letters include those to, from, or about Maude Adams, Ethel Barrymore, John Barrymore, David Belasco, Amelia Bingham, J.E. Dodson, John Drew, Maxine Elliott, Nat Goodwin, Doris Keane, Herbert Kelcey, Mary Mannering, Richard Mansfield, Julia Marlowe, Henry Miller, Modjeska, Ada Rehan, Annie Russell, Sol Smith Russell, Otis Skinner, and Blanch Walsh.

556   Ford, James L[aruen]. FORTY-ODD YEARS IN THE LITERARY SHOP. New York: E.P. Dutton and Co., 1921. 362 p. Index, illus.

> Ford drops almost every theatrical and literary name of his time. Somewhat substantial sections concern Edwin Booth, Mary Anderson, Augustin Daly, and Harrigan and Hart.

557   Frohman, Daniel. DANIEL FROHMAN PRESENTS: AN AUTOBIOGRAPHY. New York: Claude Kendall and Willoughby Sharp, 1935. New York: Lee Furman, 1935. 384 p. Index, illus.

> Frohman's chatty and rambling memoirs mention most of the leading performers of his time, with chapters devoted to Edwin Booth, E.H. Sothern, Julia Marlowe, and Joseph Jefferson III. Modjeska, William Gillette, and Dion Boucicault are treated briefly.

558   _____. MEMORIES OF A MANAGER: REMINISCENCES OF THE OLD LYCEUM AND OF SOME PLAYERS OF THE LAST QUARTER CENTURY. Garden City, N.Y.: Doubleday, Page and Co., 1911. xvii, 226 p. Index, illus. Reprint. New York: Benjamin Blom, 1969.

> Anecdotal reminiscences offering some insights into production procedures of the time. Among the players mentioned to varying degrees are Edwin Booth, William Gillette, Richard Mansfield, David Belasco, James K. Hackett, Maude Adams, Georgia Cayvan, Henry Miller, Ethel Barrymore, Margaret Anglin, Julia Marlowe, Dion Boucicault, Modjeska, John T. Raymond, Lawrence Barrett, John E. Owens, Mary Anderson, McKee Rankin, Nat Goodwin, and Hilda Spong.

559   Frohman, Daniel, and Marcosson, Isaac F. "The Life of Charles Frohman." COSMOPOLITAN 59 (September 1915): 444–57; (October 1915): 564–76; (November 1915): 791–805; 60 (December 1915): 67–80; (January 1916): 238–54; (February 1916): 411–28; (March 1916): 587–605; (April 1916): 730–41; (May 1916): 903–13; 61 (June 1916): 115–22; (July 1916): 248–56; (August 1916): 368–75. Illus.

> A heavily illustrated serialization of CHARLES FROHMAN: MANAGER AND MAN (no. 575).

560   Grau, Maurice. FORTY YEARS OBSERVATION OF MUSIC AND THE DRAMA. New York and Baltimore: Broadway Publishing Co., 1909. vi, 370 p. Illus.

> Rambling reminiscences of the entertainment industry. Among the performers mentioned in anecdotes are Mrs. John Drew, Janauschek, Nazimova, G.L. Fox, and Francis Wilson.

561   Hackett, Norman. COME MY BOYS. New York: Hackett Memorial Publication Fund, 1960. xix, 420 p. Illus.

> An autobiography of Hackett, focusing upon his work with Theta Delta Chi, but also describing his thirty-five year career in the

theatre and including his impressions of Louis James, Modjeska, Frederick Warde, E.H. Sothern, Julia Marlowe, James O'Neill, and Katharine Cornell.

562   Hart, Jerome A. IN OUR SECOND CENTURY. FROM AN EDITOR'S NOTE-BOOK. San Francisco: Pioneer Press, 1931. 450 p. Index, frontispiece.

A journalistic memoir, in which the author devotes a chapter (20) to his impressions of such performers as the Daly company, William H. Crane, Charles R. Thorne, Richard Mansfield, Stuart Robson, James O'Neill, Dion Boucicault, John Drew, Ada Rehan, Lotta Crabtree, and David Belasco.

563   Hecht, Ben. CHARLIE: THE IMPROBABLE LIFE AND TIMES OF CHARLES MacARTHUR. New York: Harper and Brothers, 1957. xii, 232 p. Index, illus.

Dedicated to Helen Hayes with considerable reference to her. Others mentioned include John Barrymore and Lenore Ulric.

564   Helburn, Theresa. A WAYWARD QUEST: THE AUTOBIOGRAPHY OF THERESA HELBURN. Boston and Toronto: Little, Brown and Co., 1960. 334 p. Index, illus.

Helburn was associated with Theatre Guild; her memoirs include observations of the Lunts, Helen Westley, Helen Hayes, Joseph Schildkraut, and others.

565   Henry, David D[odds]. WILLIAM VAUGHN MOODY: A STUDY. Boston: Bruce Humphries, 1934. 273 p. Index, bibliog.

Long considered an exemplary literary biography, this study of necessity discusses Moody's relationship with Margaret Anglin and Henry Miller.

566   Howe, M[ark]. A[nthony]. DeWolfe. MEMORIES OF A HOSTESS: A CHRON-ICLE OF EMINENT FRIENDSHIPS, DRAWN CHIEFLY FROM THE DIARIES OF MRS. JAMES T. FIELDS. Boston: Atlantic Monthly Press, 1922. 305 p. Index, illus.

Howe includes substantial sections of Mrs. Field's acquaintances with several stage stars: Edwin Booth, Joseph Jefferson III, Charlotte Cushman, and Charles Fechter.

567   Huneker, James Gibbons. STEEPLEJACK. 2 vols. New York: Charles Scribner's Sons, 1920. Published as two volumes in one by Charles Scrib-ner's Sons, 1922. 320, 309 p. Index, illus.

Huneker mentions several actors in passing, but includes more substantial sections concerning Edwin Booth, the Drews, and Richard Mansfield.

568   Irving, Pierre M. LIFE AND LETTERS OF WASHINGTON IRVING.
        4 vols. New York: G.P. Putnam, 1862-64.

        Includes descriptions of most American actors of the early nine-
        teenth century, as well as of visiting foreign stars.

569   Jessel, George. SO HELP ME. Cleveland: World Publishing Co., 1944.
        xvii, 229 p. Index, illus.

        Garrulous memoirs and anecdotal reminiscences, with comments
        on John Barrymore and George M. Cohan.

570   Krone, Charles A. "Recollections of an Old Actor." MISSOURI HISTORI-
        CAL SOCIETY COLLECTIONS 2 (1900-1906): 25-43; 3 (1908-11): 53-70,
        170-82, 275-306, 423-36; 4 (1912-23): 104-20, 209-33, 323-51, 423-
        63. Illus.

        Krone read this lengthy paper to the Missouri Historical Society
        in 1905 during several meetings. At age sixty-nine, he reminisced
        about his long stage career and recalled such performers as Law-
        rence Barrett, William Burton, Julia Dean, John Wilkes Booth,
        and Janauschek, adding little to previously published accounts.

571   Langer, Lawrence. THE MAGIC CURTAIN: THE STORY OF A LIFE IN
        TWO FIELDS, THEATRE AND INVENTION BY THE FOUNDER OF THE
        THEATRE GUILD. New York: E.P. Dutton and Co., 1951. 480 p.
        Index, illus.

        A detailed account of Langer's contributions to the Guild, in
        which the Lunts and Tallulah Bankhead figure prominently.

572   Leavitt, Michael Bennett. FIFTY YEARS OF THEATRICAL MANAGEMENT.
        New York: Broadway Publishing Co., 1912. xxii, 714 p. Index, illus.

        Leavitt's seemingly exaggerated memoirs include reminiscences
        of the Howard family, Joseph Jefferson III, Edwin Forrest, E.L.
        Davenport, Edwin Booth, Charlotte Cushman, E.A.Sothern,
        Laura Keene, G.L. Fox, the elder Booth, Maggie Mitchell,
        George M. Cohan, Lawrence Barrett, John McCullough, Lotta
        Crabtree, David Warfield, David Belasco, Harrigan and Hart,
        and Mary Anderson.

573   Macready, William Charles. THE DIARIES OF WILLIAM CHARLES MAC-
        READY, 1833-1851. 2 vols. Edited by William Toynbee. London: Chap-
        man and Hall; New York: G.P. Putnam's Sons, 1912.

        Macready makes several remarks few of them positive, about
        Edwin Forrest and Charlotte Cushman.

574   Marbury, Elisabeth. MY CRYSTAL BALL: REMINISCENCES. New York:
        Boni and Liveright, 1923. 355 p. Illus.

        The volume is dedicated to Elsie DeWolfe, who figures substantially

in the text. Also mentioned are Richard Mansfield and William
Gillette.

575 Marcosson, Isaac F., and Frohman, Daniel. CHARLES FROHMAN: MANA-
GER AND MAN. New York and London: Harper and Brothers, 1916.
440 p. Illus.

A somewhat idealized treatment of Frohman, containing substantial
references to several actors, including John Drew, Maude Adams,
Ethel Barrymore, and William Gillette.

576 Massey, Raymond. A HUNDRED DIFFERENT LIVES: AN AUTOBIOGRAPHY
BY RAYMOND MASSEY. Boston and Toronto: Little, Brown and Co.,
1979. 418 p. Index, illus.

The Canadian actor continues his autobiography which he began
with WHEN I WAS YOUNG (1976). In this volume, he describes
his film and stage career on both sides of the Atlantic, recalling
his work with Tallulah Bankhead, Ruth Gordon, and Katharine
Cornell.

577 Matthews, Brander. THESE MANY YEARS: RECOLLECTIONS OF A NEW
YORKER. New York: Charles Scribner's Sons, 1917. 463 p.

Matthews reminiscences include chapter 25, "Among the Players,"
in which he recalls his acquaintance with John Gilbert, Edwin
Booth, Joseph Jefferson III, William H. Crane, and Lester Wallack.

578 Middleton, George. THESE THINGS ARE MINE; THE AUTOBIOGRAPHY
OF A JOURNEYMAN PLAYWRIGHT. New York: Macmillan, 1947.
xii, 411 p. Index, illus.

As a playwright, Middleton describes and reacts to the work of
such players as Richard Mansfield, Ada Rehan, Lawrence Barrett,
Nazimova, David Belasco, George M. Cohan, Margaret Anglin,
the Barrymores, Edwin Booth, Ina Claire, Katharine Cornell, Arnold Daly, John Drew, Mrs. Fiske, James K. Hackett, Walter
Hampden, Eva Le Gallienne, Steele MacKaye, Julia Marlowe,
Modjeska, Otis Skinner, and E.H. Sothern.

579 Morehouse, Ward. MATINEE TOMORROW: FIFTY YEARS OF OUR THEA-
TRE. New York, London, and Toronto: McGraw-Hill Book Co., 1949.
vii, 310 p. Index, illus.

Morehouse offers an informal history of a half century of Broadway
theatre, adding his observations and comments on many players
he had seen, among them Maude Adams, Mary Anderson, Frank
Bacon, Tallulah Bankhead, the Barrymores, David Belasco, Mrs.
Leslie Carter, Ina Claire, George M. Cohan, Katharine Cornell,
Jane Cowl, John Drew, Maxine Elliott, William Faversham, Mrs.

Fiske, the Lunts, Grace George, William Gillette, Nat Goodwin, James K. Hackett, Walter Hampden, Helen Hayes, Elsie Janis, Eva Le Gallienne, Julia Marlowe, Henry Miller, Nazimova, E.H. Sothern, David Warfield, and Helen Westley.

580   Morosco, Helen M., and Dugger, Leonard P. LIFE OF OLIVER MOROSCO, THE ORACLE OF BROADWAY, WRITTEN FROM HIS OWN NOTES AND COMMENTS. Caldwell, Idaho: Caxton Printers, 1944. 387 p. Index, illus.

Undistinguished theatrical memoirs with substantial sections on Laurette Taylor and David Belasco.

581   Moses, Montrose J. "The Life Story of Clyde Fitch." McCLURE'S 52 (November 1920): 16-17, 54-57; (December 1920): 19-20, 32, 35; 53 (January 1921): 26-28, 36-37; (February 1921): 25-27, 53, 55-56; (April 1921): 25-28, 45-47; (August 1921): 35-36, 42-43. Illus.

Describes many of the players who appeared in Fitch's shows, including Henry Miller, Richard Mansfield, William J. Florence, Modjeska, Elsie DeWolfe, Viola Allen, Otis Skinner, Julia Marlowe, Amelia Bingham, Maxine Elliott, Annie Russell, Mary Mannering, and Blanche Walsh.

582   Nathan, George Jean. "George W. Lederer's Reminiscences." McCLURE'S 52 (May 1920): 12-14, 54; (June 1920): 18-19, 79-80; (July 1920): 24-25, 64-66; (August 1920): 31, 62; (September 1920): 30-31. Illus.

Although centered upon revues and their stars, this article describes the early careers of some legitimate stars, such as Elsie Ferguson, Maxine Elliott, Edna May, Lillian Russell, and Nat Goodwin.

583   Northall, William Knight. BEFORE AND BEHIND THE CURTAIN: OR FIFTEEN YEARS' OBSERVATIONS AMONG THE THEATRES OF NEW YORK. New York: W.F. Burgess, 1851. 229 p.

Interesting reminiscences with substantial accounts of the Wallacks, George Holland, William Burton, and Edwin Forrest and his place in the Astor Palace riot in 1849 (see no. 1870).

584   Oettel, Walter [Walter]. WALTER'S SKETCH BOOK OF THE PLAYERS, BY WALTER. New York: Gotham Press, 1943. 127 p. Index, illus.

Oettel served for many years as major-domo for the Players, his memoirs informally recall many of the members, including Edwin Booth, Walter Hampden, and Joseph Jefferson III.

585   Panton, Jane Ellen (Frith). LEAVES FROM A LIFE. London: Eveleigh Nash, 1908. 368 p.

Superficial remarks concerning Dion Boucicault, Joseph Jefferson

III, Charles Fechter, and E.H. Sothern.

586   Powers, James T. TWINKLE LITTLE STAR: SPARKLING MEMORIES OF
        SEVENTY YEARS. New York: G.P. Putnam's Sons, 1939. 396 p. Index,
        illus.

        Rambling, undocumented reminiscences of an active but second-
        level actor, including anecdotes concerning James K. Hackett,
        Richard Mansfield, Nat C. Goodwin, and Augustin Daly.

587   Robertson, W[alford].Graham. LIFE WAS WORTH LIVING: THE REMI-
        NISCENCES OF W[ALFORD[GRAHAM ROBERTSON. New York and
        London: Harper and Brothers, 1931. 340 p. Index, illus.

        Contains an essay (pp. 215-32), "Of Ada Rehan and Augustin
        Daly," describing a London engagement. John Drew is also men-
        tioned.

588   Rosenfeld, Sydney. "Confessions of a Playwright." THEATRE (N.Y.) 41
        (January 1925): 12-14, 16, 50, 52, 56; (February 1925): 25-26, 28, 52,
        56, 58; (March 1925): 25-26, 28, 50; (April 1925): 25-26, 62, 64; (August
        1925): 38, 40. Illus.

        Contains references to many of the performers with whom Rosen-
        feld worked, among them Dion Boucicault, Charles Fechter,
        DeWolf Hopper, Mrs. Fiske, Clara Morris, Georgie Drew Barry-
        more, Maude Adams, Ada Rehan, Maxine Elliott, and Richard
        Mansfield.

589   Seldes, Marian. THE BRIGHT LIGHTS: A THEATRE LIFE. Boston: Hough-
        ton Mifflin Co., 1978. 280 p. Illus.

        A revealing and readable theatre autobiography which includes
        reminiscences of Katharine Cornell, Tallulah Bankhead, the
        Lunts, and Zero Mostel.

590   Sims, George Robert. MY LIFE: SIXTY YEARS' RECOLLECTIONS OF
        BOHEMIAN LONDON: London: Eveleigh Nash Co., 1917. 339 p.
        Index, illus.

        While appropriately focused upon the London theatre, these
        memoirs include recollections of Dion Boucicault, Charles Fechter,
        and Adah Isaacs Menken.

591   Smith, Harry B. FIRST NIGHTS AND FIRST EDITIONS. Boston: Little,
        Brown and Co., 1931. 305 p. Index, illus.

        Rambling reminiscences with memories of DeWolf Hopper, Lillian
        Russell, and Francis Wilson.

592   Smith, Elihu Hubbard. THE DIARY OF ELIHU HUBBARD SMITH (1771-
        1798). Cronin, James E., ed. Philadelphia: American Philosophical

Society, 1973. xiii, 468 p. Index, frontispiece.

Smith was a New York physician with a lively interest in the theatre. He recorded his reactions to Mr. and Mrs. Hallam, Jr., John Hodgkinson, and Mrs. Merry in some substance, with passing references to several dozen other colonial performers.

593   Soldene, Emily. MY THEATRICAL AND MUSICAL RECOLLECTIONS. London: Downey and Co., 1897. 307 p. Index.

Soldene's rambling memoirs primarily describe her career and world tours as a singer but contain a substantial account of Dion Boucicault and Agnes Robertson, with lesser material on Harry Montague, Charlotte Cushman, Modjeska, and Augustin Daly.

594   Thomas, Augustus. THE PRINT OF MY REMEMBRANCE. New York and London: Charles Scribner's Sons, 1922. 468 p. Index, illus.

Chapter 14 deals with "Julia Marlowe and Others"; chapter 15 describes "Maurice Barrymore and THE BURGLAR."

595   _____. "The Print of My Remembrance." SATURDAY EVENING POST 194 (17 December 1921): 6-7, 66, 68, 71; (31 December 1921): 12-13, 28, 31; (14 January 1922): 12-13, 36, 39, 41-42, 44, 47; (28 January 1922): 18-19, 81, 84, 86, 89-90, 93-94, 97; (25 February 1922): 14-15, 81-82, 84-86; (11 March 1922): 14-15, 70, 73-74, 77-78; (1 April 1922): 20-21, 46, 49-50, 53, 54; (15 April 1922): 16-17, 122, 125-26, 128-29; (29 April 1922): 16, 43, 45-46, 49-50, 53-54; (13 May 1922): 30, 32, 34, 107, 110, 113-14; (3 June 1922): 26, 28, 30, 98-99, 101, 104; (8 July 1922): 24, 26, 28, 93-94, 97-98. Illus.

Serialization of Thomas's autobiography (no. 594).

596   Towse, John Rankin. SIXTY YEARS OF THE THEATER: AN OLD CRIT-IC'S MEMORIES. New York and London: Funk and Wagnall's Co., 1916. 464 p. Illus.

Towse served as drama critic for the NEW YORK EVENING POST for forty-three years. His reminiscences include comments on John Gilbert, Clara Morris, Edwin Booth, Charlotte Cushman, Modjeska, Janauschek, Mary Anderson, Lawrence Barrett, John McCullough, E.L. Davenport, Joseph Jefferson III, Lester Wallack, Richard Mansfield, Augustin Daly, Julia Marlowe, E.H. Sothern, Robert Mantell, Mrs. Fiske, Rose Coghlan, Henrietta Crosman, Margaret Anglin, and E.S. Willard.

597   Tyler, George C., and Furnas, J.C. WHATEVER GOES UP: THE HAZ-ARDOUS FORTUNES OF A NATURAL BORN GAMBLER. Intro. by Booth Tarkington. Indianapolis: Bobbs-Merrill Co., 1934. 303 p. Index, illus.

Memoirs of an active theatre manager with references to many of the stars who appeared in his theatres, among them Mary Anderson, Margaret Anglin, George M. Cohan, Augustin Daly,

Maxine Elliott, Mrs. Fiske, Lynn Fontanne, Nat Goodwin, Joseph Jefferson III, Richard Mansfield, Julia Marlowe, James O'Neill, Ada Rehan, Otis Skinner, and Laurette Taylor.

598   Wagner, Charles L[udwig]. SEEING STARS. New York: G.P. Putnam's Sons, 1940. 389 p. Index, illus.

Wagner drops practically every name in the entertainment industry at the time, but includes fairly substantial sections on David Belasco, Elsie Janis, and Maude Adams.

599   Winter, Jefferson. "As I Remember." SATURDAY EVENING POST 193 (7 August 1920): 38, 40, 42, 44; (4 September 1920): 22-23, 85-86; (30 October 1920): 34, 36, 38, 40, 43, 45. Illus.

A serialized biography of William Winter with substantial references to Joseph Jefferson III, Sol Smith Russell, and Edwin Booth, including considerable reputed correspondence.

600   _____, comp. and ed. IN MEMORY OF FRANK WORTHING, ACTOR: BORN AT EDINBURGH, SCOTLAND, OCTOBER 12, 1866, DIED AT DETROIT, MICHIGAN, DECEMBER 27, 1910. New York: "Printed for Distribution," 1911. 79 p. Illus.

A memorial volume of biography and tributes by Blanche Bates, Grace George, Julia Marlowe, Henry Miller, and Tyrone Power.

INDIVIDUAL PERFORMERS

ADAMS, EDWIN (1834-77). See nos. 399, 401, 407, 413, 489, 496, 928, 1050, and 2618.

ADAMS, MAUDE

(1872-1953)

601   Adams, Maude. "Drama as Education of the Emotions." JUNIOR COL-
LEGE JOURNAL 10 (May 1940): 615-16.

> A brief statement of Adams's educational goals and philosophies
> as an acting teacher at the college level.

602   _____. "The One I Knew Least of All." LADIES' HOME JOURNAL,
March 1926, 3-5, 206; April 1926, pp. 8-9, 213; May 1926, pp. 14-15,
150, 152, 155; June 1926, pp. 22-23, 161-62; July 1926, pp. 21, 70,
73-74; October 1926, pp. 23, 249, 259. Illus.

> A substantial autobiography by Adams, apparently intended for
> but never receiving publication in book form.

603   _____." 'Thumbs Up' for Joy and Adventure." LADIES' HOME JOUR-
NAL, May 1927, pp. 25, 226-28. Illus.

> An article containing a somewhat obtuse statement of Adams's
> theories and philosophies of the theatre.

604   Barnard, Eunice Fuller. "Peter Pan is Happy in a Land of Youth." NEW
YORK TIMES MAGAZINE, 7 November 1937, pp. 6, 21, 25. Illus.

> A brief description of Adams's work as an acting teacher at Ste-
> phens College, Columbia, Missouri, late in her life.

605   Barnes, Howard. "The Thirteen Twilight Years." THEATRE GUILD MAG-
AZINE 9 (December 1931): 32-33.

> Adams was planning to appear with Otis Skinner in THE MER-
> CHANT OF VENICE after not having appeared in New York
> since 1919 in A KISS FOR CINDERELLA. Barnes reminds the
> reader of Adams's previous theatrical contributions.

606   Brock, H.I. "Her Light Still Grows in the Theatre." NEW YORK
TIMES MAGAZINE, 8 November 1942, pp. 20-21, 37. Illus.

> A brief and adulatory tribute to Adams.

607   Cable, Lucy Leffingwell. "On the Desert with Maude Adams." LADIES'
        HOME JOURNAL, May 1907, pp. 7-8, 72. Illus.

        A description to Adams's visit to Egypt in April 1903 and her
        reactions to that country.

608   Cage, Minnie. "Maude Adams, Agricultural Expert, Inspects Her Cous-
        in's Farm." DELINEATOR 84 (March 1914): 1. Illus.

        A description of a visit to Iddenkash, a farm in Ontario, owned
        by the actress's cousin, Dr. H.S. Kiskadden.

609   Clark, Larry D. "Maude Adams at Stephens College: In Her Waning
        Years, A Philosophy of Educational Theatre." SPEECH TEACHER 14
        (March 1965): 123-27.

        Drawing upon interviews and published accounts, Clark describes
        Adams's theories and practices as an acting teacher.

610   Clemens, Cyril. "Theatreana: Some Recollections of Maude Adams."
        HOBBIES 58 (November 1953): 127-30.

        An interview in which Adams recollects Coquelin, Mary Ander-
        son, and PETER PAN.

611   Crawford, Mary Caroline. "Maude Adams in TWELFTH NIGHT." THEA-
        TRE (N.Y.) 8 (August 1908): 218-20. Illus.

        A description of a special production presented at Harvard Univer-
        sity, 3-4 June 1908.

612   Davies, Acton. MAUDE ADAMS. New York: Frederick A. Stokes Co.,
        1901. vi, 110 p. Illus.

        Similar to the Patterson biography (no. 634), undocumented and
        stylistically casual. Davies relies heavily upon Adams's mother,
        David Belasco, and his own observations of the actress.

613   _____. "Maude Adams." MUNSEY'S 33 (August 1905): 584-87. Illus.

        A list of Adams's roles up to 1905 and a discussion of her
        unique personality and theatrical appeal.

614   Dean, F. "Maude Adams." GOOD HOUSEKEEPING, May 1913, pp.
        603-8. Illus.

        An analysis of Adams's off-stage personality, emphasizing her
        efforts to retain her privacy, her love of travel, and her artistic
        and cultural tastes.

615   Dudley, Louise. "Maude Adams' Blueprint for a Campus Drama Workshop."
       THEATRE ARTS 38 (August 1954): 30-32, 92-94. Illus.

       Dudley, then head of Stephen College's division of humanities,
       recalls the actress's work there.

616   Gray, D. "Maude Adams: A Public Influence." HAMPTON'S 26 (June
       1911): 725-37. Illus.

       A substantial monograph which attempts to explain Adams's
       appeal; Gray posits that her appeal was more ethical than
       aesthetic in that the woman behind the actress struck responsive
       chords in her audiences; he also credits her industry and single-
       mindedness in her work.

617   Gray, David. "What 'Chantecler' Means to Maude Adams and What
       She Hopes to Make It Mean to the American Public." LADIES' HOME
       JOURNAL, January 1911, pp. 8, 43. Illus.

       Gray suggests that he spent a week interviewing Adams in order
       to learn how Frohman secured the rights to the script and what
       production values were intended by Adams.

618   J., W.D. "The Little Lady: An Appreciation of Maude Adams."
       BURR McINTOSH MONTHLY 19 (June 1909): n.p. Illus.

       A five-page adulatory tribute to Adams. According to the
       author, the actress's nickname was "the little lady."

619   Kiskadden, Annie Adams. "The Letters of Maude Adams to Her Mother."
       GREEN BOOK MAGAZINE 12 (December 1914): 1087-94. Illus.

       Texts of correspondence. Many of the accompanying photographs
       seem not to have been published elsewhere.

620   _____. "Maude Adams' School Days." GREEN BOOK MAGAZINE 13
       (January 1915): 176-79.

       Adams's mother's recollections.

621   Kiskadden, Annie Adams, in collaboration with Verne Hardin Porter.
       "The Life Story of Maude Adams and Her Mother." GREEN BOOK
       MAGAZINE 11 (June 1914): 11-12; 12 (July 1914): 884-900; (August
       1914): 196-212; (September 1914): 388-403; (October 1914): 596-610;
       (November 1914): 808-22. Illus.

       A substantial if understandably prejudicial account of the ac-
       tress's life and career by her mother.

622   Kobbé, Gustav. "Maude Adams and Her Long Island Farm." LADIES'
       HOME JOURNAL, November 1903, pp. 9-10. Illus.

       Kobbé describes the actress's propensity for farming and her affection for Sandygarth Farm on Long Island.

623   Leathes, Edmund. AN ACTOR ABROAD OR GOSSIP DRAMATIC, NARRATIVE, AND DESCRIPTIVE FROM THE RECOLLECTIONS OF AN ACTOR IN AUSTRALIA, NEW ZEALAND, THE SANDWICH ISLANDS, CALIFORNIA, NEVADA, CENTRAL AMERICA, AND NEW YORK. London: Hurst and Blackett, 1880. x, 317 p.

    A wandering actor's reminiscences, valuable for his description of the frontier theatre and including brief recollections of Maude Adams and Mrs. Davenport Lander.

624   Leigh, Ora V. "The Stage on Which Maude Adams First Appeared." THEATRE (N.Y.) 9 (March 1909): 88-91. Illus.

    A description of the Salt Lake Theatre in Salt Lake City and of Adams's appearance there as a child.

625   "Living Legends." HARPER'S BAZAAR 82 (September 1948): 192. Illus.

    Very brief item, but includes a late photograph of Adams.

626   Matheson, Richard. BID TIME RETURN. New York: Ballantine Books, 1975. 278 p.

    A novel involving time travel to 1896. The character of Elsie McKenna is based on Maude Adams. The story was rewritten and made into the feature film, "Somewhere in Time."

627   THE MAUDE ADAMS BOOK. New York: Charles Frohman, 1909. n.p. Illus.

    A portfolio of photographs of Maude Adams in her leading roles up to that time. No text.

628   "Maude Adams in Schiller's JOAN OF ARC." THEATRE (N.Y.) 9 (July 1909): 8-10. Illus.

    Describes preparations for staging the show in the Harvard football stadium on 22 July 1909.

629   MAUDE ADAMS IN THE LITTLE MINISTER. New York: R.H. Russell, 1899. [16 p.]

    A deluxe souvenir booklet of the production with one photograph of Adams and thirteen sketches of scenes from the play.

630   "Maude Adams's Attempt to Do the Impossible." CURRENT LITERATURE 50 (March 1911): 313-15. Illus.

    A widely varying collection of critical receptions to Adams's CHANTICLER.

631 Moses, Vivian. "Shakespeare al Fresco." COSMOPOLITAN 49 (August 1910): 375-80. Illus.

A fairly detailed description of Adams's production of AS YOU LIKE IT in the University of California Greek Theatre in Berkeley, attended by more than ten thousand spectators.

632 Nathan, George Jean. "Maude Adams' Return to the Stage." VANITY FAIR 37 (February 1932): 32, 72, 74.

Nathan discusses Adams's glamorous reputation, how she achieved it, and how it would draw customers to her intended production of THE MERCHANT OF VENICE.

633 Patterson, Ada. "At Home With Maude Adams." GREEN BOOK ALBUM 4 (December 1910): 1180-86. Illus.

A fan-oriented article, more concerned with the architecture and decor of Adams's home than with the actress.

634 _____. MAUDE ADAMS. New York: Meyer Brothers, 1907. Reprint. New York: Benjamin Blom, 1969. 109 p. Illus.

An undocumented but pleasant treatment of the actress, useful for its inclusion of cast lists from several of Adams's more successful productions.

635 _____. "Mother and I, The Combination that has Made Us See Stars." DELINEATOR 83 (October 1913): 7, 77. Illus.

Includes brief remarks on the role of their mothers in the careers of Maude Adams and Billie Burke.

636 _____. "The Real Maude Adams--A Study." THEATRE (N.Y.) 3 (September 1903): 218-23. Illus.

A fan-oriented and idealized sketch of the actress.

637 "People You Pay to Know. Maude Adams: A Perennial Peter Pan." NATIONAL MAGAZINE 47 (March 1918): 181. Illus.

A one-page tribute containing a few biographical details.

638 Pollock, Channing. "The Only Three Women I Ever Loved." GOOD HOUSEKEEPING, March 1937, pp. 34-35, 181-84. Illus.

The critic describes his admiration for Adams in THE LITTLE MINISTER, praising her air of gallantry. (The other two women were Pollock's wife and Ellen Terry.)

639 Richardson, Anna S. "Maude Adams." WOMAN'S HOME COMPANION

39 (March 1912): 8-9, 104. Illus.

Nineteen photographs and a substantial text, in part estimating the actress's income.

640 Robbins, Phyllis. MAUDE ADAMS: AN INTIMATE PORTRAIT. New York: G.P. Putnam's Sons, 1956. 298 p. Index, illus.

Robbins was a personal friend and companion of Adams, who requested her to write this comprehensive biography. The work concludes with a genealogy of Adams as well as a list of the shows in which she appeared.

641 _____. "The Wit and Wisdom of Maude Adams." THEATRE ARTS 40 (November 1956): 68-69. Illus.

Brief quotations by Adams on various subjects, culled from Robbins's MAUDE ADAMS: AN INTIMATE PORTRAIT (above).

642 _____. THE YOUNG MAUDE ADAMS. Francestown, N.H.: Marshall Jones Co., 1959. 163 p. Illus.

An undocumented account of Adams's early years, including some otherwise previously unpublished photographs.

643 Shanley, J.F. "Then and Now." NEW YORK TIMES MAGAZINE, 9 November 1952, pp. 34. Illus.

A one-page article, a tribute to the actress on her eightieth birthday.

644 Tarbell, Arthur W. " 'The Little Minister' of Maude Adams." NATIONAL MAGAZINE 9 (January 1899): 312-20. Illus.

A substantial account of how Barrie came to write the script and the production circumstances for its premiere.

645 "A Time of Years." TIME, 27 July 1953, pp. 32, 35. Illus.

A eulogistic review of Adams's career.

646 Tyrrell, Henry. "Do You Believe in Maude Adams?" COSMOPOLITAN 54 (January 1913): 266-68. Illus.

A brief, superficial article in which Tyrrell points out that Barrie had never seen Adams in any of his scripts.

647 Wagstaffe, William de. "Coining Admiration Worth Half a Million a Year." THEATRE (N.Y.) 18 (December 1913): 190-92. Illus.

The author describes Adams's appeal, then estimates her income.

648 _____. "How Maude Adams' Mood Fits Barrie's." THEATRE (N.Y.)
31 (December 1920): 356, 358.

    The author describes the long-working relationship between the
actress and the dramatist.

649 Wells, Heber M. "Recollections of Maude Adams." GREEN BOOK
MAGAZINE 14(July 1915): 164-72. Illus.

    Wells, a former Utah governor, recalls Adams as a child actress
in Salt Lake City. Some rare photographs are reproduced.

650 "What the World Is Doing: A Record of Current Events." COLLIERS 43
(10 July 1909): 20-21. Illus.

    Description and production photograph of Adams's production
of JOAN OF ARC at the Harvard football stadium.

651 Wolf, Rennold. "Maude Adams." GREEN BOOK ALBUM 8 (August
1912): 209-21. Illus.

    Wolf describes Adams as the loneliest figure on the American
stage, citing her self-inflicted obsession for privacy.

652 Woolf, S.J. "Then and Now--Maude Adams." NEW YORK TIMES
MAGAZINE, 17 October 1948, p. 17. Illus.

    A three-column biographical sketch of Adams and her career.

See also nos. 26, 28, 58, 164, 174, 177, 219, 223, 226, 245, 262, 270, 276,
278-79, 286, 294, 296-97, 314, 316, 358, 381-82, 390, 413, 427, 429-30,
436, 439-40, 444, 448, 451, 465, 469, 479, 493, 505, 508, 525, 532, 555,
558, 575, 579, 588, 598, 928, 1477, 1975, 1978, 1981, 2044, 2567, and
2984.

ADDAMS, AUGUSTUS A. (?-1851). See nos. 413 and 3168.

ADLER, STELLA
(1902-   )

653   Vandenbroucke, Russell. "Stella Adler." YALE THEATRE 8, no. 2
       (1971): 30-37. Illus.

       An interview about the possibility and nature of a uniquely
       American acting style.

See also nos. 137, 167, 291, 540, and 3052.

ALDRIDGE, IRA

(1807-67)

654   Cole, John. A CRITIQUE ON THE PERFORMANCE OF OTHELLO BY F.W. KEENE ALDRIDGE, THE AFRICAN ROSCIUS. Scarborough, Engl.: Printed for John Cole, 1831. 3 p.

    Ira Aldridge, using the forename Keene, performed at Scarborough in August 1831. Only thirty copies of Cole's response were printed. Unavailable for examination.

655   Durylin, S. "Ira Aldridge." Trans. by E. Blum. SHAKESPEARE ASSOCIATION BULLETIN 17(January 1942): 33-39.

    A capsule biography, translated from the Russian.

656   Malone, Mary. ACTOR IN EXILE: THE LIFE OF IRA ALDRIDGE. New York: Crowell-Collier, 1969. 86 p. Index, illus.

    A readable but undocumented and brief account of Aldridge's life and career with a few drawings. Requires corroboration.

657   Marshall, Herbert. FURTHER RESEARCH ON IRA ALDRIDGE, THE NEGRO TRAGEDIAN. Carbondale: Center for Soviet and East European Studies, Southern Illinois University Press, 197-. ix, 65 p.

    This monograph contains critical accounts of Aldridge, a list of his plays and roles, Marshall's additional analysis of the actor's life and art, some conclusions about Aldridge's Swedish wife, and a chronology of his appearances from 1825 to 1867.

658   Marshall, Herbert, and Stock, Mildred. IRA ALDRIDGE, THE NEGRO TRAGEDIAN. London: Rockliff, 1958. 342 p. Index, illus., bibliog.

    The only full-length and fully documented scholarly treatment of Aldridge, the result of considerable research by the authors in America and Europe. Essential to any study of Aldridge. A paperback edition was published by Southern Illinois University Press in 1968.

659   MEMOIR AND THEATRICAL CAREER OF IRA ALDRIDGE, THE AFRICAN ROSCIUS. London: Onwhyn, [1848]. 28 p. Frontispiece.

         A sensative though abbreviated treatment of the tragedian, drawing heavily upon correspondence files and published reviews, thus valuable for primary materials.

660   "Mr. Ira Aldridge." TALLIS'S DRAMATIC MAGAZINE, June 1851, pp. 14-16. Illus.

         A critical-biographical essay on Aldridge, lauding his genius and pleading for an end to racial prejudice.

661   Rollins, Charlemae. FAMOUS NEGRO ENTERTAINERS OF STAGE, SCREEN AND TV. New York: Dodd, Mead and Co., 1967. 115 p. Index, illus.

         A book of brief essays, intended for children, on Ira Aldridge (pp. 21-24) and Paul Robeson (pp. 95-99).

662   Trommer, Marie. IRA ALDRIDGE, AMERICAN NEGRO TRAGEDIAN AND TARAS SHEVCHENKO, POET OF THE UKRAINE. STORY OF A FRIEND-SHIP. New York: Marie Trommer, n.d. 14 p.

         A small pamphlet with a few of Shevchenko's poems translated by Trommer and biographical sketches of the poet and the actor.

See also nos. 190, 194, 296, 358, 367-68, 371, 385, 399-400, 461, and 551.

ALLEN, VIOLA

(1869-1948)

663   Allen, Viola. "Changing Styles in Acting." GREEN BOOK ALBUM
       1(June 1909): 1223-27.

> Allen reviews her career, suggesting she has seen a relaxation
> of theatrical traditions and a move toward a greater naturalism
> in acting.

664   _____. "The Difficulties of Playing Shakespearean Heroines." THEATRE
       (N.Y.) 6 (December 1906): 322.

> A brief, somewhat superficial essay.

665   _____. "My Beginnings." THEATRE (N.Y.) 6 (April 1906): 93-94, viii.
       Illus.

> Allen describes her early failures as an actress, then her first
> success in John McCullough's production of VIRGINIUS.

666   _____. "On the Making of an Actress." COSMOPOLITAN 31 (August
       1901): 409-14. Illus.

> Fairly abstract comments on the background, talent, and train-
> ing required for a stage career. Several photographs of Allen
> in various productions not published elsewhere are included.

667   _____. "An Optimistic View." THEATRE (N.Y.) 2 (December 1902):
       32.

> Allen views the state of the theatre at the time with a degree
> of cautious hope.

668   _____. "Plays That are Really Worth While." GREEN BOOK MAGA-
       ZINE 11 (January 1914): 81-86. Illus.

> Allen praises a series of specific scripts for their truthfulness
> and beauty while condemning others.

669 Coward, Edward Fales. "An Interview with Viola Allen." THEATRE
(N.Y.) 3 (February 1903): 44-46. Illus.

Allen describes her work in a somewhat more substantial interview than was common at the time.

670 Glover, Lyman B[eecher]. VIOLA ALLEN AS JULIA IN THE HUNCH-
BACK. New York: R.F. Seymour, [1908]. 12 p. Illus.

Glover presents a biography of the playwright, a stage history
of the script, and a few comments about Allen's performance
in the role.

671 Seymour, May Davenport. "Viola Allen." SHAKESPEARE ASSOCIATION
BULLETIN 23 (July 1948): 98-104. Illus.

A brief and undocumented overview of Allen's life and career.

672 Tyrrell, Henry. "A Modern Viola." COSMOPOLITAN 54 (February
1913): 409-11. Illus.

A brief essay publicizing Allen's appearance in THE DAUGH-
TER OF HEAVEN and praising her previous performances.

See also nos. 13, 28, 262, 270, 276, 278-79, 288, 290, 303, 367, 381-82,
413, 429, 451, 465, 506, 510, 529, 581, and 2701.

ANDERSON, MARY

(1859-1940)

673   Agate, James. THOSE WERE THE NIGHTS. London: Hutchinson, 1946; London and New York: Hutchinson, 1947. London: 1946. Reprint. New York: Benjamin Blom, 1969. 145 p. Illus.

     A collection of essays, one of which describes Anderson during her London appearance in THE WINTER'S TALE.

674   Anderson, Mary. A FEW MEMORIES. New York: Harper and Brothers, 1896. London: Osgood, McIlvaine and Co., 1896. 257 p. Index, illus.

     Anderson's somewhat sentimentalized account of her life and career up to the time of her marriage to Antonio F. de Navarro in 1890. The volume contains many anecdotes of her fellow players, including Edwin Booth, Dion Boucicault, Charlotte Cushman, Joseph Jefferson III, John McCullough, Clara Morris, and George Vandenhoff.

675   _____. A FEW MORE MEMORIES. London: Hutchinson and Co., 1936. 279 p. Index, illus.

     Anderson's sequel to A FEW MEMORIES (above), describing her life after she moved to England and retired from the stage. Two chapters (37 and 38) compare then modern with past acting, but not in significant depth.

676   _____. "The Stage and Society." NORTH AMERICAN REVIEW 148 (January 1889): 16-20.

     Anderson offers an idealized statement of theatrical motivations and the difficulties of the profession.

677   Dunsford, Alice Griffin. "Mary Anderson as a Stage Struck Girl." THEATRE (N.Y.) 5 (November 1905): 286, 288. Illus.

     The author, who was Anderson's aunt, recalls Charlotte Cushman giving encouragement to the fledgling actress.

678   Ellwanger, Mrs. E.H. "Mary Anderson as She Was Known in Kentucky." KENTUCKY REGISTER 10 (September 1912): 17-24. Illus.

A collection of newspaper notices and reviews, connected by a gushingly adulatory text describing Anderson's first appearances.

679   Farrar, J. Maurice. MARY ANDERSON: THE STORY OF HER LIFE AND PROFESSIONAL CAREER. London: David Bogue, 1884. New York: N.L. Munro, 1885. 86 p. Frontispiece.

A brief, adulatory, and systematic account of Anderson's career, drawing heavily upon published criticisms.

680   Frey, Albert R. MARY ANDERSON IN HER DRAMATIC ROLES. New York: William J. Kelly, 1892. [35 p.] Illus.

A two-page biographical sketch precedes a series of photographs of Anderson, synopses of several plays in which she appeared, plus brief excerpts from them.

681   Lytton, The Earl of. "Miss Anderson's Juliet." NINETEENTH CENTURY 16 (December 1884): 879-900.

A detailed examination of Anderson's Juliet, drawing upon published criticism as well as the author's observation of the actress at the Lyceum Theatre in London. Lytton finds himself at odds with the critics.

682   Morrissey, James W. "Some Theatrical Memories of Other Days." THEATRE (N.Y.) 12 (October 1910): 113-14, 116-17.

Morrissey, a manager, recalls meeting and working with Anderson.

683   Patterson, Ada. "Mary Anderson—Yesterday and To-Day." THEATRE (N.Y.) 14 (December 1911): 104, 106. Illus.

Patterson describes the circumstances under which Anderson made her somewhat premature retirement from the theatre.

684   _____. "Mary Anderson Comes Home." GREEN BOOK ALBUM 7 (January 1912): 215-19.

A description of Anderson's return to the United States to collaborate with Robert Hiches on THE GARDEN OF ALLAH.

685   Shaw, John. "Mary Anderson's Stratford Production of AS YOU LIKE IT." THEATRE ANNUAL 30 (1974): 40-59. Illus.

A well-researched and documented account of Anderson's engagement of the Memorial Theatre in Stratford-upon-Avon, including scenic designs, textual treatments, and critical receptions.

686   Williams, Henry Llewellyn. THE "QUEEN OF THE DRAMA!" MARY
       ANDERSON: HER LIFE ON AND OFF THE STAGE. TOGETHER WITH
       SELECT RECITATIONS FROM ALL THE GREAT PLAYS IN WHICH SHE
       HAS DELIGHTED TWO CONTINENTS. New York: Charles St. Clair,
       1885. 128 p.

       A cursory and adulatory biographical sketch comprises forty-four
       pages of text, followed by excerpts from Anderson's leading roles.

687   Winter, William. THE STAGE LIFE OF MARY ANDERSON. New York:
       George J. Coombes, 1886. 151 p. Frontispiece.

       A brief but detailed account of Anderson's early career, written
       in Winter's adulatory, somewhat turgid style.

See also nos. 13, 58, 130, 213, 245, 256, 262, 274, 277-79, 293, 316, 336,
341, 343, 346, 356, 370, 383, 398, 400, 402, 404, 406-8, 413, 417,
419, 438, 454, 459, 482, 519, 526, 534, 544, 556, 558, 572, 579, 596-97,
610, 1750, 2750, and 2987.

ANGLIN, MARGARET
(1876-1958)

688   Adams, Mildred. "Margaret Anglin." WOMAN CITIZEN 12 (June 1927): 49. Illus.

A brief sketch, praising Anglin for her productions of the Greek classic dramas.

689   Anglin, Margaret. "An Actress in the Making." HEARST'S 30 (September 1916): 168-69, 176, 178. "Some Experiences with Richard Mansfield." (October 1916): 224-25, 278-80; "With the Empire Theatre Company." (November 1916): 316-17, 370-71; "With Zira in the Great Divide." 31(January 1917): 26-27, 72-74; "My Australian Tour." (February 1917): 106-7, 122, 124; "Greek Drama and Theatrical Management." (March 1917): 206, 248. Illus.

Serialized, undistinguished memoirs, apparently never published as a separate volume. Valuable illustrations, but the text would require corroboration.

690   _____. "The Actress-Producer." DRAMA 10 (January 1920): 127-28.

A simplistic editorial on the producer's difficulties in staging productions.

691   _____. "The Ambitions of an Actress." AMERICAN MAGAZINE 79 (June 1915): 44-46, 79-81. Illus.

Somewhat idealized reminiscences of the actress's early career, including her engagement with Richard Mansfield.

692   _____. "Domesticity and the Stage: How Play-Acting and Housekeeping Work Together for Good." GOOD HOUSEKEEPING, January 1912, pp. 41-48. Illus.

Anglin suggests the strain of her touring engagements had given her a marked propensity for the domestic life.

693 _____. "Greek Drama and Theatrical Management." HEARST'S 31 (March 1917): 206, 248.

Unavailable for examination.

694 _____. "Lost--Sixty-Three Pounds." VOGUE, 1 July 1937, pp. 70-71, 78. Illus.

Anglin, who lost sixty-three pounds in three months, describes her method of dieting.

695 _____. "My Beginnings." THEATRE (N.Y.) 5 (December 1905): 314-15. Illus.

Anglin describes the slow process by which her ambition to become a public reader was transferred to acting.

696 _____. "A Run Around the World." GREEN BOOK ALBUM 2 (July 1909): 118-29.

Anglin describes a world tour with particular emphasis on her visit to Australia.

697 _____. "The 'Star' Idea." THEATRE (N.Y.) 31 (December 1920): 364.

Anglin decries the star system, complaining that money was taking precedence over artistry in the theatre.

698 _____. "Tragedy: How It Feels to Act It." HARPER'S WEEKLY 58 (6 September 1913): 14-15. Illus.

Anglin describes the exhilaration of the acting Antigone during a recent performance in California.

699 _____. "What Santa Ought to Put in Our Stockings." THEATRE (N.Y.) 24 (December 1916): 352-53, 406.

The actress pleads for "a properly balanced and intelligently conducted repertoire theatre for every one of our larger cities."

700 Eaton, Walter Prichard. "Miss Anglin in Shakespeare's Plays." AMERI-CAN MAGAZINE 77 (May 1914): 34-37.

A column devoted entirely to Anglin's Shakespearean repertory, praising her highly, but hoping that she would not desert the modern drama entirely.

701 Goddard, H.P. "Players I Have Known." THEATRE (N.Y.) 18 (August 1913): 70, vi. Illus.

Goddard, a veteran critic, recalls the performances of Margaret Anglin and Blanche Bates.

702   "Margaret Anglin with the Empire Theatre Company." HEARTS'S 30 (September 1916): 316-17, 370-71.

        Unavailable for examination.

703   "Miss Anglin in Greek Tragedy." THEATRE (N.Y.) 22 (September 1915): 116. Illus.

        A review of productions in California, but some biographical material is included as background.

704   Moses, Montrose. "New York Drama." BOOK NEWS 36 (April 1918): 302-3.

        Moses discusses Anglin's long-dreamed of productions of Greek classics in New York, giving her mixed but generally positive assessments.

705   Nathan, George Jean. "Katharine Cornell Compared with Margaret Anglin." VANITY FAIR 43 (October 1934): 45-46.

        Unavailable for examination.

706   "A New Shakespeare Portrayer." COSMOPOLITAN 55 (November 1913): 834-36. Illus.

        Anglin is quoted on her plans for a season of Shakespeare revivals for the coming season, including AS YOU LIKE IT, TWELFTH NIGHT, THE TAMING OF THE SHREW, and ANTONY AND CLEOPATRA.

707   Patterson, Ada. "At Home with Margaret Anglin." GREEN BOOK ALBUM 6 (August 1911): 418-22.

        A superficial, chatty interview of small merit.

708   _____. "A Beautiful Adventure in the Drama." COSMOPOLITAN 59 (August 1915): 352-59. Illus.

        Patterson describes the Anglin's plan to present IPHIGENIA AT AULIS, ELECTRA, and MEDEA at the University of California's Greek theatre.

709   _____. "Margaret Anglin Heads One Thousand Players." THEATRE (N.Y.) 23 (June 1916): 340-41. Illus.

        A description of Anglin's plan to stage AS YOU LIKE IT in St. Louis's Forest Park with a cast of twelve hundred.

710   P.,A. [Patterson, Ada?] "Margaret Anglin's Year as a Producer." THEATRE (N.Y.) 19 (June 1914): 290-92. Illus.

        A superficial description of Anglin's tour with a six-show repertory.

711   Stearns, Harold. "A Brilliant Shakespeare Repertory." HARPER'S WEEKLY
        58 (7 February 1914): 18-19. Illus.

        Praise for and descriptions of Anglin's TWELFTH NIGHT, AS
        YOU LIKE IT, THE TAMING OF THE SHREW, and ANTONY
        AND CLEOPATRA.

712   Wagstaff, William de. "Chats with Players." THEATRE (N.Y.) 2 (April
        1902): 12-15. Illus.

        A superficial and pointless interview.

713   White, Matthew, Jr. "Margaret Anglin." MUNSEY'S 35 (July 1906):
        504-8. Illus.

        A biographical-critical essay, largely concerned with Anglin's
        Roxanne in CYRANO DE BERGERAC and her engagement with
        E.H. Sothern.

See also nos. 28, 270, 276, 278, 294, 316, 342, 344, 381-82, 413, 430, 440,
464, 510, 512, 539, 545, 549, 558, 565, 578, 596-97, 2161, 2567, 2901, and
3177.

ASTON, ANTHONY

(c. 1682-c. 1753)

714   Aston, Anthony. A BRIEF SUPPLEMENT TO COLLEY CIBBER, ESQ: HIS LIVES OF THE LATE FAMOUS ACTORS AND ACTRESSES. [London]: Printed for the Author, [1747-48]. 24 p.

A pamphlet of extreme rarity. Unavailable for examination.

715   _____. THE FOOL'S OPERA: OR, THE TASTE OF THE AGE. London: T. Payne, 1731. 22 p.

A brief comic opera by Aston, to which he added a brief sketch of his life, from which most biographical detail is derived. Available on microprint.

716   Chetwood, W[illiam]. R[ufus]. A GENERAL HISTORY OF THE STAGE; (MORE PARTICULARLY THE IRISH THEATRE) FROM ITS ORIGIN IN GREECE DOWN TO THE PRESENT TIME. WITH THE MEMOIRS OF MOST OF THE PRINCIPAL PERFORMERS THAT HAVE APPEARED ON THE DUBLIN STAGE, FOR THE LAST FIFTY YEARS. WITH NOTES, MODERN, FOREIGN, DOMESTIC, SERIOUS, COMIC, MORAL, MERRY, HISTORICAL, AND GEOGRAPHICAL, CONTAINING MANY THEATRICAL ANECDOTES; ALSO SEVERAL PIECES OF POETRY, NEVER BEFORE PUBLISHED. London: E. Rider, 1749. 259 p. Frontispiece.

Chetwood, a prompter at Drury Lane for twenty years, has written a worthless history of the theatre, but appends brief biographical sketches of leading English actors, among them Aston (pp. 88-90), to whom he attributes a hot temper.

717   Nicholson, Watson. ANTHONY ASTON: STROLLER AND ADVENTURER, TO WHICH IS APPENDED ASTON'S BRIEF SUPPLEMENT TO COLLEY CIBBER'S LIVES: AND A SKETCH OF THE LIFE OF ANTHONY ASTON, WRITTEN BY HIMSELF. South Haven, Mich.: published by the author, 1920. 98 p.

Unavailable for examination.

718   Nickles, Mary A. "Tony Aston's 'Medleys.' " THEATRE NOTEBOOK 30, no. 2 (1976): 69-78.

While not dealing with Aston in America, this article documents some of his activity in London.

719   Wegelin, Oscar. "The Beginning of the Drama in America." LITERARY COLLECTOR 9 (June 1905): 177-81.

Includes a brief synopsis of THE FOOL'S OPERA and proposes that Aston appeared in New York sometime between 1702 and 1705.

See also nos. 29, 36, 305, and 399.

BACON, FRANK

(1864-1922)

720   "Affairs and Folks." NATIONAL MAGAZINE 50 (December 1921): 361. Illus.

> An interview with Bacon by an anonymous reporter. Contains some biographical information. Conducted during the Boston engagement of LIGHTNIN'.

721   Bacon, Frank. "Don't Get Side-Tracked." AMERICAN MAGAZINE 87 (May 1919): 34-35, 181-82, 184-86. Illus.

> A reasonably substantial autobiographical essay in which Bacon reviews his career and his eventual stardom after the age of fifty. He describes the genesis of LIGHTNIN'.

722   _____. "How I Played Capulet." THEATRE (N.Y.) 29 (March 1919): 164. Illus.

> Part of a series of articles, "The Most Striking Episode in My Life." Bacon describes having to substitute without prior warning in a San Francisco production of ROMEO AND JULIET.

723   "My Funniest Stage Experience." THEATRE (N.Y.) 31 (June 1920): 504, 565.

> Brief anecdotes by several actors, among them Frank Bacon and William Collier.

724   "New York Honors Frank Bacon--Actor." THEATRE (N.Y.) 34 (November 1921): 292, 338. Illus.

> A description of the festivities at the end of the 1,291 performance run of LIGHTNIN' in New York, then the record, as Bacon left to perform the show in Chicago.

725   Patterson, Ada. "LIGHTNIN' Breaks the Record." THEATRE (N.Y.) 31 (November 1920): 272, 312. Illus.

Bacon speculates as to the reason for his script's success as it begins it third year in New York.

726 _____. "A New Rip for the Old." THEATRE (N.Y.) 28 (November 1918): 290, 292. Illus.

Some biographical detail about Bacon, but primarily concerned with his success in LIGHTNIN'.

727 Schmidt, Karl. "There Were Liars in Those Days." EVERYBODY'S MAGAZINE 40 (January 1919): 43.

A descriptive sketch of Bacon and his characterization of Bill in LIGHTNIN'.

See also nos. 228, 377, 437, 439, 493, and 579.

BAINTER, FAY

(1892-1968)

728   Bainter, Fay. "The 'Serious' Playgoer and Lost Illusions." DRAMA (Chicago) 11 (May 1921): 272-72. Illus.

    Brief remarks pleading with actors to take their work more seriously and thus regain their straying audiences.

729   _____. "The Story of an Actress--Myself. Revealing Her Struggles from Obscurity to Stardom." FORUM 61 (May 1919): 590-99.

    Somewhat superficially, Bainter describes her childhood, her emerging interest in the theatre, her early stock company experiences, and her eventual New York successes.

730   Bloom, Vera. "Fay Bainter--A Star of Tomorrow." THEATRE (N.Y.) 26 (August 1917): 96. Illus.

    An interview shortly after Bainter's arrival in New York.

731   Roberts, Katharine. "It Takes Experience." COLLIER'S 95 (12 January 1935): 16, 34. Illus.

    An article primarily concerned with women's fashions, exemplified by Bainter's costumes as Fran Dodsworth.

732   Schmidt, Karl. "A Star of Tomorrow." EVERYBODY'S MAGAZINE 39 (August 1918): 106. Illus.

    Following her successes in ARMS AND THE GIRL and THE WILLOW-TREE, Schmidt predicts a bright future for Bainter.

See also nos. 276, 296, and 358.

BANDMANN, DANIEL

(1840-1905)

733 Bandmann, Daniel. AN ACTOR'S TOUR: OR, SEVENTY THOUSAND MILES WITH SHAKESPEARE. Edited by Barnard Gisby. Boston: Cupples, Upham, and Co., 1885. xviii, 303 p.

>   A rambling account of the German-born actor's 1879-84 world tour, with special attention paid to Hawaii. Passing mention of various performers of the time.

734 Coleman, Rufus A., ed. "Daniel E. Bandmann, 1840-1905. Shakespearean Stockman." MONTANA MAGAZINE OF HISTORY 4 (Autumn 1954): 29-43. Illus.

>   Coleman reprinted Bandmann's reminiscences from the BUTTE MINER of 21 December 1902, adding footnotes and a dozen illustrations to Bandmann's account of why he left the stage for a ranch. Useful.

735 Nobles, Milton. "Some Unwritten Stage History." THEATRE (N.Y.) 23 (August 1916): 79, 81, 94. Illus.

>   Nobles recalls the early (1870) California theatre and includes a lengthy anecdote about Bandmann.

736 Partoll, Albert J. "Bandmann's Greatest Triumph." MONTANA MAGAZINE OF HISTORY 5 (Spring 1955): 29-30. Illus.

>   A brief account of Bandmann driving a band of Indians away from his Montana ranch.

See also nos. 21, 130, 399, and 2443.

BANKHEAD, TALLULAH

(1902-68)

737   Bankhead, Tallulah. "Caught With My Facts Down." THEATRE ARTS
38 (September 1954): 22-23, 93. Illus.

> Bankhead corrects a number of factual errors in her autobiography, TALLULAH (1952).

738   _____. "My Friend, Miss Barrymore." COLLIER'S 123 (23 April 1949):
13-14, 92. Illus.

> Bankhead attests to her admiration of Barrymore, praising her barbed wit and long career.

739   _____. TALLULAH: MY AUTOBIOGRAPHY. Chicago: Sears Readers
Club, 1952. 326 p. Index, illus.

> An impudent and amusing autobiography, reflecting the qualities of the actress, but containing factual errors (no. 737) and offering little trustworthy insight.

740   _____. "Tallulah on Tallulah." LIFE, 25 June 1951, pp. 90-97. Illus.

> A highly illustrated, fan-oriented autobiographical sketch.

741   Benchley, Nathaniel. "Offstage." THEATRE ARTS 35 (November 1951):
50-51. Illus.

> Benchley describes Richard Maney's procedures in writing a biography of Bankhead.

742   Brian, Dennis. TALLULAH, DARLING: A BIOGRAPHY OF TALLULAH
BANKHEAD. New York: Pyramid, 1972. 278 p. Index, illus.

> A somewhat sensationalized biographical treatment, undocumented and requiring corroboration throughout.

743   Brando, Anna Kashfi, and Stein, E.P. BRANDO FOR BREAKFAST. New
York: Crown Publishers, 1979. viii, 273 p.

An opportunistic biography by Brando's ex-wife containing a few anecdotes about Brando's relationships with Bankhead and Lee Strasberg.

744 Carvel, Madge. "Hollywood Speaks its Mind about Tallulah Bankhead." MOVIE CLASSIC 2 (May 1932): 26, 30. Illus.

A collection of comments about Bankhead by various celebrities. Fan-oriented.

745 Cousins, E.G., ed. WHAT I WANT FROM LIFE. London: George Allen and Unwin, 1934. 112 p. Illus.

A series of brief essays, including "I Want Everything," by Bankhead, and "I Want to Be African," by Paul Robeson.

746 Cruikshank, Herbert. "Why London's in a Fog." MOTION PICTURE MAGAZINE 41(June 1931): 33, 90. Illus.

A description of Bankhead's success, professional and personal, in London.

747 Dean, Basil. SEVEN AGES: AN AUTOBIOGRAPHY 1888-1927. London: Hutchinson, 1970. 333 p. Index, illus.

The English producer devotes chapter 16 to Bankhead and her engagement at the St. Martin's Theatre.

747A Eustis, Maurice. "Tallulah Bankhead" in "Footlight Parade." THEATRE ARTS 23 (October 1939): 718-19.

A brief assessment of Bankhead's career, with the hope that her success in THE LITTLE FOXES would make better scripts available to her.

748 Frazier, George. "Tallulah Bankhead." LIFE, 15 February 1943, pp. 46, 49-50, 52. Illus.

A substantial treatment, albeit one suspects somewhat whitewashed, of Bankhead's early career.

749 Gill, Brendan. TALLULAH. New York: Holt, Rinehart and Winston, 1972. 283 p. Index, illus.

A lavishly illustrated biography which includes a chronology of Bankhead's professional career. The text is lively and evocative, but would require corroboration for scholarly purposes.

750 Grayson, C. "The Star That Has Hollywood Guessing." MOTION PICTURE MAGAZINE 43 (April 1932): 58-59, 82, 85. Illus.

Outrageous anecdotes about Bankhead upon her arrival in Hollywood.

751   Hall, Gladys. "Has Hollywood Cold-Shouldered Tallulah?" MOTION
      PICTURE MAGAZINE 44 (September 1932): 47, 86. Illus.

      Hall describes the hesitation of Hollywood hostesses to invite
      Bankhead into their homes.

752   Hicks, Sir Edward Seymour. NIGHT LIGHTS: TWO MEN TALK OF
      LIFE AND LOVE AND LADIES. London, Toronto, Sydney, and Melbourne:
      Cassell and Co., 1938. 242 p. Index, illus.

      The section "Famous Ladies of the Stage" (pp. 105-98) dis-
      cusses Bankhead and the remarkable infatuation of London audi-
      ences for her.

753   Israel, Lee. MISS TALLULAH BANKHEAD. New York: G.P. Putnam's
      Sons, 1972. New York: Dell Publishing Co., 1972. 365 p. Index,
      illus.

      Israel's biography seems well researched, is frequently bawdy,
      and reflects Bankhead's volatile personality with sensitivity.

754   Linen, James A. "A Letter from the Publisher." TIME 52 (6 December
      1948): 14. Illus.

      Linen describes his difficulties in interviewing Bankhead (see
      no. 758).

755   "THE LITTLE FOXES: Tallulah Bankhead Has Her First U.S. Hit." LIFE,
      6 March 1939, front cover, pp. 70-73. Illus.

      A photographic synopsis of the production.

756   Meade, Julian R. "Girlhood of a Star." WOMAN'S HOME COMPAN-
      ION 67 (August 1940): 23, 31. Illus.

      A somewhat romanticized and fan-oriented account of Bankhead's
      life before she entered the theatre.

757   Mosley, Leonard O. "I'm Leaving, But I'll Be Back." MOTION PIC-
      TURE MAGAZINE 45 (February 1933): 35, 79, 81, 85. Illus.

      Mosley quotes the actress as serving notice on the film colony
      in Hollywood that her departure was in no way permanent.

758   "One-Woman Show." TIME 52 (22 November 1948): cover, 76-78,
      80-83. Illus.

      Substantial biographical sketch of Bankhead, her heritage, life,
      and career.

759   Rawls, Eugenie. TALLULAH: A MEMORY. Edited by James Hatcher.
      Birmingham: University of Alabama, 1979. 97 p. Illus.

A brief biography of Bankhead, heavily illustrated and including many reproductions of letters to and from her. The volume includes a one-page biography of Rawls, who appeared with Bankhead in THE LITTLE FOXES.

760   Ray, Marie Beynon. "The Ends of Fashion." COLLIER'S 88 (19 September 1931): 17, 64. Illus.

Bankhead discusses her theories of costuming, both on and off stage.

761   "Reflecting Glory." LITERARY DIGEST 123 (29 May 1937): 22.

News item about Bankhead's triumphant return to Birmingham, Alabama, and the resultant festivities.

762   Shane, Ted. "Tallulah to You." COLLIER'S 119 (26 April 1947): 22-23, 72, 74, 76. Illus.

A brief summary of Bankhead's career, stressing her volubility, done while she was starring in THE EAGLE HAS TWO HEADS.

763   "Talullah Bankhead's House." VOGUE, 1 July 1943, pp. 56-57. Illus.

Photographs and a brief description of Bankhead's home near Bedford Village, New York, from which she commuted to Broadway.

764   "Tallulah the Actress vs. Tallulah the Tube." LIFE, 28 March 1944, pp. 36-37. Illus.

Concerns Bankhead's law suit against an advertisement agency for using Tallulah as a name for an animated tube of Prell shampoo.

765   Tunney, Kieran. TALLULAH: DARLING OF THE GODS. London: Secker and Warburg, 1972. New York: E.P. Dutton and Co., 1973. 224 p. Index, illus.

Tunney, who knew and worked with Bankhead for over twenty years, collected reminiscences of her, tending somewhat toward the more sensational aspects of Bankhead's life and career.

766   Wallace, Mike. MIKE WALLACE ASKS: HIGHLIGHTS FROM 46 CONTROVERSIAL INTERVIEWS. Edited by Charles Preston and Edward A. Hamilton. New York: Simon and Schuster, 1958. 128 p.

An excerpt from Bankhead's television interview (pp. 56-57) in which she defends the South and its ways.

767   Zolotow, Maurice. NO PEOPLE LIKE SHOW PEOPLE. New York: Random House, 1951. xii, 305 p. Also published as IT TAKES ALL

KINDS.   New York: Random House, 1952; London: W.H. Allen, 1953.

Chapter 2 (pp. 12-81) is titled "Tallulah Bankhead: The Actor As Absolute," an impression of Bankhead written for popular consumption.

See also nos. 5, 9, 26, 185, 213, 276, 296, 320, 351, 358, 413, 549, 571, 576, 579, 589, 1471, 1477, and 3071.

BARNES, CHARLOTTE (1818-63). See nos. 222 and 3168.

BARRETT, GEORGE (1794-1860). See nos. 240 and 250.

BARRETT, LAWRENCE
(1838-91)

768   Barrett, Lawrence. "Vicissitudes of the Drama." NORTH AMERICAN REVIEW 146 (February 1888): 203-10.

> Barrett proposed the American theatre was reaching its maturity at that time as "an art in harmony with other forces for man's improvement" and cites historical parallels from other nations.

769   Barron, Elwyn A. LAWRENCE BARRETT: A PROFESSIONAL SKETCH. Chicago: Knight and Leonard Co., 1889. 98 p. Illus.

> This volume offers a somewhat detailed account of Barrett's career.

770   Flory, Claude R. "Boker, Barrett and the Francesca Theme in Drama." PLAYERS 50 (February-March 1975): 58-61, 80.

> Primarily concerned with dramaturgy, but the article includes some information about Barrett's production of FRANCESCA DA RIMINI.

771   Goddard, Henry P. "Some Players I Have Known." THEATRE (N.Y.) 6 (November 1906): 295-96. Illus.

> A few personal reminiscences of Barrett and E.L. Davenport.

772   Nolan, Paul T. "William's DANTE: The Death of Nineteenth Century Heroic Drama." SOUTHERN SPEECH JOURNAL 25 (Summer 1960): 255-63.

> Espy Williams wrote a stage version of THE DIVINE COMEDY and hoped to have Barrett perform Dante, which he did not do.

773   White, Melvin R. "Lawrence Barrett and the Role of Cassius." QUARTERLY JOURNAL OF SPEECH 50 (October 1964): 293-98.

> The article posits Barrett as the greatest Cassius of his time, drawing heavily upon published newspaper accounts and reviews.

774   Williams, Edith Barrett. "The Real Lawrence Barrett." THEATRE (N.Y.)
       5 (March 1905): 61, xvii. Illus.

       Fourteen years after his death, the actor's daughter fondly
       recalls her father's home life and his friendship with Edwin
       Booth.

See also nos. 58, 130, 163-65, 204, 222, 227-28, 245, 262-63, 336, 341,
343, 352, 356, 370, 383, 387, 399, 400, 402-6, 408, 413, 417, 419, 438,
442, 454, 460, 489, 503, 511, 516, 519, 530, 548, 558, 570, 572, 578,
596, 1050, 1077-78, 1094, 1120, 1124, 1548, 1851, 2301, 2585, 2618,
2622, 2750, 2932, and 3146.

THE BARRYMORES

Entries for Ethel, John, Lionel, and Maurice Barrymore follow this section.

775   Alpert, Hollis. THE BARRYMORES. New York: Dial Press, 1964.
       xviii, 390 p. Index, illus., bibliog.

       An exceptionally objective volume on the entire Barrymore
       family. Minimal documentation.

776   Barnes, Howard. "Daughter of the Royal Family." THEATRE (N.Y.)
       52 (November 1930): 15-16. Illus.

       Publicity and puffery for the stage debut of Ethel Barrymore
       Colt in SCARLET SISTER MARY; the family heritage is highly
       touted.

777   Barrymore, John. "Lionel, Ethel, and I." AMERICAN MAGAZINE
       115 (February 1933): 12-15, 70, 72, 74; (March 1933): 20-23, 114-19;
       (April 1933): 26-29, 77-78; (May 1933): 58-61, 78, 80, 82. Illus.

       Serialized memoirs of the entire family, somewhat laundered
       for popular acceptance at the time.

778   _____. WE THREE: ETHEL--LIONEL--JOHN. Akron, Ohio, and
       New York: Saalfield Publishing Co., 1935.

       Verified in the NATIONAL UNION CATALOG, but unavaila-
       ble for examination.

779   Broeck, Helen Ten. "The Barrymores and Augustus Thomas." THEATRE
       (N.Y.) 27 (April 1918): 210.

       A survey of the three siblings' appearances in scripts by Thomas.

780   Crowther, Bosley. THE LION'S SHARE: THE STORY OF AN ENTER-
       TAINMENT EMPIRE. New York: E.P. Dutton, 1957. 312 p. Index,
       illus.

       A volume dealing primarily with the film industry and describing the work of John, Ethel, and Lionel in that medium.

781   Flagg, James Montgomery. ROSES AND BUCKSHOT. New York: G.P.
      Putnam's Sons, 1946. 224 p. Illus.

      A gossipy and undistinguished autobiography by a friend of John
      Barrymores, with references to Ethel and Lionel. Of minimal
      value.

782   Hall, Gladys. "Those Barrymore Traditions." MOVIE CLASSIC 11
      (October 1936): 38-39, 56-57. Illus.

      A collection of anecdotes recalling the Barrymore and Drew
      talent for the bon mot.

783   Harriss, John. "An Apple a Début." THEATRE (N.Y.) 53 (April 1931):
      14. Illus.

      A description of the origins of the Drew-Barrymore tradition
      of sending an apple to any of the family opening a show.

784   Hopkins, Arthur. REFERENCE POINT. New York: Samuel French,
      1948. 135 p.

      A survey of theatrical practices of the time. One chapter is
      devoted to John Barrymore, another to John, Ethel, and Lionel
      and their acting techniques.

785   _____. TO A LONELY BOY. New York: Book League of America,
      1937. 250 p.

      Hopkins touches briefly in his memoirs upon the Barrymores with
      some incidental anecdotal material.

786   Kotsilibas-Davis, James. THE BARRYMORES: THE ROYAL FAMILY
      IN HOLLYWOOD. New York: Crown Publishers, 1981. 369 p. Index,
      illus., bibliog, filmographies.

      A heavily illustrated description of Lionel, John, and Ethel
      Barrymore and their careers in the cinema. Seemingly well-
      researched, but undocumented. A valuable treatment of the
      migration of legitimate stage stars to the West Coast.

787   Schallert, Elza. "They're the 'Royal Family' of Hollywood Now."
      MOTION PICTURE MAGAZINE 44 (September 1932): 34-35, 85. Illus.

      A description of the filming of RASPUTIN, the only film in
      which Ethel, John, and Lionel appeared together.

788   Smith, H. Allen. THE LIFE AND LEGEND OF GENE FOWLER. New
      York: William Morrow and Co., 1977. 314 p. Index, illus.

Smith includes many references to John and Lionel Barrymore in this gracefully written biography of their good friend, Fowler.

See also nos. 23, 116, 135, 142, 185, 276, 278, 293, 347, 390, 417, 525, 578-79, 793, 1268, and 2907.

BARRYMORE, ETHEL

(1879-1959)

789 Barrymore, Ethel. "The Actor's Strike." OUTLOOK 123 (3 September 1919): 11-12. Illus.

  The actress explains her reasons for striking in support of Actors Equity, citing managerial abuses.

790 _____. "How Can I Be a Great Actress?" LADIES' HOME JOURNAL, 15 March 1911, p. 6. Illus.

  Barrymore discusses the requisites for a successful stage career.

791 _____. "A Little Philosophy Out of 'Tante.'" HARPER'S BAZAAR 48 (November 1913): 14-15. Illus.

  The actress's analysis of the Chambers script in which she was appearing at the time.

792 _____. MEMORIES: AN AUTOBIOGRAPHY. New York: Harper and Brothers, 1955. 224 p. Index, illus.

  Barrymore goes into considerable detail about her career, while avoiding the more lurid aspects of her family's history. Valuable photographs are included, and the work remains a basic source of information on the family.

793 _____. "My Reminiscences." DELINEATOR 103 (September 1923): 6-7, 64-65; (October 1923): 12-13, 77-78; (November 1923): 8-9, 54; (December 1923): 14-15, 80-81; 104 (January 1924): 16-17, 65; (February 1924): 12-13, 89-90. Illus.

  Serialized memoirs, written at age forty-five. Also useful for materials on William Gillette, the Drews, and the other Barrymores.

794 _____. "My Stage Life Up to Date." METROPOLITAN MAGAZINE, June 1901, pp. 838-44. Illus.

  A light-hearted autobiographical sketch covering Barrymore's

life and career through her playing in CAPTAIN JINKS AND
THE HORSE MARINES (1901).

795 _____. "Our Changing Stage." WORLD'S WORK 56 (June 1928):
220-24. Illus.

An interview with Keyes Porter in which Barrymore contrasts
the current conditions with those past, finding acting to have
become more specialized, theatres more comfortable, and the
road more satisfying.

796 _____. "Why I Want to Play Emma McChesny." AMERICAN MAGA-
ZINE 80 (November 1915): 40-42, 96-97. Illus.

The actress considered the role in the stage version of Edna
Ferber's ROAST BEEF MEDIUM especially appropriate to her
talents and personality.

797 Collins, Frederick L. "Ethel Barrymore's Successor." WOMAN'S HOME
COMPANION 56 (April 1929): 9, 60. Illus.

Speculation as to who might succeed Barrymore as America's
most popular actress. Among those advanced are Helen Hayes,
Katharine Cornell, and Lynn Fontanne.

798 Dale, Alan. [Pseud.] "The Most Interesting People of the Theatre." GREEN
BOOK MAGAZINE 14 (December 1915): 1065-72. Illus.

Dale admired Barrymore and began a series of theatrical profiles
with this essay. Well illustrated.

799 _____. "The New Ethel Barrymore." COSMOPOLITAN 56 (April 1914):
697-99. Illus.

Dale felt that Barrymore's work in TANTE, in which she was
then appearing, marked a new direction in her career.

800 _____. "The Star of the Barrymores." COSMOPOLITAN 52 (April
1912): 693-97. Illus.

A superficial interview by the adulatory Dale. Excellent illustrations.

801 Downing, Robert. "Ethel Barrymore, 1879-1959." FILMS IN REVIEW
10 (August-September 1959): 385-89. Illus.

A tribute written shortly after the actress's death; Downing
makes general remarks about the entire family.

802   Eaton, Walter Prichard. "The New Ethel Barrymore." AMERICAN MAGAZINE 72 (September 1911): 631-40. Illus.

A critical assessment of the actress, praising her work but decrying the "juvenility" of the U.S. stage at that time.

803   "Ethel Barrymore." PEARSON'S MAGAZINE 17 (January-June 1904): 488, 495. Illus.

An early interview with the actress while she was ill. She describes New York audiences as most provincial.

804   "Ethel Barrymore, A Star for Forty-Two Years." VOGUE, 1 April 1943, pp. 50-53, 91. Illus.

A brief and superficial account of Barrymore's lengthy career. Well illustrated.

805   "Ethel Barrymore's Stage Views." THEATRE (N.Y.) 1 (October 1901): 22.

A description of Barrymore early in her career.

806   Ford, James L. "The Ethel Barrymore Following." APPLETON'S MAGAZINE 12 (November 1908): 546-50.

Ford attempts to analyze the degree and nature of Barrymore's early popularity, to which he had been an eyewitness.

807   Fox, Mary Virginia. ETHEL BARRYMORE: A PORTRAIT. Chicago: Reilly and Lee, 1970. 135 p.

Undocumented biography written in the style of a novel. Useless without corroboration.

808   Grey, Daniel. "Ethel Barrymore's Little Son." LADIES' HOME JOURNAL, 1 April 1911, pp. 13, 76. Illus.

Fan-oriented discussion of the child and Barrymore's difficulty being both a mother and an actress.

808A   Halbert, Delancey M. "Ethel Barrymore: A Sketch." FRANK LESLIE'S POPULAR MONTHLY 56 (May 1903): 62-63.

A brief essay predicting a bright future for Barrymore in the theatre.

809   Heylbut, Rose. "An Interview with Ethel Barrymore." ETUDE 60 (February 1942): 79, 128. Illus.

Barrymore is quoted on her early wish to become a concert pianist and discourses on the value of a sense of rhythm and tempo in the theatre.

810   Jamison, Barbara Berch. "Ethel Barrymore--In Mid-Career at 75." NEW
       YORK TIMES MAGAZINE, 15 August 1954, pp. 25, 32. Illus.

       A tribute to the actress's longevity after fifty years on stage.

811   Kirkland, Alexander. "The Matterhorn at Twilight." THEATRE ARTS
       33 (November 1949): 26-29. Illus.

       A biographical sketch and laudatory tribute of no great distinc-
       tion.

812   Kobbé, Gustave. "The Girlishness of Ethel Barrymore." LADIES' HOME
       JOURNAL, June 1903, pp. 3-4. Illus.

       Kobbé describes Barrymore's enthusiasm for fashion, music, art,
       dancing, swimming, and various other forms of recreation.

813   Moses, Montrose J. "Miss Barrymore to Our Girls." DELINEATOR 96
       (May 1920): 5, 96, 110. Illus.

       Moses quotes the actress on inheriting acting talent, on enter-
       ing the theatrical profession, and on recent developments in the
       theatre.

814   Newman, Shirlee Petkin. ETHEL BARRYMORE GIRL ACTRESS. Indianap-
       olis and New York: Bobbs-Merrill Co., 1966. 197 p. Illus.

       A biography written for children or adolescents, lacking docu-
       mentation.

815   "One Who Knows Her." "The Real Ethel Barrymore." GREEN BOOK
       ALBUM 1(May 1909): 1020-22.

       A friendly but not especially insightful tribute to the actress.

816   Porter, Keyes. "The Changing Stage: An Authorized Interview Given
       to Keyes Porter by Ethel Barrymore." WORLD TODAY 52 (November
       1928): 589-93. Illus.

       Contrasting 1928 to her past experiences, Barrymore is quoted
       as considering the theatres of 1928 more comfortable, acting
       more specialized, long runs dreadful, the movies of no influence,
       and stage speech awful.

817   St. Johns, Adela Rogers. "Ethel Barrymore, The Cosmopolite of the
       Month." HEARST'S 115 (September 1943): 8, 12-13. Illus.

       St. Johns describes the ups and downs of Barrymore's career,
       as well as describing her personal life, such as her divorce
       from Russell Colt.

817A   Shaw, Winifield. "Ethel Barrymore." COSMOPOLITAN 37 (June 1904): 327. Illus.

> An account of the actress's career to date, following her appearance in COUSIN KATE.

818   W., W. "The Heartbreak of Acting." THEATRE (N.Y.) 34 (July 1921): 32, 62, 64.

> An assessment of Barrymore's work and a few comments by her on the psychic aspects of acting.

819   Wagstaff, William de. "Ethel Barrymore--An Impression." THEATRE (N.Y.) 2 (November 1902): 20-23. Illus.

> An interview of little value, accompanied by a series of specially posed photographs.

820   _____. "The Painted Heart of an Actress." THEATRE (N.Y.) 23 (February 1916): 80-81, 96. Illus.

> Barrymore discusses the role of emotion in acting in an insubstantial interview.

821   White, Matthew, Jr. "Ethel Barrymore." MUNSEY'S 36 (October 1906-March 1907): 218-21. Illus.

> Brief comments on Barrymore's theatrical heritage and her rise to stardom in CAPTAIN JINKS OF THE HORSE MARINES in 1901.

822   Wilson, John S. "Queen of the American Stage." THEATRE ARTS 38 (December 1954): 28-31, 95. Illus.

> An affectionate summary of Barrymore's long career.

823   Wolf, Rennold. "Ethel Barrymore." SMITH'S MAGAZINE 6 (November 1907): 288-94. Illus.

> A fan-oriented essay describing Barrymore's charm as the main reason for her popularity.

824   _____. "Ethel Barrymore as Her Friends Know Her." GREEN BOOK MAGAZINE 9 (April 1913): 640-65.

> An insubstantial interview showing the actress at home as a dutiful wife and a doting mother.

825   Wood, Philip Emerson. "Ethel Barrymore Had Stage Fright." DELINEATOR 109 (August 1926): 8, 60-61. Illus.

> A detailed description of performance anxiety in Barrymore, who suffered severely from it.

826   Woolf, S.J.   "Miss Barrymore Refuses to Mourn the 'Good Old Days.'"
        NEW YORK TIMES MAGAZINE, 13 August 1939, pp. 10-11, 19.   Illus.

> An interview done just before the actress turned sixty, in which
> she reminiscences about her career and the changes in the thea-
> tre during that time.   Well illustrated.

See also nos. 5, 9, 26, 28, 151, 172, 242, 256, 270, 275, 296, 306, 314,
316, 321, 332, 342, 351, 354, 358, 377, 412-13, 420, 425, 427, 444, 464-65,
492, 510, 547, 555, 558, 575, 738, 776, 846, 1471, 1477, 1981-82, 2044,
and 2907.

BARRYMORE, JOHN

(1882-1942)

827   "Barrie-Barrymore." LITERARY DIGEST 122 (21 November 1936): 6-7.

News item describing the failure of Barrymore's career and marriage.

828   Barrymore, Diana, and Frank, Gerald. TOO MUCH, TOO SOON. New York: Henry Holt and Co., 1957. 380 p. Illus.

Barrymore's daughter wrote a detailed, undocumented account of her tempestuous life with considerable reference to her father.

829   Barrymore, Elaine, and Dody, Sanford. ALL MY SINS REMEMBERED. New York: Appleton-Century, 1964. 274 p. Illus.

Barrymore's last wife, who was seventeen when she met him, offers an exploitive account of his last days from her prejudicial point of view.

830   Barrymore, John. CONFESSIONS OF AN ACTOR. Indianapolis: Bobbs-Merrill Co., 1926. n.p. Illus.

Useful for its many photographs. Barrymore avoids most of the major issues of his life and career.

831   _____. "The Confessions of an Actor." LADIES' HOME JOURNAL, October 1925, pp. 3-5, 40; November 1925, pp. 12-13, 56, 59; December 1925, pp. 14-15, 42; January 1926, pp. 12, 133-34; February 1926, pp. 17, 178, 181-82. Illus.

Serialization of no. 830.

832   _____. "Hamlet in Hollywood." LADIES' HOME JOURNAL, June 1927, pp. 6-7, 59, 61-62; July 1927, pp. 17, 84, 86. Illus.

Barrymore discusses his reasons for leaving the stage for film and the contrast in acting techniques for the two fields.

833 _____. "John Barrymore Writes on the Movies." LADIES' HOME JOURNAL, August 1922, pp. 7, 80, 82. Illus.

Barrymore, admitting the cinema's youth, takes the medium to task for lack of imagination and paltry art.

834 _____. "Up Against It in Hollywood." LADIES' HOME JOURNAL, January 1928, pp. 15, 76, 79. Illus.

A rambling essay, primarily concerned with the techniques of filmmaking.

835 _____. "What is a Juvenile Lead?" THEATRE (N.Y.) 19 (June 1914): 304, 317.

Barrymore describes the difficulty of sustaining such roles through a long run and the lack of challenge they represented to him.

836 "Barrymores Meet." LIFE, 9 March 1942, pp. 35-36, 38. Illus.

On his sixtieth birtday, Barrymore coached his daughter, Diana, for her first film, EAGLE SQUADRON.

837 Boyesen, Hjalmar Hjorth, II. "John Barrymore's Work." COSMOPOLI-TAN 32 (January 1902): 305-8. Illus.

A critical assessment of Barrymore's drawing and painting, some of which is reproduced in black and white.

838 Broeck, Helen Ten. "From Comedy to Tragedy." THEATRE (N.Y.) 24 (July 1916): 23, 38. Illus.

An interview with Barrymore in which he discusses his various roles and their differing demands upon him.

839 Card, James. THE FILMS OF JOHN BARRYMORE. Rochester, N.Y.: George Eastman House, 1969.

Unavailable for examination.

840 Carnegie, Dale B. DALE CARNEGIE'S BIOGRAPHICAL ROUNDUP; HIGHLIGHTS IN THE LIVES OF FORTY FAMOUS PEOPLE. New York: Greenberg, 1945. Toronto: Ambassador Books; Cleveland: World Publishing Co., 1946. 233 p.

Includes a brief, undocumented essay on Barrymore (pp. 97-102) titled, "He Earned Five Thousand Dollars a Day, Yet He Searched Garbage Cans for Food for his Pet Vulture."

841 Collins, Frederick L. "John Barrymore's Successor." WOMAN'S HOME COMPANION 56 (April 1929): 10, 59. Illus.

Collins speculates on who might inherit Barrymore's popularity as a stage star and nominates Alfred Lunt, Walter Hampden, and Richard Bennett.

842   ____. "The Loves of John Barrymore." In GREAT STARS OF HOLLY-WOOD'S GOLDEN AGE, compiled by Frank C. Platt, pp. 120–75. New York: Signet Books, 1966. Illus.

Collins offers a substantial, undocumented, somewhat sensationalized biographical sketch, stressing Barrymore's escapades in Hollywood.

843   Delehanty, Thorton. "Barrymore Redivivus." THEATRE ARTS 16 (January 1930): 315–16. Illus.

Barrymore discusses his work in the film GENERAL CRACK and comments upon the innovation of talking movies.

844   Fairbanks, D[ouglas?]., Jr. "John Barrymore." VANITY FAIR 35 (September 1930): 67. Illus.

A brief and affectionate tribute to the actor, with a caricature by the author.

845   French, William F. "'Wild Jack' Is Back Again!" MOTION PICTURE MAGAZINE 47 (July 1934): 40–41, 89. Illus.

A description of Barrymore's return to Hollywood to film THE TWENTIETH CENTURY.

846   Fowler, Gene. GOOD NIGHT, SWEET PRINCE: THE LIFE & TIMES OF JOHN BARRYMORE. New York: Viking Press; Philadelphia: Blakeston, 1944. New York: Ballantine, 1971. 525 p. Index, illus.

Fowler, a long-time friend of Barrymores, wrote what was then considered the definitive biography of him. The volume also contains material on Lionel and Ethel, William Collier, John Drew, and Mrs. Drew.

847   ____. MINUTES OF THE LAST MEETING. New York: Viking Press, 1954. 277 p. Illus.

An insightful biography of Sadakichi Hartmann, a friend of Barrymores, containing considerable material on the actor.

848   Fowler, Will. THE YOUNG MAN FROM DENVER. Garden City, N.Y.: Doubleday and Co., 1962. 310 p. Illus.

A biography of Gene Fowler, written by his son. Barrymore is mentioned frequently in the section on Fowler's Hollywood period.

849 Furness, Horace Howard, Jr. "The Hamlet of John Barrymore." DRAMA (Chicago) 13 (March 1923): 207-8, 230.

Describes the acting and staging of the production and compares Barrymore to other actors who had played the role of Hamlet. In some cases, Furness considers Barrymore inferior.

850 Gabriel, Gilbert W. "John Barrymore as Hamlet." WORLD'S WORK 50 (September 1925): 498-501. Illus.

A somewhat superficial account of Barrymore's career up to his performance of Hamlet, emphasizing his work in THE JEST.

851 "Great Profile Set in Cement." LIFE, 30 September 1940, p. 63. Illus.

A dutiful recording of a publicity stunt at Grauman's Chinese Theatre.

852 Hammond, Percy. BUT--IS IT ART. Garden City, N.Y.: Doubleday, Page and Co., 1927. vi, 186 p.

Includes an essay (pp. 168-73) in a light tone on Barrymore's Hamlet, Hammond concluding that "John Barrymore's Hamlet was not so interesting as Hamlet's John Barrymore."

853 Hecht, Ben. "A Last Performance." THEATRE ARTS 38 (June 1954): 26-28, 89-90. Illus.

An article taken from Hecht's autobiography, A CHILD OF THE CENTURY, in which he recalls the last days of Barrymore's life.

854 Jessel, George. THIS WAY, MISS. New York: Henry Holt and Co., 1955. xv, 229 p. Illus.

Chapter 28, a eulogy for Barrymore, is subtitled, "What Price Girdle?," in reference to an auction of Barrymore's personal effects after his death.

855 "John Barrymore Arrives--A Great Man." EVERYBODY'S 35 (July 1916): 122-24.

Observations about Barrymore's success and methods in playing William Falder in Galsworthy's JUSTICE, an early success for the actor.

856 "John Barrymore's Ad Lib Clowning in MY DEAR CHILDREN Wows Theatre Audiences in Chicago." LIFE, 4 December 1939, pp. 50-52. Illus.

Accounts of Barrymore's shenanigans on stage toward the end of his career.

857   Kanin, Garson. HOLLYWOOD: STARS AND STARLETS, TYCOONS AND FLESH-PEDDLERS, MOVIEMAKERS, FRAUDS AND GENIUSES, HOPEFUL AND HAS-BEENS, GREAT LOVERS AND SEX SYMBOLS. New York: Viking Press, 1967. 393 p.

         Chapter 2 (pp. 23-55) contains Kanin's recollections of Barrymore in Hollywood near the end of his career and his life.

858   Kobler, John. DAMNED IN PARADISE: THE LIFE OF JOHN BARRY-MORE. New York: Antheneum, 1977. 401 p. Index, illus., bibliog.

         Kobler includes considerable material unavailable to Gene Fowler when he wrote GOOD NIGHT SWEET PRINCE. The biography is clearly written and well documented, includes a valuable bibliography, and supersedes Fowler's work.

859   Lahue, Kalton C. GENTLEMEN TO THE RESCUE: THE HEROES OF THE SILENT SCREEN. South Brunswick, N.J.: A.S. Barnes and Co., New York: Thomas Yoseloff, 1972. 244 p. Illus.

         A brief essay on Barrymore's film career is included on pages 17-23. Of minimal value.

860   Lardner, Ring. "Onward and Upward--Or, Jack Barrymore's Revenge." COLLIER'S 86 (16 February 1929): 18, 49. Illus.

         A tongue-in-cheek analysis of Barrymore's career with reference to his family background.

861   McEvoy, J.P. "Barrymore--Clown Prince of Denmark." STAGE (N.Y.) 1 (January 1941): 27-28.

         McEvoy affectionately describes Barrymore's various bizarre antics a few years before his death.

862   Mercer, Jane. GREAT LOVERS OF THE MOVIES. London, New York, Sydney, and Toronto: Hamlyn Publishing Group, 1975. 176 p. Illus.

         Includes a three-page biographical sketch of Barrymore, plus a filmography.

863   Merritt, Peter. "John and Lionel." EVERYBODY'S MAGAZINE 41 (August 1919): 31. Illus.

         Brief remarks, more concerning John Barrymore than Lionel.

864   Power-Waters, Alma. JOHN BARRYMORE, THE LEGEND AND THE MAN. New York: Julian Messner, 1941. London: S. Paul, 1942. xiv, 282 p. Index, illus.

         Written by the wife of Barrymore's company manager for the MY DEAR CHILDREN tour. A somewhat restrained account of Barrymore's life, useful if supplemented by more recent works.

865 Roberts, W. Adolph. "Confidences Off-Screen." MOTION PICTURE MAGAZINE 30 (August 1925): 70-71, 80. Illus.

Barrymore describes his success as Hamlet in London.

866 Schallert, Elza. "What Happened to Caliban and Ariel." MOTION PICTURE MAGAZINE 53 (April 1937): 34, 90. Illus.

Fan-oriented account of Barrymore's separation from Elaine Barrie.

867 Sermolino, Maria. "John Barrymore's Barber." THEATRE (N.Y.) 30 (July 1919): 22.

Indicative of Barrymore's immense popularity at the time. His barber, Signor Conti, reveals that the actor wears a false moustache on stage.

868 Smith, Rex. "John Barrymore: An Amazing Personality." THEATRE (N.Y.) 47 (April 1928): 23, 70, 72. Illus.

An early, somewhat idealized, assessment of Barrymore, describing him as a "crusading iconoclast."

869 Strange, Michael. WHO TELLS ME TRUE. New York: Charles Scribner's Sons, 1940. 396 p. Illus.

Strange describes her marriage to and separation from Barrymore in a prejudicial narrative.

870 "The Strange Case of John Barrymore: Back on Broadway." LIFE, 12 February 1940, pp. 86-87. Illus.

An illustrated account of Barrymore in MY DEAR CHILDREN in New York and his reconciliation with Elaine Barrie.

871 Sumner, Keene. "The Hidden Talents of 'Jack' Barrymore." AMERICAN MAGAZINE 87 (June 1919): 36-37, 149-50, 153-54.

Sumner describes Barrymore's early irresponsibility as an actor and his eventual rise to fame and reputation as a serious performer in JUSTICE and PETER IBBETSON.

872 Ten Eyck, John. "John Barrymore's Idea of Resting." GREEN BOOK MAGAZINE 13 (January 1915): 25-26, 29. Illus.

A superficial interview with Barrymore and his wife at the beach.

873 Thomas, Bob. "Young Profile." COLLIER'S 124 (10 September 1949): 27, 72. Illus.

A description of the debut of John Barrymore, Jr., comparing his looks and talent to that of his father.

874   Thomas, Tony. CADS AND CAVALIERS: THE GENTLEMEN ADVEN-
TURERS OF THE MOVIES. South Brunswick, N.J., and New York:
A.S. Barnes and Co.; London: Thomas Yoseloff, 1973. 237 p. Illus.

> The author describes Barrymore's film career in an undocumented
> essay on pages 40-59. A brief article, "Barrymore: A Personal
> Recollection," is appended.

875   Woollcott, Alexander. "The Two Barrymores." EVERYBODY'S MAGA-
ZINE 42 (June 1920): 31. Illus.

> Woolcott describes Barrymore's "coming of age," maturing from
> a young, aimless comedian to the later, more commanding figure,
> as two separate careers.

876   Young, S. "A Terrible Thing." NEW REPUBLIC 52 (14 September 1927):
98-99.

> Young laments Barrymore's desertion of the stage for film, which
> Young calls "rotten, vulgar, empty, in bad taste, dishonest,
> noisome with a silly and unwholesome exhibitionism, and odious
> with a kind of stale and degenerate adolescence."

See also nos. 127, 130-31, 204, 213, 231, 270, 272, 287, 291, 296, 306,
310, 315, 325, 351, 354, 358, 377, 392, 413, 418, 425, 464, 483, 537,
542, 544, 555, 563, 569, 1471, 2481, and 3212.

BARRYMORE, LIONEL
(1878-1954)

877   Antrim, Doron K. "How Music Has Helped in My Life." ETUDE 59 (December 1941): 805, 848, 859.

An interview with Barrymore in which he claims to have a strong interest in music as an amateur.

878   Barrymore, Lionel. "Introduction." In A CHRISTMAS CAROL IN PROSE, BEING A GHOST STORY OF CHRISTMAS, by Charles Dickens. xiii-xxi. Philadelphia and Chicago: John C. Winston Co., 1938. Illus.

In an eight-page introduction, Barrymore fancifully describes how he created his characterization of Scrooge.

879   _____. "The Present State of the Movies." LADIES' HOME JOURNAL, September 1926, pp. 25, 205-6. Illus.

Barrymore blames the low quality of motion pictures on the audience's unchallenging acceptance of them.

880   _____. WE BARRYMORES. New York: Appleton-Century-Crofts, 1951. viii, 311 p. Index, illus.

Barrymore includes his entire family in his memoirs, but focuses upon his own failed career as a painter, as well as his work in the theatre and films. The front papers are a family tree of the Drew-Barrymore theatrical dynasty.

881   Carnegie, Dale B. FIVE MINUTE BIOGRAPHIES. New York: Sothern Publishers, 1937. Toronto: McLeod; Garden City, N.Y.: Blue Ribbon Books, 1939. Surrey, Engl.: World's Work, 1946. 256 p. Illus.

Barrymore is the subject of a three-page essay, "At 26 He Was a Star; at 53 a Has-been; at 57 the Greatest Actor in America." Of minimal value.

882   Crichton, Kyle. "Barrymore, The Lionhearted." COLLIER'S 123 (26 March 1949): 20-21, 36-37. Illus.

Barrymore denigrates acting as a profession after a fifty-five year career. He includes a few biographical details, such as John Barrymore's admiration for his older brother.

883   Mullett, Mary R. "Lionel Barrymore Tells How People Show Their Age." AMERICAN MAGAZINE 93 (February 1922): 36-39, 84-85. Illus.

Having been especially successful in playing older roles, Barrymore describes his observation techniques for use in his characterizations.

884   Pringle, Henry F. "Late-Blooming Barrymore." COLLIER'S 90 (1 October 1932): 27-28. Illus.

A biographical sketch, describing Barrymore as the last of the three siblings to achieve success in Hollywood and expressing doubt that he would ever return to the stage.

885   Reid, James. "The Barrymore You Don't Know." MOTION PICTURE MAGAZINE 54 (September 1937): 26-27, 66, 94. Illus.

An undistinguished accolade, suggesting Barrymore's career had been overshadowed by his brother and sister.

886   Revere, F. Vance de. "Facts I Can Read in the Faces of Film Stars." MOTION PICTURE MAGAZINE 29 (April 1925): 42, 113. Illus.

A psuedo-scientific analysis of Barrymore's face.

See also nos. 5, 306, 325, 354, 413, 549, 846, and 863.

BARRYMORE, MAURICE

(1847-1905)

887   Kotsilibas-Davis, James. GREAT TIMES GOOD TIMES: THE ODYSSEY OF MAURICE BARRYMORE. Garden City, N.Y.: Doubleday and Co., 1977. 514 p. Index, illus., bibliog.

Kotsilibas-Davis did exemplary research for this richly detailed and perceptive work, which is a valuable depiction of theatrical conditions at the time and the definitive study of this Barrymore. The bibliography reflects the author's meticulous approach.

888   Miller, Henry. "Maurice Barrymore--Actor, Scholar, and Wit." THEATRE (N.Y.) 5 (May 1905): 130.

Miller recounts a few examples of Barrymore's penetrating and frequently caustic wit.

889   "Mrs. Fiske and Maurice Barrymore." MUNSEY'S 22 (January 1900): 594, 596-98.

A brief commentary on the two stars when they were appearing together in BECKY SHARP.

890   Scherer, Barrymore Laurence. "The Purloined Plot: Did Sardou Steal His Plot for LA TOSCA from American Playwright Maurice Barrymore?" OPERA NEWS 43, no. 8(1978): 10-13. Illus.

Scherer describes but does not resolve the controversy aroused by the similarities between Barrymore's NADJEZDA and LA TOSCA.

891   Tracy, Virginia. "The First of the Barrymores." NEW YORKER 6 (11 October 1930): 29-32. Illus.

In these somewhat idealized reminiscences, Tracy, who toured with Barrymore in ARISTOCRACY, recalls him and his concern for his numerous pets.

See also nos. 112, 131, 279, 288, 386, 413, 453, 455, 526, 543-44, 548, 594, 1699, 1707-08, 2149-50, 2585, 2879, 2973, and 3146.

BATES, BLANCHE

(1872-1941)

892   Bates, Blanche. "An Actress and Her Farm, How a Well-Known Theatrical Star Lives the Genuine Country Life on an Old Farm That Pays for Itself." COUNTRY LIFE 16 (September 1909): 491-94, 538, 540.

> The seventy-eight acre farm was the "Ira Bailey place" in Westchester County, some six miles back from Ossining-on-Hudson.

893   _____. "Children and Careers." WOMAN'S HOME COMPANION 43 (October 1916): 13. Illus.

> A lively statement suggesting that married women need not remain totally domestic.

894   _____. "I Want to Be an Old-Fashioned Woman." GREEN BOOK ALBUM 7 (June 1912): 1113-19. Illus.

> Bates professes to deny the woman's liberation of her time.

895   _____. "The Luck of Nora." GREEN BOOK ALBUM 7 (January 1912): 186-90.

> A short story.

896   _____. "Sidelights of Two Generations." GREEN BOOK ALBUM 3 (March 1910): 557-62.

> Bates describes her mother, Eliza Wren, and the beneficial effects she had on the actress's career.

897   _____. "Their Beginnings." THEATRE (N.Y.) 5 (June 1905): 138-39. Illus.

> Bates describes the early struggles in her career.

898   _____. "A Triumph of the Theatre." THEATRE (N.Y.) 28 (November 1918): 270. Illus.

> One of a series of articles titled "The Most Striking Episode in

My Life." Bates recalls addressing five thousand women war workers during World War I.

899   "Blanche of the Golden West." COSMOPOLITAN 55 (October 1913): 689-91. Illus.

Bates contrasts acting in serious drama and comedy on a fairly superficial level.

900   Broeck, Helen Ten. "Motherhood and Art." THEATRE (N.Y.) 24 (December 1916): 372, 402.

Bates describes raising her two children in this interview and adheres to then modern views on child-rearing.

901   Coward, Edward Fales. "Blanche Bates and Her Stage Ideals." THEATRE (N.Y.) 3 (July 1903): 164-66. Illus.

A few reminiscences about her career and her work with David Belasco, whom she admired greatly.

902   Dale, Alan. [Pseud.] "Enthusiastic Blanche Bates." GREEN BOOK MAGAZINE 15 (May 1916): 929-33. Illus.

Dale expresses delight that Bates forsook "the pointlessness of Ibsen" for marriage.

903   Dodge, Wendell Phillips. "A Chat with Blanche Bates." THEATRE (N.Y.) 18 (July 1913): 22-24, viii. Illus.

The author and the actress reminisce about some of her more successful roles.

904   Files, Vanderheyden. "A Triple Alliance of the Stage." THEATRE (N.Y.) 20 (November 1914): 214-16, 218, 240. Illus.

A description of the circumstances surrounding Charles Frohman's revival of DIPLOMACY, starring Bates, Marie Doro, and William Gillette.

905   Lowenberg, Walter A. "How They Landed Their First Part." THEATER (N.Y.) 32 (July-August 1920): 8.

Bates and William Collier are treated.

906   Mullett, Mary B. "Blanche Bates Gives Her Secret of Happiness." AMERICAN MAGAZINE 99 (May 1925): 34-35, 184-89. Illus.

Bates describes her early career, her rise to stardom, and what she felt she had learned about people as a result.

907   Patterson, Ada. "At Home with Blanche Bates." GREEN BOOK ALBUM 5 (April 1911): 794-800.

>   Bates describes how she moved from romantic to modern drama in her roles, with emphasis on Ibsen.

908   White, Matthew, Jr. "Blanche Bates." MUNSEY'S 35 (April-September 1906): 600-604. Illus.

>   Brief biographical sketch describing how Bates came to be a member of Daly's company and her later departure to work for Belasco.

See also nos. 13, 28, 163, 270, 276, 297, 381, 408, 413, 429, 449, 464, 492, 499, 600, 701, 928, 1002, and 1471.

BELASCO, DAVID

(1859-1931)

909   Albert, Dora. "A Power in the Theatre at Seventy-five." FORECAST
       36 (November 1929): 315-24. Illus.

       Albert interviews Belasco on his eating habits and health regimes.
       FORECAST is a health-food publication.

910   "The Apprentice-Years of David Belasco." CURRENT OPINION 56 (June
       1914): 436.

       Belasco is quoted recollecting his childhood and early theatrical
       training in California.

911   Barnitz, Wirt W. "Going to the Theatre with Belasco." THEATRE (N.Y.)
       38 (July 1923): 10, 64.

       Barnitz describes seeing SIX CYLINDER LOVE with Belasco.
       Superficial.

912   Belasco, David. "About Acting." SATURDAY EVENING POST 194
       (24 September 1921): 11, 93-94, 97-98. Illus.

       Belasco describes acting as both a science and an art, lists the
       qualities requisite for an actor, discusses the place of emotion
       in acting, and describes the actor's personality as a fundamental
       consideration.

913   _____. "Advice to the Girl with Dramatic Ambitions." WOMAN'S
       HOME COMPANION 31 (October 1904): 7. Illus.

       Belasco attempts to destroy the concept of the overnight success
       in the theatre.

914   _____. "Aids to the Actor's Art." MUNSEY'S 63 (March 1918):
       265-79. Illus.

       Belasco describes his realistic scenery as being supportive of the
       actor, suggesting all concerned must sublimate their egos to
       the production as a whole.

915   _____. "Art for Business' Sake." COSMOPOLITAN 40 (December
1905): 231-39. Illus.

The director decries art's subservience to financial considerations, especially with regard to productions imported from London.

916   _____. "The Beginner." AMERICAN PLAYWRIGHT 3 (January 1914):
16-17.

A few remarks taken from Belasco's January 1914 article in
MUNSEY'S, "The Meaning of the Theatre."

917   _____. "Dramatic Schools." COSMOPOLITAN 35 (August 1903):
359-68. Illus.

Belasco reflects upon the demise of stock companies and the
rise of dramatic schools for actor training, concluding "To
other times, other methods." He advocates the founding of an
American version of the Paris Conservatoire.

918   _____. "Dramatizing the Present." HARPER'S WEEKLY 57 (12 April
1913): 18, 26. Illus.

Rambling theoretical statements and observations about the drama
and the theatre as Belasco muses over his career.

919   _____. "Edwin Booth, The Actor." CENTURY 95 (April 1918): 881-83.
Illus.

Belasco commemorates the twenty-fifth anniversary of Booth's
death by recalling several roles in which he had seen him.

920   _____. "Forward." In THEATRE LIGHTING: A MANUAL OF THE
STAGE SWITCHBOARD, by Louis Hartmann, pp. i-xiii. New York and
London: D. Appleton and Co., 1930. 131 p. Index, illus., bibliog.

Belasco pays tribute to Hartmann, who was his electrician for
twenty-eight seasons. This volume describes many effects used
in Belasco's productions, including a light plot for MIMA.

921   _____. "The Gamboling Lambs." THEATRE (N.Y.) 19 (May 1914):
230. Illus.

A description of the Lambs' Club and their annual galas.

922   _____. "The Great Opportunity of the Woman Dramatist." GOOD
HOUSEKEEPING, November 1911, pp. 627-32. Illus.

Belasco encourages female playwrights by offering them advice
and citing past examples of success.

923 _____. "How I Stage My Plays." THEATRE (N.Y.) 2 (December 1902):
31-32. Illus.

Superficial comments on production techniques.

924 _____. "Keeping Faith with the Public." MUSE 3 (April 1903): 201-3.

Belasco supports the star system in the theatre, suggesting their
use makes the audiences believe they are getting their money's
worth.

925 _____. "The Meaning of the Theatre." MUNSEY'S 50(January 1914):
645-48.

A plea for artistry in the theatre, which Belasco felt was being
sublimated by financial concerns.

926 _____. "The Movies--My Profession's Flickering Bogy." MUNSEY'S
63(April 1918): 593-604. Illus.

Belasco sees no danger to the living theatre from the motion
pictures and discounts them as trivial.

927 _____. "My Best Play, How I Wrote It, and Why." GREEN BOOK
ALBUM 5 (February 1911): 434-38.

Belasco describes his work on THE GIRL OF THE GOLDEN WEST.

928 _____. "My Life Story." HEARST'S 25 (March 1914): 296-306; (April
1914): 481-89; (May 1914): 641-52; (June 1914): 767-79; 26 (July
1914): 42-54; (August 1914): 187-200; (September 1914): 344-53; (October 1914): 454-65; (November 1914): 601-15; (December 1914): 784-97;
27 (January 1915): 41-53; (February 1915): 154-68; (March 1915): 286-
87, 319-21; (April 1915): 353-54; (May 1915): 422-23, 456; (June 1915):
500-501, 545; 28 (July 1915): 22-23, 70-72; (August 1915): 106-7, 156-58;
(September 1915): 178-79, 226-27; (October 1915): 248-49, 296-97;
(November 1915): 326-27, 370-71; (December 1915): 397-99, 434-35.
Illus.

A substantial memoir with many illustrations. Somewhat idealized
and not completely trustworthy, but still of value. Includes references to all of Belasco's many stars (William Warfield, Mrs.
Carter, Frances Starr, Blanche Bates) as well as Edwin Booth,
Edwin Adams, Lotta Crabtree, and Maude Adams.

929 _____. "Opinions on the Drama." CURRENT OPINION 23 (March
1898): 248.

One and one-half columns of Belasco's opinions on the nature
of excellence in the drama and distinctions between American
and European dramatists.

930   . "Plagiarism." GREEN BOOK MAGAZINE 13 (April 1915): 609-17. Illus.

Belasco speculates on how World War I might affect American drama and considers the conditions propitious for literary theft.

931   . "The Playwright and the Box Office." CENTURY 84 (October 1912): 883-90.

A substantial article, considering the profit-seeking aspects of theatrical production upon dramaturgy.

932   . PLAYS PRODUCED UNDER THE STAGE DIRECTION OF DAVID BELASCO. New York: privately printed, 1925. 47 p. Illus.

A list of scripts produced by Belasco followed by a list of roles he acted.

933   . "Presentation of the National Drama." HARPER'S WEEKLY 48 (December 1904): 1844-45. Illus.

The first of three articles by various authors, "Three Views of the Stage To-Day." Belasco again suggests the theatre must avoid commercialism to survive.

934   . "Stagecraft." GREEN BOOK MAGAZINE 14 (August 1915): 353-61. Illus.

Belasco describes his philosophies of casting and the place of illusion in the art of the theatre.

935   . "Stage Realism of the Future." THEATRE (N.Y.) 18 (September 1918): 86-90, ix. Illus.

Belasco predicts the theatre's future developments.

936   . THE THEATRE THROUGH ITS STAGE DOOR. Edited by Louis V. Defoe. New York and London: Harper and Brothers, 1919. 246 p. Illus.

Belasco describes and seeks to justify his theatrical methods, especially as regards his realistic staging. Material is included on David Warfield, Mrs. Carter, and Frances Starr.

937   . "The Theatrical Syndicate: One Side." COSMOPOLITAN 38 (December 1904): 193-98. Illus.

A companion piece to an article by Marc Klaw supporting the Theatre Syndicate. Belasco attacks the group as uncultured and merely profit seeking.

938 _____. "The Truth about the Theatre." LADIES' HOME JOURNAL, September 1917, pp. 19, 52, 54; October 1917, pp. 13, 114-15; November 1917, pp. 19, 108; December 1917, pp. 21, 109-10. Illus.

Part 1 is subtitled, "How I Helped Ruth St. Denis to Learn to Dance and Mrs. Leslie Carter to Become a Star"; part 2, "What It Requires of the Player as the Price of Success" (using Frances Starr and Richard Mansfield as examples); part 3, "How I Made Mrs. Carter into an Actress and How I Rehearsed Caruso to Be an American"; part 4, "How I Got Frances Starr to Scream and Taught a Stageful of Actors Not to See a Ghost" (includes material on Nance O'Neil).

939 _____. "What I Am Trying to Do." WORLD'S WORK 24 (July 1912): 291-99. Illus.

Belasco's description of his actor-training methods, written somewhat abstractly. Includes some unusual photographs.

940 _____. "Why I Believe in the Little Things and How They Have Made Successes of My Plays." LADIES' HOME JOURNAL, September 1911, pp. 17, 73. Illus.

Belasco seeks to justify the minutiae of realistic staging as he practiced it.

941 _____. "Why I Produce Unprofitable Plays." THEATRE (N.Y.) 49 (March 1929): 22, 68. Illus.

Belasco insists his theatrical motivations are neither self-aggrandizement or profit and cites his staging of MIMA at considerable cost.

942 _____. "Women and the Stage." LADIES' HOME JOURNAL, November 1920, pp. 12-13, 108, 110. Illus.

Belasco outlines the history of the actress on the English-speaking stage and includes a paragraph each on many of America's leading actresses. He concludes that the theatre is an appropriate profession for women.

943 _____. "Yesterday, To-Day and Tomorrow." THEATRE (N.Y.) 31 (May 1920): 378, 380.

Superficial speculations about the theatre's future.

944 Bell, Archie. "David Belasco Attacks Stage Tradition." THEATRE (N.Y.) 13 (May 1911): 164, 166, 168. Illus.

Bell quotes Belasco as considering theatrical tradition often untruthful, hence Belasco's preference for realism.

945   Bloom, Vera. "Belasco's Little Girls." THEATRE (N.Y.) 28 (July 1918): 14-15. Illus.

Bloom describes Belasco's beneficial effects upon the careers of Ina Claire and Lenore Ulric and predicts comparable success for Jeanne Eagels.

946   Busch, Niven, Jr. TWENTY-ONE AMERICANS, BEING PROFILES OF SOME PEOPLE FAMOUS IN OUR TIME, TOGETHER WITH SILLY PICTURES OF THEM DRAWN BY DE MISKEY. Garden City, N.Y.: Doubleday, Doran and Co., 1930. 332 p. Illus.

Frivolous essays, including one on Belasco at age seventy-one (pp. 131-54.)

947   Chapple, Joe Mitchell. "David Belasco." NATIONAL MAGAZINE 45 (September 1916): 16-32. Illus.

A substantial and well-illustrated, if somewhat overly adulatory, monograph on Belasco's contributions to the American theatre as a director and playwright.

948   Cole, Toby, and Chinoy, Helen Krich. DIRECTORS ON DIRECTING: A SOURCE BOOK OF THE MODERN THEATRE. Indianapolis and New York: Bobbs-Merrill Co., 1953. xv, 456 p. Index, bibliog.

A valuable work, containing Belasco's "Creating Atmosphere," excerpted from his THE THEATRE THROUGH THE STAGE DOOR.

949   Collins, Charles W. "When Belasco Accepts Your Play." GREEN BOOK MAGAZINE 9 (February 1913): 222-34.

A description of the results of the success of Frederic and Fanny Hatton after Belasco produced their script, YEARS OF DISCRETION.

950   Dale, Alan. [Pseud.] "The Belasco Starr." COSMOPOLITAN 53(June 1912): 121-25. Illus.

Starr describes her rise to stardom and Belasco's contribution to her career in most glowing terms.

951   "David Belasco at Work." DRAMA (Chicago) 14 (December 1923): 93. Illus.

An anonymous and brief interview quoting Belasco on his working methods as a playwright and his approach to production as a director.

952   Davies, Acton. "David Belasco: Star Maker." GOOD HOUSEKEEPING, November 1911, pp. 624-26. Illus.

A brief review of Belasco's accomplishments at age fifty-two, serving as an introduction to his article, "The Great Opportunity of the Woman Dramatist," no. 922.

953   De Foe, Louis V. "Where David Belasco Works." MUNSEY'S 43 (September 1910): 803-10. Illus.

> A description and six photographs of Belasco's "studio" in his theatre on West Forty-fourth Street in New York.

954   DeMille, Cecil B[lount]. THE AUTOBIOGRAPHY OF CECIL B. DeMILLE. Edited by Donald Hayne. Englewood Cliffs, N.J.: Prentice-Hall, 1959. viii, 446 p. Index, illus.

> The early portions of this volume contain many references to Belasco, with whom DeMille collaborated in his youth.

955   DeMille, William C. "A Letter to David Belasco from William C. deMille." STAGE 13 (August 1936): 55. Illus.

> A theatrical reminiscence of twenty-five years earlier, written for a special issue of STAGE.

956   Dodge, Wendell Phillips. "Staging a Popular Restaurant." THEATRE (N.Y.) 16 (October 1912): 104, x-xi.

> A description of Belasco's staging of the Child's Restaurant scene in THE GOVERNOR'S LADY, a realistic ultimate.

957   Dransfield, Jane. "Behind the Scenes with Belasco." THEATRE (N.Y.) 35 (April 1922): 228-30, 260. Illus.

> An insubstantial tribute, late in Belasco's life.

958   Eaton, Walter Prichard. "Concerning David Belasco." AMERICAN MAGAZINE 75 (January 1913): 61-67. Illus.

> A substantial assessment of Belasco's productions. While Eaton admires Belasco's talents, he decries his taking of "the easiest way" to success and fame.

959   _____. "Madame Butterfly's Cocoon: A Sketch of David Belasco." AMERICAN SCHOLAR 5 (Spring 1936): 172-82.

> A relatively fair treatment of Belasco by a leading critic, offering an overview of Belasco's life and career, unfortunately neither illustrated or documented.

960   THE FIRST NIGHT IN DAVID BELASCO'S STUYVESANT THEATRE. New York: n.p., n.d. 22 p. Illus.

> A hard-cover memorial volume, apparently for the premiere on

16 October 1907 for A GRAND ARMY MAN. Many of the decorations of the theatre are illustrated.

961   [Ford, James Lauren.] MRS. LESLIE CARTER IN DAVID BELASCO'S DU BARRY, WITH PORTRAITS OF MRS. CARTER BY JOHN CECIL CLAY, TOGETHER WITH PORTAIT OF DAVID BELASCO, AND NUMEROUS ENGRAVINGS OF PHOTOGRAPHS AND SKETCHES IN BLACK AND WHITE. New York: Frederick A. Stokes Co., 1902. 59 p. Illus.

A description of the production, lavishly illustrated, stressing the historical accuracy of settings, costumes, and properties. Mrs. Carter is mentioned briefly.

962   "Greatest Players in the World Appear in Screen Plays." THEATRE (N.Y.) 29 (February 1919): 122.

Describes plans for a motion picture, A STAR OVERNIGHT, to be made for the Stage Women's War Relief. Belasco and Hilda Spong were to appear in the film.

963   Hamilton, Clayton. "Belasco and the Independent Theatre." BOOKMAN 45 (March 1917): 8-12.

Hamilton suggests that Belasco's hostility to experimental theatre began only when such productions began to cut into Belasco's profits for his productions.

964   Harris, H.A. "David Belasco--The Man and His Work." COSMOPOLI-TAN 47 (November 1909): 755-64. Illus.

Personal insights into Belasco from an adulatory point of view. Harris describes Belasco's work with Rose Coghlan, Richard Mansfield, Georgia Cayvan, Mrs. Carter, and William Warfield.

965   Herford, Oliver. "The Importance of Being Belasco." HARPER'S WEEKLY 58 (2 May 1914): 12. Illus.

An irreverant page about Belasco, questioning the authorship of his dramas. Stimulated in part by Belasco's autobiography, "My Life Story," in HEARST'S MAGAZINE, 1914-15.

966   Hornblow, Arthur. TRAINING FOR THE STAGE: SOME HINTS FOR THOSE ABOUT TO CHOOSE THE PLAYER'S CAREER. Foreword by David Belasco. Philadelphia and London: J.B. Lippincott Co., 1916. 193 p. Illus.

This is a "how to succeed in theatre" book, which describes theatrical conditions in American theatre in 1916.

967   Huneker, James Gibbons. "David Belasco." OUTLOOK 127 (16 March 1921): 418-22. Illus.

Published posthumously, this adulatory monograph lauds Belasco's career and contributions to the American stage.

968 _____. "David Belasco." THEATRE ARTS 5 (October 1921): 259-67.

A condensed version of no. 967.

969 "An Indictment of David Belasco as the Evil Genius of the Theatre." CURRENT OPINION 58 (February 1915): 96-97. Illus.

Sheldon Cheney is quoted at length, attacking Belasco for his realistic staging and extolling the new stagecraft.

970 "An Interesting Example of Belasco's Stagecraft." AMERICAN PLAY-WRIGHT 4 (March 1915): 69-70.

A brief description of a staging device used in MARIE-ODILE.

971 Isaacs, Edith J.R., and Gilder, Rosamond. "David Belasco, The Playwright and the Producer." THEATRE ARTS 27 (August 1943): 492-502. Illus.

A brief overview of Belasco's major contributions to the American theatre.

972 Jenkins, Ruth Lord. "The Costume Dramatic: An Interview with David Belasco." HARPER'S BAZAAR 56 (April 1921): 58-59, 126. Illus.

Jenkins describes a visit to Belasco's chambers in his theatre, where he described his theories of costuming and exemplified them with specific examples.

973 Lanston, Aubrey. "A Rehearsal Under Belasco." THEATRE (N.Y.) 5 (February 1905): 42-43. Illus.

A brief description of a rehearsal held Christmas day for ADREA, a Belasco production starring Mrs. Carter.

974 Lardner, Ring. "Adrift in New York." COLLIER'S 83 (12 January 1929): 15, 43. Illus.

A humorous description of Belasco, Lardner suggesting that the director is approaching his 104th birthday.

975 La Verne, Sister Mary, O.S.F. "Belascoism." PLAYERS 20 (December 1943): 6, 8, 17.

A somewhat oversimplified tribute to Belasco for his contributions to the American drama.

976   Loring, Janet. "Belasco: Preface to a Re-evaluation." WESTERN
      SPEECH JOURNAL 23 (Fall 1959): 207-11.

      A brief essay, proposing that Belasco's contributions to the
      U.S. theatre have been misconstrued and that a reexamination
      of his work is in order.

977   McGee, Thomas R., Jr. "Belasco's Realism." WESTERN SPEECH JOUR-
      NAL 21 (Fall 1957): 218-21.

      An undistinguished essay describing Belasco's staging.

978   McGlinchee, Claire. "Belasco Magic." PLAYERS 43 (October-November
      1967): 12-15. Illus.

      A brief account of some of Belasco's more elaborate and spec-
      tacular staging effects.

979   Mantle, Burns. AMERICAN PLAYWRIGHTS OF TODAY. New York:
      Dodd, Mead, and Co., 1929. 313 p. Index, illus.

      Mantle briefly discusses the dramaturgy of Belasco (pp. 231-40)
      and George M. Cohan (pp. 136-43).

980   Marker, Lise-Lone. DAVID BELASCO: NATURALISM IN THE AMERICAN
      THEATRE. Princeton, N.J.: Princeton University Press, 1975. xiv,
      238 p. Index, illus., bibliog.

      A highly regarded, well-researched, and fully documented
      study of Belasco's staging and direction. Essential to any study
      of Belasco and an example of outstanding scholarship.

981   _____. "Shakespeare and Naturalism: David Belasco Produces THE
      MERCHANT OF VENICE." THEATRE RESEARCH 10, no. 1 (1969):
      17-32. Illus.

      An especially lucid and descriptive account of one of Belasco's
      more important pieces of staging.

982   "Matters and Opinions of a Playwright." CURRENT LITERATURE 23
      (March 1898): 248.

      An anonymous interview with Belasco, reprinted from the Colo-
      rado Springs TELEGRAPH, in which Belasco describes his working
      habits and techniques as a dramatist.

983   Morris, Lloyd. "He Built a Theatre, Stars, and a Legend." THEATRE
      ARTS 37 (November 1953): 29-32. Illus.

      An excerpt from Morris's CURTAIN TIME. At the time of pub-
      lication, the Belasco Theatre in New York had just been re-
      claimed from television as a legitimate theatre.

984   Moses, Montrose J. "Belasco: Stage Realist." INDEPENDENT 86 (29 May 1916): 336-37. Illus.

Moses analyzes and applauds Belasco's realistic style of staging.

985   _____. "David Belasco, Dramatist." BOOK NEWS MONTHLY 26 (June 1908): 759-65. Illus.

A substantial essay with considerable biographical data, concluding with a positive assessment of Belasco as a dramatist.

986   _____. "David Belasco: The Astonishing Versatility of a Veteran Producer." THEATRE GUILD MAGAZINE 7 (November 1929): 27-30, 51. Illus.

Moses attempts to place Belasco's work in historical perspective, suggesting he fell short of the mark, but giving him credit for the pursuit of artistry as he saw it.

987   _____. "The Psychology of the Stage." THEATRE (N.Y.) 10 (August 1909): 64-65, vii. Illus.

A useful description of stage lighting in 1909, using Belasco's practices as examples of excellence.

988   "Mr. Belasco's Quarrel with the Experimental Theatres." CURRENT OPINION 62 (March 1917): 184.

Belasco excoriates the amateur theatres for staging "the diseased output of diseased minds."

989   Nathan, George Jean. COMEDIANS ALL. New York: Alfred A. Knopf, 1919. 267 p.

Nathan offers a brief criticism of Belasco as a producer (see pp. 70-72).

990   _____. THE THEATRE THE DRAMA THE GIRLS. New York: Alfred A. Knopf, 1921. 361 p.

On pages 216-18 Nathan lauds Belasco's lighting effects in THE SON-DAUGHTER, and on pages 60-63 presents a condemnation of Nance O'Neil's talents as an actress.

991   Patterson, Ada. "David Belasco Reviews His Life Work." THEATRE (N.Y.) 6 (September 1906): 247-50, viii-ix. Illus.

Belasco pontificates on his career with a humility that does not ring true.

992   _____. "David Belasco the Man." GREEN BOOK ALBUM 7 (May 1912): 961-66. Illus.

An adulatory interview of little merit, accompanied by otherwise unpublished photographs of some interest.

993   Pierce, Francis Lamont. "Art, Youth, and Mr. Belasco." DRAMA (Chicago) 7 (May 1917): 176-91.

Pierce suggests that Belasco's time has passed, however innovative he once was, and that younger producers have taken the theatre's leadership away from him.

994   PLAYS PRODUCED UNDER THE STAGE DIRECTION OF DAVID BELASCO. ILLUSTRATED WITH TWELVE CRAYON SKETCHES BY WILLIAM F. KURZE. New York: n.p., 1925. 47 p. Illus.

A chronological list of Belasco's production; useful, if corroborated.

995   Savage, Richard. "David Belasco's Family of Dramatic Artists." THEATRE 9 (November 1909): 149-51. Illus.

Savage describes the unusual happiness and compatability of Belasco's company as they rehearsed IS MATRIMONY A FAILURE?

996   Skolsky, Sidney. "Meet the Governor." THEATRE (N.Y.) 50 (October 1929): 22. Illus.

An idealized description of Belasco's personality and work habits.

997   "This Great Dramatist Lives and Works in the Midst of Dramatic Mementoes." NATIONAL MAGAZINE 53 (September 1924): 120. Illus.

A bit of puffery about Belasco's collection of theatrical memorabilia.

998   Timberlake, Craig. THE LIFE AND WORK OF DAVID BELASCO, THE BISHOP OF BROADWAY. New York: Library Publishers, 1954. 463 p. Index, illus., bibliog.

Long considered the best work on Belasco. A well-researched and documented biography which includes many useful photographs. Belasco's work with various performers is well described: David Warfield, Mrs. Carter, Frances Starr, and Lenore Ulric are treated.

999   "A Tribute to David Belasco." THEATRE (N.Y.) 15 (April 1912): 124.

A description of some of the various commendations and awards received by Belasco for his staging of THE GIRL OF THE GOLDEN WEST.

1000 Warfield, David. "David Belasco." GREEN BOOK ALBUM 1 (February 1909): 364-75.

Warfield has the highest possible praise for Belasco and his effect upon the actor's career. Adulatory.

1001 West, Magda Frances. "Belasco's Views on Love, Women and the Play of Tomorrow." GREEN BOOK ALBUM 8 (October 1912): 577-90. Illus.

Somewhat idealized observations by the author, derived mainly from examining roles in scripts by Belasco.

1002 Winter, William. THE LIFE OF DAVID BELASCO. 2 vols. New York: Moffat, Yard and Co., 1918. Reprint. Freeport, N.Y.: Books for Libraries, 1970; New York: Benjamin Blom, 1972. Index, illus., chronology.

Winter and Belasco were good friends for thirty years; this biography is more valuable for its scope and detail than for its objectivity. Winter died during the final preparation of the manuscript; his son finished the work. Substantial material is included on Belasco's performers, among them Blanche Bates, Mrs. Carter, Francess Starr, and David Warfield.

1003 Young, Stark. "An Estimate of Belasco." NEW REPUBLIC 67 (17 June 1931): 123-24.

Young gives begrudging credit to Belasco for holding his position in the theatre for two generations in spite of his flawed tastes and old-fashioned techniques.

See also nos. 9, 112, 135, 150, 153, 163, 166, 178, 185, 211, 214, 216, 228-29, 235, 242, 256, 291, 294, 300, 348, 376, 388, 410, 448, 451, 458, 464, 483, 525, 531, 547-48, 555, 558, 562, 572, 578-80, 598, 612, 901, 908, 1308, 1471, 1477, 1503, 1521, 1975, 1981, 2115, 3013, 3152, 3161, 3177, and 3212.

BENNETT, RICHARD

(1872-1944)

1004 Beckley, Zoe. "The Home of a Player." THEATRE (N.Y.) 29 (April 1919): 222-23. Illus.

Bennett did a vigorous business in real estate in addition to acting. Beckley describes his mania and examines his residence at the time, "Gardenholm."

1005 _____. "Temperament!" THEATRE (N.Y.) 44 (October 1926): 12-13, 53. Illus.

Bennett describes theatrical stresses for actors that cause tempers to explode, especially noisy audiences for whom he had a particular loathing.

1006 Bennett, Joan, and Kibbee, Lois. THE BENNETT PLAYBILL. New York, Chicago, and San Francisco: Holt, Rinehart and Winston, 1970. xi, 332 p. Illus

Although basically an autobiography of the film actress, Joan Bennett, much material on Bennett, her father, is included in the early chapters.

1007 Manners, Dorothy. "The Stormy Petrel of Broadway." MOTION PICTURE MAGAZINE 42 (October 1931): 39, 84. Illus.

The irascible Bennett gives a particularly blunt interview when interrupted while sun-bathing.

1008 Patterson, Ada. "Richard Bennett--An Actor to Be Reckoned With." THEATRE (N.Y.) 9 (February 1909): 64-65. Illus.

Bennett describes his theatrical ambition, which was to become the greatest actor in America.

See also nos. 276, 377, 413, and 841.

BERNARD, JOHN
(1756-1828)

1008A. Bernard, John. RETROSPECTIONS OF AMERICA 1797-1811. New York: Harper and Brothers, 1887. xiii, 374 p. Illus.

Mrs. Bayle Bernard, the widow of John Bernard's son, edited chapters 1-10, while the introduction, notes, and index were supplied by Laurence Hutton and Brander Matthews. Chapter 11 is taken from Bayle Bernard's "Early Days of the American Stage," and chapters 12-15 are derived from another of the elder Bernard's manuscripts, which she published in MANHATTAN MAGAZINE, 1884, again with notes by Hutton and Matthews. The work is somewhat more readable than usual for this period and includes valuable primary descriptions of the early theatre and such performers as John Hodgkinson, James Fennell, Thomas Wignell, Mrs. Merry, Mrs. Melmouth, Thomas Abthorpe Cooper, and William Warren I.

1009 _____. RETROSPECTIONS OF THE STAGE. 2 vols. in 1. Edited by Bayle Bernard. Boston: Carter and Hendee, 1832. 235, 215 p.

This work is a detailed account of Bernard's life and career in England up to the year of his departure for the United States, 1797. It is a valuable primary source, although Bernard's editing may have distorted minor facts.

1010 [J.] "Sketch of the Life of Mr. John Bernard." POLYANTHOS 2 (April 1806): 2-13.

A biographical sketch of minimal distinction, available in the American Periodical Series, reel 39.

See also nos. 123, 180, 413, and 421.

179

BINGHAM, AMELIA

(1869-1927)

1011   "Amelia Bingham's Famous Home." GREEN BOOK MAGAZINE 13 (April 1915): 679-80. Illus.

Primarily a description and photographs of 103 Riverside Drive in New York City, Bingham's residence at the time.

1012   Bingham, Amelia. "Labor and Capital on the Stage." GREEN BOOK ALBUM 4 (December 1910): 1316-19.

Operating as both an actress and a manager, Bingham gives a fairly complete picture of the financial operation of a theatre at the time.

1013   Coward, Edward Fales. "Amelia Bingham--An Actress with Ambition." THEATRE (N.Y.) 3 (April 1903): 90-93.

Bingham describes several of her ideals in the theatre and vows to achieve at least most of them.

See also nos. 28, 314, 382, 464, 555, and 581.

BLACKMER, SIDNEY

(1898-1973)

1014   Morehouse, Ward. "The First Forty Years are the Toughest." THEATRE
        ARTS 43 (September 1959): 76-77.

   A brief interview with Blackmer, who reminisces about his early
   career.

1015   Patterson, Ada. "Sidney Blackmer--New Broadway Favorite." THEATRE
        (N.Y.) 35 (February 1922): 106. Illus.

   A biographical interview following Blackmer's success in THE
   MOUNTAIN MAN.

See also no. 276.

BLAKE, WILLIAM RUFUS (1805-63). See nos. 250, 313, 319, 396, 433, and 2235-36.

BLINN, HOLBROOK
(1872-1928)

1016   Barrell, Charles W. "Holbrook Blinn--An Actor of the Realistic School." THEATRE (N.Y.) 9 (May 1909): 144-45. Illus.

        Barrell traces Blinn's career, the actor having just attracted favorable attention in SALVATION NELL. Barrell attributes much of Blinn's success to his intellectual approach to his art.

1017   Baur, Eva E. vom. "A Theatre of Thrills." THEATRE (N.Y.) 17 (June 1913): 186, 188. Illus.

        Baur describes the opening of the Princess Theatre in New York under Blinn's direction. He planned to produce a series of one-act plays.

1018   Blinn, Holbrook. "How I Create My Bad Men." THEATRE (N.Y.) 44 (October 1926): 22, 64. Illus.

        Blinn posits that the stage villian must be investigated by the actor for sympathy, sincerity, humor, plausability, and charm.

1019   _____. "Picking Types." GREEN BOOK ALBUM 5 (May 1911): 987-91.

        Blinn decries the tendency toward type casting, feeling he had suffered from the practice.

See also no. 276.

BONSTELLE, JESSIE

(1872-1932)

1020   Adams, Mildred. "Jessie Bonstelle and her Playhouse." WOMAN CITI-
ZEN 11(July 1926): 13, 40-41. Illus.

> A biographical sketch describing Bonstelle's work in Detroit and
> her Bonstelle Theatre which had opened eighteen months earlier.

1021   Bennett, Helen Christine. "God Made the Heavens But 'Bonnie' Makes
the Stars." AMERICAN MAGAZINE 104 (December 1927): 36-37,
169-73. Illus.

> A glorified treatment of Bonstelle's career as a producer.

1022   Golden, Sylvia B. "America's First Civic Theatre." THEATRE (N.Y.)
48 (October 1928): 20-21, 72. Illus.

> A description of the Detroit Civic Theatre, formerly the Bon-
> stelle Theatre, under the direction of the actress.

1023   Lincoln, Nannette. "Ladies Behind the Scenes." EVERYBODY'S MAGA-
ZINE 54 (April 1926): 88-93, 172-73. Illus.

> An article describing four female Broadway producers, one of
> them Bonstelle, whom Lincoln described as "the most unusual
> personality in the American theatre."

1024   "A Municipal Theatre." OUTLOOK 102 (21 December 1912): 852-54.

> A description of the Northampton, Massachusetts, municipal
> theatre which hired Bonstelle to select and direct a permanent
> company.

1025   Storey, Margaret, and Gillis, Hugh. "Players' Nursery." Stanford,
Calif.: Dramatic Alliance, Stanford University, 1940. lxxv, 40 p.
Bibliog.

> A mimeographed publication prepared in conjunction with an ex-
> hibition of Bonstelle memorabilia at the Stanford Library in
> 1940. Considerable material on Bonstelle's career is included.

1026 Thorne, Clifford. "The Stars That Shine." DRAMA (Chicago) 16 (March 1926): 216. Illus.

> A brief and undistinguished summary of Bonstelle's career to that time.

See also nos. 13, 1460-61, and 1577.

BOOTH, AGNES (1841?-1910). See nos. 13, 279, 290, 293, 328, 356, 387, and 471.

BOOTH FAMILY

Entries on Edwin, John Wilkes, and Junius Brutus Booth, Sr., follow this section.

1027   Cate, Wirt Armistead. "Ford, the Booths, and Lincoln's Assassination."
        EMORY UNIVERSITY QUARTERLY 5 (March 1949): 11-19.

        The article describes the various Booths' reactions to the murder,
        but adds little to traditional accounts.

1028   Clarke, Asia Booth. THE ELDER AND THE YOUNGER BOOTH. Boston:
        James R. Osgood; London: David Bogue, 1882. 194 p. Index, frontis-
        piece.

        The elder Booth's youngest daughter wrote a somewhat distorted
        account of the career of her father and her brother Edwin. She
        implies legitimacy for the Maryland Booths and makes no men-
        tion of the Lincoln assassination. Still a useful primary source.

1029   Connell, Christopher T., and Patterson, James A. "The Booth Brothers'
        Benefit." PLAYERS 44 (April-May 1969): 148-50. Illus.

        An undocumented account of the appearance in 1864 of
        Edwin, John Wilkes, and Junius Brutus Booth, Jr., in JULIUS
        CAESAR to raise funds for a memorial statue of Shakespeare.

1030   Estavan, Lawrence, ed. MONOGRAPHS: IX: JUNIUS BRUTUS BOOTH,
        THE ELDER; X: JUNIUS BRUTUS BOOTH, THE YOUNGER; XI: EDWIN
        BOOTH. San Francisco: Works Project Administration, 1934. 155 p.
        Illus., bibliog.

        A series of poorly documented and inaccurate monographs (the
        elder Booth is said to have married Mary Ann Holmes before
        leaving England for America). Contains lists of representative
        roles for all three men. Superseded by more resent publications.

1031   "The Four Booths." GREEN BOOK MAGAZINE 14 (July 1915): 34-45.
        Illus.

An undocumented and rambling account of the family, surpassed by more recent and substantial treatments.

1032   Kimmel, Stanley. THE MAD BOOTHS OF MARYLAND. Indianapolis and New York: Bobbs-Merrill Co., 1940. Rev. ed. in paper. New York: Dover Publications, 1969. 400 p. Index, illus., notes.

A meticulously researched and documented treatment of the family with considerable attention paid to the aftermath of the Lincoln assassination. Indispensable for any Booth investigation. Contains many otherwise unpublished photographs and a useful Booth family tree. The 1969 edition contains an additional eighteen pages, mostly about John Wilkes Booth.

1033   Mahoney, Ella V. SKETCHES OF TUDOR HALL AND THE BOOTH FAMILY. Belair, Md.: Tudor Hall, 1925. 59 p. Illus.

The author's husband purchased the Booth home in Maryland from Mary Ann Holmes Booth in 1878. Her description of the house is evocative, although her capsule biographies of the elder Booth, John Wilkes, and Edwin, are somewhat idealized.

1034   Stacton, David. THE JUDGES OF THE SECRET COURT. New York: Pantheon Books, 1961. 255 p.

A fictionalized account of the assassination and the last days of Edwin Booth's life. Of minimal value.

1035   Traubel, Horace. WITH WALT WHITMAN IN CAMDEN. MARCH 28-JULY 14, 1888. 5 vols. Boston: Small, Maynard, 1906. New York: Mitchell Kennerley, 1915. Carbondale: Southern Illinois University Press, 1959. xiv, 408 p. Index, illus.

Whitman considers the relative talents of Edwin Booth and his father and voices a preference for the latter in volume 1. He scatters references to the Booths throughout the remaining volumes.

See also nos. 118, 148, 154, 163, 182, 203, 224, 250, 347, 373, 399, 417, 442, 1120, 1124, 1521, 1749, 2235-36, and 2330.

BOOTH, EDWIN
(1833-93)

1036   Abbott, Lyman. SILHOUETTES OF MY CONTEMPORARIES. New York: Doubleday, Page, 1922. x, 361 p. Frontispiece.

        Chapter 2, pages 16-27, is titled "Edwin Booth, Interpreter," and describes the actor's high degree of Christian virtue.

1037   _____. "Snap-Shots of My Contemporaries. Edwin Booth--Interpreter." OUTLOOK 127 (20 April 1921): 634-37. Illus.

        See no. 1036.

1038   Aldrich, Mrs. Thomas Bailey. CROWDING MEMORIES. Boston and New York: Houghton Mifflin Co., 1920. 286 p. Index, illus.

        Written by the widow of Booth's good friend and permeated with anecdotal material about the actor. Includes a photograph of Booth's home at Dorcester, Massachusetts.

1039   Aldrich, Thomas Bailey. "The Grave of Edwin Booth." CENTURY 60 (June 1900): 174. Illus.

        Brief comments and a drawing of Booth's grave.

1040   [B., T.] "Edwin Booth in Germany." NATION 36 (26 April 1883): 358-60.

        A report from Leipzig on Booth's great success there, a description of him as Othello, and excerpts from German reviews of him.

1041   Badeau, Adam. "Edwin Booth On and Off the Stage, Personal Recollections." McCLURE'S 1 (August 1893): 255-67. Illus.

        A gracefully written tribute to Booth by a friend and colleague.

1042   Bispham, William. "Memories and Letters of Edwin Booth." CENTURY 25 (November 1893): 132-39; 25 (December 1893): 240-50. Illus.

        The publication of Bispham's correspondence from Booth, accompanied by an unusual drawing of Booth as Shylock (page 249).

1043   Blake, Rodney. "How Success First Came to Edwin Booth." THEATRE (N.Y.) 17 (February 1913): 60. Illus.

       An undocumented account of Booth's activities in California around 1852.

1044   Booth, Edwin. THE BREAK BETWEEN PLAYER AND POET: LETTERS FROM EDWIN BOOTH TO RICHARD HENRY STODDARD. New York: 1903.

       Unavailable for examination.

1045   Booth, Ken Jon. "Everybody Knows Tom Fool!" PLAYERS 42 (Spring-Summer 1966): 92-94.

       A popularized, undocumented, highly speculative account of Booth's life.

1046   "Booth's Theatre." HARPER'S WEEKLY 13 (9 January 1869): 21-22, 29. Illus.

       A brief description and illustration.

1047   BOOTH'S THEATRE BEHIND THE SCENES. New York: Henry L. Hinton, 1872. 16 p. Illus.

       A detailed description of the storage facilities and stage machinery, much of it innovative at that time. Ten drawings of the backstage facilities are included.

1048   Bradford, Gamaliel. AS GOD MADE THEM: PORTRAITS OF SOME NINETEENTH CENTURY AMERICANS. Boston and New York: Houghton Mifflin Co., 1929. 287 p. Index, illus., notes.

       Seven essays, one (pp. 167-201) a glowing tribute to Booth, albeit Bradford does not describe his acting.

1049   Brereton, Austin. THE LIFE OF HENRY IRVING. 2 vols. New York: Longman, Green, 1908. Index, illus., bibliog. Reprint. 2 vols in 1. New York: Benjamin Blom, 1969.

       A detailed biography of the English star, including an account of Booth's engagement with him at the Lyceum (1, pp. 329-37).

1050   Bronson, Edgar Beecher. "Edwin Booth's Opinion of the Players of His Day." THEATRE (N.Y.) 11 (May 1910): 162-66. Illus.

       Booth's candid opinions are quoted on Lester Wallack, Edwin

Adams, Lawrence Barrett, E.L. Davenport, John S. Clarke, and Charles Fisher.

1051   Brush, Edward Hale. "Statues of Booth and Beecher." ART AND PROGRESS 6 (March 1915): 158-60. Illus.

An illustrated description of the Quinn statue of Booth as well as one by Gutzon Borglum of Henry Ward Beecher.

1052   Bryan, George B. "Edwin Booth's RICHARD II (1875)." SHAKESPEARE QUARTERLY 24 (Autumn 1973): 383-89.

Booth produced RICHARD II just as his managerial career was closing; Bryan suggests the actor was trying to raise theatrical tastes in America with its production.

1053   Calhoun, Lucia Gilbert. "Edwin Booth." GALAXY 7 (January 1869): 76-87. Illus.

A description of Booth in many of his major roles and a prediction of success for Booth's Theatre, which had not yet opened.

1054   Chapman, John. "The Players: Club and Treasure House of the Theatre." THEATRE ARTS 39 (June 1955): 62-64, 95-96. Illus.

A description and brief history of the club founded by Booth at 16 Gramercy Park in New York with several anecdotes about the members.

1055   Clapp, Henry Austin. "Edwin Booth." ATLANTIC 72 (September 1893): 307-17.

Written shortly after Booth's death, this article describes some of the actor's technical effects as well as eulogizes him.

1056   _____. "Edwin Booth in Some Non-Shakespearean Roles." OUTING: SPORT, ADVENTURE, TRAVEL, FICTION 6 (June 1885): 343-49.

Clapp describes Booth as Sir Giles Overreach in A NEW WAY TO PAY OLD DEBTS, Pescara in THE APOSTATE, Sir Edward Mortimer in THE IRON CHEST, Claude Melnotte in THE LADY OF LYONS, and the title roles in RUY BLAS and DON CAESAR DE BAZAN.

1057   Cohen, Richard. "Hamlet as Edwin Booth." THEATRE SURVEY 10 (May 1969): 53-74. Illus.

Cohen posits the controversial observation that "the secret of Booth's performance was that while he played Hamlet as sane, he himself, in a manner of speaking, was mad. His madness gave the performance its edge of excitement."

1058   Cole, Susan S. "Edwin Booth in THE FOOL'S REVENGE." SOUTHERN THEATRE 22 (Spring 1979): 3-6.

        Cole examined traditional sources to analyze an important but overlooked role of Booth's.

1059   Copeland, Charles Townsend. EDWIN BOOTH. Boston: Small, Maynard and Co., 1901. 157 p. Frontispiece, bibliog.

        A small work, somewhat whitewashing the more lurid aspects of the Booth family. Of minimal value.

1060   Daly, Augustin, and Palmer, A.M. EXCERPTS FROM THE MANY GOOD WORDS UTTERED IN HONOR OF EDWIN BOOTH AT THE SUPPER GIVEN ON SATURDAY NIGHT, MARCH 30, 1889, BY AUGUSTIN DALY AND A.M. PALMER. New York: Printed for the Players, 1889. 23 p.

        Includes a letter from George William Curtis, a salute from Constant Coquelin, an address by Stephen Henry Olin, and a tribute by William Winter.

1061   Doremus, R. Ogden. "Edwin Booth and Ole Bull." CRITIC 48 (March 1906): 234-44. Illus.

        Doremus once arranged a reading of Byron's MANFRED by Booth; Bull performed a concert at Booth's Theatre when the reading was repeated there.

1062   "Edwin Booth." CRITIC 22 (10 June 1893): 384-86. Illus.

        Although basically an obituary, this item includes much reprinted critical acclaim and biographical data.

1063   "Edwin Booth and Lincoln." CENTURY 77 (April 1909): 919-20.

        Text and discussion of a letter from Booth to General Adam Badeau after the Lincoln assassination.

1064   "The Edwin Booth Memorial Window." CRITIC 33 (July-August 1898): 33, 61-63. Illus.

        A description of the dedication of the Booth Memorial Window in the Church of Transfiguration in New York on 24 June 1898. Joseph Jefferson III's brief remarks are included.

1065   "Edwin Booth's Real Self." THEATRE (N.Y.) 24 (December 1916): 360, 400. Illus.

        A gracefully written tribute to Booth, ascribed to "An Intimate for Twenty-Five Years."

1066   Eaton, Walter Prichard. "Edwin Booth." THEATRE ARTS 16 (November 1932): 888-94.

> Eatons recalls seeing the "Curse of Rome" speech by Booth as Richelieu and contrasts his acting to that of the 1920s and 1930s.

1067   "Edmond T. Quinn." AMERICAN IRISH HISTORICAL SOCIETY JOURNAL 14 (1915): 319. Illus.

> A half-page biographical sketch of Quinn, who sculpted the statue of Booth as Hamlet for Gramercy Park.

1068   Fauntleroy, A.M. "The Romance of Mary Devlin Booth." WOMAN'S HOME COMPANION 21 (September 1904): 10.

> A popularized and brief account of Booth's first marriage.

1069   "First Fifty." TIME 33 (9 January 1939): 24-25. Illus.

> A description of the Players Club and Booth upon the club's fiftieth anniversary.

1070   Foreman, Edward R. "Edwin Booth in Rochester." ROCHESTER HISTORICAL SOCIETY PUBLICATION 5 (1926): 113-19.

> A minimally documented account of Booth's engagements in Rochester, New York, between 1860 and 1889. Foreman saw Booth's 1889 engagement.

1071   Frenz, Horst. "Edwin Booth in Polyglot Shakespearean Performances." GERMANIC REVIEW 18 (December 1943): 280-85.

> An examination of Booth's German tour and his Shakespearean performances there, in which he performed in English and the supporting players spoke German.

1072   [Frothingham, O.B.] "The Acting of Mr. Edwin Booth." NATION 2 (29 March 1866): 395-96.

> An analysis of Booth in several roles, including his Hamlet, which the critic does not find totally successful. Published shortly after Booth's return to the stage after the Lincoln assassination.

1073   Fuller, Charles F., Jr. "Edwin and John Wilkes Booth, Actors at the Old Marshall Theatre in Richmond." VIRGINIA MAGAZINE OF HISTORY AND BIOGRAPHY 79 (October 1971): 477-83.

> Describes how this theatre "provided a showcase for the early talents of these two American actors between 1856

and 1859." Includes a complete list of their engagements taken from newspaper accounts.

1074   Gale, Minna. "If Booth Were to Come Back to Life." GREEN BOOK ALBUM 7 (June 1912): 1132-36. Illus.

Speculation concerning Booth's possible reactions to the changes in theatrical techniques since 1893.

1075   Gallegly, J.S. "Edwin Booth in Galveston and Houston." RICE INSTITUTE PAMPHLETS 44 (April 1957): 52-64.

A brief and superficial examination of the subject.

1076   Godwin, Parke. COMMEMORATIVE ADDRESSES: GEORGE WILLIAM CURTIS; EDWIN BOOTH; LOUIS KOSSUTH; JOHN JAMES AUDUBON; WILLIAM CULLEN BRYANT. New York: Harper and Brothers, 1895. 239 p.

Publication (pp. 65-104) of Godwin's tribute to Booth given at the Players Club on 14 November 1893. The address is also published in MEMORIAL CELEBRATION OF THE SIXTIETH ANNIVERSARY OF THE BIRTH OF EDWIN BOOTH (no. 1103).

1077   Goodale, Katherine [Kitty Molony]. BEHIND THE SCENES WITH EDWIN BOOTH. Boston and New York: Houghton Mifflin Co., 1931. 317 p. Index, illus.

Goodale, who acted under the name Kitty Molony, joined Booth's company in 1886-87 for a national tour; she later wrote this chatty and adulatory account of her experiences during the season. Additional material on Lawrence Barrett, Joseph Jefferson III, Modjeska, and Frank Mayo.

1078   Grossman, Edwina Booth. EDWIN BOOTH: RECOLLECTIONS BY HIS DAUGHTER AND LETTERS TO HER AND TO HIS FRIENDS. New York: Century Co., 1894. 284 p. Index, illus. Reprint. New York: Benjamin Blom, 1969. Freeport, N.Y.: Books for Libraries, 1970.

Booth's daughter wrote a twenty-eight page recollection of her father to precede several hundred of his letters to various friends and acquaintances, which offer insights into Booth at different stages of his career. Considerable reference is made to Lawrence Barrett and Booth's father.

1979   _____. "The Real Edwin Booth." CENTURY 48 (October 1894): 803-15. Illus.

An item primarily consisting of the texts of correspondence with a connecting text by Grossman, who was Booth's daughter. Several illustrations, including one of Booth as Macbeth.

1080   Hall, Florence Marion Howe. "The Friendship of Edwin Booth and Julia Ward Howe." NEW ENGLAND MAGAZINE 15, n.s. 9 (November 1893): 315-21. Illus.

A description of a long friendship, with several reprinted letters and Hall's comments about Booth after the loss of his first wife.

1081   Hennessy, W.J. MR. EDWIN BOOTH IN HIS VARIOUS CHARACTERS. Boston: James R. Osgood, 1872. 102 p. Illus.

A large volume of engravings of Booth in various starring roles. A brief biography of Booth by William Winter is included.

1082   House, E.H. "Edwin Booth in London." CENTURY 55, n.s. 33 (December 1897): 269-79.

A sympathetic treatment of Booth's disappointing engagement in 1880.

1083   Hufstetler, Loren. "A Physical Description of Booth's Theatre." THEATRE DESIGN AND TECHNOLOGY 43 (Winter 1976): 8-18, 38. Illus.

A detailed analysis of extant materials leading to a conjectural floor plan of the theatre. Does not consider BOOTH'S THEATRE BEHIND THE SCENES (no. 1047).

1084   Hutton, Laurence. "Edwin Booth." HARPER'S WEEKLY 37 (17 June 1893): 577-81. Illus.

A moving tribute by a close personal friend, written shortly after Booth's death.

1085   _____. EDWIN BOOTH. New York: Harper and Brothers, 1893. 59 p. Illus.

A memorial volume written by Booth's good friend and fellow actor, in which is included Booth's reminiscence of his father.

1086   _____. "Edwin Booth, Man and Actor." LIVING AGE 216 (8 January 1898): 129-31.

Reprinted from Hutton's "A Group of Players" from HARPER'S MAGAZINE (no. 460), an adulatory compendium of anecdotes.

1087 "In the Gallery of the God." STAGE 14 (August 1937): 101. Illus.

Written "as if by William Winter," this is an imaginary
account of Booth in JULIUS CAESAR and HAMLET.

1088 Irvin, Eric. "Laura Keene and Edwin Booth in Australia." THEATRE
NOTEBOOK 23 (Spring 1969): 95-100. Illus.

Using Australian newspapers, Irvin gives an account of an
engagement which is largely overlooked in most biographies
of the two stars.

1089 [F., F.A.] "Memories of Booth Evoked by Centenary." LITERARY
DIGEST 116 (2 December 1933): 21. Illus.

A description of ceremonies held 13 November 1933 in
New York.

1090 Kellogg, Elizabeth R. "Old Theatre Programs." HISTORICAL AND
PHILOSOPHICAL SOCIETY OF OHIO BULLETIN 6 (July 1948): 66-68.

Superficial eyewitness accounts of Edwin Booth and Julia
Marlowe engagements in Cincinnati between 1880 and the
turn of the century.

1091 King, Rolf. "Edwin Booth's First Appearance in Rochester." ROCHES-
TER HISTORICAL SOCIETY 18 (1940): 215-18.

A brief description of Booth's 1856-57 tour, including a
performance in Rochester.

1092 Kinne, Wisner Payne. GEORGE PIERCE BAKER AND THE AMERICAN
THEATRE. Cambridge, Mass.: Harvard University Press, 1954. 335 p.
Index, Illus., bibliog.

A biography including a brief description by Baker of
Booth's King Lear.

1093 Kyle, Howard. THE HISTORY OF THE EDWIN BOOTH MEMORIAL,
APRIL 2ND, 1906, TO NOVEMBER 13TH, 1918. New York: Corlies,
Macy and Co., [1918]. 63 p. Illus.

A detailed account of the memorial statue of Booth in
Gramercy Park, including several photographs of the
dedication and transcripts of the speeches given on that
occasion.

1094 Lockridge, Richard. DARLING OF MISFORTUNE: EDWIN BOOTH:
1833-1893. New York and London: Century Co., 1932. 345 p.
Index, illus.

A sensitive and substantial biography of Booth, drawing heavily upon letters and newspapers. Superseded by later works, but still useful. Includes material on Lawrence Barrett, the elder Booth, John Wilkes Booth, Charlotte Cushman, Edwin Forrest, and Joseph Jefferson III.

1095 Lows, J.R. "Edwin Booth." NATION 56 (15 June 1893): 434-36.

An especially graceful tribute to Booth written shortly after his death.

1096 McCloskey, J.J. "Edwin Booth in Old California." GREEN BOOK ALBUM 6 (June 1911): 1322-27. Illus.

McCloskey was acting at the Jenny Lind Theatre when Booth first arrived on the West Coast; he describes seeing the actor in his first roles there.

1097 MacDougall, Sally. "Edwin Booth Counted His Ducats." CENTURY 107 (December 1928): 198-204.

Interesting and detailed account of Booth's financial circumstances, illustrating the theatrical practices of the time.

1098 Malone, John. "An Actor's Memory of Edwin Booth." FORUM 15 (July 1893): 594-603.

A charming reminiscence of Booth by a colleague.

1099 Marker, Lise-Lone, and Frederick J. "Edwin Booth's JULIUS CAESAR: A Promptbook Study." NINETEENTH CENTURY THEATRE RESEARCH 4 (Spring 1976): 1-21. Illus.

A meticulous account of the production, appropriately illustrated, using the prompt scripts held by the Players Club.

1100 Matthews, Brander. "Memories of Edwin Booth." MUNSEY'S 67 (July 1919): 240-50. Illus.

Gracefully written anecdotes and personal reminiscences, accompanied by some unusual photographs of Booth.

1101 _____. "The Players." CENTURY 21 (November 1891): 28-34.

A history and description of the club and its policies.

1102 _____. THE PRINCIPLES OF PLAYMAKING AND OTHER DESCRIPTIONS OF THE DRAMA. New York: Charles Scribner's Sons, 1919. Reprint. Freeport, N.Y.: Books for Libraries Press, 1970. 306 p.

A collection of essays primarily concerned with dramaturgy, but including "Memories of Edwin Booth" (pp.
286-306). Matthews had seen Booth as Hamlet in 1865,
attended the opening of Booth's Theatre in 1869, and met
him in 1884. An insightful essay.

1103 MEMORIAL CELEBRATION OF THE SIXTIETH ANNIVERSARY OF THE
BIRTH OF EDWIN BOOTH. New York: Gilliss Press, 1893. 60 p.
Illus.

A record of the ceremony held in the Madison Square
Garden Concert Hall on 13 November 1893 by the Players,
shortly after Booth's death. Contains texts of addresses by
Joseph Jefferson III, Tomasso Salvini, Henry Irving, Parke
Godwin, and others.

1104 Moray, John S. BOOTH'S RICHELIEU REVIEWED. New York: S. Torrey
and Co., 1871.

Verified in NATIONAL UNION CATALOG, but unavailable for examination. It is apparently a critical and historical essay on Booth's representation of Edward Bulwer-
Lytton's script and originally appeared in THE SEASON
for 14 January 1871.

1105 "New York Honors Edwin Booth." THEATRE (N.Y.) 29 (January 1919):
34. Illus.

A description of the unveiling of the Booth Memorial
statue in Gramercy Park.

1006 Oggel, L. Terry. "The Edwin Booth Promptbook Collections at the
Players: A Descriptive Catalog." THEATRE SURVEY 14 (May 1973):
72-111. Illus.

A list of some eighty-nine such prompt scripts, appropriately
indexed.

1007 _____. "A Guide to the Edwin Booth Literary Materials at the New
York Public Library." BULLETIN OF RESEARCH IN THE HUMANITIES
82 (Spring 1979): 90-104. Illus.

A listing of Booth materials in the following categories:
holograph messages to and from Edwin and Mary Devlin
Booth (876 items), promptbooks (2), scrapbooks (4), ledgers
(2), manuscripts (7), legal documents (3), and miscellaneous
items (1). A valuable resource for Booth research.

1008 _____. "A Short Guide to the Edwin Booth Literary Materials at the
Players." PERFORMING ARTS RESOURCES 3 (1976): 98-142.

Oggel lists the holograph messages to or by Edwin Booth (2,485 items), promptbooks (89), scrapbooks (34), ledgers (35), manuscripts (9), legal documents (26), miscellaneous items (15), and printed volumes (over 1,000). A valuable guide to America's oldest theatre collection.

1109   Oxford, John. "Three Men Who Touched the Heart." BURR McINTOSH MONTHLY 16 (April 1908): n.p. Illus.

A two-page article comparing Lincoln, Edwin Booth, and Henry Ward Beecher, describing the appeal of each.

1110   Pallette, Drew B. "Garland and the Prince of Players." WESTERN SPEECH 21 (Summer 1957): 160-63.

A brief article describing Garland's attempts to describe Booth's acting, drawn primarily from Garland's A SON OF THE MIDDLE BORDER (1917) and ROADSIDE MEETINGS (1930).

1111   Partridge, Edward L. "Edwin Booth to John E. Russell: Some Hitherto Unpublished Letters." OUTLOOK 127 (20 April 1921): 637-39. Illus.

Texts of nine letters from Booth to Russell, who was at one time the New York SUN drama critic and a friend of Booth.

1112   Phillips, John S. OUR INHERITANCE: THE FOUNDER'S NIGHT ADDRESS MADE ON DECEMBER 31, 1931, BY JOHN S. PHILLIPS. New York: The Players, 1932. 19 p.

A recounting of Booth's conception and execution of the Players.

1113   "The Players' Club Monument to Booth." VANITY FAIR 3 (January 1915): 26. Illus.

A brief account of the selection of Quinn's statue which was erected in Gramercy Park.

1114   "The Players' Tribute to Edwin Booth." CRITIC 23 (18 November 1893): 327-29.

A description of a memorial service held in the Madison Square Garden Concert Hall (see no. 1103), attended by some fifteen hundred people. A long elegaic poem is included.

1115   Power-Waters, Alma. THE STORY OF YOUNG EDWIN BOOTH. Foreward by Eva Le Gallienne. New York: E.P. Dutton and Co., 1955. 192 p. Illus., bibliog.

The author has freely adapted Booth material into a popularized and romanticized account of Booth up to his stage debut. Of little use.

1116   "Quotations from Papers about Booth." PUBLIC OPINION 15 (17 June 1893): 248-49.

Extracts from editorial tributes from the New York EVENING POST, the Springfield REPUBLICAN, and the Minneapolis TIMES.

1117   Roge, Charlotte F. Bates. "A Memorable Letter of Edwin Booth's." CENTURY 67 (January 1904): 414.

Trivial.

1118   Royle, Edwin Milton. "Edwin Booth as I Knew Him." HARPER'S MAGAZINE 132 (May 1916): 840-49. Illus.

Royle spent two years in Booth's company and draws upon that experience to present a few unique anecdotes in an otherwise undistinguished biographical sketch.

1119   _____. EDWIN BOOTH AS I KNEW HIM. New York: The Players, 1933. 36 p. Frontispiece.

An expansion of no. 1118, in which Royle describes Booth's theories and practices of acting.

1120   Ruggles, Eleanor. PRINCE OF PLAYERS: EDWIN BOOTH. New York: W.W. Norton and Co., 1953. 386 p. Index, illus., bibliog.

A well-researched and especially gracefully written treatment of Booth, eventually made into a feature film starring Richard Burton as Booth. Includes material on the rest of the Booth family, Lawrence Barrett, Edwin Forrest, Joseph Jefferson III, Otis Skinner, and Francis Wilson.

1121   Salvini, Tommaso. LEAVES FROM THE AUTOBIOGRAPHY OF TOMMASO SALVINI. New York: Century Co., 1893. 240 p. Illus.

Salvini offers his perceptions of Booth's acting, especially in OTHELLO.

1122   Shattuck, Charles H. "Edwin Booth's First Critic." THEATRE SURVEY 7 (May 1966): 1-14.

A useful account of Booth's reviews by Ferdinand Cartwright Ewer, a San Francisco theatre critic befriended by Booth in his youth.

1123 _____ . "Edwin Booth's HAMLET: A New Promptbook." HARVARD LIBRARY BULLETIN 15 (January 1967): 20-48. Illus.

Shattuck describes Charles Clarke's long manuscript description of Booth's production and correlates it with Booth's 1870 promptscript. This material was later incorporated into Shattuck's THE HAMLET OF EDWIN BOOTH (below).

1124 _____ . THE HAMLET OF EDWIN BOOTH. Urbana: University of Illinois Press, 1969. 309 p. Index, illus., notes.

In an outstanding example of modern theatre scholarship, Shattuck draws upon a wealth of materials to present a detailed account of "the most famous impersonation in the history of the American theatre." Includes supplementary material on the other Booths, Lawrence Barrett, Edwin Forrest, Charles Fechter, and Modjeska.

1125 Skinner, Otis. "After Booth." THEATRE ARTS 10 (July 1926): 446-48. Illus.

Skinner describes Booth and his work in contrast to the acting of the 1920s.

1126 _____ . THE LAST TRAGEDIAN: BOOTH TELLS HIS OWN STORY. New York: Dodd, Mead, 1939. xi, 213 p. Illus.

An insightful and gracefully constructed account, Skinner having appeared in Booth's company as a young actor. Contains considerable amounts of Booth's correspondence, some of it especially revealing.

1127 Sprague, Arthur Colby. "Edwin Booth's Iago: A Study of a Great Shakespearean Actor." THEATRE ANNUAL, 1947, pp. 7-17.

A well-documented treatment which Sprague includes as Chapter 8 in his SHAKESPEAREAN PLAYERS AND PERFORMANCES (no. 246).

1128 Stedman, Edmund Clarence. "Edwin Booth." ATLANTIC 16 (May 1866): 585-93.

Gushing adulation. An introductory section describes the elder Booth, followed by a tribute to Booth as Hamlet.

1129 _____ . GENIUS AND OTHER ESSAYS. New York: Moffat, Yard, and Co., 1911. 288 p.

Sixteen essays reprinted from ATLANTIC MONTHLY, one being a reprint of no. 1128.

1130   Stoddard, Richard. "A Costume Inventory in Booth's Bankruptcy Papers." THEATRE SURVEY 16 (November 1975): 185–88.

> A list of books and costumes which Booth tried to sell in 1875.

1131   _____. "Thomas Joyce, Edwin Booth's Costumer." EDUCATIONAL THEATRE JOURNAL 22 (March 1970): 71–77.

> A well-documented account of Joyce's application of historical research to costuming Booth.

1132   Waterman, Arthur E. "The Acting of Edwin Booth." JOURNAL OF POPULAR CULTURE 3 (Fall 1969): 333–44.

> The essayist draws an interesting parallel between the development of Booth's acting and the growth of the United States.

1133   Watermeier, Daniel J., ed. BETWEEN ACTOR AND CRITIC, SELECTED LETTERS OF EDWIN BOOTH AND WILLIAM WINTER. Princeton, N.J.: Princeton University Press, 1971. ix, 316 p. Index, illus., bibliog.

> A useful volume containing 118 letters from Booth to Winter, excerpts from twenty more, and six letters from Winter to Booth. Substantial bibliography.

1134   West, E.J. "A Note on Historical Styles in American Acting: Edwin F. and Edwin B." WESTERN SPEECH JOURNAL 20 (Summer 1956): 159–66.

> An undocumented essay contrasting the styles of Booth and Edwin Forrest, seemingly drawn from traditional sources, adding little.

1135   Winter, William. "Edwin Booth." HARPER'S 63 (June 1881): 61–68. Illus.

> An adulatory essay, describing Booth's acting to a certain extent.

1136   _____. EDWIN BOOTH IN TWELVE DRAMATIC CHARACTERS. Boston: James R. Osgood and Co., 1872. n.p. Illus.

> A commemorative volume with a fifty-one page tribute by Winter and twelve black and white portraits of Booth by W.J. Hennessy. The illustrations are not widely reproduced.

1137   _____. THE EDWIN BOOTH PROMPT BOOKS. 6 vols. New York: J.H. Magonigle, 1890.

Winter replicates Booth's cuts in various scripts, but adds practically no critical comments, making the set of limited value.

1138 _____. LIFE AND ART OF EDWIN BOOTH. New York and London: Macmillan and Co., 1894. New edition, rev. Boston: Joseph Knight; New York: Macmillan, 1894. Reprint. New York: Greenwood, 1968. 437 p. Frontispiece.

Winter's treatment of Booth is based on a long friendship with the actor, but it is not completely trustworthy or objective. It contains descriptions of Booth in many of his major roles and a long series of tributes made after Booth's death. Some errors in the first edition were corrected in the revisions.

See also nos. 6, 8, 12, 19, 58, 120, 127, 130, 141, 145-46, 162-63, 165-66, 171, 176, 183, 187, 195, 200-201, 204, 210-11, 216, 219, 221-22, 231, 233, 236, 238, 242, 245, 247, 262-63, 279, 288, 291, 296, 302, 307, 315, 328, 336, 338, 341, 343, 346, 352, 358, 363, 366-68, 370, 375, 383, 386-87, 389-90, 400-404, 406-7, 413, 417, 419, 423-25, 435, 438, 454, 456, 460, 463, 466, 468, 470, 489, 507, 511, 516-18, 524, 534, 538, 548, 556-58, 566-67, 570, 572, 577-78, 584, 596, 599, 674, 774, 919, 928, 1169, 1471, 1531, 1599, 1624, 1750, 1822, 1885, 2102, 2115, 2225, 2233, 2235-36, 2239, 2337, 2443, 2461, 2585, 2591, 2599-2600, 2618, 2626, 2670, 2750, 2768, 2896, 2930, 2932, 2949, 2955, 2984, 3027, 3127, 3146, and 3185.

BOOTH, JOHN WILKES

(1839-65)

1139   Baker, L. B. "An Eyewitness Account of the Death and Burial of J. Wilkes Booth." JOURNAL OF THE ILLINOIS STATE HISTORICAL SOCIETY 39 (December 1946): 425-46. Illus.

Baker was a member of the U. S. Detective Bureau in 1865; most of this article was used as testimony during the congressional investigation, but was not printed in its entirety till this publication. His account agrees with accepted versions.

1140   Baker, Ray Stannard. "Capture, Death, and Burial of John Wilkes Booth." McCLURE'S 9 (May 1897): 574-85. Illus.

Baker was related to soldiers who directed the pursuit of Booth and the disposal of the body; this article is based on reminiscences of those men. Eventually published separately in Chicago by Richard Booker in 1940.

1141   Bates, Finis L. THE ESCAPE AND SUICIDE OF JOHN WILKES BOOTH OR THE FIRST TRUE ACCOUNT OF LINCOLN'S ASSASSINATION CONTAINING A COMPLETE CONFESSION BY BOOTH MANY YEARS AFTER THE CRIME . . . WRITTEN FOR THE CORRECTION OF HISTORY. Memphis: Historical Publishing Co., 1907. 309 p. Illus.

Bates proposes that Booth escaped into the West and died by his own hand in Enid, Oklahoma, on 14 January 1903.

1142   Beall, J. Ninian. "Why Booth Killed Lincoln." COLUMBIA HISTORICAL SOCIETY 48 (1949): 127-41. Illus.

Beall, in a paper presented to the society on 7 May 1946, describes eight theories of the assassination, concluding Booth's hatred of radical Republicanism was his chief motivation.

1143 Bishop, Jim. THE DAY LINCOLN WAS SHOT. New York: Harper and Brothers, 1955. 301 p. Index, illus., bibliog.

> A popularized account of the assassination with little biographical material on Booth or his family.

1144 Clarke, Asia Booth. THE UNLOCKED BOOK: A MEMOIR OF JOHN WILKES BOOTH. Toronto: Ryerson Press; New York: G.P. Putnam's Sons, 1938. Reprint. New York: Benjamin Blom, 1971. 205 p. Illus.

> Booth's sister wrote an understandably subjective account, but supplies many details of Booth's early life. She appends an excerpt from her LIFE OF THE ELDER BOOTH, a poem about John Wilkes Booth, clippings, and letters.

1145 Coleman, John Winston. ASSASSINATION OF PRESIDENT LINCOLN AND THE CAPTURE OF JOHN WILKES BOOTH. Lexington, Ky.: Privately printed, 1969. 10 p. Frontispiece.

> The text of a speech delivered to the Chevy Chase Coffee Club in Lexington on 10 February 1969. A brief account, adding nothing to accepted versions.

1146 Doherty, Edward P. "Pursuit and Death of John Wilkes Booth." CENTURY 39, n.s. 17 (January 1890): 443-49.

> A description of the events by two participants, the author and Major M.B. Ruggles.

1147 Ferguson, W.J. I SAW BOOTH SHOOT LINCOLN. Boston: Houghton Mifflin Co., 1930. 63 p. Illus.

> Ferguson was a call-boy at Ford's Theatre during some of Booth's engagements there and describes him, both on and off stage. Ferguson appeared as Lt. Vernon in OUR AMERICAN COUSIN and was waiting in the wings when Lincoln was murdered.

1148 Forrester, Izola. THE ONE MAD ACT, THE UNKNOWN STORY OF JOHN WILKES BOOTH AND HIS FAMILY. Boston: Hale, Cushman and Flint; Toronto: T. Allen, 1937. 494 p. Index, illus.

> Booth's granddaughter proposes that the assassin lived in exile till 1879. Controversial.

1149 French, J.M. "Was the Enid Suicide John Wilkes Booth?" NEW HAMPSHIRE 61 (September 1929): 340-49. Illus.

> French examines the evidence about this controversy (see no. 1141) and concludes the man in Enid was an imposter.

1150   George, Joseph, Jr. "The Night John Wilkes Booth Played Before
        Lincoln." LINCOLN HERALD 59 (Summer 1957): 11-15. Illus.

> George proposes that Lincoln saw Booth as Raphael in
> Selby's THE MARBLE HEART on 9 November 1863.

1151   Harvey, James R., and Harvey, Mrs. James R. "Recollections of the
        Early Theatre, As Told by Eliza Logan Burt to Mr. and Mrs. James R.
        Harvey." COLORADO MAGAZINE 17 (September 1940): 161-67.
        Illus.

> Logan is quoted as having witnessed as a child the Lincoln
> assassination and describing Booth and Laura Keene's re-
> actions at the time.

1152   Herron, Robert. "How Lincoln Died in Cincinnati." HISTORICAL AND
        PHILOSOPHICAL SOCIETY OF OHIO BULLETIN 17 (January 1959):
        19-37. Illus.

> An account of Cincinnati's reactions to the assassination,
> drawn from area newspapers between 10 April and 1 May
> 1865. Not altogether trustworthy; Junius Brutus Booth,
> Jr., is referred to as John Wilkes Booth's half-brother.

1153   Holding, Charles E. "John Wilkes Booth Stars in Nashville." TENNES-
        SEE HISTORICAL QUARTERLY 23 (March 1964): 73-79.

> Holding describes a two-week engagement by Booth in that
> city in February 1864.

1154   Jones, Thomas A. J. WILKES BOOTH: AN ACCOUNT OF HIS
        SOJOURN IN SOUTHERN MARYLAND AFTER THE ASSASSINATION
        OF ABRAHAM LINCOLN, HIS PASSAGE ACROSS THE POTOMAC,
        AND HIS DEATH IN VIRGINIA. Chicago: Laird and Leo, 1893.
        126 p. Illus.

> An extremely rare volume in which Jones, a Southern
> sympathizer, claims to have assisted Booth after the assas-
> sination, for which Jones was arrested and jailed. No
> biographical information on Booth as an actor.

1155   Jordan, Jan. DIM THE FLARING LAMPS: A NOVEL OF THE LIFE
        OF JOHN WILKES BOOTH. Englewood Cliffs, N.J.: Prentice-Hall,
        1972. vi, 282.

> A novel which the author considers "based on actual
> events" as a result of his research into Booth's life.

1156   Lane, Yoti. THE PSYCHOLOGY OF THE ACTOR. New York: John
        Day Co., 1960. 224 p.

Lane attempts to present a psychological profile of actors
in general and in chapter 16 (pp. 170-79) presents an
analysis of John Wilkes Booth. Not widely accepted.

1157 Mason, Victor Louis. "Four Lincoln Conspiracies." CENTURY 51
(April 1896): 889-911. Illus.

A speculative account of the assassination by Booth, as
well as other, unsuccessful attempts.

1158 Miller, Ernest Conrad. "John Wilkes Booth in the Pennsylvania Oil
Region." WESTERN PENNSYLVANIA HISTORICAL MAGAZINE 31
(March-June 1948): 26-47.

Booth apparently spent much of 1864 in Franklin, Pennsylvania, attempting to become a successful oil producer.
This article consists of notes from some thirty-five interviews by Louis J. Mackey.

1159 _____. JOHN WILKES BOOTH--OILMAN: A PREVIOUSLY UN-
KNOWN PART OF THE ASSASSIN'S LIFE. New York: Exposition
Press, 1947. 78 p. Illus., notes.

Miller relies heavily upon notes by Louis J. Mackey, who
was especially interested in Booth's oil speculation; an
interesting treatment of a facet of Booth's personality
usually overlooked.

1160 Mosby, John S., Jr. "The Night That Lincoln Was Shot." THEATRE
(N.Y.) 17 (June 1913): 179-80, ix. Illus.

Supposed eyewitness account, forty-eight years after the
fact.

1161 Nichols, John Benjamin. "John Wilkes Booth's Physicians." COLUM-
BIA HISTORICAL SOCIETY RECORDS 46-47 (1947): 121-30.

Brief biographical sketches of Dr. Samuel Alexander Mudd
and John Frederick May and their interactions with Booth.

1162 Norcross, A.F. "A Child's Memory of the Boston Theatre." THEATRE
(N.Y.) 43 (May 1926): 37, 72. Illus.

Superficial reminiscences, chiefly concerning Booth.

1163 Poore, Ben Perley. THE CONSPIRACY TRIAL FOR THE MURDER OF
THE PRESIDENT AND THE ATTEMPT TO OVERTHROW THE GOVERN-
MENT BY THE ASSASSINATION OF ITS PRINCIPAL OFFICERS. Boston:
J.E. Tilton and Co., 1865. 552 p.

A lengthy account of the trial, with considerable discussion of Booth and his background. Useful.

1164 Russell, Pamela Redford. THE WOMAN WHO LOVED JOHN WILKES BOOTH. New York: G.P. Putnam's Sons, 1978. 379 p.

A novel depicting the relationship between Booth and Mary E. Surratt. Romantically sentimental, although perhaps stimulated by some research.

1165 Shepherd, William G. "Shattering the Myth of John Wilkes Booth's Escape." HARPER'S 149 (November 1924): 702-19. Illus.

An attempt to end the ongoing legend that Booth escaped into Oklahoma and died there many years after the murder.

1166 Stern, Philip Van Doren. THE MAN WHO KILLED LINCOLN: THE STORY OF JOHN WILKES BOOTH AND HIS PART IN THE ASSASSI-NATION. New York: Literary Guild of America, 1939. 408 p. Illus., bibliog.

A substantial volume, concerned only with the events surrounding the assassination with only a few references to Booth's career in the theatre.

1167 Townsend, George Alfred. "How Wilkes Booth Crossed the Potomac." CENTURY n.s. 5 (November 1883-April 1884): 822-32.

Speculation on the aftermath of the assassination and Booth's attempted escape.

1168 _____. THE LIFE, CRIME AND CAPTURE OF JOHN WILKES BOOTH WITH A FULL SKETCH OF THE CONSPIRACY OF WHICH HE WAS THE LEADER, AND THE PURSUIT, TRIAL AND EXECUTION OF HIS AC-COMPLICES. New York: Dick and Fitzgerald, 1865. 80 p. Illus.

The publication of a series of letters by Townsend to the New York WORLD concerning his perceptions of the assassination. Very little relates to Booth's career in the theatre.

1169 Wilson, Francis. JOHN WILKES BOOTH: FACT AND FICTION OF LINCOLN'S ASSASSINATION. Boston and New York: Houghton Mifflin Co., 1929. 311 p. Index, illus.

A detailed account of the assassination, preceded by a brief account of Booth's earlier life and career, with some material on Edwin Booth. Superseded by Kimmel (no. 1032), but still of interest.

See also nos. 131, 185, 222, 308, 400, 407, 413, 570, 1073, 1094, 1750, 2294, 2618, 2622, 2782, and 2937.

BOOTH, JUNIUS BRUTUS, SR.

(1796-1852)

1170 THE ACTOR; OR, A PEEP BEHIND THE CURTAIN. BEING PASSAGES
IN THE LIVES OF BOOTH AND SOME OF HIS CONTEMPORARIES.
New York: William H. Graham, 1846. xi, 180 p.

> This anonymously written biography is at variance with
> accepted scholarship on several important aspects of Booth's
> career and life. Incidental coverage and descriptions of
> Thomas Hamblin, William Mitchell, Charlotte Cushman,
> and Edwin Forrest.

1171 Aldrich, Thomas Bailey. "Poor Yorick." CENTURY 66 (September
1903): 710-11.

> A brief anecdote about the origins of a skull used by
> Booth as Hamlet.

1172 Booth, Junius Brutus. MEMOIRS OF JUNIUS BRUTUS BOOTH, FROM
HIS BIRTH TO THE PRESENT TIME; WITH AN APPENDIX, CONTAINING
ORIGINAL LETTERS FROM PERSONS OF RANK AND CELEBRITY; AND
COPIOUS EXTRACTS FROM THE JOURNAL, KEPT BY MR. BOOTH,
DURING HIS THEATRICAL TOUR OF THE CONTINENT. London:
Chapple, Miller, Rowden, and E. Wilson, 1817. vii, 86 p.

> Verified in the NATIONAL UNION CATALOG, but un-
> available for examination. A journal kept by Booth on
> his early tour of the continent is held by the Players Club
> in New York.

1173 Clarke, Asia Booth. BOOTH MEMORIALS: PASSAGES, INCIDENTS
AND ANECDOTES IN THE LIFE OF JUNIUS BRUTUS BOOTH. New
York: Carleton Publishers, 1886. xii, 184 p. Frontispiece.

> According to Moses in FAMOUS ACTOR-FAMILIES, a
> fuller account than the edition in 1882, this edition con-
> taining a memorandum of Booth's 1814 voyage to Holland

and an appendix of old playbills. Admittedly prejudicial, this account by Booth's daughter is in error as to his marital relation to Mary Anne Holmes.

1174 Dickens, Charles, ed. "A Gentleman of the Name of Booth." ALL THE YEAR ROUND 36, n.s. 16 (8 April 1876): 77-84.

An anonymous article describing Thomas R. Gould's THE TRAGEDIAN (below) and speculating upon Booth's rank as an actor. A bit condescending and chauvinistic.

1175 Gould, Thos. Ridgeway. THE TRAGEDIAN: AN ESSAY ON THE HISTRIONIC GENIUS OF JUNIUS BRUTUS BOOTH. New York: Hurd and Houghton, 1868. 190 p. Frontispiece. Reprint. New York: Benjamin Blom, 1969.

Writing in a turgid nineteenth-century style, Gould presents a thirty-six page biographical sketch of Booth, then analyzes many of his leading roles in a series of short essays. Requires corroboration.

1176 Hazlitt, William. THE COLLECTED WORKS OF WILLIAM HAZLITT. Edited by Alfred Rayney Waller and Arnold Glover. 12 vols. New York: McClure, Phillips; London: J.M. Dent and Co., 1903.

Included in volume 8, Section 2, "A View of the English Stage," are three critical essays on the elder Booth as the Duke of Gloucester, Iago, and Richard III, pages 354-58.

1177 MEMOIRS OF THE LIFE OF MR. BOOTH, CONTAINING A TRUE STATEMENT OF ALL THE CIRCUMSTANCES ATTENDING HIS ENGAGEMENTS AT THE RIVAL THEATRES, WITH A FEW REMARKS UPON HIS CONDUCT, BY AN OLD ACTOR. London: Printed for T. Keys, [1817]. 27 p.

Very early memoirs, chiefly concerned with Booth's rivalry with Edmund Kean following Booth's provincial success.

1178 Pray, Isaac C. "The Elder Booth." GALAXY 2 (15 September 1866): 158-63.

The author uses a review of Clarke's BOOTH MEMORIALS (1866) as an opportunity to assess the elder Booth's rank as an actor.

1179 Rourke, Constance. THE ROOTS OF AMERICAN CULTURE AND OTHER ESSAYS. New York: Harcourt, Brace and Co., 1942. xii, 296 p. Index.

Includes a long essay, "The Rise of Theatricals," with a section on Booth (pp. 141-60). A useful overview.

1180   Ryan, Thomas. RECOLLECTIONS OF AN OLD MUSICIAN. New York:
        E.P. Dutton and Co., 1899. xvi, 274 p. Illus.

> A musician's memoirs about a long career in America, in-
> cluding reminiscences about the elder Booth and John
> Brougham. Of minor value.

1181   Sage, Abby. "The Hamlets of the Stage." ATLANTIC 23-24 (June
        1869-August 1869): 665-75, 188-98.

> After surveying English actors in the role, Sage devotes
> a few pages to the elder Booth, but omits Edwin Booth
> to save space. Several personal items about the Booths
> appear to be in error.

1182   Wilson, Calvin Dill. "Through an Old Southern County (Belair)."
        NEW ENGLAND MAGAZINE n.s. 20 (April 1899): 161-76. Illus.

> Some description of the elder Booth's home in Harford
> County, Maryland.

See also nos. 36, 101, 120-21, 130, 146, 204, 211, 217, 221-22, 231-32,
244-46, 248, 250, 281, 292, 296, 338, 341, 353, 356, 358, 363, 366-
67, 371, 396, 402, 405, 407, 413, 423, 435, 456, 468, 489, 502, 517, 520,
524, 551, 572, 1078, 1085, 1094, 1128, 1822, 1993, 2235-36, 2348, 2670,
2920, 2939, 2954, 2958, and 3193.

BOUCICAULT, DION
(1822-90)

1183 Appleton, William W. MADAME VESTRIS AND THE LONDON STAGE. New York and London: Columbia University Press, 1974. x, 221 p. Index, illus., bibliog.

> An outstanding biography which contains an account of Boucicault and his relationship with Vestris when she produced his LONDON ASSURANCE.

1184 Archer, William. ENGLISH DRAMATISTS OF TODAY. London: Sampson Low, Marston, Searle, and Rivington, 1882. 380 p. Illus.

> Archer treats Boucicault on pages 41-48 of the first chapter, "Playwrights of Yesterday," focusing upon his dramaturgy rather than his acting.

1185 Boucicault, Dionysus. THE ART OF ACTING. Introduction by Otis Skinner. Notes by Brander Matthews. New York: Columbia University Press, 1926. 63 p.

> After a fifteen-page introduction on the profession of acting, the transcript of a pragmatic speech by Boucicault on the subject completes the volume.

1186 _____. "The Art of Dramatic Composition." NORTH AMERICAN RE-VIEW 126 (January-February 1878): 40-52.

> Boucicault's theories of playwriting, useful as a historical document on the subject.

1187 _____. "At the Goethe Society." NORTH AMERICAN REVIEW 148 (March 1889): 335-43.

> Boucicault describes a debate on "The Influence of the Newspaper upon Art," held at the Goethe Society, the author speaking in opposition to newspaper criticism of theatrical productions.

1188 _____ . "Coquelin and Hading." NORTH AMERICAN REVIEW 147 (November 1888): 581-83.

> Brief remarks on the ability of the two French stars, then touring the United States for the first time. He also contrasts French and Anglo-American acting styles.

1189 _____ . "Coquelin-Irving." NORTH AMERICAN REVIEW 145 (August 1887): 158-61.

> Boucicault's response to the famous paper debate between the French and English stars on the role of emotion in acting.

1190 _____ . "The Debut of a Dramatist." NORTH AMERICAN REVIEW 148 (April 1889): 454-63; "Early Days of a Dramatist." 148 (May 1889): 584-93; "Leaves from a Dramatist's Diary." 149 (August 1889): 228-36.

> The combined articles form something of an idealized and untrustworthy autobiography.

1191 _____ . "The Decline and Fall of the Press." NORTH AMERICAN REVIEW 145 (July 1887): 32-39.

> Boucicault attacks the newspaper critics, citing various specific examples of their injustices to the theatre.

1192 _____ . "The Decline of the Drama, An Epistle to Cxxxxx Rxxxe from Dion Boucicault." NORTH AMERICAN REVIEW 125 (September 1877): 235-45.

> Perhaps directed to Charles Reade, the article primarily concerns Boucicault's difficulty in earning a living.

1193 _____ . "The Future of American Drama." ARENA 2 (November 1890): 641-52.

> Boucicault posits the United States has no drama, but that a topical and utilitarian drama was emerging and would succeed.

1194 _____ . "Mutilation of Shakespeare; The Poet Interviewed." NORTH AMERICAN REVIEW 148 (February 1889): 266-68.

> A brief essay in which the author imagines Shakespeare taking umbrage at the alterations of his scripts by actor-managers of the time.

1195 _____. "My Pupils." NORTH AMERICAN REVIEW 147 (October 1888): 435–40.

Concerns Boucicault's work in both acting and dramaturgy.

1196 _____. "Opera." NORTH AMERICAN REVIEW 144 (April 1887): 340–48.

Boucicault describes opera as having nothing to do with the drama, nor opera singers with acting.

1197 _____. "Parnell and the TIMES." NORTH AMERICAN REVIEW 144 (June 1887): 648–49.

Boucicault's observations about a political dispute triggered by a controversial letter to the London TIMES.

1198 _____. "Shakespeare's Influence on the Drama." NORTH AMERICAN REVIEW 147 (December 1888): 680–85.

Vague and rambling remarks, of minimal interest.

1199 _____. "Spots on the Sun." ARENA 1 (December 1889): 131–40.

Boucicault, claiming to take the lead of Ben Jonson, discourses on the dramatistic shortcomings of Shakespeare.

1200 _____. THE STORY OF IRELAND. Boston: James R. Osgood and Co., 1881. 24 p.

A brief history of Ireland, decrying England's occupation.

1201 _____. "Theatres, Halls, and Audiences." NORTH AMERICAN REVIEW 149 (October 1889): 429–36.

Recollections of various theatres in which Boucicault had worked and speculations upon the effect of architecture on acting.

1202 Calthrop, Christopher. "Dion Boucicault and Benjamin Webster." THEATRE NOTEBOOK 32, no. 1 (1978): 28–32.

Calthrop describes the controversies surrounding the first production of THE COLLEEN BAWN.

1203 Casamajor, George H. "Beauty on the London Stage." COSMOPOLITAN 31 (October 1901): 574–83.

Boucicault's daughter, Nina, is one of the beauties described by Casamajor.

1204   Chinoy, Helen Krich. "The Profession and the Art: Directing in America, 1860-1920." In THE AMERICAN THEATRE: A SUM OF ITS PARTS, edited by Henry B. Williams, pp. 125-51. New York: Samuel French, 1971. Bibliog.

>Chinoy's essay includes a description of Boucicault's contributions to the profession.

1205   Coleman, John. CHARLES READE AS I KNEW HIM. London: Treherne and Co., 1903. 422 p. Index, Illus.

>Some passing references to the London careers of Boucicault and Agnes Robertson, Boucicault's wife.

1206   Dalton, Frank. "Small-Change and Boucicault." DUBLIN MAGAZINE 1 (November 1923): 280-85.

>An essay on Boucicault's early schooling in Dublin and his ability as a stage manager.

1207   Degen, John A. "How To End THE OCTOROON." EDUCATIONAL THEATRE JOURNAL 27 (May 1975): 170-78.

>Degen addresses the problem of the multiple versions of Boucicault's script.

1208   "Dion Boucicault." ONCE A WEEK 26 (11 May 1872): 430-31. Illus.

>A brief overview of Boucicault's career, minimally informative.

1209   Faulkner, Seldon. "The Octoroon War." EDUCATIONAL THEATRE JOURNAL 15 (March 1963): 33-38.

>A description of the circumstances surrounding the opening of Boucicault's controversial script, taken from the dramatist's point of view.

1210   Fawkes, Richard. DION BOUCICAULT: A BIOGRAPHY. Foreword by Donald Sinden. London, Melbourne, and New York: Quartet Books, 1979. xviii, 266 p. Index, illus., bibliog., notes.

>A somewhat adulatory treatment, Fawkes considering his subject "the greatest dramatist of the Victorian Age." Based in part on private papers and materials recently acquired by Christopher Calthrop, the playwright's great-grandson.

1211   Ford, James L. "Rip Van Winkle." MUNSEY'S 35 (April 1906): 72-75.

>Describes how Boucicault came to write the script.

1212   Harrison, A. Cleveland. "Boucicault on Dramatic Action: His Confirmation of the POETICS." QUARTERLY JOURNAL OF SPEECH 56 (February 1970): 45-53.

        Draws upon Boucicault's articles in the NORTH AMERICAN REVIEW to describe his requirements for dramatic literature.

1213   _____. "Boucicault on Dramatic Character." SOUTHERN SPEECH JOURNAL 37 (Fall 1971): 73-83.

        Harrison posits that Boucicault's early successes with character development foreshadowed the twentieth-century "mood play."

1214   _____. "Boucicault's Formula: Illusion Equals Pleasure." EDUCATIONAL THEATRE JOURNAL 21 (October 1969): 299-309.

        A description of Boucicault's aesthetic of dramaturgy as he described it.

1215   Hogan, Robert [Goode]. DION BOUCICAULT. New York: Twayne Publisher, 1969. 139 p. Index, bibliog.

        A scholarly biography focused upon Boucicault as a playwright, but covering all aspects of his career. Impressive bibliography and documentation; includes a complete list of Boucicault's dramas.

1216   Johnson, Albert. "The Birth of Dion Boucicault." MODERN DRAMA 11 (September 1968): 157-63.

        Speculation based on newly discovered evidence concerning Boucicault's parentage and birth.

1217   _____. "Dion Boucicault Learns to Act." PLAYERS 48 (December-January 1973): 78-85. Illus.

        A useful and well-documented account of Boucicault's early career.

1218   _____. "Fabulous Boucicault." THEATRE ARTS 37 (March 1953): 26-30, 90-93. Illus.

        Johnson outlines the highlights of Boucicault's career without documentation, describing him as a total man of the theatre who enjoyed unusual success.

1219   _____. "Real Sunlight in the Garden: Dion Boucicault as a Stage Director." THEATRE RESEARCH 12, no. 2 (1972): 119-25.

        A brief description of Boucicault's directorial and scenic techniques, drawn from traditional sources.

1220 Kavanagh, P. IRISH THEATRE: BEING A HISTORY OF THE DRAMA IN IRELAND FROM THE EARLIEST PERIOD TO THE PRESENT DAY. Tralee, Ire.: Kerryman, 1946. 465 p. Index, illus., bibliog.

A useful history, in which part 5 of chapter 3 is devoted to a brief description of Boucicault's career.

1221 Kenney, Charles Lamb. THE CAREER OF DION BOUCICAULT. New York: Graphic Co., n.d.

Unavailable for examination. Boucicault's third wife, Louise Thorndyke, is said to have maintained that Dion Boucicault wrote the volume himself.

1222 Krause, David, ed. THE DOLMEN BOUCICAULT. Chester Springs, Pa.: Durfour Editions, 1965. 253 p. Illus., bibliog.

An anthology consisting of THE COLLEEN BAWN, ARRAH NA POGUE, and THE SHAUGHRAUN. The editor includes his essay, "The Theatre of Dion Boucicault: A Short View of His Life and Art," (pp. 9-47) focused on his scripts.

1223 Entry deleted.

1224 MacQueen-Pope, Walter James. GAIETY: THEATRE OF ENCHANTMENT. London: Greenberg, in association with W.H. Allen, n.d. 481 p. Index, illus.

A history of the Gaiety Theatre in London, in which the author gives considerable attention to Boucicault and his impact and influence upon the London stage.

1225 Mathews, Charles James. THE LIFE OF CHARLES JAMES MATHEWS CHIEFLY AUTOBIOGRAPHICAL WITH SELECTIONS FROM HIS CORRESPONDENCE AND SPEECHES. Edited by Charles Dickens. 2 vols. London: Macmillan and Co., 1879. Index, frontispieces.

Some detailed remarks on the premiere of Boucicault's LONDON ASSURANCE.

1226 "Mr. Dion Boucicault on Himself." THEATRE (Engl.) 3 (November 1879): 186-88.

An anonymous essayist flays Boucicault for his self-esteem, calling him "ludicrous and contemptible."

1227   Morris, Clara. "A Memory of Dion Boucicault." COSMOPOLITAN 38 (January 1905): 273-78. Illus.

The actress describes meeting Boucicault backstage after having appeared in several of his scripts.

1228   Morris, Constance. "Dion Boucicault's School of Acting." GREEN BOOK ALBUM 6 (August 1911): 401-7.

The actress describes taking acting classes from Boucicault.

1229   Moses, Montrose J. THE AMERICAN DRAMATIST. Boston: Little, Brown and Co., 1925. xviii, 459 p. Index, illus., bibliog.

Moses focuses on Boucicault's dramaturgy in depth and includes a substantial bibliography.

1230   Nicoll, Allardyce. A HISTORY OF ENGLISH DRAMA, 1660-1900. 5 vols. Cambridge, Mass.: Cambridge University Press, 1965.

In volume 4, Nicoll discusses Boucicault's early work on pages 188-90 and lists his early scripts on pages 269-70. In volume 5, he offers a positive assessment of his later dramaturgy and lists his remaining scripts on pages 267-69 and 779.

1231   Pemberton, T. Edgar. CHARLES DICKENS AND THE STAGE: A RECORD OF HIS CONNECTION WITH THE DRAMA AS PLAYWRIGHT, ACTOR, AND CRITIC. London: George Redway, 1888. 254 p.

Pemberton quotes Dickens as he discusses several of the major actors of his period, among them Boucicault and Charles Fechter.

1232   Rahill, Frank. "Dion Boucicault and Royalty Payments for Playwrights." THEATRE ARTS 23 (November 1939): 807-13.

Rahill describes Boucicault's considerable contributions to the U.S. playwrights' economic gains in the nineteenth century.

1233   Reade, Charles L. READIANA: COMMENTS ON CURRENT EVENTS. London: Chatto and Windus, 1886. 359 p.

Contains a long discussion of stage copyrights in which Boucicault figures prominently with a description of plagiarism in the theatre.

1234   Reade, Charles L., and Reade, Rev. Compton. CHARLES READE, DRAMATIST, NOVELIST, JOURNALIST: A MEMOIR COMPILED CHIEFLY

FROM HIS LITERARY REMAINS. 2 vols. London: Chapman and Hall, 1887.

Contains many passing references to Boucicault as a playwright.

1235 Roman, Diane P., and Hamilton, Mary T. "Boucicault and the Anne Jordan Affair." JOURNAL OF IRISH LITERATURE 1, no. 2 (1972): 120-27.

A brief account, drawing mainly upon published documents, of a farcical and scandalous trial involving Boucicault.

1236 Rossman, Kenneth R. "The Irish in American Drama in the Mid-Nineteenth Century." NEW YORK HISTORY 21 (January 1940): 39-53. Illus.

The text of a paper read before the New York State Historical Association on 28 September 1939. Rossman describes and evaluates the contributions of Boucicault and John Brougham, considering both men positive cultural forces of their time.

1237 Rowell, George. THE VICTORIAN THEATRE, 1792-1914: A SURVEY. London: Oxford University Press, 1956; New York and Melbourne, 1978. xiii, 196 p. Index, illus., bibliog.

Includes a brief discussion (pp. 54-57) of Boucicault as a dramatist.

1238 Scott, Genio C. "Mr. Dion Boucicault." SPIRIT OF THE TIMES 5 (1 February 1862): 339-40.

A substantial account of the premiere and early productions of LONDON ASSURANCE.

1239 Vanbrugh, Irene. TO TELL MY STORY. London: Hutchinson and Co., n.d. 210 p. Index, illus.

The author was Boucicault's daughter-in-law and includes several references to him, although she never met him.

1240 Voegele, M. "Our Omnibus-Box." THEATRE (Engl.) o.s. 13, n.s. 4 (1 September 1884): 16 152-55.

A brief article in which Boucicault is taken vigorously to task for living in the United States and for calling London "dirty and worn out."

1241 Walsh, Townsend. THE CAREER OF DION BOUCICAULT. New York:

Dunlap Society, 1915. xviii, 224 p. Illus. Reprint. New York: Benjamin Blom, 1967.

> A balanced, albeit undocumented, account of Boucicault's fluctuating career as a dramatist and actor, cóntaining a chronological list of his dramatic works. Later scholars have suggested this work contains several errors of fact.

1242   Watson, Ernest Bradlee. SHERIDAN TO ROBERTSON: A STUDY OF THE NINETEENTH CENTURY LONDON STAGE. Cambridge, Mass.: Harvard University Press, 1926. xi, 455 p. Index, illus., bibliog. Reprint. New York: Benjamin Blom, 1963.

> A reasonably documented account in which Boucicault and Charles Fechter are each allotted a chapter.

1243   Wheeler, A.C. "Dion Boucicault." ARENA 3 (December 1890): 47-60.

> An assessment of Boucicault's dramaturgy by a leading critic, written in a somewhat obscure style.

See also nos. 21, 118-19, 130, 156, 162-64, 183, 199, 203, 208, 211, 214, 227, 233, 236, 248, 255, 262-63, 271, 291, 296, 299-300, 313, 327-28, 334, 336, 338, 341, 345, 347, 358, 365, 398, 402, 417, 433, 507, 519, 521-23, 526, 531, 557-58, 562, 585, 588, 590, 593, 674, 1750, 2235-36, 2569, 2599-2600, 2617, 2984, 3027, and 3140.

BRADY, ALICE

(1892-1939)

1244   "Alice in Stageland." COSMOPOLITAN 57 (October 1914): 702-3. Illus.

       Fan-oriented puffery about Brady's sudden success.

1245   Brady, Alice. "This Business of Dressing." GREEN BOOK MAGAZINE 14 (September 1915): 484-90. Illus.

       Fashion notes.

1246   _____. "Movies and Mummers." DRAMA (Chicago) 14 (November 1923): 46-47. Illus.

       Brady compares the stage to the cinema and finds various virtues to both.

1247   _____. "Sorry, You're Not the Type!" THEATRE (N.Y.) 50 (December 1929): 30, 78. Illus.

       Brady recalls her experiences with type casting and expresses her preference for repertory companies.

1248   _____. "Youth and the Stage." WOMAN'S HOME COMPANION 41 (November 1914): 22. Illus.

       Includes a few biographical notes in a description of the uses of children on the stage.

1249   Fletcher, Adele Whitely. "Alice the Efficient." MOTION PICTURE MAGAZINE 20 (August 1920): 32-33, 95. Illus.

       Fletcher admiringly describes Brady's skills at managing her time while pursuing a hectic schedule.

1250   Hall, Gladys. "No Young Generation is Knocking at the Door." MOTION PICTURE MAGAZINE 24 (October 1922): 24-25, 103. Illus.

Brady is quoted as speculating on the future of the film
industry and film acting.

1251   Randolph, Ann. "A Paradoxical Person." NATIONAL MAGAZINE
        41 (December 1914): 464-65. Illus.

        Randolph describes Brady as a well-balanced, normal
        American girl who is also young, pretty, and fascinating,
        which Randolph considers a paradox.

See also nos. 9, 13, 276, 469, 498, 508, 532, and 544.

BROUGHAM, JOHN
(1810-80)

1252   Brougham, John. A BASKET OF CHIPS. New York: Bunce and Brother, 1855. vi, 407 p. Frontispiece.

> A collection of humorous essays, including "Every-Day Drama--The Pigeon and the Hawks" (pp. 143-47) and "Dramas of the Day--Revenge; or, The Medium" (pp. 191-99).

1253   _____. HUMOROUS STORIES. New York: Derby and Jackson, 1857. viii, 298 p. Illus.

> An alternate title page reads THE BUNSBURY PAPERS. IRISH ECHOES BY JOHN BROUGHAM. The volume consists of nine Irish short stories of varying length, none apparently dealing with theatrical subjects.

1254   Hawes, David S. "John Brougham as Playwright." EDUCATIONAL THEATRE JOURNAL 9 (October 1957): 184-93.

> An insightful examination of Brougham's career as a playwright.

1255   LOTOS LEAVES. ORIGINAL STORIES, ESSAYS AND POEMS BY THE GREAT WRITERS OF AMERICA AND ENGLAND: MARK TWAIN, WILKIE COLLINS, PETROLEUM V. NASBY, WHITELAW REID, ALFRED TENNYSON, JOHN HAY, AND OTHERS. Edited by John Brougham and John Elderkin. Boston: W.F. Gill and Co.; London: Chatto and Windus, 1875. xv, 411 p. Illus.

> Among the stories is Brougham's "Fairy Gold" (pp. 115-27). The profits from this volume were to be donated to the American Dramatic Fund, according to the editors' preface.

1256   Plotnicki, Rita. "John Brougham: The Aristophanes of American Burlesque." JOURNAL OF POPULAR CULTURE 12 (Winter 1978): 422-31.

Plotnicki treats Brougham exclusively as a playwright, using synopses and quotations from his scripts. She considers Brougham's work the best of the nineteenth-century burlesques and extravaganzas.

1257 Ryan, Pat M., Jr. "John Brougham: The Gentle Satirist, A Critique with a Handlist and Census." BULLETIN OF THE NEW YORK PUBLIC LIBRARY 63 (December 1959): 619-40.

Ryan devotes ten pages to a biographical treatment of Brougham, then lists his complete output as a playwright.

1258 Winter, William, ed. LIFE, STORIES, AND POEMS OF JOHN BROUGHAM, COMPRISING: I. HIS AUTOBIOGRAPHY--A FRAGMENT. II. A SUPPLEMENTARY MEMOIR. III. SKETCH OF HIS CLUB LIFE. IV. SELECTIONS FROM HIS MISCELLANEOUS WRITINGS. Boston: James R. Osgood and Co., 1881. x, 461. Illus.

Winter includes Brougham's incomplete autobiography and adds a supplementary memoir. Various testimonials are included as well.

See also nos. 21, 197, 211-12, 222, 313, 319, 339, 341, 356, 375, 396, 401-2, 405, 408, 413, 450, 475, 519, 1180, 1236, 2235-36, and 2782.

BURKE, BILLIE

(1885-1970)

1259   Burke, Billie. "Billie Burke Remembers." DELINEATOR 104 (May 1924): 10-11, 84; (June 1924): 12-13, 78. Illus.

An early autobiographical sketch containing much material on Burke's stage career. Corroboration is advised.

1260   _____. "The High Purpose of the American Stage." DRAMA (Chicago) 12 (April 1922): 230-32. Illus.

A short essay in which Burke calls for a rededication to theatrical ideals.

1261   _____. "How the Red-Haired Woman Should Dress." GREEN BOOK MAGAZINE 12 (July 1914): 21-28. Illus.

Fashion advice from the actress.

1262   _____. "On Acting and Babies." AMERICAN MAGAZINE 86 (August 1918): 58-59. Illus.

Burke describes the difficulties of maintaining a family and a career simultaneously.

1263   _____. "Personal Reminiscences." THEATRE (N. Y.) 24 (September 1916): 122-25. Illus.

A well-illustrated article outlining Burke's career to that time.

1264   _____. "Saved from Anglophobia." GREEN BOOK ALBUM 3 (March 1910): 543-46.

Burke recalls living in London during her teen-age years, succeeding there as a performer, and then being accepted in the United States.

1265   . "Under My Own Vine and Fig Tree." HARPER'S BAZAAR
48 (August 1913): 19, 45. Illus.

> Burke describes her country home near New York.

1266   . "Your Daughter on the Stage--Why Not?" THEATRE (N.Y.)
51 (February 1930): 30, 60. Illus.

> Burke proposes that the theatre is no more morally danger-
> ous than any other profession.

1267   Burke, Billie, and Lackaye, Wilton. "Do Players Seldom Marry?"
THEATRE (N.Y.) 26 (September 1917): 144, 146.

> A pair of articles, Burke suggesting love will find a way
> and Lackaye suggesting that performers should only marry
> performers.

1268   Burke, Billie, with Cameron Shipp. WITH A FEATHER ON MY NOSE.
New York: Appleton-Century-Crofts, 1949. 268 p. Index, illus.

> A chatty, idealized, and superficial autobiography, con-
> taining a complete list of Burke's roles. Frequent mention
> of John Drew, the Barrymores, Charles Frohman, and
> Burke's husband, Florence Ziegfeld.

1269   "Burkeley Crest." THEATRE (N.Y.) 34 (September 1921): 186-87.
Illus.

> A pictorial entry on Burke's home.

1270   Calhoun, Dorothy. "A Vale of Tears." MOTION PICTURE MAGA-
ZINE 49 (March 1935): 51, 71. Illus.

> Burke recalls the difficulty she had assisting the producers
> of the film, THE GREAT ZIEGFELD.

1271   "Charming Billie." COSMOPOLITAN 55 (July 1913): 263-64. Illus.

> Fan-oriented puffery, in part considering the advisability
> of marriage for actresses.

1272   Cole, Celia Caroline. "Topknots and Souls." DELINEATOR 97
(September 1920): 30, 57. Illus.

> Rambling remarks from an interview with Burke about her
> life-style and health habits.

1273   Courtlandt, Roberta. "Billie Burke at Home." MOTION PICTURE
MAGAZINE 13 (April 1917): 91-94, 158. Illus.

Primarily a description of the architecture of Burke's
Hollywood home.

1274   Dale, Alan. [Pseud.] "Billie Burke, Comedienne." COSMOPOLITAN 56
(May 1914): 842-44. Illus.

A very brief and flimsy interview of minimal value.

1275   _____. "Bonnie Billie Burke." COSMOPOLITAN 52 (February 1912):
412-18. Illus.

A superficial article, praising Burke's charm and quoting
her light banter with the interviewer.

1276   Farnsworth, Marjorie. THE ZIEGFELD FOLLIES. Introduction by Billie
Burke. London: Peter Davies, 1956. 189 p. Index, illus., appendixes.

Burke wrote an introduction for this history of the Follies,
in which her own career is described but not documented.

1277   Hall, Gladys. "Piquancy and Practicality Blend in Billie Burke." MO-
TION PICTURE MAGAZINE 18 (September 1919): 52-53, 110. Illus.

A few biographical details in an otherwise pointless interview.

1278   "The Nursery in Her Home at Hastings-on-Hudson." HOUSE AND
GARDEN 35 (April 1919): 35. Illus.

Illustration's of interior decoration in Burke's house.

1279   Patterson, Ada. "At Home with Billie Burke." GREEN BOOK ALBUM
5 (May 1911): 961-66.

A chatty and frivolous interview of minimal worth.

1280   _____. "The Lady of Burkeleigh Crest." THEATRE (N.Y.) 17
(January 1913): 28-30. Illus.

More descriptive of Burke's home in Hastings-on-Hudson
than of the actress.

1281   _____. "A Sunday Morning Chat with Billie Burke." THEATRE (N.Y.)
8 (November 1908): 300-304. Illus.

An inconsequential and rambling interview.

1282   Shipp, Cameron. "Billie Burke--Her Story." COLLIER'S 122 (25
September 1948): 18-19, 73-74, 76, 78; (2 October 1948): 19, 38,
41-42; (9 October 1948): 28, 66-69. Illus.

A serialization of no. 1268.

1283   Walsh, Townsend. "Billie Burke's Clever Father." THEATRE (N.Y.)
       22 (September 1915): 138. Illus.

       Townsend traces the career of Burke's father, a successful
       circus clown.

1284   Wolf, Rennold. "Billie Burke, Married and at Home." GREEN BOOK
       MAGAZINE 12 (November 1914): 843-54. Illus.

       A description of the domestic tranquility at Ziegfeld's
       estate, Burkeley Crest.

1285   [X.] "Billie Burke--John Drew's New Leading Woman." THEATRE
       (N.Y.) 7 (September 1907): 230.

       A very brief biographical sketch shortly after Burke began
       to attract attention as an actress.

See also nos. 9, 270, 276, 354, 444, 464, 509, 542, 635, and 1981.

BURTON, WILLIAM EVANS

(1804-60)

1286   Burton, William Evans, ed. BURTON'S COMIC SONGSTER; BEING
ENTIRELY A NEW COLLECTION OF ORIGINAL AND POPULAR
SONGS, AS SUNG BY MR. BURTON, MR. TYRONE POWER, MR.
JOHN REEVE, MR. HADAWAY, ETC. ETC. Philadelphia: James Kay,
Jun. and Brother; Pittsburgh: John I. Kay and Co., 1837. 320 p.
Philadelphia: Kay and Troutman, 1846.

A substantial collection of song lyrics.

1287   _____. BURTON'S GENTLEMAN'S MAGAZINE AND AMERICAN
MONTHLY REVIEW. Philadelphia: Vols. 1-7; July 1837-December
1840.

A general magazine, for a time edited by Edgar Allan
Poe. Burton's "A Cape Codder among the Mermaids"
is included in the issue for December 1839 on pages
287-92. Volume 6 (1840): 59-62 contains Burton's
recollections of George Vandenhoff, as volume 4 (1839):
9-16 does of James W. Wallack. The entire run is included on reel 311 of the American Periodical Series.

1288   _____. THE CYCLOPAEDIA OF WIT AND HUMOR: CONTAINING
CHOICE AND CHARACTERISTIC SELECTIONS FROM THE WRITINGS
OF THE MOST EMINENT HUMORISTS OF AMERICA, IRELAND,
SCOTLAND, AND ENGLAND. ILLUSTRATED WITH PORTRAITS ON
STEEL, AND MANY HUNDRED WOOD ENGRAVINGS. New York:
Appleton and Co., 1870. xii, 1,124 p. Indexes, illus.

An enormous compendium of literary humor, divided by
nationality. Works by Burton and Sol Smith are included.
According to the NATIONAL UNION CATALOG, this
work went through seventeen editions.

1289   _____. THE LITERARY SOUVENIR, A CHRISTMAS AND NEW YEAR'S
PRESENT FOR 1838, 1840, 1844-45. Philadelphia: E.L. Carey and
A. Hart, 1838-45.

An irregular serial, edited by Burton, composed of various literary forms: poetry, essays, short stories, and others. Rarely does the material relate to the theatre.

1290 _____. WAGGERIES AND VAGARIES. A SERIES OF SKETCHES, HUMOROUS AND DESCRIPTIVE. Philadelphia: Carey and Hart, 1848. 192 p. Illus.

A series of humorous "articles," many written in Yankee dialogue and illustrative of that character's thoughts on various subjects.

1291 _____. THE YANKEE AMONG THE MERMAIDS AND OTHER WAG-GERIES AND VAGARIES. Philadelphia: T.B. Peterson, 1843. 192 p. Illus.

Humorous monologues on various subjects, including the Yankee character.

1292 Keese, William L. WILLIAM E. BURTON: A SKETCH OF HIS CAREER OTHER THAN THAT OF ACTOR, WITH GLIMPSES OF HIS HOME LIFE, AND EXTRACTS FROM HIS THEATRICAL JOURNAL. New York: Dunlap Society, 1891. Reprint. New York: Burt Franklin, 1970. 56 p. Illus.

A brief analysis of Burton, valuable for the appended extracts more than for biographical treatment.

See also nos. 197, 222, 245, 312, 341, 356, 363, 383, 396, 413, 433, 488, 570, 583, 2235-36, 2920, 3133, and 3168.

CAHILL, MARIE

(1870-1923)

1293   Cahill, Marie. "If I Had Alladin's Lamp." GREEN BOOK ALBUM
        1 (May 1909): 1100-05.

> Cahill expresses her desire for authors and composers to
> create better musical comedies.

1294   "From Texas to Broadway." COSMOPOLITAN 58 (January 1915): 263.
        Illus.

> A description of how Cahill came to appear in UNDER
> COVER.

1295   Patterson, Ada. "A Serious Talk with a Funny Woman." THEATRE
        (N.Y.) 6 (December 1906): 331-33, x. Illus.

> Cahill describes her feeling of love for the audience during
> performance, which she suggests enables her to dominate
> them.

See also nos. 13, 270, 276, 297, and 490.

CALDWELL, JAMES H.

(1793-1863)

1296 Gafford, Lucille. A HISTORY OF THE ST. CHARLES THEATRE OF NEW ORLEANS, 1835-43. Chicago: University of Chicago Libraries, 1932. 38 p.

> This account is a separately published portion of a dissertation; Caldwell's operations in New Orleans are described in some detail.

See also nos. 101, 133, 146, 166, 196, 244, and 2348.

CARNOVSKY, MORRIS
(1897-   )

1297   Carnovsky, Morris. "Design for Acting." TULANE DRAMA REVIEW
5 (Spring 1961): 68-85.

> In a paper originally presented in 1960 to the Northwest
> Drama Conference at the University of Oregon, Carnovsky
> offers substantial remarks on acting technique, drawing
> heavily upon Stanislavski's writings.

1298   _____. "Mirror of Shylock." TULANE DRAMA REVIEW 3 (October
1958): 35-45.

> A detailed analysis of the actor's approach to the role,
> originally written for the Laurel Shakespeare edition of
> THE MERCHANT OF VENICE.

See also nos. 137, 167, 291, 298, 366, 413, and 3052.

CARTER, MRS. LESLIE
(1862-1937)

1299　Carter, Mrs. Leslie. "Portrait of a Lady with Red Hair," "The Record of a Flaming Life, Written in Fire." LIBERTY 3 (15 January 1927): 14-18, 21; (22 January 1927): 11-15; (29 January 1927): 24, 27, 31-32, 35-36; (5 February 1927): 45-54; (12 February 1927): 47-55; (19 February 1927): 55-61; (26 February 1927): 59-66; (5 March 1927): 55, 57-58, 61-67; (12 March 1927): 57-62; (19 March 1927): 83-90. Illus.

>　The illustrations are many and useful, but the text is lurid and theatrical rather than reliable. To be used with caution.

1300　_____. "The Secret of Success on the Stage." BROADWAY MAGAZINE, March 1902.

>　Unavailable for examination.

1301　_____. "The Value of the Painter's Genius in Stage Productions." BURR McINTOSH MONTHLY 19 (May 1909): n.p. Illus.

>　A five-page article in which Carter extolls both the virtues of scene painting and her own production of KASSA.

1302　_____. "What My Career Means to Me." GREEN BOOK ALBUM 2 (November 1909): 1044-48.

>　Carter describes having to overcome great obstacles to win success in the theatre, but makes no mention of Belasco.

1303　Ford, James L. THE STORY OF DU BARRY. New York: Frederick A. Stokes, 1902. 288 p. Illus.

>　While this volume is a historical narrative of the actual Du Barry, it is heavily illustrated with production photographs of the Belasco-Carter production.

1304　"Mrs. Carter's Career." MUNSEY'S 30 (November 1903): 293-302.

The anonymous author remarks on the suddenness of Carter's
rise to theatrical fame.

1305   MRS. LESLIE CARTER AS ZAZA; WITH A HISTORY OF HER STAGE
        CAREER, AND THE SUCCESSFUL PRODUCTION OF THE PLAY; ILLUS-
        TRATED WITH HALF-TONE ENGRAVINGS OF THE PRINCIPAL SCENES
        IN WHICH MRS. CARTER APPEARS. New York: 1899. 8 p. Illus.

        Confirmed in NATIONAL UNION CATALOG, but unavail-
        able for examination.

1306   Wagstaff, William de. "Mrs. Leslie Carter--A Summer Study." THEATRE
        (N.Y.) 2 (October 1902): 20-23. Illus.

        Superficial and fan-oriented puffery.

1307   Wayne, Palma. "Mrs. Leslie Carter Resurgent." HARPER'S BAZAAR
        56 (November 1921): 46, 118. Illus.

        A somewhat overwritten sketch of Carter, who was returning
        to the stage after thirteen years of absence.

1308   White, Matthew, Jr. "Mrs. Leslie Carter." MUNSEY'S 35 (April-
        September 1906): 226-31. Illus.

        A description of Carter's divorce, her meeting with and
        training from Belasco, and her emergence as a star in ZAZA.

See also nos. 13, 28, 213, 262, 270, 276, 279, 297, 377, 381-82, 408, 413,
482, 579, 928, 936, 938, 961, 964, 973, 998, 1002, and 1471.

CAYVAN, GEORGIA (1857-1906). See nos. 112, 279, 290, 293, 328, 413, 558, and 964.

CHANFRAU, FRANK

(1824-84)

1309   Dorson, Richard M. "Mose the Far-Famed and World Renowned." AMERICAN LITERATURE 15 (November 1943): 288-300.

      More descriptive of the role of Mose than of the actor in it, but useful.

1310   Minnigerode, Meade. FABULOUS FORTIES, 1840-1850, A PRESENTATION OF PRIVATE LIFE. New York and London: G.P. Putnam's Sons, 1924. xii, 345 p. Illus.

      The author includes a brief (pp. 164-66) description of Chanfrau in A GLANCE AT NEW YORK.

1311   Rinear, Dave. "F.S. Chanfrau: The Rise and Fall of an Urban Folk Hero." THEATRE JOURNAL 33 (May 1981): 199-212. Illus.

      Rinear describes Chanfrau's managerial procedures and reconstructs his almost overnight success, with particular attention to his A GLANCE AT NEW YORK.

See also nos. 101, 222, 300, 375, 387, 413, 472, and 1762.

CHAPMAN, WILLIAM
(1764-1839)

1312   Ford, George D. THESE WERE ACTORS: A STORY OF THE CHAP-
MANS AND THE DRAKES. New York: Library Publishers, 1955.
xxiv, 307 p. Index, illus.

        A useful account of the frontier theatre in the United
States, minimally documented and somewhat speculative.

1313   Graham, Philip. SHOWBOATS: THE HISTORY OF AN AMERICAN
INSTITUTION. Austin and London: University of Texas Press, 1969.
210 p. Index, illus., bibliog.

        The outstanding work on the subject, containing a brief
account of Chapman and his career on the river. Well
researched and documented.

1314   Pratt, Helen Throop. "Souvenirs of an Interesting Family." CALI-
FORNIA HISTORICAL SOCIETY QUARTERLY 7 (September 1928): 282-85.

        Pratt briefly sketches the history of the Chapman family
in California, but documents nothing. The article was
written in conjunction with a small Chapman collection
at the California Historical Society.

1315   Taylor, J.H. JOE TAYLOR, BARNSTORMER: HIS TRAVELS, TROUBLES
AND TRIUMPHS DURING FIFTY YEARS IN FOOTLIGHT FLASHES. New
York: William R. Jenkins Co., 1913. 248 p. Illus.

        Rambling and charming memoirs which include idealized
recollections of the Chapmans and Lotta Crabtree. Evocative of the frontier theatre, but requires corroboration.

See also nos. 13, 148, 154, 163, 166, 180, 203, 1521-22, 2330, 2348,
2461, 2957-58, and 3168.

CHASE, ILKA

(1900-1978)

1316   Chase, Ilka. "Are You Attractive to Women?" VOGUE, 15 November 1942, pp. 52, 92. Illus.

    A humorous if inconsequential test, consisting of twenty-five questions and answers about sex appeal.

1317   ____. AROUND THE WORLD AND OTHER PLACES. Garden City, N.Y.: Doubleday, 1970. 300 p. Illus.

    An autobiographical travel book, focused on North Africa, India, Nepal, Hong Kong, and Tokyo.

1318   ____. THE CARTHAGINIAN ROSE. Garden City, N.Y.: Doubleday and Co., 1961. 429 p. Illus.

    The most substantial of Chase's many travel books, written in a breezy style. She describes visiting several theatres in Europe.

1319   ____. ELEPHANTS ARRIVE AT HALF-PAST FIVE. Garden City, N.Y.: Doubleday and Co., 1963. London: W.H. Allen, 1964. 270 p. Illus., bibliog.

    A detailed description of Chase's travels in Africa and her reactions to the trip.

1320   ____. FREE ADMISSION: MEMOIRS. Garden City, N.Y.: Doubleday and Co., 1948. 319 p.

    Autobiographical sequel to PAST IMPERFECT (no. 1325) covering her career in Hollywood.

1321   ____. FRESH FROM THE LAUNDRY. Garden City, N.Y.: Doubleday and Co., 1967. 230 p. Illus.

    Another of Chase's travel books, this one describing her

visits to Czechoslovakia, Hungary, Romania, Yugoslavia, Bulgaria, and Greece.

1321A _____. I LOVE MISS TILLI BEAN. Garden City, N.Y.: Doubleday and Co., 1946.

Unavailable for examination.

1321B _____. IN BED WE CRY. Garden City, N.Y.: Doubleday, Doran and Co., 1947. 308 p.

A novel set in a nontheatrical environment.

1322 _____. "The Lexicographer's Loyal Opposition." VOGUE, 15 September 1943, pp. 82-83, 126. Illus.

A humorous piece quarreling with dictionary publishers.

1323 _____. "Me and My Clothes." VOGUE, 15 March 1946, pp. 142-43, 205. Illus.

Fashion notes.

1324 _____. NEW YORK 22. Garden City, N.Y.: Doubleday and Co., 1951. 308 p.

A novel, the title of which refers to that section of New York City bounded by Fiftieth Street, Sixteenth Street, Fifth Avenue, and the East River.

1325 _____. PAST IMPERFECT. New York: Doubleday, Doran, and Co., 1942. 278 p. Melbourne, Australia: Lothian, 1942.

A chatty autobiography, concerned more with Chase's film career than her work on the stage. Includes some discussion of her brief marriage to Louis Calhern.

1326 _____. "The Philosophy of Being a Woman." VOGUE, 15 November 1941, pp. 78-79, 101-2. Illus.

A tongue-in-cheek piece, concerning fashions and charm for the female.

1327 _____. SECOND SPRING AND TWO POTATOES. Garden City, N.Y.: Doubleday and Co., 1965. 302 p. Illus.

A description of Chase's trip around the world with tips for travelers.

1328 _____. THE SOUNDS OF HOME. Garden City, N.Y.: Doubleday
and Co., 1971. 264 p.

    A novel of New York's high society.

1329 _____. THE VARIED AIRS OF SPRING. Garden City, N.Y.: Doubleday and Co., 1969. 262 p. Illus.

    A description of Chase's travels in Africa, Italy, Greece,
Spain, Sicily, Sardinia, Corsica, Elba, and East Africa.

1330 _____. WORLDS APART. Garden City, N.Y.: Doubleday and Co.,
1972. 273 p. Illus.

    Chase's further travels in Russia, South America, and
Africa.

1331 Gordon, James. "Silky Ilka." AMERICAN MAGAZINE 137 (April
1944): 26-27. Illus.

    Fan-oriented puffery.

1332 Pringle, Henry F. "Hungarian for Helen." COLLIER'S 106 (26 October
1940): 12, 62. Illus.

    A light article quoting several of Chase's retorts and wise-
cracks.

See also nos. 5 and 413.

CHATTERTON, RUTH

(1893-1961)

1333   "Ambition's Daughter." COSMOPOLITAN 58 (February 19.15): 328-
29. Illus.

>   Chatterton is quoted describing her continuing self-
improvement program to increase her worth as an actress.

1334   Burden, Janet. "Ruth Chatterton Helps Husband Buy Play--Forbes Asks
Her to Direct It." MOVIE CLASSIC 2 (May 1932): 34. Illus.

>   The script described in the title was COUNSEL'S OPINION,
although Chatterton planned to retitle it LET US DIVORCE.

1335   Chatterton, Ruth. "Nature as a Guide to Dress." GREEN BOOK
MAGAZINE 14 (August 1914): 261-66. Illus.

>   Fashion advice.

1336   Collins, Charles W. "The Girl Who Made Good." GREEN BOOK
MAGAZINE 12 (September 1914): 413-16. Illus.

>   A description of Chatterton's sudden and phenomenal
success in DADDY LONG LEGS.

1337   Conti, Marie. "Shopping with Ruth Chatterton." MOTION PICTURE
MAGAZINE 38 (November 1929): 68-69, 92. Illus.

>   A discussion of stationery, the object of the shopping
trip. Trivial.

1338   Grant, Jack. "Ruth and Ralph and George--One for All, and All for
One." MOVIE CLASSIC 4 (March 1933): 26, 74-75. Illus.

>   Hollywood marital gossip concerning Chatterton, Ralph
Forbes, and George Brent.

1339   Hall, Gladys. "I am a Renegade in Hollywood." MOTION PICTURES
MAGAZINE 37 (July 1929): 50, 94. Illus.

Hall suggests that Chatterton's notorious candor did not always win her friends in California.

1340 _____. "Ruth Chatterton's Own Story of Her Second Marriage." MOTION PICTURE MAGAZINE 44 (January 1933): 50-51, 64. Illus.

Chatterton's optimistic observations after marrying George Brent.

1341 Lee, Sonia. "Ruth Chatterton Tells What's Wrong with the Movies." MOTION PICTURE MAGAZINE 45 (June 1933): 50-51, 74-75. Illus.

Chatterton is quoted as suggesting most of Hollywood's ills at the time were economic, for which she suggested various remedies.

1342 [P., A.] [Ada Patterson?] "'Judy' On and Off the Stage." THEATRE (N.Y.) 21 (January 1915): 50. Illus.

Superficial comments about Chatterton's role as Judy in DADDY LONG LEGS.

1343 Pryor, Nancy. "Contented--And How!" MOTION PICTURE MAGAZINE 44 (August 1932): 56-57, 91. Illus.

Despite a failing marriage, Chatterton describes the joys of being a star.

1344 Waite, Edgar. "Sometimes It Pays to Jump Overboard." AMERICAN MAGAZINE 111 (June 1931): 72-73, 127-28.

Chatterton describes her professional comeback after it appeared her career was finished.

See also nos. 235, 276, 311, 449, 469, and 2567.

CLAIRE, INA

(1895-   )

1345   Brown, John Mason.   "Peg Woffington to Ina Claire."   THEATRE ARTS
17 (December 1933):   955-65.   Illus.

A hypothetical letter in which "Woffington" asks Claire
to consider playing the roles of classic comedy.

1346   Busch, Noel F.   "Ina Claire."   LIFE, 10 February 1947, pp. 51-54,
56.   Illus.

A summary of Claire's career, well-illustrated, to which
is appended a complimentary essay by Busch.

1347   Calhoun, Dorothy.   "The Embarrassed Embalmer."   MOTION PICTURE
MAGAZINE   38 (September 1929):   50, 112.   Illus.

A description of Claire's marriage to John Gilbert.

1348   _____.   "Ina and John Reach Parting of the Ways."   MOVIE CLASSIC
1 (October 1931):   36.   Illus.

A gossipy explanation of Claire's divorce.

1349   _____.   "Why the Gilbert-Claire Marriage has Failed."   MOTION
PICTURE MAGAZINE   42 (November 1931):   28-29, 86.   Illus.

Marital speculations in which Calhoun suggests Claire
tried to preserve the relationship.

1350   Claire, Ina.   "Discreet Words from a Discreet Actress."   GREEN BOOK
MAGAZINE   10 (October 1913):   559-63.   Illus.

Claire's somewhat idealized view of musical comedy as a
profession.

1351   Claire, Ina, as told to Katherine Roberts.   "A Dress for Cinderella."
COLLIER'S   84 (27 July 1929):   23, 57.   Illus.

A discussion of women's fashions and theories of how to fit clothing to one's personality.

1352　"The Dainty Quaker Girl." COSMOPOLITAN 55 (November 1913): 837-38. Illus.

A thin interview in which Claire describes the dangers of being too charming and praises the London managers of her recent engagement there.

1353　Dodge, Wendell Phillips. "The Quaker Girl a Star in 'THE FOLLIES.'" THEATRE (N.Y.) 23 (August 1916): 70. Illus.

Dodge describes Claire's immense success in THE ZIEGFELD FOLLIES of 1915.

1354　Hall, Gladys. "She Wanted To Be Wicked." MOTION PICTURE MAGAZINE 38 (August 1929): 58-59, 102. Illus.

Hall uses Claire to exemplify the differences between stage and cinema stars.

1355　"Ina Claire's Victorian House in San Francisco." VOGUE, 15 October 1945, pp. 118-19. Illus.

Architectural notes.

1356　Morehouse, Ward. "At Home with Ina Claire." THEATRE ARTS 42 (September 1958): 12-13, 80. Illus.

Morehouse speculates that Claire would return to Broadway if the right script appeared. Much of the article describes Claire's home in Hillsborough, California.

1357　_____. "Ina Claire of Nob Hill." THEATRE ARTS 35 (August 1951): 26-27, 91. Illus.

An account of the actress's life in San Francisco and a statement of hope that she would return to the theatre.

1358　Morley, Frank. "What Does Ina Claire Say about John Gilbert Now?" MOTION PICTURE MAGAZINE 43 (April 1932): 34-35, 90, 94. Illus.

Fan-oriented interview in which Claire says she hopes to remain on friendly terms with her ex-husband.

1359　Patterson, Ada. "Personality Portraits. No. 2. Ina Claire." THEATRE (N.Y.) 31 (March 1920): 168. Illus.

A brief and insubstantial treatment of the actress.

1360   Sumner, Keene. "People Who Are Easy to Imitate." AMERICAN
MAGAZINE 89 (February 1920): 36-37, 207-8. Illus.

> Claire describes her mimic techniques and her use of
> close observation of her subjects.

See also nos. 5, 9, 135, 275-76, 284, 295, 377, 413, 420, 441, 452, 464,
486, 495, 508, 527, 578-79, 946, and 1477.

CLARE, ADA

(c. 1836-74)

1361 Loggins, Vernon. WHERE THE WORLD ENDS: THE LIFE OF LOUIS MOREAU GOTTSCHALK. Baton Rouge: Louisiana State University Press, 1958. xii, 261 p. Index, illus., bibliog.

> Memoirs in which a ten-page chapter is devoted to Clare.

1362 Parry, Albert. GARRETS AND PRETENDERS: A HISTORY OF BO-HEMIANISM IN AMERICA. New York: Covici-Friede, 1933. xvi, 369 p. Index, illus., bibliog. Rev. ed., 1960.

> A substantial treatment of Clare as the "Queen of Bohemia," Henry Clapp being the king. Numerous drawings. More concerned with Clare's life-style than her acting.

1363 Stoddard, Charles Warren. "Ada Clare, Queen of Bohemia." NATIONAL MAGAZINE 22 (September 1905): 637-45. Illus.

> Stoddard enthusiastically defends Clare's unusual life-style and recalls her novel, ONLY A WOMAN'S HEART (1886), from which he quotes.

1364 Walker, Franklin Dickerson. SAN FRANCISCO'S LITERARY FRONTIER. New York: Alfred A. Knopf, 1939. vii, 400 p. Index, illus., bibliog.

> Contains substantial sections on Clare and Ada Isaacs Menken and describes their work when playing San Francisco.

See also nos. 13, 222, 401, and 1750.

CLARK, MARGUERITE

(1883-1940)

1365 Bodeen, DeWitt. "Marguerite Clark." FILMS IN REVIEW 15 (December 1964): 611-25. Illus.

> Bodeen sketches Clark's life and career, including a bit about her stage work. He appends a filmography and includes several theatrical photographs.

1366 Clark, Marguerite. "The Disadvantages of Being Girlish." THEATRE (N.Y.) 19 (April 1914): 188-90, 192. Illus.

> Clark's very thin philosophic speculations on fantasy versus reality in theatre and life.

1367 _____. "From Comic Opera to Moving Pictures." AMERICAN MAGAZINE 84 (December 1917): 42-43, 84-87. Illus.

> While professing to prefer the stage, Clark explains the economic advantages of working in film.

1368 _____. "How I Got In." MOTION PICTURE MAGAZINE 14 (August 1917): 79-80. Illus.

> Clark recollects Daniel Frohman's assistance in her early film career.

1369 _____. "How to Get In!" MOTION PICTURE MAGAZINE 12 (August 1916): 125-26. Illus.

> Clark suggests a "screen personality," a knowledge of the drama, and practical experience are required for a successful career in film.

1370 _____. "Just Like Play." COSMOPOLITAN 59 (June 1915): 72. Illus.

> Clark compares stage work with filmmaking, finding the latter far easier.

1371 _____. "A Little of My Life." MOTION PICTURE MAGAZINE 15 (July 1918): 60–63, 114. Illus.

> A somewhat idealized autobiographical sketch of minimal substance.

1372 _____. "The Most Critical Audience: Children." GREEN BOOK MAGAZINE 9 (May 1913): 879–83. Illus.

> Clark describes responses to her from children as she played the title role in SNOW WHITE.

1373 Dale, Alan. [Pseud.] "Petite Marguerite." COSMOPOLITAN 53 (September 1912): 547–48. Illus.

> Dale quotes Clark briefly about her early career on stage.

1374 _____. "Sensible, Sensible Marguerite Clark." GREEN BOOK MAGAZINE 16 (July 1916): 161–66. Illus.

> Dale interviews Clark after her defection to the cinema and predicts her early return to the New York stage.

1375 Eyck, John Ten. "Mr. Ten Eyck Calls on Miss Clark." GREEN BOOK MAGAZINE 11 (March 1914): 390–95. Illus.

> An insubstantial interview with Clark while she was playing the title role in PRUNELLA.

1376 "Marguerite Clark, The Girl that Is Different." MOTION PICTURE MAGAZINE 9 (July 1915): 113–15. Illus.

> An autobiographical letter to Gladys Hall in which Clark outlines the highlights of her career to date.

1377 May, Lillian. "Why Marguerite Clark is Going to Stay in Pictures." MOTION PICTURE MAGAZINE 13 (February 1917): 103–6, 162–63. Illus.

> Fan-oriented puffery in which Clark suggests she prefers the enormous exposure of films.

1378 "One Reason for the Short Life of the Movie Press Agent." THEATRE (N.Y.) 26 (November 1917): 322. Illus.

> Clark is quoted briefly about her difficulties in the early part of her film career.

1379 Phelps, T.A. "How It Feels to Be a Widow." THEATRE (N.Y.) 30 (August 1919): 112. Illus.

A brief interview with Clark about an upcoming role in the film WIDOW BY PROXY.

1380   Piquet, Alice de. "When Marguerite Hit Town." MOTION PICTURE MAGAZINE 18 (August 1919): 64-65, 103. Illus.

A description of Clark's house-hunting techniques upon her arrival in Hollywood.

1381   Washburn, Beatrice. "Marguerite Clark--Today." PHOTOPLAY 27 (April 1925): 28-29, 132-43. Illus.

Washburn describes Clark's circumstances in Patterson, Louisiana, and the estate to which she retired after her film career.

1382   Zukor, Adolph, with Kramer, Dale. THE PUBLIC IS NEVER WRONG: THE AUTOBIOGRAPHY OF ADOLPH ZUKOR. New York: G.P. Putnam's Sons, 1953. 298 p. Index, illus.

A few sections are primarily concerned with Clark's film career.

See also nos. 13 and 280.

CLARKE, JOHN SLEEPER
(1833-99)

1383   SKETCH OF THE LIFE OF MR. JOHN S. CLARKE, COMEDIAN. London: [1872]. 8 p.

        A complimentary pamphlet on Clarke, tracing his professional career, but offering very little information about his off-stage life.

1384   Stuart, William. "John S. Clarke, Comedian." LIPPINCOTT'S 28 (November 1881): 497-502.

        A critical-biographical essay, describing Clarke's appeal and lauding his high moral character.

1385   _____. SKETCHES AND REMINISCENCES OF JOHN S. CLARKE, COMEDIAN, WITH THE JOURNALISTIC AND PUBLIC OPINIONS OF AMERICA AND GREAT BRITAIN. New York: 1881. 24 p. Illus.

        A reprint of no. 1384.

See also nos. 21, 236, 336, 341, 431, 433, 1032, and 1050.

CLAXTON, KATE

(1848-1924)

1386 Cone, William Whitney. SOME ACCOUNT OF THE CONE FAMILY IN AMERICA, PRINCIPALLY THE DESCENDANTS OF DANIEL CONE, WHO SETTLED IN HADDAM, CONNECTICUT, IN 1662. Topeka, Kans.: Crane and Co., 1903. 496 p. Index, illus.

>   Claxton's genealogy, but contains no biographical data on her.

See also nos. 13, 21, 112, 222, 279, 290, 387, 413, and 471.

COGHLAN, ROSE
(1851-1932)

1387 Patterson, Ada. "The Stage Honors Rose Coghlan." THEATRE (N.Y.)
      36 (July 1922): 36. Illus.

   A description of a benefit held at the Apollo Theatre in
   New York on 23 April 1922. Various tributes were made
   to the actress, and a total of $10,000 was raised.

See also nos. 21, 112, 270, 278-79, 290, 293, 296, 328, 346, 356, 381,
387, 399, 413-14, 596, and 964.

COHAN, GEORGE M.

(1878-1942)

1388   "Broadway Boy." TIME, 9 October 1933, pp. 26-27. Illus.

       A brief biographical sketch of Cohan, then appearing in
       AH, WILDERNESS!; a sort of progress report on his career.

1389   Broeck, Helen Ten. "How George Cohan Picks Winners." THEATER
      (N.Y.) 28 (July 1918): 40.

       The interviewer tries unsuccessfully to gain Cohan's secret
       for his string of theatrical successes.

1390   Clark, Barrett H. A STUDY OF THE MODERN DRAMA: A HAND-
      BOOK FOR THE STUDY AND APPRECIATION OF THE BEST PLAYS,
      EUROPEAN, ENGLISH, AND AMERICAN, OF THE LAST CENTURY.
      New York and London: D. Appleton and Co., 1925. 486 p.

       Pages 393-99 are devoted to Cohan and his BROADWAY
       JONES.

1391   Cohan, George M. "The American Play." THEATRE (N.Y.) 31
      (November 1920): 254, 316, 324. Illus.

       Cohan suggests melodrama is the most appropriate form of
       drama for the United States.

1392   . "The Art of Adapting Plays." THEATRE (N.Y.) 26 (November
      1917): 284.

       Cohan's observations on converting novels into stage plays,
       a practice against which he advises as a general rule.

1393   . "Cohan Revue--1903-38." STAGE 15 (August 1938): 47-50.
      Illus.

       A summation of Cohan's career to date, written in the
       form of a musical comedy script, using his songs. Includes
       photographs of Cohan in his most famous roles.

1394 _____. "The Flavor of Cities: New York." AMERICAN MAGAZINE
84 (November 1917): 36–37, 124–25. Illus.

> Cohan offers a noncommittal description of New York, con-
> sidering it no worse than other metropolises of the time.

1395 _____. "George M. Cohan Interviews Himself." GREEN BOOK
ALBUM 7 (June 1912): 1220–24.

> A gimmicky article in which Cohan describes his youth.

1396 _____. "The Happiest Days of My Life." STAGE 14 (January 1937):
105–7. Illus.

> Cohan recalls his vaudeville days when he was "the fourth
> Cohan."

1397 _____. "My Beginnings." THEATRE (N.Y.) 7 (February 1907): 52,
54. Illus.

> Cohan reviews his stage career at age twenty-eight.

1398 _____. "My Most Successful Play." GREEN BOOK ALBUM 6
(November 1911): 1117.

> Cohan describes his writing and production of FORTY-FIVE
> MINUTES FROM BROADWAY.

1399 _____. "Preface of a Play to Come." STAGE 13 (January 1936):
29–30. Illus.

> A brief and chatty article on playwriting as practiced by Cohan.

1400 _____. "Some Curious Persons We Meet and Hear From." BURR
McINTOSH MONTHLY 19 (July 1909): n.p. Illus.

> A four-page article in which Cohan describes his fan mail,
> both positive and negative.

1401 _____. "The Stage as I Have Seen It." GREEN BOOK MAGAZINE
13 (January 1915): 38–49; (February 1915): 246–57; (March 1915):
421–31; (April 1915): 708–13; (May 1915): 785–89; (June 1915):
1056–62; 14 (July 1915): 30–34. Illus.

> An early, serialized biography by Cohan. Useful.

1402 _____. "To Whom It May Concern." GOOD HOUSEKEEPING,
November 1938, p. 19. Illus.

> A half-page of shallow reminiscences about his fifty years
> in the theatre.

1403 _____. TWENTY YEARS ON BROADWAY AND THE YEARS IT TOOK TO GET THERE: THE TRUE STORY OF A TROUPER'S LIFE FROM THE CRADLE TO THE "CLOSED SHOP." New York and London: Harper and Brothers, 1924. 263 p. Illus. Reprint. Westport, Conn.: Greenwood, 1971.

> Cohan describes his purpose for writing by saying "My idea in this story is to appeal to the general public. To me the college professor with the tall forehead is of no more importance than the ordinary buck dancer or dramatic critic . . . . the most thrilling, daring, and at the same time truthful exposé of a 'charmed life' ever written by an American song–and–dance man." Requires corroboration throughout.

1404 _____. "What the American Flag Has Done for Me." THEATRE (N.Y.) 19 (June 1914): 286, 288, 318-19. Illus.

> Superficial comments on playwriting.

1405 _____. "Why American Plays Succeed in London." THEATRE (N.Y.) 47 (March 1928): 17-18, 76. Illus.

> Cohan uses his own London successes as examples of excellence in dramaturgy.

1406 _____. "Why I am Leaving the Stage." GREEN BOOK MAGAZINE 9 (May 1913): 852–54.

> Cohan proposes to retire from acting so he can devote more time to writing.

1407 _____. "Why My Plays Succeed." THEATRE (N.Y.) 39 (May 1924): 9, 58.

> Cohan attributes his success to his credo of "speed and pep."

1408 Cohan, George M., and Nathan, George Jean. "The Mechanics of Emotion." McCLURE'S 42 (November 1913): 69-77. Illus.

> Cohan lists thirty situations that will cause an audience to cry, fifteen that would make them laugh, and twelve that would thrill them. A revealing look into the mechanics of Cohan's dramaturgy and theatrical philosophy.

1409 Cohan, Mrs. Helen Costigan. "Bringing up Georgie Cohan." THEATER (N.Y.) 35 (May 1922): 312, 314, 316. Illus.

> Recollections of the young Cohan by his mother.

1410 "Cohan's Return." LIFE, 27 March 1940, pp. 72-74, 76, 79-80. Illus.

The first part of this article concerns Cohan in RETURN OF THE VAGABOND; the second a production at Catholic University of YANKEE DOODLE BOY, a musical biography of Cohan written by Walter Kerr, then a twenty-seven year old theatre professor.

1411   "Cohan Writes a Play about Cohan." LITERARY DIGEST 121 (25 January 1936): 18. Illus.

Publicity puffery about Cohan's DEAR OLD DARLING.

1412   Dale, Alan. [Pseud.] "The Real George M. Cohan." COSMOPOLITAN 54 (March 1913): 547-49. Illus.

Dale quotes Cohan as preferring writing to performing.

1413   Dodge, Walter Phillips. "The Actor in the Street." THEATRE (N.Y.) 13 (February 1911): 60, 62, vii. Illus.

Dodge describes Cohan's methods of creating stage characters by observing people in real life.

1414   Eustis, Morton. "Portrait of a Producer: Presenting Sam Harris." THEATRE ARTS 22 (October 1938): 745-55. Illus.

Eustis describes Harris's producing collaboration with Cohan, a partnership which lasted fourteen years.

1415   Garland, Robert. "The Cosmopolite of the Month: George M. Cohan." HEARST'S 104 (June 1938): 8, 144-45. Illus.

An adulatory survey of Cohan's career, citing his various accomplishments as a performer and writer.

1416   "George M. Cohan, The Song and Dance Man Who Sets the Pace on Broadway." NATIONAL MAGAZINE 52 (April 1924): 451-52. Illus.

A brief sketch of Cohan of little substance.

1417   "Is George M. Cohan to Be Regarded as a Joke or a Genius?" CURRENT OPINION 56 (March 1914): 192-93. Illus.

Various quotations selected by an anonymous compiler, most of them in support of Cohan as a dramatist.

1418   Jessel, George. THE WORLD I LIVED IN. Chicago: Henry Regnery Co., 1975. 204 p. Index, illus.

Rambling reminiscences with frequent references to Cohan.

1419   Johnson, Julian. "Cohan and the Movies." PHOTOPLAY 15 (February 1919): 27-28. Illus.

   Cohan is quoted as expounding on the distinctions between theatre and film, especially in regard to acting.

1420   Kennedy, John B. "Broadway Knight." COLLIER'S 90 (8 October 1932): 14, 30, 32. Illus.

   Cohan recalls the previous twenty-five years, mourning the old days of "sentimental actors, pal producers, and stage family spirit."

1421   McCabe, John H. GEORGE M. COHAN: THE MAN WHO OWNED BROADWAY. Garden City, N.Y.: Doubleday, 1973. xii, 287 p. Index, illus.

   A readable, nicely illustrated, and well-researched treatment of Cohan, useful in conjunction with other similar works.

1422   Macfarlane, Peter Clark. "George M. Cohan." EVERYBODY'S MAGAZINE 30 (January 1914): 107-20. Illus.

   The author speculates on Cohan's rise to fame in a thoughtful, well-illustrated essay. Not a scholarly piece, but offers some unique insights.

1423   Mantle, Burns. CONTEMPORARY AMERICAN PLAYWRIGHTS. New York: Dodd, Mead and Co., 1938. x, 328 p. Index.

   Mantle includes a short critical biography of Cohan on pages 140-49.

1424   Morehouse, Ward. GEORGE M. COHAN: PRINCE OF THE AMERICAN THEATRE. Philadelphia and New York: J.B. Lippincott Co., 1943. 240 p. Illus.

   A largely undocumented and sycophantic treatment of Cohan, written in the "show biz" tradition of biography. Contains a chronology of Cohan's career. Requires corroboration.

1425   _____. "George M. Cohan: The Man Who Owned Broadway." THEATRE ARTS 28 (January 1944): 53-58.

   The first chapter, somewhat condensed, of the previous entry (no. 1424).

1426   Mullett, Mary B. "George Cohan's Definition of One Who is 'On the Level.'" AMERICAN MAGAZINE 88 (August 1919): 19-21, 125-26, 129-30. Illus.

Mullett extolls Cohan's simplistic philosophies and observations on life. Of minor value.

1427   Porter, Verne Hardin. "The Story of George M. Cohan." GREEN BOOK MAGAZINE 12 (December 1914): 964-80. Illus.

An introduction to Cohan's autobiography, serialized in following issues. (See no. 1401)

1428   Rhodes, Harrison. "Cohan, an Appreciation." METROPOLITAN MAGAZINE 41 (March 1915): 43-45.

Rhodes considers Cohan a dramatist who gives the public what it wants, but considers this a dangerous practice, suggesting the "high-brows" (Howells, Matthews, and James) will get him if he doesn't watch out.

1429   Roseman, Ethel. "George M. Cohan Hits the Trail of the Midnight Movie Crew." MOTION PICTURE MAGAZINE 16 (August 1918): 64-65, 123. Illus.

A description of the circumstances surrounding the filming of HIT THE TRAIL.

1430   [T., W.H.] "Mr. Cohan of Broadway." THEATRE (N.Y.) 52 (July 1930): 24-25, 67-68. Illus.

An adulatory appreciation of Cohan, the author calling him the theatre's most characteristic figure.

1431   "What a Man!" TIME 23 (5 February 1934): 29-30. Illus.

A brief summary of Cohan's career as a songwriter.

1432   Winders, Gertrude Hecker. GEORGE M. COHAN: BOY THEATRE GENIUS. Indianapolis: Bobbs-Merrill Co., 1968. 200 p. Illus.

A children's book, idealized and undocumented.

1433   Wolf, Rennold. "George Michaels Cohan." GREEN BOOK MAGAZINE 9 (January 1913): 40-51. Illus.

A verbose examination of how the performer Cohan became a successful playwright.

1434   _____. "William Collier 'On and Off.'" GREEN BOOK MAGAZINE 9 (May 1913): 786-96.

A substantial study of the friendship between Collier and Cohan.

Cohan, George M.

See also nos. 150, 172, 178, 208, 213, 217, 228, 243, 270, 294, 327, 348, 376, 390, 413, 430, 464, 484, 506, 508-9, 536, 543-44, 569, 572, 578-79, 597, 979, 1975, 2567, and 3094.

COLLIER, WILLIAM

(1866-1944)

1435   Collier, William. "Personality." GREEN BOOK ALBUM 7 (March 1912): 652-59.

> Collier considered himself a personality actor and describes the necessity of such appeal for success in theatre.

1436   _____. "Some Truths I Have Met." THEATRE (N.Y.) 25 (April 1917): 226, 248. Illus.

> Collier advocates truthfulness in the drama at a time when he was starring in NOTHING BUT THE TRUTH.

1437   Macfarlane, Peter Clark. "William Collier: Laugh-Builder." EVERYBODY'S MAGAZINE 32 (January-June 1915): 474-84. Illus.

> Macfarlane focuses upon Collier's instinctive comic sense.

1438   Patterson, Ada. "William Collier--the Man and the Comedian." THEATRE (N.Y.) 7 (July 1907): 184, 186-87. Illus.

> A somewhat fatuous interview containing a bit of information about Collier's early career.

See also nos. 28, 270, 276, 377, 723, 846, 905, 1434, and 1975.

COLLINGE, PATRICIA

(1894-1974)

1439   Collinge, Patricia. "Explanation for ALBERT." STAGE 15 (March 1938): 32.

      Collinge explains the practice of visiting stars backstage after the opening performance, a practice she considered unrelated to the production's quality.

1440   _____. "I Just Can't Make My Plays Behave." STAGE 14 (November 1936): 46.

      The actress recalls her unsuccessful attempts at playwriting.

1441   _____. "That Was the Sixty Club." STAGE 14 (February 1937): 72.

      Collinge fondly recalls the night life of her youth.

1442   _____. "They Also Serve--." STAGE 15 (December 1937): 80.

      Collinge describes her agony in learning lines and going to rehearsals, considering her sympathetic spouse as essential to her success.

1443   _____. "What Ever Happened to Love?" STAGE 15 (October 1937): 58.

      Collinge decries the absence of "good old-fashioned love scene[s]" in the current Broadway season.

1444   Dickinson, Justus. "Patrician Collinge." GREEN BOOK MAGAZINE 13 (May 1915): 929-31. Illus.

      The author describes the ingenue as a serious young woman making a concentrated study of the art of acting.

1445   "Patricia Tells Her Story." COSMOPOLITAN 58 (May 1915): 680-81. Illus.

A brief and superficial description of Collinge's personality.

See also nos. 276, 377, and 1463.

CONQUEST, IDA
(1876-1937)

1446   Conquest, Ida. "The Romance of the Stage." GREEN BOOK ALBUM 3 (May 1910): 1032-35.

        Conquest describes the magnetic appeal of the theatre for performers.

See also nos. 28, 270, 381-82, and 444.

COOPER, THOMAS ABTHORPE
(1776-1849)

1447 Ireland, Joseph N. A MEMOIR OF THE PROFESSIONAL LIFE OF
THOMAS ABTHORPE COOPER (1888). Philadelphia: 1888. Reprint.
New York: Benjamin Blom, 1969. x, 96 p. Index, illus.

> A brief and business-like treatment of Cooper, including
> a list of his roles. The only full-length work on this
> performer.

1448 "Life of Mr. Cooper." MIRROR OF TASTE AND DRAMATIC CENSOR
1 (January 1810): 28-44.

> A substantial if undocumented account with considerable
> biographical detail.

1449 "Mr. Cooper." MIRROR OF TASTE AND DRAMATIC CENSOR 1
(March 1810): 223-25.

> A substantial critical analysis of Cooper's repertory of roles
> at that time.

1450 "Sketch of the Life and Critical Remarks on the Theatrical Performances
of Mr. T.A. Cooper With a Portrait." POLYANTHOS 1 (January
1806): 72-86. Illus.

> A substantial but undocumented and unsigned biographical
> and critical sketch of Cooper's work in the United States.

1451 Wilmeth, Don B. GEORGE FREDERICK COOKE: MACHIAVEL OF THE
STAGE. Westport, Conn., and London: Greenwood Press, 1980. xv,
350 p. Index, illus., bibliog.

> The definitive biography of Cooke, which includes docu-
> mentation of Cooke's relationships with Cooper from 1810
> to Cooke's death in 1812. Wilmeth corrects many errors
> in William Dunlap's various accounts of this period.

1452   Woodbury, Lael J. "The American Theatre's First Star: Thomas Abthorpe Cooper." THEATRE ANNUAL 4 (1957-58): 7-14. Illus.

        The author attempts to describe Cooper's acting style, drawing upon available primary evidence. Useful.

See also nos. 101, 120-21, 123, 130, 139, 145-46, 148, 161, 182, 188, 192, 210, 213, 222, 244-45, 250, 305, 341, 399, 400, 402, 413, 456, 462, 517, 535, 541, 554, 1008, 1672, 1993, 2348, 2958, and 3168.

CORNELL, KATHARINE
(1898-1974)

1453   Adams, Mildred. "Katharine Cornell Presents--." DELINEATOR 122 (February 1933): 34, 64, 68. Illus.

        A brief biographical sketch, stressing Cornell's unique career as a producer.

1454   _____. "Mrs. Browning on Broadway." WOMAN CITIZEN 15 (March 1931): 12-13, 37-38. Illus.

        A brief history of the genesis of the script, THE BARRETTS OF WIMPOLE STREET, how Cornell first encountered it, and the subsequent production.

1455   Aherne, Brian. A PROPER JOB. Boston: Houghton Mifflin Co., 1969. 355 p. Illus.

        Aherne devotes considerable space in his memoirs to his appearance with Cornell in THE BARRETTS OF WIMPOLE STREET.

1456   "Antony and Cleopatra." LIFE, 1 December 1947, pp. 76-78. Illus.

        A photographic synopsis of the Cornell production followed by a brief descriptive essay.

1457   Beranger, Clara. "Katharine Cornell." WOMAN'S HOME COMPANION 63 (December 1936): 12-13, 51, 53; 64 (January 1937): 20-21, 57. Illus.

        An interview with considerable biographical detail, superseded by later publications, but accompanied by photographs not otherwise widely published. Useful.

1458   Brown, John Mason. "Sarah Siddons to Katharine Cornell." VANITY FAIR 40 (August 1933): 32-33, 49. Illus.

A fictitious letter from the English tragedienne to Cornell, describing parallels in their careers.

1459   Cornell, Katharine, as told to Alice Griffin. "A Good Play Will Always Find a Good Audience." THEATRE ARTS 38 (May 1954): 26-29, 90. Illus.

Cornell refuses to distinguish between audiences in New York and those on the road, but extolls the virtues of the latter.

1460   Cornell, Katharine, as told to Ruth W. Sedgewick. "I Wanted to Be an Actress." STAGE 15 (September 1938): 6-13, 50-54; 16 (October 1938): 28-29, 34, 73-76; (November 1938): 40-44, 64-66; (December 1938): 42-45, 74-77; (January 1939): 43-46, 68-70; (February 1939): 42-46, 72-73. Illus.

Serialization of the actress's memoirs; see no. 1461.

1461   _____. I WANTED TO BE AN ACTRESS. New York: Random House, 1938. 361 p. Illus.

A somewhat unrealistic autobiography which stresses the positive to the point of distortion. Includes 180 pages of carefully selected reviews of Cornell's more successful roles. See no. 1460.

1462   _____. "My Luckiest Day." HEARST'S 120 (June 1946): 98. Illus.

Cornell recalls having been chosen as an unknown actress to play Sydney in A BILL OF DIVORCEMENT, her first break toward stardom.

1463   Gilmore, Margalo (Mrs. Robert Ross), and Collinge, Patricia. B.O.W.S. New York: Harcourt, Brace and Co.; Toronto: McLeod, 1945. 173 p. Illus.

An account of the overseas tour of THE BARRETTS OF WIMPOLE STREET, which went out as a USO show during World War II.

1464   Hall, Gladys. "Why Broadway's Greatest Star--Katharine Cornell--Won't Act for the Movies." MOTION PICTURE MAGAZINE 44 (October 1932): 34-35, 92. Illus.

Cornell is quoted as preferring the immediate audience contact unique to the theatre.

1465   Harvey, Jackson. "--To the Ladies." THEATRE (N.Y.) 51 (April 1930): 24, 58, 60. Illus.

Harvey contrasts the acting styles of Cornell and Hope
Williams.

1466 Herendeen, Anne. "The Lady of Two Legends." THEATRE GUILD
MAGAZINE 8 (April 1931): 18-21. Illus.

An assessment of Cornell's work through THE BARRETTS OF
WIMPOLE STREET. Extremely adulatory rather than objective.

1467 Johns, Eric. "Actress by Design." THEATRE WORLD 34 (May 1941):
102-3, 112. Illus.

An extended appreciation of Cornell from a British point
of view, quoting published criticism of her more successful roles on the London stage.

1468 Kimbrough, Emily. "Stagecraft in the Home." LADIES' HOME JOUR-
NAL, September 1934, pp. 16-17. Illus.

A description of the McClintic-Cornell apartment.

1469 "Lucrece's Tragedy Miss Cornell's Triumph." STAGE 10 (February 1933):
16-17. Illus.

A brief assessment of Cornell's work, accompanied by eight
photographs of the production.

1470 McClintic, Guthrie. "Kit and I." AMERICAN MAGAZINE 120
(November 1935): 22-23, 164-67. Illus.

A brief biographical sketch of Cornell, by her husband.

1471 _____. ME AND KIT. Boston and Toronto: Little, Brown and Co.,
1955. 330 p. Index, illus.

Theatrical reminiscences by Cornell's husband; after their
marriage in 1921 he directed all her productions. Numerous
references to other performers of the time, among them
Tallulah Bankhead, Ethel and John Barrymore, Blanche
Bates, David Belasco, Edwin Booth, Mrs. Carter, Jane
Cowl, Mrs. Fiske, Grace George, Julia Marlowe, and
Laurette Taylor.

1472 Malvern, Gladys. CURTAIN GOING UP! THE STORY OF KATHARINE
CORNELL. New York: Julian Messner, 1943. 239 p. Index,
frontispiece.

An undocumented and adulatory treatment of Cornell, pur-
porting to capture the actress as a woman rather than as
a star.

1473   Merrill, Flora. FLUSH OF WIMPOLE STREET AND BROADWAY. New York: Robert McBride and Co., 1933. 120 p. Illus.

A children's book, illustrated with line drawings by "Edwina." Written in the first-person singular, as if by Flush, the canine who appeared as Elizabeth Barrett's pet in Cornell's production of THE BARRETTS OF WIMPOLE STREET. References by Barrett and Browning to Flush are interpolated.

1474   Morehouse, Ward. "Katharine Cornell." HEARST'S 118 (June 1945): 8, 12-13, 142. Illus.

An appreciation, Cornell being named the cosmopolite of the month. Morehouse includes an account of Cornell's tour of Europe during World War II with THE BARRETTS OF WIMPOLE STREET and briefly describes her entire career to that time.

1475   _____. "Queen Katharine." THEATRE ARTS 42 (June 1958): 9-11. Illus.

Morehouse sympathetically assesses Cornell's place in the theatre and briefly reviews her career to date.

1476   Morrow, Anne. "Katharine Cornell: A Sketch and a Prophecy." WOMAN CITIZEN 10 (October 1925): 17, 45. Illus.

A critical essay with some biographical details; Morrow predicts future greatness for the young actress.

1477   Mosel, Tad, with Gertrude Macy. LEADING LADY: THE WORLD AND THEATRE OF KATHARINE CORNELL. Boston and Toronto: Little, Brown and Co., 1978. x, 522. Index, illus.

A labor of love, exhaustively researched, albeit undocumented, and adulatory in tone. The most detailed treatment of Cornell to date. Includes references to Maude Adams, Tallulah Bankhead, Ethel Barrymore, David Belasco, Jessie Bonstelle, Ina Claire, Jane Cowl, Jeanne Eagels, Lynn Fontanne, Ruth Gordon, and Helen Hayes.

1478   Mullett, Mary B. "Unhappiness Has Its Own Magic." AMERICAN MAGAZINE 101 (June 1926): 34-35, 191-95. Illus.

Cornell describes her miserable childhood and its effect upon her acting in later years.

1479   "Off Islanders--The Guthrie McClintics." HARPER'S BAZAAR 76 (September 1942): 64-65. Illus.

The McClintic-Cornell home in Martha's Vineyard is illustrated and briefly described.

1480 Patterson, Ada. "Two Innocents on Broadway." THEATRE (N.Y.) 41
(June 1925): 22, 56. Illus.

> A superficial interview conducted shortly after Cornell's
> marriage to McClintic.

1481 "A Portrait of Katharine Cornell by Eugene Speicher." LIFE, 29 April
1940, p. 47. Illus.

> A color reproduction of the Speicher portrait plus a brief
> biographical sketch.

1482 "Queen of the Theatre." NEWSWEEK 31 (19 January 1948): cover,
82-83. Illus.

> A survey and analysis of Cornell's career to that time.

1483 Rathbone, Basil. IN AND OUT OF CHARACTER. Garden City, N.Y.:
Doubleday and Co., 1962. x, 278 p. Illus.

> Rathbone devotes Chapter 9 (pp. 119-26) to his tour with
> Cornell in ROMEO AND JULIET.

1484 "Who's Who Among the Producers." THEATRE ARTS 26 (October 1942):
620-24. Illus.

> Includes a few remarks about Cornell's work as a producer.

1485 Woollcott, Alexander. LONG, LONG AGO. New York: World
Book Co., 1943. 280 p.

> Chapter 2 (pp. 13-28) is titled "Miss Kitty Takes the Road,"
> an anecdotal tribute to Cornell's willingness and ability to
> tour, which Woollcott likens to Bernhardt's. See no. 1486.

1486 _____. "Miss Kitty Takes to the Road." In THESE WONDERFUL
PEOPLE: INTIMATE MOMENTS IN THEIR LIVES, compiled by Noel
Ames, pp. 441-55. Chicago: Peoples Book Club, 1947.

> See no. 1485.

See also nos. 5, 9, 116-17, 213, 275-76, 283-85, 295-96, 298, 351, 358, 369,
390, 394, 411, 413, 441, 447, 464, 486-87, 504, 508, 525, 527, 536, 547,
549, 561, 576, 578-79, 589, 797, 1981-82, 2369, and 3212.

COWELL, JOE

(1792-1863)

1487   Bristow, Eugene K. "'Tapping the Pockets' in 1860: An Economic Portrait of Sam Cowell's American Tour." THEATRE ANNUAL 22 (1965-66): 48-64.

An extremely detailed and documented account of Cowell's 1860-61 tour, which was a financial disaster.

1487A   Cowell, Joe. THIRTY YEARS PASSED AMONG THE PLAYERS IN ENGLAND AND AMERICA. New York: Harper and Brothers, 1844. 103 p. Reprint. Hampden, Conn.: Archon, 1979. viii, 103 p.

Cowell in the second half of this volume describes his career as a popular entertainer in the United States; he returned to England after this work was published.

1487B   Disher, M. Willson, ed. THE COWELLS IN AMERICA BEING THE DIARY OF MRS. SAM COWELL DURING HER HUSBAND'S CONCERT TOUR IN THE YEARS 1860-61. London: Oxford University Press, 1934. lxv, 409 p. Index, illus.

A detailed treatment of the engagement, rich in detail concerning American theatre at the time.

1488   Fairbrother, Sydney (Parselle). THROUGH AN OLD STAGE DOOR; WITH AN APPRECIATION BY SYDNEY CARROLL, AND AN INTRO-DUCTION BY STEPHEN GWYNN. London: Frederick Muller, 1939. Toronto: S.J.R. Saunders. 254 p. Index, illus.

Fairbrother's grandparents were the Sam Cowell's; her parents the Joe Cowells, thus she includes considerable biographical data on both. Most of the volume is devoted to Fairbrother's career in England.

See also nos. 180, 413, 2348, and 3168.

COWL, JANE
(1885-1950)

1489   Broeck, Helen Ten. "Actresses Who Write Plays." THEATRE (N.Y.) 25 (June 1917): 354. Illus.

       Broeck interviews Cowl about her writing of LILAC TIME.

1490   Cowl, Jane. "Beauty and Old Age on the Stage." GREEN BOOK MAGAZINE 8 (November 1912): 825-30. Illus.

       Cowl suggests that one's mental attitude is far more important than youth for success in either life or the theatre.

1491   _____. "Beauty in Its Relation to Stage Success." McCALL'S, October 1911, pp. 20-21. Illus.

       Cowl describes physical beauty as a desirable quality for an actress, but by no means indispensable for success in the theatre.

1492   _____. "A Bernhardt Memorial." DRAMA 14 (October 1923): 11, 35.

       A plea for a more tangible tribute to the French actress.

1493   _____. "Education and Acting." GREEN BOOK ALBUM 5 (January 1911): 210-13.

       Cowl suggests the four years needed for a degree would be better spent in the theatre gaining experience at one's craft.

1494   _____. "The Fabulous Invalid." STAGE 16 (November 1938): 34.

       Idealistic remarks about the New York commercial stage.

1495   _____. "How I Kept Myself from Being a Failure." LADIES' HOME JOURNAL, June 1919, p. 35.

Cowl describes and advocates her professional philosophy as "Don't wait for opportunities--create them!"

1496 _____. "Is Stage Emotion Real?" THEATRE (N.Y.) 23 (March 1916): 145-46, 158.

Drawing upon her own experiences, Cowl posits that real emotion is required for excellence in acting.

1497 _____. "Jane Cowl's Story." DELINEATOR 104 (April 1924): 10-11, 92, 94, 96. Illus.

Somewhat brief reminiscences of Cowl's childhood and early career.

1498 _____. "Personal Reminiscences." THEATRE (N.Y.) 24 (November 1916): 270-71. Illus.

An autobiographical sketch of no great distinction.

1499 _____. "Sex on the Stage." THEATRE (N.Y.) 29 (April 1919): 210.

The actress suggests sexual themes in the theatre retard the dignity of the profession.

1500 _____. "The Sob Part." GREEN BOOK MAGAZINE 11 (March 1914): 441-46. Illus.

A description of roles Cowl had played in which pathos was the major element.

1501 _____. "The Stage as a Career for Women." THEATRE (N.Y.) 31 (April 1920): 274, 276. Illus.

Cowl considers theatre perfectly acceptable and offers advice to those seeking employment there.

1502 _____. "Watch Sharply--The Next Time You Go to the Theatre." AMERICAN MAGAZINE 88 (September 1919): 36-37, 175-79. Illus.

Cowl describes the various staging techniques and illusions then used to focus an audience's attention.

1503 _____. "When Belasco Slapped Me." THEATRE (N.Y.) 29 (April 1919): 228. Illus.

Part of a series entitled "The Most Striking Episode in My Life." Cowl recalls Belasco driving her onto the stage once when she had very bad opening-night nerves.

1504　　　　. "Why a Reputation for Beauty is a Handicap." AMERICAN MAGAZINE 84 (August 1917): 50-51, 90-92. Illus.

Cowl suggests beauty interferes with one's artistic reputation and thus hinders an actress's growth.

1505　　　　. "With Sound Effects." THEATRE (N.Y.) 50 (September 1929): 12. Illus.

Cowl argues against stage realism, suggesting that it is probably a form of "degrading retrogression."

1506　Cowl, Jane, as told to Philip Wood. "An SOS for the Theatre." THEATRE (N.Y.) 46 (November 1927): 11-12, 58. Illus.

The actress decries the state of the theatre at that time, attributing the decline to inertia and indifference and calling for strong leadership in the future.

1507　Gaige, Crosby. FOOTLIGHTS AND HIGHLIGHTS. New York: E.P. Dutton and Co., 1948. 311 p. Index.

Theatrical reminiscences with substantial references to Cowl and Margaret Illington, with whom the author had performed.

1508　Kennedy, John B. "Jane Cowl's Only Job." COLLIER'S 78 (3 June 1926): 9. Illus.

Short interview in which Cowl recalls seeking a job as an actress upon the illness of her widowed mother and her subsequent success upon the stage.

1509　Patterson, Ada. "Jane Cowl's Approach to Juliet." THEATRE (N.Y.) 38 (October 1923): 22, 56. Illus.

Cowl is quoted as claiming to have read everything ever printed about ROMEO AND JULIET and recalls having seen Julia Marlowe in the role fifteen years earlier.

1510　Reed, Joseph Verner. THE CURTAIN FALLS. New York: Harcourt, Brace and Co., 1935. 282 p. Illus.

Chapter 7 is about Cowl and describes her performance in TWELFTH NIGHT.

1511　"A Romantic Realist." COSMOPOLITAN 54 (April 1913): 703-4. Illus.

A brief and vapid interview in which Cowl defends the romantic drama and suggests she tries to avoid being typed in her roles.

1512   "The Stars of Tomorrow."   THEATRE (N.Y.) 9 (November 1909): 156.
Illus.

An early description of Cowl as a rising young actress.

See also nos. 9, 13, 115, 256, 276, 320, 351, 377, 413, 483, 494, 500,
547, 579, 1471, 1477, and 3212.

CRABTREE, LOTTA

(1847-1924)

1513   "An Actress Who Gives Millions to Crippled Veterans." LITERARY DIGEST 83 (18 October 1924): 30-31. Illus.

     An appreciation of Crabtree and her estimated $4 million bequest, compiled largely from various newspapers.

1514   Baker, Mabella. "The Lotta I Knew." GREEN BOOK ALBUM 6 (August 1911): 385-87.

     Baker describes appearing with Crabtree in her final years on stage and their continuing friendship after retirement.

1515   Bates, Helen Marie. LOTTA'S LAST SEASON. Brattleboro, Vt.: Privately printed, 1940. 306 p. Frontispiece.

     Bates describes the reasons for Crabtree's retirement and suggests she was the last living person who had accurate knowledge of the time.

1516   Dempsey, David, with Raymond P. Baldwin. THE TRIUMPHS AND TRIALS OF LOTTA CRABTREE. New York: William Morrow and Co., 1968. 321 p. Index, illus., bibliog.

     A carefully researched, thinly documented, gracefully written account of Crabtree, which includes a chronology of her career and a list of her roles.

1517   Golden, Sylvia. "The Romance of Lotta, the Unapproachable." THEATRE (N.Y.) 53 (February 1931): 18-19, 64, 66. Illus.

     A well-written, but undocumented, appreciation and biographical sketch.

1518   Jackson, Phyllis W[ynn]. GOLDEN FOOTLIGHTS: THE MERRYMAKING CAREER OF LOTTA CRABTREE. New York: Holiday House, 1949. 310 p. Illus.

A highly speculative and undocumented treatment, written in the style of a novel. Romanticized and useless without corroboration.

1519   Kidder, Augusta Raymond. "Intimate Memories of Lotta." THEATRE (N.Y.) 40 (December 1924): 26, 68. Illus.

Anecdotal reminiscences compiled shortly after Crabtree's death.

1520   Page, Will A. "America's Richest Actress." THEATRE (N.Y.) 16 (October 1916): 114-16, viii-ix. Illus.

Page describes the process by which Lotta accumulated a fortune estimated at $4 million.

1521   Rourke, Constance. TROUPERS OF THE GOLD COAST; OR, THE RISE OF LOTTA CRABTREE. New York: Harcourt, Brace and Co., 1928, 1937. 275 p. Illus.

Although this substantial work is undocumented, the "Salutation," or preface, lists important collections of relevant material and thus inspires confidence. Also contains material on David Belasco, the Booths, the Chapmans, Julia Dean, Laura Keene, and Catherine Sinclair. See no. 1522.

1522   _____. "Troupers of the Gold Coast; or, The Rise of Lotta Crabtree." WOMAN'S HOME COMPANION 55 (May 1928): 7-10, 156-58, 162-63; (June 1928): 18-20, 82, 85-86, 88, 91; (July 1928): 15-17, 114-17; (August 1928): 31-33, 44, 46; (September 1928): 30-31, 100-102; (October 1928): 13-14, 175-75, 178, 180. Illus.

Serialization of no. 1521.

1523   Walsh, Thomas. "America's Queen of Comedy." THEATRE (N.Y.) 3 (July 1903): 176-77. Illus.

Walsh complains that Crabtree's early career had not been documented and offers a brief essay on the subject.

See also nos. 13, 153-54, 163, 166, 222, 262, 277, 279, 293, 328, 356, 413, 489, 493, 562, 572, 928, 1315, 1817, 1822, 2337, and 2599-2600.

CRANE, WILLIAM HENRY
(1845-1928)

1524   Ashby, Clifford. "William H. Crane: The Old School of Acting and the New." DRAMA SURVEY 3 (Winter 1964): 402-8.

An analysis of an article by Crane; see no. 1528.

1525   Crane, William H. "The Evolution of Stage Comedy." GREEN BOOK ALBUM 1 (May 1909): 1026-31.

Crane reviews his career, suggesting comedy had changed from physical to mental in the past four decades.

1526   _____. FOOTLIGHTS AND ECHOES. New York: Curtis Publishing Co., 1925, 1926. New York: E.P. Dutton and Co., 1927. ix, 224 p. Index, illus.

A detailed and readable autobiography, rich in anecdotal material. It includes substantial references to Stuart Robson and Joseph Jefferson III, with whom Crane appeared frequently. See no. 1527.

1527   _____. "Footlights and Echoes." LADIES' HOME JOURNAL, September 1925, pp. 8-9, 165-66, 168, 171; October 1925, pp. 23, 144, 147-48, 151, 153; November 1925, pp. 23, 167-68, 171, 173; January 1926, pp. 21, 139; February 1926, pp. 39, 131. Illus.

Serialization of no. 1526.

1528   _____. "The Old School and the New." INDEPENDENT 57 (December 1904): 1263-66.

Crane muses on changing styles in the theatre, disapproving of most of them. See no. 1524.

1529 _____ . "Some Developments of the American Stage During the Past Fifty Years." UNIVERSITY OF CALIFORNIA CHRONICLE 15 (April 1913): 207-20.

> Crane cites the emergence of native types in American drama, recalls production conditions in the early part of his career, and offers advice to those seeking jobs in the theatre. The text suggests that this was a public address, but the audience is not identified.

1530 _____ . "The Theatric Art of Make-Up." PHILHARMONIC 2 (February 1902): 6-13. Illus.

> Crane describes the changing techniques and demands of makeup over the course of his career. Seven photographs of Crane in various makeups are included.

1531 _____ . "Would We Laugh at Edwin Booth?" GREEN BOOK MAGA-ZINE 13 (June 1915): 1121-30. Illus.

> Crane contrasts and compares old and new styles of acting in the United States.

1532 Patterson, Ada. "At Home with William H. Crane." GREEN BOOK ALBUM 7 (April 1912): 872-77.

> Patterson describes Crane's home, the "Crib at Cohasset in Cape Cod County."

1533 _____ . "'The Need of the Stage is Plays!' Says Mr. Crane." THEATRE (N.Y.) 6 (August 1906): 213-15. Illus.

> Among several theatrical anecdotes, a plea for better dramaturgy in the United States.

1534 _____ . "William H. Crane--An Actor Who Loves His Art." THEATRE (N.Y.) 15 (January 1912): 8-10. Illus.

> Crane reminisces over his forty-nine year career in the theatre.

1535 Petty, Anne. "Robson and Crane." PLAYERS 48 (February-March 1973): 132-35. Illus.

> A sketchy overview of the collaboration of the two actors with some documentation.

See also nos. 28, 112, 176, 270, 279, 288, 328, 356, 379-80, 387, 413, 448, 501, 510-11, 513, 562, and 577.

CREWS, LAURA HOPE

(1879-1942)

1536   Bird, Carol. "Scarlet Roles Objectionable to Women." THEATRE (N.Y.) 34 (December 1921): 390, 432.

     Crews describes several roles she rejected because of their immorality.

1537   Patterson, Ada. "The Merry Wives of Gotham." THEATRE (N.Y.) 39 (April 1924): 12-13, 56. Illus.

     A joint interview of no great depth with Crews and Grace George, then co-starring in THE MERRY WIVES OF GOTHAM.

See also nos. 5, 13, 316, 437, 481, and 1691.

CROSMAN, HENRIETTA

(1861-1944)

1538   Crosman, Henrietta. "After the Matinee." GREEN BOOK ALBUM 3 (May 1910): 1085-89.

> Crosman describes her need for rest and spiritual rejuvenation between performances.

1539   _____. "The Gentle Art of Comedy." THEATRE (N.Y.) 25 (March 1917): 160-61. Illus.

> Crosman describes her career choices which led to her specialization in comedy.

1540   _____. "The Hardships of Stage Life." THEATRE (N.Y.) 2 (December 1902): 18-19.

> A brief essay on the trials and tribulations of acting as a career.

1541   _____. "My Stage Struggles and Triumphs." METROPOLITAN, December 1900, pp. 661-67. Illus.

> A brief and highly idealized autobiographical sketch, covering Crosman's career through her appearance in MISTRESS NELL IN 1900.

1542   _____. "The Plays an Actress Never Plays." GREEN BOOK ALBUM 3 (January 1910): 98-103.

> The actress describes some of the impossibly poor scripts submitted to her by amateur playwrights.

1543   _____. "Stage-Struck Youth and the Dramatic School." HAMPTON'S MAGAZINE 25 (August 1910): 239-48. Illus.

> Crosman's advice to stage aspirants with descriptions of various available training opportunities.

1544 _____. "The Story of 'Mistress Nell.'" HARPER'S 176 (February 1938): 279-90.

> Crosman relates how she became acquainted with George Hazelton and his script, MISTRESS NELL, in which she appeared successfully.

1545 Lorraine, Hollis. "With Rosalind in Arden, An Interview with Henrietta Crosman." THEATRE (N.Y.) 3 (August 1903): 195-97. Illus.

> An interview focused upon Crosman's work in AS YOU LIKE IT.

1546 Patterson, Ada. "Henrietta Crosman." GREEN BOOK MAGAZINE 10 (August 1913): 313-20. Illus.

> A fan-oriented and superficial interview conducted in the actress's home.

See also nos. 13, 28, 270, 276, 382-83, 413, 448, 480-81, 550, and 596.

CUSHMAN, CHARLOTTE

(1816-76)

1547   Abbott, Willis J. NOTABLE WOMEN IN HISTORY: THE LIVES OF WOMEN WHO IN ALL AGES, ALL LANDS, AND IN ALL WOMANLY OCCUPATIONS HAVE WON FAME AND PUT THEIR IMPRINT ON THE WORLD'S HISTORY. Philadelphia: John C. Winston Co., 1913. 448 p. Illus.

        Includes a five-page essay on Cushman, citing her as America's greatest tragedienne. Of minor value.

1548   Barrett, Lawrence. CHARLOTTE CUSHMAN: A LETTER. New York: Dunlap Society, 1889. Reprint. New York: Burt Franklin, 1970. 44 p. Frontispiece.

        In a very abbreviated treatment, Barrett devotes twenty-four pages to Cushman's life, the rest of the volume being a list of characters performed by the actress.

1549   Bradford, Gamaliel. BIOGRAPHY AND THE HUMAN HEART. Boston: Houghton Mifflin Co., 1932. 276 p. Index, illus., bibliog.

        Chapter 4 is a brief biographical sketch of Cushman. Of minimal value.

1550   Brewster, Annie H. "Miss Cushman." BLACKWOOD'S EDINBURGH MAGAZINE 124 (August 1878): 170-75.

        Chatty reminiscences of Cushman in several of her leading roles.

1551   Carr, Cornelia, ed. HARRIET HOSMER, LETTERS AND MEMORIES. New York: Moffat, Yard and Co., 1912. 377 p. Index, illus.

        Hosmer became a close friend of Cushman and makes frequent references to her, admittedly prejudicial.

1552   Clement, Clara Erskine. CHARLOTTE CUSHMAN. Boston: James R. Osgood, 1882. 193 p. Index.

An adulatory and detailed biography of Cushman, arranged chronologically. Useful, although superseded by later works. See no. 1581.

1553   Coats, Dorothy E. "The Masculine Repertoire of Charlotte Cushman." SOUTHERN SPEECH JOURNAL 11 (January 1946): 67-75.

The author skims traditional sources in this brief sketch of Cushman's career.

1554   Cushman, Charlotte. "Extracts from My Journal: The Actress." LADY'S BOOK AND MAGAZINE OF BELLES LETTRES, FASHIONS, MUSIC, ETC. 14 (February 1837): 70-73.

Excerpts from the first four chapters, covering the early stages of her career.

1555   _____ . ODE, RECITED BY MISS CHARLOTTE CUSHMAN AT THE INAUGURATION OF THE GREAT ORGAN IN BOSTON, NOVEMBER 2, 1863. Cambridge, Mass.: Welch, Bigelow and Co., 1863. 11 p.

A turgid bit of poetry, apparently written by Cushman.

1556   Cushman, Henry Wyles. A HISTORICAL AND BIOGRAPHICAL GENE-ALOGY OF THE CUSHMANS: THE DESCENDANTS OF ROBERT CUSHMAN, THE PURITAN, FROM THE YEAR 1617 TO 1855. Boston: Little, Brown and Co., 1855. 644 p. Index, illus.

A tribute to the entire family; pages 497-511 are devoted to the actress.

1557   Elkins, Hervey. FIFTEEN YEARS IN THE SENIOR ORDER OF SHAKERS: A NARRATION OF FACTS, CONCERNING THAT SINGULAR PEOPLE. Hanover, N.H.: Dartmouth Press, 1853. New York: AMS Press, 1973. 136 p.

The volume includes Cushman's "Lines suggested by a visit to the Shaker settlement near Albany, N.Y." on pages 4-5. The brief poem is followed by an anonymous poetic reply on pages 6-7.

1558   Ferris, George T. "Charlotte Cushman." APPLETON'S JOURNAL 11 (21 March 1874): 353-58. Illus.

A biographical tribute to Cushman, outlining the circumstances of her rise to fame.

1559 Fletcher, Edward G. "Charlotte Cushman's Theatrical Debut." In STUDIES IN ENGLISH, University of Texas Publication, no. 4026. Austin, 8 July 1940, pp. 166-75.

>A compendium of newspaper reviews and accounts of Cushman's first engagement.

1560 Goddard, Henry P. "Some Actresses I Have Known." THEATRE (N.Y.) 6 (August 1906): 206-7. Illus.

>Goddard describes his meetings with Cushman and Janauschek, among others. Minor piece.

1561 Hope, Frances. "Miss Marlowe's Hamlet, and Some Others." GREEN BOOK ALBUM 3 (May 1910): 1021-24.

>Marlowe planned to play Hamlet the following year; Hope describes other actresses who had played the Dane, including Cushman.

1562 Howitt, Mary. "The Miss Cushmans." PEOPLE'S AND HOWITT'S JOURNAL 2 (18 July 1846): 29-33, 47-49. Illus.

>A brief biographical sketch of Cushman's career to that time, prejudicially supportive.

1563 Leach, Joseph. BRIGHT PARTICULAR STAR: THE LIFE & TIMES OF CHARLOTTE CUSHMAN. New Haven, Conn., and London: Yale University Press, 1970. 442 p. Index, illus., bibliog.

>A detailed and documented treatment of Cushman, reflecting extensive research and careful scholarship. The most useful work on Cushman to date, essential to any study.

1564 Macready, William Charles. THE DIARIES OF WILLIAM CHARLES MACREADY 1833-1851. Edited by William Toynbee. 2 vols. New York: G.P. Putnam's Sons, 1912. London: Chapman and Hall, 1912. Index, illus.

>An edition of William Charles Macready's diary, with frequent references to Cushman and Edwin Forrest. See also editions by Sir Frederick Pollock (no. 1566) and J.C. Trewin (no. 1565).

1565 ____. THE JOURNAL OF WILLIAM CHARLES MACREADY 1832-1851. Edited by J.C. Trewin. London: Longmans, Green, and Co., 1967. xxxiii, 298 p. Index, illus.

>Trewin's excellent abridgements add to the usefulness of this volume. Cushman and Edwin Forrest are frequently mentioned. See editions by William Toynbee (no. 1564) and Sir Frederick Pollock (no. 1566).

1566 _____ . MACREADY'S REMINISCENCES, AND SELECTIONS FROM HIS DIARIES AND LETTERS. 2 vols. Edited by Sir Frederick Pollock. New York: Macmillan and Co., 1875. Published as one volume in 1876.

> The memoirs of William Charles Macready contain many references to Cushman and Edwin Forrest and their various relationships. See also Macready's material as edited by William Toynbee (no. 1564) and J.C. Trewin (no. 1565).

1567 Mearns, David C. "Charlotte Cushman's 'True and Faithful' Lincoln: Some Documents with Some Observations." LINCOLN HERALD 59 (Summer 1957): 3-10. Illus.

> Mearns describes the considerable impression Lincoln had made upon Cushman.

1568 "Miss Cushman." TALLIS'S DRAMATIC MAGAZINE 4 (February 1851): 100-103.

> The essay is the fourth part of a series entitled "Portrait Gallery." Stimulated by Cushman's London engagement, it is both biographical and critical.

1569 Parton, James. DAUGHTERS OF GENIUS: A SERIES OF SKETCHES OF AUTHORS, ARTISTS, REFORMERS, AND HEROINES, QUEENS, PRINCESSES, AND WOMEN OF SOCIETY, WOMEN ECCENTRIC AND PECULIAR FROM THE MOST RECENT AND AUTHENTIC SOURCES. Philadelphia: Hubbard Brothers, 1887. 563 p.

> Parton includes a brief and adulatory chapter on Cushman, pages 311-21, the only American actress included in the work.

1570 _____ . NOTED WOMEN OF EUROPE AND AMERICA, AUTHORS, ARTISTS, REFORMERS, AND HEROINES. QUEENS, PRINCESSES, AND WOMEN OF SOCIETY. WOMEN ECCENTRIC AND PECULIAR. FROM THE MOST RECENT AND AUTHENTIC SOURCES. Hartford, Conn.: Phoenix Publishing Co., 1883. 646 p. Illus.

> Forty-eight essays, of which number forty-six deals with Cushman. The essay is undocumented and adds little. See no. 1569.

1571 Pond, Major J.B. ECCENTRICITIES OF GENIUS: MEMORIES OF FAMOUS MEN AND WOMEN OF THE PLATFORM AND STAGE. New York: G.W. Dillingham Co., 1900. xxvi, 554 p. Index, illus.

> Among the subjects included are Cushman and Joseph Jefferson III, in brief and superficial essays.

1572   Price, W[illiam]. T[hompson]. A LIFE OF CHARLOTTE CUSHMAN.
New York: Brentano's, 1894. 180 p. Index, frontispiece.

> Adulatory in tone, this work has separate chapters on
> several of Cushman's more successful roles, such as Meg
> Merrilies, Nancy Sykes, Romeo, Wolsey, Queen Katherine,
> Lady Macbeth, and Bianca.

1573   Punkat, Elisabeth M. "Romeo was a Lady: Charlotte Cushman's London
Triumph." NEW YORK THEATRE ANNUAL 9 (1951): 59-69.

> A brief, documented description of Cushman's London debut.

1574   Smither, Nelle. "'The Bright Particular Star': Charlotte Cushman in
Albany." NEW YORK PUBLIC LIBRARY BULLETIN 71 (November 1967):
563-72. Illus.

> Smither, drawing heavily upon newspaper accounts, describes
> and documents Cushman's Albany engagement in 1836-37.

1575   _____. "Charlotte Cushman's Apprenticeship in New Orleans." LOUISI-
ANA HISTORICAL QUARTERLY 31 (October 1948): 973-80.

> Smithers describes Cushman's first full season as an actress
> and seeks to correct errors in previous treatments.

1576   _____. "A New Lady-Actor of Gentlemen. Charlotte Cushman's
Second New York Engagement." NEW YORK PUBLIC LIBRARY BULLETIN
74 (June 1970): 391-95.

> An assessment of Cushman's season at the National Theatre
> in 1837.

1577   Stebbins, Emma, ed. CHARLOTTE CUSHMAN; HER LETTERS AND
MEMORIES OF HER LIFE, EDITED BY A FRIEND. Boston: Houghton,
Osgood and Co., 1879. Reprint. New York: Benjamin Blom, 1969.
303 p. Index, illus.

> An adulatory but detailed account of Cushman by a close
> personal friend. Still useful, but superseded by more
> recent works. Sometimes cited as being by Cushman in
> some bibliographies and listings.

1578   Stockton, John D. "Charlotte Cushman." SCRIBNER'S 12 (June 1876):
262-66.

> A glowing critical account of Cushman's career, written
> as a tribute after her death.

1579   Walker, Mrs. Dr. REMINISCENCES OF THE LIFE OF THE WORLD-

RENOWNED CHARLOTTE CUSHMAN, COMPILED FROM VARIOUS RECORDS, BY MRS. DR. WALKER, HER CHOSEN MEDIUM: TOGETHER WITH SOME OF HER SPIRIT EXPERIENCES, EXPRESSIONS OF REGRET, ETC. Boston: William P. Tenney, 1876. 96 p. Illus.

> Walker claims to have communicated with Cushman's spirit after the actress's death in 1876. A brief and undistinguished biographical sketch precedes various bits of spiritualistic propaganda and supposed messages from beyond.

1580 Warner, William Frederic. "Charlotte Cushman in Lancaster." LANCASTER COUNTY HISTORICAL SOCIETY PAPERS 34, no. 8 (1930): 169-75.

> An assessment of Cushman as an actress in June and July 1841.

1581 Waters, Mrs. Clara Clement. CHARLOTTE CUSHMAN. American Actor Series. Edited by Laurence Hutton. Boston: J.R. Osgood, 1882. vi, 193. Illus. London: Brogue, 1882. Reprint. New York: Benjamin Blom, 1969.

> A chronological presentation of Cushman's career with sections of published critiques, letters, and the reminiscences of William T.W. Ball. See no. 1552.

1582 [White, R.G.] "Charlotte Cushman." NATION 19 (12 November 1874): 314.

> An appreciation of Cushman upon her retirement and an assessment of her talent and contributions to the theatre.

1583 Wiggins, James Henry. "Some Interesting But Little Known Facts About Charlotte Cushman." COMING AGE 3 (March 1900): 217-31. Illus.

> Wiggins met Cushman in Rome in 1864, late in her career. He recalls his acquaintance with her, describes her acting, and quotes several critical assessments of her playing.

1584 Wilson, Garff B. "Consider Theatrical Biographies." YALE THEATRE 5, no. 1 (1973): 139-45.

> Wilson reviews three theatrical biographies, among them Joseph Leach's BRIGHT PARTICULAR STAR (no. 1563), about which he makes several pages of comments.

See also nos. 6, 13, 19, 101, 119, 130, 166, 183, 195, 204, 210, 213, 222, 238, 245, 249, 262, 278, 292, 296, 307, 313, 332, 335, 337, 341, 352, 356, 357-58, 364-65, 367, 370, 383, 385, 395, 399-402, 404-5, 408, 413, 419, 425, 433, 442, 502, 519, 521, 538, 546, 566, 572-73, 593, 596, 674, 677, 1094, 1170, 2337, 2670, 2782, 2878, 2954, 3127, and 3168.

DALY, ARNOLD
(1875-1927)

1585   Daly, Arnold. "I Don't Like It." GREEN BOOK ALBUM 4 (October 1910): 880–82.

> Just before agreeing to play Hamlet, Daly castigates the Broadway critics as inept.

1586   _____. "My Beginnings." THEATRE (N. Y.) 8 (January 1908): 25–26, iv. Illus.

> Daly describes his entrée into the theatre by joining a company of Frank Mayo's.

1587   _____. "My Life--So Far." GREEN BOOK ALBUM 1 (January 1909): 157–59.

> The actor describes the early part of his career, including an engagement with Frank Mayo.

1588   _____. "Should the Doctor Order Laughter or Tears?" GREEN BOOK MAGAZINE 13 (February 1915): 346–48.

> Daly discourses on the therapeutic value of theatre-going.

1589   _____. "Why I Prefer European Playwrights." THEATRE (N. Y.) 25 (February 1917): 98, 118.

> While professing admiration for American playwrights, Daly accuses his managers of not allowing him to act in their scripts.

1590   Dodge, Wendell Philipps. "The Actor in the Street." THEATRE (N. Y.) 8 (December 1908): 326. Illus.

> Daly attests to the value of observing people in real life as an aid to role preparation.

1591   Goldsmith, B[erthold]. H. ARNOLD DALY. New York: James T. White and Co., 1927. 57 p. Illus.

> A concise and undocumented account, written with apparent objectivity. It includes a chronology of Daly's roles. The only substantial treatment of the subject.

1592   Patterson, Ada. "An Office Boy Who Became a Star." THEATRE (N.Y.) 4 (June 1904): 141–42, 144. Illus.

> An undistinguished interview in which Daly recalls his early production of CANDIDA.

See also nos. 219, 270, 377, 578, and 2589.

DALY, AUGUSTIN
(1839-99)

1593 "Augustin Daly." DONAHOE'S MAGAZINE 42 (1899): 35-41. Illus.

A memorial tribute published shortly after Daly's death.
The accompanying illustrations have not been widely published.

1594 "The Augustin Daly Library." ATHENAEUM, no. 3778 (24 March 1900):
371-72.

A detailed description of the Daly personal library, taken
from the sale catalog.

1595 Austin, W.W. "The American Stage a Generation Ago." THEATRE
(N.Y.) 14 (August 1911): 64-66, 68-70, vii. Illus.

Austin laments the passing of the stock companies such as
those run by Daly and Lester Wallack.

1596 Caffin, Charles H. "The Augustin Daly Collection." HARPER'S WEEKLY
44 (10 March 1900): 227-28. Illus.

A description of Daly's library and theatrical memorabilia,
then slated for the auction block. Fifteen thousand volumes
were included.

1597 Coleman, A.I. Du P. "Augustin Daly: An Appreciation." CRITIC
35 (August 1899): 712-20. Illus.

A memorial tribute and resume of Daly's career.

1598 Daly, Augustin. "American Drama." NORTH AMERICAN REVIEW 142
(May 1886): 485-92.

An optimistic statement about the state of the American
theatre in 1886.

1599   Daly, Joseph Francis. THE LIFE OF AUGUSTIN DALY. New York: Macmillan Co., 1917. 660 p. Index, illus.

A detailed biography prepared by the subject's brother. Contains considerable information on Daly's company and contemporary performers such as Edwin Booth, John Drew, Mrs. Gilbert, James Lewis, Richard Mansfield, and Ada Rehan.

1600   [Dithmar, Edward Augustus.] MEMORIES OF DALY'S THEATRES, WITH PASSING RECOLLECTIONS OF OTHERS, INCLUDING A RECORD OF PLAYS AND ACTORS AT THE FIFTH AVENUE THEATRE AND DALY'S THEATRE, 1869-95. New York: Privately printed, 1896. 143 p. Illus.

An adulatory tribute to Daly, including a breakdown of his productions by season. Includes numerous references to Daly's company members, especially Ada Rehan.

1601   Felheim, Marvin. "Daly's Ghost and the Rake of Avon." THEATRE ARTS 40 (October 1956): 66-68, 90-91. Illus.

Excerpts from the author's THE THEATRE OF AUGUSTIN DALY (no. 1602), dealing with Daly's Shakespearean productions.

1602   _____. THE THEATRE OF AUGUSTIN DALY: AN ACCOUNT OF THE LATE NINETEENTH CENTURY AMERICAN STAGE. Cambridge, Mass.: Harvard University Press, 1956. ix, 308 p. Index, illus. Reprint. New York: Greenwood Press, 1969.

A well-researched and comprehensive study, written in an engaging style; essential to any study of Daly or his company, especially Ada Rehan, John Drew, James Lewis, and Mrs. Gilbert.

1603   Forbes-Winslow, D. DALY'S: THE BIOGRAPHY OF A THEATRE. London: W.A. Allen and Co., 1944. 210 p. Index, illus.

A history of Daly's London operations, liberally sprinkled with incidents concerning American performers, especially Ada Rehan, although the rest of the "Big Four" (John Drew, James Lewis, and Mrs. Gilbert) are barely mentioned.

1604   Hall, Margaret. "Personal Recollections of Augustin Daly." THEATRE (N.Y.) 5 (June 1905): 150-53; (July 1905): 174-78; (August 1905): 188-91; (September 1905): 213-15. Illus.

Hall did not intend to write a biography of Daly, but to give her impressions of him as a friend for many years. Also contains material on Ada Rehan, Mrs. Gilbert, Fanny Davenport, John Drew, and May Irwin.

1605 Hibbert, H.G. FIFTY YEARS OF A LONDONER'S LIFE. London: Grant Richards, 1916. viii, 284 p. Index, illus.

> Daly and Edna May are featured in Chapter 16, "American Cousins." Hibbert mentions his reactions to various other visiting American performers.

1606 Horton, Judge William Ellis. ABOUT STAGE FOLKS. Detroit: Free Press Printing, 1902. 160 p. Illus.

> An anecdotal, episodic, and undocumented collection of brief essays, some of them vaguely biographical. Daly is the subject of one such treatment.

1607 Isaacs, Edith J.R., and Gilder, Rosamond. "Augustin Daly: The End of the Resident Company." THEATRE ARTS 27 (August 1943): 465–69. Illus.

> A brief tribute to Daly's as the best of the resident stock companies of his time.

1608 Kobbé, Gustav. "Augustin Daly and His Life-Work." COSMOPOLITAN 27 (1899): 405–18. Illus.

> A memorial tribute containing condensed biographical data, accompanied by exceptional illustrations. The company is described, but not in depth.

1609 Lathrop, George Parsons. "An American School of Dramatic Art. The Inside Workings of the Theatre." CENTURY 56 (June 1898): 265–75. Illus.

> A substantial account of the working conditions and procedures of Daly and his company just before the turn of this century.

1610 Lowenberg, Walter A. "The Passing of Daly's." THEATRE (N.Y.) 31 (October 1920): 166, 168. Illus.

> A description of Daly's successful methods for eliminating ticket speculation and a few remarks about his career in general.

1611 McCabe, L.R. "A Group of Rare Lambs." BOOK BUYER 20 (February 1900): 33–40. Illus.

> A description of Daly's library of some fourteen thousand volumes, 85 percent of which were theatrically oriented.

1612 O'Connor, Evelyn. "The Diary of a Daly Debutant." THEATRE (N.Y.) 15 (February 1912): 57–58. Illus.

The article identifies Dora Ranous as the author of the DIARY OF A DALY DEBUTANTE. See no. 1615.

1613   Osmun, Thomas Embley   [Alfred Ayres].   "The Stagecraft of Augustin Daly." THEATRE (N.Y.) 2 (December 1902): 26-27. Illus.

Brief and generalized remarks about Daly's accomplishments during his career.

1614   Phelan, Florence V. "A Child's Memory of Augustin Daly." THEATRE (N.Y.) 21 (March 1915): 136, 138, 140, 149. Illus.

Phelan's family and Daly were close friends, and Daly often visited their home. The essay also contains a few letters by Ada Rehan.

1615   [Ranous, Dora Knowlton.] DIARY OF A DAILY DEBUTANTE: BEING PASSAGES FROM THE JOURNAL OF A MEMBER OF AUGUSTIN DALY'S FAMOUS COMPANY OF PLAYERS. New York: Duffield, 1910. 249 p. Illus. Reprint. New York: Benjamin Blom, 1972.

A chatty and somewhat romanticized account of the theatre of the time. John Drew and Ada Rehan figure somewhat prominently in the text. See no. 1612.

1616   Schaal, David. "The Rehearsal Situation at Daly's Theatre." EDUCATIONAL THEATRE JOURNAL 14 (March 1962): 1-14.

Schaal draws upon numerous sources to present a detailed account of rehearsal procedures in the company.

1617   Shipman, C. "Treasures of the Daly Library." CRITIC 36 (March 1900): 213-19. Illus.

Shipman describes some of Daly's collection of theatrical memorabilia, such as the manuscript for THE SCHOOL FOR SCANDAL, David Garrick's will, and an autographed copy of Milton's PARADISE LOST.

1618   Towse, J. Ranken. "An American School of Dramatic Art. A Critical Review of Daly's Theatre." CENTURY 56 (June 1898): 261-64.

Towse praises Daly highly, citing his excellent taste and substantial accomplishments in the American theatre.

1619   Ventimiglia, Peter James. "The William Winter Correspondence and the Augustin Daly Shakespearean Productions of 1885-1898." EDUCATIONAL THEATRE JOURNAL 30 (May 1978): 220-28. Illus.

The author examines the twenty-year working relationship

between the critic and director, suggesting that Winter's
role has been overlooked.

1620   Wayne, Palma. "Mr. Daly." THEATRE ARTS 38 (August 1954): 67–
69, 93–96. Illus.

Wayne recalls a short-lived career in Daly's company and
describes the dedicated spirit of his players.

1621   Welch, Deshler. "Augustin Daly--Dramatic Dictator." BOOKLOVER'S
3 (1904): 490–504. Illus.

A detailed assessment of Daly as a manager-director, insightful and revealing, if perhaps a bit idealized. Includes several minor references to Ada Rehan.

See also nos. 17, 128, 163–64, 177, 211, 214, 228, 243, 300, 406, 432, 451,
488, 518, 529, 531, 548, 556, 562, 586–87, 593, 596–97, 908, 1060, 1750,
1903–04, 2115, and 2880.

DAVENPORT FAMILY
Davenport, Edward Loomis (1829-91)
Davenport, Fanny Elizabeth Vining (1829-91)

1622 Bayle, Bernard [B., B.]. "Mr. Davenport." TALLIS'S DRAMATIC MAGAZINE, no. 8 (June 1851): 11-12.

> A biographical and critical essay, suggesting Davenport showed promise, however flawed. Bayle considered the U.S. theatre of the time inherently inferior to that of England.

1623 Briscoe, Johnson. "The Daring Davenports." GREEN BOOK MAGAZINE 9 (March 1913): 471-77. Illus.

> Briscoe praises the family for essaying a wide range of roles.

1624 Davenport, Fanny. "Some Childish Memories." LIPPINCOTT'S 42 (October 1888): 565-67.

> A brief recollection of Davenport's first encounter with the theatre and her subsequent attraction to it. She includes some comments upon Edwin Booth, who was a frequent visitor in her home.

1625 _____. "Recollections of Fanny Davenport." THEATRE (Engl.), o.s. 12, n.s. 3 (March 1884): 164.

> Quotations from THE SPIRIT OF THE TIMES of relative insignificance.

1626 Edgett, Edwin Francis, ed. EDWARD LOOMIS DAVENPORT, A BIOGRAPHY. New York: Dunlap Society Publications, 1901. x, 131 p. Index, illus. Reprint. New York: Burt Franklin, 1970.

> The only substantial study of Davenport, covering his entire theatrical career by examining correspondence, reviews, and cast lists.

1627 Goddard, Henry P. "Recollections of E.L. Davenport." LIPPINCOTT'S 21 (April 1878): 463-68.

> A biographical eulogy, citing several reminiscences of the actor by the author and quoting his observations on the art of the theatre.

1628 Row, Arthur. "Great Moments in Great Acting." POET LORE 29 (May-June 1918): 358-63.

> Includes brief remarks about Fanny Davenport as Gismonde; not especially descriptive.

See also nos. 28, 58, 120, 171, 203, 210, 222, 227, 245, 247, 250, 262-63, 277, 279, 288, 293, 302, 313, 328, 337, 341, 346-47, 356, 383, 385, 387, 399-400, 413, 417, 426, 433, 489, 516, 530, 572, 596, 771, 1050, 1604, 1749-50, 2337, 2618, 2622, 2649, and 2880.

DAVIDGE, WILLIAM PLEATER

(1814-88)

1629 Davidge, William. THE DRAMA DEFENDED. ADDRESSES, WITH
RESPECT, TO THE PUBLIC GENERALLY, AND WITH COMMISERATION
TO MESSRS. THE REV. STRICKLAND T·L· CUYLER, &C·, &C·, &C·
New York: Samuel French, 1859. 22 p·

> A pamphlet of Davidge's replies and counterattacks on
> ministers who had either published letters or given sermons
> opposing the theatre.

1630 _____. FOOTLIGHT FLASHES. New York: American News Co·,
1866. 274 p· Illus·

> Davidge combines a reasonably detailed autobiography with
> descriptions of staging techniques and production circum-
> stances of the time·

See also nos· 245, 313, 334, and 399·

DAWN, HAZEL

(1894-   )

1631   Dawn, Hazel. "First Aids to Loveliness." GREEN BOOK MAGAZINE 13 (April 1915): 673-78. Illus.

> Fashion advice; one of a series of such articles by various celebrities.

1632   _____ . "Naughty Parts in Naughty Plays." THEATRE (N. Y.) 29 (May 1919): 278, 280. Illus.

> A fairly thoughtful essay in which Dawn recommends playing racy lines and roles with innocence in order to put the "responsibility for moral delinquency upon the audience."

1633   "Dawn of a Bright Era." THEATRE ARTS 43 (September 1959): 29-32. Illus.

> An interview in which Dawn reviews her career and vows to return to the stage, although she had not appeared in New York since 1931.

1634   "The Roseate Dawn." COSMOPOLITAN 55 (October 1913): 694-95. Illus.

> A brief description of Dawn's outstanding success in THE PINK LADY.

1635   "A Rose from Utah." COSMOPOLITAN 57 (October 1914): 698-99. Illus.

> An interview in which Dawn discusses female equality and the Mormon religion.

See also nos. 276 and 1981.

DEAN, JULIA
(1830-68)

1636 Grisvard, Larry E. "Julia Dean with Ludlow and Smith in St. Louis: 1847, 1848, and 1850." MISSOURI SPEECH JOURNAL 8 (1977): 18-21.

A brief and documented account of Dean's engagements, based primarily upon newspaper accounts.

1637 Henderson, Myrtle E. A HISTORY OF THE THEATRE IN SALT LAKE CITY FROM 1850 TO 1870. Evanston, Ill.: n.p., 1934. 161 p. Illus., bibliog.

A history which contains a bit of material about Dean's career in the West.

1638 Howard, Paul. "The Julia Deans--Yesterday and Today." THEATRE (N.Y.) 5 (September 1905): 228, 230. Illus.

A memorial tribute with some speculations on Dean's private life. Comparison is made to the later actress of the same name.

1639 Lindsay, John S[hanks]. THE MORMONS AND THE THEATRE, OR, THE HISTORY OF THEATRICALS IN UTAH, WITH REMINISCENCES AND COMMENTS HUMOROUS AND CRITICAL. Salt Lake City: Century Printing, 1905. 178 p. Frontispiece.

A somewhat mechanical treatment of the subject, studded with factual data. Chapter 7 (pp. 43-55) describes the 1865-66 season, including Dean's engagement.

1640 Maugham, Ila Fisher. PIONEER THEATRE IN THE DESERT. Salt Lake City: Deseret Book Co., 1961. xii, 165 p. Index, illus., bibliog.

A history based on research done for a graduate degree at the University of Utah in which the author includes some material on Dean's engagements in Salt Lake City.

See also nos. 13, 146, 153, 182, 196, 203, 222, 224, 226-27, 276-77, 302, 313, 400-401, 413, 492, 530, 570, 1521-22, 1672, 1750, 2235-36, 2330, 2337, and 2954.

DeANGELIS, JEFFERSON
(1889-1944)

1641   DeAngelis, Jefferson. "How I Returned to the Stage." THEATRE (N.Y.) 48 (September 1928): 17, 62. Illus.

> DeAngelis describes his decision to foresake comic opera and light opera for the legitimate stage; some autobiographical material is included.

1642   ———. "My Beginnings." THEATRE (N.Y.) 5 (August 1905): 205-6. Illus.

> DeAngelis describes his family and his early difficult days in variety entertainment.

1643   ———. "Science and the Stage." GREEN BOOK ALBUM 2 (November 1909): 1084-88.

> The actor speculates on technological innovations in the theatre.

1644   DeAngelis, Jefferson, and Harlow, Alvin F. A VAGABOND TROUPER. New York: Harcourt, Brace and Co., 1931. 325 p. Illus.

> A useful volume in which the actor describes his early days in the West through UNCLE TOM'S CABIN to his work in THE ROYAL FAMILY.

See also nos. 28, 112, 243, 279, and 378.

DeWOLFE, ELSIE

(1865-1950)

1645   DeWolfe, Elsie. "After All." LADIES' HOME JOURNAL, October
      1934, pp. 8-9, 68-69, 71-72, 74; November 1934, pp. 12-13, 72-74,
      76; December 1934, pp. 30-31, 94-96, 98-100; February 1935, pp. 34,
      48, 50, 52; April 1935, pp. 62, 104, 106, 108-9, 111, 121, 123-24,
      126, 128-29; May 1935, pp. 16, 72-74, 76. Illus.

> Serialized memoirs. See no. 1646.

1646   _____. AFTER ALL. New York and London: Harper and Brothers;
      Toronto: Ryerson Press; London: Heinemann, 1935. 278 p. Illus.

> An obviously idealized autobiographical treatment, more
> concerned with DeWolfe's social escalation than with her
> theatrical career. See no. 1645.

1647   _____. THE HOUSE IN GOOD TASTE. New York: Century Co.,
      1920. 322 p. Illus.

> A guide to interior decoration, offering advice to the
> designer-homemaker and describing the history and evolu-
> tion of modern houses. Irrelevant to DeWolfe's career in
> the theatre.

1648   Goodnow, Ruby Ross. "The Story of Elsie DeWolfe." GOOD HOUSE-
      KEEPING, June 1913, pp. 762-64. Illus.

> A brief biographical sketch focused upon DeWolfe's retire-
> ment from the stage for a career as an interior decorator.

1649   Moats, Alice-Leone. "The Elsie Legend." HARPER'S BAZAAR 83
      (May 1949): 110-11, 168-72, 177, 180. Illus.

> A biographical sketch of some substance, although fan
> and fashion oriented.

See also 13, 279, 303, 381, 574, and 581.

DIGGES, DUDLEY

(1879-1947)

1650   Digges, Dudley. "Theatre Guild Two Years Afterwards." THEATRE (N.Y.) 33 (April 1921): 266-67, 296. Illus.

> Digges, although not actually a member of the Guild, praises it highly as an exemplary production unit.

1651   Strauss, Theodore. "Dudley Digges." THEATRE ARTS 25 (October 1941): 712-20. Illus.

> An interview with Digges at age sixty-one; he reminisces about his long career and the changes in the theatre during that time.

1652   "Who's Who on Broadway." THEATRE (N.Y.) 31 (June 1920): 520, 566.

> Brief biographies of outstanding performers of the time, among them Digges.

See also nos. 413 and 464.

DODSON, J.E.

(1857-1931)

1653   Dodge, Wendell Phillips. "The Actor in the Street." THEATRE (N.Y.) 9 (July 1909): 20, 22-24. Illus.

       A substantial interview outlining Dodson's career, both in England and the United States.

1654   _____. "'Making Up' a Successful Character Actor." THEATRE (N.Y.) 10 (January 1910): 20-22. Illus.

       A detailed description of Dodson's make-up for the role of Sir John Cotswold in THE HOUSE NEXT DOOR.

1655   Dodson, J.E. "Some Memories of Irving." GREEN BOOK ALBUM 3 (January 1910): 176-83.

       Dodson reminisces about Sir Henry Irving, with whom he was a personal friend.

1656   Patterson, Ada. "Behind the Mask of a Great Character Actor." THEATRE (N.Y.) 5 (May 1905): 125-26, 128. Illus.

       Patterson describes Dodson not as a star, but as an "actor's actor."

See also nos. 28, 112, 270, 379, and 555.

DORO, MARIE
(1882-1956)

1657   Dale, Alan. [Pseud.] "Doro the Demure." GREEN BOOK MAGAZINE 15 (June 1916): 1121-26. Illus.

        Fan-oriented puffery, of minimal interest.

1658   Gannon, Marie Louise. "Dainty Marie Doro." GREEN BOOK MAGAZINE 9 (January 1913): 89-92.

        Doro, then noted for her beauty, is quoted as desiring character roles.

1659   Pollock, Arthur. "Doro and the Cold Eye of the Camera." MOTION PICTURE MAGAZINE 13 (April 1917): 38-40, 160. Illus.

        Doro compares and contrasts the different acting techniques required in film as opposed to the stage.

1660   Warwick, Anne. "Two Girls--The Story of Marie Doro." GREEN BOOK MAGAZINE 11 (May 1914): 733-36. Illus.

        Warwick describes her friendship with Doro, the result of an accidental meeting.

1661   "Winsome Marie Doro." COSMOPOLITAN 54 (May 1913): 844-45. Illus.

        The actress describes her work in OLIVER TWIST, A BUTTERFLY ON THE WHEEL, PATIENCE, and THE NEW SECRETARY, albeit in no significant depth.

See also nos. 270, 276, and 904.

DOUGLAS, MELVYN
(1901-81)

1662   Douglas, Melvyn. "How Do You Like Pictures?" STAGE 14 (December 1936): 110-11.

        Douglas admits to much absurdity in the film industry, but sees hope for substantial improvement.

1663   Millstein, Gilbert. "Melvyn Douglas." THEATRE ARTS 44 (January 1960): 30-32. Illus.

        Millstein quotes Douglas as he describes playing Clarence Darrow and reminisces about his career.

1664   Parish, James Robert, and Stanke, Don E. THE DEBONAIRS. New Rochelle, N.Y.: Arlington House, 1975. 475 p. Index, illus.

        Includes a film-oriented, undocumented chapter on Douglas, (pp. 71-130), which includes a complete filmography of the star.

1665   Spensley, Dorothy. "Hollywood's Most Civilized Marriage." MOTION PICTURE MAGAZINE 52 (November 1936): 34-35, 78. Illus.

        The story of Douglas's marriage to Helen Gahagan, written in fan-oriented style.

See also nos. 325 and 413.

DOUGLASS, DAVID

(?-1786)

1666   Graydon, Alexander. MEMOIRS OF HIS OWN TIME WITH REMINIS-
        CENCES OF THE MEN AND EVENTS OF THE REVOLUTION. Edited
        by John Stocton Littell. Philadelphia: Lindsay and Blakiston, 1846. xxiv,
        487 p. Index. Originally published as MEMOIRS OF A LIFE, CHIEFLY
        PASSED IN PENNSYLVANIA, WITHIN THE LAST SIXTY YEARS; WITH
        OCCASIONAL REMARKS ON THE GENERAL OCCURRENCES, CHARACTER
        AND SPIRIT OF THAT EVENTFUL PERIOD. Harrisburgh, Pa.: John
        Wyeth, 1811. Reprint. Edinburgh: W. Blackwood, 1822.

        Superficially indexed, but a brief section beginning on
        page 86 describes the theatre of the time, specifically
        the Douglass company. Graydon was not a regular theatre-
        goer and warns the reader that the "topic may be disgust-
        ing to persons of gravity."

1667   McNamara, Brooks Barry. "David Douglass and the Beginnings of Ameri-
        can Theatre Architecture." WINTERTHUR PORTFOLIO 3 (1967): 112-
        35. Illus.

        While the article is focused upon theatre architecture
        and scenery, McNamara describes Douglass's contributions
        in some detail with exceptional research and documentation.

1668   Mays, David D. "On the Authenticity of the 'Moral Dialogues' Playbill."
        THEATRE SURVEY 20 (November 1979): 1-14.

        Mays questions the validity of Douglass's supposed playbill
        for a thinly disguised production of OTHELLO in 1761.

See also nos. 121, 123, 138, 143, 148, 183, 225, 230, 238, 241, 253, 259,
266, 399, 445, and 2016.

DRAKE, SAMUEL

(1769-1854)

1669 Trollope, Frances. DOMESTIC MANNERS OF THE AMERICANS. Edited by Donald Smalley. New York: Alfred A. Knopf, 1949. lxxxiii, 455 p. Index, illus., bibliog.

> One of several editions of Trollope's work. She encountered the Drake family in the United States and describes their circumstances.

1670 Weisert, John Jacob. THE CURTAIN ROSE: A CHECKLIST OF PER-FORMERS AT SAMUEL DRAKE'S CITY THEATRE AND OTHER THEATRES AT LOUISVILLE FROM THE BEGINNING TO 1843. Louisville: n.p., 1958. vi, 176 p. Index.

> Lists of dates of productions, scripts given, and players' appearances. No connective or descriptive text.

1671 _____. "An End and Several Beginnings: The Passing of Drake's City Theatre." FILSON CLUB HISTORY QUARTERLY 50 (January 1976): 5-28.

> Drawing upon the Louisville newspapers for the period, Weisert describes the termination of Drake's managerial career in that city.

1672 _____. "The First Decade at Sam Drake's Louisville Theatre." FILSON CLUB HISTORY QUARTERLY 39 (October 1965): 287-310.

> A carefully researched study, drawing heavily upon published accounts from the Louisville PUBLIC ADVERTISER for the time. Engagements by Thomas Abthorpe Cooper and Julia Dean are described in passing.

1673 _____. "Golden Days at Drake's City Theatre, 1830-1833." FILSON CLUB HISTORY QUARTERLY 43 (July 1969): 255-70.

> Drawing heavily upon local newspaper accounts, Weisert

offers a detailed description of Drake's managerial activities for the specified period of time.

See also nos. 133, 146, 166, 180, 413, 1307, 1487, 2348, and 2957.

DRAPER, RUTH
(1884-1956)

1674 Canfield, Mary Cass. GROTESQUES AND OTHER REFLECTIONS. New York and London: Harper and Brothers, 1927. 238 p.

> The volume contains two essays dealing with American actresses, both admired greatly by the author. Mrs. Fiske is treated on pages 132–40; Draper on pages 196–203. Both essays are adulatory.

1675 Grenfell, Joyce. JOYCE GRENFELL REQUESTS THE PLEASURE. London: Macmillan, 1976; New York: St. Martin's Press, 1976. 288 p. Index, illus.

> Draper is the subject of chapter 17, "Monologues, Ruth Draper, and How I Learned by Doing," in which Grenfell describes Draper's influence upon her.

1676 Origo, Iris. "Ruth Draper and Her Company of Characters." ATLANTIC 202 (October 1958): 56–60. Illus.

> A reprint of no. 1677.

1677 _____. "Ruth Draper and Her Company of Characters." CORNHILL MAGAZINE, no. 1014 (1957–58), pp. 383–93. Illus.

> An adulatory description of Draper's monologues. See no. 1676.

1678 Rogers, Neville, with Dr. William Draper. "The Art of Ruth Draper." OHIO REVIEW 20 (Winter 1978): 6–23. Illus.

> Rogers reminiscences about Draper and a description of her recital before Mussolini. The author was assisted by Draper's nephew, Dr. Draper.

1679 Warren, Neilla, ed. THE LETTERS OF RUTH DRAPER 1920–1956: A SELF-PORTRAIT OF A GREAT ACTRESS. Foreward by John Gielgud.

New York: Charles Scribner's Sons, 1979. xxi, 358 p. Index, illus., bibliog., discography.

> An invaluable study of Draper, containing a genealogy as well as a descriptive list of her most successful monologues. The letters are connected by biographical material by Warren.

1680 Woolcott, Alexander. GOING TO PIECES. New York and London: G.P. Putnam's Sons, 1928. 256 p.

> "Ruth Draper," pages 99-109, is a tribute to the actress and a brief biographical sketch.

1681 [X.] "Miss Ruth Draper." SPECTATOR 135 (24 October 1925): 692-93.

> A brief description of Draper's "Original Character Sketches."

1682 Zabel, Morton Dauwen. THE ART OF RUTH DRAPER. New York: Doubleday and Co.; London: Oxford University Press, 1960. 373 p. Illus.

> A memoir of the actress with the text of thirty-seven of her best-known monologues.

See also nos. 525 and 2886.

DRESSLER, MARIE
(1869-1934)

1683 Beery, Wallace. "Her." MOTION PICTURE MAGAZINE 41 (April 1931): 32-33. Illus.

> An article praising Dressler after the author and she had an immense success in MIN AND BILL. See no. 1686.

1684 Dibble, Sue. "Marie Dressler Knows Her Cook-Book." MOTION PICTURE MAGAZINE 42 (November 1931): 78, 80. Illus.

> Recipes for a few of Dressler's more successful dishes.

1685 Dressler, Marie. THE EMINENT AMERICAN COMEDIENNE MARIE DRESSLER IN THE LIFE STORY OF AN UGLY DUCKLING: AN AUTOBIOGRAPHICAL FRAGMENT IN SEVEN PARTS, ILLUSTRATED WITH MANY PLEASING SCENES FROM FORMER TRIUMPHS AND FROM PRIVATE LIFE, NOW FOR THE FIRST TIME UNDER THE MANAGEMENT OF ROBERT M. McBRIDE. New York: Robert M. McBride, 1924. x, 234 p. Illus. London: Hutchinson, n.d.

> Chatty reminiscences, containing little factual data, but evoking the hardships of Dressler's vaudeville and early theatrical career. Some impressions of Lillian Russell are included.

1686 _____. "Him." MOTION PICTURE MAGAZINE 41 (April 1931): 32-33. Illus.

> See no. 1683.

1687 _____. "What We Want Today." GREEN BOOK ALBUM 4 (October 1910): 730-34.

> Dressler muses on the theatre's function as a diversion from mundane matters.

1688 Dressler, Marie, as told to Mildred Harrington. MY OWN STORY.

Foreward by Will Rogers. Boston: Little, Brown and Co., 1934. ix, 290 p. Illus. London: Hurst, 1935. Toronto: McClelland; Garden City, N.Y.: Blue Ribbon Books, 1936.

> While the bulk of the volume deals with Dressler's film career, several early chapters describe her work in comic opera and the legitimate theatre. Some discussion of Lillian Russell.

1689 Ergenbright, Eric L. "Marie Dressler 'Fatally Ill,' Fights to Live." MOVIE CLASSIC 7 (September 1934): 40. Illus.

> A dutiful reporting of Dressler's last illness.

1690 Kennedy, John B. "Working Girl." COLLIER'S 86 (1 November 1930): 16, 68-69. Illus.

> In a somewhat superficial essay, Dressler is quoted as she describes her early stage career and subsequent move to films.

1691 Klauber, Adolph. "Plays of Yesterday: Marie Dressler's Success in TILLIE'S NIGHTMARE." PEARSON'S 24 (July 1910): 88-95. Illus.

> Klauber describes a production starring Laura Hope Crews and Dressler in 1910.

1692 L., R. "By a Homely Man, about a Homely Woman, for other Homely Folks." HEARST'S 89 (November 1930): 19. Illus.

> A brief description of Dressler's waning fortunes on Broadway, her move to Hollywood, and her eventual success.

1693 Lee, Sonia. "Immortals of the Screen." MOTION PICTURE MAGAZINE 46 (October 1933): 32-33, 72. Illus.

> Lee includes Dressler and gives a brief tribute to her.

1694 Ruth, Jay W. "Marie Dressler--A Venture in Coming Back." THEATRE (N.Y.) 52 (October 1930): 39, 62. Illus.

> A brief article describing Dressler's move from stage to screen and back.

1695 Service, Faith. "How It Feels to Be Hollywood's First Citizen." MOTION PICTURE MAGAZINE 47 (February 1934): 52-53, 74. Illus.

> A fan-oriented treatment of Dressler's sixty-second birthday and the resultant celebration.

1696   Sherman, John. "Miss Marie. . . ." MOVIE CLASSIC 7 (October 1934): 44-45, 74. Illus.

> Fond recollections of Dressler by her long-time maid, Mamie Cox.

1697   Spensley, Dorothy. "Marie Dressler--Grand Old Fire Horse." MOTION PICTURE MAGAZINE 43 (April 1932): 26-27, 102, 104. Illus.

> Spensley records Dressler's reactions to winning the Academy Award for Best Actress.

1698   Walker, Helen Louise. "Wise to the Game." MOTION PICTURE MAGAZINE 41 (May 1931): 55, 106. Illus.

> Dressler describes her plans for the future, on the assumption her fame will not last.

See also nos. 13, 28, 142, 178, 276, 287, 311, 354, 384, 448, 481, and 490-91.

DREW FAMILY

Entries for John I, John II, Georgie, and Louisa Lane Drew follow this section.

1699 Judson, Alice. "A Child's Recollections of the Drews." METROPOLI-
TAN MAGAZINE, January 1901, pp. 32-41. Illus.

> Judson's parents evidently ran a rooming house at which
> the Drews stayed while on tour. She describes with
> considerable charm Mrs. Drew's generosity, John Drew's
> star qualities, and Maurice and Georgie Barrymore's
> humor.

1700 Patterson, Ada. "Unto the Fourth Generation of Players." THEATRE
(N.Y.) 22 (August 1915): 72-74, 91. Illus.

> Some general family reminiscences by Georgie Drew Mendum,
> the only child of Mrs. Drew who didn't go on the stage.

See also nos. 164, 347, 390, 417, 526, 567, 782-83, and 793.

DREW, JOHN I
(1827-62)

1701 Rogers, Benjamin G. "Recollections of John Drew, Sr." THEATRE
(Engl.) 3 (1887-88): 152-55.

> A memorial article which describes the elder Drew in most
> of his major roles, such as Sir Lucius O'Trigger and Handy
> Andy.

See also nos. 222, 396, 413, and 2235-36.

DREW, JOHN II
(1853-1927)

1702   Abbott, Lawrence F. "John Drew and his Art." OUTLOOK 145 (30 March 1927): 396-98. Illus.

> An assessment of Drew's stylistic contributions to the acting of his time, stimulated by his revival of TRELAWNEY OF THE WELLS.

1703   Davies, Acton. "John Drew." MUNSEY'S 34 (February 1906): 630-36. Illus.

> A relatively brief description of Drew's personality and career, Davies considering him perhaps the most popular actor then on the American stage.

1704   Dithmar, Edward A. JOHN DREW. New York: Frederick A. Stokes Co., 1900. 137 p. Illus.

> A somewhat prosaic but detailed account of Drew's career to that time by a leading critic who had been an eyewitness to most of Drew's major performances.

1705   Drew, John. "The Actor." SCRIBNER'S MONTHLY 15 (January 1894): 32-47. Illus.

> A substantial article, as much concerned with the social aspects of being a performer as with the artistic concerns.

1706   _____. "Changes and Tendencies of the American Stage." INDE-PENDENT 51 (9 November 1899): 3018-19.

> Drew suggests that although theatre architecture had improved greatly during his career, the art of acting had not. He cites examples of both.

1707   _____. MY YEARS ON THE STAGE. New York: E.P. Dutton and Co., 1922. 233 p. Index, illus.

> While Drew writes in a rather restrained and pedantic style, the volume is valuable for insights into the operation of Daly's company and several of his players: Maurice Barrymore, Ada Rehan, and James Lewis, for example. Drew's focus is upon his career; he mentions very little of his personal life.

1708   _____. "My Years on the Stage." LADIES' HOME JOURNAL, October 1921, pp. 8-9, 36, 38, 40; November 1921, pp. 6-7, 40, 43, 44-46; December 1921, pp. 14-15, 139-40, 143; January 1922, pp. 12-13,

105, 107; February 1922, pp. 21, 119, 121-22; March 1922, pp. 25, 147-49. Illus.

Serialization of no. 1707 with copious illustrations.

1709   . "What My Career Has Meant to Me." GREEN BOOK ALBUM 1 (May 1909): 1000-1003.

Drew reminisces with obvious relish about his thirty years upon the stage.

1710   "John Drew and His Plays." MUNSEY'S 26 (December 1901): 308-20.

Primarily a chronological list of Drew's major performances to that time.

1711   Kennedy, John B. "John Drew, Mummer's Boy." COLLIER'S 79 (12 March 1927): 10, 39-40. Illus.

In a fan-oriented interview, Drew recalls his theatrical debut in Mrs. Drew's company and his subsequent success, including his favorite roles.

1712   Kobbé, Gustave. "John Drew and His Daughter." LADIES' HOME JOURNAL, July 1903, pp. 7-8. Illus.

A description of Drew's home life at his cottage in East-hampton and the career of his daughter up to that time.

1713   Masterson, Kate. "John Drew." THEATRE (N.Y.) 1 (December 1901): 17-20. Illus.

A superficial description of Drew, the article being the first in a series, "Chats with Players."

1714   Wood, Peggy. A SPLENDID GYPSY: JOHN DREW. New York: E.P. Dutton and Co., 1927. 64 p.

A very brief account of Drew's last U.S. tour, in which the author replaced Pauline Lord as Imogen Parrot in a revival of TRELAWNEY OF THE WELLS.

See also nos. 28, 58, 112, 128, 131, 151, 213, 270, 276, 279, 287, 314, 321, 328, 345, 347, 356, 377, 379-80, 410, 412-13, 425, 427, 430, 432, 444, 448, 479, 555, 562, 575, 578-79, 587, 846, 1268, 1285, 1599, 1602, 1604, 1615, 1903, 1975, 2044, 2062, 2896, and 3177.

DREW, GEORGIE (1856-93). See nos. 13, 293, 451, 588, and 1699.

DREW, LOUISA LANE
(1820-97)

1715   Drew, Louisa Lane. AUTOBIOGRAPHICAL SKETCH OF MRS. JOHN
DREW. New York: Charles Scribner's Sons, 1899. 200 p. Reprint.
New York: Benjamin Blom, 1971.

> The basic source of information for Mrs. Drew's early
> career, in which she describes her work as a child star
> and her eventful management of the Arch Street Theatre
> in Philadelphia. The volume is well-illustrated and con-
> tains several anecdotes about leading players of the time.

1716   Gilder, Rosamond. "Mrs. John Drew." THEATRE ARTS 27 (May 1943):
310-19. Illus.

> A succinct biographical sketch of Mrs. Drew by a leading
> theatrical scholar.

1717   Malone, John. "What Are They That Do Play?" BOOK BUYER 20
(February 1900): 41-44. Illus.

> A review of Mrs. Drew's autobiography, containing
> additional biographical information and critical comments.

See also nos. 13, 112, 183, 222, 249, 279, 328, 340, 356, 413, 478, 513,
560, 846, 1711, 1750, 1803, 2149-50, 2234, 2614, and 2955.

DUFF, MARY ANN
(1794-1857)

1718   Ireland, Joseph N. MRS. DUFF. Boston: James R. Osgood, 1882.
188 p. Index.

> Although frequently at odds with later scholarship, this
> work contains a detailed chronology of Duff's career and
> considerable primary quoted material in praise of the
> actress. Useful if corroborated.

1719   Kendall, John Smith. "The American Siddons." LOUISIANA HISTORI-
CAL QUARTERLY 28 (July 1945): 922-40.

> A substantial monograph, undocumented, but extremely
> informative. Kendall quotes several published reviews
> in support of Duff.

1720   Wilson, Garff B. "The Forgotten Queen of the American Stage."
EDUCATIONAL THEATRE JOURNAL 7 (March 1955): 11-15.

> In a well-documented and highly descriptive article,
> Wilson proposes Duff as the greatest actress upon the
> U.S. stage prior to Charlotte Cushman.

See also nos. 13, 101, 210, 245, 341, 383, 399-400, 405, 449, and 2348.

DURANG, JOHN
(1768-1822)

1721   Durang, John. THE MEMOIR OF JOHN DURANG, AMERICAN ACTOR
        1785-1816. Edited by Alan S. Downer. Pittsburgh: University of
        Pennsylvania Press, 1966. xix, 166 p. Index, illus., bibliog.

>   Durang's memoirs, which were lost for a time, have been
>   meticulously edited by Downer, who added notes, references,
>   and an appendix. Durang's watercolor illustrations are in-
>   cluded in color. A valuable primary source.

1722   Kieffer, Elizabeth Clarke. "John Durang: The First Native American
        Dancer." PENNSYLVANIA FOLKLORE 21 (1954): 26-38. Illus.

>   A substantial account of Durang's career, well-researched
>   and illustrated, based in large part upon his MEMOIR.

1723   Moore, Lillian. "John Durang, the First American Dancer." In CHRONI-
        CLES OF THE AMERICAN DANCE, edited by Paul Magriel, pp. 15-37.
        New York: Henry Holt and Co., 1948. xii, 268 p. Illus., bibliog.

>   Although primarily concerned with Durang as a dancer,
>   this essay provides an overview of his entire career.

See also 123, 188, 192, 206, 241, 296, 358, and 434.

EAGELS, JEANNE

(1890-1929)

1724   Cruikshank, H. "The Hot-Spot." MOTION PICTURE MAGAZINE 38
(January 1930): 8, 123. Illus.

> A brief and undistinguished biographical sketch published
> shortly after the actress's death.

1725   Doherty, Edward. THE RAIN GIRL: THE TRAGIC STORY OF JEANNE
EAGELS. Philadelphia: Macrae Smith Co., 1930. 313 p. Illus.

> Described in NOTABLE AMERICAN WOMEN as a "jour-
> nalistic, undocumented biography, reliable in aspects
> which can be checked." An exploitive volume of little
> value without extensive corroboration.

1726   Eagels, Jeanne. "The Actor is More Important than the Play." THEATRE
(N.Y.) 47 (January 1928): 20, 72. Illus.

> Eagels contrasts the techniques required for film and stage
> acting, suggesting the performer is the most important
> element in both.

1727   _____. "My Greatest Tragedy." THEATRE (N.Y.) 29 (February
1919): 98. Illus.

> Part of a series, "The Most Striking Episode in My Life."
> Eagels describes a hostile reception in a small Kansas
> town when she was thirteen.

1728   Kennedy, John B. "Alias Sadie Thompson." COLLIER'S 80 (1 October
1927): 14, 32. Illus.

> A fan-oriented and somewhat superficial survey of Eagels's
> career and success in RAIN.

1729   McIntyre, O.O. "Ah, for the Girls of Yesteryear." HEARST'S 99
(October 1935): 74-75, 90. Illus.

A light-hearted article in which the author recalls
several beauties of his youth, among them Eagels.

1730   Morehouse, Ward. FORTY-FIVE MINUTES PAST EIGHT.   New York:
Dial Press; Toronto: McClelland, 1939. 267 p.

Morehouse describes his recollections of Eagels and recalls an account of her sudden death.

1731   Mullett, Mary B.   "From 'Hick' Town Tent Shows to the Lights of Broadway." AMERICAN MAGAZINE 96 (November 1923): 34, 184-90.
Illus.

At the height of her success in RAIN, Eagels is quoted
as she recalls being a child star in such midwestern tent
shows as BUFFALO BILL, JUNIOR.

1732   Patterson, Ada. "How Jeanne Eagels Became 'Sadie Thompson.'"
THEATRE (N.Y.) 38 (September 1923): 19, 68.

Patterson describes Eagels's techniques of observing real
people in order to delineate the role in RAIN.

See also nos. 9, 13, 185, 276, 296, 358, 413, 464, 945, and 1477.

ELLIOTT, MAXINE
(1871-1940)

1733   A., W.B. "Evolution of a Stage Beauty." THEATRE (N.Y.) 5 (April 1905): 100-101. Illus.

> The author likens Elliott to the ugly duckling with regard to the maturation of her appearance.

1734   Abthorpe, Ray. "Some Unique Performances." THEATRE (N.Y.) 30 (August 1919): 102.

> A few anecdotal remarks about Elliott; of minimal value.

1735   Broeck, Helen Ten. "Three Impressions of Maxine Elliott." THEATRE (N.Y.) 25 (February 1917): 74-75. Illus.

> Broeck discusses having seen Elliott in three roles and compares her reactions.

1736   Dale, Alan. [Pseud.] "Maxine the Magnificent." COSMOPOLITAN 52 (May 1912): 847-51. Illus.

> Dale quotes Elliott's comments on acting technique and the necessity for it in a successful career.

1737   "The Drama and a Dream of Fair Women: Miss Maxine Elliott's New Theatre in New York." BURR McINTOSH MONTHLY 19 (April 1909): n.p. Illus.

> A four-page description of the Maxine Elliott Theatre with several photographs of the interior.

1738   Elliott, Maxine. "How I Built My Theatre." WOMAN'S HOME COMPANION 36 (April 1909): 11, 78. Illus.

> Elliott's theatre, just off Broadway on Thirty-ninth Street in New York, opened 30 December 1908. In this article, the actress describes the financing, construction, and decoration of the building.

1739 ———. "Maxine Elliott's Advice to Stage-Struck Girls: 'Don't.'" THEATRE (N.Y.) 8 (August 1908): 202-3. Illus.

> Elliott describes the odds against theatrical success as prohibitive.

1740 Forbes-Roberston, Diana. MY AUNT MAXINE: THE STORY OF MAXINE ELLIOTT. New York: Viking Press, 1964. 297 p. Index, illus.

> Elliott's niece (the daughter of Gertrude Elliott) takes her aunt to task for her social snobbery as she focuses on Elliott's personal rather than professional life. Nat Goodwin is mentioned substantially.

1741 Hughes, Carol. "The Strange Story of Maxine Elliott." CORONET 33 (December 1952): 55-58. Illus.

> An undocumented and superficial biographical sketch; of minimal value.

1742 "Maxine Elliott's Villa." VOGUE, 1 October 1932, pp. 44-45. Illus.

> Three black-and-white photographs and a brief paragraph on Elliott's real estate holdings in Cannes, France.

1743 Patterson, Ada. "At Home with Maxine Elliott." GREEN BOOK ALBUM 5 (January 1911): 219-24.

> A superficial interview, concerned mostly with Elliott's propensity for buying and selling real estate.

1744 ———. "Beautiful Maxine Elliott: An Interview." THEATRE (N.Y.) 3 (November 1903): 270-72. Illus.

> A rambling interview of the most superficial nature.

1745 Pierce, Lucy France. "Will Maxine Elliott Return to Us?" GREEN BOOK ALBUM 8 (December 1912): 945-52. Illus.

> No prediction is made; Pierce supplies only a description of the actress and her estate at that time.

1746 Scherer, Ionia. "America's Only Actress-Manager." GREEN BOOK ALBUM 1 (April 1909): 812-17.

> Elliott is quoted as she discusses the vicissitudes of theatrical management and outlines her hopes for the future.

1747 White, Matthew, Jr. "Maxine Elliott." MUNSEY'S 35 (April-September 1906): 762-66. Illus.

White recounts how Elliott, beginning as merely a stage beauty, slowly rose to fame as an actress of some merit.

1748 Woollcott, Alexander. "The Truth about Jessica Dermot." COSMO-POLITAN 95 (October 1933): 62-63, 173-74. Illus.

A biographical sketch of Elliott, whose real name was Jessica Dermot, after her retirement to a villa at Cannes in southern France. Reprinted in Woollcott's THE PORTA-BLE WOOLLCOTT, no. 411.

See also nos. 28, 270, 276, 279, 303, 381-82, 413, 438, 482, 555, 579, 581-82, 588, and 597.

ELLSLER, EFFIE

(1854?-1942)

1749   Ellsler, John A. THE STAGE MEMORIES OF JOHN A. ELLSLER.
Cleveland: Rowfant Club, 1950. iv, 159 p. Illus.

> The author was Effie Ellsler's father; his memoirs offer
> little about the actress, but supplies family background
> and describes managerial and acting practices of the
> time. He includes many anecdotes about the Booths,
> Edwin Forrest, and E.L. Davenport.

See also nos. 13, 28, 256, 279, 293, and 493.

EYTINGE, ROSE

(1835-1911)

1750   Eytinge, Rose. THE MEMORIES OF ROSE EYTINGE: BEING RECOL-
LECTIONS AND OBSERVATIONS OF MEN, WOMEN, AND EVENTS,
DURING HALF A CENTURY. New York: Frederick A. Stokes Co.,
1905. 311 p. Illus.

> A volume especially useful for its evocation of frontier
> theatre history. Eytinge also describes her many col-
> leagues over her long career, among them Julia Dean,
> Ada Clare, Edwin Booth, John Wilkes Booth, E.L. Daven-
> port, J.W. Wallack, Fanny Davenport, George Holland,
> Augustin Daly, W.J. Florence, Mrs. Gilbert, Dion
> Boucicault, Steele Mackaye, Mrs. Drew, John McCullough,
> Mary Anderson, and Adah Isaacs Menken.

See also nos. 13, 222, 264, 290, 387, 400, 413, and 2585.

FAVERSHAM, WILLIAM

(1868-1940)

1751 Eaton, Walter Prichard. "Concerning William Faversham." AMERICAN
MAGAZINE 75 (April 1913): 61-66. Illus.

> Eaton expresses admiration for Faversham's industry and
> perserverance in the theatre, including some biographical
> data along the way.

1752 Faversham, William. "How I Found My Iago." HARPER'S WEEKLY
58 (28 February 1914): 22. Illus.

> The actor describes how a short story by Poe and a play
> by Knoblauch provided the keys for his character analysis.

1753 _____. "My First Hit." THEATRE (N.Y.) 29 (January 1919): 14.
Illus.

> Part of a series, "The Most Striking Episode in My Life."
> Faversham recalls his early success as Prince Emil in
> Bronson Howard's ARISTOCRACY.

1754 _____. "The Poetic Drama in America." GREEN BOOK ALBUM 3
(April 1910): 773-79.

> Faversham predicts a splendid future for the poetic drama,
> considering the need for the poetic as basic to mankind.

1755 _____. "That Fellow in the Box Office." GREEN BOOK ALBUM 8
(August 1912): 278-83. Illus.

> The actor describes financial abuses in the ticket offices,
> calling upon managers to reform their personnel.

1756 Fyles, Vanderheyden. "A Letter from Mrs. Faversham." GREEN BOOK
MAGAZINE 13 (April 1915): 634-35.

> The actor's wife corrects an earlier article by Fyles
> in which he gave her credit for her husband's successes.

1757   Goudiss, C. Houston. "How the Artist Keeps Fit from William Faver-
        sham's Point of View." THEATRE (N.Y.) 27 (March 1918): 178, 182.
        Illus.

> An article primarily concerned with Faversham's diet and
> the need for physical fitness in acting.

1758   Kronshage, Ernst H. "Novelty in Shakespeare." PLAYBOOK 1
        (October 1913): 28-30.

> A brief discussion of Faversham's staging of the balcony
> scene in ROMEO AND JULIET, in which he did away
> with the balcony.

1759   Lincks, Peggy. "Welcome William Faversham." MOTION PICTURE
        MAGAZINE 16 (December 1918): 42. Illus.

> A brief sketch of Faversham, outlining the high points
> of his career.

1760   Patterson, Ada. "At Home with the Favershams." GREEN BOOK
        ALBUM 6 (July 1911): 94-99.

> A superficial interview, focusing upon the Favershams'
> place in high society.

1761   _____. "William Faversham--An Interview." THEATRE (N.Y.) 4
        (September 1904): 221-23. Illus.

> A fan-oriented and superficial treatment of the actor.

See also nos. 28, 131, 151, 270, 276, 279, 379-80, 413, 455, 506, 525,
579, and 2955.

FECHTER, CHARLES
(1824-79)

1762   Burnham, Charles. "Charles Fechter's Debut in America." THEATRE (N.Y.) 25 (January 1917): 7-8, 62.

Burnham describes seeing Fechter's debut, as well as the newspaper quarrel involving Fechter, Frank Chanfrau, and James Wallack, from which he quotes letters by each.

1763   Coleman, John. PLAYERS AND PLAYWRIGHTS I HAVE KNOWN: A REVIEW OF THE ENGLISH STAGE FROM 1840 TO 1880. 2 vols. Philadelphia: Gebbie and Co., 1890. 328, 399 p. Illus.

Coleman deals almost exclusively with English actors and playwrights. Chapter 4 of volume 2 (pp. 295-322) describes Fechter as a popular sensation when he first appeared in London.

1764   Dickens, Charles. "On Mr. Fechter's Acting." ATLANTIC MONTHLY 24 (August 1869): 242-44.

A brief essay praising Fechter, especially his Hamlet, just before his American debut.

1765   Field, Kate. CHARLES ALBERT FECHTER. Boston: James R. Osgood, 1882. 193 p. Index, illus. Reprint. New York: Benjamin Blom, 1969.

After chronicling Fechter's career in Europe and America, Field presents detailed descriptions of his Hamlet and Claude Melnotte, shorter accounts of four other roles, and concludes with a series of newspaper reviews and tributes to the actor, one by Charles Dickens.

1766   _____. "Charles Albert Fechter: A Biographical Sketch." ATLANTIC MONTHLY 26 (September 1870): 285-307.

A substantial monograph, undocumented and adulatory in tone. Superseded by the previous entry.

1767   ____. "Fechter as Hamlet." ATLANTIC MONTHLY 26 (November 1870): 558-70.

> Field describes Fechter's playing of the role, attempting to explain and support his various innovations in staging and characterization.

1768   Hamley, Sir Edward B. SHAKESPEARE'S FUNERAL AND OTHER PAPERS. Edinburgh and London: William Blackwood and Sons, 1889. 311 p.

> Includes a ten-page essay, "Mr. Fechter's Othello," in which Hamley proposes that Fechter is better suited to several other Shakespearean roles than Othello.

1769   Lewes, George Henry. ON ACTORS AND THE ART OF ACTING. London: Smith, Elder and Co., 1875. New York: H. Holt and Co., 1878, 1880, 1892. New York: Grove Press, n.d. 237 p. Index.

> Chapter 11, "Foreign Actors on Our Stage," includes a detailed description and criticism of Fechter as Hamlet and Othello.

1770   Mills, John A. "The Modesty of Nature: Charles Fechter's Hamlet." THEATRE SURVEY 15, no. 1 (1974): 59-78.

> Mills cites Scott, Dickens, and Collins to support his premise that Fechter "deserves a more prominent niche in the pantheon of stage Hamlets than he has hitherto been assigned."

1771   "Mr. Charles Fechter." GALAXY 9 (April 1870): 554-61.

> The anonymous critic considers Fechter without peer in romantic or sentimental acting, but considers him unfit for high tragedy, either French or English.

1772   Ottley, Henry. FECHTER'S VERSION OF OTHELLO, CRITICALLY ANALYSED, BY HENRY OTTLEY, WITH PREFATORY OBSERVATIONS ON THE STAGE, THE AUDIENCE, AND THE CRITICS. London: T.H. Lacy, 1861. 32 p.

> Ottley takes Fechter to task in no uncertain terms for his nontraditional playing, decrying his repudiation of past generations of players. Reprinted from the MORNING CHRONICLE.

1773   [Ottley, Henry?] "Shakespeare Travestied." DUBLIN UNIVERSITY MAGAZINE, February 1862, pp. 170-82.

> An analysis of Fechter's Shakespearean roles, for which the author finds him totally unsuited and incapable of understanding.

1774   "Shakespeare and His Latest Stage Interpreters." FRASER'S MAGAZINE
64 (December 1861): 772-86.

> The anonymous critic discusses the state of the English-
> speaking stage in general, discusses Charles Kean for a
> few pages, then focuses upon Fechter and his Shakespear-
> ean innovations, finding them, if not brilliant, worthy
> of study.

1775   [White, R.G.] "The New Hamlet." NATION 10 (24 February 1870):
118-19.

> An analysis of Fechter's Hamlet, which the critic con-
> siders intolerable.

1776   Whiting, Lilian. KATE FIELD: A RECORD. Boston: Little, Brown
and Co., 1899. 577 p. Index, illus.

> A number of references are made to various foreign stars,
> among them Fechter, about whom Field had written re-
> views and a biography (see nos. 1765-67).

1777   Wilmot. A RETROSPECTIVE GLANCE AT MR. FECHTER'S IAGO, AND
ACTING EDITION OF OTHELLO. London: Thomas Hailes Lacy, 1862.
31 p.

> The author takes Fechter to task for breaking tradition
> and misconceiving OTHELLO.

1778   Woods, George B. "The New Tragedian." OLD AND NEW 1 (April
1870): 514-19.

> The author gives Fechter a very mixed review for his
> work in America, although he admits that the actor's
> best roles had not yet been performed and bases most
> of his evaluation upon his Hamlet.

1779   Yates, Edmund Hodgson. FIFTY YEARS OF LONDON LIFE: MEMOIRS
OF A MAN OF THE WORLD. New York: Harper and Brothers, 1884,
1885. xvii, 444 p. Illus.

> A meandering and undistinguished autobiography which includes
> brief observations on Fechter during his London engagements.

See also nos. 21, 119, 127, 130-31, 141, 204, 221, 231, 236, 245, 247,
281, 292, 325, 337, 341, 345, 356, 363, 368, 371, 399, 401, 408, 413,
474, 489, 521, 523, 538, 566, 585, 588, 590, 1124, 1231, 1242, 1885,
and 2235-36.

FENNELL, JAMES
(1766-1816)

1780   Entry deleted.

1781   Fennell, James. AN APOLOGY FOR THE LIFE OF JAMES FENNELL
WRITTEN BY HIMSELF. 1814. Reprint. New York: Benjamin Blom,
1969. xiii, 510 p.

> Fennell's autobiography is undisciplined and erratic; his
> self-inflicted vicissitudes after his arrival in America
> (p. 333 f.) evoke the early days of the American theatre.

1782   _____. DESCRIPTION OF THE PRINCIPLES AND PLAN OF PROPOSED
ESTABLISHMENTS OF SALT WORKS; FOR THE PURPOSE OF SUPPLYING
THE UNITED STATES WITH HOME MADE SALT. Philadelphia: Printed
by John Bioren, 1798. 60 p.

> A detailed description of Fennell's ill-fated desalination
> project.

1783   _____. A REVIEW OF THE PROCEEDINGS AT PARIS DURING THE
LAST SUMMER. INCLUDING AN EXACT AND PARTICULAR ACCOUNT
OF THE MEMORABLE EVENTS, ON THE 20TH OF JUNE, THE 14TH OF
JULY, THE 10TH OF AUGUST, AND THE 2ND OF SEPTEMBER; WITH
OBSERVATIONS AND REFLECTIONS ON THE CHARACTERS, PRINCIPLES
AND CONDUCT OF THE MOST CONSPICUOUS PERSONS CONCERNED
IN PROMOTING THE SUSPENSION AND DETHRONEMENT OF LOUIS
THE SIXTEENTH. London: E. and T. Williams, 1792. vi, 492 p.

> An eyewitness account of the early stages of the French
> Revolution.

1784   _____. A STATEMENT OF FACTS OCCASIONAL OF AND RELATIVE
TO THE LATE DISTURBANCES AT THE THEATRE-ROYAL, EDINBURGH.

Edinburgh: John and James Ainslies, 1788. London: John Bell, 1788. 56 p.

> Fennell's version of his altercation with John Jackson over the casting of Jaffier in VENICE PRESERVED.

1785 "Memoirs of Mr. Fennell." POLYANTHOS 4 (March 1807): 216-28. Illus.

> A substantial biographical sketch of Fennell, unsigned and undocumented.

1786 "Sketch of the Life of Mr. Fennell, the Celebrated Tragedian." POLYANTHOS 1 (February 1806): 187-90.

> A brief tribute, undocumented and unsigned.

See also nos. 101, 123, 188-89, 225, 238, 245, 399, 402, 413, 517, 553-54, and 1008.

FERGUSON, ELSIE
(1883-1961)

1787   Craig, Ralph H. "The Unguessed Riddle." COSMOPOLITAN 54 (January 1913): 269-70. Illus.

> A meandering interview with Ferguson as she prepared her role in PRIMROSE for opening. It includes a discussion of her qualities as an emotional actress.

1788   "Elsie and the Starry Way." COSMOPOLITAN 58 (March 1915): 458-59. Illus.

> A very brief and superficial overview of Ferguson's career to that time.

1789   Ferguson, Elsie. "After a Year of Real Success." GREEN BOOK MAGAZINE 14 (August 1915): 295-99. Illus.

> The actress reminisces about her training, trials, and tribulations while achieving star status.

1790   _____. "Backgrounds for Personality." GREEN BOOK MAGAZINE 13 (May 1915): 833-37. Illus.

> Fashion notes for women.

1791   _____. "Do You Yearn to Go on the Stage?" GREEN BOOK MAGAZINE 9 (April 1913): 599-604. Illus.

> Unavailable for examination; volume in the New York Public Library is mutilated.

1792   _____. "Helping Our Heroes Thru the Red Cross." MOTION PICTURES MAGAZINE 17 (June 1919): 28-29, 109. Illus.

> Ferguson describes her volunteer war efforts.

1793   _____. "How I Became a Star." GREEN BOOK ALBUM 3 (February 1910): 382-89.

Ferguson describes working as a chorus girl, supporting
player, and a leading lady before achieving star status.

1794   Hall, Gladys. "An Orchid Speaks." MOTION PICTURE MAGAZINE
19 (February 1920): 30-32. Illus.

Unabashed puffery.

1795   Naylor, Hazel Simpson. "Real Folk: Marshall Nielan and Elsie
Ferguson." MOTION PICTURE MAGAZINE 15 (September 1918): 34-
37, 121. Illus.

Brief remarks on working conditions and backgrounds of
the two performers; Ferguson was filming a western at
the time.

1796   P., A. [Ada Patterson?] "A Little Queen of the Stage in Real Life."
THEATRE (N.Y.) 9 (November 1909): 152-54. Illus.

The author describes Ferguson as unusually intelligent
and sensible.

1797   Patterson, Ada. "Personality Portraits No. 4: Elsie Ferguson." THEATRE
(N.Y.) 32 (July-August 1920): 20.

A description of Ferguson's qualities as an actress which
had led to considerable imitation.

1798   Sears, Gwen. "Elsie Ferguson, America's Own Actress." THEATRE
(N.Y.) 29 (May 1919): 298, 302.

Ferguson contrasts her life as a film actress and a stage
star.

1799   "The Stars of Tomorrow." THEATRE (N.Y.) 9 (February 1909): 69.
Illus.

Two paragraphs of an anonymous article predict a bright
future for Ferguson on the New York stage.

1800   "We Interview Miss Ferguson." MOTION PICTURE MAGAZINE 22
(October 1921): 22-24. Illus.

In a fan-oriented interview, Ferguson describes her plans
for vacation travel and the pace of life in America.

See also nos. 5, 270, 276, 377, and 582.

FISHER, CHARLES
(1816-91)

1801   "Departed Stage Favorites." ILLUSTRATED AMERICAN 2 (18 July 1891): 401.

Fisher is given a brief memorial tribute.

See also nos. 128, 319, 328, 404, 432-33, and 1050.

FISHER, CLARA

(1811-98)

1802   THE BIOGRAPHY OF THE BRITISH STAGE; BEING CORRECT NARRA-
TIVES OF THE LIVES OF ALL THE PRINCIPAL ACTORS & ACTRESSES
AT DRURY-LANE, COVENT-GARDEN, THE HAYMARKET, THE LYCEUM,
THE SURREY, THE COBURG, AND THE ADELPHI THEATRES. INTER-
SPERSED WITH ORIGINAL ANECDOTES AND CHOICE AND ILLUSTRA-
TIVE POETRY. TO WHICH IS ADDED, A COMIC POEM, ENTITLED
"THE ACTRESS." London: Sherwood, Jones, and Co., 1824. 295 p.
Illus.

      Pages 71-78 are a discussion of Fisher as a fourteen year-
      old child prodigy on the London stage.

1803   Maeder, Clara Fisher. AUTOBIOGRAPHY OF CLARA FISHER MAEDER.
Edited by Douglas Taylor. New York: Dunlap Society, 1897. Reprint.
New York: Burt Franklin, 1970. xlviii, 138 p. Illus.

      A charming and modest autobiography, mentioning most
      of the leading players of the time, albeit briefly. Basic
      to any study of Fisher.

1804   A SKETCH OF THE LIFE OF MISS CLARA FISHER, THE LILLIPUTIAN
ACTRESS OF THE THEATRES-ROYAL, DRURY-LANE AND COVENT
GARDEN. London: 1818. London: Lowe, 1819. 54 p. Glasgow:
Printed by William Tait, 1820.

      The first item on microfilm reel no. MW p.v. 132 in the
      Lincoln Center Theatre Collection, although not so indexed.
      It consists of ten pages of general background on Fisher,
      followed by a collection of critiques from various published
      sources.

1805   "Theatrical Portraits." NEW YORK MIRROR AND LADIES' LITERARY
GAZETTE 6 (20 September 1828): 87; 7 (12 September 1829): 76-77.

      Brief analysis with few biographical facts about the actress.

See also nos. 13, 101, 112, 121, 186, 210, 222, 261, 296, 341, 358, 399,
400, 413, 2330, 2348, and 3168.

FISKE, MINNIE MADDERN

(1865-1932)

1806   Arliss, George. UP THE YEARS FROM BLOOMSBURY: AN AUTO-
BIOGRAPHY. New York: Blue Ribbon Books, 1927. 312 p. Index,
frontispiece.

        The English actor includes a description of his seasons
        with Fiske in chapter 11, "Mrs. Fiske as a Producer."

1807   Ashby, Clifford. "Minnie Maddern Fiske: The Imperfect Ibsenite."
THEATRE SURVEY 4 (1963): 41-50.

        In a well-documented article, Ashby suggests Fiske's
        contributions to American realism in the theatre have
        been exaggerated and that she became a champion of
        Ibsen only by default.

1808   Binns, Archie, in collaboration with Olive Kooken. MRS. FISKE AND
THE AMERICAN THEATRE. New York: Crown Publishers, 1955. x,
426 p. Index, illus.

        A comprehensive and laudable biographical treatment,
        but undocumented. Much of the material apparently
        came from the Minnie Maddern Fiske-Harrison Grey Fiske
        Collection. Essential to any Fiske study.

1809   Booth, Alice. "Minnie Maddern Fiske." GOOD HOUSEKEEPING,
November 1931, pp. 34-35, 106, 108. Illus.

        Fiske was selected by the magazine as one of America's
        twelve most distinguished women. This tribute stresses
        her excellence as Becky Sharp.

1810   Bragdon, Claude. "Mrs. Fiske: Off the Stage and On." THEATRE
GUILD MAGAZINE 9 (April 1932): 32-35. Illus.

        A shallow critical account of the actress with a few
        personal memories. Of minimal value.

1811   Calder, Chester T. "Mrs. Fiske--Our Intellectual Actress." THEATRE
       (N.Y.) 17 (June 1913): 182, 184. Illus.

       Calder describes Fiske's more successful roles in terms
       of her intellectual analysis of them.

1812   Dale, Alan. [Pseud.] "Mrs. Fiske--Artiste." COSMOPOLITAN 54 (April
       1913): 698-700. Illus.

       Dale compares the career of Minnie Maddern to that of
       Mrs. Fiske, as though a dual personality were being
       considered.

1813   Dickinson, Thomas H. "The Record of Mr. and Mrs. Fiske." PLAY-
       BOOK 1 (August 1913): 3-9.

       The author praises the couple for being theatrically well
       ahead of their time and includes a list of their produc-
       tions.

1814   Dodge, Wendell Phillips. "Mrs. Fiske, America's Intellectual Actress."
       STRAND (N.Y.) 44 (October 1912): 382-92. Illus.

       An extended tribute with considerable biographical detail.
       Fiske is quoted on several theatrical topics, such as
       Ibsen, the Theatre Syndicate, and her artistic preferences.

1815   Eaton, Walter Prichard. "Mrs. Fiske and Her Influence on the American
       Stage." CENTURY 81 (April 1911): 866-69. Illus.

       Eaton considered Fiske, "though she be a woman," the
       leader of the American theatre because of her excellent
       acting and directing.

1816   _____. "The Theatre Mrs. Fiske Knew." THEATRE ARTS 16 (May
       1932): 371-76.

       Eaton recalls the high points of Fiske's career in a
       memorial tribute shortly after her death. He also
       describes the production circumstances under which she
       worked.

1817   Fiske, Minnie Maddern. "The Gift of Comedy." DRAMA (Washington,
       D.C.) 10 (May 1920): 249-50.

       Brief and unsubstantial remarks praising Duse and Lotta
       Crabtree as examples of excellence in comic acting.

1818   _____. "Ibsen's Influence on the Drama." THEATRE (N.Y.) 2
       (December 1902): 28.

Fiske castigates Ibsen for having what she considered a
pernicious influence on the theatre.

1819 _____. "The Ideal Play." PHILHARMONIC 2 (November 1902):
239-40. Illus.

Fiske calls for a return to "nobility of emotion" in
American drama, which she feels is lacking at the time.

1820 _____. "The Matter of the Play." INTERNATIONAL MONTHLY 5
(May 1904): 629-44.

Fiske discusses drama as a social force and acting as an
art, finding both of potential value to society.

1821 _____. "Plays of Stage Life." HARPER'S WEEKLY 58 (23 August
1913): 12. Illus.

Fiske offers a bit of pro-theatre propaganda, citing the
high moral standards of most theatre workers.

1822 _____. "Stage Child." GOOD HOUSEKEEPING, April 1932, pp. 48-
49, 212, 215-17. Illus.

The first chapter of Fiske's autobiography and the only
one she completed before her death. She describes her
rise to theatrical eminence and includes a few anecdotes
about the elder Booth, Edwin Booth, and Lotta Crabtree.

1823 Griffith, Frank Carlos. MRS. FISKE. New York: Neale Publishing
Co., 1912. 146 p. Illus.

The author was Fiske's manager from 1897 to 1910. His
biography of her, while undocumented, is insightful,
especially with regard to the later periods of her career.

1824 Henderson, Elliott. "Mrs. Fiske and Her New Theatre." HARPER'S
WEEKLY 45 (19 October 1901): 1061.

A brief article describing Fiske's difficulties securing
and opening the Manhattan Theatre on 24 September 1901.

1825 "How Mrs. Fiske Posed for the Movies." THEATRE (N.Y.) 19 (February
1914): 86-87, 90. Illus.

A description of the circumstances surrounding the filming
of TESS OF THE D'URBERVILLES.

1826 McM., F.H. "The Art of Mrs. Fiske." THEATRE (N.Y.) 2 (June
1902): 9. Illus.

A brief and adulatory essay. Of minimal value.

1827 "The Manhattan Stock Company." THEATRE (N.Y.) 1 (September 1901): 10. Illus.

> Harrison Grey Fiske is quoted about his plans to open the Manhattan Theatre.

1828 "Mrs. Fiske Dissects and Ridicules Sex-Nonsense on the Stage." CURRENT OPINION 72 (January 1922): 69.

> Fiske contends that the male playwrights of the time tended to exploit sex-ridden heroines.

1829 "Mrs. Fiske Surpasses Herself. "As if by Alexander Woollcott." STAGE 14 (August 1937): 73. Illus.

> A satire on Woollcott's style with Fiske as the supposed subject.

1830 Mullett, Mary B. "Mrs. Fiske Talks about Life on Both Sides of the Footlights." AMERICAN MAGAZINE 88 (October 1919): 37, 210, 212, 214-16. Illus.

> A substantial interview made late in Fiske's career. The actress describes her vegetarianism and repeats several of her theories about the theatre.

1831 Nathan, George Jean. ART OF THE NIGHT. Rutherford, Madison, Teaneck, N.J.: Fairleigh Dickinson University Press, 1928. 296 p.

> On pages 51-54 Nathan offers his observations on Mrs. Fiske's production of GHOSTS.

1832 _____. MR. GEORGE JEAN NATHAN PRESENTS. New York: Alfred A. Knopf, 1917. Rutherford, Madison, Teaneck, N.J.: Fairleigh Dickinson University Press, 1971. 310 p.

> Chapter 14, "America's Most Intellectual Actress," (pp. 183-204) is a substantial assessment of Fiske's career.

1833 "Note. Minnie Maddern Fiske Papers." THEATRE NOTEBOOK 15 (Summer 1961): 115.

> A note describing the acquisition of some 23,000 items concerning Fiske by the Library of Congress.

1834 "Noted American Actress a Winning Personality in Private Life." NATIONAL MAGAZINE 52 (January-February 1924): 366. Illus.

> An interview of no great distinction, describing Fiske's long career in the theatre.

1835   Patterson, Ada. "Mrs. Fiske's Tribute to her Mentor." THEATRE (N.Y.)
        39 (February 1924): 64.

        Fiske describes and praises the influence of her husband,
        Harrison Grey Fiske, editor of the NEW YORK DRAMATIC
        MIRROR.

1836   Schwab, Arnold T. "Minnie Maddern Fiske's Birthdate: A Correction."
        NINETEENTH CENTURY THEATRE RESEARCH 8 (Autumn 1980): 87–90.

        Schwab suggests that the traditional date of 19 December
        1865 is wrong and that Fiske was actually born in 1864.

1837   "The Stage Honors Mrs. Fiske." THEATRE (N.Y.) 29 (June 1919): 360.

        A description of a banquet held in honor of the actress
        at the Hotel Biltmore on 6 April 1919.

1838   Towne, Charles Hanson. "There Was Only One Mrs. Fiske." STAGE
        14 (January 1937): 110–12. Illus.

        An adulatory tribute of no distinction.

1839   Tyrrell, Henry. "Minnie Maddern Fiske: An Impression." THEATRE
        (N.Y.) 3 (October 1903): 246–50. Illus.

        An interview with Fiske at the time she was preparing
        HEDDA GABBLER and thus championing the work of Ibsen.

1840   W., W. "Sex Nonsense on the Stage." THEATRE (N.Y.) 34 (November
        1921): 294.

        Fiske is quoted as decrying some of the more lurid de-
        velopments in American drama.

1841   Woollcott, Alexander. MRS. FISKE: HER VIEWS ON ACTORS, ACTING,
        AND THE PROBLEMS OF PRODUCTION. New York: Century Co.,
        1917. Reprint. MRS. FISKE: HER VIEWS ON THE STAGE RECORDED
        BY ALEXANDER WOOLLCOTT. New York and London: Benjamin
        Blom, 1968. 229 p. Illus.

        An assessment by a leading critic of Fiske's approaches
        and philosophies of the theatre and drama. Essential to
        any Fiske study; considerable biographical data is in-
        cluded.

1842   _____. "Mrs. Fiske Punctures the Repertory Idea." CENTURY 93
        (November 1916–April 1917): 321–32; "Mrs. Fiske on Ibsen the Popular,"
        529–38; "Mrs. Fiske to the Actor-in-the-Making," 714–23; "Mrs. Fiske

Builds a Theatre in Spain," 909-18; "Mrs. Fiske Goes to the Play," 94 (May-October 1917): 71-82. Illus.

A heavily illustrated serialization of no. 1841.

1843 _____. "The Story of Mrs. Fiske." COLLIER'S 76 (7 November 1925): 5-6, 43; (14 November 1925): 9-10, 43; (21 November 1925): 20-21. Illus.

A substantial biographical treatment, partially related to the previous two entries.

1844 _____. "What the Public Got." EVERYBODY'S 44 (June 1921): 42-43. Illus.

Woollcott celebrates Fiske's four decades in the theatre and includes a few biographical details in his survey of her work.

1845 Young, Stark. "Estimate of Mrs. Fiske's Work." NEW REPUBLIC 70 (2 March 1932): 71-72.

A memorial tribute, but also an analytical overview of Fiske's career and its deterioration toward the end.

See also nos. 8, 13, 28, 58, 150-51, 164, 177, 213, 219, 261, 270, 272, 276, 279, 285, 288, 291, 294, 296-97, 303, 316, 323, 328, 332, 358, 377, 381-83, 400, 408, 410-11, 413, 430, 436, 440, 448, 464, 512, 525, 545, 578-79, 588, 596-97, 889, 1077, 1471, 1674, 1981, 2115, 2161, 2879, and 3094.

FLORENCE, WILLIAM J.

(1831-91)

1846   Goddard, Henry P. "Players I Have Known--Jefferson and Florence."
        THEATRE (N·Y·) 7 (April 1907): 100, 102, ix.

> Reminiscences of both players, with the bulk of the article
> devoted to Florence.

See also nos· 58, 112, 222, 302, 328, 336, 341, 343, 356, 375, 383, 396,
399, 404, 413, 419, 460, 468, 472, 496, 581, 1750, 2270, and 3136.

FONTANNE, LYNN
(1887-)

See also LUNT, ALFRED.

1847 Corathiel, Elisabethe. "How They Began. 8.--Lynn Fontanne."
THEATRE WORLD 21 (March 1934): 113. Illus.

A brief interview by a London reporter. Fontanne discusses taking acting lessons from Ellen Terry, her tours
of America, and her marriage to Alfred Lunt.

See also nos. 5, 9, 276, 291, 298, 376-77, 394, 415, 464, 486, 498, 504,
597, 797, 1477, 1981, 2044, and 3092.

FORREST, EDWIN

(1806-72)

1848 ACCOUNT OF THE TERRIFIC AND FATAL RIOT AT THE NEW YORK
ASTOR PLACE OPERA HOUSE, ON THE NIGHT OF MAY 10, 1849;
WITH THE QUARRELS OF FORREST AND MACREADY. New York:
H.M. Ranney, 1849. 32 p. Frontispiece.

A detailed account of the riot, including later testimony.
The volume also describes James H. Hackett, the manager
of the theatre at the time.

1849 Alden, Barbara. "Edwin Forrest's Othello." THEATRE ANNUAL 14
(1956): 7-18.

A well-documented study based on published critiques
and Forrest's promptbook. The frontispiece of this volume
is of Forrest.

1850 Alger, William Rounseville. LIFE OF EDWIN FORREST, THE AMERI-
CAN TRAGEDIAN. 2 vols. Philadelphia: J.B. Lippincott Co., 1877.
Reprint. New York: Benjamin Blom, 1972. Index, illus.

Alger was Forrest's official biographer, but the work
contains several substantial errors and the entire treatment
is sentimental and romantic. For a more detailed account
of the matter, see Gary Scharnhorst's "A Note on the
Authorship of Alger's LIFE OF EDWIN FORREST," no.
1879.

1851 Barrett, Lawrence. EDWIN FORREST. Boston: James R. Osgood and
Co., 1881; Houghton Mifflin, 1893. Reprint. New York: Benjamin
Blom; St. Clair Shores, Mich.: Scholarly Press, 1969. 158 p. Index.

Barrett dates the Astor Place Riot on 16 May 1848 rather
than 10 May 1849 and deals with Forrest's lurid divorce
case in only two pages, but the volume contains many
useful anecdotes. Requires corroboration.

1852   Dahl, Curtis. ROBERT MONTGOMERY BIRD. New York: Twayne
        Publishers, 1963. 140 p. Index, bibliog.

        Chapters 4 and 5 describe the relationship between
        Forrest and the playwright.

1853   Eaton, Walter Prichard. "Edwin Forrest." ATLANTIC 162 (August
        1938): 238-47.

        A thoughtful essay, evaluating Forrest's style while ad-
        mitting his excesses. Eaton decries the lack of exciting
        actors in 1938.

1854   Fife, Iline. "Edwin Forrest: The Actor in Relation to His Times."
        SOUTHERN SPEECH JOURNAL 9 (March 1944): 107-11.

        A quick sketch of Forrest based on traditional sources.

1855   Fleming, Arthur. "Behind the Scenes." HARPERS' 34 (December 1866):
        114-18.

        The author describes having seen Forrest as Spartacus and
        George Vandenhoff as Brutus.

1856   Forrest, Edwin. ORATION DELIVERED AT THE DEMOCRATIC REPUBLI-
        CAN CONVENTION OF THE SIXTY-SECOND ANNIVERSARY OF THE
        INDEPENDENCE OF THE UNITED STATES, IN THE CITY OF NEW
        YORK, FOURTH JULY, 1838. New York: Jared W. Bell, 1838. 24 p.

        The transcription of a patriotic speech given by Forrest
        in which he sets the tone by referring to the American
        Revolution as "the most august event which ever con-
        stituted an epoch in the political annals of mankind."

1857   THE FORREST DIVORCE CASE. CATHERINE N. FORREST AGAINST
        EDWIN FORREST. FULLY AND CORRECTLY REPORTED BY THE
        REPORTER OF THE NATIONAL POLICE GAZETTE; WITH OPENING
        AND CONCLUDING ARGUMENTS OF COUNSEL, CHARGE OF THE
        COURT, LETTERS FROM MR. AND MRS. FORREST, AND OTHER
        PERSONS OF STANDING AND INFLUENCE, TOGETHER WITH THE
        CONSUELO LETTER, AND OTHER INTERESTING DETAILS, LEADING
        TO THIS CONTROVERSY. New York: Stringer and Townsend, 1852.
        112 p. Illus.

        A day-by-day description of the proceedings, much of it
        in the form of a transcription. Includes two steel en-
        gravings of Forrest and Sinclair.

1858   THE FORREST DIVORCE SUIT: REPORT OF THE TRIAL OF CATHERINE
        N. FORREST VS. EDWIN FORREST FOR DIVORCE, HELD IN THE

SUPERIOR COURT OF NEW YORK, DEC., 1851 BEFORE CHIEF JUSTICE OAKLEY AND A SPECIAL JURY. New York: Herald Book and Job Office, 1851. 185 p.

> A detailed account of the trial, almost verbatim, gathered by the law reporter for the New York HERALD.

1859 Forster, John, and Lewes, George Henry. DRAMATIC ESSAYS, RE-PRINTED FROM THE EXAMINER AND THE LEADER, WITH NOTES AND AN INTRODUCTION BY WILLIAM ARCHER AND ROBERT W. LOWE. London: Walter Scott, 1896. xliv, 280 p. Index, frontispiece.

> A compendium of reviews, including essays on Forrest as Othello, Lear, Macbeth, and Richard III, including some discussion of his quarrel with Macready.

1860 Foust, Clement Edgar. THE LIFE AND DRAMATIC WORKS OF ROBERT MONTGOMERY BIRD. New York: Knickerbocker Press, 1919. Reprint. New York: Burt Franklin, 1971. x, 722 p. Index, frontispiece, bibliog.

> The first 159 pages of part 1 are a biographical treatment of the playwright with chapters 3 and 4 describing his association with Forrest.

1861 Frohman, Daniel. "Where Players Await Their Last Cue." THEATRE (N.Y.) 48 (December 1928): 30-31, 76. Illus.

> Frohman describes three theatrical retirement homes, including the Edwin Forrest Home in Philadelphia.

1862 Harrison, Gabriel. EDWIN FORREST: THE ACTOR AND THE MAN. CRITICAL AND REMINISCENT. Brooklyn: Brooklyn Eagle Book Printing Department, 1889. 210 p. Illus.

> Harrison was a personal friend of Forrest, who asked him to prepare this work. Harrison describes Forrest as Virginius, Metamora, Othello, Lear, and Damon, as well as his personal and professional life. A prejudicial treatment, useful if corroborated.

1863 Hartley, Randolph. "The Heirs of Edwin Forrest." THEATRE (N.Y.) 2 (April 1902): 16-19. Illus.

> A description of Forrest's retirement home for actors in Philadelphia.

1864 THE HISTORY OF EDWIN FORREST, THE CELEBRATED AMERICAN TRAGEDIAN, FROM HIS CHILDHOOD TO HIS PRESENT ELEVATED STATION AS A PERFORMER. WRITTEN BY AN INDIVIDUAL WHO HAS KNOWN HIM FROM HIS BOYHOOD. New York: Printed and published by the author, at No. 29 Ann Street, 1837. 24 p.

The author suggests he was stimulated to write this brief and early treatment because of an 1836 pamphlet on Forrest published by Warner and Fisher of Philadelphia. The volume praises Forrest throughout in most abstract language. The author does not identify himself.

1865   Jackson, Allan S. "Disaster Strikes: or Trouble at the Wampanoag's Camp." PLAYERS 43 (June-July 1968): 160-63. Illus.

A description of a mishap during a production of META-MORA largely quoted from Joseph Jefferson's AUTO-BIOGRAPHY.

1866   King, Emmett. "A Great Actor's Legacy." MUNCEY'S 44 (October 1910): 101-7. Illus.

An illustrated description and history of Forrest's home for retired actors.

1867   Lippincott, Henry F., Jr. "Tate's 'Lear' in the Nineteenth Century: The Edwin Booth Promptbooks." LIBRARY CHRONICLE OF THE UNIVERSITY OF PENNSYLVANIA 36 (Winter 1970): 67-75. Notes.

The essaysist suggests Forrest used the Tate version of KING LEAR in the United States long after it had been abandoned elsewhere because of the actor's virtual monopoly in the role.

1868   Mennen, Richard E. "Edwin Forrest's 'Improved' King Lear." THEATRE SOUTHWEST 7 (April 1981): 25-31. Illus., notes.

Mennen examines Forrest's promptscripts for annotations describing the evolution of his Lear, citing specific staging and performance techniques and alterations.

1869   Monaghan, Jay. [James]. THE GREAT RASCAL: THE LIFE AND AD-VENTURES OF NED BUNTLINE. Boston: Little, Brown and Co., 1952. 336 p. Index, illus., bibliog.

A well-documented biography of Forrest's friend, including a few remarks about the actor and a brief and derivative description of the Astor Place Riot. Extensive bibliography.

1870   Moody, Richard. ASTOR PLACE RIOT. Bloomington: Indiana University Press, 1958. x, 243 p. Illus.

An objective and scholarly account of the 1849 altercation and the quarrel between Forrest and the English actor, William Charles Macready.

1871 _____. EDWIN FORREST, FIRST STAR OF THE AMERICAN STAGE.
New York: Alfred A. Knopf, 1960. viii, 416 p. Index, illus.,
bibliog.

> An exemplary work of modern scholarship by an outstanding
> theatre historian. By far, the most useful single source
> on Forrest at the present time, basic to any study of the
> actor.

1872 Moses, Montrose. THE FABULOUS FORREST: THE RECORD OF AN
AMERICAN ACTOR. Boston: Little, Brown and Co., 1929. xviii,
355 p. Index, illus., bibliog.

> Moses does well in conjuring up the spirit of the times,
> but seems not to have great affection for the subject of
> his biography. Considerable material is overlooked in
> this treatment.

1873 Nardin, James T. "Forrest and Macready: A Note on Contrast."
THEATRE ANNUAL 15 (1957-58): 44-54.

> A comparison of the two actors' productions of DAMON
> AND PYTHIAS.

1874 Newton, Alfred Edward. EDWIN FORREST AND HIS NOBLE CREATION.
Philadelphia: Managers of the Edwin Forrest Home, 1928. 11 p. Illus.

> A description of the Edwin Forrest Home for Aged Actors
> as prescribed by Forrest's will and the circumstances under
> which it was founded.

1875 Rees, James [Colley Cibber]. THE LIFE OF EDWIN FORREST WITH
REMINISCENCES AND PERSONAL RECOLLECTIONS. Philadelphia:
T.B. Peterson and Brothers, 1874. 524 p. Frontispiece.

> Although a lengthy volume, Moody suggests it was some-
> what hastily written. Rees strains the evidence to justify
> Forrest's various eccentricities.

1876 REPORT OF THE FORREST DIVORCE CASE, CONTAINING THE FULL
AND UNABRIDGED TESTIMONY OF ALL THE WITNESSES, THE AFFI-
DAVITS AND DEPOSITIONS, TOGETHER WITH THE CONSUELO AND
FORNEY LETTERS. New York: Robert M. DeWitt, 1852. 187 p.

> A publication, described as the only version containing
> the "Suppressed Testimony," prepared by the "law reporter
> for the New York HERALD."

1877 Rosenberg, Marvin. "Othello to the Life." THEATRE ARTS 42 (June
1958): 58-61. Illus.

A description and assessment of Forrest's Othello, un-documented but highly evocative.

1878   Sabin, Joseph, comp. CATALOGUE OF THE LIBRARY OF EDWIN FORREST. Philadelphia: Collins, 1863. 165 p. Index, frontispiece.

A topically organized list of Forrest's extensive library.

1879   Schamhort, Gary. "A Note on the Authorship of Alger's LIFE OF EDWIN FORREST." THEATRE SURVEY 23 (1976-77): 53-55.

See no. 1850.

1880   Starr, Stephen Z. "William Charles Macready vs. Edwin Forrest." HISTORICAL AND PHILOSOPHICAL SOCIETY OF OHIO BULLETIN 7 (July 1959): 167-80.

An undocumented account of the Astor Place Riot and the events leading up to it. Superseded by later works.

1881   SUPERIOR COURT OF THE CITY OF NEW YORK: CATHERINE N. FORREST, RESPONDENT, AGAINST: EDWIN FORREST, APPELLANT, CASE. New York: Wm. C. Bryant, 1855. 467 p. Index.

The official transcript of the trial, including all relevant documents, summons, and other documents. The most useful and complete of the various accounts.

1882   Wikoff, Henry. THE REMINISCENCES OF AN IDLER. New York: Fords, Howard and Hulbert, 1880. 591 p. Index, frontispiece.

Wikoff was well acquainted with Forrest and describes his conversations with the actor as well as Forrest's engagements in several major cities.

1883   Wilson, Garff B. "The Acting of Edwin Forrest." QUARTERLY JOURNAL OF SPEECH 36 (December 1950): 483-91.

A carefully reasoned and well-documented analysis of Forrest's uniquely powerful style of acting.

1884   Wilson, Rufus Rockwell. "The Centenary of Edwin Forrest." THEATRE (N.Y.) 6 (March 1906): 73-76. Illus.

A memorial biographical sketch on the hundreth anniversary of Forrest's birth, the author considering Forrest "a very Lear among players."

See also nos. 101, 119-21, 127, 132-33, 141, 146, 148, 154, 166, 171, 183,

210-11, 213, 216, 221-22, 227, 231, 238, 245-47, 249, 261, 291, 296, 302, 313, 318, 337, 341, 352, 356, 358, 363, 366-68, 370, 373, 375, 383, 389-90, 395-96, 399, 400-402, 405, 408, 413, 417, 425, 434, 446, 456, 462-63, 468, 489, 502, 507, 517, 520, 524, 546, 570, 572-73, 583, 1094, 1120, 1124, 1134, 1170, 1564-66, 1749, 1993, 2107, 2235-36, 2249, 2337, 2348, 2461, 2670, 2750, 2782, 2920, 2954, 2957, 3127, and 3168.

FOX, GEORGE WASHINGTON LAFAYETTE
(1825-77)

1885   Draper, Walter H.   "George L. Fox's Burlesque--HAMLET." QUARTERLY
JOURNAL OF SPEECH 50 (December 1964): 318-84.

> Draper describes Fox's satires of both Edwin Booth and
> Charles Fechter in his satire.

1886   Senelick, Laurence.   "George L. Fox and American Pantomime." NINE-
TEENTH CENTURY THEATRE RESEARCH 7 (Spring 1979): 1-25. Illus.

> A well-researched and documented account of Fox's
> development in the field of pantomime. Includes specu-
> lation as to the cause of Fox's insanity and death.

See also nos. 187, 243, 333, 375, 560, and 572.

FREDERICK, PAULINE
(1883-1938)

1887   "A Biblical Heroine." COSMOPOLITAN, May 1913, pp. 846-47. Illus.

> Frederick discusses her role of Zuleika in JOSEPH AND
> HIS BRETHREN, insisting she was more than a mere stage
> beauty and was struggling to perfect her art.

1888   Bryers, Leslie. "Charms--and the Woman." MOTION PICTURE MAGA-
ZINE 23 (February 1922): 46-47, 95. Illus.

> A rambling interview in which Frederick describes her
> dislike for "society" films.

1889   Darnell, Jean. "Unusual Pauline Fredericks." NATIONAL MAGAZINE
41 (January 1915): 705-7. Illus.

> Darnell proposes that Frederick is unusual in her normalcy.

1890   Elwood, Muriel. PAULINE FREDERICK ON AND OFF THE STAGE.
Chicago: A. Kroch, 1940. 220 p. Index, illus.

> Only the first forty pages of this undocumented and adula-
> tory biography treats Frederick's stage career; the volume
> focuses upon her work in Hollywood.

1891   Frederick, Pauline. "From the Chorus to Legitimate Dramatic Star."
THEATRE (N.Y.) 17 (June 1913): 172-74, vii. Illus.

> The actress recalls the early days of her career and her
> break into stardom.

1892   _____. "Playing the Part of the Temptress." GREEN BOOK MAGA-
ZINE 9 (May 1913): 825-30. Illus.

> Frederick describes her preparation and playing of the role
> of Zuleika in JOSEPH AND HIS BRETHREN.

1893 _____ . "The Story of My Life." MOTION PICTURE MAGAZINE December 1918, pp. 63-65, 126. Illus.

> A brief and not especially informative autobiographical essay.

1894 _____ . "Why I Forsook the Stage for the Screen." THEATRE (N.Y.) 22 (November 1915): 241. Illus.

> The actress cites wider audience exposure and less restrictive contracts as her main reasons.

1895 Libby, Charles T. THE LIBBY FAMILY IN AMERICA 1602-1881. Portland, Maine: B. Thurston and Co., 1882. 616 p. Index, illus.

> A genealogical study of Frederick's paternal ancestors.

1896 Squier, Emma Lindsay. "Hello, Eddie Foy!" MOTION PICTURE MAGAZINE 18 (October 1919): 32-33, 126. Illus.

> A rambling interview in which the actress describes her reaction to stardom.

1897 "A Sympathetic Siren." COSMOPOLITAN, December 1914, p. 95. Illus.

> A one-page description of Frederick in her role in INNOCENT.

See also nos. 13, 198, and 464.

GEORGE, GRACE
(1878-1961)

1898   Crichton, Kyle. "Life on the Strand." COLLIER'S 95 (9 March 1935): 19, 39. Illus.

> George is quoted on her early career and her path to stardom while she is appearing in PERSONAL APPEARANCE.

1899   George, Grace. "The Appeal of the Theatre." FORUM 58 (November 1917): 571-78.

> An idealistic description of the theatre from the actress's point of view.

1900   _____. "My Stage Life and Why It Is Worth While." THEATRE (N.Y.) 23 (June 1916): 337-39, 366. Illus.

> George suggests that the audience is the theatrical element that most attracts her to her work.

1901   "A Grace of the Stage." COSMOPOLITAN, March 1913, pp. 550-51. Illus.

> Fan-oriented puffery, attempting an overview of George's career to that date.

1902   Patterson, Ada. "Grace George Analyzes Kitty Ashe." THEATRE (N.Y.) 6 (January 1906): 14, 16-18. Illus.

> George describes her preparation for her seventh starring role, that of Kitty Ashe in THE MARRIAGE OF WILLIAM ASHE.

See also nos. 28, 270, 276, 316, 382, 413, 427, 429, 499, 525, 532, 539, 544, 549, 579, 600, 1471, and 1537.

GILBERT, MRS. GEORGE H.

(1821-1904)

1903   Gilbert, Anne Hartley. THE STAGE REMINISCENCES OF MRS. GILBERT. Edited by Charlotte M. Martin. New York: Charles Scribner's Sons, 1901. 248 p. Illus.

> A charming if somewhat idealized autobiography with exceptional illustrations. Useful for Augustin Daly and the rest of the "Big Four," with passing references to various other performers of the time.

1904   _____. "The Stage Reminiscences of Mrs. Gilbert." Edited by Charlotte M. Martin. SCRIBNER'S 29 (1901): 167-84, 312-23, 460-71. Illus.

> Serialization of the previous entry with additional illustrations.

1905   Le Soir, George. "A Fellow Player's Tribute." THEATRE (N.Y.) 5 (January 1905): 8. Illus.

> A memorial tribute to the actress.

See also nos. 13, 128, 279, 340, 356, 404, 407-8, 413, 432, 446, 471, 476, 518, 1599, 1602, 1604, and 1750.

GILBERT, JOHN
(1810-89)

1906   Towse, J. Ranken. "John Gilbert." Illustrations by J.W. Alexander. CENTURY n.s. 13 (January 1888): 378-84.

An appreciation of the actor in Towse's usual style.

1907   Winter, William. THE LIFE OF JOHN GILBERT TOGETHER WITH EX-TRACTS FROM HIS LETTERS AND SOUVENIRS OF HIS CAREER. New York: Dunlap Society, 1890. Reprint. New York: Burt Franklin, 1970. 55 p.

Winter draws heavily upon correspondence and newspaper accounts for his brief treatment of Gilbert. The actor's own autobiographical sketch is included, reprinted from the New York HERALD, 5 December 1878.

See also nos. 261, 328, 356, 383, 387, 399, 405, 413, 471, 489, 577, 596, 1347, and 3027.

GILLETTE, WILLIAM

(1855-1937)

1908   Burton, Percy, as told to Lowell Thomas. ADVENTURES AMONG IM-
MORTALS; PERCY BURTON--IMPRESARIO. New York: Dodd, Mead
and Co., 1937. 330 p.

> While most of Burton's career was spent with British com-
> panies, he offers reminiscences of working with Richard
> Mansfield and William Gillette.

1909   Burton, Richard. "William Gillette." BOOK BUYER 16 (February
1898): 26-30. Illus.

> A positive critical assessment of Gillette as a dramatist
> in mid-career.

1910   Coburn, Charles. "Playing Opposite 'Our Youngest Actor.'" STAGE 13
(March 1936): 42. Illus.

> Coburn recalls rehearsals and performances with Gillette
> in THREE WISE FOOLS, at which time Gillette was
> eighty years old.

1911   Cook, Doris E., comp. "The Library of William Gillette." BULLETIN
OF BIBLIOGRAPHY 22 (September-December 1957): 89-93; (January-
April 1958): 116-20; (May-August 1958): 137-42.

> A list of the materials removed from Gillette's castle
> at Hadlyme, Connecticut, around 1945, and taken to
> the Connecticut State Library in Hartford. Some 595
> items are listed.

1912   _____. SHERLOCK HOLMES AND MUCH MORE, OR SOME OF THE
FACTS ABOUT WILLIAM GILLETTE. Hartford, Conn.: Connecticut
Historical Society, 1970. vi, 112 p. Illus., notes.

> A slight volume, well-illustrated and documented, treating
> Gillette's professional career as actor and dramatist.

1913   Dodge, W. P. "William Gillette." STRAND (N. Y.) 42 (October 1911): 304-13. Illus.

>An insightful description of Gillette's playwriting techniques and his off-stage personality.

1914   Garland, Hamlin. MY FRIENDLY CONTEMPORARIES, A LITERARY LOG. New York and London: Macmillan, 1932. xvi, 544 p. Frontispiece.

>Briefly describes Garland's acquaintance with William Gillette and E. H. Sothern during the period between 1913 and 1923.

1915   Gillette, William. THE ILLUSION OF THE FIRST TIME IN ACTING. Introduction by George Arliss. New York: Dramatic Museum of Columbia University, 1915. 58 p.

>Gillette's essay was originally delivered to a joint session of the American Academy of Arts and Letters and the National Institute of Arts and Letters in Chicago on 14 November 1913 and was later published by those organizations. Gillette discusses the theatre in general and the problem of the actor's spontaneity in this still highly regarded essay.

1916   "A Great Actor's Explanation of the Decay of Acting." CURRENT OPINION 57 (December 1914): 406. Illus.

>Gillette is quoted from a New York TIMES interview in which he described the requisities for excellence in acting, qualities which he found lacking at the time.

1917   Hamilton, Clayton. "The Final Episode of Sherlock Holmes." THEATRE (N. Y.) 51 (January 1930): 36. Illus.

>An appreciation of Gillette upon his return to the stage after twelve years of retirement.

1918   _____. "William Gillette: Theatrical Craftsman." COLLIER'S 56 (18 December 1915): 9, 23. Illus.

>Hamilton lavishly praises Gillette's skill as a director, suggesting his fame as such would long outlive his reputation as an actor.

1919   Hooker, Edward. THE DESCENDANTS OF REV. THOMAS HOOKER, HARTFORD, CONNECTICUT, 1586-1908. Rochester, N. Y.: Printed for Margaret Huntington Hooker, 1909. 476 p. Index, illus.

>Gillette's ancestry.

1920   Keddie, James, Jr.   "About a William Gillette Collection."   BAKER STREET JOURNAL 12, no. 1, n.s. (1962): 17-21.

> Keddie describes his personal and extensive collection of Gillette materials.

1921   Kobbé, Gustav.   "The Real William Gillette."   LADIES' HOME JOURNAL, September 1903, pp. 3-4.   Illus.

> A description of Gillette's home in Hartford and his houseboat, "Aunt Polly."   Gillette is described as a family man with great affection for children.

1922   LaBorde, Charles B.   "Sherlock Holmes on the Stage after William Gillette."   BAKER STREET JOURNAL, 24, no. 2 (1974): 109-19.   Illus.

> A survey of attempts to dramatize the Holmes stories, contrasted with Gillette's version.

1923   Lynch, Gertrude.   "The Real William Gillette."   THEATRE (N.Y.) 13 (April 1901): 122-24.   Illus.

> A thoughtful essay describing Gillette's work habits and attitudes about his work in the theatre.

1924   Macfarlane, Peter Clark.   "The Magic of William Gillette."   EVERYBODY'S MAGAZINE 32 (February 1915): 257-68.   Illus.

> The author, seemingly in awe of Gillette, offers a positive, enthusiastic, and substantial assessment of his work.   Insightful, undocumented.

1925   Moses, Montrose.   "William Gillette Says Farewell."   THEATRE GUILD MAGAZINE 7 (January 1930): 30-35, 56.   Illus.

> Moses extolls Gillette's virtues, stressing his importance to an earlier generation of theatregoers.

1926   Nichols, Harold J.   "William Gillette--Innovator in Melodrama."   THEATRE ANNUAL 31 (1975): 7-15.   Illus.

> A survey of Gillette's dramatic methods, suggesting he contributed greatly to the rise of realism by his pantomimic action, detailed settings, dramatic structure, and rapid-fire diction.

1927   Payne, George Henry.   "William Gillette's Personal Side."   GREEN BOOK ALBUM 2 (September 1909): 573-78.

> A shallow and adulatory article by one of Gillette's friends, describing his life and personality off stage.

1928 Perkins, Henry A. "William Gillette, the Man." CONNECTICUT WOODLANDS 10 (February 1945): 3-6.

> The transcript of an address given at the opening of the Gillette Castle on 7 October 1944; general remarks and positive assessments of the actor.

1929 Schuttler, Georg W. "Sherlock Holmes as Hamlet." THEATRE SURVEY 18 (November 1977): 72-85.

> Schuttler describes Gillette's intended production of HAMLET, which never reached the stage.

1930 Shafer, Yvonne [Bonsall]. "A Sherlock Holmes of the Past: William Gillette's Later Years." PLAYERS 46 (June-July 1971): 229-34. Illus.

> A well-documented account of Gillette's continuing, almost legendary success as Sherlock Holmes.

1931 Shepstone, Harold J. "Mr. Gillette as Sherlock Holmes." STRAND (N.Y.) 22 (December 1901): 613-21. Illus.

> A substantial and thoughtful article, describing Gillette's personal life as well as his characterization of Holmes. Several production photographs are included.

1932 Stone, P.M. "William Gillette's Stage Career." BAKER STREET JOURNAL 12, no. 1, n.s. (1962): 8-16.

> A brief and undocumented treatment of Gillette's career.

1933 _____. "William Hooker Gillette." BAKER STREET JOURNAL (SUPPLEMENT) n.s. 3 (July 1953): [14].

> Stone discusses Gillette's genealogy, then describes his characterization of Holmes.

1934 _____. "Mr. William Gillette." SHERLOCK HOLMES JOURNAL 4 (1960): 115-18. Illus.

> A brief overview of the critical receptions in New York and London to SHERLOCK HOLMES.

1935 Tucker, Florence L. "The North Carolina Home of William Gillette." THEATRE (N.Y.) 6 (February 1906): 51-52. Illus.

> A description, including photographs, of Gillette's "Thousand Pines," his retreat in North Carolina.

See also nos. 28, 58, 112, 166, 177, 199, 211, 214, 228-29, 270, 276, 279, 288, 291, 300, 321, 338, 379-80, 410, 413, 427, 458, 533, 557-58, 574-75, 579, 793, 904, 1975, 2065-66, 2907, and 3177.

GILPIN, CHARLES S.

(1878-1930)

1936   Hart, Moss. ACT ONE: AN AUTOBIOGRAPHY. New York: Random House, 1959. 444 p.

>Hart, at the beginning of his theatrical career, played Smithers opposite Gilpin in a revival of THE EMPEROR JONES, as described on pp. 98 f.

1937   L., W. A. "A Negro Genius in Greenwich Village." THEATRE (N. Y.) 33 (January 1921): 8. Illus.

>A short sketch stimulated by Gilpin's success in THE EMPEROR JONES.

See also nos. 190, 194, and 413.

GISH, DOROTHY

(1898-1968)

1938   Carr, Harry.   "Three Little Girls Who Came Back."   MOTION PICTURE
MAGAZINE 26 (August 1923): 21-22, 102. Illus.

Carr describes the return to the screen of three actresses,
among them Dorothy Gish.

1939   Cheatham, Maude S.   "Gatling Gun Gish."   MOTION PICTURE MAGA-
ZINE 18 (August 1919): 30-31, 102. Illus.

The author stresses Gish's vivacity on and off the screen.

1940   Gletcher, Adele Whitely.   "A Flapper with Philosophy."   MOTION
PICTURE MAGAZINE 24 (December 1922): 34-35, 92. Illus.

A rambling interview containing a few remarks about the
Gish family.

1941   Gish, Dorothy.   "And So I am a Comedienne."   LADIES' HOME JOUR-
NAL, July 1925, pp. 7, 57-58. Illus.

A brief autobiographical sketch, describing her early
career on the stage and defending her choice of film
for her subsequent work.

1942   _____. "My Sister Lillian." THEATRE (N.Y.) 46 (December 1927):
32. Illus.

The second of a pair of articles by the sisters, both
mutually complimentary.

1943   _____, et al. "Why We Are Glad to Get Back Home." MOTION PIC-
TURE MAGAZINE 28 (October 1924): 24-25, 109. Illus.

The Gish sisters were in Florence for eight months filming
ROMOLA; they wrote these articles upon their return.

1944   Hall, Gladys.   "Mrs. Dorothy Gish Rennie."   MOTION PICTURE
        MAGAZINE 21 (July 1921): 39, 86. Illus.

> Fan-oriented puffery about Gish's recent marriage.

1945   Hall, Gladys, and Fletcher, Adele W.   "We Interview the Two Orphans."
        MOTION PICTURE MAGAZINE 23 (May 1922): 47-49, 97. Illus.

> Written in the form of a script; the Gish sisters discuss
> their various films in the most general of terms.

1946   Keefe, W. E.   "Dorothy Gish."   MOTION PICTURE MAGAZINE 9
        (June 1915): 109-11. Illus.

> An interview in which Gish describes her entry into the
> motion picture industry.

1947   Klumph, Inez, and Klumph, Helen.   SCREEN ACTING: ITS REQUIRE-
        MENTS AND REWARDS. New York: Falk Publishing Co., 1922.
        243 p. Illus.

> The Gish sisters were advisors for this volume and offered
> some advice for those seeking careers in the silent films.

1948   Revere, F. Vance de.   "What I Can Read in the Faces of the Film
        Stars." MOTION PICTURE MAGAZINE 28 (November 1924): 49, 88.
        Illus.

> Revere presents a facial analysis of the actress, claiming
> to determine personal characteristics by so doing.

1949   Roberts, W. Adolphe.   "Confidences Off-Screen." MOTION PICTURE
        MAGAZINE 29 (June 1925): 44.

> Puffery of the most fan-oriented type.

1950   Slide, Anthony. THE GRIFFITH ACTRESSES. South Brunswick, N.J.,
        and New York: A. S. Barnes and Co.; London: Tantivy Press, 1973.
        181 p. Illus., bibliog.

> The Gish sisters are treated in chapters 5 and 6 (pp. 77-
> 109); the sections are undocumented and heavily illus-
> trated.

1951   Williams, Richard L.   "The Gallant Gish Girls." LIFE, 20 August
        1951, pp. 115-16, 118, 121-22, 124, 127. Illus.

> A substantial sketch describing the Gish's popular appeal
> and film careers.

1952 Wilson, Beatrice. "A Broken Set of Gishes." MOTION PICTURE
      MAGAZINE 37 (April 1929): 55, 94. Illus.

      Wilson describes three distinct careers in the backgrounds
      of the Gish sisters and their mother.

1953 Wright, Edna. "Dot Gish: Studio Star and Home Tomboy." MOTION
      PICTURE MAGAZINE 13 (June 1917): 78-81. Illus.

      An adulatory and pointless interview.

See also nos. 5, 9, 23, 276, 376, 413, 1962, 1966, and 1981.

GISH, LILLIAN
(1893-)

1954 Bowers, Ronald. "Lillian Gish's Bicentennial Proposal." FILM IN REVIEW 25 (October 1974): 467-69. Illus.

> Gish wrote the governors of each of the fifty states to propose that film students at each state university film the history of their state.

1955 Carr, Harry. "The Girl Who is Different." MOTION PICTURE MAGA-ZINE 30 (December 1925): 1, 27. Illus.

> Accolades for Gish's acting ability and her careful role study.

1956 Collins, Frederick L. "What Happened to Lillian Gish?" NEW MOVIE, June 1933, pp. 36-37, 97-101. Illus.

> An adulatory, fan-oriented article extolling Gish's acting prowess in film.

1957 Fletcher, Adele W. "The White Sister in a Bright Red Coat." MOTION PICTURE MAGAZINE 26 (December 1923): 21-22. Illus.

> A rambling description of Gish's film, THE WHITE SISTER.

1958 Gish, Lillian. "Beginning Young." LADIES' HOME JOURNAL, September 1925, pp. 19, 117-18, 120.

> An autobiographical sketch describing the actress's affinity for acting, her early career, and her entrance into films.

1959 _____. "Birth of an Era." STAGE 14 (January 1937): 100-102. Illus.

> Gish recollects the filming of THE BIRTH OF A NATION.

1960 _____. DOROTHY AND LILLIAN GISH. Edited by James E. Frasher.

New York: Charles Scribner's Sons, 1973. 312 p. Illus.

A lavishly illustrated account of the Gish sisters' careers from the beginning to Lillian Gish's return to the legitimate stage.

1961 _____. "How To Get In!" MOTION PICTURE MAGAZINE 12 (August 1916): 128-29. Illus.

Gish recommends patience, willingness to work, and originality as essential to a successful film career.

1962 _____. LILLIAN GISH: THE MOVIES, MR. GRIFFITH AND ME. Englewood Cliffs, N.J.: Prentice-Hall, 1969. xii, 372 p. Index, illus.

Although the Gish sisters' careers were primarily cinematic, their mother was a sometime stage actress, and they both had brief stage careers as children, as described by the first four chapters of this volume. Both appeared in the legitimate theatre as adults from time to time.

1963 _____. "My Sister and I." THEATRE (N.Y.) 46 (November 1927): 14-15.

Brief and complimentary remarks.

1964 _____. "A Universal Language." In "Motion Pictures," ENCYCLO-PEDIA BRITANNICA (1929 ed.) volume 15, pp. 865-66.

A brief essay in which Gish describes an idealized future for film, likening the medium to an international language.

1965 _____. "Would I Do It Over Again? Lillian Gish Said--." PHOTO-PLAY 21 (May 1922): 39. Illus.

Gish suggests she would not pursue an acting career if she had a second chance.

1966 Hall, Gladys. "'Lights!' Say Lillian!" MOTION PICTURE MAGAZINE 19 (April-May 1920): 1, 30-31, 102. Illus.

A description of Lillian Gish directing her sister Dorothy in a film.

1967 Hergesheimer, Joseph. "Lillian Gish." AMERICAN MERCURY 1 (April 1924): 397-402.

An appreciation of Gish's film career to that time, stressing her vision of the film as a force for good.

1968   Paine, Albert Bigelow. LIFE AND LILLIAN GISH. New York: Mac-
        millan Co., 1932. 303 p. Illus.

        An undocumented account of Gish's early career, lavishly
        illustrated.

1969   Roberts, W. Adolphe. "Mary Astor." MOTION PICTURE MAGAZINE
        30 (October 1925): 54–55, 94. Illus.

        Astor describes her admiration of Gish.

1970   Seidman, Benjamin. "The Lily of Denishawn." MOTION PICTURE
        MAGAZINE 12 (October 1916): 134–36. Illus.

        A description of Denishawn, the Gishs' woodland estate
        near Los Angeles.

1971   Slide, Anthony, comp. LILLIAN GISH: ACTRESS. London: National
        Film Theatre, 1969. 14 p.

        Unavailable for examination.

1972   Wagenknecht, Edward. LILLIAN GISH: AN INTERPRETATION. Edited
        by Glenn Hughes. Seattle: University of Washington Chapbooks, 1927.
        27 p. Frontispiece.

        A meandering monograph of limited value, to which is
        appended a one-page biographical note.

1973   Wagenknecht, Edward, and Slide, Anthony. THE FILMS OF D.W.
        GRIFFITH. New York: Crown Publishers, 1975. 271 p. Index, illus.,
        bibliog.

        A heavily illustrated history of Griffith's films with brief
        notes on their critical reception. The Gish sisters are
        mentioned frequently as actresses for Griffith.

See also nos. 59, 23, 142, 198, 235, 276, 413, 545, 1943, 1948, 1950–52,
and 1981.

GOODWIN, NAT C.

(1857-1919)

1974　Goodwin, Nat.　"A Century of Comedy."　PHILHARMONIC　2 (December 1902): 295-97.　Illus.

> Goodwin describes the changes in comedy on stage during his career and predicts the future of the genre.

1975　_____.　NAT GOODWIN'S BOOK.　Boston: Richard G. Badger, 1914. ix, 357 p.　Index, illus.

> Goodwin describes his career in a somewhat turgid and superficial style, devoting chapters to various of his colleagues, among them Stuart Robson, John McCullough, Joseph Jefferson III, Sol Smith Russell, Richard Mansfield, Maude Adams, Tyrone Power, DeWolf Hopper, George M. Cohan, John Drew, Wilton Lackaye, David Warfield, Lillian Russell, William Gillette, William Collier, Henry Miller, and David Belasco.

1976　Patterson, Ada.　"Nathaniel C. Goodwin--An Interview."　THEATRE (N. Y.)　4 (February 1904): 40, 42-43.　Illus.

> Goodwin describes his growing disenchantment with the theatre and his acting methodologies.

See also nos. 28, 58, 174, 177, 270, 276, 279, 288, 303, 328, 339, 356, 377, 379-80, 409, 413, 448, 451, 475, 513, 555, 558, 579, 582, 586, 597, and 1740.

GORDON, RUTH
(1896-   )

1977   Crighton, Kyle. "Gifted Gordon." COLLIERS' 113 (27 May 1944):
       75. Illus.

>   A one-page description of Gordon's early career and her
>   writing of OVER TWENTY-ONE.

1978   Gordon, Ruth. "A Great Lady in the Grand Manner." STAGE 14
       (January 1937): 90-91. Illus.

>   Gordon recalls working with Maude Adams in PETER PAN
>   in the early days of her career.

1979   _____. "Legitimate Laughton." THEATRE ARTS 34 (November 1950):
       30-31, 92. Illus.

>   Gordon recalls Charles Laughton's attempts to form a
>   stock company for live theatre in Hollywood.

1980   _____. MYSELF AMONG OTHERS. New York: Atheneum, 1971.
       389 p.

>   A rambling and chatty set of memoirs with a minimum of
>   autobiographical data.

1981   _____. MY SIDE: THE AUTOBIOGRAPHY OF RUTH GORDON. New
       York, Hagerstown, San Francisco, and London: Harper and Row, 1976.
       488 p. Index, illus.

>   A strangely impressionistic work, evocative rather than
>   factual, but highly readable, offering unusually penetrating
>   insights into the author. Substantial references to David
>   Belasco, Katharine Cornell, Maude Adams, Ethel Barrymore,
>   Billie Burke, Hazel Dawn, Mrs. Fiske, Lynn Fontanne,
>   Dorothy and Lillian Gish, and Helen Hayes.

1982   _____. RUTH GORDON: AN OPEN BOOK. Garden City, N.Y.:
       Doubleday and Co., 1980. 373 p. Index.

Reminiscences and anecdotes, many of them concerning Gordon's colleagues, such as Katharine Cornell, the Lunts, Ethel Barrymore, and Helen Hayes.

1983 _____. YEARS AGO. New York: Viking Press, 1947. 173 p.

A three-act play script in which Gordon depicts the parental objection to her becoming an actress.

1984 Houghton, Norris. "The Kanins on Broadway." THEATRE ARTS 30 (December 1946): 731-33.

An assessment of the several talents of Gordon and her husband, Garson Kanin.

1985 Kanin, Garson. IT TAKES A LONG TIME TO BECOME YOUNG. AN ENTERTAINMENT IN THE FORM OF A DECLARATION OF WAR ON THE MINDLESS YOUTH CULT THAT HAS OUR TIME IN ITS GRIP: DEMORALIZING OUR PEOPLE, WEAKENING OUR SYSTEM, DEPLETING OUR ENERGY, FEEDING OUR DEPRESSION, WASTING OUR EXPERIENCE, BETRAYING OUR DEMOCRACY, AND BLOWING OUR BRAINS. Garden City, N.Y.: Doubleday and Co., 1978. 185 p.

A diatribe, humorous to a degree, but containing a substantial section on Gordon's career and her attitude toward her age.

1986 [Playgoer.] "Open Letter." THEATRE GUILD 9 (March 1932): 14. Illus.

A letter complaining about Gordon's appearance in A CHURCH MOUSE, a script the writer considered beneath the actress's talents.

1987 Reed, Rex. CONVERSATIONS IN THE RAW: DIALOGUES, MONOLOGUES, AND SELECTED SHORT SUBJECTS. New York: World, 1969. 312 p. New York: New American Library, 1970.

Pages 18-24 describe Gordon's social life and style, then her opinions on various subjects.

1988 "Years Ago." LIFE, 6 January 1947, pp. 58-60. Illus.

A photographic synopsis of Gordon's autobiographical script, plus one column on the actress and her early career.

1989 Young, Stark. "Ruth Gordon Compared with Helen Hayes." NEW REPUBLIC 69 (23 December 1931): 163.

A brief review of Hayes in THE GOOD FAIRY; the critic

considers Gordon Hayes's only rival, but places Hayes in
first place for having a wider range.

See also nos. 5, 117, 242, 275-76, 351, 508, 525, 576, 1477, and 3071.

HACKETT, JAMES HENRY
(1800-1871)

1990 Durand, John. "Souvenirs of Hackett the Actor." GALAXY 14 (October 1872): 550-56.

> Durand had planned a biographical sketch of Luman Reed, a merchant and friend of Hackett's; this article presents Hackett's anecdotal memories of Reed, plus a few observations about the Yankee character.

1991 Hackett, James Henry. FALSTAFF: A SHAKESPEAREAN TRACT. London: Thomas C. Saville, 1840. 11 p.

> A brief analysis of one of Hackett's more successful roles. Also appended to AN ESSAY ON THE DRAMATIC CHARACTER OF SIR JOHN FALSTAFF by Maurice Morgann (London: Wheatley and Adlard, 1825. 189 p.).

1992 _____. "Hamlet's Soliloquy on Suicide." TOWN AND COUNTRY, November-December 1860.

> A brief and superficial analysis of the "To be or not to be" soliloquy from HAMLET.

1993 _____. NOTES, CRITICISM, AND CORRESPONDENCE UPON SHAKESPEARE'S PLAYS AND ACTORS. New York: 1864. Reprint. New York: Benjamin Blom, 1968. x, 353 p.

> Hackett presents his own character analyses of Hamlet and King Lear, then describes various other performers in the role of Hamlet: Thomas Abthorpe Cooper, James W. Wallack, the elder Booth, John Vandenhoff, Edwin Forrest, William Augustus Conway, and Thomas S. Hamblin. Hackett also analyses the character of Falstaff.

1994 _____. OXBERRY'S 1822 EDITION OF KING RICHARD III, WITH THE DESCRIPTIVE NOTES RECORDING EDMUND KEAN'S PERFORMANCE MADE BY JAMES H. HACKETT. Edited by Alan S. Downer. London: Society for Theatre Research, 1959. xxiii, 100 p., xxiv-xxxii. Illus., bibliog.

Hackett left a detailed description of Kean which Downer edited with his usual meticulousness, adding a useful introduction and notes. Hackett had seen the performance at least a dozen times during November 1826.

1995　Hackett, James Henry, and Adams, John. THE CHARACTER OF HAMLET. Edited by a Lady. New York: J. Mowatt, 1844. 7 p.

Unavailable for examination.

1996　Hodge, Francis. "Biography of a Lost Play: LION OF THE WEST." THEATRE ANNUAL 12 (1954): 48-61.

Hodge reconstructs the early history of this script and describes Hackett's playing the leading role in it.

1997　_____. "Yankee in England: James Henry Hackett and the Debut of American Comedy." QUARTERLY JOURNAL OF SPEECH 45 (December 1959): 381-90.

Hodge presents Hackett's 1832 production of WHO WANTS A GUINEA? as an important battle in America's struggle for cultural independence from England. An early version of a section of Hodge's YANKEE THEATRE (no. 181).

1998　Lawrence, W.J. "Stage Falstaffs." GENTLEMAN'S MAGAZINE n.s. 42 (May 1889): 425-38.

A stage history of the fat knight, primarily concerning English actors, but including a brief section on Hackett.

1999　"Mr. James Henry Hackett." TALLIS'S DRAMATIC MAGAZINE, June 1851, pp. 35-57. Illus.

A biographical-critical essay, praising Hackett's Falstaff and comparing him to Garrick.

2000　Sprague, Arthur Colby. "Falstaff Hackett." THEATRE NOTEBOOK 9 (April-June 1955): 61-67. Illus.

A thorough description of the characterization, based on five promptscripts in the Enthoven Collection at the Victoria and Albert Museum in London.

See also nos. 130, 146, 148, 181-83, 211, 222, 227, 245, 296, 341, 347, 356, 383, 385, 401, 405, 413, 433, 472, 489, 501-2, 1848, 2348, 2461, 2782, 3127, and 3168.

HACKETT, JAMES KETELTAS
(1869-1926)

2001   "The Clever Son of a Famous Father." MUNSEY'S 28 (March 1903): 935-44.

> A lead article in MUNSEY'S regular feature, "The Stage," in which a hereditary basis for Hackett's skill is posited.

2002   Flower, B.O. "A Representative Young American Actor." ARENA 25 (February 1901): 220-24.

> Flower lauds Hackett's work in THE PRIDE OF JENNICO and suggests he embodies the best of American youth, predicting a bright future in the theatre for him.

2003   Hackett, James K. "Macbeth." GREEN BOOK MAGAZINE 15 (June 1916): 1107-09. Illus.

> Hackett defends his somewhat novel interpretation of the script.

2004   _____. "My Beginnings." THEATRE (N.Y.) 6 (October 1906): 275-76. Illus.

> In spite of having a famous name, Hackett encountered difficulties breaking into the profession.

2005   _____. "Some Accidents and Others." GREEN BOOK ALBUM 2 (August 1909): 368-73.

> Hackett describes various onstage accidents he had experienced during his career.

2006   _____. "The Stage Villain." GREEN BOOK ALBUM 1 (January 1909): 201-2.

> Hackett addresses the moral objections to presenting evil on the stage.

2007 _____. "A University for the Drama." INDEPENDENT 55 (23 April 1903): 973-74.

> Noting that every other branch of art has degree programs, Hackett proposes a bachelor of dramatic art program for colleges and universities.

2008 Woollcott, Alexander. "When Birnam Wood Did Come to Dunsinane." VANITY FAIR 27 (January 1927): 58, 108.

> A rambling discourse on Hackett's personal life.

See also nos. 28, 131, 183, 270, 276, 279, 303, 347, 367, 379, 413, 451, 455, 459, 558, 578-79, 586, and 3094.

HALLAM FAMILY
Hallam, Lewis Sr. (1714-56)
Hallam, Lewis Jr. (1740-1808)
Hallam, Eliza Lewis Tuke (fl. 1785)

2009   Dexter, Elisabeth Anthony. COLONIAL WOMEN OF AFFAIRS: A STUDY OF WOMEN IN BUSINESS AND THE PROFESSIONS IN AMERICA BEFORE 1776. Boston and New York: Houghton Mifflin Co., 1924. 204 p. Illus., bibliog., glossary.

> A brief essay is included on pre-Revolution actresses, including Mrs. Hallam, drawing heavily upon Seilhamer and Graydon. An illustration of Mrs. Hallam as Marianne in Fielding's MISER is located on pages 158-59.

2010   Dye, William. "Pennsylvania versus the Theatre." PENNSYLVANIA MAGAZINE OF HISTORY AND BIOGRAPHY 55, no. 4 (1931): 333-72. Bibliog.

> A carefully researched and lucid examination of early theatricals with particular emphasis upon the Hallam company.

2011   Gelb, George W. "Playhouses and Politics: Lewis Hallam and the Confederation Theatre." JOURNAL OF POPULAR CULTURE 5 (Fall 1971): 324-39.

> A description of Lewis Hallam, Jr.'s, career, drawing upon nontraditional sources. Useful, although some dates might be questioned.

2012   Harbin, Billy J. "The Role of Mrs. Hallam in the Hodgkinson-Hallam Controversy: 1794-1797." THEATRE JOURNAL 32 (May 1980): 213-22.

> Harbin proposes that Mrs. Hallam's alcoholism was at the core of the problem and that Hodgkinson has been poorly treated by historians of the incident.

2013   Highfill, Philip, Jr. "The British Background of the American Hallams." THEATRE SURVEY 11 (May 1970): 1-35.

> A well-researched and documented attempt to clarify the

genealogy and professional background of the family prior
to their arrival in North America in 1752.

2014   Hogan, Charles Beecher.   "The New Wells."   THEATRE NOTEBOOK 3
(July-September 1949):   67-72.

A detailed and documented account of the Hallams in
London prior to 1752.   Useful background.

2015   Ritter, Charles C.   "The Hallam Females."   SOUTHERN SPEECH JOUR-
NAL   25 (Spring 1960):   167-71.

Ritter tries without notable success to clear up the
genealogical confusion about the Hallams.

2016   Turner, Vivian.   "Our Colonial Theatre."   QUARTERLY JOURNAL OF
SPEECH   27 (December 1941):   559-73.

Based on secondary sources, this article offers an overview of the early theatre in North America, mentioning
the Hallams and David Douglas [sic].   Of minimal value.

See also nos. 101, 121, 123, 138, 143, 146, 148, 158, 166, 183, 188, 192,
206, 210, 216, 222, 225, 227, 230, 238, 240-41, 253, 259, 266, 296, 317,
341, 358, 399, 400, 413, 423, 428, 434, 445, 462, 485, 535, 541, 592, 1666,
and 3208.

HAMBLIN, THOMAS SOWERBY (1800-1853). See nos. 222, 399, 502, 1170, 1993, 2348, 2958, and 3168.

HAMPDEN, WALTER

(1879-1956)

2017 Bird, Carol. "The Tragic Mask." THEATRE (N.Y.) 34 (August 1921): 104, 132.

> Hampden discusses the techniques of playing Shakespeare's tragic leading roles while starring in MACBETH.

2018 Bragdon, Claude. "The Scenery for Walter Hampden's HAMLET." THEATRE ARTS 3 (July 1919): 194-95. Illus.

> A one-page description of the setting, accompanied by one sketch and one photograph.

2019 Brown, Frank Chouteau. "Shakespeare, Hampden, and Bragdon." DRAMA 11 (March 1921): 196-99. Illus.

> A description of arriving at the scenic design for Hampden's HAMLET.

2020 Hamilton, Clayton. "An Idealist of the Stage: The Intimate Story of a Fine Actor." RED CROSS MAGAZINE 15 (June 1920): 27-32, 70. Illus.

> Written when Hampden was only forty years old, but had played over seventy Shakespearean roles. This substantial article suggests Hamden's idealism, both personal and professional, was a major factor in his success.

2021 _____. "New York Hails a New Hamlet." THEATRE (N.Y.) 27 (June 1918): 360-61.

> Hamilton considers Hampden's the finest Hamlet since Edwin Booth's, with the possible exception of Forbes-Robertson's.

2022 _____. "Walter Hampden--Actor, Manager." WORLD'S WORK 47 (February 1924): 410-17. Illus.

An appreciation of the actor, especially for his work in
CYRANO DE BERGERAC. A few biographical details are
included.

2023   Hampden, Walter. "The Changing Drama." DRAMA 11 (March 1921):
184-86.

A few idealistic remarks asking for the theatre's self-
improvement.

2024   _____. "Pretense." AMERICAN MAGAZINE 119 (April 1935): 11.

A quest editorial by Hampden in which he describes on
and off stage pretense.

2025   _____. "Wanted--A Leader in Our Theatre." THEATRE (N.Y.) 40
(July 1924): 9, 54. Illus.

Hampden deplores the rising costs of production and calls
for a modified repertory theatre, claiming audiences would
support such a venture.

2026   Hampden, Walter, as told to Harold Bolce. "Neglect Shakespeare and
the Theatre Dies." THEATRE (N.Y.) 47 (April 1928): 19, 62. Illus.

The actor extolls the virtues of the Bard and speculates
on the future of Shakespearean production in America,
maintaining a classical repertory company would do much
to solve the theatre's ills.

2027   Parker, Henry T. "Walter Hampden on the Stage as Seen by H.T.
Parker." THEATRE ANNUAL 7 (1948-49): 7-26. Illus.

Henry Taylor Parker was drama critic for the Boston
EVENING TRANSCRIPT. Elinor Hughes, drama critic
for the Boston HERALD, collected his evaluations of
Hampden as Hamlet, Macbeth, and Cyrano for this
publication.

2028   Stratton, Clarence. "Walter Hampden, A New Hamlet." DRAMA 9
(February 1919): 82-88.

A description and assessment of Hampden's Dane, positive
but not without some criticism.

2029   "Walter Hampden and the American Stage." OUTLOOK 128 (18 May
1921): 100. Illus.

Very brief remarks on Hampden's season of repertory.

2030   Young, Stark.   "Walter Hampden's Acting."   NEW REPUBLIC   45 (27
       January 1926):   272.

       A general evaluation of Hampden in CYRANO and
       OTHELLO with serious reservations as to the actor's
       talent.

See also nos. 5, 9, 120, 127, 204, 213, 245–46, 276, 285, 296, 358, 367,
412–13, 464, 578–79, 584, 841, and 2567.

HARNED, VIRGINIA

(1868-1946)

See also E.H. Sothern.

2031 Patterson, Ada. "Virginia Harned--A 'Material' Actress." THEATRE (N. Y.) 4 (April 1904): 93-95. Illus.

> An article containing an account of the actress's first meeting with E.H. Sothern, whom she later married.

See also nos. 28, 270, 279, 303, 321, 381, 429, 493, and 2976.

HARRIGAN, EDWARD

(1845-1911)

2032   Ford, James L. "The Days of Harrigan and Hart. Annie Mach, Now Appearing in KICK IN, Recalls Old Times." VANITY FAIR 3 (February 1915): 53. Illus.

        Mach played Mrs. Lochmuller for Harrigan and Hart, whom she joined after leaving Edwin Booth's company. She reminisces briefly about her experiences with the comedians.

2033   Harrigan, Edward. "Holding the Mirror up to Nature." PEARSON'S 16 (November 1903): 499-506. Illus.

        A substantial monograph, describing the process by which Harrigan created his "East Side" characters.

2034   Kahn, Ely Jacques, Jr. THE MERRY PARTNERS: THE AGE AND STAGE OF HARRIGAN AND HART. New York: Random House, 1955. xiii, 302 p. Illus.

        A lively, seemingly well-researched, but undocumented account of Harrigan and Hart's unique association. Details are plentiful and many sources are described, but none are cited. At present, the foremost source of information on the partnership.

2035   "The Last of the Hogans." ILLUSTRATED AMERICAN 9 (23 January 1892): 443-46. Illus.

        A thoughtful description of the script, seeking to put Harrigan's work into perspective, accompanied by several drawings of various characters from the work.

2036   Moody, Richard. NED HARRIGAN: FROM CORLEAR'S HOOK TO HERALD SQUARE. Chicago: Nelson-Hall, 1980. x, 270 p. Index, illus., bibliog., notes.

Moody gained access to hitherto unknown Harrigan materials and with his usual exemplary scholarship produced an outstanding biography. Mandatory for any study of Harrigan or the period.

2037 Moses, Montrose J. "Edward Harrigan." THEATRE ARTS 10 (March 1926): 176-88. Illus.

Moses offers a very brief overview of Harrigan's career and appends a scene from Harrigan's script, SQUATTER SOVEREIGNTY.

2038 _____. "Harrigan, American." THEATRE GUILD 7 (June 1930): 24-29, 64. Illus.

A substantial if undocumented description of Harrigan's unique contribution to the evolution of native types on the American stage.

2039 P., A. [Ada Patterson?] "Harrigan Recollections." STAGE 11 (February 1934): 40-41. Illus.

Nedda Harrigan reminisces about her father in a series of anecdotes.

See also nos. 112, 129, 163, 208, 213, 229, 243, 279, 300, 328, 413, 548, 556, and 572.

HAWORTH, JOSEPH

(1855-1903)

2040 Ogden, Vivia. "Early Memories of John Ellsler and Joseph Haworth."
THEATRE (N. Y.) 3 (October 1903): 258–61. Illus.

> Ogden recalls a few details of having acted with Haworth
> and Ellsler many years before.

See also nos. 28, 112, 256, 263, 279, 379, 399, and 454.

HAYES, HELEN

(1900-   )

2041 Arell, Ruth. "Flaws That Made Fortunes." DELINEATOR 130 (March 1937): 46-47. Illus.

> Hayes's theatrical start is attributed to a pigeon-toed left foot which prohibited dancing; her mimic gift was therefore encouraged.

2042 Babcock, Muriel. "Star Annoyed by Wisecrack." MOVIE CLASSIC 1 (September 1931): 40. Illus.

> Hayes is quoted as never planning to allow her daughter to become an actress.

2043 Beckley, Zoe. "Little Helen Hayes." THEATRE (N.Y.) 44 (November 1946): 32, 56. Illus.

> Beckley describes the childhood and early theatrical training of Hayes.

2044 Brown, Mrs. Catherine Estelle (Hayes). LETTERS TO MARY. New York: Random House; Toronto: Macmillan (limited autographed ed.), 1940. x, 337. Index, illus.

> The title refers to Mary MacArthur, Hayes's daughter, to whom Hayes's mother wrote the letters. The New York TIMES said of the book, "All through the crassness and silliness of this book we keep looking for glimpses of the Helen Hayes we know." Includes substantial sections on Alfred Lunt, John Drew, Lynn Fontanne, Maude Adams, and Ethel Barrymore.

2045 Chandler, Julia. "Movies Have Done More for Me than the Stage." MOTION PICTURE MAGAZINE 47 (April 1934): 59, 98-99.

> Quotes Hayes as appreciating the wider variety of roles available to her in the motion pictures.

2046 "Concerning Helen Hayes." DRAMA 19 (February 1929): 136-37. Illus.

>The anonymous author, in a brief biographical sketch, recalls Hayes's New York debut in OLD DUTCH with Lew Fields.

2047 "Cue for Baby." AMERICAN MAGAZINE 141 (February 1946): 108. Illus.

>A minor incident in Hayes's marriage to Charles MacArthur.

2048 Cushman, Wilhela. "Mother and Daughter (Mary MacArthur) Have Similar Tastes in Dress Fashions." LADIES' HOME JOURNAL, July 1947, pp. 60-61. Illus.

>Fashion notes.

2049 Dody, Sanford. GIVING UP THE GHOST: A WRITER'S LIFE AMONG THE STARS. New York: M. Evans and Co., 1980. 334 p.

>Dody, a professional ghost writer, recalls working with various celebrities, among them Hayes.

2050 "Dressing a Personality--Helen Hayes." GOOD HOUSEKEEPING, March 1934, pp. 62-66. Illus.

>Fashion notes and Hayes's observations on the subject.

2051 Franklin, Rebecca. "First Lady's Fond Memories." THEATRE ARTS 43 (September 1959): 17-20. Illus.

>Hayes reminisces about some of her colleagues in the past and the changes in the profession during her career.

2052 Frost, David. THE AMERICANS. New York: Stein and Day, 1970. 250 p.

>A series of interviews, one of which, "How Does It Feel to Be a First Lady Longer than Eleanor Roosevelt?" (pp. 56-61), is with Hayes, who discusses various roles, her theatre, and how fame has affected her life.

2053 Funke, Lewis, and Booth, John E. "On Acting." SHOW 1 (October 1961): 88-95. Illus.

>Interviews which were later published in ACTORS TALK ABOUT ACTING. The first, "You Can't Depend on God," is with Hayes.

2054   Goldbeck, Elisabeth. "Look Out, Hollywood! Here Comes Helen Hayes!"
MOTION PICTURE MAGAZINE 42 (October 1931): 26-27, 93.

> Goldbeck lists Hayes's stage triumphs and predicts a
> bright future in film.

2055   "Greatest Living Actress." LIFE, 23 November 1936, pp. 32-35. Illus.

> A pictorial tribute to Hayes upon beginning the VICTORIA
> REGINA tour of the United States. Several early photo-
> graphs of Hayes and her daughter Mary are included.

2056   "Happy, Happy Birthday." NEWSWEEK 28 (11 November 1946): 92-
94. Illus.

> A tribute and overview of Hayes's career to that time.

2057   "Happy Birthday, Dear Helen." THEATRE ARTS 39 (December 1955):
14-15.

> THEATRE ARTS congratulates Robert W. Dowling for re-
> naming his Fulton Theatre as the Helen Hayes Theatre,
> as suggested by John D. MacArthur, editor and publisher
> of the magazine.

2058   Harriman, Margaret Case. "Helen Hayes and Mr. MacArthur." LADIES'
HOME JOURNAL, October 1939, pp. 28, 72. Illus.

> A fan-oriented article on Hayes's home life.

2059   _____. TAKE THEM UP TENDERLY: A COLLECTION OF PROFILES.
New York: Alfred A. Knopf; Toronto: Ryerson Press, 1944. xiii,
266 p.

> Chapter 6, "Veni, Vidi, Vicky," (pp. 110-34) is a re-
> print of a NEW YORKER profile on Hayes. Considerable
> biographical, descriptive, and critical material is in-
> cluded, especially with regard to Hayes as Queen Victoria.

2060   Hayes, Helen. "ANTA." THEATRE ARTS 31 (October 1947): 33-34.

> The actress briefly describes the operation of ANTA, which
> she hoped would be the beginning of a national theatre in
> this country.

2061   _____. "Discipline." AMERICAN MAGAZINE 122 (August 1936):
11. Illus.

> A guest editorial on the benefits of self-control.

2062   _____. "Just Living." LADIES' HOME JOURNAL, April 1936, pp. 8-9, 75-76, 78, 80-81. Illus.

        Hayes offers her formula for happiness and describes the influence of Lillian Russell and John Drew upon her career.

2063   _____. "The Things I Learned from Lew Fields." STAGE 14 (January 1937): 102-4. Illus.

        Hayes fondly recalls her first New York appearance in Field's OLD DUTCH.

2064   _____. "Where Are the New Stars?" THEATRE ARTS 33 (October 1949): 49-51. Illus.

        Hayes berates the profession for not encouraging out-standing performers, although she considered talent plentiful at the time.

2065   Hayes, Helen, with Sanford Dody. ON REFLECTION: AN AUTO-BIOGRAPHY. New York: M. Evans and Co., 1968. New York: Fawcett World Library, 1969. 224 p. Illus.

        One of Hayes's two volumes of autobiography, this one a bit more concerned with her personal life than with her professional career. See next entry.

2066   Hayes, Helen, with Lewis Funke. A GIFT OF JOY. New York: M. Evans and Co., 1965. 254 p. Illus. New York: Fawcett, 1966.

        A revealing autobiography, although dealing minimally with the actress's career. An incisive view of the times and Hayes's reactions to them.

2067   Hecht, Ben. A CHILD OF THE CENTURY. New York: Simon and Schuster, 1954. 633 p. Index, illus.

        A sprawling autobiography of Hecht, who collaborated with MacArthur on FRONT PAGE. Hayes and other players are mentioned frequently.

2068   "Helen Hayes' and Charles MacArthur's Small-Town Life." VOGUE, July 1939, pp. 44-47. Illus.

        A description of Hayes's home life at Nyack, New York, in her home, "Pretty Penny."

2069   "Helen Hayes' Anniversary Album." THEATRE ARTS 40 (February 1956): 32-35. Illus.

A collection of photographs of Hayes in various roles, published in honor of her fiftieth year on the stage.

2070 "Helen Hayes Ends Her Screen Career." LITERARY DIGEST 120 (20 July 1935): 21. Illus.

Hayes, after winning the Academy Award for THE SIN OF MADELON CLAUDET, declared she would appear exclusively on the stage from then on.

2071 "Helen Hayes Gives Creed for Living." LITERARY DIGEST 121 (9 May 1936): 22. Illus.

A succinct survey of Hayes's career to that time and her situation in 1936, including some financial difficulties and her plans for eliminating them.

2072 "Helen Hayes on the Air." NEWSWEEK 33 (14 February 1949): 46-47. Illus.

A review of Hayes's career on radio and in the film industry.

2073 "Helen Hayes Returns to Radio in the Electric Theatre." LIFE, 8 November 1948, p. 77. Illus.

An advertisement for the electric light and power companies of America, in which Hayes describes three of her favorite roles, Viola in TWELFTH NIGHT, Queen Victoria in VICTORIA REGINA, and Maggie in WHAT EVERY WOMAN KNOWS.

2074 "Helen Millennial." TIME 26 (30 December 1935): cover, 22-24. Illus.

A tribute and survey of Hayes's career to that time.

2075 Heylbut, Rose. "My Life with Music." ETUDE 64 (August 1946): 425-26. Illus.

Heylbut quotes Hayes describing her love of music and hoping for a wider recognition of the interrelationship of the arts.

2076 Janeway, Doris. "Helen Hayes Sued for $100,000 By Her Husband's Former Wife." MOVIE CLASSIC 2 (August 1932): 32. Illus.

Carol Frink, a Chicago drama critic, filed the suit against Hayes almost four years after her divorce from Charles MacArthur.

2077 Kennedy, John B. "Lucky Lady." COLLIER'S 83 (30 March 1929): 33, 42. Illus.

> A somewhat frivolous interview in which Hayes deplores her emotionalism and her inability to write a play.

2078 Lee, Sonia. "Helen Hayes . . . Dynamite De Luxe." MOVIE CLASSIC 8 (May 1935): 42, 78-79. Illus.

> Lee describes Hayes as one of Hollywood's great funsters.

2079 "LIFE Goes Calling on Helen Hayes." LIFE, 13 November 1939, pp. 82-85. Illus.

> A fan-oriented photographic essay on the MacArthur home in Nyack, New York.

2080 "LIFE Goes on the Road with Helen Hayes in VICTORIA REGINA." LIFE, 11 April 1938, pp. 62-64. Illus.

> Backstage photographs, including six of Hayes's makeup for the title role.

2081 Patterson, Ada. "Personality Portraits No. 5: Helen Hayes." THEATRE (N.Y.) 33 (January 1921): 26. Illus.

> An early and positive assessment of the actress.

2082 Roberts, Katherine. "A Front-Page Family." COLLIER'S 87 (13 June 1931): 30, 59. Illus.

> An interview of no great depth with Hayes and Charles MacArthur at a time when their daughter, Mary, was one year old.

2083 Service, Faith. "Helen Hayes Keeps a Marriage Ledger." MOTION PICTURE MAGAZINE 44 (October 1932): 31, 80. Illus.

> Hayes light-heartedly discusses the ups and downs of life with Charles MacArthur.

2084 Smalley, Jack. "I've Never Belonged to Myself." MOTION PICTURE MAGAZINE 49 (April 1935): 34-35, 80.

> Hayes describes the trials and tribulations of stardom.

2085 [Spelvin, George.] "To London with Love, or A Haymaker by Helen." THEATRE ARTS 40 (December 1956): 62-63, 92. Illus.

> "Spelvin" describes the furor caused in London by Hayes's

suggestion that American actors and playwrights were superior to those in England.

2086   Sumner, Keene. "A Star at Nineteen." AMERICAN MAGAZINE 91 (March 1921): 34, 152, 154. Illus.

A substantial interview shortly after Hayes began to attract attention in New York; she describes her career as a child star.

2087   "Whispers from the Wings." THEATRE WORLD (London) 49 (September 1948): 33-34. Illus.

An essay filled with praise for Hayes, both as a person and as Amanda Wingfield in THE GLASS MENAGERIE, in which she was then appearing at the Theatre Royal, Haymarket.

2088   "The Wisteria Trees." LIFE, 24 April 1950, pp. 68-70. Illus.

A photographic essay about the production of THE WISTERIA TREES.

2089   Woollcott, Alexander. "The Child-Actor Grows Up." EVERYBODY'S 42 (February 1920): 57-58. Illus.

Woollcott speculates on Hayes's future, saying, "Helen Hayes is a marvel at eighteen. What will she be at twenty-five--great or nothing?"

See also nos. 5, 9, 117, 135, 276, 283, 295-96, 298, 320, 349, 358, 377, 390, 394, 413-14, 441, 452, 484, 486, 525, 532, 545, 549, 563-64, 579, 797, 1477, 1981-82, 1989, and 3071.

HENRY, JOHN (1738-94). See nos. 101, 121, 123, 158, 225, 230, 238, 240-41, 266, 399-400, 423, 428, 445, and 554.

HERNE, CHRYSTAL KATHERINE
(1882-1950)

2090 "Chrystal Herne--A Versatile Actress." THEATRE (N. Y.) 21 (April 1915): 176. Illus.

A very brief overview of the actress's career to date.

2091 Herne, Chrystal. "How the Slender Woman Should Dress." GREEN BOOK MAGAZINE 12 (August 1914): 219-24. Illus.

Fashion notes.

2092 _____. "The Normal Actress." GREEN BOOK ALBUM 6 (July 1911): 174-78.

Herne suggests the "normal" life as being most productive for an actress.

2093 _____. "Playing the Shrew." THEATRE (N. Y.) 44 (October 1926): 9, 62.

Herne describes her preparation for and playing of CRAIG'S WIFE.

2094 _____. "Some Memories of My Father." GREEN BOOK ALBUM 1 (April 1909): 744-49.

A filial tribute, focused upon James A. Herne's ability to inspire love.

See also nos. 13, 270, 417, 2102, 2110, and 2115.

HERNE, JAMES A.

(1839-1901)

2095 Bucks, Dorothy S., and Nethercot, Arthur H. "Ibsen and Herne's MARGARET FLEMING: A Study of the Early Ibsen Movement in America." AMERICAN LITERATURE 17 (January 1946): 311-33.

> The authors conclude that Herne does not deserve the credit he has received for his originality in developing the American drama of ideas, his work being inspired by and derivative of Ibsen and other foreign playwrights. This article stimulated Quinn to pen a rejoinder (no. 2118).

2096 Edwards, Herbert. "Herne, Garland, and Henry George." AMERICAN LITERATURE 28 (November 1956): 359-67.

> An essay describing George's influence through Garland upon Herne on the single tax issue and Herne's efforts for that cause.

2097 _____. "Howells and Herne." AMERICAN LITERATURE 22 (January 1951): 432-41.

> Edwards suggests Howells, realizing he could not write the realistic drama he championed, proclaimed and fought for those who could, such as Herne.

2098 Edwards, Herbert J., and Herne, Julie A. JAMES A. HERNE: THE RISE OF REALISM IN THE AMERICAN DRAMA. Orono: University of Maine Press, 1964. vi, 176 p. Index, illus., bibliog.

> A well-researched, articulate account of Herne's career, stressing his dramaturgy more than his acting. Includes a valuable newspaper bibliography.

2099 "An Epoch-Making Drama." ARENA 4 (July 1891): 247-49.

> An editorial lauding MARGARET FLEMING, which the

author suggests "points to the woman of today her stern and inexorable duty."

2100   Garland, Hamlin. "Mr. and Mrs. Herne." ARENA 4 (October 1891): 542-60. Illus.

Using photographs and sections of scripts, Garland assesses Herne's contributions to a "truthful drama."

2101   _____. "On the Road with James A. Herne." CENTURY 88 (August 1914): 575-81. Illus.

Garlin worked with Herne for a time and recalls their friendship.

2102   _____. ROADSIDE MEETINGS. New York: Macmillan, 1930. vi, 474 p.

Chapter 2 recalls an Edwin Booth engagement in Boston; chapter 7 describes James A. and Katherine Herne in DRIFTING APART; and additional material on James A. Herne is included in chapter 8.

2103   Garland, Hamlin; Enneking, J.J.; and Flower, B.O. "James A. Herne: Actor, Dramatist, and Man." ARENA 26 (September 1901): 282-91.

An appreciative tribute, consisting of three sections: Garland's "His Sincerity as a Playwright"; Enneking's "Mr. Herne as I Knew Him"; and Flower's "The Man and His Work."

2104   Hatlen, Theodore. "Margaret Fleming and the Boston Independent Theatre." EDUCATIONAL THEATER JOURNAL 8 (March 1956): 17-21.

A description of critical and popular receptions to the Hernes and to the script.

2105   Herne, James A. "Act III of James A. Herne's GRIFFITH DAVENPORT." AMERICAN LITERATURE 24 (November 1952): 330-51.

The original manuscript of GRIFFITH DAVENPORT was lost in a fire at Herne Oaks. Act 4 surfaced in William Archer's papers; act 3 was found in Herne's. Included is a floor plan, a prefatory paragraph by A.H. Quinn, and a commentary by Julie A. Herne.

2106   _____. "Art for Truth's Sake in the Drama." ARENA 17 (February 1897): 361-70.

Herne seeks to justify his dramas by proposing that the

theatre has a responsibility to instruct equal to the responsibility to amuse.

2107 _____. "Forty Years Behind the Footlights." COMING AGE 2 (July-December 1899): 121-29.

The anonymous interviewer asks Herne to recall his early days on the stage; in so doing, Herne recalls Edwin Forrest and compares him to John McCullough.

2108 _____. "Old Stock Days in the Theatre." ARENA 6 (September 1892): 401-16.

Herne reminisces about his early years, describing the lines of business still in use and some of the other conventions of the theatre of the time.

2109 _____. "The Present Outlook for the American Drama." COMING AGE 1 (March 1899): 250-55.

The first four pages are an editorial sketch of Herne and his career, followed by an extremely optimistic interview with the playwright in which he suggests the future of the American drama has never been so bright.

2110 _____. SHORE ACRES AND OTHER PLAYS. New York: Samuel French, 1928. xxix, 329. Illus.

Julie Herne's "biographical note" on James A. and Chrystal Herne, pages ix-xxix, precedes an anthology of three of Herne's scripts.

2111 Herne, Julie. "Two Important Qualities of James A. Herne's Plays." PHILHARMONIC 2 (April 1902): 65-71. Illus.

The text is prejudicial in praising Herne's verisimilitude. Included are several illustrations of Herne Oaks.

2112 Howells, William Dean. THE STORY OF A PLAY. New York and London: Harper and Brothers Publishers, 1898. 312 p.

A novel of little distinction, but widely considered a roman à clef about Herne.

2113 Morton, Frederick. "James A. Herne." THEATRE ARTS 24 (December 1940): 899-902.

A brief tribute on the centenary of Herne's birth in which Morton stresses the relationship between Herne's acting and his playwriting.

2114   Moses, Montrose J.   "James A. Herne and Realistic Drama."   BOOK
NEWS 26 (August 1908): 917-24. Illus.

A thoughtful biographical-critical sketch by a leading
critic, including a biographical sketch and a positive
assessment of Herne's realistic dramaturgy.

2115   Perry, John. JAMES A. HERNE, THE AMERICAN IBSEN. Chicago:
Nelson-Hall, 1978. x, 326 p. Index, illus., notes.

Originally a dissertation, this biographical and critical
study seems well researched and documented. Material
is included on David Belasco, Edwin Booth, Augustin Daly,
Mrs. Fiske, Chrystal Herne, Joseph Jefferson III, and
Richard Mansfield. A substantial study of basic importance
to any Herne work.

2116   Pizer, Donald.   "An 1890 Account of MARGARET FLEMING." AMERI-
CAN LITERATURE 27 (May 1955): 264-67.

A reprint of a detailed review of the opening (4 July
1890) from the 8 July 1890 Boston EVENING TRANSCRIPT,
signed "H. G." (Hamlin Garland).

2117   _____.   "The Radical Drama in Boston 1889-1891."   NEW ENGLAND
QUARTERLY 31 (September 1958): 361-74.

Pizer suggests that while unsuccessful, Garland, Herne,
and the First Independent Theatre Association pointed
the way for the radical drama and independent theatre
in the United States.

2118   Quinn, Arthur Hobson.   "Ibsen and Herne--Theory and Facts." AMERI-
CAN LITERATURE 19 (May 1947): 171-77.

Quinn's reply to Bucks and Nethercot's article (no. 2095);
they reply to Quinn on pages 177-80 of this volume.

2119   Robinson, Alice M.   "James A. Herne and His 'Teatre Libre' in Boston."
PLAYERS 48 (Summer 1973): 202-9. Illus.

A useful study, well-researched and documented, of
Herne's early attempts to establish the independent
theatre here.

2120   Saraceni, Gene Adam.   "Herne and the Single Tax: An Early Plea for
an Actor's Union."   EDUCATIONAL THEATRE JOURNAL 26 (October
1974): 315-25.

The author draws heavily upon the Hamlin Garland papers
at the University of Southern California to document
Herne's attempts to improve the actors' circumstances.

2121 Tiempo, Marco. "Workers at Work: VI, James A. Herne in GRIFFITH
DAVENPORT." ARENA 22 (September 1899): 375-82.

> One of a series, this essay compares Herne as an artist
> to Eastman Johnson in the "plastic arts," to Bret Harte
> and James Whitcomb Riley in literature, and praises the
> truthfulness of GRIFFITH DAVENPORT.

2122 Waggoner, Hyatt Howe. "The Growth of a Realist: James A. Herne."
NEW ENGLAND QUARTERLY 15 (March 1942): 62-73.

> Waggoner suggests Herne's ongoing interest in science
> influenced his realistic drama to a great degree.

2123 Wilson, J.H. "Independent Theatre in Boston." HARPER'S WEEKLY
35 (7 November 1891): 874-75.

> A description of the opening of MARGARET FLEMING.

See also nos. 17, 28, 153, 199, 208, 211-12, 214, 219, 228, 279, 288, 299-
300, 327, 379-80, 413, 417, 451, and 2094.

HERON, MATILDA
(1830-77)

2124   HISTORY OF CAMILLE AS PERFORMED BY MATILDA HERON FOR
       OVER ONE THOUSAND NIGHTS. Cincinnati: Wrightson and Co.,
       1864.

> A reprint in pamphlet form of an article which originally
> appeared in the MISSOURI REPUBLICAN, a St. Louis
> newspaper. A copy is in the California State Library in
> Sacramento, but the volume was unavailable for examina-
> tion.

2125   Perkins, Merle L. "Matilda Heron's CAMILLE." COMPARATIVE
       LITERATURE 7, no. 4 (1955): 338-43.

> A brief stage history of Heron in the title role, dealing
> primarily with her alterations of the script as she created
> her own unique version.

See also nos. 13, 203, 222, 261, 277, 313, 337, 341, 401, 407, 413, 507,
2567, and 2782.

HILL, GEORGE HANDEL

(1809-49)

2126   Collier, Gaylan.   "George Handel Hill: The Yankee of Them All."
SOUTHERN SPEECH JOURNAL 24 (Winter 1958): 91-93.

> An extremely brief reprint of a portion of the author's
> dissertation on the subject.

2127   Hill, George Handel.   SCENES FROM THE LIFE OF AN ACTOR.
COMPILED FROM THE JOURNALS, LETTERS, AND MEMORANDA OF
THE LATE YANKEE HILL.   New York: Garrett and Co., 1853. viii,
246 p. Illus. Reprint. New York: Benjamin Blom, 1969.

> Hill's widow, Cordelia, with the help of their son,
> arranged her husband's manuscripts for publication three
> years after Northall had published LIFE AND RECOL-
> LECTIONS (below). Hill had intended to publish his
> memoirs at age fifty. A valuable source.

2128   Northall, William Knight.   LIFE AND RECOLLECTIONS OF YANKEE
HILL: TOGETHER WITH ANECDOTES AND INCIDENTS OF HIS
TRAVELS.   New York: W.F. Burgess, 1850. vii, 203. Illus.

> A detailed account of Hill's Yankee characters, drawing
> heavily upon newspaper criticism. Pages 1-97 are a
> biographical sketch of Hill; the rest of the volume con-
> sists of anecdotes and incidents. Useful.

See also nos. 181, 222, 413, 2461, and 3168.

HITCHCOCK, RAYMOND

(1865-1929)

2129　Hitchcock, Raymond. "Bursting the Strait-Jacket." GREEN BOOK
ALBUM 2 (October 1909): 804-9.

> Hitchcock refers to the mental straitjackets of the anti-
> theatrical forces then in evidence.

2130　_____. "Just Life." GREEN BOOK MAGAZINE 11 (June 1914):
987-89.

> Hitchcock celebrates his easy-going life-style in a some-
> what superficial essay of minimal value.

See also nos. 270, 276, and 377.

HODGKINSON, JOHN
(c. 1765-1805)

2131   [Carpenter, Cullen.] "Sketch of the Life of the Late Mr. John Hodgkin-son." MIRROR OF TASTE AND DRAMATIC CENSOR 1 (March 1810): 202-12; (April 1810): 283-97; (May 1810): 368-80; (June 1810): 457-66; 2 (July 1810): 15-22; (August 1810): 99-109; (November 1810): 235-45.

A substantial if undocumented account of Hodgkinson's life and career, basic to any study of the actor.

2132   Harbin, Billy. "Hodgkinson and His Rivals at the Park: The Business of Early Romantic Theatre in America." EMERSON SOCIETY QUARTERLY 20 (3d quarter 1974): 148-69.

Unavailable for examination.

2133   _____. "Hodgkinson's Last Years: At the Charleston Theatre, 1803-05." THEATRE SURVEY 13 (November 1972): 20-43. Illus.

A detailed and documented account, stressing the actor's immense popularity.

2134   _____. "John Hodgkinson in the English Provinces, 1765-1792." THEATRE NOTEBOOK 28, no. 3 (1974): 106-16.

A well-researched and documented account of Hodgkinson's career prior to his arrival in the United States.

2135   Hodgkinson, John. A NARRATIVE OF HIS CONNECTION WITH THE OLD AMERICAN COMPANY FROM THE FIFTH SEPTEMBER, 1972, TO THE THIRTY-FIRST OF MARCH, 1797. New York: J. Oram, 1797. 23 p.

A very rare volume in which Hodgkinson relates his side of the many quarrels which beset the company at this time. The work is reprinted in the second edition of Dunlap's HISTORY OF THE AMERICAN THEATRE (1833).

See also nos. 101, 121, 123, 139, 147, 188, 192, 206, 238, 399, 402, 413, 428, 485, 517, 535, 541, 554, 592, 1008, and 2012.

HOLLAND FAMILY

See nos. 146, 183, and 347.

Entries for George, Edmund Milton, and Joseph Jefferson Holland follow.

HOLLAND, GEORGE
(1791-1870)

2136   Morrell, T.H.   HOLLAND MEMORIAL.   SKETCH OF THE LIFE OF
GEORGE HOLLAND, THE VETERAN COMEDIAN, WITH DRAMATIC
REMINISCENCES, ANECDOTES, &C.   New York: T.H. Morrell,
1871.   124 p.   Frontispiece.

> Limited to 250 copies, fifty on quarto paper. A memorial
> tribute written shortly after the actor's death. As such,
> the first half of the volume is biographical, the latter
> half a compendium of tributes by the leading members of
> the profession. Considerable description of the Church of
> the Transfiguration (The Little Church around the Corner)
> is included; Holland's funeral was held there.

See also nos. 201, 222, 244, 319, 401, 408, 413, 450, 583, 1750, 2235-36,
3027, and 2959.

HOLLAND, EDMUND MILTON
(1848-1913)

2137   Holland, Edmund M.   "Personality vs. Technique."   GREEN BOOK
ALBUM 5 (February 1911): 373-76.

> Holland describes his approach to role preparation and
> characterization in his work.

See also nos. 28, 112, 261, 270, 328, 379, 451, and 513.

HOLLAND, JOSEPH JEFFERSON (1860-1926). See nos. 112, 188, and 279.

HOPPER, DeWOLF

(1858-1935)

2138   Bird, Carol. "When Should the Actor Quit?" THEATRE (N.Y.) 33 (April 1921): 242, 294.

        Hopper is quoted on the subject of retirement, holding that performers quit when their powers begin to fade.

2139   "DeWolf Hopper Discusses Light Opera." ETUDE 45 (December 1927): 941.

        A brief extract from ONCE A CLOWN (no. 2150).

2140   Gardner, Martin. "Casey at the Bat." AMERICAN HERITAGE 18 (October 1967): 64-68. Illus.

        Although primarily a history of the poem by Ernest Lawrence Thayer, considerable mention of Hopper is made.

2141   Hopper, DeWolf. "Art of the Operatic Comedian." PHILHARMONIC 3 (March 1903): 73-77. Illus.

        Hopper describes the skills requisite for such roles, drawing upon his own experience.

2142   ————. "DeWolf Hopper, Actor, vs. DeWolf Hopper, Man." GREEN BOOK ALBUM 6 (October 1911): 763-70.

        Hopper describes his own opinion of himself, which was fairly high, both on and off stage.

2143   ————. "Elephants and Thrills." THEATRE (N.Y.) 28 (November 1918): 270. Illus.

        Part of a series, "The Most Striking Episode in My Life." Hopper recalls an incident involving Jennie, a five-ton Hippodrome elephant.

2144 _____. "If I Had Never Been an Actor." THEATRE (N.Y.) 19 (January 1914): 9-10, 44. Illus.

> Hopper describes the tribulations of his early career, but never mentions an alternative occupation.

2145 _____. "My Beginnings." THEATRE (N.Y.) 5 (November 1905): 284-85. Illus.

> Hopper maintains his first experience in the commercial theatre cost him his inheritance of $50,000.

2146 _____. "Personal Reminiscences." THEATRE (N.Y.) 26 (October 1917): 194-95, 256. Illus.

> A somewhat thin autobiographical sketch.

2147 _____. "Some True Stories." PEARSON'S 26 (September 1911): 392-400. Illus.

> A collection of theatrical anecdotes, several of them involving Richard Mansfield.

2148 _____. "A Thousand Years in a Flat." GREEN BOOK ALBUM 2 (September 1909): 617-21.

> The comedian bemoans the "four-rooms and bath" life of the actor and recounts anecdotes of his experiences.

2149 Hopper, DeWolf, and Stout, Wesley W. "Myself When Young." SATURDAY EVENING POST 198 (10 October 1925): 10-11, 88, 90, 92, 94, 96; "Once a Clown, Always a Clown," (24 October 1925): 20-21, 82, 84; "Casey at the Bat" (14 November 1925): 8-9, 148-49; "How Not to Act," (5 December 1925): 26, 226, 229-30, 233-34; "Came Dawn at Hollywood," (12 December 1925): 14, 50, 52, 54, 56; "Wolfie Loves the Lambs," 199 (17 April 1926): 45-46, 141, 145-46. Illus.

> Serialization of the next entry, with additional illustrations.

2150 _____. ONCE A CLOWN, ALWAYS A CLOWN: REMINISCENCES OF DE WOLF HOPPER. Boston: Little, Brown, and Co., 1927. 238 p. Illus. Also published as REMINISCENCES OF DE WOLF HOPPER; ONCE A CLOWN, ALWAYS A CLOWN. Garden City, N.Y.: Garden City Publishing Co., 1932. 245 p. Illus.

> A chatty recollection of Hopper's career, anecdotal and minimally factual. In the "show biz" tradition of autobiographies, with many good-natured reminiscences of Louis James, Mrs. Drew, Joseph Jefferson III, and Maurice Barrymore. See previous entry.

2151   Schmidt, Karl.   "Stage Drift."   HARPER'S WEEKLY   60 (15 May 1915): 466.   Illus.

>   Schmidt applaudes Hopper's impressive accomplishments in revivals of Gilbert and Sullivan works.

2152   Wolf, Rennold.   "DeWolf Hopper, That Justly Celebrated Husband." GREEN BOOK MAGAZINE   11 (March 1914):   396-404.

>   A substantial examination of Hopper, stressing his vigor and morality.

See also nos. 28, 112, 191, 243, 270, 272, 276, 279, 346, 378, 413, 492, 588, 591, 1975, and 3094.

HOWARD FAMILY
Howard, George C. (1818-87)
Macdonald, Cordelia Howard (1848-1941)

2153   Birdoff, Harry.   THE WORLD'S GREATEST HIT: UNCLE TOM'S CABIN.
New York: S. F. Vanni, 1947.   440 p.   Illus.

> Birdoff's readable and lively production history of the
> script(s) includes a description of the Howards' various
> productions of it.

2154   Drummond, A. M., and Moody, Richard.   "The Hit of the Century:
Uncle Tom's Cabin--1852-1952. "   EDUCATIONAL THEATRE JOURNAL
4, no. 4 (1952): 315-22.

> Some observations about the Howard family are included
> in this brief production history.

2155   Kaye, Joseph.   "Famous First Nights: UNCLE TOM'S CABIN. "
THEATRE (N. Y.)   50 (August 1929): 26, 65.   Illus.

> A description of and excerpts from reviews for the opening
> of the production at the National Theatre in New York
> on 26 July 1853.

2156   Judd, Dr.   "The Pioneer Uncle Tomers. "   THEATRE (N. Y.)   4 (February
1904): 44.   Illus.

> A brief reminiscence of the Howard family by a member
> of one of their companies.

2157   Macdonald, Cordelia Howard.   "Memoirs of the Original Little Eva. "
Edited and foreword by George P. Howard.   EDUCATIONAL THEATRE
JOURNAL 8, no. 4 (1956): 267-82.

> Howard edited his aunt's manuscript, written in 1928 and
> published for the first time here.   Mrs. Macdonald gives
> a detailed account of her experiences with the production.

2158   Moody, Richard.   "Uncle Tom, the Theatre, and Mrs. Stowe. "   AMERI-
CAN HERITAGE   6 (October 1955): 28-33, 102-3.   Illus.

Moody includes a brief account of the Troy, New York, production and the Howards. Several color illustrations of posters are included.

2159 Rahill, Frank. "America's Number One Hit." THEATRE ARTS 36 (October 1952): 18-24. Illus.

A popularized stage history of UNCLE TOM'S CABIN with a bit of material on the Howard's original production of the script.

See also nos. 13, 222, and 229.

HULL, HENRY

(1890-1977)

2160 Hull, Henry. "Silence is the Most Effective Censorship." THEATRE
(N.Y.) 49 (February 1929): 35, 74. Illus.

Hull suggests that audiences take responsibility for the
"immoral" drama when creating controversy in America.

See also nos. 276 and 412.

HULL, JOSEPHINE

(1886-1957)

2161 Carson, William Glasgow Bruce. DEAR JOSEPHINE: THE THEATRICAL CAREER OF JOSEPHINE HULL. Norman: University of Oklahoma Press, 1963. xii, 297 p. Index, illus., bibliog.

> A pleasant biographical exercise by an outstanding scholar, with substantial material on Margaret Anglin and the Fiskes.

2162 Gresham, William Lindsay. "Comedienne from Radcliffe: Josephine Hull." THEATRE ARTS 29 (June 1945): 346-52. Illus.

> Hull recalls with great fondness her collegiate training for the stage.

See also nos. 5 and 276.

HUSTON, WALTER

(1884-1950)

2163 Grant, J. "Walter Huston Says, 'If I Were Roosevelt--.'" MOVIE CLASSIC 4 (May 1933): 30, 68. Illus.

> A publicity puff for Huston's film, GABRIEL OVER THE WHITE HOUSE, in which he played Jud Hammond, U.S. president.

2164 Huston, John. AN OPEN BOOK. New York: Alfred A. Knopf, 1980. 373 p. Index, illus.

> An autobiography by the actor's son, a film director, with considerable biographical material in the early portion.

2165 Huston, Walter. "In and Out of the Bag: Othello Sits Up in Bed the Morning After and Takes Notice." STAGE 14 (March 1937): 54-55, 57.

> Huston staged an unsuccessful OTHELLO and describes his reactions to the negative criticism.

2166 _____. "There's No Place Like Broadway." STAGE 16 (September 1938): 22-25. Illus.

> A light and anecdotal essay on the lure of the Great White Way.

2167 "The Hustons--Son and Father." HARPER'S BAZAAR 80 (March 1946): 182-83. Illus.

> A brief description of John and Walter Huston, the latter appearing in APPLE OF HIS EYE.

2168 Kennedy, John B. "Shrinking Star." COLLIER'S 87 (2 May 1931): 19, 46. Illus.

> Kennedy describes Huston's departure from the stage to

become an electrical engineer, his subsequent return, and his eventual success in films and on the stage.

2169   Service, Faith. "Walter Huston Won't Live in Hollywood." MOTION PICTURE MAGAZINE 52 (December 1936): 40, 80. Illus.

Huston is quoted as saying, "Hollywood is the most idiotic place in the world to live," and adding several other reasons to avoid it.

See also nos. 5, 276, 291, 310, 325, 413, 437, and 484.

ILLINGTON, MARGARET

(1879-1934)

2170   Illington, Margaret. "One Way to Compel Good Plays." GREEN BOOK MAGAZINE 10 (July 1913): 25-32. Illus.

>The actress laments the lack of American classic dramas, but predicts they will come to pass in the future.

2171   _____. "The Theatre I Should Like to Build." GREEN BOOK ALBUM 5 (May 1911): 1094-96.

>Illington suggests if she ran a theatre she would specialize in American scripts, but might do a few from Germany.

2172   Patterson, Ada. "A Chat with Margaret Illington." THEATRE (N. Y.) 15 (May 1912): 141-43, xiii. Illus.

>A discussion of Illington's considerable success in KINDLING, just after her first retirement from the stage.

2173   _____. "Margaret Illington: An Interpreter of Life as It Is." GREEN BOOK ALBUM 7 (April 1912): 755-59.

>A very thin interview; Illington is quoted as believing happiness is a requisite for success.

See also nos. 316, 444, 509, and 1507.

IRVING, ISABEL

(1871-1944)

2174   Irving, Isabel.   "How the Blonde Woman Should Dress."   GREEN BOOK
       MAGAZINE 12 (September 1914): 456-61. Illus.

       Fashion advice.

2175   _____. "A Little Chapter of Memories." GREEN BOOK ALBUM 3
       (April 1910): 832-37.

       Irving describes some of her more successful vacations.

2176   Patterson, Ada.   "Isabel Irving--The Eternal Ingenue." THEATRE (N. Y.)
       10 (April 1910): 124, 126-28. Illus.

       A particularly fatuous interview of minimal value.

See also nos. 28, 270, 279, 381, 444, 448, and 480.

IRWIN, MAY

(1862-1938)

2177   Ewen, David. THE LIFE AND DEATH OF TIN PAN ALLEY: THE
GOLDEN AGE OF AMERICAN POPULAR MUSIC. New York: Funk
and Wagnall's, 1964. xv, 346 p. Index, bibliog.

> Includes considerable material on Irwin as a musical
> comedy performer.

2178   Irwin, May. "The Business of the Stage as a Career." COSMOPOLITAN
28 (April 1900): 655-60. Illus.

> Irwin muses over her twenty-five year career and the
> changes she has seen in the theatre, most of which she
> supports. Several otherwise unpublished photographs
> accompany the text.

2179   _____. "I Want to Live to be a Hundred." GREEN BOOK MAGA-
ZINE 10 (September 1913): 441-46. Illus.

> Irwin notes that humorists improve with age and hopes that
> as a comedienne she can do the same.

2180   _____. "My Views on Women." GREEN BOOK MAGAZINE 8
(December 1912): 1057-63. Illus.

> Irwin calls for women to liberate themselves from home-
> making and child rearing.

2181   _____. "Nursing the Nerves." GREEN BOOK ALBUM 2 (July 1909):
152-56.

> Irwin's observations and advice on dealing with stage
> fright, which she never considered a problem for herself.

2182   P., A. [Ada Patterson]. "May Irwin on Popularity." THEATRE (N.Y.)
17 (June 1913): 175. Illus.

Irwin posits that her success has been a result of her respect for and honesty with her audiences.

2183   Patterson, Ada. "At Home with May Irwin." GREEN BOOK ALBUM 5 (March 1911): 520–25.

An interview focused on household cleaning and budgets.

2184   _____. "May Irwin on Humor, Home and Business." THEATRE (N. Y.) 5 (October 1905): 258, 260–61. Illus.

Irwin proposes her surprisingly modern theories on comedy and the playing thereof.

2185   _____. "Twenty Years a Star." THEATRE (N. Y.) 22 (November 1915): 236, 253. Illus.

The actress reminisces over her career and describes the vicissitudes of fame.

2186   Randolph, Ann. "Comedienne and Cook: May Irwin." NATIONAL MAGAZINE 38 (September 1913): 1101–02. Illus.

Randolph assures the reader that although Irwin was an outstanding comic actress, she could and did perform household chores satisfactorily.

2187   Spaeth, Sigmund. A HISTORY OF POPULAR MUSIC IN AMERICA. New York: Random House, 1948. xv, 662 p. Index, bibliog.

An undistinguished history with scattered references to Irwin.

See also nos. 13, 28, 129, 168, 261, 270, 276, 279, 288, 381, 413, 448, 491–92, 509, and 1604.

JAMES, LOUIS
(1842-1910)

2188   Balance, John. "Two Actors: A Comparison." MASK 1 (August
        1908): 121-23.

>   The author compares James and the elder Sothern, stimulated
>   by their published remarks on acting techniques, and finds
>   Sothern the superior of the two.

2189   Hackett, Norman. "The Louis James I Knew." GREEN BOOK ALBUM
        3 (May 1910): 984-89.

>   A tribute by a young actor who had worked with and
>   befriended James.

2190   Wagstaff, William de. "Louis James--An Actor of Tradition." THEATRE
        (N.Y.) 2 (September 1902): 22-25. Illus.

>   Wagstaff evaluates James's acting within the tradition of
>   Shakespearean stock company performances.

See also nos. 112, 165, 176, 245, 263, 270, 279, 386, 399, 446, 501, 561,
2149-50, 3142, and 3146.

JANAUSCHEK, FRANCESCA

(1830-1904)

2191   Knepler, Henry W. "MARIA STUART in America." THEATRE ANNUAL 16 (1959): 30-50. Illus.

        In tracing the script's production history, Knepler describes productions by Janauschek and Modjeska.

2192   Knight, Joseph. THEATRICAL NOTES. London: 1893. Reprint. New York: Benjamin Blom, 1972. xvi, 309 p. Index, frontispiece.

        Published reviews of Janauschek as Mary Stuart and in THE GOLDEN FLEECE.

2193   Leuchs, Frederich Aldoph Herman. THE EARLY GERMAN THEATRE IN NEW YORK. New York: Columbia University Press, 1928. xxi, 281 p. Index, bibliog.

        A description and history of Janauschek's various New York engagements.

2194   Wallison, L.R. "America's Queen of Tragedy." THEATRE (N.Y.) 3 (September 1903): 228-29. Illus.

        A tribute to Janauschek after her retirement, describing her successes in the United States and elsewhere.

See also nos. 13, 112, 163, 222, 233, 245, 261, 263, 279, 328, 356, 367, 387, 400, 413, 417, 419, 451, 474, 493, 548, 560, 570, 596, 1560, 2585, 2625, and 2932.

JANIS, ELSIE
(1889-1956)

2195 B., H. T. [Broeck, Helen Ten?] "The New Lady of Philipse Manor."
THEATRE (N. Y.) 23 (July 1916): 16-17. Illus.

>Janis had just bought this mansion, once associated with
>George Washington.

2196 Craig, Ralph H. "The Incorrigible Elsie." COSMOPOLITAN 54
(February 1913): 412-13. Illus.

>A frivolous attempt to review Janis's career to that time,
>adding little of substance.

2197 Duggan, Marion. "Romance No Stranger to Elsie Janis, Who Weds at
Forty-Two." MOVIE CLASSIC 2 (April 1932): 34. Illus.

>An account of Janis's wedding to Gilbert Wilson, "sixteen
>years her junior."

2198 "Elsie Janis--Dramatic Star." GREEN BOOK MAGAZINE 14 (October
1915): 716. Illus.

>A one-column tribute, citing Janis's recently successful
>London tour.

2199 "Elsie Janis--'The Lady of a Million Laughs.'" NATIONAL MAGAZINE
53 (September 1924): 128, 133. Illus.

>A brief essay stressing Janis's many talents and wide
>popularity.

2200 "The Girl Who 'Got' London." HARPER'S BAZAAR 49 (July 1914):
13. Illus.

>A brief description of Janis's London successes, plus
>seven photographs.

2201   Janis, Elsie. THE BIG SHOW. MY SIX MONTHS WITH THE AMERICAN
        EXPEDITIONARY FORCES. New York: Cosmopolitan Book Corp., 1919.
        xii, 227 p. Illus.

>   Light-hearted reminiscences of World War I and Janis's
>   tour of the front lines to entertain the troops. See no. 2202.

2202   _____. "The Big Show, My Six Months in France with the A.E.F."
        HEARST'S 35 (February 1919): 15-16, 71. "To-Night at Seven-Thirty,"
        (March 1919): 24-25; "Such Rain-Such Mud!" (April 1919): 14-15;
        "Oh, for a Young Chateau!" (May 1919): 21, 62; "No Wonder the
        Church-Bells Rang!" (June 1919): 28-29, 58; "Exit Queen Nurse!"
        (July 1919): 22-23, 71; "I Meet General Pershing," (August 1919):
        28, 74. Illus.

>   A serialized version of Janis's book of the same title.
>   See no. 2201.

2203   _____. "Flirting with the Famous." COLLIER'S 77 (19 June 1926):
        7-8. Illus.

>   Janis describes meeting various celebrities, most of them
>   politicians or athletes.

2204   _____. "Home Again." GOOD HOUSEKEEPING, September 1919,
        pp. 27-29, 185-86. Illus.

>   Janis recalls her experiences while performing for the
>   troops in Europe during World War I.

2205   _____. "How I Do My Imitations." THEATRE (N.Y.) 25 (June 1917):
        336, 374. Illus.

>   Janis, who had a reputation for mimicry, describes not so
>   much her technique as her subjects.

2206   _____. IF I KNOW WHAT I MEAN. New York: G.P. Putnam's
        Sons, 1925. iv, 132 p. Illus.

>   A series of humorous essays by Janis on various subjects
>   none of them dealing with the theatre or acting.

2207   _____. "I Interview Myself." GREEN BOOK ALBUM 1 (April 1909):
        776-81.

>   A gimmicky essay; of minimal value.

2208   _____. "Is Imitation the Sincerest Flattery?" SATURDAY EVENING
        POST, 26 September 1925, pp. 14-15, 194, 197. Illus.

>   A justification by Janis of her mimicry, suggesting she
>   could not imitate anyone whom she did not admire greatly.

2209 _____. "The Slacker." THEATRE (N. Y.) 26 (October 1917): 210-11. Illus.

> A patriotic poem of slight literary value written by the actress.

2210 _____. SO FAR, SO GOOD! AN AUTOBIOGRAPHY BY ELSIE JANIS. New York: E. P. Dutton and Co., 1932. London: Long, 1933. 344 p. Illus.

> A self-indulgent autobiography, largely anecdotal, but surprisingly specific as to dates.

2211 _____. "A Star for a Night." GREEN BOOK ALBUM 6 (August 1911): 257-99.

> Janis's novelization of her play of the same name.

2212 _____. "The Story of My Life." AMERICAN MAGAZINE 84 (November 1917): 33-35, 126-30. Illus.

> A thin account of the actress's early career, describing her skill and propensity for mimicry.

2213 L., R.I. "Elsie Janis Gives a Concert." NATIONAL MAGAZINE 52 (December 1923): 319, 326. Illus.

> A description of Janis's one-woman show of impressions, after she left musical comedy.

2214 "The Lady of a Million Laughs." NATIONAL MAGAZINE 51 (February 1923): 413-15. Illus.

> A fan-oriented but substantial interview, including one of Janis's poems, "Blind," and several photographs.

2215 Tyrrell, Henry. "Elsie Janis--The Inimitable Child." THEATRE (N. Y.) 5 (August 1905): 208. Illus.

> A description of Janis at age sixteen when she first began to attract substantial attention as a performer.

2216 Young, Z. Z. "Elsie Janis and Her Manor-House." GREEN BOOK MAGAZINE 15 (January 1916): 104-9. Illus.

> Janis brought her dream house after her successes in the theatre, the Philipse Manor House at Tarrytown-on-the-Hudson.

See also nos. 168, 270, 276, 377, 413, 422, 509, 536, 543, 579, and 598.

JEFFERSON FAMILY

JEFFERSON, JOSEPH I (1774-1832). See nos. 101, 118, 180, 192, 206, 347, 399, 413, 417, and 541.

JEFFERSON, JOSEPH III
(1829-1905)

2217   Albert, A.D., Jr. "Mrs. Joseph Jefferson as a Painter." CRITIC 39 (July 1901): 32-36. Illus.

> Jefferson's art work is evaluated and four paintings re-
> produced in black and white; the critic is not impressed
> with the actor's work.

2218   Bacheller, Morris. "The Dean of the American Stage." MUNCEY'S 12 (1895): 497-502. Illus.

> A sketch of the career and personality of Jefferson, his
> early adventures and successes as Rip Van Winkle and Bob
> Acres.

2219   Ballou, William Hosea. "Joseph Jefferson at Home." COSMOPOLITAN 7 (June 1889): 120-27. Illus.

> Ballou describes a visit to Jefferson's retreat in New
> Iberia, Louisiana, in the midst of "Evangeline" country.
> Jefferson is presented as a benificent squire of this domain.

2220   Bradford, Gamaliel. AMERICAN PORTRAITS, 1875-1900. Boston and New York: Houghton Mifflin Co., 1920. xiii, 242 p. Index, illus., notes.

> Chapter 7, pages 199-223, is a biographical sketch of

Jefferson, drawing heavily upon William Winter, Francis
Wilson, and Jefferson's AUTOBIOGRAPHY.

2221 _____. "Joseph Jefferson." ATLANTIC 129 (January 1922): 85-95.

A graceful, albeit undocumented assessment of Jefferson's
career and personality, praising both highly.

2222 Curtis, Isabel Gordon. "An Inherited Autograph." LIPPINCOTT 76
(November 1905): 574-76. Illus.

Curtis owned a playscript with Joseph Jefferson I's autograph in it, which closely resembled that of Jefferson III.
A few biographical bits of information are added.

2223 Davis, L. Clarke. "Jefferson and Rip Van Winkle." LIPPINCOTT 24
(July 1879): 57-75. Illus.

A history of the Jeffersons, focused on Jefferson III,
with steel engravings of him as Rip Van Winkle.

2224 Dole, Nathan Haskell. JOSEPH JEFFERSON AT HOME. Boston: Estes
and Lauriat, 1898. 110 p. Illus.

A brief and undocumented biography of Jefferson with
rarely published photographs.

2225 Farjeon, Eleanor. PORTRAIT OF A FAMILY. New York: Frederick A.
Stokes Co.; Toronto: McClelland, 1935. xiv, 456 p. Illus. Published
also as NURSERY IN THE NINETIES. London: Gollancz; Toronto:
Ryerson Press, 1935. 528 p. Illus.

The Farjeon family was related to the Jeffersons; this
volume contains numerous anecdotal references to Jefferson III and to Edwin Booth, a frequent visitor.

2226 Gilder, Joseph B. "Career of Joseph Jefferson." REVIEW OF REVIEWS
31 (June 1905): 674-77. Illus.

A brief overview of minimal value.

2227 Gilder, R.W. "The Passing of Jefferson." CENTURY n.s. 48 (July
1905): 474.

A eulogistic poem.

2228 Gilder, Rosamond. "Joseph Jefferson." THEATRE ARTS 27 (June 1943):
375-84. Illus.

A biographical sketch, gracefully written, stressing the
affection of the public for the actor.

2229   Graf, LeRoy P. "Soldier Entertainment a Hundred Years Ago." THEATRE ANNUAL 5 (1946): 48–61.

> Drawing heavily upon THE AMERICAN FLAG, a U.S. Army newspaper published in Matamoros, Mexico, during the occupation in 1846–48, Graf describes an engagement there by Jefferson.

2230   Grossman, C. Edwin Booth. "A Morning Fishing with Joseph Jefferson." THEATRE (N.Y.) 5 (July 1905): 179–80. Illus.

> Anecdotal reminiscences written by the grandson of Edwin Booth.

2231   Huneker, James. "Joseph Jefferson." WORLD'S WORK 10 (June 1905): 6317–20.

> An undistinguished eulogy and overview.

2232   Hutton, Laurence. "Recollections of Joseph Jefferson." HARPER'S WEEKLY 49 (6 May 1905): 656–57, 661, 663. Illus.

> Hutton wrote, at Jefferson's request, this tribute in November 1898 while the actor was ill. Jefferson asked that it be published after his death.

2233   Jefferson, Eugenie Paul. INTIMATE RECOLLECTIONS OF JOSEPH JEFFERSON. New York: Dodd, Mead and Co., 1909. 366 p. Illus. Reprint. New York: Benjamin Blom, 1969.

> A somewhat rambling, but nevertheless useful, reminiscence of Jefferson and various of his colleagues in the theatre. Edwin Booth is mentioned frequently.

2234   _____. "Joseph Jefferson at Home." CENTURY 77 (April 1909): 886–89. Illus.

> Chatty reminiscences, including descriptions of visits to the Jefferson home by Mrs. Drew.

2235   Jefferson, Joseph. THE AUTOBIOGRAPHY OF JOSEPH JEFFERSON. New York: Century Co.; London: Unwin, 1890. New York: Century Co., 1897, 1917. Published as "RIP VAN WINKLE": THE AUTOBIOGRAPHY OF JOSEPH JEFFERSON. London: Reinhardt and Evans, 1949; New York: Appleton-Century-Crofts, 1950. Edited by Alan S. Downer as THE AUTOBIOGRAPHY OF JOSEPH JEFFERSON. Cambridge, Mass.: Belknap Press of Harvard University Press, 1964. xxv, 361 p. Index, illus., notes.

> Jefferson wrote an especially charming account of his career, one of the more readable such accounts. It con-

tains many accounts and insights about his fellow players:
the elder Booth, Edwin Forrest, John E. Owens, Laura
Keene, William Warren, Jr., Edwin Booth, Dion Boucicault,
William Rufus Blake, John Brougham, William Evans Burton,
Julia Dean, John Drew I, Charles Fechter, George Holland,
James Murdoch, John Howard Payne, Henry Placide, E. A.
Sothern, James W. Wallack, and others. As Francis Wilson
said of this work, "Jefferson lived a full, rich, finely
ordered life, and he wrote a full, rich, charming autobiography, albeit he found it tedious at times to adhere
to statistics." See no. 2236.

2236   . "The Autobiography of Joseph Jefferson." CENTURY n.s. 39
(November 1889-April 1890): 3-25, 184-203, 367-84, 494-504, 643-
57, 803-11; n.s. 40 (May-October 1890): 135-43, 263-68, 406-18,
538-56, 704-23, 803, 814-37. Illus.

The serialization of Jefferson's AUTOBIOGRAPHY with
additional illustrations. See no. 2235.

2237   . "From My Autobiography." THEATRE WORKSHOP 1 (January-
March 1937): 60-64.

Four pages reprinted from Jefferson's AUTOBIOGRAPHY in
which he describes how some actors achieve great effects.

2238   . "Is Acting Art?" PHILHARMONIC 1 (January 1901): 1-2.
Illus.

Jefferson holds that acting is as much an art as any other.

2239   . "Jefferson on Edwin Booth." CRITIC 25 (29 September 1894):
210.

A transcript of Jefferson's address to the Players Club
on Founder's Night, 1894, in which he recalls his friendship with Booth. This was the first address given by
Jefferson to the Players as their president.

2240   . "Jefferson on His Art." CRITIC n.s. 25 (13 June 1896): 432.

Brief remarks by Jefferson on acting as an art and the
effects upon it of the starring system.

2241   Entry deleted.

2242   . "Joseph Jefferson, Chicagoan." In REMINISCENCES OF
CHICAGO DURING THE FORTIES AND FIFTIES, edited by Mabel
McIlvaine, pp. 77-91. Chicago: R. R. Donnelley and Sons Co., 1913.
xxiii, 137 p. Frontispiece.

Describes Jefferson's early experiences in and around

Chicago, reprinted from his AUTOBIOGRAPHY.

2243 _____. "Origin of Rip Van Winkle." CURRENT LITERATURE 19 (February 1896): 138.

An article reprinted from the Boston HERALD in which the actor describes his attraction to the role of Rip.

2244 _____. RIP VAN WINKLE AS PLAYED BY JOSEPH JEFFERSON. New York: Dodd, Mead and Co., 1902. 199 p. Illus.

Contains substantial stage directions, a preface to each act, many illustrations, and an introduction by Jefferson.

2245 _____. "Speech at Dinner in Honor of Tolstoy." CRITIC n.s. 30 (October 1898): 285-87.

Jefferson appeared in New York at a dinner on 8 September 1898 in honor of the Russian author, but his remarks were all theatrical anecdotes, having nothing to do with Tolstoy.

2246 "Joseph Jefferson." OUTLOOK 79 (April 1905): 1027-29.

A eulogistic assessment, stressing the public's strong affection for the actor.

2247 "Joseph Jefferson as the Spectators Knew Him." OUTLOOK 80 (May 1905): 17-18. Illus.

A summation of Jefferson's career with several seldom published photographs of the actor.

2248 "Joseph Jefferson Enshrined." LITERARY DIGEST 85 (4 April 1925): 37-38. Illus.

The background of the memorial window to Jefferson in the Little Church around the Corner in New York City.

2249 Kendall, John Smith. "Joseph Jefferson in New Orleans." LOUISIANA HISTORICAL QUARTERLY 26 (1943): 1150-67.

Kendall describes the importance of New Orleans to Jefferson's career in an undocumented article. He includes an anecdote of Jefferson's appearance with Edwin Forrest there.

2250 Lauriston, Henri. "America's Greatest Actor." NEW ENGLAND MAGAZINE n.s. 32 (June 1905): 395-98. Illus.

A extended tribute to Jefferson, adding little.

2251   McVicker, James H. THE THEATRE; ITS EARLY DAYS IN CHICAGO.
Chicago: Knight and Leonard, 1884. 88 p.

> The text of a paper read before the Chicago Historical
> Society, 19 February 1884. Chiefly of interest for
> material on Jefferson's father and his early work in that
> city.

2252   Malvern, Gladys. GOOD TROUPERS ALL: THE STORY OF JOSEPH
JEFFERSON. Philadelphia: Macrae Smith Co., 1945. 282 p. Illus.,
bibliog.

> A chatty biography, written in the form of a novel, in-
> ferior to other works, but well illustrated.

2253   "Mr. Jefferson and the Decadent Stage." STAGE 14 (August 1937):
100. Illus.

> Written in the style of Mark Twain, offering an assess-
> ment of Jefferson with high praise.

2254   "Mr. Jefferson in His Best Role." CRITIC n.s. 29 (2 April 1898): 238.

> The role referred to is that of himself. Jefferson had
> been the guest of the Aldine Club; this article reports
> his remarks there.

2255   "Mr. Jefferson on the Psychology of Rip." CURRENT LITERATURE 38
(June 1905): 485-86.

> Jefferson is quoted on his approach to creating Rip Van
> Winkle and to acting in general.

2256   Mudd, A.I. "Jefferson's Debut as Rip." THEATRE (N.Y.) 5 (July
1905): 180.

> A brief essay drawn from Jefferson's AUTOBIOGRAPHY.

2257   "The Old Cabinet." "Jefferson's Rip." SCRIBNER'S 1 (December 1870):
216-17.

> A brief and fanciful account of Jefferson's Rip Van
> Winkle.

2258   "Origin of Rip Van Winkle." CURRENT OPINION 19 (February 1896):
138.

Part of a column, apparently quoted from the Boston HERALD; of minimal value.

2259 Overstreet, Robert. "Joseph Jefferson, RIP VAN WINKLE, and Savannah." GEORGIA SPEECH JOURNAL 3 (Fall 1971): 28-39.

The author combines sections of Jefferson's AUTOBIOG-RAPHY with newspaper accounts to describe engagements between 1873 and 1903.

2260 Pierce, Gilbert A. "A Good-Bye to Rip Van Winkle." ATLANTIC 52 (November 1883): 695-703.

Pierce laments that Jefferson's age is causing him to near the end of his career as Rip, then describes the script and characterization in some detail.

2261 Reamer, Lawrence. "The Drama." HARPER'S WEEKLY 44 (12 May 1900): 442.

Reamer suggests that Jefferson is the world's greatest actor at that time.

2262 Remington, Frederic. "Jefferson as a Painter." HARPER'S WEEKLY 49 (13 May 1905): 684-85. Illus.

A description of Jefferson's painting techniques, with a reproduction of one landscape.

2263 "Rip Van Winkle." APPLETON'S n.s. 4 (February 1878): 146-51.

A detailed critical description of the role as performed by Jefferson, quoting him extensively.

2264 Robb, Josephine. "'Rip Van Winkle' as He is at Home." LADIES' HOME JOURNAL, May 1898, p. 2. Illus.

A brief description of Jefferson at "Crow's Nest," the home into which he moved in July 1894. Two interior photographs are included.

2265 Runnion, James B. "Joseph Jefferson." LIPPINCOTT'S 4 (August 1869): 167-76.

A early and positive assessment of Jefferson, noting his theatrical heritage and predicting a successful future.

2266 Scanlan, Tom. "The Domestication of Rip Van Winkle. Joe Jefferson's Play as Prologue to Modern American Drama." VIRGINIA QUARTERLY REVIEW 50 (Winter 1974): 51-62.

Scanlan posits twentieth-century American drama as domestic drama, and he proposes RIP VAN WINKLE as an anticipation of later family drama.

2267 [Sedgwick, A. G.] "Jefferson as Rip Van Winkle." NATION 9 (23 September 1869): 247-48.

The critic considered Jefferson too great an actor to waste time with this script which he despised.

2268 Shaw, Mary. "The Human Side of Joseph Jefferson." CENTURY 85 (January 1913): 379-85. Illus.

Amusing anecdotes about the actor by a fellow player.

2269 _____. "The Stage Wisdom of Joseph Jefferson." CENTURY 83 (March 1912): 731-73. Illus.

Personal insights and reminiscences by a member of Jefferson's company.

2270 Sothern, E. H. "Joseph Jefferson." LESLIE'S MONTHLY 55 (February 1903): 422-24.

A brief tribute to Jefferson's industry as a performer, exemplified by an anecdote involving W. J. Florence.

2271 Towse, J. Ranken. "Joseph Jefferson as Caleb Plummer." CENTURY 5 (January 1884): 476-77.

A thoughtful description of the characterization.

2272 Waterman, Arthur E. "Joseph Jefferson as Rip Van Winkle." JOURNAL OF POPULAR CULTURE 1 (Spring 1968): 371-78.

The author suggests Jefferson's Rip grew out of favor as realism emerged in the late nineteenth century, although the role retained its appeal in the small towns of the South and the Midwest.

2273 Watson, Ernest Bradlee. "Joseph Jefferson." THEATRE ARTS 13 (June 1929): 420-30. Illus.

A gracefully written tribute, emphasizing his popularity as Rip Van Winkle.

2274 Wilson, Francis. JOSEPH JEFFERSON: REMINISCENCES OF A FELLOW PLAYER. New York: Charles Scribner's Sons, 1906. 346 p. Index, illus.

Wilson's expressed purpose in this work was "merely to
set down the remembrances, mostly anecdotal, which
were his over a number of years in connection with the
subject of this sketch." A volume of immense charm.

2275 _____. "Joseph Jefferson at Work and Play." SCRIBNER'S 39
(February 1906): 128-44. Illus.

An affectionate memorial tribute to the actor in which
Wilson reminisces about Jefferson's Rip Van Winkle, his
recreations, and their personal relationship.

2276 Winter, William. THE JEFFERSONS. Boston: James R. Osgood and
Co., 1881. 252 p. Index. Reprint. New York: Benjamin Blom,
1969.

Winter was an avowed fan of Jefferson's and wrote an
adulatory, biased account of four generations of the
family. Studded with facts.

2277 _____. "Joseph Jefferson." HARPER'S MAGAZINE 73 (August 1886):
391-97.

A tribute, with a few details of Jefferson's family tree,
but adding nothing to other similar works.

2278 _____. "Joseph Jefferson--A Great Actor Gone." THEATRE (N. Y.)
5 (June 1905): 139. Illus.

Extracts from William Winter's tribute in the New York
TRIBUNE upon Jefferson's death.

2279 _____. LIFE AND ART OF JOSEPH JEFFERSON TOGETHER WITH
SOME ACCOUNT OF HIS ANCESTRY AND OF THE JEFFERSON
FAMILY OF ACTORS. American Actor Series. New York and London:
Macmillan and Co., 1894. xi, 313 p. Index, illus.

A complete revision of Winter's 1881 volume on the family.
Contains detailed descriptions of Jefferson's leading roles,
such as Rip Van Winkle and Bob Acres.

2280 _____. "Tribute to Jefferson." CRITIC 46 (June 1905): 502-5.

Winter's eulogy reprinted from the New York TRIBUNE,
including two poems, one by Winter and one ("Immortality")
by Jefferson.

2281 _____. A WREATH OF LAUREL, BEING SPEECHES ON DRAMATIC
AND KINDRED OCCASIONS. New York: Dunlap Society, 1898.
Reprint. New York: Benjamin Blom, 1970. xiii, 149 p. Illus.

Most of the addresses are extremely theoretical, but one
(pages 59–67) is a tribute to Jefferson given at the
Colonial Club in New York, 31 March 1898, concluding
with one of Winter's poems.

See also nos. 8, 12, 21, 58, 118–19, 129–30, 132, 146, 148, 155, 165–66,
177, 183, 188, 200–201, 211, 213, 219, 222, 236, 279, 287–88, 291, 296,
300, 302–3, 307, 313, 328, 336, 341, 343, 346, 356–58, 370, 379, 383,
387, 389–90, 399, 402–4, 409, 413, 417, 425, 430–31, 433–34, 438–39, 466,
468, 472–73, 478, 503, 507, 513–14, 517, 519, 526, 544, 557, 566, 568,
572, 577, 584–85, 596–97, 599, 674, 1064, 1077, 1094, 1103, 1120, 1211,
1526, 1571, 1846, 1865, 1975, 2115, 2149–50, 2294, 2337, 2443, 2585, 2711,
2750, 2932, 2936, 2984, 3168, and 3185.

KALICH, BERTHA

(1874-1939)

2282   Archbald, Anne. "Types--Bertha Kalich--Polish." THEATRE (N. Y.) 29 (February 1919): 104-5. Illus.

> A brief description of Kalich followed by a page and a half about her clothing fashions.

2283   Dale, Alan. [Pseud.] "A Modern Rachel." COSMOPOLITAN 56 (March 1914): 552-54. Illus.

> Dale recalls having seen Kalich as Hamlet in Yiddish twelve years earlier and describes her transformation into an English-speaking actress.

2284   Kalich, Bertha. "Do Audiences Want Serious Plays?" THEATRE (N. Y.) 28 (October 1918): 214. Illus.

> Kalich, then starring in a serious play, THE RIDDLE-WOMAN, posits that U. S. audiences are the most sympathetic in the world.

2285   _____. "Managers and the Theatre in America." GREEN BOOK ALBUM 7 (April 1912): 823-25.

> Kalich had been criticized for appearing in vaudeville; she defends and rationalizes her position.

2286   Tyrrell, Henry. "Bertha Kalich--The Yiddish Duse." THEATRE (N. Y.) 5 (July 1905): 161-62. Illus.

> A somewhat more thoughtful interview than usual at the time, useful for its evocation of ethnic theatre then.

2287   X., X. "Mme. Kalich Deplores Low Theatrical Standards." THEATRE (N. Y.) 8 (November 1908): 306-7. Illus.

> Kalich deplores New York audiences and the star system.

See also nos. 13, 270, 413, and 459.

KEANE, DORIS
(1885-1945)

2288   Baur, Eva Elise Vom. "Doris Keane—An Actress of Serious Purpose." THEATRE (N. Y.) 17 (April 1913): 112-13, viii-ix. Illus.

> Keane describes her early training and compares European and U. S. theatre.

2289   Dale, Alan. [Pseud.] "A Star of Romance." COSMOPOLITAN 55 (June 1913): 121-23. Illus.

> A few rambling and superficial remarks about Keane's career and acting.

2290   Eyck, John Ten. "Talking Art with Doris Keane." GREEN BOOK MAGAZINE 10 (October 1913): 627-34. Illus.

> The actress's remarks on the subjects of the artistic personality and the functions of art.

2291   Hall, Gladys. "Flavor of Fame." MOTION PICTURE MAGAZINE 20 (August 1920): 54-55, 107. Illus.

> Keane is interviewed on the director's function in film-making and the nature of artistic truth.

2292   Sumner, Keene. "More than 2,000 Nights in One Play." AMERICAN MAGAZINE 92 (November 1921): 34-35, 133-36. Illus.

> Keane played about eight years in ROMANCE in New York and London; she describes her early career and the problems of the long run.

2293   Young, Stark. "Doris Keane." NEW REPUBLIC 113 (10 December 1945): 798.

> An especially gracefully written appreciation of Keane and a brief review of her career.

See also nos. 270, 276, 436, 525, and 555.

KEENE, LAURA

(c. 1820-73)

2294   Crehan, John. THE LIFE OF LAURA KEENE: ACTRESS, ARTIST, MANAGER, AND SCHOLAR. TOGETHER WITH SOME INTERESTING REMINISCENCES OF HER DAUGHTERS. Philadelphia: Rodgers Publishing Co., 1897. 249 p. Index, illus.

> Written by a friend of the family, a volume requiring corroboration in almost every case. Several colleagues are described substantially, among them Joseph Jefferson III, John Wilkes Booth, J.W. Wallack, and Kate Reignolds.

2295   Harbin, Billy J. "Laura Keene at the Lincoln Assassination." EDUCATIONAL THEATRE JOURNAL 18 (March 1966): 47-54.

> Harbin attempts to separate myth from fact concerning Keene's actions after the murder. Well documented.

See also nos. 13, 164, 203, 247, 261, 277, 313, 400-401, 407, 413, 433, 572, 1088, 1151, 1521, 2235-36, 2984, and 3027.

KELCEY, HERBERT

(1855-1917)

2296 Kelcey, Herbert. "Pushed Upon the Stage." GREEN BOOK ALBUM 1 (June 1909): 1251-53.

> The actor describes his theatrical debut.

2297 Wagstaff, William de. "Chats with Players." THEATRE (N.Y.) 2 (May 1902): 20-23. Illus.

> Wagstaff supposedly interviews a pair of players, but focuses his interview on Kelcey's co-star, Effie Shannon.

See also nos. 28, 270, 279, 379, 399, and 555.

LACKAYE, WILTON

(1862-1932)

2298   Dodge, Wendell Phillips. "The Actor in the Street." THEATRE (N. Y.)
9 (February 1909): 49-50. Illus.

      A biographical sketch of Lackaye with a few remarks from
him about his role preparation techniques.

2299   Lackaye, Wilton. "Endowed Theatre and the Actor." THEATRE (N. Y.)
1 (August 1909): 13-14. Illus.

      Lackaye argues for a subsidized theatre in the United
States.

2300   _____. "Is the Stage of Today Worth While?" THEATRE (N. Y.) 30
(July 1919): 32, 34.

      Half of a two-part article, the other half being written
by a clergyman, John Talbot Smith, who predicts the
demise of the theatre. Lackaye is more optimistic.

2301   _____. "My Beginnings." THEATRE (N. Y.) 5 (October 1905): 250,
252. Illus.

      Lackaye was first employed in the theatre by Lawrence
Barrett for twenty dollars a week, having overcome considerable parental opposition.

2302   Morgan, M. "Svengali's Impersonator Talks of 'Trilby's' First Night."
THEATRE (N. Y.) 21 (May 1915): 242-43, 274. Illus.

      Lackaye was a perennial Svengali and reminisces about
the original production.

2303   Patterson, Ada. "At Home with Wilton Lackaye." GREEN BOOK
ALBUM 6 (December 1911): 1333-37.

      Lackaye had an estate on Shelter Island, which Patterson
describes.

2304 _____ . "'The Stage a Terrible Business,' Says Lackaye." THEATRE
(N. Y.) 35 (April 1921): 216. Illus.

> After thirty-nine years of acting, Lackaye condemns the
> profession, especially the financial aspects of it.

2305 _____ . "Wilton Lackaye Talks of the Actor's Art." THEATRE (N. Y.)
4 (May 1904): 119-20, 122. Illus.

> Lackaye advocates technique as preferable to inspiration
> or "psychology" in acting.

2306 White, Frank Marshall. "About Wilton Lackaye." GREEN BOOK
ALBUM 1 (June 1909): 1254-59.

> White, a personal friend of Lackaye, presents a very
> positive description of his personality and acting ability.

See also nos. 28, 112, 131, 270, 279, 361, 379, 492, 506, 1267, and 1975.

LANDER, JEAN MARGARET DAVENPORT (1829-1903). See nos. 222, 405, 413, 623, and 2782.

LARRIMORE, FRANCINE

(1898-1975)

2307 Harper, Carleton. "Women Achieving New Stellar Glory." NATIONAL
MAGAZINE 58 (June 1930): 402, 412. Illus.

> Harper traces the careers of Evelyn Herbert and Larrimore
> up to their recently achieved stardom in LET US BE GAY.

See also no. 276.

Le GALLIENNE, EVA

(1899-   )

2308   Benchley, Robert. "Eva Le Gallienne's Civic Repertory Theatre." LIFE, 11 January 1929, p. 21.

A column of praise and congratulations for the Civic Repertory Theatre a year and one-half after its opening.

2309   Bird, Carol. "Stage Mary an Extinct Species." THEATRE (N. Y.) 35 (May 1922): 286, 288.

Le Gallienne is quoted as preferring "hectic" roles to the "goody goody" kind.

2310   Carb, David. "Eva Le Gallienne." THEATRE GUILD MAGAZINE 8 (February 1931): 36-40. Illus.

A graceful account of Le Gallienne's theatrical philosophies, praising her high standards and industry.

2311   F., C. "Miss Le Gallienne Remembers." STAGE 11 (February 1934): 47-48. Illus.

Reminiscences of the actress's childhood.

2312   Hall, Gladys. "Why I Detest Broadway." METROPOLITAN 58 (February 1924): 44, 68. Illus.

Hall quotes Le Gallienne on the materialism of the Broadway theatre and the need for beauty in one's life.

2313   Langer, Lawrence. "Miss Le Gallienne Fights it through." STAGE 10 (April 1933): front cover, 32.

Langer bemoans the economic conditions which forced the actress to close her repertory theatre.

2314   Lee, Mrs. Amy. A CRITIC'S NOTEBOOK. Boston: Manthorne and Burack, 1943. 334 p. Illus.

Pages 132-34 describe a Le Gallienne engagement in San
Antonio, but presents her theatrical philosophies rather
than merely reviewing her productions.

2315   Le Gallienne, Eva. AT 33. New York and Toronto: Longmans, Green
and Co., 1934. 262 p. Illus.

Le Gallienne traces her career through the demise of her
Civic Repertory in 1932 and includes a record of the 1581
productions by that company.

2316   _____. "My Adventures in Repertory." THEATRE (N.Y.) 45 (April
1927): 12, 52B. Illus.

Le Gallienne explains the success of the first season of
her Civic Repertory Theatre by contrasting it to the
sexually oriented and controversial plays then in the
commercial theatre.

2317   _____. THE MYSTIC IN THE THEATRE: ELEONORA DUSE. New
York: Farrar, Straus and Giroux, 1965. 185 p.

Although an excellent biography of Duse, the volume
contains considerable material on Le Gallienne's career
and her theories of the theatre.

2318   _____. "Repertory . . . When?" THEATRE ARTS 42 (September
1958): 14-16, 76-77. Illus.

Le Gallienne pleads for a repertory theatre, hoping the
projected Lincoln Center operation would succeed.

2319   _____. "S. B. Quand-Même." FORUM 11 (Summer, 1973-Winter,
1974): 32-42. Illus.

An adulatory article about Sarah Bernhardt, recalling
Le Gallienne's first observation of her in 1906; she
describes her impressions of the French actress then and
through 1917.

2320   _____. "Sarah Bernhardt and Eleonora Duse." STAGE 14 (January
1937): 96-99.

Le Gallienne describes her first meetings with the two
stars, both of whom she admired greatly.

2321   _____. "Sir James Barrie, 'Peter Pan,' and I." THEATRE (N.Y.) 49
(January 1929): 15-16, 68. Illus.

Le Gallienne recalls seeing PETER PAN as a child and

describes her production of it at the Civic Repertory
Theatre.

2322 _____. "We Believe. . . ." THEATRE ARTS 30 (March 1946): 176–
78.

Le Gallienne writes two columns of praise for the American
Repertory Theatre.

2323 _____. "What is Wrong with the Theatre?" WOMAN CITIZEN 11
(April 1921): 22–23, 45. Illus.

The actress promotes repertory theatre as a cure for most
of the American theatre's ills, having just opened her
Civic Repertory Theatre.

2324 _____. WITH A QUIET HEART. New York: Viking Press, 1953.
viii, 303 p. Index, illus.

A sequel to AT 33, covering in some detail the next
two decades of the actress's life and career.

2325 Mullett, Mary B. "The Story of a Stubborn Girl." AMERICAN MAGA-
ZINE 95 (June 1923): 18–19, 78, 80. Illus.

Mullett expresses amazement at the actress's intellectual
abilities and her dedication to success and high standards.

2326 Patterson, Ada. "Eva Le Gallienne--A Cerebral Actress." THEATRE
(N. Y.) 39 (February 1924): 20, 58. Illus.

In a somewhat superficial interview, Le Gallienne describes
her substantial library and her early career.

2327 Pennybacker, Ruth. "Eva Le Gallienne, Rebel Actress." WOMAN
CITIZEN 10 (March 1926): 17, 42–43. Illus.

A biographical sketch stressing the actress's idealism in
matters theatrical.

2328 Sarton, May. "The Genius of Eva Le Gallienne. Acting as a Criticism
of Life." FORUM 11 (Summer 1973–Winter 1974): 43–49. Illus.

A thoughtful and well-illustrated analysis of Le Gallienne's
acting as a reflection of her vision of reality.

2329 Schanke, Robert A. "Eva Le Gallienne: The Comeback of a Star."
SOUTHERN THEATRE 21 (Fall 1978): 3–12. Illus., notes.

An adulatory article describing the actress's tour in
THE ROYAL FAMILY.

See also nos. 5, 9, 130, 135, 174, 204, 213, 235, 247, 276, 285, 376, 413, 512, 578–79, 1115, and 2691.

LEMAN, WALTER M.

(1810-90)

2330   Leman, Walter M. MEMORIES OF AN OLD ACTOR. San Francisco: A. Roman Co., 1886. xv, 406 p. Frontispiece. Reprint. New York: Benjamin Blom; St. Clair Shores, Mich.: Scholarly Press, 1969.

        Rambling reminiscences which mention almost every leading player of the time; useful for evocation of frontier theatre of the time.

2331   McDermott, Douglas. "Touring Patterns on California's Theatrical Frontier, 1849-1859." THEATRE SURVEY 15 (May 1974): 18-28. Illus.

        McDermott typifies touring practices of the time by describing those of Catherine Sinclair and Leman.

See also no. 164.

LeMOYNE, SARAH COWELL

(1859-1915)

2332   LeMoyne, Sarah Cowell. "The Power of Imagination in the Theatre."
        GREEN BOOK ALBUM 7 (February 1912): 385-87.

>   The actress refers to the theatre as the Temple of Imagi-
>   nation, suggesting the audience should be an active
>   participant.

2333   Phelps, William Lyon. "An Actress Who Played Browning." INDE-
        PENDENT 83 (20 September 1915): 394. Illus.

>   A brief biographical sketch written shortly after the
>   actress's death.

See also nos. 28, 328, and 381-82.

LEWIS, JAMES (c. 1838-96). See nos. 128, 245, 279, 356, 404, 407-8, 432, 471, 518, 1599, 1602, 1707-8, 1903, and 2624.

LOFTUS, CECILIA

(1876-1943)

2334 Anderson, John. "Miss Cecilia Loftus." HARPER'S BAZAAR 72 (June 1938): 52-53, 114-15, 120, 126.

> A substantial article tracing Loftus's career in London and the United States and her considerable financial difficulties.

See also nos. 13, 270, and 276.

LOGAN, OLIVE

(1839-1909)

2335   Logan, Olive. "American and Foreign Theatres." GALAXY 5 (January 1868): 22-27.

>   Logan contrasts theatre architecture and customs in the United States with those in Europe, decrying many recent changes in this country.

2336   _____. APROPOS OF WOMEN AND THEATRES. WITH A PAPER OR TWO ON PARISIAN TOPICS. New York: Carleton; London: S. Low, Son and Co., 1869. 240 p.

>   Much of this volume had appeared previously in various periodicals; some of it was written specifically for this publication. Logan decries the immorality of the stage in the 1860s, recalls her early career, and describes experiences in Paris.

2337   _____. BEFORE THE FOOTLIGHTS AND BEHIND THE SCENES: A BOOK ABOUT "THE SHOW BUSINESS" IN ALL ITS BRANCHES: FROM PUPPET SHOWS TO GRAND OPERA; FROM MOUNTEBANKS TO MENAGERIES; FROM LEARNED PIGS TO LECTURERS; FROM BURLESQUE BLONDES TO ACTORS AND ACTRESSES: WITH SOME OBSERVATIONS AND REFLECTIONS (ORIGINAL AND REFLECTED) ON MORALITY AND IMMORALITY IN AMUSEMENTS: THIS EXHIBITING THE "SHOW WORLD" AS SEEN FROM WITHIN, THROUGH THE EYES OF THE FORMER ACTRESS, AS WELL AS FROM WITHOUT, THROUGH THE EYES OF THE PRESENT LECTURER AND AUTHOR. Philadelphia, Cincinnati, and Middletown, Conn.: Parmelee and Co., 1870. 612 p. Illus.

>   Partially autobiographical and partially a critical description of theatrical conditions, this volume includes reminiscences of Julia Dean, Stuart Robson, E. L. Davenport, Lotta Crabtree, Joseph Jefferson III, Edwin Booth, Edwin Forrest, and Charlotte Cushman. Logan attacks THE BLACK CROOK and other "leg-shows" of the time. Republished in 1871 as THE MIMIC WORLD, no. 2339.

2338 _____. "The Leg Business." GALAXY 4 (August 1867): 440-44.

Logan fulminates against what she calls "naked drama," predicting the public would reject it in the near future.

2339 _____. THE MIMIC WORLD AND PUBLIC EXHIBITIONS: THEIR HISTORY, THEIR MORALS, AND EFFECTS. Philadelphia: New-World Publishing Co., 1871. 590 p.

A republication of no. 2337 with the first chapter excised.

2340 _____. "The Secret Regions of the Stage." HARPER'S 47 (April 1874): 628-42. Illus.

An explanation of various staging effects then in use, such as disappearances, fires, sound effects, and others.

2341 Wills, J. Richard. "Olive Logan vs. the Nude Woman." PLAYERS 47 (October-November 1971): 36-43. Illus.

A documented description of Logan's various pleas for higher morality on the New York stage during her life.

See also nos. 13 and 459.

LORD, PAULINE
(1890-1950)

2342   Bird, Carol. "A Chat with Anna Christie." THEATRE (N.Y.) 35
        (March 1922): 162, 192, 194.

        Lord is quoted contrasting Christie to other roles she
        had played, especially "fallen" women.

2343   "Concerning Pauline Lord." THEATRE GUILD 9 (February 1932): 9-
        10, 12. Illus.

        An extremely brief biographical sketch.

2344   Lord, Pauline. "My Anna Christie." METROPOLITAN MAGAZINE 55
        (June 1922): 36-37. Illus.

        Lord praises O'Neill for the character as written and
        describes her own approach to the character in a reason-
        ably insightful essay.

2345   Rohe, Alice. "The Poignant Women of Pauline Lord." THEATRE (N.Y.)
        41 (April 1925): 20, 58.

        Lord discusses the role of Anna Christie and describes
        other types of roles she hoped to play.

2346   Sergeant, Elizabeth Shepley. FIRE UNDER THE ANDES: A GROUP
        OF NORTH AMERICAN PORTRAITS. New York: Alfred A. Knopf,
        1927. 331 p. Illus.

        Chapter 8, "One Stung by the Gadfly," describes Lord's
        career, especially her ability to create images of "femi-
        nine desolation."

2347   _____. "Pauline Lord, Once Stung by the Gadfly." NEW REPUBLIC
        48 (22 September 1926): 112-15.

        See no. 2346.

See also nos. 13, 276, 285, 377, 410, 413, 447, 542-43, and 1714.

LUDLOW, NOAH MILLER

(1795-1886)

2348   Ludlow, Noah M. DRAMATIC LIFE AS I FOUND IT: A RECORD OF
PERSONAL EXPERIENCE; WITH AN ACCOUNT OF THE RISE AND
PROGRESS OF THE DRAMA IN THE WEST AND SOUTH, WITH ANEC-
DOTES AND BIOGRAPHICAL SKETCHES OF THE PRINCIPAL ACTORS
AND ACTRESSES WHO HAVE AT TIMES APPEARED UPON THE STAGE
IN THE MISSISSIPPI VALLEY. St. Louis, 1880. Reprint. Introduction
by Francis Hodge. Edited by Richard Moody. New York: Benjamin
Blom, 1966. Index, frontispiece.

> While Ludlow's text is not completely trustworthy, the
> volume is a valuable source of information about the
> frontier theatre up to 1852. As the title implies, many
> brief biographical sketches are included for such performers
> as Mrs. Duff, the Caldwells, the elder Booth, the Chap-
> mans, Thomas Abthorpe Cooper, Joe Cowell, the Drakes,
> Clara Fisher, Edwin Forrest, James H. Hackett, Thomas
> Hamblin, Anna Cora Mowatt, the Placides, the Wallacks,
> William Wood, and Ludlow's partner, Sol Smith.

See also nos. 132-33, 146, 148, 166, 180, 244, and 318.

LUNT, ALFRED

(1893-1977)

2349   "Alfred Lunt Presents: Penny Plain and Tuppence Colored." THEATRE
        ARTS 31 (January 1947): 48-49. Illus.

        A description of Lunt's passion for and collection of toy
        theatres, his collection then being exhibited at the Museum
        of the City of New York.

2350   Armstrong, Sargent. "Colloquy in Wisconsin." STAGE 13 (October
        1935): 29. Illus.

        An imaginary conversation with the Lunts on the validity
        of their repertory.

2351   Brown, John Mason. "Children of Skelt." SATURDAY REVIEW OF
        LITERATURE 30 (4 January 1947): 20-23. Illus.

        A description of Lunt's toy theatre collection, then on
        display at the Museum of the City of New York.

2352   Dukes, Ashley. "The Lunts in London: The English Scene." THEATRE
        ARTS 28 (April 1944): 209-10, 213-14.

        An account of the Lunts' production of Sherwood's THERE
        SHALL BE NO NIGHT and their reasons for selecting it.

2353   Eustis, Morton. "On the Road with the Lunts." THEATRE ARTS 23
        (June 1939): 414-23.

        Eustis describes touring conditions in the South as the
        Lunts presented AMPHITRYON 38 and IDIOT'S DELIGHT.

2354   Freedley, George. THE LUNTS. London: Rockliffe, 1957. 134 p.
        Illus. Also published as THE LUNTS: AN ILLUSTRATED STUDY OF
        THEIR WORK, WITH A LIST OF THEIR APPEARANCES ON STAGE AND
        SCREEN. New York: Macmillan, 1958. 134 p.

A biographical treatment written with considerable affection; well-illustrated, undocumented, and including a chronological list of roles played by the Lunts.

2355   "Glamour and the Lunts." VOGUE, 15 November 1932, pp. 42-43. Illus.

Fashion notes on Fontanne's glamorous outfits; of minimal informative value.

2356   Goodman, Randolph, ed. DRAMA ON STAGE. New York: Holt, Rinehart and Winston, 1961. 475 p.

Includes an article, "The Actor Attacks His Part," an interview by Morton Eustis, originally published in THEATRE ARTS in 1936. See no. 441.

2357   Hark, Ann. "Side by Side with Their Husbands." LADIES' HOME JOURNAL, February 1930, pp. 14, 161. Illus.

A brief article on successful marriage, including those by the Lunts and Peggy Wood. Of minimal value.

2358   "The Home of Lynn Fontanne at Genesee Depot, Wis." VOGUE, 1 November 1933, pp. 50-53. Illus.

Fan-oriented architecture and interior decoration notes.

2359   Lunt, Alfred. "An Editorial." THEATRE ARTS 34 (February 1950): 57-58. Illus.

Very brief remarks on the nature of touring at the time.

2360   _____. "Why Make Up?" THEATRE GUILD MAGAZINE 6 (November 1928): 15-17. Illus.

A brief essay on illusion in the theatre and the vogue of experimental bare staging at the time.

2361   "The Lunts, World's Greatest Acting Team, Make Fun of Married Love." LIFE, 1 November 1937, pp. 106-9. Illus.

A pictorial essay on the Lunts in many of their more successful roles and in their Genesee home.

2362   "The Lunts Celebrate 25 Triumphant Years." LIFE, 7 November 1949, pp. cover, 134-38, 141. Illus.

A pictorial tribute with a brief text accompanied by photographs of key scenes from the Lunts' major hits.

2363 Maxwell, Elsa. "Alfred Lunt . . . Cook." VOGUE, 15 June 1942, pp. 26-27, 72-73. Illus.

> A tribute to Lunt's culinary skills, with eight of his more successful recipes.

2364 Moats, Alice Leone. "Mr. & Mrs. Alfred Lunt." LADIES' HOME JOURNAL, December 1940, pp. 14-15, 105-17. Illus.

> A superficial sketch with minimal informative value.

2365 Morehouse, Ward. "Lynn Fontanne and Alfred Lunt, of Genesee, Wisconsin." VOGUE, 1 May 1940, pp. 70-73, 108, 110. Illus.

> Fan-oriented trivia concerning the Lunt's home life.

2366 "Mr. & Mrs." TIME 30 (8 November 1937): front cover, 25-26, 28, 30. Illus.

> A sketch of the Lunts in AMPHITRYON 38 with biographical descriptions.

2367 Mullett, Mary B. "Jealous? We Should Say Not!" AMERICAN MAGAZINE 106 (December 1928): 42-43, 124-28. Illus.

> The Lunts are quoted describing how they successfully combined careers with marriage.

2368 Patterson, Ada. "The Guardsman and His Wife." THEATRE (N.Y.) 41 (March 1925): 23, 52. Illus.

> A fan-oriented interview describing why the Lunts chose to appear in THE GUARDSMAN.

2369 Pringle, Henry, and Pringle, Helena. "Why Don't They Fight?" LADIES' HOME JOURNAL, July 1936, pp. 8-9, 45. Illus.

> A superficial examination of the marriages of the Lunts and of Katharine Cornell, both considered extraordinary combinations of careers and domesticity.

2370 "Reunion in Genesee." VOGUE, 1 November 1935, pp. 50-53. Illus.

> Six photographs of the Lunt's Genesee home and farm, accompanied by a brief interview of little substance.

2371 Sedgwick, Ruth Woodbury. "God Plays Solitaire." STAGE 13 (April 1936): 26-28. Illus.

> An account of the preparation and early rehearsals by the Lunts for IDIOT'S DELIGHT.

2372   Sherwood, Robert E. "The Lunts." STAGE 13 (May 1936): 36–39. Illus.

> An appreciative essay stressing the Lunts' contributions to the playwright's successes in New York.

2373   Woollcott, Alexander. "Luck and Mr. Lunt." HEARST'S 94 (April 1933): 56–57, 84, 86. Illus.

> Although Woollcott considers Lunt the best actor in New York since the Barrymore's departure, the critic feels that Lunt has been exceptionally lucky, to which Lunt agrees.

2374   Young, Stark. "Important Variety." NEW REPUBLIC 87 (17 June 1936): 180.

> An appreciation of the Lunts' body of work to that time, praising their versatility and willingness to serve the play rather than their own reputations.

2375   Zolotow, Maurice. "Alfred Lunt, Director." THEATRE ARTS 38 (April 1954): 26–29, 95–96. Illus.

> Lunt is quoted as saying he had been directing sub rosa for some years, but his staging of ONDINE was the first official directing assignment.

2376   _____. STAGESTRUCK: THE ROMANCE OF ALFRED LUNT AND LYNN FONTANNE. New York: Harcourt, Brace and World, 1964. x, 272 p. Index, illus.

> A breezy and undocumented account of the Lunts by a close friend who had seen most of their work.

See also nos. 5, 9, 117, 135, 185, 213, 235, 275–76, 285, 291, 295–96, 298, 351, 358, 390, 394, 413, 420, 425, 441, 504, 508, 527, 540, 542, 545, 549, 564, 571, 579, 589, 841, 1847, 1982, 2044, 2901, and 3212.

McCLENDON, ROSE

(1884-1936)

2377   "Dramatis Personae. Rose McClendon." CRISIS 34 (April 1927): 55,
66-67. Illus.

A brief appreciation of McClendon, largely drawn from
published reviews in various sources.

See also nos. 13, 190, and 194.

McCULLOUGH, JOHN
(1832-85)

2378   Clark, Susie C.   JOHN McCULLOUGH AS MAN, ACTOR, AND
        SPIRIT. Boston: Murray and Emery, 1905. 359 p. Index, illus. New
        York: Broadway Publishing Co., 1914. 368 p. Illus.

> A turgidly written, gushing account of the actor's life
> and afterlife, including several descriptions of the author's
> supposed psychic contacts with the deceased player.

2379   Robbins, Kenneth R.   "John McCullough: Pigmy Giant of the American
        Stage." SOUTHERN SPEECH JOURNAL 38 (Spring 1973): 244-54.

> Robbins draws from traditional sources for this sketch,
> concluding that McCullough was an actor of dubious
> ability.

2380   Winter, William, ed. IN MEMORY OF JOHN McCULLOUGH. New
        York: DeVinne Press, 1889. 66 p. Illus.

> A memorial volume, consisting of a brief biography and
> elegy by Winter, the funeral oration by Henry Edwards,
> an address by W. F. Johnson, an oration by Steele
> MacKaye, and an anonymous chapter on the McCullough
> monument.

See also nos. 154, 164, 171, 176, 222, 238, 245, 261, 296, 337, 341, 343,
356, 358, 366, 370, 383, 387, 399, 401-2, 404, 408-9, 413, 417, 454, 460,
489, 503, 519, 526, 539, 570, 572, 596, 665, 674, 1750, 1975, 2107, 2585,
2599-2600, and 2984.

MacKAYE, JAMES MORRISON STEELE
(1842-94)

2381   Corbin, John. "Dawn of American Drama." ATLANTIC 99 (May 1907): 632-44.

> A critical assessment of MacKaye as a dramatist; Corbin considered him of primary importance.

2382   Curry, Wade. "Steele MacKaye: Producer and Director." EDUCATIONAL THEATRE JOURNAL 18 (October 1966): 210-15.

> Curry drew upon the MacKaye collection at Dartmouth as well as more traditional sources for this assessment of MacKaye's production efforts.

2383   Grover, Edwin Osgood. ANNALS OF AN ERA: PERCY MacKAYE AND THE MacKAYE FAMILY 1826-1932. Washington, D.C.: Pioneer Press, 1932. 534 p. Frontispiece.

> Some biographical material is included, most of it focused on Percy MacKaye, but several sections deal with his father. The volume draws heavily upon the MacKaye Collection at the Dartmouth College Library.

2384   MacKaye, Percy. EPOCH: THE LIFE OF STEEL MacKAYE, GENIUS OF THE THEATRE IN RELATION TO HIS TIMES & CONTEMPORARIES. 2 vols. New York: Boni and Liveright, 1927. Index, illus.

> A detailed and comprehensive treatment, admittedly prejudicial in its attitude. Quoting heavily from letters, manuscripts, and publications, it is indispensable for any study of MacKaye.

2385   _____. "Steele MacKaye, Dynamic Artist of the American Theatre." DRAMA 4 (November 1911): 138-61; 5 (February 1912): 153-73. Illus.

> An adulatory sketch, later expanded greatly into EPOCH by the subject's son. See no. 2384.

2386 _____. The Theatre of Ten Thousand: Steele MacKaye's Spectatorium."
THEATRE ARTS 7 (April 1923): 116-26. Illus.

> A condensed version of the account in EPOCH. Illustra-
> tions include a floor plan and side elevations of the huge
> theatre, plus conjectural drawings for THE WORLD FINDER,
> the intended opening production.

2387 MacKaye, Mrs. Steele. "Steele MacKaye and François Delsarte."
WERNER'S VOICE MAGAZINE 14 (July 1892): 187-89.

> In a letter to the editors of WERNER'S, MacKaye's wife
> describes the relationship, both personal and professional,
> between the two artists.

2388 MacKaye, Steele. "Safety in Theatres." NORTH AMERICAN REVIEW
135 (November 1882): 461-70.

> MacKaye examines public safety in theatre architecture,
> especially with regard to fire hazards, and makes a
> series of recommendations.

2389 Moses, Montrose. "Percy MacKaye and His Father." BOOK NEWS
30 (October 1911): 99-105.

> An especially graceful biographical sketch of MacKaye,
> contrasting his qualities and talents with those of his son.

2390 Patterson, Ada. "Steele MacKaye's Poet-Playwright Son." THEATRE
(N. Y.) 7 (December 1907): 338-40. Illus.

> Includes substantial observations on the elder MacKaye,
> admittedly prejudicial.

2391 Ruyter, Nancy Chalfa. "American Delsartism: Precursor of an American
Dance Art." EDUCATIONAL THEATRE JOURNAL 25 (December 1973):
421-35. Illus.

> The author devotes the first section of her article to
> MacKaye and his importation of Delsartism to the United
> States.

2392 Shaver, Claude L. "Steele MacKaye and the Delsartian Tradition."
In THE HISTORY OF SPEECH EDUCATION IN AMERICA, edited by
Karl R. Wallace, pp. 202-18. New York: Appleton-Century-Crofts,
1954. Index, illus.

> The essay, based on the author's dissertation, outlines
> MacKaye's transfer of the Delsarte system to this country.

See also nos. 214, 261, 300, 388, 544, 578, 1750, and 2380.

MANN, LOUIS

(1865-1931)

2393   Mann, Louis. "In Defense of Revivals." THEATRE (N. Y.) 50 (July 1929): 19, 64. Illus.

> Mann defended revivals by suggesting most dramas of the day were recreations of older scripts.

2394   Patterson, Ada. "Where the Smile Meets the Tear." THEATRE (N. Y.) 38 (July 1923): 27. Illus.

> Mann is quoted comparing and contrasting the playing of comedy and tragedy.

See also nos. 28, 270, 380, and 529.

MANNERING, MARY

(1876-1953)

2395   "How Mary Mannering Came to be Janice Meredith." MUNSEY'S 23 (September 1900): 845-47.

> A brief description of casting techniques.

2396   Mannering, Mary. "The Home, the Stage, and the Woman." GOOD HOUSEKEEPING, February 1912, pp. 201-8. Illus.

> Mannering has no regrets for choosing a stage career, but warns others of the hardships of the profession and the difficulties of combining a marriage with a career.

2397   [Sartoris, Mlle.] "Mary Mannering's New Frocks." THEATRE (N. Y.) 9 (December 1909): xxiii-xxiv, xxvi, xxviii, xxx. Illus.

> Fashion notes.

2398   Wagstaff, William de. "Mary Mannering and her Views Regarding Stage and Other Ideals." THEATRE (N. Y.) 2 (July 1902): 9-12. Illus.

> The actress describes beauty as the theatre's ideal in a superficial interview, distinguished only by specially posed photographs.

2399   White, Matthew, Jr. "Mary Mannering." MUNSEY'S 36 (October 1906-March 1907): 104-8. Illus.

> A brief description of Mannering's early life, her discovery by Daniel Frohman, and her rise to stardom.

See also nos. 28, 270, 276, 303, 381-82, 413, 465, 555, and 581.

MANSFIELD, RICHARD

(1857-1907)

2400   Bell, Archie. "Were Mansfield's Eccentricities Proof of Genius?" THEATRE (N.Y.) 7 (December 1907): 323. Illus.

> A somewhat pointless comparison of Mansfield to other eccentrics.

2401   Bennett, James O'Donnell. "Richard Mansfield." MUNSEY'S 36 (October 1906-March 1907): 770-76. Illus.

> Bennett describes Mansfield as an eccentric both on and off stage, suggesting he thus triumphed over the tendencies of the time.

2402   Case, Paul T. "The Real Richard Mansfield." THEATRE (N.Y.) 20 (August 1914): 58, 60-62, 88. Illus.

> Case describes Mansfield's methods and personality, drawing on his experience as a member of the Mansfield company.

2403   Corbin, John. "The Greatest English Actor." APPLETON'S 9 (March 1907): 287-94. Illus.

> Corbin considers Mansfield the greatest English-speaking actor since the death of Henry Irving; he describes the highlights of Mansfield's career in the process.

2404   Dale, Alan. [Pseud.] "Who is Our Worst Actor?" COSMOPOLITAN 40 (April 1906): 683-90.

> Dale attacks Mansfield, saying, "There is no living actor who is so obstrusively the man, apart from the role he essays, as Richard Mansfield. That is why I say he is the worst actor I know."

2405   Eaton, Walter Prichard. "Richard Mansfield." THEATRE ARTS 11 (February 1927): 111-20. Illus.

Eaton compares Mansfield first to the actors of the critic's youth, then to those of the 1920s.

2406   Faett, L. A. "Richard Mansfield." DIXIE: A MONTHLY MAGAZINE, December 1899, pp. 617-24. Illus.

A general descriptive essay on Mansfield's personality, stressing his intellect and describing his approach to CYRANO DE BERGERAC.

2407   Ferguson, William J. "Reminiscences of Richard Mansfield." AMERICAN PLAYWRIGHT 2 (March 1913): 96-97.

Brief anecdotes about Mansfield's production of BEAU BRUMMELL.

2408   Fyles, Franklin. "What Was the Influence of Richard Mansfield on the American Drama?" REVIEW OF REVIEWS 36 (October 1907): 424-28. Illus.

Writing shortly after the actor's death, Fyles describes Mansfield's influence as beneficial, citing his productions of new scripts.

2409   Glover, Lyman B. "Richard Mansfield." WORLD TO-DAY 13 (October 1907): 973-76. Illus.

A eulogistic remembrance of Mansfield, describing his unique qualities as an artist and person.

2410   Greene, Clay M. "Henry Irving's Successor." MUNSEY'S 35 (May 1906): 191-95.

Greene compares Mansfield to several English actors, including Irving and E. H. Sothern, and finds Mansfield superior to them all.

2411   Hamilton, Clayton. "The Last of the Titans: Richard Mansfield." STAGE 14 (January 1937): 108-9. Illus.

A brief memorial tribute of no great distinction. Eleven photographs of Mansfield in various roles are included.

2412   Hanna, N. D. "Mansfield and King Henry V." GUNTON'S MAGAZINE, October 1900, pp. 324-32.

Hanna lauds Mansfield for staging one of Shakespeare's lesser known works and describes his restoration of the text more than the actual production.

2413 _____ . "Richard Mansfield, Actor." MUNSEY'S 21 (September 1899): 881-88. Illus.

> An appreciation of no particular insight, but accompanied by some uncommon photographs.

2414 Hillhouse, Lewis J. "Richard Mansfield--His Hopes and Disappointments." THEATRE (N. Y.) 6 (July 1906): 190-93. Illus.

> Mansfield rarely granted interviews, but gave this one in order to argue for a nationally endowed theatre for the United States.

2415 "Is Mr. Mansfield to Direct the 'New Theatre'?" THEATRE (N. Y.) 6 (April 1906): 88.

> An editorial speculating on the coincidental retirement of Mansfield and the opening of the New Theatre.

2416 Kobbé, Gustave. "Richard Mansfield and His Little Boy." LADIES' HOME JOURNAL, January 1903, pp. 9-10. Illus.

> A description of Mansfield's home life, the interview taking place shortly after the birth of his son, Georgie.

2417 Mansfield, Mrs. Richard. "Metropolitan Audiences." COSMOPOLITAN 36 (April 1904): 667-76. Illus.

> A discussion of the public, their tastes and behavior, written in the form of a dialogue between an optimist, a pessimist, and a girl who knows.

2418 Mansfield, Richard. "Concerning Acting." NORTH AMERICAN RE-VIEW 159 (September 1894): 337-40.

> Mansfield describes his various theories on the art of acting.

2419 _____ . "Man and the Actor." ATLANTIC 97 (May 1906): 577-85.

> Mansfield philosophizes about the theatre as a profession, ending with a plea for a national theatre.

2420 _____ . "More Sketches Out of the Life of a Great Singer." THEATRE (London), February 1879, pp. 31-33.

> A continuation of Mansfield's "Sketches Out of the Life of a Great Singer," no. 2423.

2421 _____ . "My Audiences--And Myself." COLLIER'S 26 (6 October 1900): 13. Illus.

A rambling discourse on the actor's relationship with
his public, expressing the doubt that the audience had
ever seen all he attempted to include in his work.

2422 _____. "Plain Talk on the Drama." NORTH AMERICAN REVIEW
155 (September 1892): 308-14.

Mansfield begs the press to support young actors and
actresses.

2423 _____. "Sketches Out of the Life of a Great Singer." THEATER
(London), 1 November 1878, pp. 272-74.

Chatty anecdotes about Madame Rudersdorff, an opera
singer. See no. 2420.

2424 _____. "The Story of a Production." HARPER'S WEEKLY 34 (24
May 1890): 407-8.

Mansfield describes the genesis of his production of
RICHARD III, especially the scenery.

2425 Mawson, Henry P. "Richard Mansfield's True Rank as an Actor."
THEATRE (N.Y.) 7 (October 1907): 282-84, ix-x. Illus.

A memorial tribute and assessment of the actor's major
roles.

2426 Moses, Montrose J. "Richard Mansfield." PEARSON'S 18 (November
1905): 449-55. Illus.

A highly complimentary overview of Mansfield's career,
including descriptions and assessments of most of his
major roles and productions by a leading critic of the
time.

2427 Parker, C.A. "An Impressionistic Sketch of Richard Mansfield's Career."
PHILHARMONIC 1 (April 1901): 97-103. Illus.

A monograph praising the actor for his work to that time
(through his HENRY V) and predicting great success in
the future.

2428 Payne, George Henry. "The Personal Side of Richard Mansfield."
SATURDAY EVENING POST 171 (14 January 1899): 456-57. Illus.

Undocumented biographical anecdotes stressing the actor's
human nature and sympathy.

2429 Phelps, William Lyon. "Shakespeare in New York." INDEPENDENT
55 (5 February 1903): 298-300. Illus.

E. H. Sothern and Mansfield are among the players described, both in their productions of HAMLET.

2430   "Richard Mansfield--Actor and Man." THEATRE (N. Y.) 4 (March
1904): 67-68. Illus.

Puffery within a brief biographical sketch.

2431   "Richard Mansfield: Prophet of Modernism." THEATRE ARTS 27 (August
1943): 461. Illus.

A one-page assessment of Mansfield as Beau Brummell,
citing several critics.

2432   "Richard Mansfield and Hans von Bülow." ETUDE 33 (October 1915):
747.

An anecdote about the two men in 1875, prior to
Mansfield's stage career, when he was a music critic
in Boston.

2433   Ruhl, Arthur. "Richard Mansfield, A Review of His Work." COLLIER'S
39 (14 September 1907): 21. Illus.

A eulogistic tribute penned shortly after the actor's death,
describing many of his mannerisms and eccentricities.

2434   Seibel, George. "Memories of Richard Mansfield." THEATRE GUILD
8 (October 1930): 30-33, 53. Illus.

Several of Mansfield's letters are quoted in a brief
biographical sketch of no distinction.

2435   Sherry, Laura. "The Art of Richard Mansfield." PLAY BOOK 1
(November 1913): 16-20.

An adulatory description of Mansfield and his theatrical
theories and practices, stressing his intellectual side.

2436   "The Solitary Genius of Richard Mansfield." CURRENT LITERATURE 48
(April 1910): 433-36. Illus.

Largely made up of quotations from Winter's biography
of the actor.

2437   Stanley, W. A. "Richard Mansfield's Real Self." THEATRE (N. Y.) 26
(September 1917): 126, 162; (October 1917): 200, 202, 256. Illus.

Stanley was a boyhood friend of Mansfield's; his articles
stress how unhappy the actor was with his career.

2438   Tacchella, B.   "Richard Mansfield, an Old Darbeian." DERBY SCHOOL MAGAZINE, April 1908.

A biographical sketch; Mansfield was one of the Derby (Engl.) School's more famous graduates. The material was later printed separately by the author for private circulation.

2439   Vassault, F.I.   "Mansfield and Ibsen." BELLMAN, 15 December 1906, pp. 559-60. Illus.

Vassault praises Mansfield's production of PEER GYNT, although he deplores the script itself.

2440   Wagenknecht, Edward.   "Richard Mansfield: Portrait of an Actor." SEWANEE REVIEW 38 (April 1930): 150-60.

A prejudicial assessment of the actor's work, extolling his virtues in the most general of terms.

2441   West, Kenyon.   "Richard Mansfield." ARENA 35 (January 1906): 2-15. Illus.

An adulatory essay, highlighting Mansfield's career. West suggests that Mansfield leads the English-speaking stage after the death of Irving.

2442   Wilson, Garff B.   "Richard Mansfield: Actor of the Transition." EDUCATIONAL THEATRE JOURNAL 14 (March 1962): 38-43.

A brief analysis of Mansfield's art and personality.

2443   Wilstach, Paul.   RICHARD MANSFIELD: THE MAN AND THE ACTOR. New York: Charles Scribner's Sons, 1909. xvii, 490 p. Index, illus., bibliog. Reprint. Freeport, N.Y.: Books for Libraries, 1970.

The most complete of the Mansfield studies, based on the author's acquaintances with the actor and his wife and his access to Mansfield's papers. Includes a valuable bibliography and references to most of Mansfield's contemporaries, such as Daniel Bandmann, Edwin Booth, and Joseph Jefferson III.

2444   _____.   "Richard Mansfield--The Man and the Actor." THEATRE (N.Y.) 9 (January 1909): 31-37. Illus.

Quotations from Wilstach's biography of Mansfield (no. 2443).

2445   Winter, William.   LIFE AND ART OF RICHARD MANSFIELD WITH SELECTIONS FROM HIS LETTERS. 2 vols. New York: Moffat, Yard and Co., 1910. Index, illus. Reprint. Freeport, N.Y.: Books for Libraries; Westport, Conn.: Greenwood, 1970.

> Written at Mansfield's request, this massive work includes a forty-four page chronology of the actor's career. Volume 2 consists of twenty-seven chapters devoted to Mansfield's major roles.

2446 _____. "Shakespeare in New York." HARPER'S WEEKLY 34 (11 January 1890): 33-35. Illus.

> Winter describes major players and their more important productions, among the performers being Mansfield and Ada Rehan.

2447 Wolfe, Thomas. "Portrait of a Player." THEATRE ANNUAL, 1947, pp. 43-54.

> Originally published in ATLANTIC MONTHLY, June 1939, as "The Winter of Our Discontent," and, slightly re-arranged and supplemented, as chapter 26 of Wolfe's THE WEB AND THE ROCK (1939). A short story in which the actor Brandell is a representation of Mansfield, as described in the preface to this article.

2448 Wood, Douglas. "The Last of the Giants." SHOW 3 (September 1963): 84-85. Illus.

> Wood recalls having seen Mansfield on stage. The article is an excerpt from Wood's unpublished memoirs, ON STAGE: AN ACTOR'S STORY.

2449 [Z., X.Y.] "The Actor and the Critics." THEATRE (N.Y.) 10 (June 1910): 195-97, vi. Illus.

> Reprints of correspondence, some of it rather testy, be-tween Mansfield and the critic, William Winter.

See also nos. 12, 28, 58, 165-66, 177, 201, 213, 219, 223, 228, 233, 245, 256, 261, 263, 276, 279, 288, 291, 296, 303, 321, 328, 346, 356, 358, 379-80, 386, 389, 399, 402, 404-6, 413, 419, 425, 438, 446, 451, 510, 519, 529, 533, 539, 542-44, 555, 558, 562, 567, 574, 578, 581, 586, 588, 596-97, 691, 938, 964, 1599, 1908, 1975, 2115, 2147, 2585, 2589, and 2973.

MANTELL, ROBERT BRUCE

(1854-1928)

2450   Bulliet, Clarence J. "A Tragedian as a Country Gentleman." SUBUR-
BAN LIFE 17 (November 1913): 256. Illus.

> A half-page description and a half-page photograph of
> Mantell's "Brucewood" in the village of Atlantic High-
> lands.

2451   _____. ROBERT MANTELL'S ROMANCE. Boston: John W. Luce and
Co., 1918. viii, 256 p. Illus.

> Although containing a good deal of information about
> Mantell's career, this volume seems excessively adulatory
> and gushing. Lack of documentation makes corroboration
> necessary, although Bulliet was a personal friend of
> Mantells.

2452   Dodge, Wendell Phillips. "Robert B. Mantell. The Actor Who Makes
Shakespeare Pay." STRAND (N.Y.) 43 (June 1912): 591-603. Illus.

> An extended tribute, Dodge praising Mantell's successful
> Shakespearean productions in the face of commercialism,
> sensationalism, and the star system, then contaminating
> the New York stage. Biographical and critical accounts
> are included.

2453   Favorini, Attilio. "'Richard's Himself Again!' Robert Mantell's Shakespearean Debut in New York City." EDUCATIONAL THEATRE JOURNAL
24 (December 1977): 402-14. Illus.

> A well-researched and documented account, attempting to
> assess Mantell's rank among U.S. Shakespearean actors.

2454   Govier, Georgia Bowen. "At Home with the Mantells." GREEN BOOK
ALBUM 6 (November 1911): 1072-77.

> A description of Mantell's "Brucewood," a farm in New
> Jersey, used as a retreat from the pressures of touring.

2455 Keightley, Mabel S. "Robert Mantell--Last of the Heroic Shakespearean Actors." THEATRE (N.Y.) 21 (March 1915): 122-23. Illus.

> A summation of the actor's career with emphasis upon his leading tragic roles in Shakespeare.

2456 Mantell, Robert. "My Adventures with Shakespeare." GREEN BOOK ALBUM 5 (March 1911): 577-84.

> Various anecdotes from the actor's career with little biographical value.

2457 _____. "Personal Reminiscences." THEATRE (N.Y.) 24 (October 1916): 194-96. Illus.

> A brief autobiographical sketch; well-illustrated.

2458 _____. "Playing Lear Under the Stars." THEATRE (N.Y.) 29 (April 1919): 228. Illus.

> Part of a series, "The Most Striking Episode in My Life." Mantell recalls playing in the Greek theatre in Berkeley, California.

2459 Moses, Montrose J. "Robert Mantell as an Interpreter of Shakespeare." BOOK NEWS 30 (March 1912): 505-7. Illus.

> Moses considers Mantell the preeminent Shakespearean tragedian in America at the time, superior to Sothern.

2460 "Robert Mantell's Country Home." THEATRE (N.Y.) 34 (August 1921): 118-19. Illus.

> A pictorial study of "Brucewood," Mantell's New Jersey farm.

See also nos. 28, 131, 150, 247, 270, 276, 279, 290, 366, 379, 399, 413, and 596.

MARBLE, DAN

(1810-49)

2461   [Falconbridge.] DAN MARBLE; A BIOGRAPHICAL SKETCH OF THAT
FAMOUS AND DIVERTING HUMORIST, WITH REMINISCENCES,
COMICALITIES, ANECDOTES, ETC., ETC. New York: Dewitt and
Davenport, 1851. 234 p. Illus.

> A largely anecdotal and evocative rather than factual
> coverage of the bulk of Marble's career. Passing mention
> is made of Sol Smith, Edwin Booth, Edwin Forrest, George
> Hill, James H. Hackett, William B. Wood, the Chapmans,
> Francis Wemyss, and James W. Wallack, Jr. A valuable
> source for the period.

See also nos. 146, 181, and 413.

MARCH, FREDRIC

(1897-1975)

2462   Brownfield, Lloyd. "With Fredric March on a South Seas Isle." MOVIE CLASSIC 8 (April 1935): 24-25, 78. Illus.

> An account of March's vacation in Tahiti.

2463   Burrows, Michael. CHARLES LAUGHTON AND FREDRIC MARCH. Cornwall, Engl.: Primestyle, 1969. 41 p. Illus.

> Pages 22-40 are a biographical sketch of March, heavily illustrated and focused upon his film career.

2464   Calhoun, Dorothy. "Fredric March Lives in a French 'Farmhouse.'" MOTION PICTURE MAGAZINE 49 (February 1935): 52-53, 79. Illus.

> Architectural details of March's home in Beverly Hills.

2465   THE FILM FAN'S BEDSIDE BOOK NO. 2. Edited by J.J. Lynx. London: Co-Ordination (Press and Publicity), 1949. 136 p. Illus.

> Pages 118-20 is a fan-oriented essay, "Hollywood's Happiest Marriage," about March and Florence Eldridge.

2466   Gay, Valerie. "Hollywood Hero No. 1--Frederic March." MOVIE CLASSIC 8 (August 1935): 33, 76. Illus.

> Accolades for March's successes in the film industry.

2467   Gehman, Richard. "Theatre Arts Gallery." THEATRE ARTS 45 (December 1961): 14-16, 72-74. Illus.

> March is honored in the Theatre Arts Gallery; some biographical detail emerges as he muses over his career to that time.

2468   Hall, Gladys. "Who Will Be King of the Movies?" MOTION PICTURE MAGAZINE 38 (December 1929): 30, 103. Illus.

Hall suggests March would probably replace John Gilbert
as the leader of the industry.

2469 Isaacs, Hermine Rich. "Two Girls and Fredric March." THEATRE ARTS
28 (April 1944): 243-46.

>An account of March's wartime visit to Ascension Island
>and the material he chose to entertain troops there.

2470 Lang, Harry. "Forward, March!" MOVIE CLASSIC 10 (May 1936):
46-47, 68. Illus.

>A publicity puff for ANTHONY ADVERSE, which March
>had just filmed.

2471 Lee, Sonia. "Fredric March Gambled with Death--and Won." MOTION
PICTURE MAGAZINE 46 (December 1933): 60, 70.

>A description of March's heart trouble and how he over-
>came it.

2472 Manners, Dorothy. "Fredric March Defends Hollywood's Morals."
MOTION PICTURE MAGAZINE 48 (November 1934): 31, 64. Illus.

>March condemns certain indecent and immoral films, but
>considers the majority of films as wholesome.

2473 _____. "Why We Have Adopted a Baby." MOTION PICTURE MAGA-
ZINE 44 (January 1933): 58-59, 75. Illus.

>How and why the March's chose to adopt their daughter,
>Penelope.

2474 Osborn, Kay. "March--Not a Pedestal-Percher." MOTION PICTURE
MAGAZINE 52 (October 1936): 35, 74. Illus.

>Osborn quotes March on his attempts to avoid the ego-
>centricity of star status.

2475 Paxton, John. "This Militant March." STAGE 16 (15 May 1939):
front cover, 20-23, 54. Illus.

>An account of March's appearance in THE AMERICAN
>WAY and of various political accusations made against
>him.

2476 Quirk, Lawrence J. THE FILMS OF FREDRIC MARCH. New York:
Citadel Press, 1971. 255 p. Illus.

>Pages 13-36, "Fredric March: His Life and Career,"

> while undocumented, briefly describes March's stage career.

2477   Service, Faith. "I've Faced These Temptations in Hollywood." MOTION PICTURE MAGAZINE 46 (August 1933): 49, 66-67. Illus.

> March offers moral advice to Hollywood newcomers.

2478   Tozzi, Romano. "Fredric March." FILMS IN REVIEW 9 (December 1958): 545-71. Illus.

> Tozzi offers a substantial biographical treatment, a positive critical assessment, and a complete list of March's films. Heavily illustrated.

2479   Tully, Jim. "Jim Tully Reveals Real Fredric March." MOTION PICTURE MAGAZINE 50 (December 1935): 27, 74-75. Illus.

> A biographical sketch about March's youth.

2480   Vandour, Cyril. "Freddie Marches On." MOTION PICTURE MAGAZINE 54 (December 1937): 31, 78-79. Illus.

> Vandour attempts to describe March's combined careers in films and on stage.

2481   Walker, Helen Louise. "Fredric March's Ahead." MOTION PICTURE MAGAZINE 37 (May 1929): 76, 108. Illus.

> A report of John Barrymore's reaction to seeing March in THE ROYAL FAMILY.

See also nos. 5, 276, 369, and 413.

MARLOWE, JULIA
(1866-1950)

2482   "An Actress' Favorite Books." THEATRE (N.Y.) 1 (September 1901): 15. Illus.

        Marlowe's literary preferences and library.

2483   "Another Woman Hamlet." LITERARY DIGEST 39 (31 July 1909): 169-70. Illus.

        An announcement of Marlowe's intention to play Hamlet to E.H. Sothern's Claudius, and a reprint of T. Allston Brown's history of the role as played by women, reprinted from the New York DRAMATIC MIRROR.

2484   Barry, John D. JULIA MARLOWE. Boston: Richard G. Badger and Co., 1899. 87 p. Illus. Boston: E.H. Bacon, 1907. 117 p. Illus.

        A truncated biographical treatment, relying heavily upon critiques in periodicals, to which Barry adds his own brief remarks.

2485   Bell, Archie. "Sothern and Marlowe are Quitting the Stage." GREEN BOOK ALBUM 8 (September 1912): 393-402. Illus.

        The acting team discusses retirement possibilities.

2486   Bradford, Margaret. "A Chat with Julia Marlowe and Susan B. Anthony." THEATRE (N.Y.) 13 (March 1911): 78. Illus.

        Brief anecdotes of little substance or insight.

2487   Corbin, John. "Julia Marlowe." COSMOPOLITAN 37 (July 1904): 361-62. Illus.

        A brief and highly adulatory essay.

2488   Dale, Alan. [Pseud.] "Julia and Juliet." COSMOPOLITAN 57 (July 1914): 257-59. Illus.

Superficial remarks on Marlowe's Shakespearean repertory.

2489 _____. "Julia Marlowe--A Famous Career." GREEN BOOK ALBUM 16 (September 1916): 523-28. Illus.

Dale surveys Marlowe's career to that time, but in no significant depth.

2490 Dodge, Wendell Phillips. "Julia Marlowe." STRAND (N.Y.) 45 (July 1913): 733-43. Illus.

A well-illustrated appreciation and survey of Marlowe's career. E.H. Sothern is quoted extensively.

2491 Firkins, Oscar W. "Sothern and Marlowe--An Estimate." THEATRE (N.Y.) 18 (October 1913): 118-22, viii-ix. Illus.

A substantial and thoughtful critical reaction to the team in seven Shakespearean productions.

2492 Hovey, Carl. "Playing Shakespeare." METROPOLITAN 37 (January 1913): 32-35. Illus.

A superficial interview in which Sothern and Marlowe describe the joys of playing Shakespeare and the lines between success and failure.

2493 Herrmann, Karl von. "How Julia Marlowe Climbed Vesuvius." LADIES' HOME JOURNAL, November 1905, pp. 7, 75. Illus.

An eyewitness account of Marlowe's 1903 visit to the volcano.

2494 "Julia Marlowe's Greatest Roles." WOMAN'S HOME COMPANION 38 (November 1911): 9. Illus.

A photographic resume of Marlowe in six roles.

2495 Kobbé, Gustav. "The Actress We Know as Julia Marlowe." LADIES' HOME JOURNAL, February 1903, pp. 7-8. Illus.

A description of Marlowe's life at "Highmount," her four hundred acre estate in the western Catskill Mountains. Kobbé describes the actress's training for the stage as well.

2496 Laughlin, Clara E. "Back of the Footlights with 'Juliet.'" LADIES' HOME JOURNAL, May 1907, pp. 13, 76. Illus.

A not especially detailed description of the Sothern-Marlowe company's process of setting up for an engagement.

2497   McCracken, Elizabeth.   "Julia Marlowe."   CENTURY 73 (November 1906): 46-55. Illus.

A critical assessment, including the actress's opinions on the major characters she had played.

2498   _____. "When the Public Does Not See the Actress--Behind the Scenes with Julia Marlowe." LADIES' HOME JOURNAL, April 1913, pp. 21, 78-81. Illus.

A superficial description of backstage activity, adulatory and lacking precision.

2499   Marlowe, Julia.   "The Eloquence of Silence."   GREEN BOOK MAGA- ZINE 9 (March 1913): 393-401. Illus.

The actress cites examples of performers whose strongest points were made without speaking.

2500   _____. "The Essentials of Stage Success." THEATRE (N.Y.) 1 (December 1901): 13-15. Illus.

Idealized advice for beginning performers.

2501   _____. "The Future of the Historical Romance for the Stage." INDE- PENDENT 54 (26 June 1902): 1531-35. Illus.

Marlowe proposes that "mental action" was superseding physical action in the drama, a change she approved.

2502   _____. "Julia Marlowe's Farewell to Shakespeare's Women." THEATRE (N.Y.) 23 (July 1916): 7. Illus.

A poem by Marlowe, recited by her at her farewell from the stage, 27 May 1916.

2503   _____. "Reminiscences of an Actress." PHILHARMONIC 1 (July 1901): 137-50. Illus.

Autobiographical notes, gracefully written in a somewhat restrained tone, focusing upon the actress's early career.

2504   _____. "Stage Work and the Stage Aspirant." GOOD HOUSEKEEP- ING, March 1912, pp. 325-32. Illus.

Marlowe describes the nature of a stage career, the neces- sity for hard work, and the potential rewards.

2505   _____. "Why I Am Leaving the Stage." LADIES' HOME JOURNAL, January 1916, p. 20. Illus.

Marlowe claims physical and mental exhaustion and a lack of worlds to conquer as her primary reasons.

2506 _____. "Women, Marriage, and the Art of the Theatre." GREEN BOOK MAGAZINE 11 (January 1914): 135-39. Illus.

Somewhat pointless remarks on the life of an actress, especially combined with marriage.

2507 Morris, A.R. "A Note on the Inflection of Julia Marlowe." QUARTER- LY JOURNAL OF SPEECH 20 (April 1934): 200-202.

A technical appraisal and analysis of Marlowe in ROMEO AND JULIET with graphs of her inflections of several key lines.

2508 Moses, Montrose J. "Two Interpreters of Shakespeare." INDEPENDENT 76 (9 October 1913): 76, 79.

A positive assessment of Marlowe and E.H. Sothern by a leading critic.

2509 Patterson, Ada. "At Home with Julia Marlowe." GREEN BOOK ALBUM 5 (February 1911): 335-40.

A fan-oriented interview of minimal value or insight.

2510 _____. "Julia Marlowe--The Actress and Woman." THEATRE (N.Y.) 3 (December 1903): 297, 300. Illus.

A superficial interview, primarily concerning Marlowe's work in Shakespearean repertory.

2511 Russell, Charles Edward. JULIA MARLOWE: HER LIFE AND ART. New York and London: D. Appleton and Co., 1926. xxv, 567 p. Index, illus.

A substantial but undocumented life of Marlowe, including a chronological list of her roles. The author served as Marlowe's business manager for over thirty years.

2512 _____. "Miss Marlowe and Mr. Sothern in Shakespeare." CRITIC 45 (December 1904): 525-31. Illus.

An extended description and analysis of the performers in ROMEO AND JULIET, HAMLET, and MUCH ADO ABOUT NOTHING.

2513 Sogliuzzo, A. Richard. "Edward H. Sothern and Julia Marlowe on the Art of Acting." THEATRE SURVEY 11 (November 1970): 187-200. Illus.

The author draws upon newspaper accounts and various
unpublished documents for this essay, concluding that
Sothern and Marlowe tended toward realism without ever
achieving it.

2514 Sothern, E.H. JULIA MARLOWE'S STORY. Edited by Downey Fairfax.
New York: Rinehart and Co., 1954. x, 237 p. Illus.

Sothern had completed this manuscript by the time he died
in 1933; Marlowe stipulated in her will that it be published. It is in fact an autobiography as told to Sothern,
later edited by Fairfax, who added occasional notes for
clarification.

2515 Symons, Arthur. "Great Acting in English." MONTHLY REVIEW 28
(April-June 1907): 12-17.

A laudatory description of Marlowe and Sothern's ROMEO
AND JULIET and HAMLET during a London engagement.

2516 Tyrrell, Henry. "Julia of Avon." COSMOPOLITAN 54 (December
1912): 119-21. Illus.

Marlowe describes her visits to Stratford-upon-Avon and
their influence upon her Shakespearean roles.

2517 Wagenknecht, Edward Charles. SEVEN DAUGHTERS OF THE THEATRE:
JENNY LIND, SARAH BERNHARDT, ELLEN TERRY, JULIA MARLOWE,
ISADORA DUNCAN, MARY GARDEN, MARILYN MONROE. Norman:
University of Oklahoma Press, 1964. x, 224 p. Index, illus., bibliog.

A series of biographical-critical essays, more useful for
their bibliographies than their texts; one deals with Marlowe.

2518 Winter, William. "The Art of Julia Marlowe." CENTURY 90 (June
1915): 209-16.

Winter expresses great admiration for Marlowe's acting
ability, especially in Shakespeare.

See also nos. 13, 28, 58, 130, 245, 256, 261, 270, 276-79, 288, 291, 296,
303, 314, 316, 321, 328, 342, 344, 352, 356, 358, 367, 377, 381-83, 390-91,
400, 407-8, 413, 430, 440, 448, 464-65, 493, 505, 509-10, 513, 531, 539, 547,
555, 557-58, 561, 578-79, 581, 594, 596-97, 600, 1090, 1471, 1509, 1561,
2973, 2975, and 2989.

MASON, JOHN B.

(1857-1919)

2519   Dodge, Wendell Phillips. "The Best Dressed Actor on the Stage."
THEATRE (N.Y.) 16 (November 1912): 150, 152, vi. Illus.

> Mason is quoted as he discourses on his attention to de-
> tail, especially regarding costuming.

2520   Mason, John. "Do You Want to Be an Actor?" GREEN BOOK MAGA-
ZINE 9 (May 1913): 761-70. Illus.

> Well-meaning advice to would-be performers.

2521   _____. "Personal Reminiscences." THEATRE (N.Y.) 24 (December
1916): 350-51. Illus.

> A brief autobiographical sketch, concluding with a salute
> to the actor's fellow performers.

2522   Mason, William Lyman. A RECORD OF THE DESCENDANTS OF ROBERT
MASON OF ROXBURY, MASS. Milwaukee: Burdick, Armitage and
Allen, 1891. 39 p.

> A straightforward listing of birth and death dates with
> no substantial biographical material on Mason or any of
> his ancestors.

2523   Savage, Richard. "John Mason--An Actor of Strong Personality."
THEATRE 8 (July 1908): 182-85. Illus.

> A brief sketch of Mason's career with some remarks on his
> theatrical philosophies.

See also nos. 270, 290, 379-80, and 594-95.

MAY, EDNA

(1878-1948)

2524   Baker, Graham. "The Belle of New York." MOTION PICTURE MAGA-
ZINE 11 (March 1916): 144-46. Illus.

> Baker quotes May's reminiscences of the opening of the
> comic opera, THE BELLE OF NEW YORK, in which May
> rose to fame.

2525   Matthews, Richard. "Actresses Who Have Made Notable Marriages."
MUNSEY'S 40 (January 1909): 543-51. Illus.

> Matthews congratulates May on her marriage to Oscar
> Lewisohn.

2526   Patterson, Ada. "The Ambition of Miss Edna May." THEATRE (N.Y.)
5 (November 1905): 276, 278-79. Illus.

> A superficial interview in which May describes her hopes
> to marry and have children.

2527   White, Matthew, Jr. "Edna May." MUNSEY'S 37 (April-September
1907): 340-44. Illus.

> White proposes that May, although having little talent,
> achieved stardom by her demure beauty and unaffected
> manner.

See also nos. 28, 314, 324, 582, and 1605.

MAYO, FRANK

(1839-96)

2528 Lewis, W. A. "Frank Mayo--Man and Artist." THEATRE (N. Y.) 6
(June 1906): 149-51, iii. Illus.

> Lewis quotes Mayo as planning to abandon the role of
> Davy Crockett for a more classical repertory.

See also nos. 112, 131, 164, 222, 279, 300, 399, 472, 489, 550, 1077, and
1587.

MENKEN, ADAH ISAACS
(1835-68)

2529   Barclay, George Lippard, ed.   THE LIFE AND REMARKABLE CAREER OF ADAH ISAACS MENKEN, THE CELEBRATED ACTRESS: AN ACCOUNT OF HER CAREER AS A DANSEUESE, AN ACTRESS, AN AUTHORESS, A POETESS, A SCULPTOR, AN EDITRESS, AS CAPTAIN OF THE "DAYTON LIGHT GUARD," AS THE WIFE OF THE PUGILIST JOHN C. HEENAN, AND OF "ORPHEUS KERR." Philadelphia: Barclay and Co., 1868. 63 p. Illus.

   A turgidly written, undocumented, and speculative pamphlet, useless without corroboration.

2530   Coleman, Marion Moore.   MAZEPPA POLISH AND AMERICAN: A TRANSLATION OF SLOWACKI'S MAZEPPA, TOGETHER WITH A BRIEF SURVEY OF MAZEPPA IN THE UNITED STATES. Chesire, Conn.: Cherry Hill Books, 1966. 73 p. Illus., notes.

   A copy of the script, to which Coleman appends a stage history, a large portion of which describes Menken and her portrayal.

2531   Edwards, Samuel.   QUEEN OF THE PLAZA. Folkestone, Engl.: Alvin, Redman; London: Mayflower, 1969.

   Originally published in 1964 under the same title with the author listed as Paul Lewis, a pseudonym for Noel Bertram Gerson. See no. 2534.

2532   Falk, Bernard.   NAKED LADY: OR, STORM OVER ADAH: A BIOGRAPHY OF ADAH ISAACS MENKEN. London: Hutchinson, 1934. 295 p. Index, illus.

   A substantial, well-researched, and documented treatment, basic to any study of Menken. Well-illustrated.

2533   Fleischer, Nat.   RECKLESS LADY: THE LIFE STORY OF ADAH ISAACS MENKEN. New York: C.J. O'Brien, 1941. 36 p. Illus.

The author was editor of RING MAGAZINE; his interest in Menken grew out of her relationship with the pugilist, John Heenan. The work is brief, speculative, and completely undocumented.

2534   Gerson, Noel Bertram [Lewis, Paul]. QUEEN OF THE PLAZA: A BIOGRAPHY OF ADAH ISAACS MENKEN. New York: Funk and Wagnalls Co., 1964. 296 p. Index, bibliog.

While substantial, based on Menken's autobiographical fragments, and partially documented, the volume is not completely trustworthy without corroboration.

2535   Gorman, Herbert. THE INCREDIBLE MARQUIS: ALEXANDRE DUMAS. New York: Farrar and Rinehart, 1929. 452 p. Index, frontispiece.

Menken is treated in passing on page 432 f.

2536   Hibbert, Henry George. A PLAYGOER'S MEMORIES. London: Grant Richards, 1920. 290 p. Index, illus.

While primarily concerned with the British actors of the time, Hibbert describes Menken briefly in chapter 21, "Horse-Play."

2537   James, Ed[win]., ed. BIOGRAPHY OF ADAM ISAACS MENKEN. WITH SELECTIONS FROM "INFELECIA." New York: Edwin James, [1881]. 24 p. Illus.

A biographical treatment by a friend of Menken's, the first sixteen pages describing her life and career, the remaining eight consisting of some of the actress's poetry.

2538   Kendall, John Smith. "'The World's Delight': The Story of Adah Isaacs Menken." LOUISIANA HISTORICAL QUARTERLY 21, no. 3 (1938): 846-68.

In an undocumented monograph, Kendall seeks to correct some misconceptions about Menken, especially concerning her parentage and childhood.

2539   Krich, John F. "The Amiable Lady Charms the Iron City: Adah Isaacs Menken in Pittsburgh." WESTERN PENNSYLVANIA HISTORICAL MAGAZINE 51 (July 1968): 259-78. Illus.

Krich's well-documented essay describes Menken's successful engagements in Pittsburgh, with a complete list of scripts performed there.

2540   Lafourcade, Georges. SWINBURNE, A LITERARY BIOGRAPHY. London: G. Bell and Sons, 1932. xiv, 307 p. Index, illus., bibliog.

Menken's relationship with Swinburne was covered briefly
in this biography, as it is in many Swinburne studies.

2541   Lesser, Allen F. "Adah Isaacs Menken: A Daughter of Israel." AMERI-
CAN JEWISH HISTORICAL SOCIETY 34 (1937): 143-47.

Lesser attempts to separate fact from Menken's "unblush-
ing fabrications," devised and written solely for their
value as theatrical publicity. Lesser concludes Menken
was of Jewish ancestry.

2542   _____. ENCHANTING REBEL: THE SECRET OF ADAH ISAACS MEN-
KEN. New York: Beechhurst Press, 1947. 273 p. Index, illus.,
bibliog.

A lively, undocumented (although Lesser includes a three-
page bibliography) account of Menken, stressing the more
scandalous aspects of her life and career.

2543   _____. WEAVE A WREATH OF LAUREL: THE LIVES OF FOUR JEWISH
CONTRIBUTORS TO AMERICAN CIVILIZATION. New York: Coven
Press, 1938. x, 72 p. Index, illus., bibliog.

Pages 21-35 offer an undistinguished biographical sketch
of Menken; a short bibliography is appended.

2544   Lucas-Dubreton, Jean. THE FOURTH MUSKETEER: THE LIFE OF
ALEXANDER DUMAS. Trans. by Maida Castelhun Darnton. New York:
Coward-McCann, 1928. 276 p. Bibliog.

A highly speculative work, written in novel form, containing scattered references to Menken and her relationship with Dumas.

2545   Lyman, George D. THE SAGA OF THE COMSTOCK LODE: BOOM
DAYS IN VIRGINIA CITY. New York: Charles Scribner's Sons, 1934.
399 p. Illus., notes.

Chapters 52-53 (pp. 270-84) describe Menken as Mazeppa
in a lively but documented style.

2546   Mayne, Ethel Colburn. ENCHANTERS OF MEN. New York and
London: G.P. Putnam's Sons, 1925. 358 p. Index, illus.

Mayne concludes this volume of short biographical
sketches with a sixteen-page chapter on Menken; of little
value.

2547   Morrison, Ian. THE SENSATION: A NOVEL BASED ON THE LIFE OF
ADAH ISAACS MENKEN. New York: New American Library, 1963.
158 p.

A fanciful and fictionalized treatment of Menken; of little value to the scholar.

2548   Northcott, Richard. ADAH ISAACS MENKEN: AN ILLUSTRATED BIOGRAPHY. London: Press Printers, 1921. 53 p. Illus.

A small volume, drawing heavily upon reviews, letters, poems, and other material published elsewhere, but including several photographs of Menken rarely published elsewhere.

2549   Parsons, Bill. "The Debut of Adah Isaacs Menken." QUARTERLY JOURNAL OF SPEECH 46 (February 1960): 8-13.

Parsons suggests that Menken's first appearance was at least six months earlier than most biographers have reported.

2550   Shpall, Leo. "Adah Isaacs Menken." LOUISIANA HISTORICAL QUARTERLY 26 (1943): 162-63.

A brief biographical treatment of Menken, speculating on the more problematic details, such as her parentage.

2551   Stoddard, Charles Warren. "La Belle Menken." NATIONAL MAGAZINE 21 (February 1905): 477-88. Illus.

A substantial and well-illustrated essay, somewhat overly enthusiastic about Menken, whom the author had seen when he was a child.

2552   Sykes, William. "Excursions through an Old Scrap Book." THEATRE (N.Y.) 24 (November 1916): 294. Illus.

A brief biographical sketch of Menken, adding little.

2553   Wyndham, Horace. VICTORIAN SENSATIONS. London: Jarrolds, 1933. 279 p. Index, illus.

Pages 167-205, subtitled "Poetry and Passion," is a fairly sympathetic treatment of Menken's European escapades.

See also nos. 13, 154, 164, 222, 277, 333, 392, 413, 459, 482, 590, 1364, 1750, and 2330.

MENKEN, HELEN

(1901-66)

2554 Menken, Helen. "Don't Envy Me!" WOMAN'S HOME COMPANION 50 (July 1923): 12, 103. Illus.

> An autobiographical essay in which Menken, although she had just won plaudits for THREE WISE FOOLS, proclaims she finds the theatre less than satisfactory.

2555 _____. "Jack Appears in HEAVEN." AMERICAN MAGAZINE 137 (May 1944): 64. Illus.

> A minor incident recalled from Menken's early career.

2556 _____. "'To the Ladies'--God Help Them!" THEATRE (N.Y.) 49 (March 1929): 37, 76.

> Menken describes the different status of women in the Orient and the West, having researched and played several Eastern roles.

2557 Mullett, Mary B. "A Star at 22--But after 17 Years of Preparation." AMERICAN MAGAZINE 96 (September 1923): 34-35, 138, 142, 144. Illus.

> An "overnight success" in SEVENTH HEAVEN, Menken recalls being a child dancer at age five and a nearly continuous stage career thereafter.

2558 Patterson, Ada. "Helen Menken: Philosopher and Player." THEATRE (N.Y.) 37 (May 1923): 26, 56. Illus.

> Menken had just won rave reviews in SEVENTH HEAVEN and describes her preparation for stardom.

2559 _____. "Miss Menken Defends THE CAPTIVE." THEATRE (N.Y.) 45 (February 1927): 22-23, 60. Illus.

Menken defends the value of the controversial script, a modern version of the Laocoon legend.

See also nos. 464 and 512.

MERRY, ANN BRUNTON

(1768-1808)

2560   Adams, M. Ray. "Robert Merry and the American Theatre." THEATRE
SURVEY 6 (May 1965): 1-11.

> A carefully prepared article describing the arrival of
> the Merrys in America in 1796 and their careers until
> Robert Merry's death in 1798.

2561   "Biographical Sketch of Mrs. Warren." MIRROR OF TASTE AND DRA-
MATIC CENSOR 1 (February 1810): 118-33.

> An undocumented biographical sketch with considerable
> detail; a useful primary source needing corroboration.

2562   Condie, Thomas. "Biographical Anecdotes of Mrs. Merry of the Theatre,
Philadelphia." PHILADELPHIA MONTHLY MAGAZINE, OR UNIVERSAL
REPOSITORY OF KNOWLEDGE AND ENTERTAINMENT 1 (April 1798):
185-88. Illus.

> A useful biographical and critical account of the actress
> by the magazine's editor after Merry had been in this country
> two years.

2563   Doty, Gresdna Ann. "Anne Merry and the Beginning of Stardom in
the United States." QUARTERLY JOURNAL OF SPEECH 55 (December
1968): 383-91.

> A preliminary to Doty's later book-length work on the
> actress (see no. 2564).

2564   _____. THE CAREER OF MRS. ANNE BRUNTON MERRY IN THE
AMERICAN THEATRE. Baton Rouge: Louisiana State University Press,
1971. xiii, 165 p. Index, illus., bibliog.

> The outstanding work on Merry now available; Doty has
> combined careful research, meticulous documentation,
> graceful writing, and logical thinking into this biographi-
> cal work.

2565   Genest, John. SOME ACCOUNT OF THE ENGLISH STAGE FROM
         THE RESTORATION IN 1660 TO 1830. 10 vols. Bath: H. E. Carring-
         ton, 1832.

              Mrs. Merry's career at Covent Garden before her arrival
              in the United States is described.

See also nos. 13, 29, 123, 139, 188, 192, 413, 462, 592, 1008, and 3208.

MILLER, HENRY
(1860-1926)

2566   "Henry Miller's Onslaught Upon the New Theatre." CURRENT OPINION 48 (March 1910): 318-19.

>   Miller predicted disaster for the recently founded New Theatre, considering it elitist, while calling for a national theatre devoted only to American scripts.

2567   Morse, Frank P. BACKSTAGE WITH HENRY MILLER. New York: E. P. Dutton and Co., 1938. 283 p. Index, illus.

>   At present, the only full-length treatment of Miller; a lively and undocumented account of his career with references to Maude Adams, Margaret Anglin, Ruth Chatterton, George M. Cohan, Matilda Heron, Walter Hampden, and Nazimova.

2568   Patterson, Ada. "At Home with Henry Miller." GREEN BOOK ALBUM 5 (June 1911): 1247-52.

>   Primarily a description of Miller's farm near New York.

2569   _____. "A Morning Call on Henry Miller." THEATRE (N.Y.) 5 (June 1905): 154-56. Illus.

>   Patterson quotes Miller reminiscing about his career, including having learned acting from Dion Boucicault.

See also nos. 28, 131, 150, 242, 270, 276, 279, 290, 297, 342, 379-80, 413, 448, 451, 455, 464, 555, 558, 565, 579, 581, 600, 1975, and 2589.

MILLER, MARILYN
(1898-1936)

2570   Carr, Harry. "The New House of Pickford." MOTION PICTURE MAGA-
ZINE 26 (October 1923): 26-27, 85. Illus.

> A description of Miller and Jack Pickford's home in
> southern California after Miller began her film career.

2571   Chapple, Joe Mitchell. "Affairs at Washington." NATIONAL MAGA-
ZINE 53 (December 1924): 195-96. Illus.

> A brief description of Miller in the title role of PETER
> PAN.

2572   "A Dainty Debutante." COSMOPOLITAN 57 (November 1914): 806-
7. Illus.

> A description of Miller's success in New York at age
> sixteen.

2573   Hall, Gladys. "Bees from Broadway." MOTION PICTURE MAGAZINE
38 (October 1929): 58-59, 100. Illus.

> Hall suggests Broadway was losing its major stars to the
> film industry, citing Miller as an example.

2574   _____. "Marilyn Miller--The New 'It' Girl of Hollywood." MOTION
PICTURE MAGAZINE 42 (September 1931): 46-47, 98. Illus.

> A fan-oriented article in which Hall suggests Miller's
> appeal brought her marriage proposals in unprecedented
> numbers.

2575   Mullett, Mary B. "Here is a Girl Who Can Make You Forget Your
Troubles." AMERICAN MAGAZINE 91 (May 1921): 19, 141-44.
Illus.

> Mullett describes Miller as quite optimistic in spite of
> her early widowhood and various other personal calamities.

2576 Perkins, Jeanne. "Mary Martin." LIFE, 27 December 1943, pp. 98-102, 104, 106, 108. Illus.

> The article features Martin, but describes a projected tribute to Miller and includes a brief sketch of her life and career.

See also no. 437.

MILLS, FLORENCE

(1895-1927)

2577   Bogle, Donald. BROWN SUGAR: EIGHTY YEARS OF AMERICA'S
BLACK FEMALE SUPERSTARS. New York: Harmony Books, 1980. 205 p.
Index, illus., bibliog.

> Mills is the subject of a separate if superficial biographi-
> cal sketch on pages 40-43.

2578   Levinson, André. "The Negro Dance." THEATRE ARTS 11 (April
1927): 282-93. Illus.

> An essay including a brief assessment of Mills.

See also no. 543.

MITCHELL, MAGGIE (1832-1918). See nos. 13, 222, 290, 328, 356, 387, 413, 433, 503, 572, and 2750.

MITCHELL, WILLIAM
(1798-1856)

2579   Rinear, David L. "Burlesque Comes to New York: William Mitchell's First Season at the Olympic." NINETEENTH CENTURY THEATRE RE-SEARCH 2 (Spring 1974): 23-34. Illus.

> In a well-researched and gracefully written article, Rinear describes Mitchell's first season in 1839-40 as highly successful despite considerable adversity.

See also nos. 261, 488, 1170, and 3027.

MODJESKA, HELENA
(1840-1909)

2580   Altemus, Jameson Torr. HELEN MODJESKA. New York: J.S. Ogilvie, 1883. Reprint. New York: Benjamin Blom, 1969. 217 p. Illus.

> A brief biographical sketch, followed by reprints of published criticisms of Modjeska's major roles and a reprint of her article, "Success on the Stage," from the NORTH AMERICAN REVIEW, December 1882.

2581   "A Brilliant Career Closes for Helena Modjeska." THEATRE (N.Y.) 9 (May 1909): 139. Illus.

> A brief memorial tribute.

2582   Coleman, Arthur Prudden, and Coleman, Marion Moore. WANDERERS TWAIN: MODJESKA AND SIENKIEWICZ: A VIEW FROM CALIFORNIA. Chesire, Conn.: Cherry Hill Books, 1964. ix, 102 p. Index, illus., bibliog.

> Based on information supplied by Modjeska's niece, Marylka Modjeska Pattison. Modjeska's theatrical career is only tangentially mentioned; most of the book concerns Modjeska's attempt to create a utopian society in Anaheim, California.

2583   Coleman, Marion Moore. "American Debut." BOOKS AND THINGS n.s. 6-7 (Winter 1964-Spring 1965): 1-40.

> Source material on the first appearance of Modjeska on the U.S. stage, including letters and dispatches by Henry Sienkiewicz.

2584   _____. AMERICAN DEBUT: SOURCE MATERIALS ON THE FIRST APPEARANCE OF THE POLISH ACTRESS HELENA MODJESKA OF THE AMERICAN STAGE INCLUDING LETTERS AND DISPATCHES BY HENRYK SIENKIEWICZ. Chesire, Conn.: Cherry Hill Books, 1965. 37 p. Illus.

A reprint of no. 2583, including the letters mentioned in the title and newspaper reviews of the debut.

2585 _____. FAIR ROSALIND: THE AMERICAN CAREER OF HELENA MODJESKA. Chesire, Conn.: Cherry Hill Books, 1969. 990 p. Index, notes.

> An enormous work, well-documented and extremely detailed, containing an appendix of every known appearance by the actress in the United States (pp. 881-968). No bibliography is supplied, but the footnotes are explicit and frequent. Substantial references to Maurice Barrymore, Edwin Booth, Rose Eytinge, Janauschek, Joseph Jefferson III, John McCullough, Richard Mansfield, Clara Morris, Cora Urquhart Potter, Otis Skinner, and Lawrence Barrett.

2586 _____. "To Play or Not to Play; Modjeska and the St. Petersburg Engagement." POLISH REVIEW 12 (1967): 44-56.

> An account based primarily on Modjeska's correspondence of an unsuccessful attempt to tour Russia.

2587 Collins, Mabel. THE STORY OF HELENA MODJESKA (MADAME CHLAPOWSKA). London: W. H. Allen and Co., 1883. 296 p.

> Totally undocumented and unillustrated biography, somewhat gushing in tone, to be used only with caution.

2588 Dithmar, Edward A. "Helena Modjeska." HARPER'S BAZAAR 23 (11 January 1890): 31.

> The critic assesses Modjeska's first twelve years of performances in English, focusing on nine Shakespearean heroines.

2589 Garland, Hamlin. COMPANIONS ON THE TRAIL: A LITERARY CHRONICLE. New York: Macmillan, 1931. 539 p. Frontispiece.

> Chapter 24 describes the author's first meeting with Modjeska and an assessment of her work. Garland also offers brief comments on Henry Miller, Arnold Daly, and Richard Mansfield.

2590 Gilder, Rosamond. "The Many Triumphs of Mme. Modjeska." THEATRE ARTS 45 (July 1961): 66-67, 74-75. Illus.

> Gilder draws upon her parents' friendship with Modjeska for personal insights in this tribute to the actress, as well as quoting from several previously unpublished letters.

2591 Gronowicz, Antoni. MODJESKA, HER LIFE AND LOVES. New York: Thomas Yoseloff, 1956. 254 p. Illus.

> An undocumented and luridly sensationalized biography, useless without corroboration, but including sections of Modjeska's diary while she was on tour with Edwin Booth in 1889-90.

2592 Hinds, William Alfred. AM. COMMUNITIES AND CO-OPERATIVE COLONIES. Chicago: H. Kerr and Co., 1908. 599 p. Index.

> A history of attempts to create utopian communities, including Modjeska's ill-fated attempt in Anaheim, California.

2593 "How Madame Modjeska's Career Was Saved by Zagloba." CURRENT LITERATURE 46 (June 1909): 667-68. Illus.

> Zbigniew Brodowski is quoted as describing in his memoirs the actress's San Francisco debut and her language difficulties there.

2594 Kay, Charles de. "Modjeska." SCRIBNER'S 17 (March 1879): 665-71. Illus.

> A brief and adulatory biographical sketch, adding little.

2595 Krythe, Maymie Richardson. "Madame Modjeska in California." HISTORICAL SOCIETY OF SOUTHERN CALIFORNIA QUARTERLY 35 (March 1953): 29-40.

> Using traditional sources previously published, the author describes the actress's arrival and residence on the West Coast. A bibliography is appended.

2596 Kyle, Howard. "On Tour with Modjeska." METROPOLITAN 31 (January 1910): 445-54. Illus.

> Kyle recalls his experiences with Modjeska on the road; he has high praise for the actress. As well as personal insights, he describes her in several of her more successful roles.

2597 "Modjeska, Dramatic Artist and Patriot." REVIEW OF REVIEWS 31 (June 1905): 678-79. Illus.

> A brief assessment; of little value.

2598 Modjeska, Helena. LETTERS TO EMILIA: RECORD OF A FRIENDSHIP. SEVEN LETTERS OF HELENA MODJESKA TO A FRIEND BACK HOME.

Edited and annotated by Marion Moore Coleman. Chesire, Conn.: Cherry Hill Books, 1967. 39 p. Illus., notes.

> The letters are to Emilia Sierzputowska, describing Modjeska's experiences while on tour. Coleman's notes are valuable and clarifying.

2599 _____. MEMORIES AND IMPRESSIONS OF HELENA MODJESKA: AN AUTOBIOGRAPHY. New York: Macmillan Co., 1910. ix, 562 p. Index, illus. Reprint. New York: Benjamin Blom, 1969.

> Basic to Modjeska studies; the actress described her life and career in considerable detail, including her impressions of most of the leading performers of the time, including Edwin Booth, Clara Morris, Dion Boucicault, Lotta Crabtree, and John McCullough. See no. 2600.

2600 _____. "Modjeska's Memoirs: The Record of a Romantic Career." CENTURY. "The Beginnings of a Great Actress," 79 (December 1909): 185-205; "The Author's Triumphant Rise and Sudden Abandonment of her Profession for a Home in the New World," (January 1910): 360-80; "Failure of the Polish Colony in California, and Return to the Stage," (February 1910): 549-65; "Success, and Friendship in New York and Boston," (March 1910): 697-712; "Success in London," (April 1910): 877-90; "Last Tours," 80 (May 1910): 85-103. Illus.

> A serialization of no. 2599.

2601 Ritter, Charles C. "Helena Modjeska: The Story of a Journey." WESTERN SPEECH 24 (Summer 1980): 155-60.

> A brief and unadorned account of Modjeska's first tour in the United States.

2602 Sienkiewicz, Henryk. PORTRAIT OF AMERICA: LETTERS. Edited and trans. by Charles Morley. New York: Columbia University Press, 1959. xix, 291 p. Index.

> Includes brief passing remarks about Modjeska.

2603 _____. "Sienkiewicz's Tribute to Helena Modjeska." THEATRE (N.Y.) 10 (March 1910): 90, 92.

> The text of Sienkiewicz's funeral address, given in Warsaw.

2604 Skinner, Constance. "The Modjeska I Knew." GREEN BOOK ALBUM 2 (July 1909): 174-78.

> Reminiscences by Skinner, who lived on Modjeska's California ranch and assisted the actress with her memoirs.

2605　Skinner, Maud.　"Modjeska."　THEATRE ARTS　11 (1927):　423-37. Illus.

> The author recalls appearing with Modjeska in such scripts as MAGDA and includes several quotations from their correspondence.

2606　Towse, J. Rankin.　"Madame Modjeska."　CENTURY　5 (November 1883):　22-26.　Illus.

> An appreciation, filled with praise and including some description of the actress as Viola and Rosalind.

See also nos. 28, 58, 112, 166, 171, 245, 247, 261, 263, 274, 277, 279, 288, 293, 316, 336, 341, 356, 367, 370, 381, 383, 398-400, 405, 408, 413, 417, 419, 450, 454, 503, 542, 555, 557-58, 561, 578, 581, 593, 596, 1077, 1124, 2191, 2613, 2701, 2879, 2896, 2912, 2932, and 3177.

MONTAGUE, HENRY JAMES (1844-78).   See nos. 131, 201, 343, 401, 407, 453, 460, and 593.

MORRIS, CLARA

(1848-1925)

2607   Ashby, Clifford. "The Technique of Clara Morris." EDUCATIONAL THEATRE JOURNAL 16 (May 1964): 134-41.

Ashby describes Morris's achievements in an acting style considered at the time the ultimate in reality.

2608   "Benefit for Clara Morris." THEATRE (N. Y.) 9 (April 1909): iv. Illus.

Plans for a 16 April benefit to raise money to pay off the mortgage on Morris's home.

2609   "Clara Morris." SUCCESS MAGAZINE AND THE NATIONAL POST 14 (November 1911): 23. Illus.

A recollection of Morris as the last of the Daly company of her day, written after the actress's retirement.

2610   "Clara Morris's Unique Interpretation of Lady Macbeth." CURRENT OPINION 41 (August 1906): 184-87. Illus.

The article draws heavily upon THE LIFE OF A STAR (no. 2617) in describing Morris's Lady Macbeth, a characterization softer and more emotional than prior interpretations.

2611   Morris, Clara. "A Damp Christmas." THEATRE (N. Y.) 2 (December 1902): 17-18. Illus.

A brief account of having been stranded on a train for the holiday.

2612   _____ . "The Drama as an Educator." THEATRE (N. Y.) 4 (August 1904): 206. Illus.

An idealistic essay about the theatre's function in society.

2613 _____. "A Dressing Room Reception." BURR McINTOSH MONTHLY 11 (October 1906): n.p. Illus.

> A seven-page description of Morris's work in L'ARTICLE 47, as played with Modjeska and Wilson Barrett in the audience, with an account of their backstage meeting after the performance.

2614 _____. "The Dressing-Room Reception, Where I First Met Ellen Terry and Mrs. John Drew." McCLURE'S 22 (December 1903): 204-11. Illus.

> A short article, recounting Morris's backstage meeting with the two stars.

2615 _____. "Has the Drama Degenerated?" THEATRE (N.Y.) 3 (December 1903): 313-16. Illus.

> Morris builds a somewhat flimsy case for the theatre of the time.

2616 _____. "Is Stage Emotion Real or Simulated?" THEATRE (N.Y.) 4 (December 1904): 303-4.

> Morris examines both sides of the question, quoting Diderot, but suggesting her emotion while playing was real.

2617 _____. THE LIFE OF A STAR. New York: McClure, Phillips, and Co., 1906. vii, 363 p.

> Rambling reminiscences of Morris's career, including a chapter (21) on Dion Boucicault. Evocative rather than descriptive of the actress's era.

2618 _____. LIFE ON THE STAGE: MY PERSONAL EXPERIENCES AND RECOLLECTIONS. New York: McClure, Phillips, and Co., 1901. 399 p. Frontispiece.

> A rambling but detailed account of the actress's career with anecdotal material about John Wilkes Booth, Edwin Booth, E.L. Davenport, Edwin Adams, Lawrence Barrett, and John E. Owens. See no. 2622.

2619 _____. "My Best Remembered Christmas." SUBURBAN LIFE 7 (December 1908): 271-72. Illus.

> The actress recalls at age seven explaining Santa Claus to an eighty-two year old woman who had never heard of him.

2620 _____ . "My Debut in JANE SHORE." BURR McINTOSH MONTHLY 10 (April 1906): 36-39.

> Morris describes preparing her costume for the title role and a subsequent on-stage battle with a flea.

2621 _____ . A PASTEBOARD CROWN; A STORY OF THE NEW YORK STAGE. New York: Charles Scribner's Sons, 1904. 370 p.

> An undistinguished novel by the actress, set in a theatrical milieu.

2622 _____ . "Recollections of the Stage and its People." McCLURES. "My First Appearance in New York," 16 (January 1901): 201-14; "Some Recollections of John Wilkes Booth," (February 1901): 299-304; "Mr. and Mrs. Charles Kean," 17 (May 1901): 53-59; "Recollections of the Comedian John E. Owens," (June 1901): 149-52; "Recollections of E. L. Davenport," (July 1901): 256-61; "The Wild Horse of Tartary," (August 1901): 324-27; "Recollections of Lawrence Barrett," (September 1901): 443-49; "Staging 'Miss Milton,'" (October 1901): 529-33. Illus.

> A serialization of LIFE ON THE STAGE (no. 2618) with additional illustrations.

2623 _____ . STAGE CONFIDENCES: TALKS ABOUT PLAYERS AND PLAY ACTING. Boston: Lothrop Publishing Co., 1902. 316 p. Illus.

> Morris has very little to say about anyone except herself in various roles. Profusely illustrated.

2624 _____ . "Strapped." BURR McINTOSH MONTHLY 10 (July 1906); 11 (August 1906): n.p.

> A short essay in two parts, describing Morris's first trip abroad, in the company of Mr. and Mrs. James Lewis and E. A. Sothern.

2625 _____ . "Two Famous Actresses." BURR McINTOSH MONTHLY. "Jane Hading," 8 (October 1905): 39-42; "Fanny Janauschek," 8 (November 1905): 40-45. Illus.

> In the first essay, Morris describes a backstage visit by Hading, a French actress, and their difficulty with the language barrier; in the second she recalls seeing Janauschek in an inferior script, meeting her backstage, and discussing Janauschek's career.

2626 _____ . "Two Great Othellos." MUNSEY'S 42 (November 1909): 271-78. Illus.

> The actress compares Edwin Booth and Salvini in the role,

considering Booth the more refined, Salvini the more powerful.

2627 _____. "An Unwelcome Hit." GREEN BOOK ALBUM 1 (January 1909): 160-65.

An undistinguished short story on the pitfalls of theatrical management.

2628 _____. "When We Stage Folk Grow Old." DELINEATOR 80 (September 1912): 134.

Very brief remarks on the fleeting qualities of fame.

2629 _____. "A Word of Warning to Young Actresses." CENTURY 60 (May 1900): 41-46. Illus.

Morris describes some of the pitfalls of work in the commercial theatre.

2630 Ogden, Vivia. "Childish Recollections of Clara Morris." THEATRE (N.Y.) 2 (June 1902): 14-20. Illus.

Recollections of Morris's early career by an intimate.

2631 Wilson, Garff B. "Queen of Spasms: The Acting of Clara Morris." SPEECH MONOGRAPHS 22 (November 1955): 235-42.

While Wilson does not consider Morris a great actress, he analyzes her work with compassion and precision. A valuable essay.

See also nos. 58, 112, 130, 165, 213, 247, 256, 277, 279, 288, 290, 293, 302, 336, 340-41, 356, 367, 383, 387, 398, 405, 407, 413, 449, 471, 473, 476, 492, 588, 596, 674, 2585, and 2599-2600.

MORRIS, OWEN (1759-90) AND MRS. (ELIZABETH) (1753-1826). See nos. 225 and 230.

MOSTEL, ZERO

(1915-77)

2632   Butterfield, Roger.   "Zero Mostel."   LIFE, 18 January 1943, pp. 61-64, 67. Illus.

> A substantial and useful essay outlining the early part of Mostel's career.

2633   "Hail of Conquering Hero."   NEWSWEEK 64 (19 October 1964): 94-96, 98. Illus.

> A biographical and critical sketch of Mostel, reviewing most of his major roles in New York to that time.

2634   Kerr, Walter. JOURNEY TO THE CENTER OF THE THEATRE.   New York: Alfred A. Knopf, 1979. 320 p. Index.

> Pages 235-37 offer an assessment of Mostel as a performer, specifically his work in FIDDLER ON THE ROOF.

2635   Mendoza, George. SESAME STREET BOOK OF OPPOSITES.   New York: Platt and Munk, 1974. n.p. Illus.

> A collection of photographs of Mostel portraying opposites (light-heavy, up-down, etc.), designed for children.

2636   Mostel, Kate, and Gilford, Madeline, with Jack Gilford and Zero Mostel. 170 YEARS OF SHOW BUSINESS. New York: Random House, 1978. xi, 175 p. Illus.

> Anecdotal reminiscences, seemingly somewhat romanticized, but with considerable charm and substance.

2637   Mostel, Zero. "Opening Nights." THEATRE ARTS 45 (March 1961): 57-61. Illus.

> A collection of photographs of Mostel protraying various theatrical workers on opening nights. No text.

2638   _____ . ZERO. New York: Horizon Press, 1965. Unpaged.

> A loosely conducted interview prefaces a portfolio of
> photographs of Mostel. Minimally informative.

2639   Mostel, Zero, with Israel Shenker. ZERO MOSTEL'S BOOK OF VIL-
LAINS. Illus. by Alex Gotfryd. Garden City, N.Y.: Doubleday and
Co., 1976. [94 p.]

> Forty-three portraits of Mostel as various historical villains,
> such as Benedict Arnold, Attila the Hun, Lady Macbeth,
> and the Loch Ness monster.

2640   Prince, Hal. CONTRADICTIONS: NOTES ON 26 YEARS IN THE
THEATRE. New York: Dodd, Mead and Co., 1974. x, 231 p.
Index, illus.

> Prince recalls Mostel's work in several productions of his.
> Anecdotal.

See also nos. 5, 296, 358, 369, 413, and 589.

MOWATT, ANNA CORA
(1819-70)

2641 Barnes, Eric Wollencott. THE LADY OF FASHION: THE LIFE AND THE THEATRE OF ANNA CORA MOWATT. New York: Charles Scribner's Sons, 1954. xi, 308 p. Illus., bibliog.

A scholarly and well-documented treatment of Mowatt, relying heavily on primary materials; indispensable for any study of Mowatt.

2642 [Bernard, Bayle.] "Mrs. Mowatt." TALLIS'S DRAMATIC MAGAZINE, June 1851, pp. 9-11. Illus.

A biographical-critical assessment of Mowatt, positive in nature.

2643 Butler, Mildred Allen. ACTRESS IN SPITE OF HERSELF: THE LIFE OF ANNA CORA MOWATT. New York: Funk and Wagnalls Co., 1966. 188 p.

An undocumented and speculative account of Mowatt's life and career, relying heavily upon Barnes's LADY OF FASHION (no. 2641). Written in the style of a novel, requiring corroboration.

2644 Harland, Marion. MARION HARLAND'S AUTOBIOGRAPHY: THE STORY OF A LONG LIFE. New York and London: Harper and Brothers, 1910. 498 p.

Chapter 29 contains a brief account of the author's meeting with and impressions of Mowatt.

2645 _____. "Personal Recollections of a Christian Actress." OUR CONTINENT 1 (15 March 1882): 73-74.

Harland was a friend and neighbor of Mowatt's at the time of her second marriage; she attests to the actress's Christian virtues in adulatory terms.

2646   Howitt, Mary. "Memoir of Anna Cora Mowatt." HOWITT'S JOURNAL, 4 March 1848, pp. 146-49; 11 March 1848, pp. 167-70; 18 March 1848, pp. 181-5.

        A biographical sketch, adulatory in tone, including fairly detailed observations of Mowatt's acting.

2647   Kellock, Harold. "The Simpering 'Forties.'" FREEMAN MAGAZINE 8 20 February 1924): 567-68.

        In reviewing the Provincetown Players' production of FASHION, Kellock describes the circumstances under which Mowatt wrote the script.

2648   Moses, Montrose J. "Early American Dramatists." THEATRE (N. Y.) 25 (March 1917): 142, 188. Illus.

        The fourth in a series of such articles, Moses dealing with FASHION in this essay.

2649   Mowatt, Anna Cora. AUTOBIOGRAPHY OF AN ACTRESS: OR, EIGHT YEARS ON THE STAGE. Boston: Ticknor, Reed, and Fields, 1853. 488 p. Frontispiece.

        A lengthy and detailed work, written shortly before the actress's retirement, indispensable for Mowatt studies. Includes some discussion of her leading man, E. L. Davenport.

2650   _____. "Chapters from Some Unwritten Memoirs." MacMILLAN'S MAGAZINE. "My Witches' Cauldron," 66 (May 1892): 17-22; "My Witches' Cauldron," (August 1892): 265-70; (no title), (September 1892): 344-49; "Mrs. Kemble," 68 (May 1893): 190-96; "At Mennecy," 69 (April 1894): 443-50; "In Italy," 70 (October 1894): 429-34.

        Rambling and disconnected reminiscences, the section on Mrs. Kemble being most useful to students of acting. Various Roman numerals are assigned to the separate articles, but no continuity is evident.

2651   _____. MIMIC LIFE; OR, BEFORE AND BEHIND THE CURTAIN. A SERIES OF NARRATIVES. Boston: Ticknor and Fields, 1856. xiv, 408 p.

        A unique and useful volume, seemingly slightly idealized, of reminiscences, offering insights into Mowatt's perceptions of theatrical conditions at the time.

2652   Poe, Edgar Allan. THE COMPLETE WORKS OF EDGAR ALLAN POE. Edited by James A. Harrison. 17 vols. New York: Thomas Y. Crowell, 1902.

Poe wrote a brief essay assessing Mowatt, which is here reprinted from GODEY'S LADY'S BOOK, June 1846.

2653 Wheeler, William O. THE OGDEN FAMILY IN AMERICA. Philadelphia: Printed for private circulation by J. B. Lippincott Co., 1907. 472 p. Index, illus. 1907.

A genealogical study of some bulk, including brief account of Mowatt on pages 156-57.

See also nos. 17, 101, 146, 210-13, 222, 227, 337, 341, 383, 385, 400-401, 413, 2348, and 3168.

MUNI, PAUL
(1895-1967)

2654 Beatty, Jerome. "The Man Who Is Always Somebody Else." AMERICAN MAGAZINE 125 (February 1938): 42-43, 86-88. Illus.

> A description of Muni's film career, plus some of his personal characteristics.

2655 Best, Katherine. "Danger: Man at Work." STAGE 16 (1 April 1939): 28-31. Illus.

> Best describes Muni's role preparation as conscientious, relentless, and exasperating.

2656 Cooley, Donald G. "They Tried to Make a Chaney out of Muni." MOVIE CLASSIC 8 (April 1935): 30, 64. Illus.

> Cooley posits that Hollywood didn't take advantage of Muni's considerable acting talents.

2657 Druxman, Michael B. PAUL MUNI: HIS LIFE AND HIS FILMS. South Brunswick and New York: A.S. Barnes and Co.; London: Thomas Yoseloff, 1974. 227 p. Illus.

> Focused upon Muni's film career, but includes a sketchy treatment of his work on stage.

2658 Eustis, Morton. "Paul Muni." THEATRE ARTS 24 (March 1940): 194-205. Illus.

> In an interview made during Muni's appearance in KEY LARGO, he purports to know nothing of acting technique, either for film or stage.

2659 Hall, Gladys. "Farewell for Muni?" MOTION PICTURE MAGAZINE 54 (September 1937): 31, 86, 88.

> Speculation about rumors of Muni's retirement from the screen.

2660   Lang, Harry. "Great Actor--Great Hermit." MOVIE CLASSIC 9
(February 1936): 48, 66.

Lang proposes that Muni literally became the characters
he played.

2661   Lawrence, Jerome. ACTOR: THE LIFE AND TIMES OF PAUL MUNI.
New York: G. P. Putnam's Sons, 1974. 370 p. Index, illus.

A seemingly well-researched, if relatively undocumented,
biography of considerable substance; the outstanding work
to date on this performer.

2662   Muni, Paul, as told to Gladys Hall. "Hollywood is the World's Melting
Pot." MOVIE CLASSIC 11 (November 1936): 28-29, 84. Illus.

Muni notes with pleasure that he has performed with actors
of almost every nationality and has considered the experience highly educational.

2663   Parish, James Robert. THE TOUGH GUYS. New Rochelle, N.Y.:
Arlington, 1976. 610 p. Index, illus.

Includes a chapter devoted to Muni, including a filmog-
raphy.

2664   Service, Faith. "Paul Muni Interviews Himself." MOTION PICTURE
MAGAZINE 46 (December 1933): 54, 88-90. Illus.

A more substantial interview than usual in the film fan
magazine, Muni managing to avoid the usual cliches.

2665   Zeitlin, Ida. "The Man Who Couldn't Be Typed." MOTION PICTURE
MAGAZINE 52 (August 1936): 50-51, 89. Illus.

A description of how Muni's expertise with makeup served
him well in the early part of his career.

See also nos. 5, 298, 413, and 415.

MURDOCH, JAMES EDWARD

(1811-93)

2666　Murdoch, James Edward.　ANALYTIC ELOCUTION, CONTAINING
STUDIES, THEORETICAL AND PRACTICAL OF EXPRESSIVE SPEECH.
New York and Cincinnati:　Van Antwerp, Bragg and Co.; New York:
American Book Co., 1884.　500 p.　Index.

> A highly detailed and mechanical approach to expressive
> speaking, based in large part on the work of Benjamin
> Rush.　Contains numerous pieces of material for drill.

2667　_____.　"Introductory Observations."　ORTHOPHONY; OR THE
CULTIVATION OF THE VOICE, IN ELOCUTION: A MANUAL
OF ELEMENTARY EXERCISES, ADAPTED TO DR. RUSH'S "PHILOSOPHY
OF THE HUMAN VOICE," AND THE SYSTEM OF VOCAL CULTURE
INTRODUCED BY MR. JAMES MURDOCH, by William Russell, pp. 7-
10.　Boston:　Ticknor, Reed, and Fields, 1846.　Boston:　Flicknor and
Fields, 1868.　300 p.

> A manual of elocution, indicative of Murdoch's analytical
> approach to acting.　Very popular.

2668　_____.　PATRIOTISM IN POETRY AND PROSE: BEING SELECTED PAS-
SAGES FROM LECTURES AND PATRIOTIC READINGS BY JAMES E. MUR-
DOCH.　Philadelphia:　J.B. Lippincott and Co., 1864.　172 p.　Frontispiece.

> Murdoch gained a considerable reputation doing readings
> during the Civil War, some of which are published in this
> volume, the proceeds from which were to be given to military
> relief committees.

2669　_____.　A PLEA FOR SPOKEN LANGUAGE.　AN ESSAY UPON COMPAR-
ATIVE ELOCUTION, CONDENSED FROM LECTURES DELIVERED THROUGH-
OUT THE UNITED STATES.　Cincinnati and New York:　Van Antwerp, Bragg
and Co., 1883.　320 p.

> Drawing upon Benjamin Rush's work, Murdoch places elocution
> in historical context, then presents his systematic approach to
> the subject.

2670   _____. THE STAGE OR RECOLLECTIONS OF ACTORS AND ACTING FROM AN EXPERIENCE OF FIFTY YEARS: A SERIES OF DRAMATIC SKETCHES. Philadelphia: J.M. Stoddart and Co., 1880. Reprint. New York and London: Benjamin Blom, 1969. 504 p. Index, illus.

> Includes a biographical sketch of the author, but the bulk of the volume consists of Murdoch's observations on acting in general and anecdotes about specific performers such as Charlotte Cushman, Edwin Forrest, the elder Booth, Edwin Booth, the Wallacks, and William Wood.

2671   White, Roberta Fluitt. "A Biographical Sketch of James Edward Murdoch." SOUTHERN SPEECH JOURNAL 9 (March 1944): 95-101.

> A brief overview, based on secondary sources.

See also nos. 130, 203, 210, 222, 228, 245, 356, 383, 399, 413, 489, 516, 2235-36, 2782, and 3168.

NAZIMOVA, ALLA

(1879-1945)

2672   Ashby, Clifford. "Alla Nazimova and the Advent of the New Acting in America." QUARTERLY JOURNAL OF SPEECH 45 (April 1954): 182-88.

A well-documented capsulation of Nazimova's life and career.

2673   Bamberger, Theron. "Nazimova Goes A-Trouping." DELINEATOR 128 (April 1936): 64-65.

A description of the forty-eight-city tour of GHOSTS, following the successful run in New York.

2674   Barnes, Djuna. "Alla Nazimova, One of the Greatest of Living Actresses, Talks of Her Art." THEATRE GUILD MAGAZINE 7 (June 1930): 32-34, 61. Illus.

A short sketch of the actress's rise to fame with a few biographical observations.

2675   Bell, Archie. "Wanted: A Successful Play--Nazimova." GREEN BOOK ALBUM 7 (March 1912): 574-78.

After her auspicious beginnings in this country, Nazimova could not find a suitable vehicle. Bell describes her search.

2676   Brush, Katherine. "Nazimova--Player of Roles." NATIONAL MAGAZINE 52 (July 1923): 58, 89. Illus.

A biographical sketch describing the actress as a feminist of the time.

2677   Dale, Alan. [Pseud.] "Nazimova and Some Others." COSMOPOLITAN 42 (April 1907): 674-76.

Dale praises Nazimova for rousing New York theatre-goers

from their complacency in accepting anything offered to them, citing her work in HEDDA GABBLER and A DOLL'S HOUSE.

2678 _____. "Nazimova the Inscrutable." GREEN BOOK MAGAZINE 15 (February 1916): 303-8. Illus.

In a somewhat condenscending interview, Dale describes the actress as enigmatic.

2679 Davies, Acton. "Mme. Alla Nazimova." COSMOPOLITAN 53 (November 1912): 835-37. Illus.

Davies interviewed the actress while she was preparing the role of Mrs. Chepstow in BELLA DONNA. The actress also describes her difficulties in learning the English language.

2680 DeFoe, Louis V. "Nazimova at Last Meets Her Big Promise." GREEN BOOK MAGAZINE 13 (May 1915): 905-14. Illus.

An account of Nazimova's success in Marion Craig Wentworth's thirty-five minute vaudeville sketch, WAR BRIDES.

2681 Erskine, Lucile. "Nazimova--The Unknowable." THEATRE (N.Y.) 16 (December 1912): 186-88, 190, vi.

Erskine contributes to Nazimova's reputation as mysterious and enigmatic. Nazimova is quoted as working on an autobiography, which seems never to have appeared.

2682 Forman, Henry James. "Nazimova." HARPER'S WEEKLY 51 (20 April 1907): 576-77. Illus.

A brief description of the actress shortly after she had arrived in New York.

2683 Fyles, Vanderheyden. "In English--More or Less." THEATRE (N.Y.) 21 (April 1915): 193-95, 201. Illus.

Fyles describes the circumstances under which Nazimova learned English and came to the United States.

2684 Graham, Jean. "A Russian Actress." CANADIAN MAGAZINE 32 (March 1909): 476.

A very brief and complimentary sketch of Nazimova, praising her work in HEDDA GABBLER.

2685 Gray, Frances. "Nazimova--and Her Language of the Soul." MOTION PICTURE MAGAZINE 20 (October 1920): 30-31, 107. Illus.

Publicity puffery, describing the actress's exotic qualities.

2686　Johnson, Owen. "Mme. Alla Nazimova." CENTURY 74 (June 1907): 219-27. Illus.

A substantial biographical sketch of Nazimova with critical descriptions of the actress in several roles. Includes a color plate of her as Hedda Gabbler.

2687　Kirkland, Alexander. "The Woman from Yalta." THEATRE ARTS 33 (December 1949): 28-29, 48, 94-95. Illus.

A biographical sketch, impressionistic rather than factual, but nevertheless strongly evocative of the actress.

2688　"Madame Nazimova's American Doll House." THEATRE (N. Y.) 10 (May 1910): 168-71. Illus.

An interview focused upon a description of Nazimova's recently completed home.

2689　Mullett, Mary B. "How a Dull, Fat Little Girl Became a Great Actress." AMERICAN MAGAZINE 93 (April 1922): 18-19, 111-12, 114. Illus.

The actress is quoted as describing an unhappy childhood and her emergence from it while at drama school.

2690　Naylor, Hazel Simpson. "My Devlish Ambition." MOTION PICTURE MAGAZINE 15 (July 1918): 54-57, 115. Illus.

Nazimova recalls her driving ambition to achieve stardom early in her career.

2691　Nazimova, Alla. "I Come Full Circle." THEATRE (N.Y.) 49 (April 1929): 18, 64, 74. Illus.

The actress describes her apprenticeship in Russia, then her affiliation with Eva Le Gallienne at the Civic Repertory Theatre in New York.

2692　_____. "A Shattered Illusion." THEATRE (N. Y.) 28 (November 1918): 270. Illus.

Part of a series, "The Most Striking Episode in My Life." Nazimova describes an incident backstage in Moscow.

2693　"Nazimova--An Apostle of the Drama." THEATRE (N. Y.) 25 (March 1917): 144.

The actress is interviewed briefly after a performance of 'CEPTION SHOALS.

2694   Peacock, Anne. "Mme. Nazimova to Enact Her Ideal Woman."
       THEATRE (N. Y.) 7 (September 1907): 231-32.

       Nazimova describes her plans for a production of THE
       MASTER BUILDER.

2695   Roberts, Katherine. "Artists Don't Need Ruffles." COLLIER'S 90
       (10 December 1932): 9, 45. Illus.

       Describing her as the "Russian Duse," Roberts surveys
       Nazimova's career, suggesting that her indifference to
       worldly possessions and her joy in creativity contributed
       to her twenty-five year success in America.

2696   West, Magda Frances. "Nazimova's Views on Love, Husbands and
       Wicked Women." GREEN BOOK MAGAZINE 9 (March 1913): 414-
       18. Illus.

       Nazimova is quoted as hoping she would not be associated
       in the public's mind with her more lurid roles, such as
       Bella Donna.

2697   X. "Russian Artist Becomes an American Star." THEATRE (N. Y.) 7
       (January 1907): 12-13, vii. Illus.

       Nazimova is quoted on her techniques of role preparation.

See also nos. 9, 13, 150-51, 217, 247, 270, 276, 291, 295-96, 316, 358,
413, 441, 495, 506, 508-9, 560, 578-79, and 2567.

NETHERSOLE, OLGA

(1863-1951)

2698   Nethersole, Olga. "Sex Dramas To-Day and Yesterday." GREEN BOOK MAGAZINE 10 (January 1914): 29-35. Illus.

>The actress, who was once arrested for enacting Sapho, muses on the shifting morality of the U.S. drama during her career.

See also nos. 58, 381, and 413.

OLCOTT, CHAUNCEY
(1860-1932)

2699 Olcott, Chauncey. "Danger Ahead--In Killarney." THEATRE (N.Y.) 29 (February 1919): 98. Illus.

> Part of a series, "The Most Striking Episode in My Life." Olcott recalls a terror-filled ride in an Irish "jaunting car."

2700 _____. "Personal Reminiscences." THEATRE (N.Y.) 25 (February 1917): 76-78, 124. Illus.

> Olcott describes his early career and entry into the theatre.

See also nos. 28, 247, 270, 276, 279, 303, and 3094.

O'NEIL, NANCE
(1874-1931)

2701   Goddard, Henry P. "Some Players I Have Known. " THEATRE (N. Y.)
8 (September 1908): 237-38. Illus.

> Brief remarks on Modjeska, O'Neil, and Viola Allen.

2702   O'Neil, Nance. "The Lure of the Tropics. " GREEN BOOK ALBUM
3 (June 1910): 1212-15.

> Reminiscences of a vacation in Hawaii.

2703   _____. "The Theatre Advancing. " DRAMA 11 (December 1920): 72-
74. Illus.

> Idealistic observations of no great distinction.

2704   _____. "The Unloved Woman on the Stage. " THEATRE (N. Y.) 31
(June 1920): 516.

> O'Neil describes her experiences while playing unsympa-
thetic roles.

2705   Patterson, Ada. "Nance O'Neil and the Mantle of Cushman. " THEATRE
(N. Y.) 5 (March 1905): 62-64. Illus.

> McKee Rankin, O'Neil's manager, dominates the interview
and the interviewer with his views.

2706   Shea, Maureen A. "Nance O'Neil: Power and Passion on the 'Modern'
American Stage. " THEATRE STUDIES 21 (1974-75): 61-68. Illus.

> A brief overview of O'Neil's career, in which Shea pro-
poses the actress as a carryover from the earlier romantic
school of acting. Heavily documented from newspaper
reviews.

See also nos. 276, 278, 413, 938, and 990.

O'NEILL, JAMES
(1847-1920)

2707 Bowen, Croswell, with the assistance of Shane O'Neill. THE CURSE OF THE MISBEGOTTEN: A TALE OF THE HOUSE OF O'NEILL. New York, Toronto, and London: McGraw-Hill, 1959. xviii, 372 p. Index.

> An eminently readable volume, focused on Eugene O'Neill, but containing much material about James O'Neill.

2708 Carpenter, Frederic I. EUGENE O'NEILL. New York: Twayne Publishers, 1964. Rev. ed., 1979. 189 p. Index, frontispiece, bibliog.

> Pages 19-26 deal with James O'Neill, drawing heavily upon LONG DAY'S JOURNEY INTO NIGHT.

2709 Clark, Barrett H. EUGENE O'NEILL, THE MAN AND HIS PLAYS. New York: Dover Publications, 1929. vi, 177 p. Index, illus., bibliog.

> A slight volume, the early sections dealing with the playwright's father in passing.

2710 Gelb, Arthur, and Gelb, Barbara. O'NEILL. New York: Harper and Brothers, 1962. New York: Harper and Row, 1973. xx, 964 p. Index, illus., bibliog.

> The most substantial of the O'Neill biographies, massive and well-researched and documented, containing much material on James O'Neill. Valuable.

2711 O'Neill, James. "Personal Reminiscences." THEATRE (N. Y.) 26 (December 1917): 338, 340, 388. Illus.

> Requires corroboration, but contains many anecdotes about Joseph Jefferson III.

2712 Patterson, Ada. "James O'Neill--The Actor and the Man." THEATRE (N. Y.) 8 (April 1908): 101-2, 104, ix. Illus.

O'Neill surveys his career after having performed in THE
COUNT OF MONTE CRISTO some 5,100 times.

2713   Sheaffer, Louis. O'NEILL: SON AND PLAYWRIGHT. Boston: Little,
Brown and Co., 1968, 1973. xviii, 728 p. Index, illus.

A major O'Neill biography with substantial information
about the playwright's father and his influence upon his
son's drama.

See also nos. 28, 112, 154, 165, 200, 270, 279, 300, 373, 379-80, 413,
548, 561-62, and 597.

OWENS, JOHN EDMOND

(1823-86)

2714   Owens, Mrs. Mary C. Stevens.   MEMORIES OF THE PROFESSIONAL
AND SOCIAL LIFE OF JOHN E. OWENS, BY HIS WIFE.   Baltimore:
John Murphy and Co., 1892.   vi, 292 p.   Illus.

> A detailed if undocumented account of Owen's career,
> obviously prejudicial, with numerous references to other
> players of the time.   The only substantial work on the
> subject.

See also nos. 129, 196, 302, 375, 383, 405, 431, 472, 489, 558, 2235-36,
2618, and 2622.

PAYNE, JOHN HOWARD
(1791-1852)

2715 Baillou, Clemens de, ed. JOHN HOWARD PAYNE TO HIS COUNTRY-MEN. Athens: University of Georgia Press, 1961. v, 61 p.

> Introduction by Baillou. Reprinting of two documents by Payne after 1828 when gold was discovered in Georgia in land occupied by the Cherokees. No theatrical references.

2716 Bass, Althea. "From the Notebooks of John Howard Payne." FRONTIER AND MIDLAND 14 (January 1934): 139-46.

> Drawing upon Payne's notebooks, Bass recounts his attempt to publish the journal JAM JEHAN NIMA and his visits to Cherokee tribes.

2717 Blakely, Sidney H. "John Howard Payne's THESPIAN MIRROR, New York's First Theatrical Magazine." STUDIES IN PHILOLOGY 46 (October 1949): 577-602.

> A substantial and well-documented account of the attitude, techniques, and contents of the MIRROR.

2718 Brainard, Charles Henry. JOHN HOWARD PAYNE; A BIOGRAPHICAL SKETCH OF THE AUTHOR OF "HOME, SWEET HOME," WITH A NARRATIVE OF THE REMOVAL OF HIS REMAINS FROM TUNIS TO WASHINGTON. Boston: Cupples, Upham and Co.; Washington, D.C.: George A. Coolidge, 1885. 144 p. Illus.

> A detailed, albeit undocumented life of Payne, focused upon his death, funeral, and subsequent events. Considerable use of manuscript material.

2719 [Carpenter, S.C.] "Master Payne's Performances." MIRROR OF TASTE AND DRAMATIC CENSOR 1 (February-March 1810): 141-57, 220-23, 241.

A collective critique, offering a contemporary's analysis of Payne in nine roles in repertory.

2720 Chiles, Rosa Pendleton. "John Howard Payne, American Poet, Actor, Playwright, Consul and the Author of 'HOME, SWEET HOME.'" COLUMBIA HISTORICAL RECORDS 31-32 (1930): 209-97. Also published as a separate volume, Washington, D.C.: Press of W.F. Roberts, 1930. 89 p.

A concise but useful treatment of Payne's life.

2721 Duffee, Francis Harold. "Reminiscences of John Howard Payne." BOOGHER'S REPOSITORY 1 (April 1883): 93-100.

An adulatory description of Payne, recalling the author's first meeting with him, being introduced by James Rees (Colley Cibber.)

2722 [Fairfield, Sumner Lincoln.] "The Captivity of John Howard Payne." NORTH AMERICAN QUARTERLY MAGAZINE 7 (January 1836): 107-24.

Payne was held by the Georgia Guard on charges of having stimulated rebellion among the Indians; the author is filled with righteous indignation and calls for revenge.

2723 _____. "Memoirs of John Howard Payne." NORTH AMERICAN QUARTERLY MAGAZINE 2 (May 1833): 25-48.

Fairfield condensed Theodore S. Fay's biography of Payne, adding only a brief introduction and conclusion.

2724 _____. "The Payne Benefit." NORTH AMERICAN QUARTERLY MAGAZINE 1 (November 1832): 128.

A brief account of a production of BRUTUS given on 29 November 1832 to celebrate Payne's return from abroad.

2725 Fay, Theodore S. SKETCH OF THE LIFE OF JOHN HOWARD PAYNE, AS PUBLISHED IN THE BOSTON EVENING GAZETTE, COMPRESSED, (WITH ADDITIONS BRINGING IT FORWARD TO A LATER PERIOD). BY ONE OF THE EDITORS OF THE NEW YORK MIRROR: NOW FIRST PRINTED IN A SEPARATE FORM, WITH AN APPENDIX, CONTAINING SELECTIONS OF POETRY AND FURTHER ILLUSTRATION. Boston: W.W. Clapp, 1833. 27 p.

An adulatory tribute of little consequence; apparently Clapp's father was a close friend of Payne.

2726 Foreman, Grant. "John Howard Payne and the Cherokees." AMERICAN HISTORICAL REVIEW 37 (July 1932): 723-30.

A brief account of Payne's interest in the Cherokees with a letter describing his visit to John Ross, a Cherokee chief.

2727　Gilbert, Vedder Morris. "John Howard Payne, The Actor." UNION ALUMNI MONTHLY 28 (May 1939): 198-202. Illus.

An undocumented essay on Payne's early career, emphasizing his performances as Hamlet and young Norval.

2728　_____. "The Stage Career of John Howard Payne, Author of 'HOME, SWEET HOME.'" WEST OHIO QUARTERLY 23 (1950-51): 59-74. Bibliog.

A brief overview superseded by later works, but including a useful bibliography.

2729　Hanson, Willis T. THE EARLY LIFE OF JOHN HOWARD PAYNE WITH CONTEMPORARY LETTERS HERETOFORE UNPUBLISHED. Boston: University Press, 1913. 226 p. Illus., bibliog. Reprint. New York: Benjamin Blom, 1971.

Hanson traces Payne's life to 1813 when he left the United States. This volume contains reprints of nos. 1, 13, and 14 of Payne's journal, THE THESPIAN MIRROR.

2730　Harrison, Gabriel. JOHN HOWARD PAYNE, DRAMATIST, POET, ACTOR, AND AUTHOR OF "HOME SWEET HOME!" HIS LIFE AND WRITINGS. Philadelphia: Lippincott, 1885. Reprint. New York: Benjamin Blom, 1969. 396 p. Index, illus.

Harrison's introduction lists his primary sources, though not as a formal bibliography. He presents Payne's life and career in some depth, with chapter 2 treating Payne as an actor. Harrison added considerable material to this revision of his 1875 biography of Payne.

2731　_____. THE LIFE AND WRITINGS OF JOHN HOWARD PAYNE, THE AUTHOR OF "HOME, SWEET HOME;" THE TRAGEDY OF BRUTUS; AND OTHER DRAMATIC WORKS. Limited ed. (250 copies and 15 large paper copies.) Albany: Munsell, 1875. ix, 410 p.

A general biography evoking much of the theatre's flavor at the time. See no. 2730 for an expanded version.

2732　Hughes, Rupert. "Man Without a Home." THIS WEEK MAGAZINE, 5 May, pp. 3-4, 16; 12 May 1935, pp. 10, 12; 19 May 1935, pp. 6-7; 26 May 1935, pp. 13, 31; 2 June 1935, pp. 12, 24; 9 June 1935, pp. 14, 31. Illus.

An apparently fictionalized treatment of Payne's love

affair with Mary Godwin, with considerable description
of Payne's activities in England.

2733   Hutton, Laurence. "John Howard Payne, the Actor." MAGAZINE OF
AMERICAN HISTORY 9 (May 1883): 335-39. Illus.

A brief and undocumented sketch of Payne, including a
list of his scripts.

2734   Leary, Lewis, and Turner, Arlin. "John Howard Payne in New Orleans."
LOUISIANA HISTORICAL QUARTERLY 31 (January 1948): 110-22.

This monograph describes Payne's return to America in
1832 after almost twenty years abroad, his proposed
magazine, JAM JEHAN NIMA, and his reception in
New Orleans in 1835, drawing heavily upon newspaper
accounts.

2735   Luquer, Thatcher T. Payne. "Correspondence of Washington Irving and
John Howard Payne." SCRIBNER'S 48 (October 1910): 461-82;
(November 1910): 597-616. Illus.

Luquer was Payne's grandnephew. A well-illustrated and
useful study, recommended for any study of Payne.

2736   _____. "Extracts from the Diary of John Howard Payne." SCRIBNER'S
69 (January 1921): 66-81; (February 1921): 237-46. Illus.

Primarily concerned with Payne's writing a script while
in debtor's prison.

2737   _____. "When Payne Wrote HOME, SWEET HOME, Letters from Paris,
1822-1823." SCRIBNER'S 58 (December 1915): 742-54. Illus.

Concerned primarily with the production of CLARI.

2738   MEMOIRS OF JOHN HOWARD PAYNE, THE AMERICAN ROSCIUS:
WITH CRITICISMS ON HIS ACTING, IN THE VARIOUS THEATRES OF
AMERICA, ENGLAND, AND IRELAND. COMPILED FROM AUTHENTIC
DOCUMENTS. London: John Miller, 1815. 131 p.

An edited compilation drawn from critical and descriptive
sources, rather than an actual memoir. A valuable source
of information.

2739   Overmeyer, Grace. AMERICA'S FIRST HAMLET. New York: New
York University Press, 1957. 431 p. Index, frontispiece, bibliog.

The most substantial modern work on Payne; exemplary research, extensive documentation, and clear writing offer

a valuable insight into the American, English, and continental theatre of the time.

2740 _____. "The Baltimore Mobs and John Howard Payne." MARYLAND HISTORICAL MAGAZINE 58 (March 1963): 54-61.

Originally written as a chapter of Overmeyer's AMERICA'S FIRST HAMLET, but omitted due to length. Describes Payne's activities during the season of 1812-13.

2741 Pennypacker, Morton. THE JOHN HOWARD PAYNE MEMORIAL "HOME, SWEET HOME" EAST HAMPTON, LONG ISLAND, NEW YORK. East Hampton, N.Y.: Board of Trustees, 1935. 32 p. Illus.

A pamphlet describing in a brief paragraph Payne's life and career, his ancestry, his home in East Hampton, and including a nine-page chronology of his life.

2742 Saxon, A.H. "John Howard Payne, Playwright with a System." THEATRE NOTEBOOK 24 (Winter 1969-70): 79-84.

Saxon proposes that Payne, like many other playwrights of the time, was something of a hack in his adaptations of others' works.

2743 Shelley, Mary Wollstonecraft. THE ROMANCE OF MARY W. SHELLEY, JOHN HOWARD PAYNE, AND WASHINGTON IRVING. Annotated by H.H. Harper. Boston: Bibliophile Society, 1907. 101 p. Illus.

A collection of correspondence suggesting the near marriage of Payne and Mrs. Shelley.

2744 Stearns, Bertha-Monica. "John Howard Payne as an Editor." AMERICAN LITERATURE 5 (November 1933): 215-28.

An assessment of Payne's various editorships for the THESPIAN MIRROR, the PASTIME, the OPERA GLASS, JAM JEHAN NIMA, and, briefly, the LADIES' COMPANION.

2745 Wegelin, Oscar. "The Writings of John Howard Payne." LITERARY COLLECTOR 9 (1905): 94-100.

A partial list of Payne material, including his serials, scripts, plays in manuscript, Payne biographies, and engraved portraits.

2746 Wood, Clarence Ashton. "Birthplace of John Howard Payne." LONG ISLAND FORUM, October 1948, pp. 183-85, 195-97. Illus.

The author proposes that Payne was not born at East

Hampton, Long Island, as thought, but in New York City at No. 4 Great Dock Street; he then cites various documents to support his case.

2747 Woolf, S.J. "The Romance of HOME, SWEET HOME and its Author." ETUDE 65 (September 1947): 484, 494, 540; (October 1947): 564. Illus.

Undocumented sketch of Payne as a musical composer.

See also nos. 101, 121, 161, 211, 214, 222, 227, 240, 341, 399, 457, and 2235-36.

PERKINS, OSGOOD

(1892-1937)

2748   Talmey, Allene. "This Amazing Fellow Perkins." STAGE 10 (October 1932): 22. Illus.

> A general assessment of Perkins as a specialist in "tough guy" roles.

2749   "The Tang of High Farce--Osgood Perkins in GOOD BYE AGAIN." STAGE 10 (June 1933): 34-35. Illus.

> Brief comments on Perkins's methods of preparing roles, heavily illustrated.

See also nos. 413 and 508.

PITOU, AUGUSTUS

(1843-1915)

2750 Pitou, Augustus. MASTERS OF THE SHOW AS SEEN IN RETROSPEC-
TION BY ONE WHO HAS BEEN ASSOCIATED WITH THE AMERICAN
STAGE FOR NEARLY FIFTY YEARS. New York: Neale Publishing Co.,
1914. 186 p. Illus.

> Anecdotal reminiscences about Edwin Booth and Edwin
> Forrest, with whom Pitou appeared, as well as Joseph
> Jefferson III, Lawrence Barrett, Mary Anderson, and
> Maggie Mitchell.

See also no. 112.

PLACIDE FAMILY
Placide, Alexandre (?-1812)
Placide, Henry (1799--1870)

2751   Moore, Lillian. THE DUPORT MYSTERY. New York: Dance Perspectives, 1960. 105 p. Illus.

> Chapter 8, "The Placide-Douvillier Duel," describes
> Alexandre Placide and his theatre. A note on page 60
> suggests that Eola Willis left to the Charleston Free
> Library an unfinished manuscript history of the Placides.

2752   Pelby, William. LETTERS ON THE TREMONT THEATRE, RESPECTFULLY ADDRESSED TO THE PRIMITIVE SUBSCRIBERS, ITS FRIENDS AND PATRONS, BY WILLIAM PELBY. Boston: Press of John H. Eastburn, 1830. 44 p.

> An early history of the Boston stage, containing several
> references to the Placides.

See also nos. 101, 146, 182, 188, 240, 244, 259, 261, 319, 341, 383, 401, 413, 2235-36, 2348, 3127, and 3168.

POE, ELIZABETH
(1787?-1811)

2753 Allen, Hervey. ISRAFEL: THE LIFE AND TIMES OF EDGAR ALLAN POE. 2 vols. New York: George H. Doran Co., 1927. Index, illus.

> The early sections of this substantial biography contain some material on Poe's mother.

2754 Fagin, N[athan]. Bryllion. THE HISTRIONIC MR. POE. Baltimore: Johns Hopkins Press; London: Oxford, 1949. xi, 275 p. Index, frontispiece, notes.

> Contains a number of passing references to Elizabeth Poe, but fewer than other biographies of the poet.

2755 Hubbell, Jay B. "Poe's Mother: With a Note on John Allen." WILLIAM AND MARY QUARTERLY 21 (July 1941): 250-54.

> A brief sketch of Elizabeth Poe, focused upon her early career with her mother after coming to the United States.

2756 Moreland, James. "The Theatre in Portland in the Eighteenth Century." NEW ENGLAND QUARTERLY 11 (June 1938): 331-42.

> Drawn mostly from newspaper accounts of the time, this article includes a few remarks about Elizabeth Arnold Poe.

2757 Quinn, Arthur Hobson. EDGAR ALLAN POE, A CRITICAL BIOGRAPHY. New York and London: D. Appleton-Century Co., 1941. 770 p. Index, illus., bibliog.

> Quinn, a major theatre scholar, describes Mrs. Poe in the text and appends "The Theatrical Career of Edgar Poe's Parents" (pp. 697-724), citing theatres, dates, scripts, and roles in the most substantial account available.

See also nos. 13, 188, 192, 240, and 259.

POTTER, CORA URQUHART

(1857-1936)

2758　Kaufman, Emma B. "Cora Urquhart Potter." COSMOPOLITAN 34 (December 1902): 185-90. Illus.

> An adulatory essay, extolling Potter's virtues as an actress and woman.

2759　Nirdlinger, Charles Frederic. MASQUES AND MUMMERS: ESSAYS ON THE THEATRE OF HERE AND NOW. New York: DeWitt Publishing House, 1899. 370 p.

> Includes a brief chapter, "The Influence of Mrs. Potter and Mr. Bellew."

2760　Potter, Cora Urquhart. "The Age of Innocence--and I." HEARST'S 94 (March 1933): 16-19, 146-53; (April 1933): 48-51, 110-14; (May 1933): 76-78, 81-82, 84, 86, 88. Illus.

> A serialized autobiography of the actress of substantial length. Well-illustrated and possibly intended for separate publication, but somewhat self-indulgent. Nevertheless, the most comprehensive single source on Potter.

See also nos. 279, 288, 413, and 2585.

POWER, TYRONE

(1869-1931)

2761   Arce, Hector. THE SECRET LIFE OF TYRONE POWER. New York: William Morrow and Co., 1979. 317 p. Illus., bibliog.

> A biography of the Hollywood star, somewhat sensational-ized, but containing in the early sections some material on the elder Power.

2762   Guiles, Fred Lawrence. TYRONE POWER: THE LAST IDOL. Garden City, N.Y.: Doubleday and Co., 1979. xvii, 371 p. Index, illus., bibliog.

> A biography of the film star, but including something of his family background and his father.

2763   Power, Tyrone. "The Actor as Gambler." GREEN BOOK ALBUM 2 (December 1909): 1214-18.

> Power decries the passing of the stock companies which he described as supplying a "home of sorts" for actors.

2764   Winter, William. LIFE OF TYRONE POWER. New York: Moffat, Yard, 1913. Reprint. New York: Benjamin Blom, 1969, 1972. 192 p. Illus.

> Written in Winter's somewhat florid style, the only sub-stantial treatment of Power, including a list of his reper-tory and a chronology of his life and career.

See also nos. 101, 296, 347, 413, 543, 600, and 1975.

RAMBEAU, MARJORIE

(1889-1970)

2765   Archbald, Anne. "Behind the Scenes with Miss Marjorie Rambeau."
THEATRE (N.Y.) 27 (February 1918): 108, 110. Illus.

      An article more concerned with clothing fashions than
with the theatre.

2766   Rambeau, Marjorie. "The Seamy Side of Life Won't Hurt You."
AMERICAN MAGAZINE 90 (July 1920): 37-38, 141-42, 145-46. Illus.

      Rambeau, who spent her childhood in Alaska, describes
various hardships and vicissitudes there before she went
into the theatre.

See also nos. 422 and 464.

RANKIN, ARTHUR McKEE
(1842-1914)

2767   Fyles, Vanderheyden. "An Apollo of Long Ago." GREEN BOOK MAGA-
ZINE 12 (July 1914): 39-42. Illus.

> Affectionate reminiscences of the actor by one who had
> seen him on several occasions.

See also nos. 352, 413, 558, and 2705.

RAYMOND, JOHN T.
(1836-87)

2768   Goddard, Henry P. "Some Players I Have Known." THEATRE (N. Y.)
7 (November 1907): 298, 300. Illus.

> Goddard reminisces about seeing Edwin Booth as Hamlet
> and Raymond as Col. Sellers.

See also nos. 176, 222, 328, 336, 339, 341, 387, 401, 405, 472, 475, and
558.

REED, FLORENCE
(1883-1967)

2769   "The Home of the Player." THEATRE (N.Y.) 33 (March 1921): 199. Illus.

> A five-photograph feature on Reed's apartment, stressing her propensity for Chinese decor.

2770   Mullett, Mary B. "Florence Reed Has Made Herself What She Preferred Not To Be." AMERICAN MAGAZINE 102 (October 1926): 18-19, 122, 125-26, 128.

> Mullett quotes Reed as wishing to be a comedienne, but allowing circumstances to lead her to emotional roles.

2771   Naylor, Hazel Simpson. "It's Great to Be a Star." MOTION PICTURE MAGAZINE 15 (February 1918): 29-33. Illus.

> Reed describes her reactions to stardom, claiming she prefers the stage to films, but prefers the higher salaries of the film industry.

2772   Reed, Florence. "The Sex Appeal." THEATRE (N.Y.) 27 (February 1918): 94. Illus.

> Reed, while admitting sex appeal exists in the theatre, advises restraint in playing "disreputable" roles.

2773   _____. "What Makes a Play 'Click' or 'Flop'?" THEATRE (N.Y.) 46 (August 1927): 32, 52. Illus.

> The actress, also a prolific playwright, suggests directing as a pivotal element in production, then comments on the currently fashionable scripts.

2774   _____. "Why I Prefer to Play the Scarlet Woman." THEATRE (N.Y.) 44 (July 1926): 22.

> Reed describes playing Mother Goddam in THE SHANGHAI GESTURE.

2775 _____. "Wicked Women on the Stage." THEATRE (N. Y.) 29 (March 1919): 146, 148. Illus.

> While decrying the difficulty of playing such roles, Reed suggests women are more wicked off the stage than on.

2776 W., M. "Florence Reed Finds Her Symphonic Background." MUSICAL COURIER 124 (1 December 1941): 77. Illus.

> Very brief remarks about the actress's background in and affection for music.

See also nos. 9, 276, 320, 464, and 500.

REHAN, ADA

(1860-1916)

2777   Golden, Sylvia. "The Romance of Ada Rehan." THEATRE (N.Y.) 53 (January 1931): 21-22, 64. Illus.

>A gracefully written appreciation and brief biographical sketch of Rehan.

2778   La Follette, Fola. "Ada Rehan: Some Personal Recollections." BOOK-MAN 43 (July 1916): 501-6. Illus.

>The author, for some time a supporting player to Rehan, recalls his admiration for her as both a performer and a person.

2779   Lawrence, Boyle, ed. CELEBRITIES OF THE STAGE. London: George Newnes, 1895. Issued in parts. 106 p. Illus.

>A portfolio of portraits and capsule biographies, primarily of English stars, but including Rehan.

2780   Winter, William. ADA REHAN: A STUDY. First printed in New York for Augustin Daly in 1891 as A DAUGHTER OF COMEDY, 80 p. Illus. 2d ed., with a new chapter and additional portraits: New York: Published for Augustin Daly: 1891. 88 p. Illus. 3d ed. New York: Privately printed for Augustin Daly, 1891-98. 211 p. Illus. Reprint. New York and London: Benjamin Blom, 1969. 211 p. Illus.

>Winter wrote an adulatory volume, but included many reviews, descriptions, and illustrations, as well as a list of Rehan's repertory and a chronology of her life. The second edition was limited to 113 copies.

See also nos. 13, 28, 58, 128, 177, 213, 236, 239, 261, 270, 277, 279, 288, 290, 293, 316, 324, 328, 340, 356, 371, 381-82, 400, 404-8, 413, 432, 438, 444, 451, 476, 482, 493, 555, 562, 578, 587-88, 597, 1599-1600, 1602-04, 1614-15, 1621, 1707-8, 1903, 2446, 2896-97, 2899, and 2932.

REIGNOLDS, CATHERINE

(1836-1911)

2781 Reignolds-Winslow, Catherine. READINGS FROM THE OLD ENGLISH
DRAMATISTS. 2 vols. Boston: Lee and Shephard, 1895. 372, 317 p.
Frontispieces.

> An anthology of English drama with brief critical introduc-
> tions to each volume.

2782 _____. YESTERDAYS WITH ACTORS. Boston: Cupples and Hurd,
1887. xv, 201 p. Illus.

> Reminiscing over her own career, Reignolds recalls many
> of her colleagues, among them Charlotte Cushman, Edwin
> Forrest, John Brougham, E.A. Sothern, Matilda Heron,
> J.H. Hackett, Mrs. John Wood, James E. Murdoch, Mrs.
> Lander, John Wilkes Booth, Mrs. J.R. Vincent, and
> William Warren, Jr.

See also nos. 13, 239, 245, 252, 278, 290, 400, and 2294.

ROBESON, PAUL

(1898-1976)

2783 Beatty, Jerome. "America's No. 1 Negro." AMERICAN MAGAZINE 137 (May 1944): 28-29, 142-44. Illus.

> A minor biographical essay suggesting that blacks can rise to any heights in America.

2784 Bradford, R. "Paul Robeson is John Henry." COLLIER'S 105 (13 January 1940): 15, 45. Illus.

> Publicity puffery prior to the opening of a music-drama about the folk hero, John Henry.

2785 Brown, Lloyd L. LIFT EVERY VOICE FOR PAUL ROBESON. New York: Freedom Associates, 1971.

> Unavailable for examination.

2786 _____. PAUL ROBESON REDISCOVERED. Occasional Papers, no. 19. New York: American Institute for Marxist Studies, 1976. 23 p. Notes.

> The transcript of an address delivered 22 April 1976 at the National Conference on Paul Robeson at Purdue University.

2787 Cripps, Thomas. "Paul Robeson and Black Identity in American Movies." MASSACHUSETTS REVIEW 11 (Summer 1970): 468-85.

> Cripps suggests that Robeson, more than any other person, bridged the gap between the race movies of the ghettos and Hollywood's commercial films.

2788 Cruse, Harold. THE CRISIS OF THE NEGRO INTELLECTUAL. New York: William Morrow and Co., 1967. 568 p. Index, bibliog.

> Pages 285-301, "Paul Robeson," discuss Robeson's activism and persecution as the most widely known and prototypical Negro in America, if not the world.

2789   Dorn, Julia. "I Breathe Freely." NEW THEATRE, July 1935, p. 5. Illus.

> Dorn quotes Robeson as he expresses his delight with the Soviet Union, which he visited in hopes of finding a serious consideration of ethnology. He also comments upon the Russian theatre of the time.

2790   DuBois, W. E. B. "Paul Robeson, Right." NEGRO DIGEST, March 1950, pp. 8–18.

> A companion piece to Walter White's "Wrong," composing a paper debate for and against Robeson and his political position.

2791   Embree, Edwin R[ogers]. 13 AGAINST THE ODDS. New York: Viking Press, 1944. 261 p. Illus.

> Includes an essay, "Voice of Freedom" (pages 243–61), about Robeson, a biographical sketch stressing his success as a singer and actor.

2792   Fast, Howard M. PEEKSKILL: U. S. A.--A PERSONAL EXPERIENCE. New York: Civil Rights Congress, 1951. Moscow: Foreign Language Publishing House, 1954. 110 p. Illus.

> A somewhat sensationalized account of the incident, an attempt on Robeson's life during a concert.

2793   Fishman, George. "Paul Robeson's Student Days and the Fight Against Racism at Rutgers." FREEDOMWAYS 9 (Summer 1969): 221–29.

> Drawn from published sources for the most part, this article describes Robeson's considerable accomplishments while in college.

2794   Foner, Philip S., ed. PAUL ROBESON SPEAKS: WRITINGS-SPEECHES-INTERVIEWS 1918-1974. New York: Brunner, Mazel Publishers, 1978. xvii, 590 p. Index, illus., bibliog.

> An annotated collection of Robeson's published works, including a twenty-page chronology of his life and career. Copiously illustrated, with a substantial bibliography.

2795   Garvey, Marcus. "Paul Robeson and His Mission." BLACK MAN 2 (January 1937): 2–3.

> Garvey attacks Robeson for appearing in films and plays that denigrated the black race.

2796   Gilliam, Dorothy Butler. PAUL ROBESON: ALL-AMERICAN. Washington, D.C.: New Republic Book Co., 1976. x, 206 p. Index, illus., bibliog.

> An adulatory, relatively shallow account of Robeson's life, superseded by subsequent biographies.

2797   Graham, Shirley. PAUL ROBESON, CITIZEN OF THE WORLD. New York: Julian Messner; Toronto: Smithers and Bonellie, 1946. 259 p. Index, illus., bibliog.

> An evocative rather than analytical biographical treatment, written in a somewhat florid style.

2798   Hamilton, Virginia. PAUL ROBESON: THE LIFE AND TIMES OF A FREE BLACK MAN. New York: Evanston, San Francisco, London: Harper and Row Publishers, 1974. xvi, 212 p. Index, illus., bibliog.

> A straightforward, reasonably documented biographical account, written in readable, if adulatory, style.

2799   Himber, Charlotte. FAMOUS IN THEIR TWENTIES. New York: Association Press, 1942. 127 p.

> Pages 91-101, "Let My People Go," is a brief, undocumented biographical sketch, somewhat idealized.

2800   Hoyt, Edwin P. PAUL ROBESON: THE AMERICAN OTHELLO. Cleveland and New York: World Publishing Co., 1967. ix, 228 p.

> A straightforward, undocumented biographical treatment, adequate only as an introduction to Robeson.

2801   Hutchens, John K. "Paul Robeson." THEATRE ARTS 28 (October 1944): 579-85. Illus.

> A biographical appreciation of the actor-singer at age forty-six; Hutchens considers him "the greatest Negro player in the theatre."

2802   James, C.L.R. "Paul Robeson: Black Star." BLACK WORLD 20 (November 1970): 106-15. Illus.

> Reminiscences of Robeson by a personal friend and playwright, who recalls him as unusually powerful and gentle at the same time.

2803   Kempton, Murray. PART OF OUR TIME: SOME RUINS AND MONUMENTS OF THE THIRTIES. New York: Simon and Schuster, 1955. 334 p.

An essay, "George" (pages 236-60), concerns Pullman car conductors and Robeson's place in their struggle for better working conditions and equality.

2804 Landay, Eileen. BLACK FILM STARS. New York: Drake Publishers, 1973. 191 p. Index, illus., bibliog.

Includes a brief essay on Robeson and several photographs.

2805 Mieirs, Earl Schenck. BIG BEN, A NOVEL. Philadelphia: Westminster Press, 1942. xiii, 238 p. Illus.

A fictional work; as the author suggests, "In spirit, if not always in fact, BIG BEN is Robeson's story."

2806 _____. "Paul Robeson: Made by America." NEGRO DIGEST 8 (October 1950): 21-24. Illus.

A brief article in which Mieirs outlines Robeson's life and civil rights activities, considering him a beneficial influence and no danger to American security.

2807 _____. "Paul Robeson--Made in America." NATION 170 (27 May 1950): 523-24. Illus.

A minor biographical sketch.

2808 Moos, Elizabeth. "Free Paul Robeson!" MASSES AND MAINSTREAM 4 (October 1951): 8-10. Illus.

Moos calls for a reversal of the government decision not to allow Robeson a passport, thus prohibiting a singing engagement he had in Scotland.

2809 Ovington, Mary White. PORTRAITS IN COLOR. New York: Viking Press, 1927. x, 241 p.

A series of adulatory biographical and critical sketches, pages 205-15 concerning Robeson.

2810 Patterson, William L. "Paul Robeson: A Giant Among Men." POLITI- CAL AFFAIRS 47 (May 1968): 18-21.

A brief tribute to Robeson on his seventieth birthday, recalling his long struggle for human equality.

2811 PAUL ROBESON: THE GREAT FORERUNNER. Chronology by Erwin A. Salk. Bibliography by Ernest Kaiser. New York: Dodd, Mead and Co., 1965. 376 p. Index, illus., bibliog.

A tribute to Robeson, prepared by the editors of FREEDOM-WAYS, originally published as a special issue. Part 1 consists of twenty articles, three by Robeson; part 2 are selections from Robeson's writings and speeches; part 3 is made up of tributes in prose and poetry to Robeson. Very useful.

2812   Pittman, John. "Mount Paul." NEW WORLD REVIEW 30 (February 1962): 24-28.

Robeson's popularity in the USSR was such that one of the peaks of the Kirghiz Pamirs was named for him. Pittman examines other aspects of Robeson's popularity as well.

2813   Redding, J. Saunders. THE LONESOME ROAD: THE STORY OF THE NEGRO'S PART IN AMERICA. Garden City, N.Y.: Doubleday and Co., 1958. 340 p. Index, bibliog.

A biographical sketch, "A Big Man Goes Far," (pages 275-88) assesses Robeson's contributions by focusing upon his Marxist ideals.

2814   Robeson, Elanda Goode. PAUL ROBESON, NEGRO. New York and London: Harper and Brothers, 1930. 178 p. Illus.

Written by Robeson's wife. An admiring volume, outlining the major events of Robeson's life and career and describing the plight of the black man in the entertainment industry of that time.

2815   _____. PAUL ROBESON GOES TO WASHINGTON. Salford, Lancashire: National Paul Robeson Committee, [1956].

Unavailable for examination.

2816   Robeson, Paul. "The Culture of the Negro." SPECTATOR 152 (15 June 1934): 916-17.

A brief account of Robeson's attempt to educate himself about his and his race's heritage.

2817   _____. HERE I STAND. New York: Othello Associates, 1958. Reprint. London: Dennis Dobson, 1958. 128 p.

Includes some autobiographical material, but primarily a plea for racial equality, Negro action, and social justice.

2818   Robeson, Rev. B.C. "My Brother--Paul Robeson--An Appraisal." QUARTERLY REVIEW OF HIGHER EDUCATION AMONG NEGROES, October 1954, pp. 159-63.

A recollection of Robeson as a child and his first attempts at singing.

2819   "Robeson in London." LIVING AGE 341 (September 1931): 85.

A brief interview in which Robeson discusses the Russian language, which he was studying, and Eugene O'Neill's work, which he admired.

2820   Rogers, Joel Augustus. WORLD'S GREAT MEN OF COLOR. 2 vols. New York: J. A. Rogers, 1947. Illus., bibliog.

Pages 513-20, "Paul Robeson, Intellectual, Musical and Histrionic Prodigy," offers a brief overview of Robeson's career with a minimal bibliography appended.

2821   Rowan, Carl T. "Has Paul Robeson Betrayed the Negro?" EBONY, October 1957, pp. 31, 36, 38-42. Illus.

A thoughtful analysis of black reaction to Robeson's struggles for racial equality. Robeson felt many blacks did not support his efforts.

2822   Scheien, Haemi. "Paul Robeson Becomes an Amateur." DRAMA (London) 16 (July-September 1938): 154-55.

Scheien quotes Robeson as he describes why he appeared in PLANT IN THE SUN at the Unity Theatre in St. Pancras in London for a month with a cast of amateurs for no salary.

2823   Sergeant, Elizabeth Shepley. FIRE UNDER THE ANDES, A GROUP OF NORTH AMERICAN PORTRAITS. New York: Alfred A. Knopf, 1927. 331 p. Illus.

Pages 193-209 present an adulatory essay on Robeson, then twenty-seven years old.

2824   Seton, Marie. PAUL ROBESON. London: Dennis Dobson, 1958. 243 p. Index, illus.

An article especially informative about Robeson's work in England. The author quotes extensively from published criticisms of Robeson.

2825   Shechter, Amy. "Paul Robeson's Soviet Journal: An Interview." SOVIET RUSSIA TODAY 17 (August 1949): 9-11, 24. Illus.

Robeson describes himself as a representative of the more progressive element of America as he discusses various political topics.

2826   Stevens, Hope R. "Paul Robeson--Democracy's Most Powerful Voice."
        FREEDOMWAYS 5 (Summer 1965): 365-68.

        The text of an address, a tribute made to Robeson on an
        unspecified occasion.

2827   Stuckey, Sterling. "'I Want to be African,': Paul Robeson and the
        Ends of Nationalist Theory and Practice, 1914-1945." MASSACHUSETTS
        REVIEW 17 (Spring 1976): 81-138.

        A substantial and well-documented analysis of Robeson's
        attempts to establish a valid black culture in America,
        written with unusual precision.

2828   Van Vechten, Carl. "All God's Chillun Got Songs." THEATRE (N. Y.)
        42 (August 1925): 24, 63. Illus.

        A complimentary overview of Robeson's career up to 1925,
        describing the difficulties he had overcome in seeking a
        career in the theatre.

2829   Weaver, Harold D. "Paul Robeson: Beleagured Leader." BLACK
        SCHOLAR 5 (December 1973-January 1974): 24-33. Illus., bibliog.

        A perceptive and sensitive biographical sketch written by
        the founding chairman of African Studies at Rutgers Uni-
        versity. A brief bibliography is appended.

2830   Woollcott, Alexander. "Ol' Man River--In Person." HEARST'S 95
        (July 1933): 54-55, 101-3. Illus.

        Woollcott recalls Jerome Kern's discovery of Edna Ferber's
        novel, SHOWBOAT, the eventual staging of the musical,
        and Robeson's part in the production.

2831   Wright, Charles H. ROBESON: LABOR'S FORGOTTEN CHAMPION.
        Detroit: Balamp Publishing, 1975. vii, 164 p. Index, frontispiece,
        bibliog.

        A paean of praise for Robeson's political activities, relying
        heavily upon quotations from articles, speeches, and books.

See also nos. 9, 296, 358, 368, 411, and 745.

ROBSON, MAY
(1858-1942)

2832 Condon, Frank. "A Lady Who Tells Her Age." COLLIER'S 95 (26 January 1935): 19, 39. Illus.

> Condon describes Robson's fifty-one years on the stage and her subsequent move to Hollywood to begin a film career.

2833 Robson, May. "My Beginnings." THEATRE (N.Y.) 7 (November 1907): 305-6, 308, 310.

> A substantial essay outlining Robson's childhood in Australia and England, then her early career in the United States.

2834 Service, Faith. "Sixty-Five, and Still a Star--May Robson." MOTION PICTURE MAGAZINE 47 (June 1934): 68, 104. Illus.

> Robson is quoted as saying her age had been no hindrance whatsoever to her career.

See also nos. 13, 381, 465, 481, and 506.

ROBSON, STUART

(1836-1903)

2835 Howard, Bronson. "The Late Stuart Robson--An Appreciation." THEATRE
(N.Y.) 3 (June 1903): 137-38.

> Howard recalls his personal and professional relationship
> with the actor.

2836 Robson, Stuart. "An Optimistic View of the Current Stage." PHILHAR-
MONIC 2 (August 1902): 183-89. Illus.

> Robson contends the theatre would grow as the United
> States grew, while reminiscing about the changes in the
> profession he had seen during his career.

See also nos. 28, 112, 176, 279, 288, 302, 328, 356, 379-80, 387, 413, 511,
562, 1526-27, 1535, 1975, and 2337.

ROWSON, SUSANNA HASWELL

(c. 1762-1824)

2837　Buckingham, Joseph T. PERSONAL MEMOIR AND RECOLLECTIONS OF
EDITORIAL LIFE. 2 vols. Boston: Ticknor, Reed, and Fields, 1852.

> Rowson is mentioned briefly in volume 1, pp. 83-85.

2838　Cobbett, William. A KICK FOR A BITE, OR REVIEW UPON REVIEW.
Philadelphia: T. Bradford, 1795. Unpaged.

> Cobbett, a journalist, attacks Rowson's patriotism in this
> pamphlet. Difficult to obtain; located in the Rare Book
> Collection of the New York Public Library.

2839　Spargo, John. ANTHONY HASWELL, PRINTER-PATRIOT-BALLADER:
A BIOGRAPHICAL STUDY WITH A SELECTION OF HIS BALLADS AND
AN ANNOTATED BIBLIOGRAPHICAL LIST OF HIS IMPRINTS. Rutland,
Vt.: Tuttle Co., 1925. xv, 293 p. Illus., bibliog.

> Rowson was Haswell's daughter; she is briefly mentioned
> in this account.

2840　Vail, Robert W. G. "Susannah Haswell Rowson, A Bibliographical Study."
PROCEEDINGS OF THE AMERICAN ANTIQUARIAN SOCIETY n.s. 42
(20 April 1932-19 October 1932): 47-160. Illus.

> A substantial index, including a brief account of the
> subject's life and career, a list of her roles from 1794
> to 1797, plus a lengthy annotated bibliography of works
> by and about her. Indispensable. Printed separately by
> the society in 1933.

See also nos. 13, 232, and 240.

RUSSELL, ANNIE
(1864-1936)

2841   Chapple, Joe Mitchell.   "Affairs at Washington."   NATIONAL MAGA-
ZINE 56 (May 1928): 385-86. Illus.

A brief and relatively insignificant interview with Russell.

2842   Dale, Alan. [Pseud.] "A Lady of Quality." COSMOPOLITAN 54 (May
1913): 841-43. Illus.

A biographical sketch of little depth.

2843   Kobbé, Gustav. "Annie Russell Out-of-Doors." LADIES' HOME JOUR-
NAL, May 1903, pp. 6-7. Illus.

A description of Russell's forty-acre estate in Pemaquid,
Maine, which she called "The Ledges." Kobbé describes
her summer vacations there and her propensity for the
outdoor life.

2844   Patterson, Ada. "Annie Russell and Her Unique Venture." THEATRE
(N.Y.) 17 (February 1913): 56-58. Illus.

A description of Russell's nine-week season of revivals
of classic comedies at the Thirty-ninth Street Theatre,
where she did such shows as SHE STOOPS TO CONQUER,
MUCH ADO ABOUT NOTHING, and THE RIVALS.

2845   Russell, Annie. "As the Player Sees the Playgoer." LADIES' HOME
JOURNAL, November 1912, pp. 16. Illus.

Russell, considering the American stage increasingly immoral, calls for a reform to be led by women theatregoers.

2846   _____. "The Point of View." GREEN BOOK ALBUM 5 (February
1911): 407-9.

A brief, superficial article describing the debilitating

effects of tradition in the theatre, especially with regard to casting.

2847 _____. "The Stage and Its People." LADIES' HOME JOURNAL, November 1909, p. 37. Illus.

A column in which Russell answered general questions about the theatre from JOURNAL readers.

2848 _____. "The Tired Business Man at the Theatre." LADIES' HOME JOURNAL, March 1914, p. 56.

Russell pleads for higher standards in the theatre, decrying the businessman's "candy appetites."

2849 _____. "What It Really Means to be an Actress." LADIES' HOME JOURNAL, January 1909, pp. 11, 49. Illus.

Russell thoughtfully describes the actress's need for self-discipline, her lack of leisure time, and the wide public misconceptions of the profession.

2850 _____. "The Woman of the Stage." THEATRE (N. Y.) 20 (October 1914): 177, 186. Illus.

Russell describes the vicissitudes of the theatre as a profession from the female point of view.

2851 Wagstaff, William. "Annie Russell." THEATRE (N. Y.) 2 (January 1902): 10-13. Illus.

An interview focused on Russell's preferences in roles.

See also nos. 13, 28, 112, 270, 279, 288, 321, 381-82, 413, 427, 448, 465, 555, and 581.

RUSSELL, LILLIAN
(1861-1922)

2852   Aronson, Rudolph. THEATRICAL AND MUSICAL MEMOIRS. New York: McBride, Nast and Co., 1913. 268 p. Index, illus.

        A rambling autobiography, including undocumented reminiscences of Russell and Francis Wilson.

2853   Brough, James. MISS LILLIAN RUSSELL: A NOVEL MEMOIR. New York: McGraw-Hill Book Co., 1978. ix, 307 p.

        A speculative treatment of Russell, more valuable for its evocation of the flavor and color of the time than for factual data.

2854   Dale, Alan. [Pseud.] "Lillian Russell and Eternal Youth." GREEN BOOK MAGAZINE 16 (August 1916): 237-42. Illus.

        Dale characterizes Russell as "a mixture of effulgent good nature, serene generosity, and superb optimism" in a somewhat fatuous profile.

2855   Day, Clarence. "Appearing with Lillian Russell." SATURDAY EVENING POST 208 (26 October 1935): 90.

        A humorous essay in which Day recalls playing a supernumerary in New Haven in order to see Russell in the 1890s appearing in THE GRAND DUCHESS.

2856   Fields, Ann. "When Lillian Russell was Glamour Queen." CORONET 30 (May 1951): 64-68. Illus.

        A popularized, undocumented biographical profile of minimal substance.

2857   Franklin, Irene. "The American Beauty." STAGE 16 (October 1938): 50-51. Illus.

Franklin, an actress in Marie Burrough's company, compares Russell to Burroughs in a shallow profile.

2858 Gibson, Ida McGlone. "Breakfast with Lillian Russell." GREEN BOOK ALBUM 6 (July 1911): 214-17.

  A tribute to the external youthfulness of the actress.

2859 "Lillian Russell Discovers Personality in Perfume." THEATRE (N.Y.) 26 (December 1917): 384.

  Journalistic filler of the most superficial type.

2860 "Lillian Russell's Path to Fame." LITERARY DIGEST 73 (24 June 1922): 40-42. Illus.

  A brief account of Russell's career, accompanied by four photographs and a cartoon.

2861 McKenzie, Ella. "Lillian Russell To-Day." GREEN BOOK ALBUM 1 (February 1909): 358-60.

  The author purports to explain how Russell retained her youth and beauty.

2862 Morrell, Parker. DIAMOND JIM: THE LIFE AND TIMES OF JAMES BUCHANAN BRADY. New York: Simon and Schuster, 1934. Reprint. New York: AMS Press, 1970. 278 p. Index, illus.

  References to Russell permeate this biography, based on much of the same material Morrell used for his later volume on the actress. See no. 2863.

2863 _____. LILLIAN RUSSELL: THE ERA OF PLUSH. Garden City, N.Y.: Garden City Publishing Co., 1943. 309 p. Index, illus.

  A popularized and undocumented biographical treatment, to be used only with corroboration.

2864 O'Connor, Richard [Burke, John]. DUET IN DIAMONDS: THE FLAMBOYANT SAGA OF LILLIAN RUSSELL AND DIAMOND JIM BRADY IN AMERICA'S GILDED AGE. New York: G.P. Putnam's Sons, 1972. 271 p. Index, illus., bibliog.

  An anecdotal account, written for popular consumption, but documented to an extent. Evocative rather than factual, but useful.

2865 Patterson, Ada. "Lillian Russell--Beauty and Philosopher." THEATRE (N.Y.) 5 (February 1905): 44-46. Illus.

Patterson quotes Russell as she discourses on beauty versus intelligence and her own sense of fatalism.

2866 _____. "Lillian Russell, Connoisseur." GREEN BOOK MAGAZINE 14 (November 1915): 864-70. Illus.

Patterson describes Russell's objects d'art, including what the interviewer calls a $100,000 Chinese restroom.

2867 Russell, Dorothy. "My Mother, Lillian Russell: An Intimate Portrait." LIBERTY 6 (19 October 1929): 9-14; (26 October 1929): 42-46; (2 November 1929): 51-59; (9 November 1929): 46-54; (16 November 1929): 58-66; (23 November 1929): 58-64. Illus.

Russell's daughter offers a prejudicial biography of her mother, tracing her career from her birth to her engagement with Weber and Fields, her later career, her war effort during World War I, and her death. Heavily illustrated.

2868 Russell, Lillian. "Is the Stage a Perilous Place for the Young Girl?" THEATRE (N. Y.) 23 (January 1916): 22. Illus.

Russell admits there are dangers in the profession, but suggests there are no more than in any other profession.

2869 _____. "Lillian Russell's Reminiscences." COSMOPOLITAN 72 (February 1922): 12-18, 92; (March 1922): 25-29, 126-29; (April 1922): 23-26, 90, 92, 94; (May 1922): 69-72, 92, 94; (June 1922): 81-83, 98, 100, 102; 73 (July 1922): 93-96, 110, 112; (August 1922): 80-82; (September 1922): 72-74, 106, 108. Illus.

A detailed autobiographical work which does not inspire trust, seeming somewhat romanticized. To be used with corroboration and care.

See also nos. 13, 191, 243, 270, 272-73, 276-77, 279, 288, 293, 384, 386, 392, 413, 443, 465, 482, 491-93, 510, 529, 547, 582, 591, 1685, 1688, 1975, and 2062.

RUSSELL, SOL SMITH

(1848-1902)

2870   Kidder, Edward E. "The Sol Smith Russell Plays." GREEN BOOK
        ALBUM 6 (September 1911): 620-23.

> Kidder, who served as Russell's "official" playwright for
> some years, recalls the relationship fondly.

2871   Mason, Bertha K. "Sol Smith Russell, Actor from Jacksonville."
        JOURNAL OF THE ILLINOIS STATE HISTORICAL SOCIETY 45 (Spring
        1952): 23-29. Illus.

> A simplistic treatment of Russell's life and career, based
> on recollections by Mason's uncle, J. R. H. King, a friend
> of the actor.

2872   Payne, George H. "The Personal Side of America's Greatest Actor."
        SATURDAY EVENING POST 171 (29 October 1898): 281-82. Illus.

> A tribute to Russell, considered by the author to be
> "the truest American actor." Thin.

See also nos. 28, 58, 112, 279, 328, 379, 413, 555, 599, and 1975.

SANDERSON, JULIA

(1887-1975)

2873   Dale, Alan. [Pseud.] "Julia Sanderson--Siren." COSMOPOLITAN 52 (March 1912): 559-65. Illus.

    A typically fan-oriented and superficial interview by Dale.

2874   "Why Stage Modesty Should Prevail in Musical Comedy." THEATRE (N.Y.) 18 (September 1913): 93-94, vi. Illus.

    Supposedly the actress's first interview, in which she reminisces about her early career before stardom.

See also nos. 270, 276, and 506.

SCHILDKRAUT, JOSEPH

(1896-1964)

2875   Bay, Dorothy. "A Mediaeval Modern." MOTION PICTURE MAGA-
ZINE 37 (April 1929): 78, 121. Illus.

>   Bay describes Schildkraut's romantic qualities as typical
>   of the Middle Ages.

2876   Belfrage, Cedric. "I Think I am Very Good." MOTION PICTURE
MAGAZINE 38 (September 1929): 74, 108-9. Illus.

>   A sketch of Schildkraut, who evaluates his recent work
>   in SHOWBOAT as his best to date.

2877   Schildkraut, Joseph, as told to Leo Lania. MY FATHER AND I. New
York: Viking Press, 1959. 288 p. Index, illus.

>   An unusually straightforward autobiography in which
>   Schildkraut describes in some detail the European career
>   of his father, Rudolph Schildkraut.

See also nos. 5, 135, 413, 464, and 563.

SHAW, MARY

(1854-1929)

2878 Patterson, Ada. "Actresses' Clubs in America." THEATRE (N. Y.) 20
(October 1914): 182-84, 187.

> Patterson describes, among others, the Charlotte Cushman
> Club in Philadelphia and Shaw's role in its inception.

2879 Shaw, Mary. "The Actress on the Road." McCLURE'S 37 (July 1911):
263-72. Illus.

> Shaw describes the hardships of touring; he relates
> anecdotes about Mrs. Fiske, Maurice Barrymore, and
> Modjeska. A useful article.

2880 _____. "The Boston Museum and Daly's Theatre." SATURDAY EVE-
NING POST 182 (20 May 1911): 14-15, 34-35. Illus.

> The actress recalls her entry into the theatre, including
> her early training, her work in William Warren's company,
> touring with Fanny Davenport, and joining Augustin Daly's
> company for a short time.

2881 _____. "My 'Immoral' Play: The Story of the First American Production of 'Mrs. Warren's Profession.'" McCLURE'S 38 (April 1912): 684-
94. Illus.

> Shaw describes her production and the resultant scandal
> and controversy.

2882 T., H. "Mary Shaw--A Woman of Thought and Action." THEATRE
(N. Y.) 2 (August 1902): 21-23. Illus.

> An interview in which Shaw discusses her preferences in
> roles.

2883 Young, Rose. "Suffrage as Seen by Mary Shaw." HARPER'S WEEKLY
60 (8 May 1915): 456.

A brief article quoting Shaw as being pro-sufferage.

See also nos. 13, 112, 278-79, 381-82, 480, and 2268-69.

SINCLAIR, CATHERINE (MRS. EDWIN FORREST) (1817-91). See entries under Edwin Forrest and nos. 13, 154, 164, 224, 277, 1521, 2331, and 3127.

SKINNER, CORNELIA OTIS

(1902-79)

2884   "The Art of Cornelia Otis Skinner." LITERARY DIGEST 119 (13 April 1935): 23. Illus.

   A brief survey of Skinner's one-woman shows.

2885   Crichton, Kyle. "Trouping Alone." COLLIER'S 93 (3 March 1934): 24, 48. Illus.

   The author seeks to describe the origins of Skinner's one-woman shows and explain the appeal thereof.

2886   "Eugénie--Once an Empress--Then a Fashion--And Now Cornelia Otis Skinner." STAGE 10 (November 1932): 34-35. Illus.

   A comparison of Skinner and Ruth Draper's one-woman productions and a plot outline of Skinner's show.

2887   Johns, Eric. "Conversation Piece." THEATRE WORLD 40 (May 1944): 25-26. Illus.

   Johns quotes Skinner as she describes how to engage an actress in conversation if one is a fan.

2888   Kimbrough, Emily. WE FOLLOWED OUR HEARTS TO HOLLYWOOD. New York: Dodd, Mead and Co., 1943. 210 p. Illus.

   An account of Emily Kimbrough and Cornelia Otis Skinner's trip to Hollywood in connection with the filming of their book, OUR HEARTS WERE YOUNG AND GAY.

2889   Mann, Arthur. "Honor of the Family." COLLIER'S 114 (16 December 1944): 19, 88. Illus.

   A description of Skinner's financial successes contrasted with those of her father, plus a few remarks about her writing habits.

2890 Nathan, George Jean. "With Regards to Guido D'Arezzo." NEWS-
WEEK 10 (20 December 1937): 31. Illus.

A brief appreciation of Skinner's work.

2891 Skinner, Cornelia Otis. THE APE IN ME. Boston: Houghton Mifflin
Co.; Cambridge, Mass.: Riverside Press, 1959. 172 p.

A compendium of humorous essays; "Stage Fright" is of
interest to acting students.

2892 _____. "The Bard and My Father." NEW YORKER 26 (18 November
1950): 45-48.

A description of Otis Skinner's attempt to perform Richard
III at a benefit.

2893 _____. BOTTOMS UP! New York: Dodd, Mead and Co., 1950.
208 p. Illus.

A series of humorous essays, the first of which is "The
Bard and My Father." See no. 2892.

2894 _____. DITHERS AND JITTERS. New York: Dodd, Mead and Co.,
1938. 168 p. Illus.

A collection of Skinner's humorous essays, none of them
relevant to the theatre.

2895 _____. EXCUSE IT, PLEASE. New York: Dodd, Mead and Co.,
1936. 225 p. Illus.

Humorous essays republished from various serials.

2896 _____. FAMILY CIRCLE. Boston: Houghton Mifflin, 1948. 310 p.
Illus.

Skinner's autobiography up to the time of her New York
debut. Anecdotal reminiscences of Otis Skinner, Edwin
Booth, John Drew, Modjeska, and Ada Rehan. See nos.
2897 and 2899.

2897 _____. "Family Circle." LADIES' HOME JOURNAL, September 1948,
pp. 3, 36-37, 74, 77-80, 82-83, 85-86; October 1948, pp. 89-90,
92-93, 95-96, 99-100, 102-6, 108, 110, 112-14, 116-20. Illus.

A serialization of no. 2896.

2898 _____. "Father." HARPER'S BAZAAR 75 (August 1941): 82-83, 135-
36. Illus.

Skinner describes a happy if peripatetic childhood, expressing great affection for both her parents.

2899 _____. HAPPY FAMILY. London: Constable and Co.; Bombay, Calcutta, Madras: Orient Longmans; Cape Town, Nairobi: Longmans, Green and Co., 1950. 309 p. Illus.

Identical to FAMILY CIRCLE (no. 2896), but with different illustrations. See no. 2897.

2900 _____. "I Saw Your Father in Kismet." THEATRE ARTS 25 (October 1941): 762-66. Illus.

A brief and humorous essay on the tribulations of being a celebrity's daughter.

2901 _____. LIFE WITH LINDSAY AND CROUSE. Boston: Houghton Mifflin Co., 1976. xiv, 234 p. Index, illus.

Biographical sketches of the playwrights and a description of their collaboration, including substantial references to the Lunts and Margaret Anglin.

2902 _____. MADAME SARAH. Boston: Houghton Mifflin Co.; Cambridge, Mass.: Riverside Press, 1967. 346 p. Index, illus., bibliog.

A readable biography of Sarah Bernhardt, reasonably if not outstandingly researched. A bibliography is appended, although the text is undocumented and some minor errors are included. Skinner had seen Bernhardt on several occasions.

2903 _____. NUTS IN MAY. New York: Dodd, Mead and Co., 1942. 188 p. Illus.

Assorted essays, some ("Actors Will Do Anything," "Opening Nights," and "Backstage Performance") theatrically oriented.

2904 _____. ONE WOMAN SHOW: MONOLOGUES AS ORIGINALLY WRITTEN AND PERFORMED BY CORNELIA OTIS SKINNER. Chicago: Dramatic Publishing Co., 1974. 125 p. Appendix.

Twenty-five monologues used by Skinner during her career.

2905 _____. POPCORN. London: Constable and Co.; Toronto: Macmillan Co. of Canada, 1943. xii, 185 p. Illus.

Another of Skinner's anthologies of humor, including "I Saw Your Father in Kismet" and "Wednesday Matinee."

2906 _____. "Pour le Sport." STAGE 14 (September 1937): 64.
Skinner's remarks on English clothing fashions.

2907 _____. "The Radiant Ethel Barrymore." McCALL'S, February 1950,
pp. 16-19, 100-109; March 1950, pp. 36-37, 110, 114, 118-19, 121-
23, 126-27, 130. Illus.

A lengthy, well-illustrated, and adulatory biographical
treatment. The article includes some descriptions of the
Barrymore family and William Gillette.

2908 _____. SOAP BEHIND THE EARS. New York: Dodd, Mead and Co.,
1943. 214 p. Illus.

Eighteen humorous essays, including "First Nights," "Long
Live the Sticks," It's Summer, But Is It Theatre?" and "I
Saw Your Father in Kismet." All are reprinted from various
serials and newspapers.

2909 _____. THAT'S ME ALL OVER. New York: Dodd, Mead and Co.,
1945. 312 p. Illus.

A collection of humorous essays, some on theatrical sub-
jects, selected from DITHERS AND JITTERS, SOAP BE-
HIND THE EARS, EXCUSE IT, PLEASE!, and TINY
GARMENTS.

2910 _____. TINY GARMENTS. New York: Farrar and Rinehart, 1931.
London: I. Nicholson and Watson, 1933. New York: Dodd, Mead
and Co., 1943. n.p. Illus.

One of Skinner's humorous essays, published as a separate
entity, concerning the care and raising of infants.

2911 Skinner, Cornelia Otis, and Kimbrough, Emily. OUR HEARTS WERE
YOUNG AND GAY. New York: Dodd, Mead and Co., 1942. 247 p.
Illus.

An amusing account of the two young women's first trip
to Europe, largely autobiographical.

2912 Skinner, Cornelia Otis, and Skinner, Otis. MAUD DURBIN SKINNER.
Binghamton, N.Y.: Vail-Ballou Press, 1939. 28 p.

A gracefully written tribute to the actor's wife and the
actress's mother. It also describes Mrs. Skinner's career
with Modjeska.

2913 Smith, H. Allen. "Cornelia Otis Skinner." COSMOPOLITAN 112
(April 1942): 8, 10-11. Illus.

A brief but well-written biographical sketch describing Skinner's childhood, education, and rise to stardom.

See also nos. 5, 242, 525, 547, and 2951.

SKINNER, OTIS
(1858-1942)

2914   Brown, John Mason. "Otis Skinner." THEATRE ARTS 13 (November 1929): 812-18. Illus.

   A tribute to the actor, describing his charisma in a wide variety of roles, both sympathetic and unsympathetic.

2915   Dodge, Wendell Phillips. "The Actor in the Street." THEATRE (N.Y.) 8 (June 1908): 156. Illus.

   Dodge describes Skinner's preparations for playing Colonel Phillippe Bridau in THE HONOR OF THE FAMILY.

2916   Glover, Lyman B[eecher]. OTIS SKINNER PRESENTING GEORGE HENRY BOKER'S TRAGEDY FRANCESCA DA RIMINI. Chicago: Ralph Fletcher Seymour, 1901. 28 p. Illus.

   A plot synopsis and analysis of the script, as well as an appreciation of Skinner and his staging. Includes eleven illustrations.

2917   "His Speech Betrayeth Him." LITERARY DIGEST 97 (19 May 1928): 24-25. Illus.

   A reprint of a speech by Skinner, taken from the New York TIMES, on America's polyglot speech.

2918   Patterson, Ada. "Otis Skinner--A 'Big' Man." GREEN BOOK ALBUM 8 (October 1912): 648-55. Illus.

   Superficial remarks, accompanied by photographs not often published in other Skinner material.

2919   _____. "Otis Skinner--America's Leading Romantic Actor." THEATRE (N.Y.) 15 (March 1912): 101-3, vii. Illus.

   Insubstantial interview conducted while Skinner was starring in KISMET, which he discusses briefly.

2920   Skinner, Maud, and Skinner, Otis. ONE MAN IN HIS HOME: THE
       ADVENTURES OF H[ARRY] WATKINS, STROLLING PLAYER 1845-1863
       FROM HIS JOURNAL. Philadelphia: University of Pennsylvania Press,
       1938. xiii, 253 p. Index, illus.

           The Skinners edited Watkins's journal, the text of which
           constitutes about half this volume, the rest being the
           Skinners' narrative. Specific chapters deal with the
           elder Booth, Edwin Forrest, and William Burton; other
           actors are mentioned.

2921   Skinner, Otis. "The Actor and His Audience." THEATRE (N. Y.) 35
       (April 1922): 242, 244.

           A few remarks on the audience's ability to judge produc-
           tion standards.

2922   _____. THE ACTOR'S ETHICAL VIEWPOINT. AN ADDRESS GIVEN
       BY OTIS SKINNER IN THE CHICAGO UNIVERSITY COURSE OF THE
       LECTURE ON THE DRAMA, JANUARY 21ST, 1908. N.p.: n.p., n.d.
       14 p.

           Skinner advocates the theatre's purpose as "holding the
           mirror up to nature" and reflecting "the very age and
           body of the time."

2923   _____. "The Art of the Actor." THEATRE (N. Y.) 2 (April 1902):
       19-20. Illus.

           Brief but pithy remarks on the profession and its demands.

2924   _____. "Bad Actors and Beginners." GREEN BOOK MAGAZINE 9
       (January 1913): 25-34. Illus.

           Advice to would-be actors and suggestions of errors to
           avoid when beginning work in the theatre.

2925   _____. "Bath and James Quin." SCRIBNER'S 75 (March 1924): 305-
       14. Illus.

           A monograph on the eccentric career of the English actor
           who retired to the city of Bath. Written in a lively
           style.

2926   _____. "The Case of the Automatic Drama." JOURNAL OF THE
       NATIONAL INSTITUTE OF SOCIAL SCIENCES 1, no. 1 (1915): 85-88.

           Skinner notes the growing popularity of film, but suggests
           the new media "must always lack the human equation and
           can never dispute the supremacy of true dramatic art or
           inflict upon it a permanent injury."

2927 _____. "The Celluloid Drama." JOURNAL OF THE NATIONAL IN-
STITUTE OF SOCIAL SERVICES 7 (1 August 1921): 62-64.

> Skinner recalls his difficulty in making the transition
> from the stage to motion pictures when he filmed KISMET,
> but he refers to film as "the greatest, the most universal
> source of amusement for people that has ever been con-
> ceived." See no. 2926.

2928 _____. "Come Let Us Play." GOOD HOUSEKEEPING, July 1912,
pp. 38-45. Illus.

> Skinner suggests the need for more leisure time and recre-
> ation for everyone, especially actors, to slow down the
> pace of life.

2929 _____. "A Conservatory of Acting." DRAMA 10 (November 1919):
43-44.

> Skinner pleads for a conservatory, possibly to be operated
> by the Drama League of America, publisher of DRAMA.

2930 _____. "'First Nights' in the Palmy Days of the Drama." THEATRE
(N.Y.) 9 (December 1909): 184.

> Skinner recalls opening night experiences while in Edwin
> Booth's company.

2931 _____. "Footlights and Spotlights: Forty-Six Years of Romance and
Adventure on the American Stage." LADIES' HOME JOURNAL, October
1923, pp. 7, 160-62, 165; "A Year in 'Stock' at Philadelphia's Walnut
Street Theatre," November 1923, pp. 15, 46, 48, 51-52; "Footlights
and Spotlights: When Booth Burned the Costumes of Lincoln's Assassin,"
December 1923, pp. 10, 126, 129-30; "The Years With Mather and
Modjeska," February 1924, pp. 23, 193-96; "Footlights and Spotlights,"
March 1924, pp. 26, 131-32, 135-37. Illus.

> Serialization of no. 2932, heavily illustrated.

2932 _____. FOOTLIGHTS AND SPOTLIGHTS: RECOLLECTIONS OF MY
LIFE ON THE STAGE. New York: Blue Ribbon Books, 1923. 354 p.
Index, frontispiece. Indianapolis: Bobbs-Merrill, 1924. Reprint.
Westport, Conn.: Greenwood, 1972.

> A charming and anecdotal autobiography with valuable
> insights into theatrical procedures of Skinner's time and
> numerous accounts of Edwin Booth, Lawrence Barrett,
> Modjeska, Janauschek, Joseph Jefferson III, and Ada
> Rehan. See no. 2931.

2933 _____. "Good Diction on the Stage." EMERSON QUARTERLY 9 (March 1929): 3-4, 12.

> The American Academy of Arts and Letters had given Skinner a gold medal for good diction on the stage. This essay is his acceptance speech, in which he describes the nature and causes of declining American speech habits.

2934 _____. "The Job of Being an Actor." THEATRE (N.Y.) 30 (July 1919): 18, 20.

> Skinner proposes that while there is no easy path to theatrical fame, success on the stage brings substantial rewards.

2935 _____. JOSEPH JEFFERSON HOLLAND; A TRIBUTE, BY OTIS SKINNER, DELIVERED AT THE FUNERAL SERVICE IN THE CHURCH OF THE TRANSFIGURATION, NEW YORK, SEPTEMBER 28, 1926. New York: Privately printed by Witherspoon and Co., 1926. 6 p.

> A gracefully written eulogy.

2936 _____. "Kindling the Divine Spark." THEATRE ARTS 22 (September 1938): 666-73. Illus.

> A somewhat rambling discourse on techniques of acting in comedy; Skinner quoting Joseph Jefferson III as an authority.

2937 _____. "The Last of John Wilkes Booth." AMERICAN MAGAZINE 67 (November 1908): 73-77. Illus.

> Skinner recounts how Edwin Booth disposed of his brother's costumes and properties after his death, as told to him by Booth's assistant, Garrie Davidson.

2938 _____. "Lost--A Romantic Actor." HARPER'S WEEKLY 58 (11 October 1913): 12. Illus.

> Skinner decries the end of the romantic tradition and expresses hope for a renaissance after the "politicians, crooks, cadets, white slaves, gunmen, grafters, gamblers, saloon keepers, and detectives" leave the stage.

2939 _____. MAD FOLK OF THE THEATRE: TEN STUDIES IN TEMPERAMENT. Indianapolis: Bobbs-Merrill Co., 1928. 297 p. Illus.

> Chapter 9 describes the quirks of the elder Booth.

2940 _____. "The Motion Pictures not an Art." LADIES' HOME JOURNAL, May 1922, pp. 7, 89, 93. Illus.

Skinner laments the overnight successes of some film performers, their dependency upon directors and cameramen,
and the general waste of talent in the film industry.

2941 _____. "My Beginnings." THEATRE (N.Y.) 6 (May 1906): 119-19,
vii.

A gracefully written essay in which Skinner suggests his
success in the theatre was a triumph over both heredity
and environment.

2942 _____. "My First Appearance in New York." GREEN BOOK ALBUM
1 (March 1909): 565-65.

Skinner describes his debut in the role of Maclou in
ENCHANTMENT at Niblo's Gardens.

2943 _____. "Otis Skinner on the Drama." THEATRE (N.Y.) 9 (February
1909): xvii.

Remarks of a general nature extracted from a lecture the
actor made at Chicago University.

2944 _____. "Otis Skinner Tells Why the Screen Drama is Not an Art."
CURRENT OPINION 73 (September 1922): 363-64.

Skinner suggests that film acting is only pantomime and
that photography itself cannot be an art in the true sense.

2945 _____. "Scandal and the Movies." LADIES' HOME JOURNAL, June
1922, pp. 8, 91-92. Illus.

Skinner expresses horror at the lurid gossip from Hollywood
concerning the film stars' lives, as well as the excessive
costs of filmmaking.

2946 _____. "Shakespeare and His Friends." THEATRE (N.Y.) 23 (April
1916): 208, 210. Illus.

In a special tercentenary edition, Skinner speculates on
Shakespeare's relationships with his fellow actors.

2947 _____. "Some Personal Experiences at Daly's Theatre." PHILHARMONIC
2 (June 1902): 133. Illus.

Skinner, who spent a part of his early career at Daly's,
recalls a few anecdotes from those days.

2948 _____. ". . . Speaking in the Talking Pictures." THEATRE (N.Y.)
52 (December 1930): 32, 70. Illus.

The actor, having just filmed KISMET, contrasts acting for the stage and screen.

2949 _____. "A Tragedian's Christmas Dinner." THEATRE (N.Y.) 4 (December 1904): 311.

Skinner recalls Christmas on the road with Edwin Booth.

2950 _____. "What I Believe." In THEY BELIEVE AS TOLD BY OTIS SKINNER, HERBERT ADAMS GIBBONS, IDA M. TARBELL, YUSUKE TSURUMI, CHARLES G. NORRIS, WILLIAM ALLEN WHITE, INEZ HAYNES IRWIN, WILL IRWIN, ALEXANDER BLACK, THOMAS A. EDISON, pp. 3-15. New York and London: Century Co., 1928.

A series of declarations of religious faith. Skinner's essay discusses his personal credo and the relationship of theatre to religion.

2951 "Speaking of Pictures . . . Here is Fun with Skinner." LIFE, 30 August 1948, pp. 8-10. Illus.

Photographic memorabilia about Skinner in support of Cornelia Otis Skinner's forthcoming publication of FAMILY CIRCLE (see no. 2896).

2952 Tyrrell, Henry. "America's Foremost Romantic Actor: An Interview with Otis Skinner." THEATRE (N.Y.) 4 (January 1904): 8-9. Illus.

Tyrrell quotes Skinner's reminiscences about his early career, prior to his stardom.

2953 Voegele, M. "Home of Otis Skinner." WESTERN ARCHITECTURE 20 (September 1914): n.p.

Two photographs and the floor plans of Skinner's home near Philadelphia.

See also nos. 9, 28, 130, 150-51, 213, 227-28, 245, 261, 270, 276, 279, 285, 287-88, 291, 296, 303, 348, 358, 361, 379, 412-13, 446, 448, 464, 479, 499, 510, 530, 546-47, 555, 578, 581, 597, 605, 1120, 1125-26, 1185, 2585, 2889, 2892-93, 2896, and 2898.

SMITH, SOLOMON FRANKLIN
(1801-69)

2954   Carson, William G. B. "Sol Smith and Theatre Folk, 1836-1865."
MISSOURI HISTORICAL SOCIETY GLIMPSES OF THE PAST 5 (July-
September 1938): 99-136.

> Texts of thirty-six of the nine hundred letters by Smith
> held by the Missouri Historical Society in St. Louis.
> Included are a few letters to and from the elder Booth,
> Edwin Forrest, Charlotte Cushman, and Julia Dean's
> father.

2955   Morgan, Mary. "The Oldest Actress on the American Stage." THEATRE
(N. Y.) 10 (April 1910): 104. Illus.

> Reminiscences by Smith's widow, with anecdotes about
> Edwin Booth, Mrs. Drew, and William Faversham.

2956   Smith, Mrs. Sol. "Reminiscences of America's Oldest Actress." THEATRE
(N. Y.) 16 (October 1912): 124, 126-28, vi. Illus.

> Excerpts from Smith's widow's proposed memoirs, written
> at age eighty-six after fifty years of performing.

2957   Smith, Solomon. THEATRICAL APPRENTICESHIP. COMPRISING A
SKETCH OF THE FIRST SEVEN YEARS OF HIS PROFESSIONAL LIFE;
TOGETHER WITH ANECDOTES AND SKETCHES OF ADVENTURE IN
AFTER YEARS. Philadelphia: T. B. Peterson, 1845. 215 p. Illus.

> Smith relates how he left his home in Albany, New York,
> to become an actor and tells of his misadventures on the
> road. He includes references and anecdotes concerning
> the Chapmans and the Drakes, as well as a minor reference
> to Edwin Forrest. A valuable primary account of condi-
> tions in the frontier theatre.

2958   _____. THE THEATRICAL JOURNEY-WORK AND ANECDOTAL RECOL-
LECTIONS OF SOL. SMITH, COMEDIAN, ATTORNEY AT LAW, ETC.,

ETC. COMPRISING A SKETCH OF THE SECOND SEVEN YEARS OF HIS PROFESSIONAL LIFE; TOGETHER WITH SKETCHES OF ADVENTURE IN AFTER YEARS. Philadelphia: T. B. Peterson, 1854. 254 p. Frontispiece.

> A companion volume to no. 2957, a valuable account of early theatre along the Mississippi Valley. Smith's professional quarrels with Noah Ludlow moved him to omit any mention of his partner from this narrative, but many others are described, among them Thomas Abthorpe Cooper, the elder Booth, Thomas Hamblin, T. D. Rice, the Chapmans, and a few minor figures.

2959 _____. THEATRICAL MANAGEMENT IN THE WEST AND SOUTH FOR THIRTY YEARS: INTERSPERSED WITH ANECDOTAL SKETCHES AUTOBIOGRAPHICALLY GIVEN. New York: Harper and Brothers, 1868. Reprint. New York: Benjamin Blom, 1968. xx, 294 p. Index, illus.

> Smith's anecdotes are lively and evocative, but require corroboration in this account of the development of the frontier theatre. A valuable primary source, nonetheless.

See also nos. 101, 132-33, 146, 148, 211, 222, 244, 318, 401, 1288, 2348, 2461, and 3168.

SOTHERN FAMILY

Entires for Edward Askew and Edward Hugh Sothern follow this section.

2960   Baker, Hettie Gray. "The Sotherns--Father and Son--as Lord Dundreary."
        THEATRE (N.Y.) 8 (February 1908): 55-56. Illus.

> More a description of the role than a comparison of the
> two actors.

See also nos. 347 and 417.

SOTHERN, EDWARD ASKEW
(1826-81)

2961   Andrews, Alan. "E.A. Sothern and the Theatre in Halifax, Nova Scotia."
        NINETEENTH CENTURY THEATRE RESEARCH 7 (Autumn 1979): 73-91.

> Andrews documents Sothern's theatrical management in
> Halifax from 1856 to 1859, proposing that Sothern gained
> experience there of some value to his later career. Well
> documented.

2962   Blunt, Jerry. "America's Amazing Lord." THEATRE ANNUAL 16
        (1959): 60-69.

> A description of the creation of Lord Dundreary in OUR
> AMERICAN COUSIN as acted by Sothern.

2963   DeFontaine, F[elix]. G[regory]., ed. BIRDS OF A FEATHER FLOCK TO-
        GETHER OR TALKS WITH SOTHERN. New York: G.W. Carleton,
        1878. xiii, 250 p. Illus.

> DeFontaine describes the volume: ". . . its contents
> were gleaned, from time to time, in conversations with
> the eminent artist and his friends." Random remarks and
> anecdotes with little specificity.

2964   Fuller, Lucy Derby. "Humour of the Elder Sothern." CENTURY 64
        (June 1902): 196-203. Illus.

       Anecdotes and reminiscences of the elder Sothern.

2965   Goddard, Henry P. "Players I Have Known." THEATRE (N.Y.) 16
        (September 1912): 82, 84. Illus.

       Reminiscences of Sothern in various roles.

2966   Pemberton, T. Edgar. A MEMOIR OF EDWARD ASKEW SOTHERN.
        London: Richard Bentley and Son, 1889. iv, 338. Index, illus.
        Later published as LORD DUNDREARY: A MEMOIR OF EDWARD
        ASKEW SOTHERN. New York: Knickerbocker Press, 1908. 291 p.
        Illus.

       Pemberton was a personal friend of Sothern's and had the
        cooperation of his family in preparing these memoirs after
        the actor's death. A valuable source of information,
        largely based on an article published in THEATRE MAGA-
        ZINE (Engl.).

2967   _____. "Some Personal Reminiscences of E.A. Sothern." THEATRE
        (Engl.), 12 April 1888, pp. 230-40.

       Published just prior to Pemberton's book-length memoir
        of Sothern.

2968   Sala, George Augustus. BREAKFAST IN BED, OR, PHILOSOPHY
        BETWEEN THE SHEETS: A SERIES OF INDIGESTIBLE DISCOURSES.
        Boston: J. Redpath; London: John Maxwell and Co., 1863. 334 p.

       Reprinted from TEMPLE BAR, the first article, "On a
        Remarkable Dramatic Performance," describes Sothern's
        Lord Dundreary in OUR AMERICAN COUSIN, while
        raising the question of good taste in concern with some
        of the byplay.

2969   Sothern, E.A. "Reminiscences." THEATRE (Engl.) n.s. 1 (1 August
        1878): 17-23.

       Sothern describes how he created Lord Dundreary in OUR
        AMERICAN COUSIN.

See also nos. 21, 156, 236, 255, 302, 313, 335, 337, 341, 356, 363, 396,
401-2, 409, 413, 439, 468, 496, 519, 522-23, 538, 572, 2188, 2235-36,
2410, 2624, 2782, and 2984.

SOTHERN, EDWARD HUGH
(1859-1933)

2970   Aldrich, Mildred. "Edward Hugh Sothern." ARENA 6 (October 1892): 516-31. Illus.

> A biographical sketch, praising Sothern's sentimentality in the face of rising "truthfulness" in acting.

2971   "The Ambition of Sothern." BOOK NEWS 32 (November 1913): 179-80. Illus.

> Sothern recalls deciding at age nineteen that he would someday play Hamlet and his eventual realization of that dream.

2972   Coward, Edward Fales. "Edward H. Sothern--An Actor with Ideals." THEATRE (N.Y.) 3 (March 1903): 66-68. Illus.

> An article focused on Sothern's techniques in preparing roles for the stage.

2973   Dodge, William Phillips. "E.H. Sothern." STRAND (N.Y.) 46 (December 1913): 602-16. Illus.

> An appreciation of Sothern, describing his rise to stardom. Dodge also describes Sothern's work with Julia Marlowe, Richard Mansfield, and Maurice Barrymore.

2974   Held, Anna, and Sothern, E.H. "When the Players Grow Tired." THEATRE (N.Y.) 22 (December 1915): 290, 323. Illus.

> A two-part article in which both stars suggest they will continue to work.

2975   Hovey, Carl. "Playing Shakespeare: A Talk with Mr. Sothern and Miss Marlowe Concerning the Line between Success and Failure." METROPOLITAN 37 (January 1913): 32-35. Illus.

> A somewhat superficial interview in which the two stars describe the efforts required to perform Shakespeare and the satisfactions gained therefrom.

2976   Kobbé, Gustave. "Edward H. Sothern and His Wife." LADIES' HOME JOURNAL, October 1903, pp. 4-5. Illus.

> A fan-oriented description of Sothern's home life and his house on West Sixty-ninth Street in New York. Mrs. Sothern's (Virginia Harned) early attempts at housekeeping are also described.

2977   McCracken, Elizabeth. "Mr. Sothern as a Producer." CRITIC 47
        (November 1905): 464-68.

        An analysis of Sothern's staging of THE SUNKEN BELL,
        IF I WERE KING, THE PROUD PRINCE, HAMLET, and
        ROMEO AND JULIET.

2978   Moses, Montrose J. "Booking Actors for 'Over There.'" THEATRE
        (N.Y.) 27 (June 1918): 346-48. Illus.

        Sothern's (and Winthrop Ames's) remarks about playing
        to soldiers, after having returned from a European tour
        to the fronts.

2979   Patterson, Ada. "Mr. Sothern in the Movies." THEATRE (N.Y.) 24
        (November 1916): 292, 321. Illus.

        Sothern describes the shift from stage to film while film-
        ing THE MAN OF MYSTERY for Vitagraph.

2980   Reamer, Lawrence. "The Drama." HARPER'S WEEKLY 44 (6 October
        1900): 946.

        Reamer offers a balanced analysis of Sothern's Hamlet.

2981   Sothern, E.H. "America's 'Over There' Theatre League: A Player on
        the Fighting Front." SCRIBNER'S MAGAZINE 64 (July 1918): 22-34,
        129-41. Illus.

        A well-illustrated description of Sothern's European en-
        gagements during World War I.

2982   _____. "The Great Shakespeare-Bacon Controversy." MUNSEY'S 46
        (January 1912): 536-42.

        Sothern rejects the arguments of the Baconians.

2983   _____. MATTERS FOR A MAY MORNING: POEMS FOND & FOOL-
        ISH. New York: Privately printed, 1929. 195 p.

        An anthology of Sothern's poetry, a few of which are on
        theatrical topics, such as "On Playing London."

2984   _____. THE MELANCHOLY TALE OF 'ME'; MY REMEMBRANCES.
        New York: Charles Scribner's Sons, 1916. 401 p. Index, illus.

        A relatively thoughtful and detailed account of the actor's
        life and career, with observations on many of his fellow-
        players, such as Maude Adams, Edwin Booth, Joseph
        Jefferson III, John McCullough, E.A. Sothern, Dion
        Boucicault, William Warren, Mrs. Vincent, and Laura
        Keene.

2985 _____. "Modernizing Shakespeare." THEATRE (N. Y.) 35 (March 1921): 178, 198, 200.

>Sothern seeks to justify some of the alterations he made in staging HAMLET, TWELFTH NIGHT, and THE TAMING OF THE SHREW.

2986 _____. "My Remembrances: The Melancholy Tale of 'Me.'" SCRIB-NER'S 59 (January 1916): 1-17; (February 1916): 133-47; (March 1916): 306-17; (April 1916): 389-402; 60 (July 1916): 38-53; (September 1916): 330-42. Illus.

>A serialization of Sothern's autobiography (see no. 2984) with additional illustrations.

2987 _____. "Playing with Mary Anderson for American Soldiers." SCRIB-NER'S 65 (January 1919): 1-13. Illus.

>An anecdotal account, primarily of their MACBETH.

2988 _____. "Raynor, J. P." SCRIBNER'S 64 (September 1918): 279-85. Illus.

>An undistinguished short story, apparently based on Sothern's experiences during World War I.

2989 _____. "Sothern and Marlowe on Inspiration." AMERICAN PLAY-WRIGHT 2 (July 1913): 233-35.

>Sothern is quoted from the July 1913 STRAND on inspiration in acting, which he considered desirable but insufficient.

2990 _____. "The Theatre May Be Better in Two Hundred Years." THEATRE (N. Y.) 45 (April 1927): 5. Illus.

>A brief and pessimistic essay on the stage of the art, paired with a rejoinder by Laurence Stallings.

2991 _____. "The Thraldom of Stage Tradition." GREEN BOOK ALBUM 7 (March 1912): 535-40.

>Sothern describes and decries the conventions involved in acting Shakespearean roles.

2992 _____. "Tradition." DRAMA (Chicago) 12 (February 1922): 150-52. Illus.

>Sothern discusses the roles of spontaneity and improvisation in acting.

2993 _____. "What is the Picture Play Going to Do to (or For) Us?" GREEN BOOK MAGAZINE 11 (June 1914): 901-6. Illus.

> Sothern posits that the human voice will continue to draw audiences into the live theatre.

2994 _____. "When I Was a Scene-Painter." THEATRE (N. Y.) 46 (July 1927): 32, 62, 64. Illus.

> A description of Sothern's early career with John O'Connor, scene painter for the Haymarket Theatre in London.

2995 Sothern, E. H., and Palmer, A. M. "An Endowed Theatre." THEATRE (N. Y.) 1 (June 1901): 10-12. Illus.

> Sothern expresses his opinions on the desirability of a subsidized company of actors.

2996 "Sothern as a Star and Before." MUNSEY'S 26 (December 1901): 320-22.

> A description of the earlier portions of Sothern's career.

2997 White, Matthew, Jr. "Edward H. Sothern." MUNSEY'S 36 (October 1906-March 1907): 383-89. Illus.

> A survey of the actor's life, culminating in his performances as Hamlet and various Shakespearean leading roles.

2998 Wilson, B. F. "The Matinee Idol--Old and New." THEATRE (N. Y.) 41 (May 1925): 22, 82. Illus.

> A slight article describing Sothern and his immense popularity at the time.

2999 Winter, William. "The Art of E. H. Sothern." CENTURY 90 (May 1915): 109-17. Illus.

> An adulatory essay of high praise for Sothern, who was one of Winter's favorite performers.

See also nos. 21, 28, 58, 112, 118, 127, 130, 150, 163, 177-78, 228, 245, 256, 261, 263, 270, 276, 278-79, 287-88, 291, 297, 303, 321, 328, 344, 367, 377, 379-80, 390-91, 407-8, 413, 430, 448-49, 455, 464, 506, 510, 531, 544, 547, 557, 561, 578-79, 585, 596, 713, 1914, 2031, 2270, 2410, 2429, 2485, 2490-92, 2496, 2508, and 2512-15.

SPELVIN, GEORGE

(1886-?)

3000   Spelvin, George, as told to Robert Downing. "I Am Not a Camera: The
        Memoirs of George Spelvin." THEATRE ARTS 40 (October 1956): 32,
        96.

> A fanciful article on the history of the Spelvin tradition.

3001   Wood, Philip. "The World's Most Versatile Actor." THEATRE (N. Y.)
        47 (April 1928): 37, 78, 80.

> A tongue-in-cheek memoir of the "official double," George
> Spelvin.

SPONG, HILDA

(1875-1955)

3002   Spong, Hilda. "The Actress and Her Critics." GREEN BOOK ALBUM 3 (March 1910): 609-13.

        Spong describes the variety of critics and criticism at the time.

3003   _____. "Working with Pinero, Barrie and Shaw." THEATRE (N. Y.) 31 (July-August 1920): 32, 34.

        The actress compares the dramaturgy of the three playwrights, in whose scripts she had appeared.

See also nos. 28, 382, 558, and 962.

STAHL, ROSE

(1870-1955)

3004   Patterson, Ada. "The Real Rose Stahl." GREEN BOOK ALBUM 7 (June 1912): 1127-31. Illus.

   Superficial observations.

3005   _____. "Rose Stahl--An Actress of Rainbow Personality." THEATRE (N.Y.) 14 (September 1911): 98-100, vii.

   Stahl discusses her role in MAGGIE PEPPER and describes her preparation for it.

3006   "Rose Stahl." BOOK NEWS 32 (April 1914): 406. Illus.

   A brief description of Charles Klein's MAGGIE PEPPER, in which Stahl starred.

3007   Stahl, Rose. "Rose Stahl Talks about Comedy." GREEN BOOK MAGAZINE 13 (February 1915): 309-11.

   A reasonably thoughtful article on the nature of comedy in the theatre.

See also nos. 270, 276, 391, 491, and 497.

STARR, FRANCES

(1881-1973)

3008 Dale, Alan. [Pseud.] "Meek and Mouse-Like Frances Starr." GREEN BOOK MAGAZINE 15 (March 1916): 431. Illus.

> A condenscending and somewhat sarcastic profile; of minimal value.

3009 "Frances Starr's Stage History." PEARSON'S 22 (July 1909): 98-100. Illus.

> A summation of Starr's career to date, with some details of her conception of Laura Murdoch in THE EASIEST WAY, in which she had just appeared.

3010 Garside, Frances L. "Why a Cook?" THEATRE (N.Y.) 29 (May 1919): 286.

> Starr describes her role in TIGER! TIGER!

3011 Patterson, Ada. "At Home with Frances Starr." GREEN BOOK ALBUM 7 (March 1912): 529-34.

> Wandering reminiscences; of minimal worth.

3012 _____. "A Drive with America's Youngest Dramatic Star." THEATRE (N.Y.) 8 (February 1908): 47-48, 50. Illus.

> Superficial puffery, fan-oriented.

3013 _____. "Frances Starr--The Cinderella of the Stage." THEATRE (N.Y.) 7 (February 1907): 50-51. Illus.

> Starr describes the early part of her career, then her affiliation with Belasco.

3014 _____. "How Frances Starr Trained for the Role of a Nun." THEATRE (N.Y.) 21 (April 1915): 174-76. Illus.

Starr is quoted describing her preparation for the title
role in MARIE-ODILE.

3015   Rodgers, John J. "Frances Starr as a Personality." GREEN BOOK
MAGAZINE 16 (November 1916): 801. Illus.

Rodgers profiles Starr, finding her no more enigmatic
than any other woman, then describes several of her
professional fears.

3016   Starr, Frances. "Drive Out Your Fear of the Shelf." THEATRE (N. Y.)
45 (January 1927): 24, 58.

Starr, then appearing in THE SHELF, suggests an actress
need not fear being discarded; her work could sustain
her indefinitely.

3017   _____. "How I Prepare a Role." DELINEATOR 96 (June 1920): 23,
96, 99. Illus.

Part of a series by Starr. In this article, she claims to
depend more on industry than inspiration for her work.

3018   _____. "My Greatest Tragedy." THEATRE (N. Y.) 29 (March 1919):
164.

Part of the series, "The Most Striking Episode in My
Life." Starr recalls Winter giving her birthdate six years
early in his LIFE OF DAVID BELASCO.

3019   _____. "My Philosophy of Clothes." GREEN BOOK MAGAZINE 13
(March 1915): 491-95. Illus.

The actress considered selecting her wardrobe as a "mathe-
matical problem in subtraction."

3020   _____. "My Stage Principles; An Actress Reveals the Personal Creed
of Her Stage Career." FORUM 61 (March 1919): 335-42.

An article in which Starr discusses such matters as the
moral responsibility of an actress, the need for self-
effacement, the power of personality, and the possibility
of a role contaminating its player.

3021   _____. "My Views on Marriage." DELINEATOR 95 (November 1919):
12, 87. Illus.

Part of a series by Starr. Although she had at this time
never been married, she offers suggestions to those considering matrimony.

3022 _____. "Personal Reminiscences." THEATRE (N. Y.) 25 (June 1917): 330-31. Illus.

> Somewhat flowery recollections of the actress's early career.

3023 _____. "Stage Beginnings." DELINEATOR 95 (October 1919): 12, 95-96. Illus.

> Part of a series by Starr. She describes her childhood and early career.

3024 _____. "A Study in Green." GREEN BOOK MAGAZINE 11 (April 1914): 657-63. Illus.

> Amateur psychology illustrated by scenes from some of Starr's roles.

3025 Starr, Frances, as told to Philip Wood. "The Theatre Will Not Perish!" THEATRE (N. Y.) 47 (January 1928): 16-18, 66. Illus.

> Starr sees no danger of film surplanting live theatre; she likens movies to "canned cooking," whereas theatre is "the real thing."

3026 "A Star Who Wants to be Different." COSMOPOLITAN 58 (May 1915): 676-77. Illus.

> Starr insists she wishes to be more than a mere "personality star," hence her wide variety of roles.

See also nos. 270, 276, 464, 495, 497-99, 928, 936, 938, 950, 998, and 1002.

STODDART, JAMES H.

(1827-1907)

3027   Stoddard, J[ames]. H[enry]. RECOLLECTIONS OF A PLAYER. New York: Century, 1902. xxi, 255 p. Illus.

> Although English, Stoddart had a considerable career in the United States. His memoirs contain substantial references to Edwin Booth, George Holland, Laura Keene, William Mitchell, John Gilbert, Lester Wallack, and Dion Boucicault.

3028   _____. "The Recollections of a Player." CENTURY 64 (May 1902): 51-62; (June 1902): 290-304. Illus.

> Extracts from Stoddart's autobiography (see no. 3027).

See also nos. 112, 288, 328, and 387.

STONE, FRED

(1873-1959)

3029   Clark, Neil M. "They Said He'd NEVER Dance Again." AMERICAN MAGAZINE 111 (May 1931): 50-51, 100-106. Illus.

        An account of Stone's air accident, his recovery, and the development of his crutch dance.

3030   Craig, Carol. "O, The Girls' Best Friend is Their Father . . . (Meaning Fred Stone)." MOTION PICTURE MAGAZINE 52 (November 1936): 52-53, 56-57. Illus.

        An interview with Stone concerning his three daughters. Fan-oriented.

3031   "Fred Stone--Beloved Actor Who Declares His Faith in Old-Fashioned Religion." NATIONAL MAGAZINE 52 (June 1924): 548. Illus.

        Interview with Stone about his fundamentalist religious beliefs.

3032   "Fred Stone, The Superclown of the American Theatre." CURRENT OPINION 56 (April 1914): 278-79. Illus.

        A brief assessment of Stone, describing his entry into show business.

3033   "Fred Stone's 'Wild West' Home in the East." NATIONAL MAGAZINE 55 (October 1926): 78-80. Illus.

        A description of Stone's 2,200 acre "ranch" in Old Lyme, Cohnecticut.

3034   Macfarlane, Peter Clark. "Clown and Superclown." EVERYBODY'S 30 (March 1914): 399-412. Illus.

        A breezy but substantial assessment of Stone's career, stressing the artistry required to do comedy well.

3035   "A Matter of Make-Up." THEATRE (N.Y.) 21 (June 1915): 310.
Illus.

> Stone's abilities with stage make-up are demonstrated by
> illustrations from several of his roles.

3036   Merritt, Peter. "Fred Stone's Becomingest Picture." EVERYBODY'S 39
(December 1918): 29. Illus.

> Insubstantial puffery.

3037   Mullett, Mary B. "Climbing a Greased Pole Was Fred Stone's First
Triumph." AMERICAN MAGAZINE 102 (December 1926): 18-19,
132, 134, 137-39.

> A biographical sketch which describes Stone's early work
> with the Sells-Renfrew Circus, his partnership with Mont-
> gomery, and his success in THE WIZARD OF OZ.

3038   "Religion Behind the Footlights." LITERARY DIGEST 76 (24 March
1923): 34-35. Illus.

> Brief remarks, mostly reprinted from various newspapers,
> concerning Stone's religious conversion.

3039   Shirk, Adam Hull. "You Can't Keep a Good Man Down." MOTION
PICTURE MAGAZINE 16 (December 1918): 37-38, 120-21. Illus.

> A substantial biographical interview, somewhat more de-
> tailed than usual for this serial.

3040   Stone, Fred. "The Clown Who Built a Skyscraper with Laughter."
AMERICAN MAGAZINE 84 (October 1917): 32-35, 88-90, 92, 94-
95. Illus.

> An autobiographical sketch of some substance, describing
> how Stone came to purchase the Pullman Building in New
> York.

3041   _____. "Let Your Costume Reflect You." WOMAN'S HOME COM-
PANION 59 (March 1932): 82. Illus.

> Fashion advice.

3042   _____. ROLLING STONE. New York and London: Whittlesey House
(McGraw-Hill), 1945. 246 p. Illus.

> Especially useful for its insights into vaudeville and the
> frontier entertainment industry of the time. A detailed
> personal memoir.

3043 Stone, Paula. "My Dad Fred Stone." MOVIE CLASSIC 10 (June 1936): 40–41, 81. Illus.

Adulatory reminiscences by one of Stone's three daughters.

See also nos. 9, 243, 272, and 276.

STRASBERG, LEE
(1901-82)

3044 "Actors Studio is Not a School." PLAYS AND PLAYERS 4 (February 1957): 9. Illus.

>   Strasberg is quoted as insisting that the Actors Studio is simply a place where professional actors could continue to do the work necessary to their craft, not an artistic movement in itself.

3045 Adams, Cindy. LEE STRASBERG: THE IMPERFECT GENIUS OF THE ACTORS STUDIO. Garden City, N.Y.: Doubleday and Co., 1980. 384 p. Index, illus.

>   Slightly sensationalized and written for the commercial rather than scholarly market, this volume is the only current full-length biography of Strasberg. The author is well acquainted with the subject and writes in a lively style, but a deeper understanding and analysis of the Strasberg system would have made the work more useful to acting theorists.

3046 Alpert, Hollis. "Autocrat of the Sweat Shirt School." ESQUIRE, October 1961, pp. 88-89, 179-83, 185. Illus.

>   A somewhat popularized treatment, assessing Strasberg's contributions to the Actors Studio and his charisma among the performers there.

3047 Aulicino, Armand. "How THE COUNTRY GIRL Came About." THEATRE ARTS 36 (May 1952): 54-57. Illus.

>   A set of interviews with those involved with the production, including the producer, Strasberg.

3048 Brady, Leo. "The Man Behind the Method." CRITIC 18 (August-September 1959): 13.

>   Unavailable for examination.

3049 Brustein, Robert. "Keynes of Times Square." NEW REPUBLIC 147 (1 December 1962): 28-30.

> Brustein takes the Actors Studio and Strasberg to task on several accounts, calling for a radical reform in the New York theatre.

3050 "Clap Hands, Here Comes Lee Strasberg." TIME 90 (6 October 1967): 78. Illus.

> An account of Strasberg in France, lecturing on the "Method" to established French performers.

3051 Dundy, Elaine. "How to Succeed in the Theatre Without Really Being Successful." ESQUIRE, May 1965, pp. 88-89, 91, 153-54, 156-58. Illus.

> An article describing the work of Harold Clurman, Cheryl Crawford, Elia Kazan, and Strasberg.

3052 Garfield, David. A PLAYER'S PLACE: THE STORY OF THE ACTORS STUDIO. New York: Macmillan Publishing Co., 1980. xii, 300. Index, illus., bibliog.

> A solidly researched history of the Actors Studio which seeks to correct many misconceptions about that organiza- tion. Strasberg figures prominently in the text; Stella Adler and Morris Carnovsky are mentioned.

3053 Gray, Paul. "Stanislavski and America: A Critical Chronology." TULANE DRAMA REVIEW 9 (Winter 1964): 21-60.

> A detailed chronology of the "System" from Stanislavski's meeting with Nemirovich-Danchenko in 1897 through the Moscow Art Theatre and Actors Studio to the publication of STANISLAVSKI'S LEGACY in 1961. Strasberg is mentioned frequently.

3054 Hager, Steven. "Lee Strasberg: The Acting Master Turns the Method on Himself." HORIZON 23 (January 1980): 18-25. Illus.

> Strasberg discusses his recent career as a film actor in "The Godfather II," "Broadwalk," "And Justice for All," and "Going in Style." Brief remarks by Estelle Parsons are included as a separate essay.

3055 Hethmon, Robert H., ed. STRASBERG AT THE ACTORS STUDIO. New York: Viking Press, 1965. vii, 413 p. Index, illus.

> A substantial and valuable work, based almost entirely upon transcripts of tape recordings made during sessions

of the Actors Unit of the Studio. Part 1 deals with the
Actors Studio; part 2 with the actor's individual work;
and part 3 with the actor's relationships to others. Four
appendixes give further information about the Actors Studio.

3056 Hewes, Henry. "The Wing--Without Feathers." SATURDAY REVIEW
OF LITERATURE 36 (25 July 1953): 26-27.

Hewes quotes Strasberg on theatrical research and how it
differs from research in other arts.

3057 Richardson, Tony. "An Account of the Actors Studio: The Method and
Why." SIGHT AND SOUND 26 (Winter 1956-57): 132-36. Illus.

An admiring assessment of the Actors Studio with Strasberg
described as the pivotal force. Richardson gives some
space to anti-Method viewpoints.

3058 Rogoff, Gordon. "Lee Strasberg: Burning Ice." TULANE DRAMA RE-
VIEW 9 (Winter 1964): 131-54.

A description of Strasberg's procedures and goals for the
Actors Studio, combining both praise and censure for the
operation.

3059 Seymour, Victor. "Directors Workshop: Six Years Activity of the Actors
Studio Directors Unit." EDUCATIONAL THEATRE JOURNAL 18, no. 1
(1966): 12-26.

A history of the development of this unit of the Actors
Studio, begun in 1960 by Crawford, Kazan, and Strasberg,
who is quoted extensively.

3060 Strasberg, Lee. "Acting and the Training of the Actor." In PRODUCING
THE PLAY, rev. ed., edited by John Gassner, pp. 128-62. New York:
Holt, Rinehart and Winston, 1953. Index, illus., bibliog.

The Strasberg essay offers a capsule version of the Stanislavski
system as employed at the Actors Studio, including affec-
tive memory and relaxation exercises.

3061 _____. Introduction to ACTING: A HANDBOOK OF THE STANISLAVSKI
METHOD, by Toby Cole. New York: Lear, 1947. 223 p. Illus.

Cole's volume is a compendium of articles on and about
the system, for which Strasberg wrote an eighteen-page
introduction. He traces the history of acting and publications about the art, considering Stanislavski's work a sharp
departure from the traditions preceding it.

3062   Entry deleted.

3063   _____. "Introductory Note." THEATRE WORKSHOP 1 (October 1936):
3-4.

   Strasberg discusses the lack of conclusive writing about
   acting technique.

3064   _____. "Lee Strasberg's Russian Notebook." DRAMA REVIEW 17, no. 1
(1973): 108-23. Illus.

   Reprinted notes by Strasberg during his visit to Russia
   in the early 1930s. Appended is an interview with
   Russian director Okhlopkov conducted by Strasberg and
   Sidney Kingsley.

3065   _____. "Looking Back." EDUCATIONAL THEATRE JOURNAL 28
(December 1976): 544-52.

   Strasberg reminisces about his work with the Group Theatre
   in an issue composed of articles by his colleagues about
   that producing agency.

3066   _____. "Past Performances." THEATRE ARTS 34 (May 1950): 39-
42. Illus.

   Strasberg uses Edmund Kean and David Garrick to illustrate
   how performances from the past may be in part rediscovered.

3067   _____. "Professional Actor Training." EDUCATIONAL THEATRE
JOURNAL 18 (November 1966): 333-35.

   Example of Strasberg's methods of acting instruction.

3068   _____. "We Don't Appreciate the Power of American Culture." U.S.
NEWS AND WORLD REPORT, 16 June 1980, p. 94. Illus.

   Strasberg describes the worldwide impact of American
   culture, the need for a national theatre, and the unique
   nature of the theatre as an art form.

3069   _____. "Working with Live Material." TULANE DRAMA REVIEW 9
(Fall 1964): 117-35.

   An interview conducted by Richard Schechner in which
   Strasberg describes many of his specific training techniques
   for actors.

3070 _____, ed. FAMOUS AMERICAN PLAYS OF THE 1950'S. New York: Dell Publishing Co., 1962. 415 p.

> Strasberg chose CAMINO REAL, THE AUTUMN GARDEN, TEA AND SYMPATHY, THE ZOO STORY, and A HATFUL OF RAIN for inclusion. He also wrote a fifteen-page introduction of considerable merit, discussing the scripts and the state of the commercial theatre in the 1950s.

3071 Strasberg, Susan. BITTERSWEET. New York: G.P. Putnam's Sons, 1980. 285 p. Illus.

> An unusually revealing autobiography by Strasberg's daughter. She includes considerable reference to her father and his work, as well as anecdotal material concerning Tallulah Bankhead, Ruth Gordon, Helen Hayes, and various film stars.

3072 Vandenbroucke, Russell. YALE THEATRE 8, nos. 2 and 3 (1976): 20-29. Illus.

> An interview with Strasberg on the subjects of the Group Theatre, the Method, and the possibilities of a national theatre in the United States.

3073 Wasserman, Debbi. "Developing an American Acting Style." NEW YORK THEATRE REVIEW 2 (February 1978): 5-9. Illus.

> Includes an essay by Strasberg (page 6) on style in acting.

3074 Weaver, Neal. "A Place to Come In Out of the Rain: The Actors Studio." AFTER DARK, May 1968, pp. 31-37. Illus.

> A brief history and description of the Actors Studio and Strasberg's function in it. Somewhat more balanced than most articles.

3075 Winters, Shelley. SHELLEY, ALSO KNOWN AS SHIRLEY. New York: William Morrow and Co., 1980. 511 p. Illus.

> Winters describes her work at the Actors Studio and her relationship with Strasberg.

See also nos. 5, 137, 167, 291, 540, and 743.

TAYLOR, LAURETTE
(1884-1946)

3076 Bird, Carol. "A Dressing Room Chat with 'Peg.'" THEATRE (N. Y.) 33 (May 1921): 322.

> In an interview during a revival of PEG O' MY HEART, the actress discusses her fear of aging and makes various observations on the state of the theatre.

3077 Carr, Harry. "Hard-Boiled Eggs with Peg O' My Heart." MOTION PICTURE MAGAZINE 24 (January 1923): 20-21, 100. Illus.

> Taylor reviews her stage career and describes the recent filming of PEG O' MY HEART.

3078 Chapman, John. "Lady with a Present." COLLIER'S 116 (10 November 1945): 85-66. Illus.

> A review of Taylor's long career, written shortly after her success in THE GLASS MENAGERIE.

3079 Courtney, Marguerite. LAURETTE. New York and Toronto: Rinehart and Co., 1955. 433 p. Illus.

> While undocumented, this volume seems to be the result of considerable research and firsthand acquaintanceship with the subject. A better than average theatre biography.

3080 Hall, Gladys. "Laurette Taylor as Seen." MOTION PICTURE MAGAZINE 27 (June 1924): 23-24, 93. Illus.

> Taylor is quoted as decrying the lack of vision in the youth of the day.

3081 Houghton, Norris. "Laurette Taylor." THEATRE ARTS 29 (December 1945): 688-96. Illus.

> A substantial essay reviewing Taylor's career, written shortly after her appearance in THE GLASS MENAGERIE.

3082 "Laurette o' My Heart." COSMOPOLITAN 54 (April 1913): 701-2. Illus.

>Anonymous recollections of Taylor's success in PEG O' MY HEART.

3083 "Laurette Taylor, Noted Actress, Made Her First Stage Appearance at Ten Years." NATIONAL MAGAZINE 54 (January 1926): 239. Illus.

>Taylor offers a few remarks about her early career and her success in PEG O' MY HEART.

3084 "Laurette Taylor--We Applaud--." HARPER'S BAZAAR 79 (February 1945): 90-91. Illus.

>A brief announcement of Taylor's return to the stage in OUTWARD BOUND.

3085 "Laurette Taylor Gets Prize for Acting in OUTWARD BOUND." LIFE, 22 May 1939, pp. 57-58. Illus.

>Photographs of the play's highlights and a list of Taylor's more unusual awards.

3086 Moses, Montrose. "Laurette Taylor in Shakespearean Roles." BOOK NEWS 36 (May 1918): 342.

>Unavailable for examination.

3087 Parker, R. A. "Laurette Taylor's Secret." INTERNATIONAL: A REVIEW OF TWO WORLDS 7 (August 1913): 230.

>Parker proposes Taylor as expert at improvisation and spontaneity and attributes her success to this quality.

3088 Patterson, Ada. "Laurette Taylor--A New Star." THEATRE (N.Y.) 17 (March 1913): 82-83. Illus.

>A somewhat superficial interview conducted during PEG O' MY HEART.

3088A _____. "Playing Under Fire." THEATRE (N.Y.) 23 (March 1916): 149-50, 158. Illus.

>Taylor describes a London engagement performed during Zeppelin raids.

3089 Taylor, Dwight. BLOOD-AND-THUNDER. New York: Atheneum, 1962. x, 232 p.

>The author was the son of Charles A. Taylor, playwright,

and Laurette Taylor. Considerable mention is made of
the actress, but little factual information is supplied.

3090　Taylor, Laurette. "The Actress Who Would Not Be Starred." COLLIERS'
49 (23 March 1912): 18, 24-25. Illus.

Taylor in a fairly articulate essay muses upon the vagaries
of theatrical fame, but suggests she would make the effort
to be a star again.

3091　_____. "Americans for America. One Flag! One Language! One
Allegiance!" DELINEATOR 93 (November 1918): 11, 52. Illus.

A plea by the actress for "controlled democracy" in
national affairs.

3092　_____. "Critics: An Actress Talks Back." TOWN AND COUNTRY
97 (March 1942): 47, 70, 85; "An Actress Talks Back to Noel Coward,"
(May 1942): 56, 82-83; "Lynn Fontanne," (August 1942): 44, 60;
"Mrs. Pat ad Libitum." 86, 98-99, 114. Illus.

A series of autobiographical articles; fan-oriented.

3093　_____. "From Seattle to Broadway." AMERICAN MAGAZINE 83
(January 1917): 26-27, 84-89. Illus.

Taylor describes her entry into the theatre and her eventual
rise to stardom.

3094　_____. "THE GREATEST OF THESE--" A DIARY WITH PORTRAITS
OF THE PATRIOTIC ALL-STAR TOUR OF OUT THERE. New York:
George H. Doran, 1918. ix, 61 p. Illus.

Taylor recalls an all-star tour which raised two-thirds
of a million dollars for the Red Cross. The cast included
Mrs. Fiske, Julia Arthur, George M. Cohan, James K.
Hackett, Chauncey Olcott, and DeWolf Hopper. The
text includes many anecdotes about the tour.

3095　_____. "Living and Play-Acting." McCLURE'S 54 (September 1922):
44-48, 86. Illus.

Taylor describes her childhood and her entry into the
theatre in a somewhat romanticized narrative.

3096　_____. "London, an Actor's Utopia." GREEN BOOK MAGAZINE
14 (September 1915): 558-61. Illus.

Taylor describes her reception during a London engagement, which was highly positive.

3097   _____. "'Peg' and My Art." NASH'S AND PALL MALL MAGA-
ZINE 54 (December 1914): 337-39. Illus.

   A few rambling autobiographical notes.

3098   _____. "The Quality You Need Most." GREEN BOOK MAGAZINE
11 (April 1914): 556-62. Illus.

   Taylor describes the role of imagination in the theatre,
   holding it to be the essential for all theatricians.

3099   _____. "Sarah Bernhardt Left Them Kneeling." VOGUE, 15 February
1941, pp. 42, 90-91.

   Taylor describes seeing Bernhardt in CAMILLE and meeting
   her backstage on two occasions, late in the French star's
   career.

3100   _____. "The 'Sex Play'--An Assassin of Youth." GREEN BOOK MAGA-
ZINE 11 (February 1914): 247-48.

   Taylor condemns erotic scripts.

3101   _____. "Some Memories--Theatrical and Otherwise." STRAND (N. Y.)
50 (November 1915): 510-14. Illus.

   The actress describes her lonely childhood and early
   struggles in the theatre, then relates them to her work
   in PEG O' MY HEART.

3102   _____. "Versatility." THEATRE (N. Y.) 27 (January 1918): 32.

   Taylor recommends character work as insurance against
   the day an actress's beauty fades.

3103   Tuttle, Day. "Recollections of Laurette Taylor." THEATRE ARTS 34
(March 1950): 42-48. Illus.

   Gracefully written personal reminiscences, largely anecdotal, of the actress.

3104   Wolf, Rennold. "Laurette Taylor." GREEN BOOK MAGAZINE 11
(May 1914): 785-96. Illus.

   A substantial interview following Taylor's success in
   PEG O' MY HEART.

3105   Woollcott, Alexander. "A Partnership of the Theatre." EVERYBODY'S
42 (May 1920): 78-79. Illus.

Woollcott celebrates the marriage of Taylor and J. Hartley Manner during the long run of PEG O' MY HEART.

See also nos. 5, 13, 117, 275-76, 291, 332, 377, 413, 447, 469, 500, 509, 543, 549, 580, 597, and 1471.

TEMPLETON, FAY

(1865-1939)

3106   Crichton, Kyle. "Lady in the Wings." COLLIER'S 93 (21 April 1934): 18, 59. Illus.

        Crichton reviews Templeton's career a few months after she turned sixty-five and describes her observations about her long career.

3107   Patterson, Ada. "Before the Matinee with Fay Templeton." THEATRE (N. Y.) 16 (July 1912): 23-24, vi. Illus.

        Patterson quotes Templeton on the requisites for playing in burlesque.

See also nos. 28, 191, 279, 288, and 3177.

THOMPSON, DENMAN

(1833-1911)

3108   Brady, James Jay. LIFE OF DENMAN THOMPSON (JOSHUA WHIT-
        COMB.) New York: E. A. McFarland and Alex. Comstock, 1888.
        88 p. Illus.

> An undocumented biography, more concerned with Thomp-
> son's writing of JOSHUA WHITCOMB and THE OLD HOME-
> STEAD than with his acting.

3109   "The Significance of Joshua Whitcomb." CURRENT OPINION 50
        (June 1911): 648-50. Illus.

> Substantial praise for Thompson in THE OLD HOMESTEAD,
> suggesting his portrayal of the New England farmer was
> definitive, comparable to Jefferson's Rip Van Winkle.

3110   Walsh, William H. "Reminiscences of Denman Thompson." NEW
        ENGLAND MAGAZINE 43 (September 1910): 43-50. Illus.

> An appreciation by an old friend of Thompson's as he
> neared the age of seventy-seven. The essay describes
> several of Thompson's roles.

See also nos. 28, 112, 200, 328, and 356.

THORNE, CHARLES R., JR. (1840-83). See nos. 328, 401, 471, 511, 562, and 3168.

TYLER, ODETTE (1869-1936). See nos. 279 and 381.

ULRIC, LENORE
(1892-1970)

3111　"Affairs and Folks." NATIONAL MAGAZINE 49 (November-December 1920): 361. Illus.

> Publicity puffery for Ulric in THE SON-DAUGHTER in Boston.

3112　"Face to Face with Celebrities." NATIONAL MAGAZINE 53 (September 1924): 123.

> Superficial remarks about the nature of Ulric's appeal.

3113　Kennedy, John B. "Naughty Girl." COLLIER'S 87 (17 January 1931): 18, 42. Illus.

> Ulric is quoted as deploring her reputation as a vamp and describes her unsuccessful attempts to obtain more wholesome roles.

3114　Manners, Dorothy. "A Flame in Furs." MOTION PICTURE MAGAZINE 38 (October 1929): 36, 116.

> A somewhat more substantial interview than usual in the film magazines of the time; Ulric compares southern California to New York, expressing a preference for the latter.

3115　Manning, Maybelle. "Portrait des Modes of Miss Lenore Ulric." THEATRE (N. Y.) 53 (January 1931): 52-53. Illus.

> Fashion notes.

3116　Pollock, Arthur. "A Girl with a Good Philosophy of Work." AMERICAN MAGAZINE 87 (March 1919): 53-54. Illus.

> Pollock praises Ulric for her high artistic standards and her personal industriousness.

3117   Schmid, Peter Gridley. "Shadows of Bernhardt." MOTION PICTURE
        MAGAZINE 12 (January 1917): 73-76. Illus.

> A biographical sketch in which Schmid predicts enormous
> success for Ulric.

3118   Ulric, Lenore. "Where I Get My 'Pep.'" THEATRE (N.Y.) 44
        (September 1926): 9, 54. Illus.

> The actress suggests her notable energy is hereditary.

See also nos. 276, 285, 413, 464, 495, 508, 563, 945, and 998.

VANDENHOFF, GEORGE

(1813-85)

3119   R., E.F. "Mr. and Mrs. Vandenhoff." TALLIS'S DRAMATIC MAGA-
ZINE, April 1851, pp. 165-69.

> The bulk of the essay is devoted to a critical and bio-
> graphical assessment of Vandenhoff.

3120   Vandenhoff, George. THE ART OF ELOCUTION, AS AN ESSENTIAL
PART OF RHETORIC: WITH INSTRUCTIONS IN GESTURE; AND AN
APPENDIX OF ORATORICAL, POETICAL, AND DRAMATIC EXTRACTS.
London: Sampson Low and Son, 1861, 1862, 1867. New York: 1888.
405 p. Index.

> A substantial treatise on Vandenhoff's extremely mechani-
> cal approach to elocution, accompanied by numerous
> pieces for illustration, practice, or study.

3121   _____. THE ART OF ELOCUTION; FROM THE SIMPLE ARTICULATION
OF THE ELEMENTAL SOUNDS OF LANGUAGE, UP TO THE HIGHEST
TONE OF EXPRESSION IN SPEECH, ATTAINABLE BY THE HUMAN
VOICE. London: Wiley and Putnam, 1846. 369 p. Index.

> An "enlargement and improvement" of Vandenhoff's
> PLAIN SYSTEM OF ELOCUTION, no. 3128.

3122   _____. THE ART OF ELOCUTION; OR, LOGICAL AND MUSICAL
READING AND DECLAMATION. New York: C. Shephard, 1847.
New York: Spalding and Shephard, 1847, 1849, 1851.

> Unavailable for examination.

3123   _____. THE ART OF READING ALOUD IN PULPIT, LECTURE ROOM,
OR PRIVATE REUNIONS WITH A PERFECT SYSTEM OF ECONOMY OF
LUNG POWER ON JUST PRINCIPLES FOR ACQUIRING EASE IN
DELIVERY AND A THOROUGH COMMAND OF THE VOICE. London:
Sampson Low, Marston, Searle, and Rivington, 1878. viii, 234 p.

Another of Vandenhoff's many elocutionary texts, mechanical and systematic.

3124 _____. THE CLAY CODE; OR, TEXT-BOOK OF ELOQUENCE, A COLLECTION OF AXIOMS, APOTHEGMS, SENTIMENTS, AND REMARKABLE PASSAGES ON LIBERTY, GOVERNMENT, POLITICAL MORALITY AND NATIONAL HONOR: GATHERED FROM THE PUBLIC SPEECHES OF HENRY CLAY. New York: C. Shephard, 1844. 144 p. Index.

A compendium of Clay's observations, with a preface by Vandenhoff, extolling Clay as a patriot.

3125 _____. THE CLERICAL ASSISTANT: AN ELOCUTIONARY GUIDE TO THE READING OF THE SCRIPTURES AND THE LITURGY; SEVERAL PASSAGES BEING MARKED FOR PITCH AND EMPHASIS: WITH SOME OBSERVATIONS ON CLERICAL BRONCHITIS. London: Sampson Low, Son, and Co., 1862. vi, 103 p.

Vandenhoff's elocutionary principles as applied to church rituals.

3126 _____. THE LADY'S READER, WITH SOME PLAIN AND SIMPLE RULES AND INSTRUCTIONS FOR A GOOD STYLE OF READING ALOUD, AND A VARIETY OF SELECTIONS FOR EXERCISE. London: Sampson Low, Son, and Co., 1862. iv, 283 p.

Vandenhoff's techniques applied to the female reader. A few chapters of theory are followed by several sections of exercises and selections.

3127 _____. LEAVES FROM AN ACTOR'S NOTE-BOOK; OR, ANECDOTES OF THE GREEN-ROOM AND STAGE AT HOME AND ABROAD. London: T.W. Cooper and Co., 1860. xvi, 318 p. Also published as LEAVES FROM AN ACTOR'S NOTE-BOOK; WITH REMINISCENCES AND CHIT-CHAT OF THE GREENROOM AND THE STAGE IN ENGLAND AND AMERICA. New York: D. Appleton and Co., 1860. vi, 347 p. Also LEAVES FROM AN ACTOR'S NOTE-BOOK; OR, THE GREEN-ROOM AND THE STAGE. London: J.C. Hotten, 1865. xvi, 318 p.

Vandenhoff's memoirs, stylistically typical of theatrical biographies of the time. He describes his career in England and the United States, including his impressions of the Placides, Charlotte Cushman, Edwin Forrest, Mrs. Sinclair, the elder Hackett, and Edwin Booth. Details seem untrustworthy and the volume contains many typographical errors, but is useful if corroborated. Titles vary somewhat with various editions.

3128 _____ . PLAIN SYSTEM OF ELOCUTION: OR, LOGICAL AND MUSICAL READING AND DECLAMATION WITH EXERCISES IN PROSE AND VERSE, DISTINCTLY MARKED FOR THE GUIDANCE OF THE EAR AND VOICE OF THE PUPIL: TO WHICH IS ADDED, AN APPENDIX, CONTAINING A COPIOUS PRACTISE IN ORATORICAL, POETICAL AND DRAMATIC READING AND RECITATION: THE WHOLE FORMING A COMPLETE SPEAKER, WELL ADAPTED TO PRIVATE PUPILS, CLASSES, AND THE USE OF SCHOOLS; BY G. VANDENHOFF, PROFESSOR OF ELOCUTION IN THE CITY OF NEW-YORK. New York: C. Shepard, 1844, 1845. 164 p.

> A mechanical approach to verbal expression, similar to that of MacKaye or Delsarte. A detailed treatise.

See also nos. 245, 252, 335, 367, 399, 413, 674, 1287, 1855, 1993, and 3168.

VINCENT, MRS. MARY ANN FARLOW

(1818-87)

3129 FIFTIETH ANNIVERSARY OF THE FIRST APPEARANCE ON THE STAGE OF MRS. J. R. VINCENT, BOSTON'S FAVORITE ACTRESS. New York: Augustin Daly, 1885. 28 p. Frontispiece.

> A brief but informative tribute to the actress, containing considerable professional and personal biographical material.

3130 Richardson, James B. MRS. JAMES R. VINCENT: A MEMORIAL ADDRESS DELIVERED AT A MEETING OF THE MANAGERS OF THE VINCENT MEMORIAL HOSPITAL, APRIL 9, 1911. Cambridge, Mass.: Riverside Press, 1911. 39 p. Frontispiece.

> A brief biographical treatment of the actress and her career.

See also nos. 13, 233, 328, 2782, and 2984.

WALLACK FAMILY

Entries for James William and Lester Wallack follow this section.
See nos. 164, 211, 222, 313, 347, 399, 457, 583, 2348, and 2670.

WALLACK, JAMES WILLIAM
(1791-1864)

3131 Burnham, Charles. "The Wallack Centennial." THEATRE (N.Y.) 28
      (September 1918): 150. Illus.

> A biographical tribute to Wallack on the occasion of the
> one-hundreth anniversary of his New York debut.

3132 Wallack, James William. A SKETCH OF THE LIFE OF JAMES WILLIAM
      WALLACK, SEN., ACTOR AND MANAGER. New York: T.H. Morrell,
      1865. 61 p.

> A brief, seemingly rushed, memorial volume, drawn from
> various sources at and around the time of Wallack's death.
> Limited to 250 copies.

See also nos. 118, 121, 146, 183, 245, 302, 328, 334-35, 341, 353, 356,
400-401, 407, 413, 433, 488-89, 1287, 1750, 1762, 1993, 2235-36, 2294, 2461,
and 3168.

WALLACK, LESTER
(1820-88)

3133 [B.] "Memoirs of the Life and Theatrical Career of James W. Wallack."
      GENTLEMAN'S MAGAZINE AND AMERICAN MONTHLY REVIEW 4
      (1939): 9-16, 78-86. Illus.

> Anecdotal reminiscences and biographical sketch, presum-
> ably written by Burton. Adulatory in tone, but reasonably
> detailed.

3134 Buchanan, Robert. "Memoriam." ACADEMY 34 (22 September 1888): 195-96.

> A brief tribute to the high professional skill, charm, grace, courtliness, and dignity of the recently deceased Wallack.

3135 Burnham, Charles. "The Passing of Wallack's." THEATRE (N. Y.) 21 (February 1915): 72-76, 94. Illus.

> A brief history of the theatre building and the career of Lester Wallack.

3136 Florence, William J. "Lester Wallack." NORTH AMERICAN REVIEW 147 (October 1888): 453-59.

> A tribute from Florence, partly biographical, partly a critical assessment.

3137 Stuart, William. "John Lester Wallack." GALAXY 6 (October 1888): 485-92.

> An adulatory tribute to Wallack, describing his theatrical philosophies and including a few biographical details.

3138 Towse, J. Ranken. "Lester Wallack." CRITIC 13 (15 September 1888): 121-22.

> A brief and descriptive tribute to the late actor.

3139 Wallack, Arthur. "Memories of Lester Wallack by His Son." THEATRE (N. Y.) 12 (July 1910): 6-8. Illus.

> Personal reminiscences of an anecdotal nature.

3140 Wallack, John Lester. MEMORIES OF FIFTY YEARS. Edited by Laurence Hutton. New York: Charles Scribner's Sons, 1889. London: S. Low, 1889. 226 p. Index, illus. Reprint. New York: Benjamin Blom, 1969.

> Wallack dictated this memoir during his last years, but did not live to correct the transcriptions. Hutton edited the volume, adding a biographical sketch of Wallack, a list of the characters he played, and various other addenda. Wallack mentions and describes practically every American actor of substance during his time in this country.

See also nos. 118, 123, 163, 227, 242, 336, 341, 343, 356, 363, 375, 386-87, 400-401, 407, 413, 433, 460, 470, 488, 577, 596, 1050, 1595, 3027, and 3143.

WALLER, EMMA (1820-99). See no. 413.

WALSH, BLANCHE

(1873-1915)

3141 Mawson, Harry P. "From Trilby to Tolstoy, Some Account of the Interesting Stage Career of Miss Blanche Walsh." THEATRE (N. Y.) 3 (June
1903): 148-50. Illus.

> A relatively insignificant interview, somewhat biographical
> in nature.

3142 Walsh, Blanche. "Their Beginnings." THEATRE (N. Y.) 5 (July 1905):
181-82. Illus.

> Walsh describes her early life and first role, that of
> Olivia in Louis James's production of THE WINTER'S
> TALE.

See also nos. 28, 270, 381, 413, 479, 550, 555, and 581.

WARD, GENEVIEVE

(1838-1922)

3143 Gustafson, Zadel Barnes [Buddington]. GENEVIEVE WARD. A BIO-
GRAPHICAL SKETCH FROM ORIGINAL MATERIALS DERIVED FROM
HER FAMILY AND FRIENDS. Boston: James R. Osgood, 1882. xv,
261 p.

> Gustafson traces Ward's family back to William the Con-
> queror before describing the actress's career, quoting
> liberally from pertinent publications and documents. An
> appendix contains additional primary material, including
> a record of a law suit against Lester Wallack.

3144 MEMOIR OF GINEVRA GUERRABELLA. New York: T.J. Crowen,
1863. 63 p.

> Ward had a substantial career as an opera singer, using
> the name Ginevra Guerrabella. Illness and overwork
> ruined her voice; she became an actress in 1873. This
> volume describes her career up to age thirty, some years
> before she became an actress.

3145 Ward, Genevieve, and Whiteing, Richard. BOTH SIDES OF THE CUR-
TAIN. New York, London, Toronto, and Melbourne: Cassell and Co.,
1918. 284 p. Index, illus.

> A rambling, self-centered memoir to be used only with
> corroboration. Well illustrated.

See also nos. 236, 245, 263, 391, and 404.

WARDE, FREDERICK BARKHAM

(1851-1935)

3146 Warde, Frederick. FIFTY YEARS OF MAKE-BELIEVE. Los Angeles: Times-Mirror Press, 1923. 314 p. Illus.

> A gracefully written, relatively detailed account of Warde's rise to stardom, which includes useful insights into various performers of the day, such as Edwin Booth, Lawrence Barrett, Maurice Barrymore, and Louis James.

3147 _____. THE FOOLS OF SHAKESPEARE: AN INTERPRETATION OF THEIR WIT, WISDOM AND PERSONALITIES. New York: McBride, Nast and Co., 1913, 1915. Los Angeles: Times-Mirror Press, 1923. 244 p. Illus.

> Warde analyses a dozen of Shakespeare's clown roles, drawing upon his own experiences of having played or watched the roles in performance. He takes some apparent delight in differing sharply from scholarly opinions.

3148 Woods, Alan. "Frederick B. Warde: America's Greatest Forgotten Tragedian." EDUCATIONAL THEATRE JOURNAL 29 (October 1977): 333-44. Illus.

> An unusually successful sketch of an actor-manager whose career flourished outside New York. Well documented.

See also nos. 28, 130, 163, 245, 263, 343, 399, and 561.

WARFIELD, DAVID
(1866-1951)

3149   Bell, Archie. "The Other Side of the Gentle Music Maker." THEATRE
        (N. Y.) 12 (July 1910): 18. Illus.

      Bell describes Warfield's expertise at card tricks.

3150   "David Warfield in 'The Auctioneer.'" HARPER'S WEEKLY 45 (21
        December 1901): 1322.

      An account of Warfield's preparation for the role, citing
      the truthfulness of it as opposed to the stereotyped stage
      Jews of the time.

3151   Eaton, Walter Prichard. "The Rise of David Warfield." AMERICAN
        MAGAZINE 55 (January 1908): 316-23. Illus.

      A gracefully written appreciation of Warfield following
      his success in THE MUSIC MASTER, Eaton nevertheless
      finding minor flaws in his acting.

3152   Hall, Lawrence. "David Warfield: The Actor and the Man." ARENA
        41 (March 1909): 258-69. Illus.

      An idealized biographical sketch, tracing Warfield's
      career and describing his views on the theatre. Some
      of his early work with Belasco is described.

3153   Patterson, Ada. "David Warfield--The Actor and the Man." THEATRE
        (N. Y.) 5 (January 1905): 17-19. Illus.

      An essay of minimal value, containing a few biographical
      details.

3154   "People You Pay to Know: David Warfield: The Music Master."
        NATIONAL MAGAZINE 47 (February 1918): 133. Illus.

      A one-page tribute containing a few biographical details.

3155   Warfield, David. "And the Blind Shall See." THEATRE (N. Y.) 28 (December 1918): 340. Illus.

>Part of a series, "The Most Striking Episode in My Life," in which Warfield describes a visit backstage by Helen Keller.

3156   _____. "Do Actors Feel the Emotion They Portray?" THEATRE (N. Y.) 6 (December 1906): 330. Illus.

>Warfield expresses his preference for the emotional school of acting.

3157   _____. "How I Created 'Simon Levi.'" THEATRE (N. Y.) 2 (March 1902): 16-17. Illus.

>A useful essay on the role of observation of reality in preparing a role.

3158   _____. "How I Play Old Men." GREEN BOOK MAGAZINE 12 (July 1914): 43-47. Illus.

>Warfield suggests he has no insights into his acting techniques and has in fact no idea how he does it.

3159   _____. "My Beginnings." THEATRE (N. Y.) 6 (February 1906): 41-42.

>Warfield describes his career prior to his first engagement with Belasco.

3160   _____. "My Friends Levi, Barwig, and Peter Grimm." AMERICAN MAGAZINE 76 (December 1913): 28-31, 95, 97-102. Illus.

>A substantial autobiographical monograph, perhaps idealized, tracing the actor's rise to stardom.

3161   _____. "My Own Story." McCLURE'S 49 (September 1917): 13-15, 42, 44; (October 1917): 16-17, 67-69. Illus.

>A detailed autobiographical treatment, part 1 describing Warfield's early days in San Francisco and his first years in New York; part 2 recounting his days with Weber and Fields and his first meeting with Belasco.

3162   _____. "Personal Reminiscences." THEATRE (N. Y.) 26 (August 1917): 84-85. Illus.

>Brief autobiographical sketch.

See also nos. 191, 270, 276, 297, 303, 377, 408, 413, 427, 439, 464, 499, 550, 572, 579, 928, 936, 964, 998, 1000, 1002, and 1975.

WARREN FAMILY

WARREN, WILLIAM I
(1767-1832)

3163 "Life of William Warren." MIRROR OF TASTE AND DRAMATIC CENSOR
3 (February 1811): 73-86; (March 1811): 140-51; (April 1811): 213-
21; (May 1811): 274-84; 4 (December 1811): 422-26.

> Although undocumented, a substantial treatment of Warren's
> work in Philadelphia with considerable biographical detail.

3164 Pritner, Calvin L. "William Warren's Financial Arrangements with
Traveling Stars--1805-1829." THEATRE SURVEY 6 (November 1965):
83-90.

> A well-researched and documented study of business condi-
> tions and their reflection upon the theatre of the time as
> exemplified by Warren's practices.

See also nos. 101, 192, 225, 413, 554, and 1008.

WARREN, WILLIAM II
(1812-88)

3165 Ball, William Thomas Winsborough. LIFE AND MEMOIRS OF WILLIAM
WARREN, BOSTON'S FAVORITE COMEDIAN, WITH A FULL ACCOUNT
OF HIS GOLDEN JUBILEE: FIFTY YEARS OF AN ACTOR'S LIFE.
Boston: Daly, 1888. 70 p. Illus.

> An undistinguished text offers only plaudits, but does
> include a season-by-season repertoire of the actor.
> Several excellent photographs are included.

3166 Clapp, Henry Austin. "William Warren." ATLANTIC 62 (December
1888): 786-96.

A tribute penned shortly after the actor's death. Includes descriptions of Warren in most of his more successful roles.

See also nos. 148, 188-89, 210, 213, 222, 233, 245, 261, 279, 328, 356, 370, 383, 407, 413, 431, 438, 454, 503, 514, 518, 524, 538, 2235-36, 2782, 2880, 2984, and 3168.

WEMYSS, FRANCIS COURTNEY

(1797-1859)

3167 Wemyss, Francis Courtney. CHRONOLOGY OF THE AMERICAN STAGE, FROM 1752 TO 1852. New York: W. Taylor and Co., O. A. Roorbach, 1852. Reprint. New York: Benjamin Blom, 1968. 191 p.

> Wemyss attempted to list all the U. S. theatres and their managers up to 1852, but the list is not altogether accurate. The bulk of the volume consists of very short entries on performers, listed in alphabetical order.

3168 _____. TWENTY-SIX YEARS OF THE LIFE OF AN ACTOR AND MANAGER. INTERSPERSED WITH SKETCHES, ANECDOTES AND OPINIONS OF THE PROFESSIONAL MERITS OF THE MOST CELE-BRATED ACTORS AND ACTRESSES OF OUR DAY. 2 vols. in 1. New York: Brugess, Stringer and Co., 1847. 402 p.

> A valuable insight into the productions' circumstances of the time. Wemyss also includes his impressions of such performers as the elder Booth, Clara Fisher, William Warren, William Wood, Thomas Abthorpe Cooper, James Wallack, Henry Placide, Edwin Forrest, Thomas S. Hamb-lin, the Chapmans, James H. Hackett, Joseph Jefferson III, George Handel Hill, Augustus Addams, Sol Smith, Frank Murdoch, Joe Cowell, Charlotte Barnes, George Vandenhoff, William E. Burton, Charlotte Cushman, Charles Thorne, and Anna Cora Mowatt.

See also nos. 146, 359, 393, 413, and 2461.

WEST, THOMAS WADE
(1745-99)

3169 Curtis, Julia. "The Architecture and Appearance of the Charleston Theatre: 1793-1883." EDUCATIONAL THEATRE JOURNAL 23 (March 1971): 1-12. Illus.

> Includes some material concerning West as a manager in Charleston.

3170 _____. "Thomas Wade West's Problematic Puffery." THEATRE SURVEY 13 (November 1972): 94-99.

> A brief overview of West's career in the theatre prior to his arrival in New York in 1790.

3171 Hoole, William Stanley. "Two Famous Theatres of the Old South." SOUTH ATLANTIC QUARTERLY 36 (July 1937): 273-77.

> Includes a description of West's attempted theatrical revival in Charleston in 1792.

3172 Sherman, Susanne Ketchum. "Thomas Wade West, Theatrical Impressario, 1790-1799." WILLIAM AND MARY QUARTERLY 9 (January 1952): 10-28.

> An exceptional essay which supplements standard sources with newspaper accounts and unpublished materials about West and his career.

See also no. 240.

WESTLEY, HELEN
(1875-1942)

3173   Bird, Carol.   "An Actress Who Plays Unusual Women. " THEATRE (N. Y.)
        36 (August 1922): 72, 124.

        Bird quotes Westley as she expresses a preference for the
        sort of roles which brought her stardom.

3174   [Search-Light.]   "Adventures with a Difference. " NEW YORKER   2 (27
        March 1926): 15-16.   Illus.

        A typical NEW YORKER profile, evocative rather than
        informative and descriptive rather than factual.

See also nos. 13, 413, 464, 564, and 579.

WHEATLEY, WILLIAM (1816-76). See nos. 396 and 405.

WHIFFEN, MRS. THOMAS

(1845-1936)

3175 Robertson, Catherine. "Is It Luck or Pluck?" THEATRE (N. Y.) 33 (April 1921): 256, 294.

> Robertson quotes Whiffen at age seventy-five as suggesting her career was more influenced by perseverance than by chance or even talent.

3176 Sumner, Keene. "A Wonderful Old Lady Who Has Been on the Stage 57 Years." AMERICAN MAGAZINE 94 (October 1922): 34-36, 169-76. Illus.

> A chatty reminiscence of Whiffen, written when she was seventy-seven, thus comprehensive, albeit undocumented.

3177 Whiffen, Mrs. Thomas. KEEPING OFF THE SHELF. New York: E. P. Dutton and Co. , 1928. 203 p. Illus.

> Somewhat idealized and romanticized memoirs, which include anecdotal material about Fay Templeton, David Belasco, Modjeska, William Gillette, John Drew, and Margaret Anglin. See no. 3178.

3178 _____. "Keeping Off the Shelf." WOMAN'S HOME COMPANION 55 (February 1928): 7-9, 86, 88, 91-92; (March 1928): 12-14, 136, 138-40, 142-43; (April 1928): 29-30, 46, 48, 50; (May 1928): 31-32, 54, 56. Illus.

> A serialized treatment of no. 3177.

3179 _____. "Then and Now in the Theatre." DRAMA 13 (May-June 1923): 286-88. Illus.

> Brief and rambling reminiscences.

See also nos. 13, 279, and 414.

WIGNELL, THOMAS (1753–1803). See nos. 101, 123, 129, 138, 158, 188, 192, 240–41, 413, 535, 541, 554, and 1008.

WILLARD, E.S.

(1853-1915)

3180   Goddard, A. PLAYERS OF THE PERIOD. A SERIES OF ANECDOTAL, BIOGRAPHICAL, AND CRITICAL MONOGRAPHS OF THE LEADING ENGLISH ACTORS OF THE DAY. 2 vols. London: Dean and Son, 1891. 368, 316 p. Illus.

> Among the players with chapters devoted to them is Willard, although only his career in England is covered.

3181   Wagstaff, William de. "Chats with Players." THEATRE (N. Y.) 2 (February 1902): 13–15.

> Wagstaff quotes Willard as he comments on the general state of the profession at the time.

See also nos. 58, 236, 279, 380, 399, 404–6, and 596.

WILSON, FRANCIS

(1854-1935)

3182 Bangs, John Kendrick. "On the Links with Francis Wilson." HARPER'S WEEKLY 45 (1901): 868-69. Illus.

>A humorous account of Wilson on the golf course at the Pelham Country Club.

3183 Kobbé, Gustav. "Francis Wilson and His Bookish Home." LADIES' HOME JOURNAL, March 1903, pp. 8-9. Illus.

>A description of Wilson's home, "The Orchard," in New Rochell, his library of over ten thousand volumes, and his extensive collection of paintings.

3184 Wagstaff, William de. "Chats with Players." THEATRE (N.Y.) 2 (March 1902): 13-15. Illus.

>A brief interview with Wilson, primarily concerning his home in New Rochelle.

3185 Wilson, Francis. FRANCIS WILSON'S LIFE OF HIMSELF. Boston and New York: Houghton Mifflin Co., 1924. 444 p. Index, illus.

>An exceptionally well-written autobiography with substantial sections on Joseph Jefferson III, Edwin Booth, the actors' strike, and the Theatre Syndicate.

3186 _____. "Keeping the Stage Clean." OUTLOOK 139 (11 March 1925): 370-72. Illus.

>Wilson condemns the attack of "sultry" plays then on Broadway, hoping that audience rejection of them would make censorship unnecessary.

3187 _____. "Memories of the Old Broadway Theatre." THEATRE (N.Y.) 49 (March 1929): 42, 81. Illus.

Wilson offers some very general remarks about the time
of the demolition of the Broadway Theatre.

3188 _____. "We Old Time Troupers." THEATRE GUILD MAGAZINE 6
(November 1928): 32-34.

Nominally a review of TROUPERS OF THE GOLD COAST,
but Wilson comments on the state of the theatre in general
at that time.

See also nos. 28, 112, 177-78, 243, 270, 276, 279, 287, 321, 361, 378,
412, 510, 513, 560, 591, 1120, 2220, 2274-75, and 2852.

WOLHEIM, LOUIS

(1881-1931)

3189   Bird, Carol. "Enter the Monkey Man." THEATRE (N.Y.) 36 (August 1922): 102, 120.

        Bird interviews Wolheim about his sudden success as Yank in O'Neill's THE HAIRY APE.

3190   Collins, F.L. "A Motion Picture Roll of Honor." GOOD HOUSE-KEEPING, August 1932, pp. 62-63, 156-58. Illus.

        Collins applauds Wolheim for his film work as he nominates Wolheim, Lon Chaney, Theodore Roberts, and John Bunny for a cinematic honor roll.

3191   Wolheim, Louis. "I Prefer the Movies to the Stage." THEATRE (N.Y.) 46 (September 1927): 41. Illus.

        Wolheim expresses his preference for more frequent work which he could obtain in film as well as for the California climate.

See also nos. 9, 377, 412, and 464.

WOOD, MRS. JOHN (1831-1915). See nos. 13, 21, 26, 203, 252, 407, 526, 2330, 2782, and 3027.

WOOD, PEGGY

(1892-1978)

3192   Cruikshank, Herbert. "The Girl with Six Careers." MOTION PICTURE MAGAZINE 38 (November 1929): 82, 129. Illus.

> A somewhat confused analysis of Wood's recent stage work. Of minimal value.

3193   "Miss Peggy Wood in Four Acts of a Dress Drama." VOGUE, 15 March 1941, pp. 78-79. Illus.

> Fashion notes.

3194   Mullett, Mary B. "Peggy Wood Seems Like Such a Nice Girl." AMERICAN MAGAZINE 102 (August 1926): 36-37, 161, 164, 166. Illus.

> A fan-oriented monograph, although containing some bits of biographical information scattered throughout.

3195   Weaver, John V.A. "My Wife Cured Me." COSMOPOLITAN 77 (November 1924): 48-49, 102. Illus.

> Weaver, Wood's husband, claims to have been a "bore and a pest" because of an inferiority complex, but suggests his wife cured him of these problems.

3196   Wood, Peggy. ACTORS--AND PEOPLE: BOTH SIDES OF THE FOOT-LIGHTS. New York and London: D. Appleton and Co., 1930. 178 p. Illus.

> Rambling and chatty theatrical reminiscences, requiring corroboration.

3197   _____. ARTS AND FLOWERS. New York: William Morrow and Co., 1963. 189 p. Illus.

> A loosely written but charming account of the author's later career in film and video.

3198 _____. "Festivals: True and False." THEATRE ARTS 44 (December 1960): 16-17.

>Wood expresses suspicion about New York theatre festivals and predicts success for the regional repertory companies.

3199 _____. "Glasses Aren't So Bad." AMERICAN MAGAZINE 114 (December 1932): 51, 78, 80. Illus.

>Wood describes her adjustment to wearing glasses.

3200 _____. "How? I Don't Know." WOMAN CITIZEN 9 (16 May 1925): 10-11, 30. Illus.

>Wood, asked how to succeed in the theatre, professes ignorance of the process, saying one "just goes on the stage."

3201 _____. HOW YOUNG YOU LOOK: MEMOIRS OF A MIDDLE-SIZED ACTRESS. New York: Farrar and Rinehart, 1941. 277 p. Illus.

>Rambling memoirs of the actress's childhood up to 1939, with scattered references to various performers in New York and London.

3202 _____. "Musical Comedy or Drama? An Alternative." DRAMA (Chicago) 15 (October 1925): 6-7. Illus.

>Wood contrasts acting techniques in both types of production and expresses her hope to continue in both.

3203 _____. "Paint!" GREEN BOOK MAGAZINE 16 (October 1916): 615-21. Illus.

>Wood describes the horror of three nontheatrical women watching her apply makeup.

3204 _____. STAR-WAGON. New York: Farrar and Rinehart, 1936. 311 p.

>A novel of borderline relevancy to the theatre.

3205 _____. "Strange Alleys." GREEN BOOK MAGAZINE 15 (March 1910): 522-29. Illus.

>Somewhat romanticized tales of being on the road and doing one-night stands.

See also nos. 5, 276, 413, 542, 1714, and 2357.

WOOD, WILLIAM BURKE

(1779-1861)

3206   "Sketch of the Life of William B. Wood." ALBION (1811): 230-35.

      Unavailable for examination.

3207   "Sketch of the Life of Mr. William B. Wood." MIRROR OF TASTE AND DRAMATIC CENSOR 2 (November 1810): 230-35.

      A brief biographical essay, undocumented but seemingly useful.

3208   Wood, William Burke. PERSONAL RECOLLECTIONS OF THE STAGE, EMBRACING NOTICES OF ACTORS, AUTHORS, AND AUDITORS, DURING A PERIOD OF FORTY YEARS. Philadelphia: Henry Carey Baird, 1855. xxi, 477 p. Frontispiece.

      Wood sought to counterpoint Dunlap's HISTORY OF THE AMERICAN THEATRE (1832, no. 147), which covered developments in the northern United States, with his own reminiscences of Philadelphia, Baltimore, Washington, D.C., and Alexandria. In so doing, he describes almost every player of note at the time in this valuable primary source. See no. 99 for index.

See also nos. 123, 130, 148, 188, 192-93, 216, 296, 358, 413, 554, 2348, 2461, 2670, and 3168.

YURKA, BLANCHE
(1893-1974)

3209   Maltin, Leonard, ed.   THE REAL STARS: ARTICLES AND INTERVIEWS
ON HOLLYWOOD'S GREAT CHARACTER ACTORS.   New York: Curtis
Books, 1973. 320 p.   Illus.

>   Includes a brief biographical sketch (pages 309-20) and
>   a filmography by Mel Schuster.   Yurka is quoted as deni-
>   grating her career in films.

3210   Row, Arthur William.   "A Pilgrimage to Stardom: An Interview with
Blanche Yurka."   DRAMA (Chicago) 18 (April 1928): 196-98.   Illus.

>   Yurka is quoted as advocating perserverance as the quality
>   most essential to achieving star status.

3211   _____.   "A Star Who is a Luminary."   POET LORE   38 (Spring 1929):
132-33.

>   A brief and adulatory essay, praising Yurka for her lack
>   of concern with the passing of her youth.

3212   Yurka, Blanche.   BOHEMIAN GIRL: BLANCHE YURKA'S THEATRICAL
LIFE.   Athens: Ohio University Press, 1970.   viii, 302 p.   Index,
illus.

>   Yurka describes her sixty-year acting career in a lucid
>   and readable style.   She also includes her reactions to
>   and work with such performers and theatricians as John
>   Barrymore, David Belasco, Katharine Cornell, Jane Cowl,
>   and the Lunts.

3213   _____.   "Speed Mania is the Curse of Modern Drama."   THEATRE (N.Y.)
49 (May 1929): 20, 58.   Illus.

>   Yurka decries the rate of output in the theatre, especially
>   that of playwrights, whose work she considers done far
>   too hastily.

3214 Zachary, Ralph. "Flowermaiden." OPERA NEWS 35 (3 April 1971):
12-13. Illus.

> Yurka recalls her failed career as a singer in opera,
> which preceded her entry into the theatre.

See also nos. 9, 26, 413, and 547.

ADDENDUM

ADDENDUM

3215 Bank, Rosemarie K. "Louisa Lane Drew at the Arch Street Theatre: Repertory and Actor Training in Nineteenth Century Philadelphia." THEATRE STUDIES, nos. 24-25 (1977-79): 36-46. Illus.

A well-researched and nicely executed account of Mrs. Drew in Philadelphia. Useful.

3216 Belasco, David. "About Play Production." SATURDAY EVENING POST 192 (10 January 1920): 17, 36, 38. Illus.

While suggesting that modern producers work too quickly and thus lost artistic potential, Belasco describes Joseph Jefferson III as Rip van Winkle and Bob Acres. Belasco also describes his concepts of dramatic structure.

3217 _____. "About Playwriting." SATURDAY EVENING POST 192 (1 November 1919): 5, 153-54. Illus.

Belasco suggests that would-be playwrights study "theatre mechanics," the practical aspects of the stage, before writing.

3218 _____. "'Atmosphere' on the Stage." AMERICAN MAGAZINE 56 (August 1903): 404-5.

Belasco defines atmosphere as the impression of reality, exemplifying his theories with THE DARLING OF THE GODS, his latest success.

3219 _____. "Beauty as I See It." ARTS AND DECORATION 19 (July 1923): 9-10, 60-61. Illus.

Belasco describes his personal and professional love and need for the beautiful, describing beauty as the awakening of the imagination.

3220 _____. "My Ideal Home." COUNTRY LIFE (USA) 40 (October 1921): 37, 39. Illus.

In a companion piece to similar articles by others, Belasco expresses his love for "all things Colonial," including architecture.

3221 Bergman, Herbert. "David Belasco's Dramatic Theory." UNIVERSITY OF TEXAS STUDIES IN ENGLISH 32 (1953): 110-22.

Bergman draws upon several published sources as well as the various files in the New York Public Library Theatre Collection and the Harvard Theatre Collection to suggest that Belasco reflected the theatrical tastes of the time, considering drama as entertainment and recreation, "not the proper medium for cranks to rant their isms." Well-documented.

3222 Berliner, Burt, ed. FIFTY FAMOUS FACES IN TRANSITION. New York: Fireside, Simon and Schuster, 1980. 96 p. Illus.

A collection of photographs of celebrities at various stages in their lives, among them Tallulah Bankhead.

3223 Bordman, Gerald. AMERICAN OPERETTA FROM H.M.S. PINAFORE TO SWEENEY TODD. New York and Oxford: Oxford University Press, 1981. Index, illus. 194 p.

A history of American operetta, with descriptions of such stars as Lillian Russell and Francis Wilson.

3224 Brenman-Gibson, Margaret. CLIFFORD ODETS: AMERICAN PLAYWRIGHT: THE YEARS FROM 1906 TO 1940. New York: Atheneum, 1981. xiv, 718 p. Index, illus., bibliog.

A massive and definitive biography of the playwright by a friend of Odets, this volume won the George Freedley Award for 1981. In the course of the book, descriptions are included of Stella Adler, Tallulah Bankhead, Morris Carnovsky, and Lee Strasberg.

3225 Bryer, Jackson R., ed. THE THEATRE WE WORKED FOR: THE LETTERS OF EUGENE O'NEILL TO KENNETH MACGOWAN. New Haven and London: Yale University Press, 1982. xiii, 267 p. Index, illus.

O'Neill's letters frequently mention John Barrymore, David Belasco, and Katharine Cornell.

3226 Chinoy, Helen Krich, and Jenkins, Linda Walsh, eds. WOMEN IN THE AMERICAN THEATRE, CAREERS, IMAGES, MOVEMENTS. AN ILLUSTRATED ANTHOLOGY AND SOURCEBOOK. New York: Crown Publishers, Inc., 1981. 364 p. Index, illus., bibliog., notes.

A collection of essays, illustrations, and sources comprising the story of women in the American theatre. Separate essays

treat Anne Brunton Merry, Charlotte Cushman, Adah Isaacs
Menken, Mary Shaw, Ruth Draper, and Eva Le Gallienne.

3227 Cole, Susan S. "Charlotte Cushman as Romeo." SOUTHERN THEATRE 24
(Fall 1981): 3-10. Illus., notes.

A brief stage history of Cushman in her most successful breeches
role, drawn for the most part from standard sources.

3228 Crane, William H. "The Modern Cart of Thespis." NORTH AMERICAN
REVIEW 154 (1891): 472-79.

Crane describes his opinions of the state of the American theatre at the time, both positive and negative.

3229 Cypkin, Diane. "Of Madame Kalich and the Kreutzer Sonata."
PASSING SHOW 6 (Winter 1982): 6-7. Illus.

This serial is the newsletter of the Shubert Archive. Cypkin
describes the materials in the archives relevant to Kalich's tour
in THE KREUTZER SONATA by Jacob Gordin.

3230 Fiske, Minnie Maddern. "Effects of a 'First Night' upon the Actor."
CRITIC 39 (October 1901): 317-18.

Fiske describes the various ways that opening performances affect performers, reaching no substantial conclusions.

3231 Goldstein, S. Ezra. "Why Is This Man Angry about High School Theatre?"
DRAMATICS 46 (January-February 1977): 10-17. Illus.

Strasberg takes high school theatre to task in no uncertain terms,
coming down heavily on the teachers. Succeeding issues include
reader responses, ranging from the reasoned to the incoherent.

3232 Gordon, Ruth. SHADY LADY. New York: Arbor House, 1981. 223 p.

A novel describing the career of a midwestern girl who rises to
fame as a Ziegfeld in the 1920s.

3233 Guthrie, Tyrone. "Is There Madness in the Method?" NEW YORK TIMES
MAGAZINE, 15 September 1957, pp. 23, 82-83. Illus.

Although Guthrie expresses his respect for Strasberg, he predicts
the Method may all too easily become a thing of the past.

3234 Hare, Arnold. GEORGE FREDERICK COOKE: THE ACTOR AND THE
MAN. London: Society for Theatre Research, 1980. viii, 248 p.
Index, illus., bibliog., notes, appendixes.

Hare describes the relationship between Cooke and Thomas Abthorpe Cooper, drawing heavily upon Dunlap's biography of Cooke.

3235 LaCasse, Don. "Edwin Booth on Dion Boucicault, Playwriting, and Play Production--a Previously Unpublished Letter." THEATRE SURVEY 21, No. 2 (November 1980): 181-84.

> LaCasse discovered a letter in the Rosenbach Museum and Library in Philadelphia in which Booth compares Boucicault and Shakespeare.

3236 "Melvyn Douglas." DRAMATICS 49 (November-December 1977): 18-21. Illus.

> An interview conducted by Thomas H. Arther, who was preparing a biography of Douglas. Douglas discusses the difference between film and theatrical acting, as well as his training for both.

3237 Miller, Tice L. BOHEMIANS AND CRITICS: AMERICAN THEATRE CRITICISM IN THE NINETEENTH CENTURY. Metuchen, N.J., and London: Scarecrow Press, 1981. x, 180 p. Index, bibliog.

> A brief but useful analysis of five of America's leading critics of the nineteenth century. In the course of the text, some mention is made of the Booths, Dion Boucicault, John Brougham, Ada Clare, Charlotte Cushman, Augustin Daly, the Davenports, Mrs. Fiske, Edwin Forrest, Edward Harrigan, Matilda Heron, Joseph Jefferson III, Laura Keene, John McCullough, Modjeska, Clara Morris, Anna Cora Mowatt, and Lester Wallack.

3238 Molin, Sven Eric, and Goodefellow, Robin. DION BOUCICAULT, THE SHAUGHRAN: A DOCUMENTARY LIFE, LETTERS AND SELECTED WORKS: PART ONE: THE EARLY YEARS. Newark, N.J.: Proscenium Press, 1979. 108 p. Illus.

> Apparently the first in a series of volumes on Boucicault. This volume concludes its coverage in 1844 with the production of OLD HEADS AND YOUNG HEARTS.

3239 Mordden, Ethan. THE AMERICAN THEATRE. New York: Oxford University Press, 1981. ix, 350 p. Index, bibliog.

> A history of the American theatre which attempts to describe the processes by which a British colonial theatre became uniquely American. Some material is included on Maude Adams, Stella Adler, Tallulah Bankhead, the Barrymores, David Belasco, Dion Boucicault, Ina Claire, Katharine Cornell, Jane Cowl, Jeanne Eagles, Minnie Maddern Fiske, Lynn Fontanne, William Gillette, Ruth Gordon, Helen Hayes, James A. Herne, Alfred Lunt, James O'Neill, John Howard Payne, and Lee Strasberg.

3240 Morris, Clara. "An Interview with Mark Twain." METROPOLITAN MAGAZINE, March 1904, pp. 867-72.

Unavailable for examination.

3241 _____. LEFT IN CHARGE. New York: G.W. Dillingham Co., 1904. 355 p.

Confirmed in the NATIONAL UNION CATALOG, but unavailable for examination.

3242 _____. LITTLE "JIM CROW," AND OTHER STORIES OF CHILDREN. New York: Century Co., 1899. 226 p. Frontispiece.

Eleven undistinguished short stories for children.

3243 _____. THE NEW "EAST LYNNE." New York: C.H. Doscher and Co., 1908. 326 p. Frontispiece.

Confirmed in the NATIONAL UNION CATALOG, but unavailable for examination.

3244 _____. "Reflections of an Actress." NORTH AMERICAN REVIEW 153 (September 1891): 329-36.

Rambling remarks on the nature of the theatre and the profession of acting.

3245 _____. A SILENT SINGER. New York: Brentano's, 1899, 1902. 302 p.

Eleven short stories of no particular merit.

3246 _____. "Stage Notes." CRITIC 36 (January 1900): 61-63; (February 1900): 148-51; (April 1900): 318-20; (May 1900): 444-46; (June 1900): 540-42; 37 (July 1900): 32-33; (October 1900): 347-49; 38 (January 1901): 25-28; (May 1901): 445-47; 39 (January 1901): 59-61.

Rambling remarks and anecdotes, mostly autobiographical. Augustin Daly is mentioned in the first article; John E. Owens in the next to last one.

3247 _____. THE TROUBLE WOMAN. New York and London: Funk and Wagnalls Company, 1904. 58 p.

Confirmed in the NATIONAL UNION CATALOG, but unavailable for examination.

3248 Nazel, Joseph. PAUL ROBESON: BIOGRAPHY OF A PROUD MAN. Los Angeles: Holloway House Publishing Co., 1980. 216 p. Bibliog.

A somewhat popularized biography, undocumented but drawn

from traditional sources. Perhaps most useful as an introduction to Robeson's controversial career and life.

3249 Peary, Danny, ed. CLOSE-UPS: INTIMATE PROFILES OF MOVIE STARS BY THEIR CO-STARS, DIRECTORS, SCREENWRITERS AND FRIENDS. New York: Galahad Books, 1978. xvi, 592 p. Index, illus., filmographies.

A fan-oriented volume, lavishly illustrated, with brief sketches of John Barrymore, Fredric March, Ruth Gordon, and Lillian Gish.

3250 Peck, S. "Temple of the Method." NEW YORK TIMES MAGAZINE, 6 May 1956, pp. 26-27, 42, 44, 47-48. Illus.

A description of the methods used at the Actors Studio as administered by Strasberg and the members' devotion to the institution.

3251 PERFORMING ARTS LIBRARIES AND MUSEUMS. Edited by Andre Veinstein and Rosamond Gilder. 2nd ed., rev. Paris: Centre National de la Recherche Scientifique, 1967. 801 p. Indexes. Published in 1960 as PERFORMING ARTS COLLECTIONS: AN INTERNATIONAL HANDBOOK.

A description of the more important collections, including those in the United States. Individual actors are indexed.

3252 Rahill, Frank. THE WORLD OF MELODRAMA. University Park: Pennsylvania State University Press, 1967. xviii, 325 p. Index, bibliog.

Chapter 22 (pages 182-92) is entitled "Boucicault and the Stage Irishman." Chapter 32 (pages 262-71), "Melodrama Comes of Age," describes the contributions of David Belasco and William Gillette to that genre.

3253 Robbins, Jhan. FRONT PAGE MARRIAGE. New York: G.P. Putnam's Sons, 1982. 224 p.

A popular biography of Helen Hayes.

3254 Robeson, Susan. THE WHOLE WORLD IN HIS HANDS: A PICTORIAL PORTRAIT OF PAUL ROBESON. Secaucus, N.H.: Citadel Press, 1981. 254 p. Illus., notes.

A heavily illustrated treatment with minimal text, prepared by Robeson's grand-daughter. The notes include several important newspaper citations.

3255 Shafer, Yvonne. "George L. Fox and the HAMLET Travesty." THEATRE STUDIES, nos. 24-25 (1977-79): 78-93. Illus.

A solidly researched and gracefully written account of Fox's travesty of Edwin Booth's HAMLET.

3256 Shipman, David. THE GREAT MOVIE STARS: THE GOLDEN YEARS. New Rev. Ed. New York: Hill and Wang, 1979. 588 p. Index, illus., bibliog.

A substantial series of brief biographical sketches of film stars, some of whom had stage careers. Included are Mary Astor, Tallulah Bankhead, John Barrymore, Billie Burke, Ruth Chatterton, Melvyn Douglas, Marie Dressler, Lillian Gish, Helen Hayes, Fredric March, Paul Muni, and Paul Robeson.

3257 Slide, Anthony. THE VAUDEVILLIANS: A DICTIONARY OF VAUDE-VILLE PERFORMERS. Westport, Conn.: Arlington House, 1981. xiv, 173 p. Illus., bibliog.

A guide to the outstanding performers of vaudeville, preceded by a brief historical overview of that form. Some of the stars covered are Marie Cahill, George M. Cohan, Marie Dressler, May Irwin, Elsie Janis, Cissie Loftus, Florence Mills, Lillian Russell, and Fred Stone.

3258 Stout, Wesley Winans. "Little Eva is Seventy-five." SATURDAY EVEN-ING POST, 8 October 1927, pp. 10-11, 191, 193, 194, 197-98, 201. Illus.

A history of the novel, UNCLE TOM'S CABIN, and the various staged versions thereof. Includes material on G.L. Fox, the Howard family, and DeWolf Hopper.

3259 Strasberg, Lee. "How To Be an Actor." SATURDAY REVIEW OF LITERA-TURE 38 (July 1955): 18.

Strasberg reviews STANISLAVSKI DIRECTS by Nikolai M. Gor-chakov, giving the volume considerable praise.

3260 TWENTIETH-CENTURY AMERICAN DRAMATISTS. Volume 7 of DIC-TIONARY OF LITERARY BIOGRAPHY. 2 vols. Detroit, Mich.: Gale Research Co., 1981. Index, illus., bibliog.

Biographical and critical sketches of this century's outstanding dramatists. Walter J. Meserve wrote a nine-page entry on Belasco, including a bibliography and a list of selected produc-tions.

3261 Vaughn, Jack A. EARLY AMERICAN DRAMATISTS FROM THE BEGINNING TO 1900. New York: Frederick Ungar Publishing Co., 1981. 193 p. Index, illus., bibliog.

A short history of U.S. dramaturgy, with chapters or sections

on several playwrights who were actors: John Howard Payne,
Anna Cora Mowatt, Dion Boucicault, and James A. Herne.
Augustin Daly and David Belasco are also treated.

3262 Weichmann, Louis J. A TRUE HISTORY OF THE ASSASSINATION OF
ABRAHAM LINCOLN AND THE CONSPIRACY OF 1865. Edited by
Floyd E. Risvold. New York: Vintage Books, 1977. xxx, 492 p.
Index, notes.

Weichmann was the chief witness for the U.S. government in
the prosecution of the conspirators and prepared this account
before he died in 1902, but neither he nor his family published
it. Risvold obtained a copy from Weichmann's neice in 1972,
adding his own notes. Booth's career is described, although his
political views are described in more detail.

3263 Young, Stark. STARK YOUNG: A LIFE IN THE ARTS--LETTERS, 1900-
1962. 2 vols. Edited by John Pilkington. Baton Rouge: Louisiana State
University Press, 1976.

The Lunts are described.

INDEXES

AUTHOR INDEX

This index includes all authors, editors, compilers, translators, and other contributors to works cited in the text. References are to entry numbers and alphabetization is letter by letter.

A

A., W.B. 1733
Abbott, Lawrence F. 1702
Abbott, Lyman 1036-37
Abbott, Willis J. 1547
Abthorpe, Ray 1734
Adams, Cindy 3045
Adams, John 1995
Adams, M. Ray 2560
Adams, Maude 601-3
Adams, Mildred 414, 688, 1020, 1453-54
Adams, William 1
Agate, James 673
Aherne, Brian 1455
Albert, A.D., Jr. 2217
Albert, Dora 909
Albert, Hollis 775
Alden, Barbara 1849
Aldrich, Mildred 2970
Aldrich, Mrs. Thomas Bailey 1038
Aldrich, Thomas Bailey 1039, 1171
Alexander, J.W. 1906
Alger, William Rounseville 1850
Allen, Hervey 2753
Allen, Viola 663-68
Alpert, Hollis 3046
Altemus, Jameson Torr 2580
Ames, Noel 1486
Amory, Cleveland 2, 272

Anderson, James R. 521
Anderson, John 115, 415, 2334
Anderson, Mary 674-76
Andrews, Alan 2961
Anglin, Margaret 689-99
Antrim, Doron K. 877
Appleton, William W. 1183
Arce, Hector 2761
Archbald, Anne 2282, 2765
Archer, William 416, 1184
Arell, Ruth 2041
Arliss, George 1806
Armstrong, Sargent 2350
Arnott, James Fullarton 36
Aronson, Rudolph 273, 2852
Arther, Thomas H. 3236
Arthur, Sir George C.A. 274
Ashby, Clifford 1524, 1807, 2607, 2672
Aston, Anthony 714-15
Atkinson, Brooks 116-19
Aulicino, Armand 3047
Austin, W.W. 1595
Ayres, Alfred 352, 489. See also Osmun, Thomas Embley

B

B. 3133
B., B. See Bayle, Barnard
B., H.T. 2195
B., T. 1040

C

Forrester, Izola 1148
Forster, John 1859
Foster, Lois M. 159
Foust, Clement Edgar 1860
Fowler, Gene 846-47
Fowler, Will 848
Fox, Dixon Ryan 160
Fox, Mary Virginia 807
Francis, John Wakefield 161
Frank, Gerald 828
Franklin, Irene 443, 2857
Franklin, Rebecca 2051
Frasher, James E. 1960
Frazier, George 748
Frederick, J. 1099
Frederick, Pauline 1891-94
Freedley, George 61, 2354
French, J.M. 1149
French, William F. 845
Frenz, Horst 1071
Frey, Albert R. 680
Frohman, Daniel 162, 557-59, 575, 1861
Fronshage, Ernst H. 1758
Frost, David 2052
Frothingham, O.B. 1072
Fuller, Charles F., Jr. 1073
Fuller, Edward 163
Fuller, Lucy Derby 2964
Funke, Lewis 298, 2053, 2066
Furnas, J.C. 597
Furness, Horace Howard, Jr. 849
Fyles, Franklin 2408
Fyles, Vanderheyden 444, 1756, 2683, 2767

G

Gabriel, Gilbert W. 850
Gafford, Lucille 1296
Gagey, Edmond M. 164
Gaige, Crosby 1507
Gale, Minna 1074
Gallegly, J.S. 1075
Gallegly, Joseph 165
Gallico, Paul 9
Gannon, Marie Louise 1658
Gard 536
Gard, Robert E. 166
Gardner, Martin 2140
Garfield, David 167, 3052
Garland, Hamlin 1914, 2100-2103, 2589

Garland, Robert 1415
Garrett, Kurt L. 445
Garside, Frances L. 3010
Garvey, Marcus 2795
Gassner, John 299, 3060
Gay, Valerie 2466
Gebbie, George 356
Gehman, Richard 2467
Gelb, Arthur 2710
Gelb, Barbara 2710
Gelb, George W. 2011
Geller, James Jacob 300
Genest, John 2565
George, Grace 1890-1900
George, Joseph, Jr. 1150
Gerson, Noel Bertram 2534
Gerson, Virginia 555
Gibson, Ida McGlone 2858
Gielgud, John 1679
Gilbert, Anne Hartley 1903-4
Gilbert, Douglas 168
Gilbert, Vedder Morris 2728
Gilder, Joseph B. 2226
Gilder, R.W. 2227
Gilder, Rosamond 60-61, 971, 1607, 1716, 2228, 2590, 3251
Gilford, Jack 2636
Gilford, Madeline 2636
Gill, Brendan 749
Gillette, William 300, 1915
Gilliam, Dorothy Butler 2796
Gillis, Hugh 1025
Gilmore, Margalo (Mrs. Robert Ross) 1463
Gish, Dorothy 1941-43
Gish, Lillian 1958-65
Glover, Arnold 1176
Glover, Lyman Beecher 169, 670, 2409, 2916
Goddard, A. 3180
Goddard, Henry P. 446, 701, 771, 1560, 1627, 1846, 2701, 2768, 2965
Godwin, Parke 1076
Gohdes, Clarence 62-63
Goldbeck, Elisabeth 2054
Golden, Sylvia B. 1022, 1517, 2777
Goldsmith, Berthold H. 1591
Goldstein, S. Ezra 3231
Goodale, Katherine [Kitty Molony] 1077

Goodefellow, Robin 3238
Goodman, Randolph 2356
Goodnow, Ruby Ross 1648
Goodrich, Marc 447
Goodwin, Nat 1974-75
Gorchakov, Nikolai M. 3259
Gordin, Jacob 3229
Gordon, James 1331
Gordon, Ruth 1978-83, 3232
Gorman, Herbert 2535
Gotfryd, Alex 2639
Gould, Thos. Ridgeway 1175
Govier, Georgia Bowen 2454
Graf, LeRoy P. 2229
Graham, Franklin 170
Graham, Jean 2684
Graham, Peter John 10
Graham, Philip 1313
Graham, Shirley 2797
Grant, J. 2163
Grant, Jack 1338
Grau, Maurice 560
Grau, Robert 448
Graves, Ralph 449
Gray, David 616, 617
Gray, Frances 2685
Gray, Giles Wilkeson 64-65
Gray, Paul 3053
Graydon, Alexander 1666
Grayson, C. 750
Grebanier, Bernard 171
Green, Abel 172-73, 301
Green, Carol Hurd 26
Greene, Clay M. 2410
Green, Roger Lancelyn 174
Grenfell, Joyce 1675
Gresham, William Lindsay 2162
Grey, Daniel 808
Grey, Katherine 451
Griffin, Alice 1459
Griffith, Frank Carlos 1823
Grisvard, Larry E. 1636
Gronowicz, Antoni 2591
Grossman, C. Edwin Booth 2230
Grossman, Edwina Booth 1078-79
Grover, Edwin Osgood 2383
Goudiss, C. Houston 1757
Guiles, Fred Lawrence 2762
Gustafson, Zadel Barnes [Buddington] 3143
Guthrie, Tyrone 3233

H

Hackett, James Henry 1991-95
Hackett, James K. 2003-7
Hackett, Norman 561, 2189
Hagan, John S.G. 175
Hager, Steven 3054
Halbert, Delancey M. 808a
Hall, Florence Marion Howe 1080
Hall, Gladys 751, 782, 1250,
1277, 1339-40, 1354, 1464,
1794, 1944-45, 1966, 2291,
2312, 2468, 2573-74, 2659,
2662, 3080
Hall, Lawrence 3152
Hall, Lillian Arrilla 66
Hall, Margaret 1604
Hall, William T. 176
Hamar, Clifford E. 67
Hamilton, Clayton 963, 1917-18,
2020-22, 2411
Hamilton, Edward A. 766
Hamilton, Virginia 2798
Hamley, Sir Edward B. 1768
Hamm, Margherita Arlina 303
Hammond, Percy 852
Hampden, Walter 2023-26
Hanaford, Harry Prescott 11
Hanna, N.D. 2412-13
Hanson, Willis T. 2729
Hapgood, Norman 177
Harbin, Billy 2132-34
Harbin, Billy J. 2012, 2295
Harding, Alfred 178
Hare, Arnold 3234
Hark, Ann 2357
Harlan, Kenneth 325
Harland, Marion 2644-45
Harlow, Alvin F. 1644
Harper, Carleton 2307
Harper, H.H. 2743
Harrigan, Edward 2033
Harriman, Margaret Case 452, 2058-59
2058-59
Harrington, John Walker 453
Harris, H.A. 964
Harrison, A. Cleveland 1212-14
Harrison, Gabriel 1862, 2730-31
Harrison, James A. 2652
Harriss, John 783
Hart, Jerome A. 562
Hart, Moss 1936

Author Index

Powers, James T. 586
Pratt, Helen Throop 1314
Pray, Isaac C. 1178
Preston, Charles 766
Price, William Thompson 1572
Prince, Hal 2640
Pringle, Helena 2369
Pringle, Henry F. 884, 1332, 2369
Pritner, Calvin L. 3164
Pryor, Nancy 1343
Punkat, Elisabeth M. 1573
Pyper, George D. 226

Q

Quinn, Arthur Hobson 227-28,
2118, 2757
Quinn, Edward G. 4, 299
Quirk, Lawrence J. 2476

R

R., E.F. 3119
Rahill, Frank 229, 1232, 2159, 3252
Rambeau, Marjorie 2766
Randolph, Ann 494, 1251, 2186
Rankin, Hugh F. 230
Ranous, Dora Knowlton 1615
Rathbone, Basil 1483
Rawls, Eugenie 759
Ray, Marie Beynon 760
Reade, Charles L. 1233-34
Reade, Rev. Compton 1234
Reamer, Lawrence 2261, 2980
Redding, J. Saunders 2813
Rede, Leman Thomas 359
Reed, Florence 2772
Reed, Joseph Verner 1510
Reed, Rex 1987
Rees, James [Colley Cibber] 1875
Reid, Erskine 360
Reid, James 885
Reignolds-Winslow, Catherine 2781-
82
Remington, Frederic 2262
Revere, F. Vance de 886, 1948
Rhodes, Harrison 1428
Rice, Edward LeRoy 361
Richardson, Anna S. 639
Richardson, James B. 3130

Richardson, Tony 3057
Rigdon, Walter 362
Rinear, David L. 1311, 2579
Risvold, Floyd E. 3262
Ritter, Charles C. 2015, 2601
Robb, Josephine 2264
Robbins, Jhan 3253
Robbins, Kenneth R. 2379
Robbins, Phyllis 640-42
Roberts, Katharine 731, 2082,
2695
Roberts, W. Adolph 865, 1949,
1969
Robertson, Catherine 3175
Robertson, Walford Graham 587
Robeson, Elanda Goode 2814-15
Robeson, Paul 2816-17
Robeson, Rev. B.C. 2818
Robeson, Susan 3254
Robins, Edward 363-64
Robinson, Alice M. 2119
Robinson, John William 36
Robson, May 2833
Robson, Stuart 2836
Rodgers, John J. 3015
Roge, Charlotte F. Bates 1117
Rogers, Benjamin G. 1701
Rogers, Joel Augustus 2820
Rogers, Neville 1678
Rogers, Will 1688
Rogoff, Gordon 3058
Rohe, Alice 2345
Rollins, Charlemae 661
Roman, Diane P. 1235
Rooker, Henry Grady 231
Roorbach, Orville Augustus 88
Roseman, Ethel 1429
Rosenberg, Charles Q. 365
Rosenberg, Marvin 366-68, 1877
Rosenfeld, Sydney 588
Ross, Claire 495
Ross, Helen 369
Ross, Lillian 369
Ross, Mrs. Robert. See Gilmore,
Margalo
Ross, Paul L. 25
Rossman, Kenneth R. 1236
Rourke, Constance 232, 1179,
1521-22
Row, Arthur William 1628, 3210-11
Rowan, Carl T. 2821

Author Index

Taylor, J.H. 1315
Taylor, Laurette 3090-3102
Ten Eyck, John 872
Thomas, Augustus 594-95
Thomas, Bob 873
Thomas, Lowell 1908
Thomas, Tony 874
Thorne, Clifford 1026
Ticknor, Howard Malcom 163
Tiempo, Marco 2121
Timberlake, Craig 998
Toll, Robert C. 251
Tompkins, Eugene 252
Towne, Charles Hanson 1838
Townsend, George Alfred 1167-68
Townsend, Margaret 386
Towse, J. Ranken 163, 596, 1618,
  1906, 2271, 2606, 3138
Toynbee, William 573, 1564
Tozzi, Romano 2478
Tracy, Virginia 891
Traubel, Horace 1035
Trollope, Frances 1669
Trommer, Marie 662
Trumble, Alfred 387
Tucker, Florence L. 1935
Tully, Jim 2479
Tunney, Kieran 765
Turner, Arlin 2734
Turner, Vivian 253, 2016
Tuttle, Day 3103
Tyler, George C. 597
Tyrrell, Henry 646, 672, 1839,
  2215, 2286, 2516, 2952

U

Ulric, Lenore 3118

V

Vail, Robert W.G. 2840
Vanbrugh, Irene 1239
Vandenbroucke, Russell 653, 3072
Vandenhoff, George 3120-28
Vandour, Cyril 2480
Van Lennep, William 254
Van Law, H.R. 505
Van Vechten, Carl 2828
Vardac, A. Nicholas 388

Vassault, F.I. 2439
Vaughn, Jack A. 3261
Veinstein, Andre 3251
Ventimiglia, Peter James 1619
Voegele, M. 1240, 2953

W

W., M. 2773-76
W., W. 818, 1840
Wagenknecht, Edward Charles 389,
  1972-73, 2440, 2517
Waggoner, Hyatt Howe 2122
Wagner, Charles Ludwig 598
Wagner, Frederick 390
Wagstaffe, William de 647-48,
  712, 819-20, 1306, 2190,
  2297, 2398, 2851, 3181, 3184
Waite, Edgar 1344
Walbrook, H.M. 391
Walker, Franklin Dickerson 1364
Walker, Helen Louise 1698, 2481
Walker, Mrs. Dr. 1579
Wallace, Amy 392
Wallace, Irving 392
Wallace, Karl R. 2392
Wallace, Mike 766
Wallace, Sylvia 392
Wallack, Arthur 3139
Wallack, James William 3132
Wallack, John Lester 3140
Wallechinsky, David 392
Waller, Alfred Rayney 1176
Wallison, L.R. 2194
Walsh, Blanche 3142
Walsh, Thomas 1523
Walsh, Townsend 1241, 1283
Walsh, William H. 3110
Ward, Genevieve 3145
Warde, Frederick 3146-47
Warfield, David 1000, 3155-62
Warner, William Frederic 1580
Warren, Neilla 1679
Warwick, Anne 1660
Washburn, Beatrice 1381
Wasserman, Debbi 3073
Waterman, Arthur E. 1132, 2272
Watermeier, Daniel J. 1133
Waters, Mrs. Clara Clement 1581
Waters, Willard W. 107

TITLE INDEX

This index includes all titles of books cited in the text. In some cases the titles have been shortened. References are to entry numbers and alphabetization is letter by letter.

G

S

SUBJECT INDEX

This index is alphabetized letter by letter, and references are to entry numbers. Main areas of interest within a subject have been underlined.

A

Acting companies. See Stock companies
Actors and acting
  bibliographies and indexes 33-113
  biographies and autobiographies 521-600
  general references, dictionaries, encyclopedias, and biographical guides 1-32, 108
  general sources: books 267-413
  general sources: serials 414-520
  histories, surveys, and regional studies 114-266
  individual actors 600-3208
  influence of heredity on 418
  portraits and photographs of 66, 68, 289, 297, 314, 358, 459
  study and teaching 601, 604, 609, 615, 917, 939, 1228, 1308, 1493, 1789, 1847, 2007, 2288, 2495, 3044-46, 3049-50, 3052-53, 3055, 3057-58, 3060-61, 3067, 3069, 3072, 3074-75
  See also names of actors and actresses
Actors Equity 25, 134, 178, 549
Actors' Fund to America 242

Actor's Studio 168, 3044-46, 3049, 3052-53, 3055, 3057-60, 3074-75
Adams, Edwin 399, 401, 407, 489, 496, 928, 1050, 2618
Adams, Maude 26, 28, 164, 174, 177, 219, 223, 226, 245, 270, 278-79, 286, 294, 296-97, 316, 358, 381-82, 390, 429-30, 436, 439-40, 444, 448, 451, 465, 469, 479, 493, 505, 508, 525, 532, 555, 575, 579, 588, 598, 601-52, 928, 1477, 1975, 1978, 1981, 2044, 2567, 2984, 3239
  autobiographical-theatrical writings by 427, 601-3
  bibliography on 58
  correspondence 619
  in fiction 626
  pictures of 314, 358, 625, 627, 639, 642
Addams, Augustus 3168
Adelphi Theatre (London) 1802
Adler, Stella 137, 167, 540, 653, 3052, 3224, 3239
  on acting 291
Albany, N.Y., theatre in 220, 222, 1574
Aldine Club 2254

H